P9-AQM-249

The Evolution of
American Educational Technology

The Evolution of American Educational Technology

PAUL SAETTLER

California State University
Sacramento

INFORMATION AGE
PUBLISHING

80 Mason Street • Greenwich, Connecticut 06830 • www.infoagepub.com

ISBN: 1-59311-139-8

Copyright © 2004 Information Age Publishing Inc.

Original copyright © 1990 Paul Saettler

All rights reserved. No part of this publication may be reproduced, stored in a
retrieval system, or transmitted, in any form or by any means, electronic, mechanical,
photocopying, microfilming, recording or otherwise, without written permission
from the publisher.

Printed in the United States of America

They're Back!

Thanks to the efforts of Information Age Publishing, seven classic publications in the field of instructional technology are once again available. These seven publications have been on my bookshelf for over 25 years, and are alongside Richard Clark's *Learning From Media*, also published by Information Age.

My copies were worn and torn, and often used. When asked for a list of publications that I considered "must" reading for those in the field, these were at the top of my list. While I do not use them every day, I use them often enough in classes, in meetings, and as references for newly written papers that I keep them close at hand. In my opinion, they are the basis for a professional library of any person in the fields of instructional technology, instructional media, instructional design, or distance education.

Extending Education Through Technology, a collection of writings by Jim Finn, long considered the "father of educational communications and technology," features articles written by Finn decades ago that are still widely quoted and directly relevant to the issues of the field today. One article alone, "Professionalizing the Audiovisual Field," is worth the price of this classic publication.

The history of the field, *The Evolution of American Educational Technology*, by Paul Saettler is *the* basic reference for how the field has grown and become the driving force in education and training that it is today. Every student of the field should read this book.

Three books on this list of classics, Ball and Barnes' *Research, Principles, and Practices in Visual Communications*, Chu and Schramm's *Learning from Television*, and Ofiesh and Meierhenry's *Trends in Programmed Instruction*, are the primary sources for research and design in our field. Some claim, and they are probably correct, that much of what are considered "best practices' today can be traced directly back to the conclusions provided by these three extremely important monographs. Change the terms visual communication, television, and programmed instruction to visual literacy, distance education, and e-learning, and you have classic publications with direct implications to the work of most of us today.

Robert Heinich's often quoted and rarely found classic, *Technology and the Management of Instruction*, is a masterpiece of writing and advice about the field that resonates strongly today. Heinich is still a leader in the field, and many consider this monograph to be his best work.

With little doubt, the 20 years of Okoboji conferences set the stage and provided a platform for leadership development and intellectual growth in the field. The Okoboji conferences have been often mimicked but never duplicated. This summary of the 20 years of conferences by Lee Cochran, the driving force behind them, is a must for every book shelf.

As Santayana noted, "Those who cannot remember the past are condemned to repeat it." These classic publications do not prevent us from making the same errors that these writers admonished us from committing. Once read however, they do help us remember, and remember well.

—Michael Simonson

To
DIAN
With much love

In memory of James D. Finn
(Courtesy of Robert J. Casey, Jr.)

Contents

Part III
GROWTH OF THEORETICAL THOUGHT
AND PRACTICE:
From Mid-Century to 1980

Part V
APPENDIXES

Foreword to the First Edition

Philosophers, commentators, schoolteachers, industrialists, and songwriters all have, in the course of time, commented on the value and usefulness of history. History has been considered as a philosophy, as a technique, as an aesthetic experience, as a sure guide to the future, as an account of the crimes of mankind, as a tissue of lies, as "bunk."

With so much comment on historical writing existing as a vast literature of its own, it is difficult to compose a foreword to Dr. Saettler's work which, in any new way, might suggest the value of his contribution. Perhaps one of the earliest historians, Thucydides, in commenting on his own work, stated my general feelings. Speaking of the history of the Peloponnesian War, Thucydides said, "But if he who desires to have before his eyes a true picture of the events which have happened, and of the like events which may be expected to happen thereafter in the order of human things, shall pronounce what I have written to be useful, then I shall be satisfied." An accurate, generalizable account of the past which may serve, at least in part, as a guide to the future is what we want from history. In this pioneering work on the history of instructional technology, Paul Saettler has given us such a tool.

The history of technology (and of science, for that matter) is a relatively new professional area for historians that, with the great explosion in technology occurring in this century, has become increasingly popular. In a large sense, Paul Saettler's work is in this new tradition. The history of technology is a difficult area to work in, as Lynn White, Jr., one of the leading historians in this field, has pointed out. Knowledge in the general area of the history of technology is as yet so sketchy that some of the existing compilations have been referred to as the "codification of error." Historical work in all aspects of technology is badly needed. Hence, the present book is especially valuable in adding to our knowledge of technology in education.

In tracing the history of instructional technology up to the present time, Dr. Saettler has had to deal with this development in the context of American education. This is especially important when American education is considered, technically, as a bureaucracy. For, as Charles Hoban has recently pointed out, we know very little about the processes of innovation within a bureaucracy. All aspects of instructional media—the *Orbus pictus*, the Keystone slide sets, the sound motion picture or television—have represented innovations thrusting into the context of a very special kind of bureaucracy. Hence, the accounts of

---

The first edition was entitled *A History of Instructional Technology*. It was published by McGraw-Hill in 1968 and was written by Paul Saettler.

committees, commissions, organization plans, and departments of various kinds, which are all, in the correct sense of the term, technological in nature, give us some insight into this little-understood process.

The result of Dr. Saettler's hard work is the book before you. We can do no better, in conclusion, than return to the quotation of Thucydides. For American education is either in the midst of, or on the verge of a great technological revolution that has penetrated from the industrial, scientific, and military sectors of our culture. The changes are sure to be great; they may be so great that the past will not prove too sound a basis upon which to predict the future; nonetheless, such insight as we can get from the past is perhaps the major path to the "like events which may be expected to happen hereafter in the order of human things." Paul Saettler has helped us a long way down that path.

James D. Finn
University of Southern California

January 1968

Donald P. Ely (Courtesy of Donald P. Ely)

Foreword to the Second Edition

There are generally two major positions taken by people confronted by historical infor-mation: one is to accept, embrace, and preserve history before it is too late and we lose our heritage; the other is to reject, downplay, and bury history before it prevents or inhibits pro-gress. Most people seem to appreciate history that is related to their own personal and pro-fessional interests, but they usually do not dwell on it or permit archaic information to dominate their thoughts. These same people like to think of themselves as forward-looking individuals, part of the information generation that has a good fix on the future. The image of a person standing with one foot in the past and one foot in the future fits the contem-porary educational technologist who wants to build on the historic substance of the field while moving ahead with new ideas, concepts, and technologies.

For being a relatively new field, educational technology has a substantial history, much of it written during the twentieth century. No one has documented that history as thoroughly as Paul Saettler. He is *the* historian of the field. His first historical volume, now out of print, is a prized possession in the libraries of many professionals. He continues to document the field's growth in this welcome volume.

Any serious professional is concerned about his/her heritage. Perhaps in the initial rush to acquire knowledge and skills to become a professional, many have placed secondary in-terest in the origins and growth of the field. Eventually, however, the reflective practitioner wants to know the sources of the definitions, concepts, and theories that have helped to shape the field. The search is somewhat akin to the recent preoccupation with genealogical "roots."

In a field that has concentrated on the practical applications of technology in solving educational problems, the emphasis has been more on the *how* than on the *why*. The techni-cian knows *how* to do something; the professional not only knows how, but also *why*. It is in the search for the *why* that Paul Saettler provides the information and perceptions that most professionals need. Where did the field originate? Who made the field? What are the theoretical and conceptual underpinnings? What mistakes were made in attempting to ex-pand the field? What inventions appeared to advance the field? —and so forth. This is the *stuff* of history.

George Santayana once said, "Those who do not remember the past are condemned to relive it." There are those today who feel educational technology has just been discovered or that it began with the microcomputer. Not so! Educational technology has been evolving since the early days of centuries past, with accelerated growth in this century. It was born in the minds and actions of visionaries who believed that learning could be improved with a variety of methods, techniques, and resources to enrich the educational environment. That vision persists today and permeates some of the best examples of contemporary educational technology.

History is not dull. It is alive with the ideas of people who believed they had solutions for some of the problems of their day, beginning with the insights of the ancient Greeks. The more we know of our heritage, the more we earn the right to lead the field forward in our own time. Several decades hence, our actions might be studied as stepping stones that moved the field toward a brighter day.

Donald P. Ely
Syracuse University

1990

Preface

Anyone proposing to write a history of educational technology has to make choices as the work is planned and executed. This work proposes to provide a basis for the historical analysis and interpretation of the diverse aspects of American educational technology and to trace its antecedents as it evolved from ancient times to the present day. The focus of this history is on the impact of educational technology in the American public schools. Except for the military experiences of World War II, this history does not specifically concern itself with its development in the industrial, military, government, or medical or public health sectors.

The primary purpose of this book is to trace the theoretical and methodological foundations of American educational technology. It must be emphasized that this work is essentially a history of the *process* of educational technology rather than of products in the form of devices or media. Although media have played an important role in educational technology, the reader should not lose sight of the central process which characterizes and underlies the true historical meaning and function of educational technology. Moreover, the assumption is made that all current theory, methodology, and practice rests upon the heritage of the past. Indeed, a common problem in the field has been the failure, in many instances, to take adequate account of past history in planning for the present or the future.

A related purpose of this book is to provide a selective survey of research in educational technology as it relates to the American public schools. Such research reviews are not intended to be comprehensive, but were included because of their historical importance and their relevance in understanding the process of educational technology.

This author's previous history published over two decades ago was the first comprehensive history of American educational technology. Much of the first portion of the earlier book has been lightly revised for inclusion in the second edition. The last third of the second edition is completely new, covering the period from 1968 to the present. The first chapter has also been completely rewritten to reflect changed views and changes in the field since 1968. What is more, the present work extends the theoretical and historical dimensions of the former work and, in fact, replaces it to a large extent.

This history has five parts. The first part explores the meaning of educational technology and provides a general introduction. Part 2, chapters 2 through 8, focuses on the theoretical and methodological foundations of educational technology from the last half of the fifth century B.C. to the middle of the twentieth century. Part 3, chapters 9 through 15, deals with the formative theoretical and methodological patterns which developed from the middle of this century to 1980. Part 4, chapters 16 through 19, covers the developments from 1980 to the present and projects about prospects for the future. Part 5 is the appendixes.

Throughout all the chapters great effort has been made by the author to use scholarly historical and research data based on the best available primary and secondary sources. At the end of each chapter, relevant notes and a select bibliography are included for further reading and research. No glossary has been provided since there are a number available in the field. A listing of these sources is given in the bibliographic section at the end of the first chapter.

Since this history has been written primarily for the professional person in the field, those most likely to read this book are those who have some familiarity with educational technology or those who have served in an active role as a practitioner or a scholar. This book should also prove useful as a text in courses in the history of educational technology or in introductory courses in educational technology or in such courses as instructional design or those concerned with new technologies of instruction. There may also be those in the related fields of educational psychology and communications as well as interested laymen who may read various portions of this history.

Many will remain unmentioned who have aided me in my historical analysis. I am grateful to all of them, but I especially want to mention a person who critically read all of the chapters in their early stages and whose comments were exceedingly helpful. This person is Professor Milad Y. Sawiris of California State University, Sacramento. Of course, any remaining flaws in this work are my responsibility.

A number of others were involved in initiating and producing a book of this kind. I received encouragement from and invaluable assistance from Dr. David V. Loertscher, Senior Acquisitions Editor for Libraries Unlimited, Inc. My deep thanks is also extended to Dr. Donald P. Ely who has long supported the publication of this history and who generously offered to write the foreword. Additional thanks go to those individuals and publishers who permitted quotations from published works and to the many unnamed persons who have made American educational technology what it is today. Finally, my greatest thanks is reserved for my wife, Dian Saettler, to whom this book is dedicated. Without her constant encouragement, love, and support, this work could not have been completed.

Paul Saettler

July 1990

Part I

Introduction

1

The Meaning of Educational Technology

Nature of Technology

Technology (the Greek form is *techne*, translated as *art, craft,* or *skill*) was conceived by the ancient Greeks as a particular activity and as a kind of knowledge.[1] Plato viewed *techne* and *episteme* (systematic or scientific knowledge) as closely associated. For Aristotle, *techne* was the systematic use of knowledge for intelligent human action. *Techne* is not only the name for the activities and skills of the craftsperson, but also for the arts of the mind and the fine arts.[2]

Some may assert that these concepts of technology may hold for the Greeks, but that they simply do not fit modern views of technology. If technology is to be completely understood, in either ancient or modern terms, it should be seen as a system of practical knowledge not necessarily reflected in things or hardware. In the past, many technological innovations have emerged that involved little or no changes in tools or machines. For example, in the three-field system of crop rotation, often called "the greatest agricultural novelty of the Middle Ages in Western Europe,"[3] no tools or machines were involved. Not only did the three-field system greatly increase the productivity of medieval agriculture, but the rotation of crops brought about improved nutrition by providing a larger variety of food in the form of natural carbohydrates and protein. For Northern Europe, this brought about "the startling expansion of population, the outreach of commerce, and the new exuberance of spirits which enlivened that age."[4] Thus, an amazing transformation took place without a single tool or piece of hardware!

Another striking example of why technology may not merely be a set of machines is vividly shown by the recent revelation of an ingenious form of agriculture that enabled ancient peoples on the high plains of the Peruvian Andes around Lake Titicaca to reap bumper crops in the face of flood, drought, and the killing frosts of 12,000-foot altitudes. Archaeologists were amazed to find a prehistoric technology of *raised field* agriculture which required no chemical fertilizer and only labor to dig canals and build up platforms.[5]

A further example of the use of technology without benefit of tools or machines is dramatically illustrated by the revolutionary innovation of division of labor.[6] Workers in a factory previously performed all the operations to manufacture a product. In the new approach, each performed only a few operations. Thus, the technological focus was on the improvement of skills and the organization of work rather than on tools and machinery.

In modern terms, technology is "any systematized practical knowledge, based on experimentation and/or scientific theory, which enhances the capacity of society to produce goods and services, and which is embodied in productive skills, organization, or machinery."[7] This definition clearly exceeds narrow conceptions of technology that equate it exclusively with hardware and machines. In fact, Mumford (1963) has pointed out that the first machines to emerge in history consisted of people as component parts and these served as prototypes for machines composed of inanimate materials.[8]

Emergence of Educational Technology

This section examines some of the primary antecedents prior to the twentieth century to demonstrate that the historical function of educational technology is a *process* rather than a product. No matter how sophisticated the media of instruction may become, a precise distinction must always be made between the process of developing a technology of education and the use of certain products or media within a particular technology of instruction.

Educational technology, as a process, emerged out of the early technological tradition when a kind of knowledge began to be systematically applied to instruction. Educational technology, despite the uncertainty of the origin of the term, can be traced back to the time when tribal priests systematized bodies of knowledge and early cultures invented pictographs or sign writing to record and transmit information. In every age, one can find an instructional technique or a set of procedures intended to implement a particular culture. The more advanced the culture, the more complex became the technology of instruction designed to reflect particular ways of thinking, acting, speaking or feeling. Over the centuries, each significant shift in educational values, goals or objectives has led to diverse technologies of instruction.

The invention of the printing press was a prime development in the history of conveying the instruction that complex and advanced-technology cultures needed. Although books were produced laboriously by hand, or by means of inked carved woodblocks upon which paper was pressed, before the printing press, it was now possible to collect and transmit information relatively inexpensively on an unprecedented scale. Moreover, this development generated experimentation with the technique of presenting subject matter. One of the manifestations was the appearance of the printed catechisms of monastic education which resembled the step-by-step procedure of programmed materials. Johann Comenius, the Moravian teacher and theologian of the seventeenth century, saw in the printed book the opportunity to organize subject matter in an optimum sequence, making it possible to teach several hundred pupils at once.[9] In fact, Comenius can be considered the forerunner, if not the inventor, of modern programmed instruction.

It is clear that educational technology is essentially the product of a great historical stream consisting of trial and error, long practice and imitation, and sporadic manifestations of unusual individual creativity and persuasion. For example, in seventeenth-century European science, the growing influence of the empirical viewpoint was reflected in a technology of instruction whereby the learner began with actual and simple observations of what he knew best and then proceeded to more complex and unfamiliar things. It was thought that learning through the senses using actual objects was far more effective than merely learning words and rules from books. In England, Locke's *tabula rasa* theory[10] advocated a shift in the conception of education from mental discipline to habit formation. As a consequence, he developed a technology of instruction focused on procedures designed to form proper habits or behavior in students or what came to be the precursor of modern behavioral modification. Meanwhile, some German schools of the day applied the empirical outlook by using actual objects, models, and pictures to illustrate lessons from books. Also, excursions were used to give students a firsthand acquaintance with farms, shops, markets, mines, and museums.[11]

Some early educators recognized that a technology of instruction must consider the developmental stages of the learner. Thus, in Jean Jacques Rousseau's (1712-1778) educational treatise, *Emile*, we find that the principal concept is that instructional method should follow the natural stages of human development from early childhood to maturity. In order to implement this concept Rousseau proposed an appropriate technology to fit each stage.[12]

An important historic development occurred in Germany when Johann Friedrick Herbart (1777-1841) developed the first *systems approach* to instruction in his famous four-steps learning design. Herbart's discussions of how sensory information was transformed, organized, stored and related to new experiences were unique and laid the foundation for a modern psychology of perception.[13]

Maria Montessori (1870-1952) exerted a dynamic impact on educational technology through her development of graded materials designed to provide for the proper sequencing of subject matter for each individual learner. Her methods possessed three principal characteristics. First, school work was adapted to each child's individuality; second, she insisted upon freedom; and third, her system emphasized sensory education.[14]

Another notable influence of nineteenth-century scientific concepts on educational technology was the work of James Sully (1842-1923) of Aberdeen, Scotland. His *Teacher's Handbook of Psychology* (1886)[15] presented one of the first complete discussions of the function of science in the teaching process. He asserted that teaching is a technological process and that instruction is both an art and a science. Sully believed that if the art of teaching were to be performed successfully, the teacher must be aware of the general nature of psychological laws and principles and be able to apply them in a systematic fashion to practical instructional situations.

Others contributed to the development of pre-twentieth-century educational technology, but the point is that much of the shape of modern educational technology evolved before research on human behavior began. Although some educators today assume educational technology is a recent development, it is clear that whatever form or direction educational technology may take, it has a long, continuous history that began in ancient times.

Definitions of Educational Technology

It is difficult to draw precise boundaries for a historical interpretation of American educational technology because the past has generated such a heterogeneous or diverse collection of definitions and statements concerning its nature and function. Inevitably, the meaning of educational technology is intertwined with certain historical conceptions and practices or bound to specific philosophical and psychological theory as well as with particular scientific orientations. Oftentimes, another level of confusion arises in the tendency in some quarters to equate the new information technology with a technology of instruction.

Some consider educational technology a branch of educational theory and practice that is concerned "primarily with the design and use of messages which control the learning process."[16] Moreover, Ely makes a clear distinction between devices and equipment or the *physical science* of educational technology and the *behavioral science* of educational technology and considers *process* as the *how to* knowledge and skills (the art and craft of the Greek concept of *techne*) and *product* as the equipment and materials used in the process.[17] Others see it "as systematic knowledge derived from scientific research" and "not the machines or the materials used for instructional presentation—the projectors, the films, the display screens, the computer programs."[18]

Heinich, et al.[19] adapted John Kenneth Galbraith's[20] definition of technology, applying it to instruction, and defined instructional technology "as the application of our scientific knowledge about human learning to the practical tasks of teaching and learning." Thus, technology of instruction "is a particular, systematic arrangement of teaching/learning events designed to put our knowledge of learning into practice in a predictable, effective manner to attain specific learning objectives."

The Commission on Instructional Technology (1970) defined instructional technology as "the media born of the communication revolution which can be used for instructional purposes alongside the teacher, textbook, and blackboard."[21] Although the Commission's report followed this definition, a second definition was offered which went beyond any particular medium or device and stated that instructional technology

> is a systematic way of designing, carrying out, and evaluating the total process of learning and teaching in terms of specific objectives, based on research in human learning and communication, and employing a combination of human and nonhuman resources to bring about more effective instruction.[22]

The Commission concluded at the time that "the widespread acceptance and application of this broad definition belongs to the future."[23] Ironically, one current definition views educational technology as "any device available to teachers for use in instructing students in a more efficient and stimulating manner than the sole use of the teacher's voice."[24]

Definitions can be contradictory. For example, one author whose purpose was "to foster understanding of educational technology" began by defining the field as "a systematic way of designing, applying and evaluating the total process of teaching and learning"[25] then proceeded to equate educational technology with devices or media. A comprehensive national study of educational technology began with a science-based definition but essentially described a media or hardware concept of educational technology.[26] In still other instances, one finds what appears to be confused or ambivalent conceptions of educational technology as either a process or a product or even a mixture of both, Wittich and Schuller[27] for example.

Some authors prefer to refer to a *theory* of instruction rather than a *technology* of instruction. Some authors in recent years have tended to use educational technology not only with reference to hardware or software, but also with reference to principles providing guidelines for the use of these devices. One of the persistent definition problems has been the use of the word *technology* to refer only to hardware rather than to the broader scientific process involved in educational technology.

While some definitions are excessively narrow, particularly those confined to devices or hardware, others are much too broad and bear little relevance to the real world of the public school. Here is an excellent example of such an omnibus definition:

> Educational technology is a complex, integrated process involving people, procedures, ideas, devices, and organizations, for analyzing problems, and devising, implementing, evaluating and managing solutions to those problems, involved in all aspects of human learning. In educational technology, the solutions to problems take the form of all the Learning Resources that are designed and/or selected as Messages, People, Materials, Devices, Techniques and Settings. The processes for analyzing problems, and devising, implementing and evaluating solutions are identified by the Educational Development Functions of Research-Theory, Design, Production, Evaluating-Selection, Logistics and Utilization. The processes of directing or coordinating one or more of these functions are identified by the Educational Management Functions or Organization Management and Personnel Management.[28]

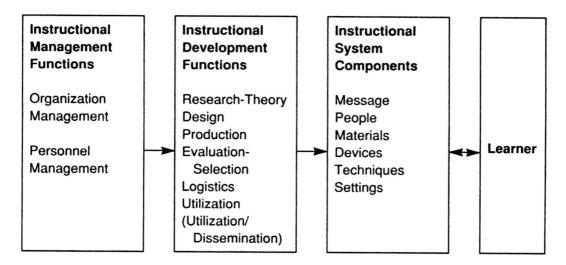

Fig. 1.1. Domain of educational technology (From AECT, *The Definition of Educational Technology.* Washington, D.C.: Association for Educational Communications and Technology, 1977. Used by permission of the publishers.)

This definition, provided by the AECT (Association for Educational Communications and Technology) Task Force on Definition and Terminology (1977), was obviously designed to include everything and to please everyone. Because of the current changes in the field, it is seriously outmoded and is in need of revision.

Paradigms of Educational Technology

Kuhn[29] proposed a perspective which suggested that science does not advance primarily by accumulating but instead by revolutionary changes, by viewing things in radically new ways. He describes these as paradigm shifts. The importance of paradigmatic elements in educational technology is that they determine to a large extent how practitioners in the field think, see, feel, and act with reference to the instructional problems they encounter. These paradigms have distinct sets of assumptions, values, and general tendencies. Moreover, these paradigms flux and conflict as each paradigm attempts to offer a response to the problems of learning and instruction in the public schools.

In this century, at least four distinct paradigms have emerged in educational technology. Each of these paradigms have quite different philosophical and theoretical orientations that have affected both the theory and practice of educational technology. These so-called paradigm shifts may be characterized as: (1) the physical science or media view; (2) the communications and systems concept; (3) the behavioral science-based view, comprising the behaviorist and neo-behaviorist concepts; and (4) the cognitive science perspective.

Physical Science or Media Approach to Educational Technology

The media or hardware approach to educational technology applies physical sciences and engineering technology, such as motion picture projectors, television, audio and video-discs, microcomputers, etc., in the presentation of materials or programs. Characteristically, this approach views the various media as aids to instruction and tends to be preoccupied with the effects of devices and procedures rather than with the differences in individual learners or the selection or design of instructional content.

The historical-theoretical notion embodied within the media concept of educational technology casts media such as graphics, films, television, videodiscs, etc., in nonverbal roles, and some traditional media (lectures, books) in verbal roles. The underlying assumption is that nonverbal media are more concrete and effective and that the perennial villain in the teaching-learning process is "verbalism."[30] Many texts and publications have justified the use of visual materials to combat verbalism in the instructional process.[31]

The media concept of educational technology was accepted quite generally by practitioners in the visual (later audiovisual) instruction movement that flourished during the first half of this century and also by the early commercial producers of slides, filmstrips and films. The modern electronic computing industry still accepts this concept.

Media concepts of educational technology began to wane in the 1960s and a number of leaders in the audiovisual instruction movement grew dissatisfied with this viewpoint. The first formal steps toward redefinition of the media concept came in 1963 when the name *audiovisual instruction* was changed to *audiovisual communications.* Simultaneously, the emphasis on audiovisual materials as aids that provided concrete experiences changed to an emphasis on the complete process of communication.[32] In 1970, the Department of Audiovisual Instruction of the National Education Association, the professional organization of the audiovisual instruction movement in the United States, changed its name to the Association for Educational Communications and Technology (AECT). Finally, in 1972, AECT published a task force report that adopted the name, "educational technology."[33]

Regardless of these name changes, the media concept of educational technology persists in many quarters of the education community and in the communications industry.[34] Even in the AECT, many still cling to the old media concept or related variations— *educational media, learning resources,* or *media technology.* Many "media specialists" view the field only from the perspective of their particular media specialty and appear to have little or no concept of the total process of educational technology.

Ambivalent theoretical conceptions of educational technology still prevail in the professional theory and research writings of AECT. The AECT journals have reflected contradictory conceptual frames, but, as Ely observed:

> There appears to be no hue and cry for a new or revised definition of educational technology. It could be that the silence connotes satisfaction with the definitions which now exist. It could be that there are more vitally important matters before the community. It could be that those who were so vitally concerned with the definitions are tired and have moved on to other projects. There is a Definition and Terminology Committee of AECT, but there does not seem to be any major issues on the agenda.[35]

However, at the May 1989 meeting of the Professors of Instructional Development and Technology (PIDT), a working group (Typology and Geography of the Field) was established for the purpose of updating the definition and domain of the field.

Further conceptual changes will occur within AECT, within professional education, and within society as a whole. This will, in turn, bring about new educational needs and demands that will affect the future development of educational technology.

Audiovisual Communications: A Synthesis of Communications and Systems Concepts

The communications approach to educational technology altered the traditional theoretical framework of the field. Instead of focusing on devices or media, the focus was shifted to the entire process of communicating information from a source (a teacher or medium) to a receiver (the learner). In addition, such communications models as those developed by Ball and Byrnes (1960)[36] and Berlo (1960)[37] were employed to describe the total teaching-learning process.

Simultaneously, the early systems concept of educational technology stressed the idea that the basic unit, or product, of the field did not involve individual materials but rather complete instructional systems. Another associated concept was that individual media or devices were viewed as components of an instructional system rather than as isolated aids. The integrating or unifying concept was *instructional design*, whereby all the components of the system were related to specific instructional problems and objectives. This was the first time in the history of educational technology that instructional design became a primary consideration. The official definition of the field by the Department of Audiovisual Instruction (DAVI) in 1963, which reflected a major paradigm change, was as follows:

> Audiovisual communications is that branch of educational theory and practice concerned primarily with the design and use of messages which control the learning process.
>
> It undertakes: (a) the study of the unique and relative strengths of both pictorial and nonrepresentation messages which may be employed in the learning process for any purpose; and (b) the structuring and systematizing of messages by men and instruments in an educational environment. These undertakings include the planning, production, selection, management and utilization of both components and entire instructional systems.
>
> Its practical goal is the efficient utilization of every method and medium of communication which can contribute to the development of the learner's full potential.[38]

Most of the concepts developed in this definition evolved out of the work of Eboch.[39] His model went beyond stating that there were components of an instructional system. Specific components were identified and defined as follows:

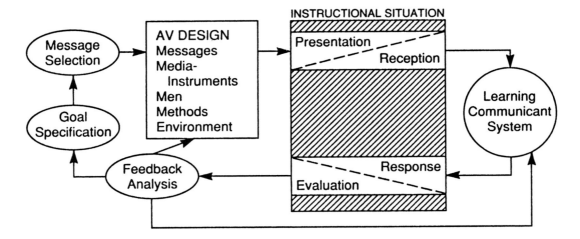

Fig. 1.2. AV relationships to educational-communication process (From Donald P. Ely, ed. *The Changing of the Audiovisual Process in Education: A Definition and a Glossary of Terms*, Monograph No. 1 of the Technological Development Project. Washington, D.C.: National Education Association, 1963, D-35. Reprinted by permission of NEA.)

Messages are the information to be transmitted—the content is the meaning.

Men indicates the personnel required to control or assist in the information-transmission or the presentation.

Media-Instrumentation indicates the transmission systems (the materials and devices) available for carrying the selected messages.

Methods are the specifications and techniques required for effective presentations.

Environment indicates the controls or requirements of the given conditions within the instructional situation.

The model and its list of elements reiterated such earlier concepts as:

there are components within a system;

the components can be classified by type, rather than listing each individual component;

the message itself is an important component which must be included in the design of audiovisual communication; and

people, as well as materials, must be included as components of the system.

The model also added these two newer concepts:

the methods of utilizing "media-instruments" are important and must be considered as components of the system, and

the environment in which the "media-instruments are used affects the presentation and response, and therefore must also be considered as a component of the system."[40]

Although this revolutionary paradigm change synthesized most of the concepts of earlier orientations as well as introducing some significant new concepts to the field, a contradictory terminology inherited from the media paradigm persisted. For example, such terms as *audiovisual communications, audiovisual, educational communications* and *instructional technology* were often used interchangeably. This created considerable confusion.

This paradigm contained the beginnings of a *systems-as-process* or *systems approach* concept, but all the components of a systems approach were never completely integrated. For example, in this paradigm, "message selection occurs outside the context of the audio-visual design system" as do goal specification and feedback analysis.[41]

In the middle 1960s the communications paradigm moved closer to a systems approach. Thus, the systems approach now required the

> ... examination of a process as an entity with cognizance of the relationships involved in and among all components. It starts with specification of objectives, proceeds through the necessary operations, and evaluates the end product in terms of these objectives and modifies the system if found wanting.[42]

The systems approach was carried a step further when educational technology was viewed as utilizing both human and nonhuman resources—the first time that the term *resources* was used to describe the products of educational technology. In using the terms *designing, carrying out*, and *evaluating*, the concept was emphasized that there were certain functions which had to be fulfilled in the practice of educational technology. The systems concept was expressed in the 1970s as follows:

> A systematic approach to the design, production, evaluation, and utilization of complete systems of instruction, including all appropriate components and a management pattern for using them; instructional development is larger than instructional product development, which is concerned with only isolated products, and is larger than instructional design, which is the one part of instructional development.[43]

Despite this advance, the systems instructional development approach did not provide an adequate definition of educational technology in terms of addressing the problems of curriculum development, the functions involved in distributing and using instructional systems once they were developed, and the activities involved in the application process concerning the noninstructional aspects of education. Moreover, it failed to deal with institutional constraints, was less specific about the types of resources that could be used and the necessary teacher-learner interaction required, and provided no way of generating or testing new theory. Unfortunately, the fragile connection with communications theory and practice began to unwind with the increasing impact of the behavioral sciences on educational technology during the 1960s and 1970s.

Behavioral Sciences Approach to Educational Technology

The study of human behavior focused on the fields of psychology, anthropology, and sociology is known as the behavioral sciences. Although the influence of behavioral sciences in educational technology is relatively new, its beginnings can be traced to the late nineteenth century. During World War I, the use of intelligence tests and statistical measurements provided an impetus for the development of psychology as a discipline. Growth of the behavioral sciences between the two world wars was stimulated largely by university research.

Great expansion occurred during World War II because of increased demand for behavioral scientists in connection with the war effort. Behavioral sciences grew so quickly that the United States became the leading practitioner, and many observers feel there is a uniquely American version of the behavioral sciences.

Behavioral sciences applied to problems of learning and instruction are fundamental to a modern concept of educational technology. The behavioral sciences concept of educational technology believes that educational practice should depend more on the methods of science as developed by behavioral scientists in the broad areas of psychology, anthropology, sociology, and in the more specialized areas of learning, group processes, language and linguistics, communications, cybernetics, perception, and psychometrics. Moreover, this approach includes the application of engineering research and development (including human factors engineering) and branches of economics and logistics related to the effective utilization of instructional personnel, buildings, etc., or management science, and computerized systems for data processing, informational retrieval, and instructional purposes.

Problems of Integration

Prior to the 1960s, it was assumed that once a behavioral-sciences-based technology had been validated in experimental classrooms, that the new technique of instructional method would be adopted. We now know that an integrative strategy is a prerequisite before the real educational situation can be transformed or some type of innovation can be expected to take place. Hilgard (1964) has described stages that must be taken to implement the transition from behavioral sciences research to an established educational technology.[44] The first three steps constitute theoretical pure-science research on learning, and are not directly relevant to the practical needs of instruction. However, Hilgard suggests,

> there may be bridges from any pure-science project to a practical one: perhaps drugs discovered in brain studies of rats may aid remedial reading, studies of interference may suggest intervals between classes or what should be studied concomitantly, and language-vocabulary results in a pure context may guide language acquisition in schools.[45]

The final three steps are directly within the domain of educational technology. Hilgard describes these steps:

Technological Research and Development

Step 4. Research conducted in special laboratory classrooms, with selected teachers, e.g., bringing a few students into a room to see whether or not instruction in set theory or symbolic logic is feasible, granted a highly skilled teacher.

Step 5. A tryout of the results of prior research in a "normal" classroom with a typical teacher. Whatever is found feasible in Step 4 has to be tried out in the more typical classroom, which has limited time for the new method, and may lack the special motivation on the part of either teacher or pupil.

Step 6. Developmental steps related to advocacy and adoption. Anything found to work in Steps 4 and 5 has to be "packaged" for wider use, and then go through the processes by which new methods of procedures are adopted by those not party to the experimentation.[46]

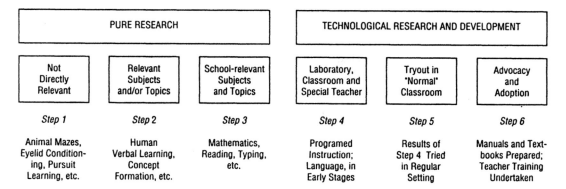

Fig. 1.3. Steps in research on learning—pure research to technological development (From Hilgard, ed., *Theories of Learning and Instruction*, Part I. Chicago: University of Chicago Press, 1964. Used by permission of the publisher.)

A basic problem of integrating educational technology and behavioral sciences is that each has its own terminology, theory, and research methodology. The behavioral sciences are more research oriented, in the "pure" rather than "applied" sense, and the behavioral scientist is more interested in developing knowledge in his own field rather than applying it to the problems of educational technology. Behavioral scientists usually receive training and practice in only one of the established disciplines, and they find it difficult to understand and keep up with the problems and findings of the others. The person combining behavioral sciences knowledge and research explorations with the problems of educational technology is rare.

Solving the problems of integrating behavioral sciences to educational technology and making the relationship a viable method of instructional design requires new and imaginative training programs. These need to provide for a systematic method of integration. Until this occurs, much of the behavioral sciences approach to educational technology is likely to be segmented and spread thin among the various specialties of educational technology.

Two Theoretical Orientations

According to Berelson, to be considered a part of the behavioral sciences, a field must satisfy two basic criteria. First, it must deal with human behavior. Second, it must study its subject matter in a scientific manner.[47] However, it is not always clearly recognized that two conflicting theoretical orientations prevail in the behavioral sciences, and these theoretical viewpoints lead to entirely different instructional approaches in educational technology.[48] One is the behaviorist concept and the other the cognitive concept of educational technology.

The Behaviorist Concept of Educational Technology

The dominant theoretical viewpoint in the behavioral sciences has until recent times been behaviorism. The radical behaviorists, led first by John B. Watson and later by B. F. Skinner, argued that science must investigate public, observable events.[49] The behaviorists concluded that mental events such as thoughts, images and consciousness had no place in the science of psychology because they could not be observed directly. From the early 1920s through the late 1950s almost all experimental psychologists focused on observable behavior, rejected the investigation of mental events, and proclaimed the effects of reinforcement on the behavior of laboratory animals and humans.

Ironically, even as the behaviorist position in psychology began to decline in the late 1950s, its impact on educational technology accelerated simultaneously. Skinner's notions of reinforcement and its application to teaching machines and programmed instruction had begun to influence the development of a science-based technology of instruction. When behavioral objectives were applied to Skinner's *contingency management* techniques, it served as a foundation to the systems approach to instruction. Simultaneously, ideas of programmed instruction reawakened the old notion of individualized instruction whereby students could proceed at their own pace.[50] Computer-assisted instruction was also influenced by this trend.

Behaviorist theory was derived from experimental work with lower organisms, namely, laboratory rats and pigeons. Skinner asserted that "in shaping the behavior of a pigeon, success depends on how the requirements for reinforcement are set" and he goes on to state that "in deciding what behavior to reinforce at any given time, the basic rule is 'Don't lose your pigeon.' "[51] When applied to human learning, the behaviorist concept of educational technology tends to be focused on the lower cognitive processes with motives being controlled through conditioning. Thus, the behaviorist orientation leads to a curriculum that is programmed step by step in small units, focused on immediately observable and measurable learning products.

According to Skinner, "a student is taught in the sense that he is induced to engage in new forms of behavior and in specific forms upon specific occasions," and "teaching is simply the arrangement of contingencies of reinforcement."[52] In recent years, the notion of the school curriculum as a production system has been embodied in the behavioristic view of specific behavioral objectives, behavior modification, systems analysis, performance contracting, and accountability.

The Cognitive Concept of Educational Technology

The cognitive approach to educational technology, unlike behaviorism, attempts to understand the internal processes of behavior and emphasize knowing rather than responding. Its focus is not upon stimulus-response bonds, but on mental events. The cognitive approach to educational technology views the learner not as passive, but as active, constructive, and playful. This is important because, in the cognitive view, the learner becomes an active participant in the process of acquiring and using knowledge. The cognitive theorist believes that any complete theory of human cognition must include an analysis of the plans or strategies that the learner uses for thinking, remembering, and understanding and using language.[53]

According to Wittrock, the cognitive approach to educational technology implies that:

> the art of instruction begins with an understanding and a diagnosis of the cognitive and affective processes and aptitudes of the learners. From these one designs different treatments for different students in different situations to actively induce mental elaborations that related previous learning and schemata to stimuli. In this conception the learners are active, responsible, and accountable for their role in generative learning.[54]

By the early 1980s, the cognitive model of learning began to replace the behaviorist model in educational technology, particularly in the instructional design process. In a cognitive model of instructional design, the organization, processing, and storage of information by the learner constitute vital elements in instructional development. The cognitive science view of educational technology has developed the concept of *learning strategies*, intellectual skills that learners use to control their internal processes of attending, perceiving, encoding, and retrieval.[55] Learning strategies may vary in their quality, origin, generality, and purpose. From a cognitive view, educational technology should be focused on activating the appropriate learning strategies during the instructional process rather than merely initiating behavioral responses.[56]

Tessmer and Jonassen point out that learning strategies selection may become an independent step in the overall design process, or may be a part of the overall plan for selecting instructional events and activities.[57] This may affect such instructional design processes as task analysis and learner strategy implementation. Moreover, in order to implement an information processing learning strategy into media such as CAI or television, the designer will have to consider the media attributes of the medium as well.

Educational Technology: A Preparadigmatic State of Development

We have examined four paradigms which have emerged in educational technology in this century. It is more than likely that the future will see the development of newer, more innovative paradigms in educational technology. At present, it is evident that educational technology is in a *pre*paradigmatic state of development with respect to an adequate and generally acceptable paradigm. Even the emergence of the cognitive science approach has generated some dissatisfaction. For example, some complaints have arisen that the cognitive science approach has led to an overemphasis upon cognition and has neglected motivation and deemphasized the affective components.

Educational technology has been traditionally considered as a change agent in educational development and design, but it has currently fallen behind other fields and disciplines. Little attention has been given by educational technologists to such frontier research areas as neuroscience, linguistics, artificial intelligence, and to bringing about a closer relationship between educational technology and semiotics, art, literature and music. Novel sources of knowledge (such as from Eastern religions) may in the future give rise to new paradigms in educational technology. Some might pose the question, "Where does one stop?" Perhaps the discipline does not stop, but continues to explore.

Some have already begun their explorations in their search for new, exciting paradigms in educational technology. For example, Guellette sees the emergency of what he calls *psychotechnology*.[58] Psychotechnology will focus on the management and control of the psychological processes of the learner and may include such supporting learning strategies as anxiety reduction, biofeedback, meditation, music, relaxation training, and yoga. Hlynka and Belland[59] have brought together a collection of critical readings from such divergent areas as semiotics and qualitative methodologies to explore their appropriateness for educational technology.

Messer, et al.[60] describe an interpretative or *hermeneutic* approach which has important implications for educational technology. The hermeneutic approach "insists upon the inseparability of fact and value, detail and context, and observation and theory" and "seeks less to generate universal laws than to understand the specific case in its historical and cultural context."[61] Moreover, this approach proposes methodological alternatives to the narrowly defined scientific approach of the behavioral sciences.

The educational technology of the next century may be totally different in terms of its methodology and outlook.[62] Other exploration will be made in the years ahead. The possibilities seem endless.

Notes

[1]C. Mitcham, "Philosophy and the History of Technology," in George Bugliarello and Dean B. Doner, eds., *The History and Philosophy of Technology*. Urbana, Ill.: University of Illinois Press, 163-201.

[2]Martin Heidegger, *The Question Concerning Technology* (translated and with an introduction by William Lovitt). New York: Harper & Row, 1977, 3-35.

[3]Lynn White, Jr., *Medieval Technology and Social Change*. London: Oxford University Press, 1964, 69.

[4]Ibid., 76.

[5]*New York Times*, November 22, 1988. B 7.

[6]Emile Durkheim, *The Division of Labor in Society* (translated by G. Simpson). New York: Free Press, 1933.

[7]Bernard Gendron, *Technology and the Human Condition*. New York: St. Martin's, 1977, 23.

[8]Lewis Mumford, *Technics and Civilization*. New York: Harcourt, Brace and World, 1963.

[9]M. W. Keatinge, *The Great Didactic of John Amos Comenius*, 2 vols. London: A & C Black, 1921.

[10]*Tabula rasa*—blank tablet—means there are no innate ideas. Locke was convinced that not only is the mind empty at birth, but also any ideas that one holds must have come originally through one's senses. See J. Locke, *Some Thoughts Concerning Education* (with introduction and notes by the Rev. R. H. Quick). 2d ed., Cambridge: The University Press, 1889.

[11]R. Freeman Butts, *A Cultural History of Education*. New York: McGraw-Hill, 1947.

[12]Jean-Jacques Rousseau, *Emile* (translated by B. Foxley). New York: Dutton, 1911.

[13]Johann F. Herbart, *Outlines of Educational Doctrine* (translated by A. F. Lange). New York: Macmillan, 1901.

[14]Maria Montessori, *The Montessori Method* (translated by A. E. George with introduction by H. W. Holmes). New York: Frederick A. Stokes, 1912.

[15]James Sully, *Teacher's Handbook of Psychology*. New York: D. Appleton, 1886.

[16]Donald P. Ely, "Educational Technology as Instructional Design," *Educational Technology*, 8 (January 1968), 4-6.

[17]Donald P. Ely, "The Definition of Educational Technology: An Emerging Stability," *Educational Considerations*, 10 (Spring 1983), 2-4.

[18]Robert M. Gagnè, ed., *Instructional Technology Foundations*. Hillsdale, N.J.: Lawrence Erlbaum, 1987, 3.

[19]Robert Heinich, et al., *Instructional Media and the New Technologies of Instruction*, 3d ed. New York: Macmillan, 1989, 24.

[20]John K. Galbraith, *The New Industrial State*. Boston: Houghton Mifflin, 1967, 12.

[21]A report by the Commission on Instructional Technology, *To Improve Learning*, vols. 1 and 2 (edited by S. G. Tickton). New York: R. R. Bowker Co., 1970, 21.

[22]Ibid., 21.

[23]Ibid., 8.

[24]Larry Cuban, *Teachers and Machines.* New York: Teachers College Press, 1986, 4.

[25]Margaret Gillett, *Educational Technology: Toward Demystification.* Scarborough, Ontario: Prentice-Hall of Canada, 1973, 2.

[26]A Report of the Carnegie Commission on Education, *The Fourth Revolution: Instructional Technology in Higher Education.* New York: McGraw-Hill, 1972.

[27]Walter A. Wittich and Charles F. Schuller, *Instructional Technology: Its Nature and Use.* New York: Harper & Row, 1979.

[28]Association for Educational Communications and Technology, *The Definition of Educational Technology.* Washington, D.C.: AECT, 1977, 1.

[29]See Thomas Kuhn, *The Structure of Scientific Revolutions,* 2d ed. Chicago, Ill.: University of Chicago Press, 1970.

[30]Those who support the abstract theoretical notion do not always make it clear that in denouncing verbalism they are not necessarily claiming to have found a superior alternative to verbal communication. A few extremists have, in fact, expressed the hope that media specialists might develop a completely nonverbal language for the purpose of exact communication. The very idea reflects the conception that so-called nonverbal media offer a true alternative to either written or spoken communication and can, therefore, be used as substitutes for written and spoken communication. An organization known as the International Visual Literacy Association, for example, reflects this nonverbal bias. See R. A. Braden, et al., eds., *About Visuals: Research, Teaching and Applications.* Readings from the 20th Annual Conference of the International Visual Literacy Association. Blacksburg, Va.: Virginia Tech University, 1989.

[31]See, for example, J. J. Weber, *Visual Aids in Education.* Valparaiso, Ind.: Valparaiso University, 1930; C. F. Hoban, et al., *Visualizing the Curriculum.* New York: Dryden Press, 1937; and Edgar Dale, *Audio-Visual Methods in Teaching.* New York: Dryden Press, 1954.

[32]See Donald P. Ely, ed., "The Changing Role of the Audiovisual Process in Education: A Definition and a Glossary of Related Terms" (TDP monograph 1), *AV Communication Review,* 11 (January/February 1963), supplement 6.

[33]It is unclear who first used the term *educational technology.* We have documented evidence that Franklin Bobbitt and W. W. Charters used *educational engineering* in the early 1920s. This author first heard *educational technology* used by W. W. Charters in an interview with this author in 1948. This author used *educational technology* in a seminar paper at the University of Southern California in 1949. The late James D. Finn used *instructional technology* in a foreword he wrote for the first publication of the NEA-sponsored Technological Development Project in 1963. However, the focus of this publication was *audiovisual communications.* As late as 1965, it was still unclear whether the new name for the NEA Department of Audiovisual Instruction (DAVI) should be *audiovisual instruction, learning resources, educational communications* or *instructional technology.* None of these names were ultimately chosen. *Audiovisual Communications* became the accepted new name. However, instructional technology began to be thought of as a subset of educational technology that is concerned with the total process of education.

[34]A vivid example of the potency of the media concept of educational technology can be seen in the report to the United States Secretary of Education by the National Task Force on Educational Technology, in which educational technology is equated with hardware or media. Throughout this report, the word *technology* is used repeatedly to mean media and, particularly, computers. Since most of the task force members were representatives of the computer industry, it is not difficult to understand why this report was focused on computers as the primary media in instruction. See "Transforming American Education: Reducing the Risk to the Nation," a report to the Secretary of Education by the National Task Force on Educational Technology, in *TechTrends,* 31 (May/June 1986), 11-24.

[35]Donald P. Ely, "The Definition of Educational Technology: An Emerging Stability," *Educational Considerations*, 10 (Spring 1983), 2.

[36]See J. Ball and F. C. Byrnes, *Research, Principles and Practice in Visual Communication*. Washington, D.C.: Department of Audiovisual Instruction, 1960.

[37]See Don Berlo, *The Process of Communication*. New York: Holt, Rinehart and Winston, 1960.

[38]Ely, "The Changing Role," 18-19.

[39]See Sidney Eboch, "The AV Specialist: Some Reflections on an Image," *Audiovisual Instruction*, 8 (January 1963), 15-17.

[40]Ely, "The Changing Role," 24-27.

[41]Ibid., 25.

[42]Robert Heinich, *The Systems Engineering of Education II: Application of Systems Thinking to Instruction*. Los Angeles: University of Southern California, Instructional Technology and Media Project, 1965, 4.

[43]Association for Educational Communications and Technology, *Educational Technology: Definition and Glossary of Terms*, vol. 1. Washington, D.C.: AECT, 1977.

[44]Ernest R. Hilgard, ed., *Theories of Learning and Instruction*. 63rd National Society for the Study of Education Yearbook. Chicago: University of Chicago Press, 1964, 407.

[45]Ibid., 490-510.

[46]Ibid., 410.

[47]Bernard Berelson, ed., *The Behavioral Sciences Today*. New York: Basic Books, 1963, 2-3.

[48]The expression *behavioral science* reflects the emphasis on behavior in the early 1950s even though all psychologists and biological and social scientists were not necessarily committed to behaviorism. J. G. Miller, then at the University of Chicago, introduced the term in 1949 and it became the name of the Committee on the Behavioral Sciences there, which he chaired from 1952 to 1955.
    There is some confusion whether one should refer to "behavioral science" or "behavioral sciences." When one speaks of an approach, the singular term may be appropriate. Most writers refer to the behavioral sciences in the plural because true unification of the behavioral sciences is still an unattained goal. With the present state of our knowledge and lack of synthesis, the plural term, as in the case of the social sciences, seems more appropriate and will be so used in this book.

[49]See John B. Watson, *Psychology from the Standpoint of a Behaviorist*, 2d ed. Philadelphia: Lippincott, 1924; and B. F. Skinner, *The Technology of Teaching*. New York: Appleton-Century-Crofts, 1968.

[50]B. F. Skinner, *Contingencies of Reinforcement*. New York: Appleton-Century-Crofts, 1969.

[51]Skinner, *The Technology of Teaching*, 158.

[52]Ibid., 5, 33.

[53]See John R. Anderson, *Cognitive Psychology and Its Implications*. New York: W. H. Freeman and Co., 1985.

[54]Merlin C. Wittrock, "The Cognitive Movement in Instruction," *Educational Researcher*, 8 (February 1979), 5.

[55]See R. R. Schmeck, ed., *Learning Strategies and Learning Styles*. New York: Plenum Press, 1988.

[56]See David Jonassen, "Learning Strategies: A New Educational Technology," *Programmed Learning and Educational Technology* 22, 1, 26-34.

[57]Martin Tessmer and David Jonassen, "Learning Strategies: A New Instructional Technology," in D. Harris, ed., *Education for the New Technologies*. World Yearbook of Education 1988. London: Kogan Page, 1988, 44.

[58]D. Guellette, "Psychotechnology as Instructional Technology: Systems for a Deliberate Change in Consciousness." Paper presented at the annual meeting of the AECT, Atlanta, Ga., 1987.

[59]D. Hlynka and J. Belland, *Educational Technology: The Critical View* (in press).

[60]Stanley Messer, et al., eds., *Hermeneutics and Psychological Theory*. New Brunswick, N.J.: Rutgers University Press, 1988, xiv.

[61]Ibid.

[62]A number of current deficiencies in educational technology have been addressed by physiologists, biologists, and philosophers. Two eminent physiologists, Eccles and Sperry, have both recently stressed values as the principal determinants of human behavior. Among biologists, Thorpe and J. Z. Young have struck similar notes, while particularly notable among philosophical contributions has been the work of Susan Langer's *Mind: An Essay in Human Feeling*, in which she defends the thesis that feeling is the starting point of a philosophy of mind. There is, in fact, a whole dimension of mind, rooted in feeling, culminating in value, and intimately related to motivation and learning, that educational technology has ignored. See J. C. Eccles, *The Human Mystery*. Berlin: Springer, 1979; R. Sperry, *Science and Moral Priority*. Oxford: Blackwell, 1983; W. H. Thorpe, *Purpose in a World of Chance: A Biologist's View*. Oxford: Oxford University Press, 1978; J. Z. Young, *Programs of the Brain*. Oxford: Oxford University Press, 1978; and Susan Langer, *Mind: An Essay on Human Feeling*. 3 vols. Baltimore, Md.: Johns Hopkins University Press, 1967.

Select Bibliography

Glossaries are listed in this bibliography for assistance in understanding technical terms in the field. Each glossary listed is marked by an asterisk. This list is not exhaustive, but is selected on the basis of general value, availability, or special interest, and appears only once in the book.

Association for Educational Communications and Technology. *The Definition of Educational Technology*. Washington, D.C.: AECT, 1977.

*Association for Educational Communications and Technology. *Educational Technology: A Glossary of Terms*. Washington, D.C.: AECT, 1979.

Bailyn, Bernard. *Education in the Forming of American Society*. New York: W. W. Norton, 1960.

Barthes, Roland. *The Semiotic Challenge*, tr. Richard Howard. New York: Hill and Wang, 1988.

Berger, Charles R., and Steven H. Chaffee, eds. *Handbook of Communication Science*. Beverly Hills, Calif.: Sage Publications, 1987.

*Blisher, E., ed. *Encyclopedia of Education*. New York: Philosophical Library, 1970.

Brubacher, John S. *A History of the Problems of Education*. New York: McGraw-Hill, 1947.

Bugliarello, George, and Dean B. Doners, eds. *The History and Philosophy of Technology*. Urbana, Ill.: University of Illinois Press, 1979.

Butts, R. Freeman. *A Cultural History of Education*. New York: McGraw-Hill, 1947.

Butts, R. Freeman, and Lawrence C. Cremin. *A History of Education in American Culture.* New York: Henry Holt, 1953.

Cantrell, Zita M., and Hortense A. Doyle, eds. *Instructional Technology: An Annotated Bibliography.* Metuchen, N.J.: Scarecrow Press, 1974.

Commission on Instructional Technology. *To Improve Learning.* Report to the President and the Congress of the United States. Washington, D.C.: GPO, 1970.

Cubberley, Ellwood P. *Public Education in the United States.* Boston: Houghton Mifflin, 1934.

*Dejnozka, Edward L. *Educational Administration Glossary.* Westport, Conn.: Greenwood Press, 1983.

*Ellington, H., and D. Harris, eds. *Dictionary of Instructional Technology.* New York: Nicholas, 1986.

Ellsbree, Willard S. *The American Teacher.* New York: American Book Co., 1939.

*Ely, Donald P., ed. "The Changing Role of the Audiovisual Process in Education: A Definition and a Glossary of Related Terms." TDP Monograph No. 1. *AV Communication Review* vol. 11, no. 1, supplement no. 6 (January/February 1963).

*Heinich, Robert, et al. *Instructional Media and the New Technologies of Instruction*, 3d ed. New York: Macmillan, 1989.

Hilgard, Ernest R. *Psychology in America: A Historical Survey.* New York: Harcourt Brace Jovanovich, 1987.

*Hills, P. J., ed. *A Dictionary of Education.* Boston: Routledge and Kegan Paul, 1982.

Knight, Edgar W. *Education in the United States*, 3d rev. ed. Boston: Ginn, 1951.

Kuhn, Thomas. *The Structure of Scientific Revolutions.* Chicago: University of Chicago Press, 1962.

Moore, E. C. *The Story of Instruction: The Beginnings.* New York: Macmillan, 1936.

Mumford, Lewis. *The Myth of the Machine: Technics and Human Development.* New York: Harcourt, Brace and World, 1967.

_____. *Technics and Civilization.* New York: Harcourt, Brace and World, 1963.

*National Center for Educational Statistics, Educational Technology. *A Handbook of Standard Terminology and a Guide for Recording and Reporting Information about Educational Technology. Handbook X.* Washington, D.C.: GPO, 1975.

Noble, Stuart G. *A History of American Education.* New York: Farrar and Rinehart, 1938.

Reisner, E. H. *The Evolution of the Common School.* New York: Macmillan, 1930.

Saettler, Paul. *An Assessment of the Current Status of Educational Technology.* Syracuse, N.Y.: ERIC Clearinghouse on Information Resources, Syracuse University, 1979.

Tylor, Edward B. *Researches into the Early History of Mankind and the Development of Civilization.* Chicago: University of Chicago Press, 1964.

*Unwin, Derick, and Ray McAleese. *The Encyclopedia of Educational Media Communications and Technology*, 2d ed. New York: Greenwood Press, 1988.

Winner, Langdon. *Autonomous Technology.* Cambridge, Mass.: MIT Press, 1977.

*Wolman, Benjamin B., ed. *Dictionary of Behavioral Sciences*, 2d ed. New York: Academic Press, 1989.

Part II
Heritage of Theoretical Thought and Practice: 450 B.C. to 1950

Part II provides a broad historical perspective to evaluate the significance of distinct theoretical and instructional methodologies and their impact on the mainstream of American educational technology.

2

Early Forerunners: Before 1900

The forerunners of educational technology can be seen in the polychromatic, lifelike bison sketched in the deep recesses of cave walls by Cro-Magnon artists. These animal paintings, often of astonishing precision and beauty, were Totemistic in the sense that they constituted a symbolic magic for the primitive hunter. But, aside from this function, these paintings marked the first step in man's need and desire to communicate.[1]

Primitive children were taught to observe, imitate, and participate in activities vital to the survival of the tribe. Dramatization and demonstration of tribal arts and skills constituted an essential part of their instruction. The oral tradition emphasized memory and training, and continued to be the primary method of instruction even after the development of a simplified and flexible alphabet led to the spread of writing and reading. The more advanced the culture, the more complex became the technology of instruction. The aim of each age or society has been to find the basic skills or subject content which offer promise of transfering cultural heritage to learner behavior. Each significant shift in cultural values over the centuries has led to new theories of knowledge and learning and to new technologies of instruction.

Methods Foreshadowing
Modern Educational Technology

Although historical instructional methods were not based on science as we understand it, they embodied many concepts that influenced the thinking, language, method, research, and development of subsequent methods or technologies. For example, some early educators (the Sophists) were aware of the problems associated with perception, motivation, individual differences, and evaluation and recognized that different instructional strategies achieved different behavioral outcomes. What is more, they analyzed modes of effective instruction and made hypotheses to take into account the factors disclosed by their analyses, just as current researchers do.

The major difference between such early inquiries and those of contemporary research lies in the invention and refinement of modern research instruments and scientific design. Even with these advances, however, we have taken only the first tentative steps toward the development of a mature science and technology of instruction.

Criteria Used to Select Educational Technology Antecedents

The choice of theoretical and methodological antecedents of educational technology for this chapter was guided mainly by two broad criteria. First, only the theories and methods of professional teachers were included, thus automatically eliminating the work of religious figures known as "great teachers" and nonteaching philosophers such as Rousseau and Locke who, nevertheless, influenced the educational practices of others. The second, and most important, criterion was to identify the most distinctive instructional techniques that were key precursors of a modern science and technology of instruction.

The Elder Sophists: Ancestors of Educational Technology

The Elder Sophists, a small group of peripatetic teachers drawn to Athens during the last half of the fifth century B.C., were probably the first instructional technologists.[2] We know that there were five Elder Sophists: Protagoras of Abdera (ca.500-410 B.C.), Gorgias of Leontini (ca.485-380 B.C.), Prodikos of Ceos, Hippias, and Thrasymachus.

The Sophists never formed a school in the institutional sense, but rather operated as freelance teachers in competition with each other, accepting fees for their work.[3] Since it was not customary to accept payment for teaching in those days, they persuaded the public to purchase their skills by resorting to publicity stunts such as donning purple robes or making proclamations from a throne. Plato referred to the Sophist as a "paid hunter of the young ... a sort of trader in intellectual disciplines of the soul"; yet in his dialogue *Protagoras*, Plato attested to the Sophists' fame in a scene in which young Hippocrates rouses Socrates from sleep to tell him that Protagoras has just arrived in Athens, and that the great Sophist teacher must be persuaded without delay to accept Hippocrates as a student.[4]

Typically, a Sophist demonstration took one of three forms: a carefully prepared lecture, an extemporized lecture on a subject suggested by a member of the audience, or a free debate with another Sophist or some other person on a subject chosen by the audience. Once he had obtained students, the Sophist taught by a modified tutorial system.[5] For the first time, the relationship was not between a tutor and a single disciple, but between a teacher and a group of pupils. This was the first recorded instance of mass instruction.

Sophist Theory

The Elder Sophists belonged to the pre-Socratic-Promethean liberal tradition in Greek thought. The basic tenets were:

1. Man evolves through technology and social organization to a state of civilization where he can guide his affairs effectively.

2. This evolutionary process is continuous. Morality and law evolve and are accepted because they have survival value, and derive their sanction from social consensus, not from a priori absolute principles or from divine authority.

3. History is a slow but forward progress in the management of human affairs, neither cyclical nor regressive.

4. Society should be democratic and egalitarian.

5. The theory of knowledge is progressive, pragmatic, empirical, and behavioristic.[6]

Not every Sophist expounded all these views, but all of them built on this common liberal tradition, which was condemned by Plato in his dialogues.

The Sophist believed all men were capable of intelligent, socially responsible self-rule, but that they could not achieve their potential without education. Plato, on the other hand, believed all men were destined for either a low or high social position, for subservience or leadership. In contrast to Plato's belief that virtue could not be taught and only aristocrats might be depended upon for right action, the Sophists believed in the value of teaching virtue and of defending a just cause. Plato also differed with the Sophists on the value of *techne* (technology). The Sophists honored all technology, which included both statecraft and handicraft, whereas Plato believed technology was unworthy of gentlemen and had no place in their education. The beginnings of the rift between culture and religion in ancient Greek education can be located in the age of the Sophists.

Instructional Method

The Sophists undertook to teach the art of politics and develop political *arête* — that is, the excellence of the individual human being in relation to an ideal that could be realized in a democratic community. This *arête*, for them, was primarily intellectual power and oratorical ability. To develop these skills was

> clearly the systematic expression of the principle of shaping the intellect, because it begins by instruction in the form of language, the form of oratory, and the form of thought. This educational technique is one of the greatest discoveries which the mind of man has ever made: it was not until it explored these three of its activities that the mind apprehended the hidden law of its own structure.[7]

Although the instructional methods of individual Sophists varied, all used the expository lecture and "Sophistic dialogue," or group discussion method (probably invented by Protagoras) of solving problems.[8] The lecture and group discussion techniques were combined by Protagoras into a third method applicable specifically in political activities, but which can also be considered an instructional technique. This technique is defined by Havelock as "the antithetical formulation of public positions and the setting of party lines which took place in any parliament or assembly where power was at stake and public policy was made."[9]

The Sophists probably invented and developed the technique of analysis in teaching of rhetoric. By analyzing exemplary models of writing and speaking, they formulated rules for effective writing and speaking. Rhetoric was the chief subject of Sophistic instruction for two reasons: (1) In ancient Greece the oral tradition reigned supreme, and (2) the Sophists found rhetoric the most effective technique for transmitting practical knowledge.

In teaching rhetoric, they combined theory and application. First, the Sophist taught his students the rules (theory) of the spoken and written word. Then he prepared a model speech for them to copy, analyze, discuss, and present in actual spoken practice. The model discourse was often on a poetic, moral, or political subject, although sometimes a fantastic subject, such as a eulogy of mice or peacocks, was used to demonstrate pure virtuosity. The final objective was not precise imitation of the model, but the development of virtuosity and the skill to use alternative formulas and accurately judge the relative merits of each according to the differing demands of each situation (application).

However, Sophist instruction was not confined to formal aspects of rhetoric. Their goal was a "polymath," a man who possessed universal competence and knowledge in every field. Consequently, Sophist instruction was a combination of form and content. The technique of applied analysis was used to formulate whole bodies of cognitive rules in various fields: geography, natural history, logic, history, painting, drawing, music, religion, sculpture, and athletics. They also evolved a branch of rhetoric devoted to ideas. Their analytical approach enabled them to develop a rather sophisticated technology of instruction that combined rhetoric with eristic (the art of disputation).

Because Sophist procedures were inherently systematic, the student always knew what was expected of him, how he might achieve his goals, and how well he was progressing. And although Sophist methods have often been considered formal and rigid, they possessed a certain amount of flexibility in that the student could choose from a variety of formulas or modes of action for application to practical situations.

Influence of the Sophists

The Sophists had enormous influence on subsequent instruction and courses of study. Their use of rhetoric, dialectic, and grammar dominated the design of the "quadrivium" and the "trivium" (the seven liberal arts, as they came to be called), which made up the curriculum of European education for a thousand years to come.[10]

Before Plato overthrew the educational success of the Sophists and became the chief influence in the Western world, the Sophists offered a bold solution to a difficult problem that has still not been satisfactorily resolved.[11] It is the current problem explored by Snow in *The Two Cultures and the Scientific Revolution*: One culture is presumed to be inhabited by people of science and another, separate, culture by people of letters. Yet, as Snow shows, science and technology do not necessarily deny art, any more than art or any of the humanities denies science.[12] The Sophist solution was to combine the two cultures in a single concept, *techne*, or technology; this is the Sophist legacy.

The Socratic Method

Socrates (470-399 B.C.) left no writings; all we know of his teaching was gleaned from the works of his students, Plato and Xenophon. In contrast to the relativism of the Sophists, Socrates sought to understand the nature of virtue as a guide to moral conduct. Perhaps his most important educational contribution was the so-called Socratic method of instruction (inquiry). The inquiry was carried on through the give-and-take of conversation, which Socrates guided by a series of leading questions. In the Socratic method, the questioner used only those facts already known to the pupil. If the pupil had to collect data in order to reach a new conclusion, the teacher had strayed from the original Socratic technique.

A dramatic example of the Socratic method is described in Plato's *Meno*. Socrates, at random, selected a boy off the street and by clever questioning led him to demonstrate a geometrical theorem despite the fact that the boy had no previous mathematical training. This story has led some current leaders in the programmed instruction movement to mistakenly claim Socrates as their educational forefather. The Socratic method was predicated, however, on the principle that knowledge is inborn and can be brought out by means of skillful questioning. Since the reinforcement schedule of the programmed text or machine is usually based on an entirely different principle (stimulus-response association), it is incorrect to claim Socrates as the forerunner of programmed instruction.

Abelard: Precursor of Scholastic Method of Instruction

Scholasticism, an intellectual movement that flourished in Europe during the twelfth and thirteenth centuries, was a vitally productive and effective method of instruction. Its name was derived from the medieval term *doctor scholasticus*, which referred to authorized teachers in monastic or cathedral schools, for these teachers, best exemplified by Pierre Abelard,[13] developed the distinctive methods of philosophical speculation that are associated with scholasticism—ultimately transforming some of these schools into universities, especially in the north of Europe.

Abelard Shapes the Pattern of Scholastic Instructional Method

The basic characteristics of the scholastic method were established by Abelard when he taught at the Notre Dame cathedral school (which became the University of Paris in 1180). By training his theology students in Aristotelian logical analysis, Abelard helped to transform theology from the mere citing of authorities into the interpretation of Scripture. His method was best represented by his famous book *Sic et Non* (Yes and No), wherein he presented the pros and cons of theological and philosophical propositions, leaving the formulation of conclusions to his students. Abelard allowed any subject or thought to be reasonably examined for the purpose of understanding, verification, or qualification. This method shocked many of his colleagues, who felt that Abelard gave his students the freedom to arrive at heretical conclusions.

Elements of Abelard's Method

In *Sic et Non* Abelard formulated 158 questions about the Trinity, Redemption, and the Sacraments. He placed the views of the authorities in one column and the opposite views in another column. His instructional procedure in reaching reconciliation was as follows:

1. The statements had to be read and studied in context to determine whether they were contradictory. Before the contexts could be fully considered, some historical research was usually required of either the teacher or other scholars.

2. Textual distortions were to be discovered and corrected. The necessary textual and criticism skills were a knowledge of etymology, grammatical form, and linguistics.

3. The next step was to judge the real meaning of each statement. Authorities could be consulted at this stage.

4. A final check was made to ensure that there was no later change by the authority of the cited passages on record.

5. Finally, an inquiry was made to discover the circumstances that led to the writing of the statements.

6. If contradictions still remained, the student could reach one of two conclusions: (a) this was a mystery to be believed, or (b) a theory was needed that could encompass both views, each of which was but a partial aspect of the truth.[14]

Influence of Abelard on Lombard and Aquinas

Abelard's method directly influenced Peter Lombard (1100-1160) and St. Thomas Aquinas (1225-1274), his successors at Paris. Lombard, a former student of Abelard, modeled his famous textbook *The Sentences* on *Sic et Non*; but for every question he posed, he was careful to supply the correct, orthodox response. As a result, Lombard's method was more generally accepted because of its less controversial approach.

The final technique of instruction that was widely employed by many generations of scholars was the scholastic method as developed by St. Thomas Aquinas. According to Aquinas, the proper instructional approach was to teach the student how to acquire knowledge using syllogisms. In his *Summa Theologiae*, Aquinas, like Abelard, introduced material in the form of questions, then proceeded, through a series of syllogisms, to propose the solutions. A thesis was formulated, the proof was given, objections were raised and refuted; the whole proposition was treated in a minutely logical procedure.

Influence of the Scholastic Method

Without question, Abelard deserves an important place among the forerunners of modern educational technology. His greatest achievement was the development and popularization of the scholastic method.[15]

It may be argued that Abelard's scholastic method degenerated into a cumbersome formalism in which Aristotelian logic became hopelessly ossified. But this instructional method played an important role in the rise of European universities and helped lay the groundwork for the later system of scientific inquiry and experimentation. Confronted with a mass of traditional and irrational doctrines, the medieval teacher used the scholastic method to examine ideas in a systematic and rational manner.

A Method of Instruction According to Comenius

Johann Amos Comenius (1592-1670) was born to modest, Protestant (Moravian Brethren) parents in Moravia (now a part of Czechoslovakia) and attended the Protestant universities of Herborn and Heidelberg in Germany.[16] As a Moravian pastor and teacher, Comenius spent a long, itinerant life in Poland, Hungary, Sweden, England, and Holland — due primarily to the disruptions of the Thirty Years' War (1618-1648) between the Catholics and the Protestants.

His period of greatest educational productivity began in 1627 at the Polish town of Leszno where, as a teacher of Latin and rector of the Moravian Gymnasium, he began to write a series of remarkable textbooks.[17] Later he directed curriculum reforms in Holland and Sweden and organized a model school in Hungary.

Fig. 2.1. Portrait of Johann Amos Comenius.

Educational Theory

The *Great Didactic*, Comenius's most important theoretical treatise, dealt with every phase of instruction.[18] One of its recurrent themes was his idea of "pansophia," or a system of universal knowledge in which a methodical procedure could be applied to all problems of humankind.[19] Further, he recommended the establishment of a college of pansophy, or scientific research.

According to Comenius, Christian philosophy should not prevent examination of the human mind by methodical and empirical observation. Thus the theory underlying the instructional system of Comenius said that the goal of education was to be derived deductively using Christian philosophy; the instructional process had to be analyzed and improved inductively, according to science.

Comenius's educational aims were knowledge, morality, and piety. He regarded education as a means of preparing men to live as human beings rather than as a means of fitting them into a predetermined occupation or station. Moreover, he wanted to end the custom of providing education according to social status rather than ability. To achieve these broad aims, Comenius proposed a system open to all that led from the kindergarten through the university—an idea some three centuries ahead of its time.

Principles of Instructional Method

Among the great mass of instructional principles advocated by Comenius were the following:

1. Instructional method should follow the order of nature. Content should be studied according to the developmental stage of each learner.

2. Instruction should begin at infancy and be designed for the age, interest, and capacity of each learner.

3. Everything that is taught should have a practical application to life and possess some value for the learner.

4. Subject matter should be organized according to its difficulty. Instruction should proceed by the inductive process from the simple to the complex.

5. A graduated series of textbooks and illustrative materials should be correlated with instruction.

6. Sequence is important. For example, it is irrational to teach a foreign language before the native language has been learned.

7. General principles should be explained and examples given before rules are learned. Nothing should be memorized until it is understood.

8. Reading and writing should be taught together; subjects should be correlated whenever possible.

9. Learning is to be approached through the senses. Actual objects and things should be studied and associated with words.

10. Content should first be presented orally by the teacher and pictorially illustrated whenever possible.

11. All parts of an object (or subject matter) must be learned with reference to their order, position, and connection with one another; only one thing should be taught at any one time. (Comenius suggested outlining all the texts specified for use on the walls of the classroom so the learner could see the entire content to be studied.)

12. Corporal punishment should not be administered when a student fails to learn.

13. Schools must be cheerful, equipped with real and illustrative materials, and staffed with sympathetic teachers. (Something of the monitorial plan was latent in Comenius's system. He believed that it was possible for one teacher to instruct several hundred children at one time. After the general presentation by the teacher, the large group was to be divided into sections of ten for further drilling and reciting to small-group student leaders.)

It is evident from these instructional principles that Comenius was the first true forerunner of modern educational technology. By applying Bacon's inductive method to education, he anticipated, to a remarkable extent, the modern concept of educational technology as an applied science in support of the practical arts. It is unfortunate that during his lifetime he was never in a position to test his own pioneering principles for any extended period of time.

The *Orbus Pictus*: Application of the Method of Comenius

Perhaps the best example of an application of Comenius's method of instruction was his own *Orbus pictus* (The World in Pictures), published in Nuremburg in 1658. This illustrated, thoroughly planned, "visual aid" textbook was written specifically for children who were studying Latin and sciences. Although it has often been referred to (erroneously) as the first illustrated book of its kind, it has been without question the most popular illustrated textbook ever written for children.[20] The book was still being purchased in the United States as late as 1810.

Organized in a series of topics (e.g., God, world, air, trees, man, flowers, vegetables, metals, birds), the *Orbus pictus* was illustrated by 150 pictures, each serving as a topic for one lesson (see figure 2.2, page 32). Thus the teaching of Latin and the sciences was accomplished by associating objective reality, or its pictorial representations, with abstract cognate word symbols.

Influence of Comenius

For nearly two centuries, Comenius was generally unknown and had little direct effect on instructional theory or practice, except through his language methods texts. The *Orbus pictus* went through an almost unlimited number of editions in many languages and became the sole link to his work. When his other works were finally rediscovered in the middle of the nineteenth century, it became clear that he had been the greatest educator of his century. Many of his ideas have since been incorporated into contemporary instructional method.

(77)

The Taylor.   LXII.   Sartor.

The *Taylor*, 1. cutteth *Cloth*, 2. with *Shears*, 3. and seweth it together with a *Needle* and *double thread*, 4.

Then he presseth the *Seams* with a *Pressing-iron*, 5. And thus he maketh *Coats*, 6.

with *Plaits*, 7.

in which the *Border*, 8. is below with *Laces*, 9.

Cloaks, 10.

with a *Cape*, 11.

and *Sleeve Coats*, 12.

Doublets, 13.

with *Buttons*, 14.

and *Cuffs*, 15.

Breeches, 16.

sometimes with *Ribbons*, 17.

Stockins, 18.

Gloves, 19.

Sartor, 1. discindit *Pannum*, 2. *Forfice*, 3. consuitque *Acu* & *Filo duplicato*, 4.

Posteâ complanat *Suturas Ferramento*, 5.

Sicque conficit *Tunicas*, 6.

Plicatas, 7.

in quibus infra est *Fimbria*, 8. cum *Institis*, 9.

Pallia, 10.

cum *Patagio*, 11.

& *Togas Manicatas*, 12.

Thoraces, 13.

cum *Globulis*, 14.

& *Manicis*, 15.

Caligas, 16. aliquando cum *Lemniscis*, 17.

Tibialia, 18.

Chirothecas, 19.

Fig. 2.2. Page from the *Orbus pictus* of Comenius (From *The Orbus pictus of Johann Amos Comenius*. Syracuse, N.Y.: C. W. Bardeen, 1887.)

Status of Instructional Method in American Schools: Before 1800

Before continuing with our survey of the forerunners of educational technology, we will briefly examine instructional method in American schools prior to the nineteenth century.

Before 1800, instruction at both the elementary and secondary levels was predominantly individual. The principal method of the village schoolmaster consisted of calling one or several pupils to his desk to hear individual, memorized recitations. Developing understanding through inductive group discussions was unknown. When teaching writing, the teacher's primary concern was with whittling goose-quill pens and "setting copies" for pupils. Much instruction was superficial and impractical, and the school term was short (one to six months). Children sometimes attended school for years without progressing beyond a smattering of reading and writing skills. The teachers were generally incompetent and so relied on fear to motivate learners and keep order in the classroom.[21]

The buildings and equipment of early American schools, not to mention their instructional materials, were primitive. The typical one-room schoolhouse prior to 1800 was a log building, with one end usually occupied by a fireplace and the room's only window at the opposite end. Sticks were inserted between the logs that formed the walls and used to hold boards that served as desks. Backless benches made of split logs ran the entire length of the board desks.

The beginning of the nineteenth century brought little improvement in these conditions. Public and free schools were generally lacking outside the New England area, and even there conditions and facilities were wretched. Illiteracy prevailed among children of the poor, and conditions intensified with the development of industry, the breakdown of the apprenticeship system, and the rapid growth of American cities. "Free school societies" (such as the Public School Society of New York) were organized in some of the larger cities to try to cope with the problems of ignorance, poverty, and crime. These semipublic, philanthropic organizations later came to regard the so-called Lancasterian system as ideal, since it offered mass education at low cost. And as the public became increasingly aware of the desperate need for mass education, legislatures saw in monitorial schools a possible solution to the school-financing problem, which had to be solved before adequate public schools could be established. The introduction of the Lancasterian system, in fact, provided the basis for the eventual support of free public schools in the United States.

Lancasterian Monitorial Instruction

The wide success of a monitorial system of instruction in the first half of the nineteenth century was chiefly due to Joseph Lancaster (1778-1838) of England, whose unique manuals included details of classroom organization and economic management, as well as subject matter organized according to a graded plan for group instruction.[22] To aid in the implementation of his method, Lancaster studied the construction of special classrooms that would make the most effective use of instructional media and student grouping. He also explored the techniques of motivation. Although it appears questionable that Lancaster's method was rooted in any systematic theory of learning, he was probably influenced by Locke's theory of learning, which prevailed at the time.[23]

Economy of the Lancasterian System

Much of the popularity of the system was due to its low cost. For example, during the period when the Lancasterian plan was operating in New York City (1806-1853), the annual cost of instruction per child ranged from $1.37 to a maximum of $5.83. The system was also adopted in Pennsylvania, where legislators were unwilling to appropriate money for free education, except for the children of paupers. A particular aspect of Lancasterian economy may be noted in the ratio of pupils to teachers. In Philadelphia in 1819, there were 10 public Lancasterian schools with 10 teachers and 2,845 pupils, or 1 teacher per 284 pupils.

School buildings were constructed to accommodate hundreds of children in a series of large, undivided rooms, with careful attention paid to lighting, ventilation, seating, and acoustics. One 50-by-100-foot room could accommodate as many as 500 pupils, with a space of 10 square feet allotted to each. Slates, sand tables, wall charts, and blackboards saved paper, ink, and pens, and made fewer books necessary. By following the principle of mass instruction at low cost, the Lancasterian schools provided the only kind of instruction that could be hoped for in what were to become free schools during the latter part of the nineteenth century.

The Lancasterian Monitorial Method of Instruction

The Lancasterian plan provided a detailed, systematic method in the following six areas: instruction (memorization and drill) and a body of content, monitor training, control, grouping, testing, and administration. Under an efficient scheme of classroom management, one teacher taught a group of fifty head pupils, or monitors, who, in turn, each drilled ten other pupils. Thus, one teacher was able to take charge of five hundred or more students at one time.[24]

In the teaching of arithmetic, for example, Lancaster had the following plan. The basis of progress was founded on a thorough knowledge of the multiplication tables. As each new rule was introduced, the examples were at first short and easy, then increased in length and difficulty as the ability of the learner increased. Each class worked a group of sample problems over and over until they could solve the problems with facility. When teaching a new rule, the monitor first dictated an example, then worked it out while the pupils copied the process on their slates. Then the slates were cleaned and examples were written on the blackboard; each pupil, in turn, solved a sample problem.[25]

The results of the Lancasterian method, when contrasted with the one-room school method of individual recitation, were revolutionary. In fact, Salmon relates an incident in which an anxious parent protested to his pastor against the practices of the monitorial school, because he was convinced that the rapid progress of his son in arithmetic resulted from an evil magic being employed by the school.[26]

Fig. 2.3. A monitorial school, 1839 (Courtesy of Pestalozzi Foundation of New York.)

Pupils were grouped according to ability, which meant a pupil might recite with one group in reading or spelling and with another group in some other subject. Economy of time was also achieved in the Lancasterian school routine. For example, to avoid calling the roll of the entire school in order to discover who was absent, each pupil was given a number, and corresponding numbers were printed in a row on the wall. The class was marked into position, each pupil took his place beneath his number, and the vacant numbers immediately indicated the absentees.

Use of Instructional Materials

Ingenuity was refreshingly displayed in the use of instructional media. For example, a thin layer of sand was spread on each desk for writing practice. The learner wrote with a pointed stick and made erasures by passing a long straight stick across the sand. This procedure was designed to save ink and paper. The text of a speller or some other book was sometimes printed in large letters and hung on the schoolroom wall, in order that one volume could serve an entire class. Through the use of slates, hundreds of learners wrote and spelled the same word at the same time, and when reciting, groups of ten gathered around the monitors.

Assessment of the Lancasterian System

As we have seen, the Lancasterian schools were not only economical but also effective, particularly when compared to the prevailing, primitive instructional conditions of the times. Influenced by Lancaster's methods, American schools began to adopt centralized management practices, improve instructional media, develop more systematic approaches to instruction, and recognize the need for trained teachers. The system was praised by such men as Governor DeWitt Clinton of New York; Governor Oliver Wolcott of Connecticut; William Russell, editor of the first *American Journal of Education*; and John Griscom, noted scientist and educator. Governor Clinton stated in 1809:

> When I perceive that many boys in our school have been taught to read and write in two months, who did not before know the alphabet, and that even one has accomplished it in three weeks—when I view all the bearings and tendencies of this system—when I contemplate the habits of order which it forms, the spirit of emulation which it excites, the rapid improvement which it produces, the purity of morals which it inculcates—when I behold the extraordinary union of celerity in instruction and economy of expense—and when I perceive one great assembly of a thousand children, under the eye of a single teacher marching with unexampled rapidity and with perfect discipline to the goal of knowledge, I confess that I recognize in Lancaster the benefactor of the human race. I consider his system as creating a new era in education, as a blessing sent down from heaven to redeem the poor and distressed of this world from the power and dominion of ignorance.[27]

Likewise, a prominent educator of the time, William Russell strongly favored the system and even edited a *Manual of Mutual Instruction* (1826), which contained directions for organizing instruction according to the Lancasterian plan and encouraged its adoption in the colleges.

The monitorial method solved a great educational emergency in the United States, but it was clearly mechanical and lacked a systematic psychology of learning. Furthermore, it encouraged the development of narrow, supposedly practical rules of thumb, which were to be used as instructional method for teacher education in the newly established normal schools. Under the monitorial influence, method became a set of standardized techniques for handling large numbers of children at one time. This practice-centered approach lacked theoretical unity and was utterly separated from a recognizable theory of learning. Lancasterian schools do, however, deserve to be called forerunners of modern instructional technology, because they introduced order and system into instructional method in American schools.[28] Indeed, their impact on subsequent educational practices, although negative in many respects, would be difficult to overemphasize. For example, in 1891, Gordy pointed out two misconceptions of the monitorial method that had not yet disappeared from teacher training: (1) that teaching is imparting knowledge; and (2) that all that is necessary to teach is simply to possess the knowledge to be taught.[29] Even today one can discover such views in much of the rationale voiced by critics of teacher education.[30]

The practice and influence of the Lancasterian system began to wane by the middle of the nineteenth century as increased financial resources enabled the people to support free public education. Moreover, the inherent defects of the Lancasterian method became more apparent as the psychological systems of Pestalozzi and, later, Froebel and Herbart were more widely implemented.

Pestalozzi and His "Psychologizing" of Instructional Method

Johann Heinrich Pestalozzi (1746-1827) developed a comprehensive system of instruction based on the educational theories expounded by Jean Jacques Rousseau (1712-1778) in his *Emile*.[31] Born in Zurich, Switzerland, Pestalozzi attended the university there to prepare himself first for the pulpit and later for law. Then, discouraged by legal conservatism and profoundly influenced by Rousseau's ideas, he decided to undertake what was to become a historic series of educational experiments. These began (1774-1780) with waifs he gathered at his home (Neuhof), near the village of Birrfield, and continued in his experimental schools at Stanz (1798), Burgdorf (1799-1804), and Yverdon (1805-1825), where he did his most significant work.

Educational Theory

Pestalozzi said, "I wish to psychologize instruction," by which he meant that he wished to organize instruction in accordance with what he believed were the laws of natural human development.[32] He felt that the moral, intellectual, and physical powers of each learner would develop, according to natural laws, in successively widening circles of experience. To Pestalozzi, this development of the learner was the supreme objective; he believed it could be accomplished by constant emphasis on sensory impression. "The most essential point from which I start is this: Sense impression of Nature is the only foundation of human instruction, because it is the only true foundation of human knowledge."[33]

Pestalozzi believed it vital for instruction to follow the stages of natural human development: It must begin with the simplest elements, advancing gradually in a series of steps connected with the learner's psychological development. Thus, Pestalozzi recognized that learners have individual differences, and saw the necessity for instructional methods that functioned with the learner as a whole. Although sensory instruction became Pestalozzi's chief method, he accepted the theory of separate faculties. As we have seen, exercising the faculties was often considered more important than acquiring knowledge. Ironically, however, Pestalozzi's followers began to concentrate on the formal discipline of the senses, similar to the formal training of the faculties undertaken by the classicists.

Fig. 2.4. Johann H. Pestalozzi.

Instructional Method

The reform of instruction had been anticipated by Comenius, who predicated his method on nature and the senses and insisted on moving from concrete to abstract concepts. But with the exception of Comenius's instructional methods, Francke's *Realschule*, and Basedow's *Philanthropinum*, little had been done to implement these insights in the classroom until Pestalozzi began his educational experiments.[34] Briefly, Pestalozzi's method focused on providing content to ideas through firsthand experience and giving significance to individual expression by means of ideas. He simplified the complicated process of cognition by giving learners threefold instruction: (1) in the elements of number (arithmetic); (2) in the elements of form (drawing, leading to writing); and (3) in names and the ideas they connote (language). According to Pestalozzi, this method led to *Anschauung*, or the development of insight. Insight is achieved when instruction follows the order of the mind's natural growth, gradually proceeding from the simple to the complex. (See figure 2.5, page 38.)

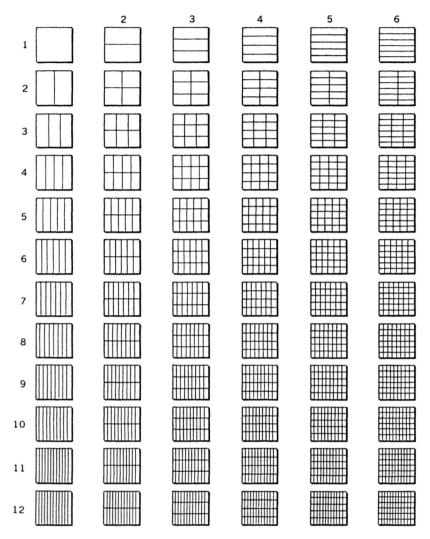

Fig. 2.5. Part of a chart for teaching fractions (From J. H. Pestalozzi, *How Gertrude Teaches Her Children*, translated by L. E. Holland and F. C. Swan. Syracuse, N.Y.: Bardeen's, 1874, 329.)

Pestalozzi elaborated his concept of the learning sequence in what he called the ABC of *Anschauung*. His approach was to break down content into its simplest elements and then develop graduated exercises based as far as possible on the study of objects rather than words. For example, in studying arithmetic the learner counted things around him—the number of steps across the room, the number of plies in the thread he was weaving, etc.—to learn what each number meant. Pestalozzi devised arithmetic boards divided into squares, on which were placed dots or lines that concretely represented each unit up to 100. By means of this arithmetic board the learner received a clear concept of the meaning of digits and the process of addition. In the study of form, objects such as sticks were placed in different directions; then lines representing the sticks were drawn until all elementary forms and angles had been mastered and could be combined into more complex figures.

In the study of words (language), the fundamental units were the elementary sounds. From articulating sounds, the learner progressed to reading syllables, words, and sentences. Pestalozzi's pupils would examine the number, form, position, and color of the designs, holes, and rents in the wallpaper of the school, and then express their observations in increasingly complex sentences.

Like the Lancasterian system, Pestalozzian instruction replaced the old recitation approach. Under Pestalozzi's method, the teacher taught the whole class as a group, framing questions according to the understanding reflected in students' answers to previous questions. This method challenged the teacher, since it demanded knowledge of subject matter as well as competence in questioning and group management.

Influence of Pestalozzi

Although Pestalozzi experimented without the aid of modern science or an empirical method, he did anticipate a science of instruction. Through introspection, he sought to understand what he should do and then attempted to use these insights to improve his method. Observers who visited Pestalozzi's experimental schools reported a program of studies that brought life closer to the learner, replaced drill with observation and learner motivation, respected the individuality of each learner, and supplanted fear of punishment with mutual cooperation.

Since the instruction principles set forth by Comenius had not yet been rediscovered, Pestalozzi's ideas seemed unique, and found champions in Europe and in the United States. His greatest contribution, however, was not his own instructional methodology, but the stimulus that his ideas provided to others in the search for better teaching methods.

Pestalozzi's major influence in Europe was in Germany. In philosopher Johann Gottlieb Fichte's (1762-1814) famous *Addresses to the German Nation* (1807-1808), in which he emphasized the regeneration of Germany following the defeat by Napoleon, he declared: "To the course of instruction which has been invented and brought forward by Heinrich Pestalozzi, and which is now being successfully carried out under his direction, must we look for our regeneration."[35] German schools became models of Pestalozzianism and were observed by many educators from other countries.

Pestalozzi also exerted an important influence on the German educator Friedrich Wilhelm Froebel, the founder of the kindergarten. Froebel incorporated Pestalozzian object-teaching into his own methodology by means of his now well-known "gifts and occupations."

Pestalozzianism in the United States

Pestalozzianism first appeared in the United States in 1809, when William MacClure (1763-1840) brought an assistant of Pestalozzi, Joseph N. Neef (1770-1854), to Philadelphia, where MacClure opened the first of a series of schools. Later, Neef opened his own "Pestalozzian" schools in Pennsylvania, Kentucky, and Indiana. Although Neef's schools did not have a significant influence, they represented the earliest American interpretation of Pestalozzi's teachings.

Another variation of Pestalozzi's method also came into vogue quite early in the United States. Philip von Fellenberg (1771-1844), a Swiss nobleman and educator, had developed a school where the objects of instruction were the tools and materials of shop and farm; Fellenberg's ideas swept the U.S. between the years 1825 and 1835. In New York City in 1831, the Society for Promoting Manual Labor in Literary Institutions was formed for the purpose of collecting and diffusing information about Fellenberg's approach, but by 1860 the movement had come full circle, and there was little respect in academic quarters for manual labor instruction.

In the meantime, Pestalozzian principles had been widely spread by early educational journals, professional textbooks, and official reports about Pestalozzian schools in Europe, including Albert Picket's *Academian* (1818-1820), William Russell's *American Journal of Education* (1826-1830), and Henry Barnard's *Connecticut Common School Journal* (1838-1842). Others praising Pestalozzi were Calvin Stowe (1802-1886), Victor Cousin (1792-1867), and Horace Mann (1796-1859), Louis Agassiz (1807-1873), and Herman Krusi, Jr. (1817-1903).

Warren Colburn (1793-1833) published his *First Lessons in Arithmetic on the Plan of Pestalozzi* (1821);[36] David P. Page (1810-1848), director of New York State Normal School at Albany, condemned mere book learning;[37] Warren Burton (1800-1866), in his charming little book *The District School as It Was* (1833), asserted that the abstract moral sentences of texts presented only faint meaning to the child;[38] Henry Barnard (1811-1900) anticipated that educational efficiency might be increased "ten-fold" by the use of "some simple apparatus so as to employ the eye in the acquisition of knowledge";[39] and Charles W. Eliot (1834-1926), president of Harvard University from 1869 to 1909, in his later years believed that the absence of sensory training was "the greatest defect in the kind of education which has come down upon us from the middle ages."[40]

After precariously maintaining itself for almost six decades, Pestalozzian object-teaching achieved its first widespread acceptance in the United States through the work of Edward A. Sheldon (1823-1897), superintendent of schools in Oswego, New York. Sheldon was first inspired to adopt new classroom methods after visiting an educational museum in Toronto, Canada, in 1859, where he saw an appealing display of pictures, color charts, models, and other object-teaching materials. He purchased various "objects" to show to his own board of education; upon his return to Oswego, Sheldon obtained approval for their use and immediately began revising the curriculum and classroom procedures of the Oswego schools.

In 1860, at Oswego, the object-lesson plan became the first major attempt by American educators to psychologize instruction. From London, Sheldon brought a teacher familiar with Pestalozzian principles and methods; shortly thereafter he engaged Herman Krusi, Jr., son of one of Pestalozzi's helpers at Yverdun. Within a few years, the Oswego system, along with the Oswego State Normal School (1867), became the great proponent of object-teaching and progressive instructional methods in the United States.[41]

The Oswego method soon assumed a formalism of its own, however, and sometimes became as verbal and mechanistic as the classical methods it was trying to reform. Many teachers shifted from the traditional concept that everything could be learned by reading to the new extreme that everything should be taught exclusively by the object method. Even Krusi observed that the lessons at Oswego sometimes had no connection with each other and failed to follow some general plan. Furthermore, in the object lessons, the objects chosen were not always used effectively.

As Oswego declined, a new variation of American Pestalozzianism was being introduced in 1875 by Francis W. Parker (1837-1902), superintendent of schools at Quincy, Massachusetts. Although the so-called Quincy methods were similar to the Oswego method in the use of concrete materials, they were actually a new form of object-teaching that employed a wider variety of materials from everyday life and the sciences. To learn about erosion, for example, the children formed hills in a sandbox and poured water on them. In an introduction to botany, they planted seeds in a box filled with earth. Local geography assumed more importance than the study of foreign lands, and the solving of common, everyday problems was of more consequence than learning abstract rules and principles.

Quincy parents soon began to criticize Parker for changing their schools into "natural history museums" and "mud-pie factories." To settle the issue, the Massachusetts State Board of Education gave the Quincy children an examination in traditional subject matter and found them superior to children educated by traditional methods. Ultimately, the Quincy methods exerted a wide influence on instructional method throughout the country.[42]

Object-teaching made a brief reappearance in the nature study movement of the late 1800s and early 1900s. L. H. Bailey of Cornell University said the movement was an effort to put the child in contact with his own environment, and insisted that "education should always begin with objects and phenomena" instead of books and museums.[43] He also insisted that nature study was itself a new instructional method rather than a subject area.

There had always been a few teachers who took their pupils on excursions or brought natural objects and specimens into the classroom for the children to study. In the United States, the father of nature study as a movement was probably Louis Agassiz, the great naturalist and Harvard professor. As early as 1847, when lecturing at teachers' institutes, he would appear with a jar of live grasshoppers and explain their structure and habits as each teacher personally examined one of the specimens. He helped his wife, also a teacher, prepare *A First Lesson in Natural History* (1859), and gave daily lectures illustrated with specimens, drawings, and models to her pupils. Agassiz and his students were also instrumental in the creation of many natural history museums, among them the American Museum of Natural History in New York City, for which one of his students, Albert Smith Bickmore, created the design.

H. H. Straight (1846-1886), a disciple of both Agassiz and Nathaniel Shaler (1841-1906), another early leader in the nature study movement, was regarded by some as the real founder of the movement. Proponents of the nature study movement denounced textbooks, dispensed with lectures, and ridiculed questions on assigned readings. They were convinced that the most effective method of learning about nature was to find a specimen and study it until it was understood.[44]

Object-teaching achieved its greatest popularity in the 1860s.[45] Some of its philosophy and method were incorporated in the kindergarten movement of the 1870s and in the learning-by-doing movement, which reached its height in the 1880s. By the end of the nineteenth century, object-teaching had begun to decline and increasingly gave way to Herbartian principles. There was no doubt, however, that Oswego had made a lasting contribution to the development of educational technology. Under the Oswego program, wherein experts demonstrated methods and explained the underlying philosophical rationale, there occurred the first synthesis of theory and practice in both action and word. Before examining the next step in the evolution of a technology of instruction, we turn first to an examination of Froebel.

A Method of Instruction According to Froebel

Friedrich Wilhelm Froebel (1782-1852) was born in Oberweissbach, Germany, and, after a haphazard education, spent several years groping for a career until Herr Gruner, headmaster of a Pestalozzian model school in Frankfurt, persuaded him to become a teacher there. Froebel later lived and worked with Pestalozzi at Yverdon,[46] where he developed a keen interest in young children that culminated in his greatest educational achievement—the kindergarten.

Educational Theory

Detailed discussion of the complicated metaphysical framework of Froebel's educational theory, as laid out in his *The Education of Man* (1826), is not within the scope of this chapter. A few words with regard to some of his key ideas are necessary, however, in order to understand his method.

The dominant idea underlying Froebel's whole view of education was the organic unity of all things in God. The forming crystal, the growing tree, the developing child all reflect God's plan of creation. The purpose of the educator was to control the growth of a child

Fig. 2.6. Portrait of Friedrich Froebel (1782-1852).

into a man, just as the gardener controlled the growth of a plant into its full flowering. Thus, according to Froebel, instruction had to be controlled development by which the learner came into the realization of life in the all-encompassing unity of which he was a part.

Froebel also espoused the recapitulation theory, which asserted that cultural epochs were relived by each learner in his transition from infancy to adulthood as he progressed to increasingly higher levels of development. Froebel believed history could therefore provide a timetable for the natural interests and activities of learners, and that the literary history of the culture could serve as a resource for materials that would be specifically appropriate for each stage of development.

There were four basic components embodied in Froebel's mystical philosophy of education: (1) free self-activity, (2) creativity, (3) social participation, and (4) motor expression. He contended that free self-activity directed the learner's growth and allowed him the active creativity and social participation necessary to merge his personality with the spirit of humanity. To Froebel, motor expression meant to learn by doing, not through verbal communication alone. What is more, individual educational activity was to take place only when the learner felt a need for it. Froebel believed this readiness was a condition of man's inner nature rather than a mere result of curiosity, interest, or past experience.

Perhaps most important to Froebel's instructional method was his notion of opposites. He believed a plant or animal or child grew by the twofold process of impressing the form of its own life on some external material while developing its inner nature in doing so; or, as Froebel put it, by making the inner outer and the outer inner. Growth was the process of overcoming differences by finding some connection between things that at first appeared opposed.

Instructional Method

The most notable application of Froebel's theoretical principles was his kindergarten system of early education, which was designed to appear to the child as play. The system, although not rigid, was methodical. It consisted of three aspects: (1) games and songs, (2) construction, and (3) gifts and occupations. The games and songs, perhaps the finest expression of the kindergarten spirit, were chiefly for acquainting children with the inner life of animals and humanity. Froebel was the first educator to grasp the value of socialization as a basic teaching method. The "morning circle" in his kindergarten, where the teacher and the children stood in a ring and joined hands for song and play, is an excellent example of this method. A visitor to almost any kindergarten anywhere may still observe a dozen children singing in a circle while they pantomime planting, watering, weeding, plucking, or smelling flowers.[47]

Construction was undertaken in such pursuits as drawing, paper cutting, pasteboard work, modeling, etc. — all familiar activities in a contemporary kindergarten. To implement his instructional method, Froebel devised a series of materials that he called *gifts and occupations.* The occupations were activities, while the gifts provided ideas for such activities. Gifts were of two types: geometric shapes, and the basic materials for modeling, drawing, sewing, and coloring. The first gift was a ball, the most universal plaything and symbolic of the unity of the universe. The second gift consisted of a ball, a cube, and a cylinder, which symbolized thesis, antithesis, and synthesis. The third gift was formed by dividing a cube into various shapes. These building blocks were specifically designed to illustrate certain relationships and teach form, number, and measurement. They also led children to compare, examine, arrange, and analyze. Today's modern school has adapted Froebel's concept of gifts by providing materials and games, miniature industrial processes, and mechanical models from the child's real world.

Froebel used objects (gifts) in a uniquely different way from Pestalozzi. While Pestalozzi used a great variety of materials and expected the learner to exercise his sensory powers to become acquainted with each object, Froebel, on the other hand, used fewer formal objects and placed more importance on the symbolic knowledge suggested by the quality of the object than on the immediate knowledge yielded by a sensory experience (observation) of it.

Influence of Froebel

Although a reactionary Prussian government closed all kindergartens in 1861,[48] a year before Froebel's death, his influence spread rapidly throughout Europe and the United States, reaching its height in the United States about 1880. The U.S. kindergarten movement was led by Mrs. Carl Schurz (a former student of Froebel), who established the first American kindergarten (German-speaking) at Watertown, Wisconsin, in 1855. By the end of the nineteenth century, there were about 1,400 English-speaking, public kindergartens in the United States, enrolling more than 95,000 pupils.[49]

The manual-training movement (not to be confused with the manual labor movement mentioned previously in connection with Pestalozzian influence) also owes much to Froebelian ideas of motor expression, or learning by doing. This method was brought to the attention of American educators during the Centennial Exposition in Philadelphia in 1876, where it was shown as it was then being practiced in postkindergarten schools in Finland and Russia.[50]

Although superficial defects of Froebel's method such as his mysticism and the crudity of his materials[51] may seem obvious, his basic doctrines have proven to be psychologically and socially sound. Through his emphases on motor expression and the social aspects of instruction, along with his advocacy of a school without set tasks, Froebel made a distinctive contribution to instructional method. His experiments not only led to the establishment of kindergartens, but also his principles of instruction were applied in later years.

The Herbartian Method of Instruction

It is appropriate to conclude this chapter with an examination of Johann Friedrich Herbart (1776-1841), in whom the various trends that had developed since the time of Comenius came to fruition. Both Comenius and Pestalozzi, as we have seen, believed sense perception was necessary in developing clear conceptualization. Herbart expanded their work to show how the teacher could assimilate new concepts with old ones. Herbart's view that moral development was the primary aim of education reflected the influence of Froebel. Perhaps not since the time of the Elder Sophists had instruction become so highly systematized, nor had such a sophisticated formula been devised for the teaching of virtue.

The brilliant son of a distinguished, middle-class family of Oldenburg, Germany, Herbart entered the University of Jena, at Bremen, to prepare for a law career. However, he left before graduation to spend two years (1797-1799) as private tutor to the sons of the governor of Interlaken, Switzerland.[52] During this period he visited Pestalozzi's school at Burgdorf, and was impressed with what he saw. Later, after completing his doctoral studies, Herbart focused on education. From 1802 to 1809, he lectured on education and philosophy at the University of Göttingen, Germany, where he published his *Science of Education* (1806). For the next twenty-four years, he held the chair of philosophy (formerly occupied by Immanuel Kant) at the University of Königsberg, Germany. Here he founded an educational seminar and a practice school for teacher education and experimentation in method teaching. In 1833, he returned to Göttingen where, in 1835, he published his famous *Outlines of Educational Doctrine*.

Educational Theory

In contrast to all of his predecessors, Herbart rooted his method in a systematic psychology of learning. His was the first modern psychology of learning to harmonize with the *tabula rasa* (blank tablet) theory formulated by Locke.[53] Not only did Herbart negate the idea of inborn faculties, which had been prevalent since classical times, but he denied that the mind itself existed at birth. Minds, according to Herbart, were simple battlegrounds and storehouses of ideas, and ideas had an active quality of their own. Ideas, he thought, could lead a life of their own in a mind, which was completely passive. On this basis, Herbart developed a systematic psychology of learning and instruction.[54]

To Herbart, all learning was apperception, or a process of relating new ideas to old ones and assimilating them into a total, apperceptive mass. Within this apperceptive process, Herbart identified three levels of learning: the first level, predominantly sensory activity; the second level, wherein previously formed ideas were reproduced; and the third, or highest, level, in which conceptual thinking or understanding occurred.

Herbart's theory suggested that the primary task of instruction was the formation of this apperceptive mass through the proper presentation of the right sequence of ideas. Psychologically, learners were formed by the world of ideas as it was presented to them from without. Thus the problem of instruction was selecting the correct ideas and materials to develop a large, apperceptive mass within learners. Herbart was particularly convinced that the history and great literature of the world, when properly selected and arranged, would develop the interests and understanding of learners at each successive period of growth.

Instructional Method

Herbart formulated a four-step, systematic method based on his concept of the mind and theory of apperception:

1. **Clearness.** The first stage concentrated on the learner's absorption of new ideas. Objects of study were broken up into elements so that the learner might focus on each fact or detail in isolation.

2. **Association.** When the learner had gained sufficient knowledge of the object, it was then associated with related objects already known. This could be done by free conversation or by sensory experiences, if these experiences would help in the foundation of generalization and abstraction.

3. **System.** When the facts were seen in their proper relationship, they could then be viewed as an interrelated whole. At this stage, a clear distinction was made between the essential and the irrelevant, thereby completing the process of apperception.

4. **Method.** In this stage, the system was tested by checking the relationship of individual facts within it. For example, once an arithmetical rule had been established (system), the learner tested his knowledge of the rule with new problems (method). Each new experience in this process then became part of the unity of the mind.[55]

In essence, the four steps of Herbart transferred Pestalozzi's method of sensory impressions to the intellectual level of learning. While Pestalozzi identified the need to begin with sensory impressions, he had neither the time nor the scholarship to construct a psychology of learning beyond what already existed. Herbart, on the other hand, was able to develop a system of learning that, while purely speculative and mechanical, provided a logical theoretical framework for educational practice.

Influence of Herbart

Herbart's ideas had surprisingly little impact on European educational practice until about a quarter of a century after his death. In Germany, Tuiskon Ziller (1817-1882) popularized Herbartian principles by applying his methods to elementary school instruction,[56] by organizing a pedagogical seminar at the University of Leipzig, and by founding the Association for the Scientific Study of Education. Wilhelm Rein (1847-1929), a student of Ziller who became head of the pedagogical seminar and of the practice schools at the University of Jena, further spread the influence of Herbart by making Jena a great center of German Herbartianism.

Aside from Germany, the United States has been influenced by Herbartianism more than any other country. Before 1880, little mention had been made of Herbart in American educational literature. The American movement was fostered largely by a few enthusiastic

American teachers, who studied with Rein at Jena and brought back with them the new science of instructional method. These included Charles de Garmo, who published *The Essentials of Method* in 1889, and Charles A. McMurry, who published his *General Method* in 1892 and also published books with Frank M. McMurry, his brother, on the special methods of teaching various subjects that were stressed by the Herbartians.

Simultaneously, Herbartians began to penetrate the entire structure of American public education. In 1892, the National Herbart Society was organized at the Saratoga Springs meeting of the National Education Association, for the purpose of translating the works of Herbart and various German Herbartians.[57] Most of the normal schools—particularly in the Midwest—were soon advocating Herbartian principles and, through the teachers they sent to every section of the country, greatly influenced the practices of the schools. For some twenty years after 1895, Herbartians wrote most of the educational texts and dominated several educational journals as well as the professional discussions and debates. Nevertheless, it was clearly evident as early as 1901 that Herbartianism was waning in the United States.

In his book of 1901, *Talks to Teachers on Psychology*, William James (1842-1910) made a distinction between the art and the science of education and proceeded to refute the Herbartians' key concept of apperception by revealing its empty verbalism and mystical origins. James was joined in his attacks by philosophers John Dewey, Wilhelm Dilthy, and Josiah Royce, all of whom pointed out the anachronisms of Herbartian rational science. More important, perhaps, than criticisms of the abstruse features of Herbart's theoretical system were criticisms of the instructional practices that system established. Herbartianism essentially committed teachers to a program of indoctrination whereby they determined precisely what their pupils would be taught. Each lesson plan included not only the questions, but all the answers as well, which the learners arrived at through a largely mechanical process that was completely dominated by the teacher. Thus, learning was seen as a process similar to the filling of a storage container.

Despite its limitations, no other system of instruction, except that of Pestalozzi, has ever had so wide an influence on American instructional method as well as on teachers' thinking. Herbart made important contributions to educational technology by emphasizing a psychological and scientific, if not experimental, approach to instruction and learning.

Recapitulation and Analysis

This survey is intended to provide only a set of concepts, selected from historical instructional theory and method, that may be considered precursors to modern educational technology. It is not a history of instructional method in any definitive sense.

Probably the first professional teachers, the Elder Sophists, appear to have been the ancestors of modern educational technology. Their systematic analyses of subject matter and organization of teaching materials laid the groundwork for a technology of instruction. More important, when teaching was not commonly considered a profession, the Sophists viewed it as *techne* in the old Greek sense, or technology, in which the theoretical is combined with the practical.

With Abelard and the scholastic method, some of the techniques of the Elder Sophists were combined with the rules of logic and the content of philosophical, theological, and other writings to create a distinctive method of instruction suited to the period. The primary emphasis was on developing an attitude toward knowledge.

For Comenius, nature offered the key to biological, cognitive, and moral development whereby the learner was led inductively to generalized knowledge by working with natural objects and studying practical things. On the basis of these convictions, Comenius devised a system of instruction that anticipated many of the modern principles of learning.

In the learning theory that was the foundation for the methods of the early forerunners, faculty psychology was implicit or openly advocated. Faculty psychology assumes that, with adequate cultivation, the human mind can know the objective reality of the world. Man, being a rational animal, is free (within limits) to act as he chooses in the light of what he understands. Instead of being a creature of instinct, he enjoys a complex and delicate faculty of "knowing" whose basic aspect is reason. In an educational context, it is assumed that knowledge is a fixed body of true principles that are handed down in the form of great books or basic subject content. Thus, specific subject matter lends itself to the exercise or training of the faculty of reason.[58]

Abelard, and later medieval Scholastics, also accepted faculty psychology as a theory of learning. The emphasis on the role of intellect in learning, at the expense of the senses, was generally stressed even more in the medieval world. Knowledge derived from sensory impression was considered highly variable and unreliable, while that of the intellect was thought to be stable and dependable.

The educator who restored the balance between intellect and sensory experience was Comenius. Although he accepted the faculty psychology of his day, he predicated his instructional method on the priority of the senses, and thereby anticipated the theoretical ideas of Locke.

From the foregoing analysis, it appears the primary function of exercising the faculties was believed to be that of acquiring knowledge. There are, however, repeated references in educational literature, from Plato onward, that illustrate the viewpoint that true learning consists in the exercise of faculties for their own sake. According to this viewpoint, exercising or strengthening the faculties is of prime importance, rather than the acquisition of knowledge and the development of understanding.

There are few aspects of current instructional practice that cannot be traced back to Lancaster, Pestalozzi, Froebel, or Herbart. The Lancasterian method segmented instruction into separate classroom packages and thus introduced a type of lockstep system that still dominates educational patterns. The prevailing concept of Lancaster's day, that instruction consisted principally of transmitting information and controlling learner behavior, was reinforced and implemented in the monitorial system.

Viewing the instructional task in more complicated terms, object-teaching, as developed by Pestalozzi and Froebel, went beyond mere practice and shifted to theoretical considerations and other things of a less immediately practical nature. With Herbart, there was a more advanced return to methods similar to those of the Elder Sophists. Instruction became highly systematized and cognitive elements once again became the central focus of the instructional process. It was a new formula for virtue through knowledge, to be acquired from the intellectual resources of the race. Moreover, Herbart developed a rational science of learning that pointed the way to the first systems instructional approach.

The next chapter begins an examination of the formative concepts that have led toward the development of a modern science and technology of instruction.

Notes

[1]See Lancelot Hogben, *From Cave Painting to Comic Strip*. London: Max Parrish, 1949.

[2]Between 450 and 350 B.C., the Greek title *sophist* or *sophistes* was used to describe any man of science or learning. But by the time of the Peloponnesian War (431-404 B.C.), the name began to acquire an equivocal ring because the conservative fathers of Athens suspected the Sophist teachers of ruining the city by leading the youth from the traditional Homeric virtues and the old religion. Plato's later denigration of the Sophists accentuated the prejudices against them. We must, however, go beyond Plato's prejudices to assess the educational role of the Elder Sophists. In this effort, we are indebted to the technical scholarship of Eric A. Havelock and his *The Crucifixion of Intellectual Man*, as well as his *The Liberal Temper in Greek Politics*, in which he endeavors to put Sophist thought and practice into proper historical perspective.

[3]Although the widespread prejudice against the Sophists was partly due to their acceptance of fees, Protagoras was quite unashamed of his profession. His fees, indeed, seem to have been high. He demanded 10,000 drachmas for a two- or three-year course of instruction at a time when 1 drachma was a skilled worker's daily wage. By 350 B.C., however, the price of such a course had fallen to about 1,000 drachmas. In spite of the liberal, democratic ideals the Sophists espoused, it is clear that only aristocrats could afford their services.

[4]Eric A. Havelock, *The Liberal Temper in Greek Politics*. New Haven, Conn.: Yale University Press, 1957, 161.

[5]The period of instruction generally seems to have lasted for three or four years.

[6]Havelock, *The Liberal Temper*, 30-80.

[7]Werner Jaeger, *Paideia: The Ideals of Greek Culture*, Vol. 1 (translated from the 2d German ed. by Gilbert Highet), Fair Lawn, N.J.: Oxford University Press, 1939, 311ff.

[8]In contrast to the so-called Socratic method, the Sophistic dialogue provided both flexibility and creativity in its free conversational exchange of ideas. Students were not expected merely to answer yes or no to questions or, in effect, to separate one syllogism from another. The theory of Sophistic dialogue viewed the student as an active, inquiring individualist who could lead the discussion down new, divergent paths.

[9]Havelock, *The Liberal Temper*, 216.

[10]The favorite subjects of the Sophists, grammar and rhetoric, occupy two-thirds of the "trivium," in which Plato is not even represented.

[11]In contrast to the democratic viewpoint of the Sophists, Plato's philosophy suggested an antidemocratic, totalitarian government in which an aristocratic and military elite of "supermen" ruled a lower-class majority who were considered to be inferior and motivated by gross appetites. This philosophy supported authoritarian tendencies and control throughout the history of the Western world. In the teaching of the Church, Platonic doctrines were wedded with the will of God as revealed in Scripture, which led to the identification of Platonism with Christianity.

[12]See C. P. Snow, *The Two Cultures and the Scientific Revolution*. New York: Cambridge University Press, 1959.

[13]Pierre Abelard (1079-1142) was born of noble stock in Brittany and died in the Priory of St. Marcel, near Chalons, France.

[14]Adapted from Harry S. Broudy and John R. Palmer, *Exemplars of Teaching Method*. Chicago: Rand McNally, 1965, 62-63.

[15]Abelard may have found a model for his method in the work of such men as Ivo of Chartres, who in the tenth century had undertaken to reconcile contradictory statements.

[16]The closer University of Prague was then controlled by the Utraquists, a Hussite sect opposed to the Moravians.

[17]Among them was the *Janua linguarum reserata* (The gate of languages unlocked), published in 1631, in which Comenius selected 8,000 of the commonest words and used them in 1,000 graded sentences.

[18]Comenius's ideas for his system of instruction were first formulated at Leszno, Poland, where he wrote his *Great Didactic*. His later texts were elaborations of this basic work. The *Great Didactic*, written in Czech, was first published in German in 1633 and in Latin in 1657.

[19]The Moravians, who had suffered severely at the hands of the Catholics during the Thirty Years' War, were secretly sympathetic to the Protestant Swedes during their invasion of Poland. After peace was declared, Comenius openly published a letter of congratulation to the Swedish king, Charles Gustavus.

In retaliation, the Poles attacked and plundered Leszno, the town where Comenius was living. He barely escaped with his life and lost his entire family and his collection of pansophic materials on which he had worked most of his life. Since he was then in his sixty-fifth year, he lacked the enthusiasm and strength to pursue the dream further.

[20]Peter Canisius, one hundred years before, had issued a child's catechism with marginal pictures and woodcuts illustrating the lives of Christ and the saints, as well as church ceremonies.

[21]The teachers included ministers, college students, indentured servants, mechanics, physicians, and even ex-convicts and tramps. In many areas, the summer sessions catered to young children who were not needed in the fields for work. Women and girls as young as sixteen were often employed to teach these sessions, since the problems of discipline were not too severe. In the winter term, men generally taught the older children.

[22]A Scot, Andrew Bell (1753-1832), simultaneously and independently developed the monitorial method. In the matter of details, Lancaster elaborated more than Bell; he also toured both Europe and the United States. The method, however, was not original with either Bell or Lancaster. It had been used by the Hindus; it had formed part of the Jesuit method; and it had been recommended to Comenius in his *Great Didactic*. Bell was primarily concerned with religious instruction while Lancaster was generally interested in secular systems. In time, laymen and educators began referring to the monitorial system as the Lancasterian method.

[23]In the seventeenth century, John Locke (1632-1704) challenged the whole notion of innate faculties or ideas, as well as the concept of learning as the development of such innate faculties. His *tabula rasa* (blank tablet) theory held that the mind is empty at birth and that any ideas a person holds must have come to him originally through his senses. Locke's theory opened the way for psychologists to emphasize environment over heredity. Locke believed teachers should develop a systematic instructional method for training the senses rather than the faculties.

[24]Schools that used the monitor method soon experienced difficulties because of competition for clerical and other kinds of literate workers in the cities. Pupils mature enough to become monitors seldom could be induced to remain after their parents discovered that they could earn more money in other occupations. About 1827, women replaced boy monitors, but at a salary of $25 for the first year. These untrained women, however, could not provide even the low-level, standardized instruction that the trained boy monitors had assumed. To improve this situation, some cities, such as New York, established Saturday classes for new women teachers. These "normal schools," which developed after 1840, became the main teacher training ground. However, these training schools were so influenced by the Lancasterian method that the adults who would replace the boy monitors were given essentially the same authoritarian perspective. This was a simple process of insisting on obedience within a hierarchical chain of command, which made rote learning the only practical type of instruction.

[25]John Gill, *Systems of Education.* Boston: D. C. Heath, 1887, 192-93.

[26]David Salmon, *Joseph Lancaster.* New York: Longmans, Green, 1904, 12.

[27]W. O. Bourne, *History of the Public School Society of New York City.* Baltimore: Wood and Company, 1870, 19.

[28]Those who support the idea of using master teachers, assisted by monitors, to instruct large groups using such a medium as television might well study the Lancasterian scheme.

[29]J. P. Gordy, *The Rise and Growth of the Normal-School Idea in the United States.* U.S. Bureau of Education, Circular of Information 8. Washington, D.C.: GPO, 24.

[30]See H. G. Rickover, *Education and Freedom.* New York: Dutton, 1959; Arthur E. Bester, *Educational Wastelands.* Urbana: University of Illinois Press, 1953; and James D. Koerner, *The Case for Basic Education.* Boston: Little, Brown, 1959. We generally agree with these critics that teachers often have been poorly educated, but this does not imply that strengthening teachers' backgrounds in the liberal arts and sciences will necessarily increase their effectiveness in the classroom. It is surprising

that, in the current teacher education controversy, the nature of instruction has not been analyzed nor has the relevance of various proposals been examined with respect to the realities of the process of instructing groups of learners.

[31]Rousseau's central theme in *Emile* was that education should be in accordance with the natural interests of the child. He divided the learner's development into definite stages and prescribed a distinct educational program for each successive period. His approach stemmed from the viewpoint that man is naturally good and is at the same time active in relation to his environment. Since man is naturally good, the teacher should let the learner develop in a natural environment, free from corruption. Pestalozzi used this same principle, under the name of "organic development," as a basis for his own educational theory and practice.

[32]J. H. Pestalozzi, *How Gertrude Teaches Her Children* (translated by L. E. Holland and F. C. Swan). Syracuse, N.Y.: Bardeen's, 1874.

[33]Ibid.

[34]August Herman Francke (1663-1727) founded the first *Realschule* at Halle, Germany, where he and his fellow teachers employed "real things" to facilitate instruction. Johann Bernard Basedow (1723-1790) established his *Philanthropinum* at Dessau, Germany, where he attempted to put Rousseau's theories into practice.

[35]Johann Gottlieb Fichte, *Die Reden an die Deutsche*. Fourteen in all; the endorsement of Pestalozzi's principles occurs in the tenth.

[36]Colburn's book ranks with the *New England Primer* and Webster's *Speller* in historical importance because it was the first to emphasize sensory objects in teaching mental arithmetic.

[37]David P. Page, *Theory and Practice of Teaching*. New York: A. S. Barnes and Co., 1893.

[38]Warren Burton, *The District School as It Was*. Boston: Phillips, Sampson, 1850, 52. (First published in 1933.)

[39]Henry Barnard, *Connecticut Common School Journal* 3 (December 15, 1840), 61.

[40]Charles W. Eliot, *The Tendency to the Concrete and Practical in Modern Education*. Boston: Houghton Mifflin, 1913, 11.

[41]For a comprehensive account, see Ned H. Dearborn, *Oswego Movement*. New York: Teachers College Press, Columbia University, 1925.

[42]See Lelia E. Patridge, *The Quincy Methods Illustrated*. New York: E. L. Kellogg and Company, 1886.

[43]L. H. Bailey, "The Nature-Study Movement," *National Education Association Proceedings*. Printed by University of Chicago Press. Winona, Minn.: The Association, 1903, 109-16.

[44]Wilbur S. Jackson carried on the work of H. H. Straight by publishing a teachers' guide entitled *Nature Study for the Common Schools* (1891).

[45]In post-Civil War years, the spread of Oswego graduates throughout normal schools all over the United States developed the first unified theoretical viewpoint in teacher training.

[46]Froebel first spent two weeks with Pestalozzi at Yverdon in 1805, and later taught there from 1807 to 1809. Thereafter he pursued a university career, first at Göttingen and then at Berlin. He founded his first school at Keilhau in 1817 and established the first kindergarten at Blankenburg in 1837.

[47]Froebel published *Mother Play and Nursery Songs* in 1843. This work consisted of an organized series of songs, games, and pictures intended to direct the educational role of the mother. Each song contained three parts: (1) a motto for the guidance of the mother; (2) a verse with the accompanying music, to sing to the child; and (3) a picture illustrating the verse.

[48]Prussian kindergartens were suspected of reflecting socialistic and liberal viewpoints dangerous to the existing government. The effects of their closing were felt in Prussia for a decade. Elsewhere, this education movement, in which women took a major part, received impetus from Baroness von Marenholtz-Bulow in Germany and spread to England, France, Italy, and the Netherlands. Henry Barnard, an American educator, witnessed a kindergarten demonstration at the Great Exhibition in London in 1854 and his description inspired Elizabeth Peabody to start a kindergarten in Boston in 1860.

[49]Nicholas Murray Butler, *Education in the United States*. New York: American Book Company, 1900, 41-42.

[50]Uno Cygnaeus (1810-1888) introduced the manual-training concept into Finnish schools in 1886. John D. Runkle, president of the Massachusetts Institute of Technology, after seeing a display of the Imperial Technical School of Moscow, recommended the establishment of manual-training workshops in the United States. His idea was further developed by Calvin M. Woodward and others. The manual-training vogue continued until about 1910.

[51]In *Mother Play and Nursery Songs*, for example, the pictorial illustrations are rough and poorly drawn, the music is crude, and the verses are lacking in rhythm, poetic spirit, and diction. The arrangement of verses is awkward and seems at times to lack consistency.

[52]Tutoring proved to be a valuable practical experience as well as an important influence on Herbart's educational views. His patron required a bimonthly written report of Herbart's methods and his students' progress; five of these letters are still extant and reveal the germs of an educational system. At this early date, Herbart already recognized individual differences in learners and attempted to adapt his instruction to their particular needs. He afterward maintained that careful study of the development of a few children was the best preparation for a teaching career.

[53]See note 23 for information on Locke's *tabula rasa* theory.

[54]Herbart's psychology was the last great system of metaphysical psychology. Although he maintained that his system was based on "metaphysics, empiricism and mathematics," he conducted no empirical studies. His entire system was based on introspection. He felt that it was appropriate for a science like physics to be experimental but equally appropriate that psychology be introspective and metaphysical.

[55]Herbart's four steps were later expanded to five by American Herbartians. Clearness became (1) preparation and (2) presentation; association became (3) comparison and abstraction; system became (4) generalization; and method became (5) application.

[56]Ziller elaborated the Herbartian principles of correlation and concentration, which unified all subjects around one or two central studies such as literature or history. Ziller also formulated the cultural epochs theory, which held that materials for a course of study should be selected to parallel the development of the individual and the race.

[57]The National Herbart Society was the predecessor of the National Society for the Scientific Study of Education, which was organized in 1895. However, the NSSS never seemed comfortable with the word *scientific*; in 1910, the official title became the National Society for the Study of Education.

[58]Plato and his student-successor, Aristotle, formulated and refined the theory of faculty psychology. Plato's entire educational structure was based on faculty psychology, directed toward producing leaders by means of a rigid choice of subject matter. He believed that training the faculties through mathematics and philosophy was the best preparation for the conduct of public affairs. Having trained his mental faculties, a philosopher-king was considered ready to solve all problems. Aristotle agreed with Plato and further contended that once a man had trained his faculties by mastering specific subject matter he would be able to transfer his power to the mastery of other subjects. Aristotle described at least five different faculties, the greatest, and the one unique to man, being that of reason.

Select Bibliography

Bourne, William O. *History of the Public School Society of New York City.* New York: Wood & Co., 1870.

Broudy, Harry S., and John R. Palmer. *Exemplars of Teaching Method.* Chicago: Rand McNally, 1965.

Burton, Warren. *The District School as It Was*, ed. Clifton Johnson. New York: Thomas Y. Crowell, 1923.

Dearborn, Ned H. *Oswego Movement.* New York: Teachers College Press, Columbia University, 1925.

Eliot, Charles W. *The Tendency to the Concrete and Practical in Modern Education.* Boston: Houghton Mifflin, 1913.

Ely, Frederick. *The Development of Modern Education*, 2d ed. New York: Prentice-Hall, 1952.

Havelock, Eric A. *The Liberal Temper in Greek Politics.* New Haven, Conn.: Yale University Press, 1957.

Herbart, Johann F. *Outlines of Educational Doctrines.* New York: Macmillan, 1904.

Livingston, R. W. *The Legacy of Greece.* New York: Oxford Press, 1928.

McMurry, Charles A. *The Elements of General Method, Based on the Principles of Herbart.* New York: Macmillan, 1903.

Page, David P. *Theory and Practice of Teaching.* New York: A. S. Barnes and Co., 1893.

Patridge, Lelia E. *The Quincy Methods Illustrated.* New York: E. L. Kellogg and Co., 1886.

Pestalozzi, Johann H. *How Gertrude Teaches Her Children*, tr. L. E. Holland and F. C. Swan. Syracuse, N.Y.: Bardeen's, 1874.

Rousseau, Jean-Jacques. *Emile*, tr. Barbara Foxley. New York: Dutton, 1911.

Salmon, David. *Joseph Lancaster.* New York: Longmans, Green & Co., 1904.

Thursfield, Richard. *Henry Barnard's Journal of Education.* Baltimore, Md.: Johns Hopkins University Press, 1946.

Ulich, Robert. *History of Educational Thought*, rev. ed. New York: American Book Co., 1968.

Waddell, Helen. *Peter Abelard.* New York: Holt, 1933.

White, Lynn, Jr. *Medieval Religion and Technology.* Berkeley: University of California Press, 1978.

Wilkins, A. S. *National Education in Greece in the Fourth Century B.C.* New York: Stechert, 1911.

Wolf, Abraham. *A History of Science, Technology, and Philosophy in the 16th and 17th Centuries.* New York: Macmillan, 1935.

3

Beginnings of a Science and Technology of Instruction: 1900–1950

No particular event or date marks the beginning of a modern science and technology of instruction. Yet it is clear that at the beginning of the twentieth century there occurred a series of related events that together might be interpreted as the beginning of a science of instruction.

William James (1842-1910), for example, in his book, *Talks to Teachers on Psychology*, made one of the first distinctions between the art and the science of teaching, calling for a scientific approach to instruction. Similarly, also in 1901, John Dewey (1859-1952) interpreted the method of empirical science in educational terms, viewing the classroom as an experimental laboratory. In 1902, Edward Thorndike (1874-1949) offered the first course in educational measurements at Columbia University and became the first to apply the methods of quantitative research to instructional problems.[1] G. Stanley Hall (1846-1924) published his *Adolescence* (1904), a landmark in the scientific study of the child. The French psychologist Alfred Binet (1857-1911) and Theodore Simon, his collaborator, published *A Method of Measuring the Intelligence of Young Children* (1905). Moreover, a true science of behavior, and especially of learning theory, began to emerge, no longer based primarily on metaphysical or philosophical speculation. This new science and learning theory would eventually be applied to a technology of instruction.

This chapter focuses on a few educators whose theories and methods either produced or fostered a modern science and technology of instruction. Two who dominated much of the thought and practice of American education during the first half of this century were Edward L. Thorndike and John Dewey. Both Thorndike and Dewey rose to eminence during roughly the same period and, for a time, both argued against those who still clung to the unscientific modes of thinking. Dewey, a philosopher, developed a comprehensive theoretical system that encompassed everything from the nature of man and learning to ethical and logical theory. Thorndike, an educational psychologist, fashioned the first scientific learning theory and established empirical investigation as the basis for a science of instruction.

By the early twenties, it was apparent that Thorndike's and Dewey's theories of instruction were incompatible. Dewey, a pragmatist and founder of the experimentalist school, built a system that had little basis in empirical data and whose hypotheses still have not been subjected to experimental investigation, despite his warnings to inquire, test, and to criticize. On the other hand, Thorndike was the exemplar of what might be achieved through empirical theorizing and investigation. His theories, however, were rejected by many educational leaders, who were attracted by Dewey's more democratic, though untested, approaches to instruction and learning.

Thorndike and the Science of Instruction

American educational psychologist Edward L. Thorndike made monumental contributions to a science and technology of instruction. The most remarkable aspect of Thorndike's work is that he dealt with every major psychological concept of his time. He either demonstrated an approach's inadequacies experimentally or incorporated it into his own system. It is well known, for example, how he refuted the mental discipline theory as a psychology of learning, as well as the recapitulation theory of psychological development.[2] Thorndike was not an ivory-tower theorist. He shuttled back and forth from his laboratory at Columbia University to countless public-school classrooms, tackling the relevant instructional problems of his day.

Thorndike's psychological career began with laboratory studies of learning in various animal species, while he was a student of William James at Harvard and of James McKeen Cattell (1860-1944) at Columbia.[3] His doctoral dissertation, *Animal Intelligence* (1898), remains a landmark in the history of psychology. Thorndike joined the faculty of Teachers College at Columbia University in 1899, where, at the suggestion of Cattell, he shifted his emphasis from animal learning to what became his lifetime concern with a science of human learning and a technology of instruction.

Thorndike's Theory of Connectionism

Thorndike's studies of animals led to the first scientific theory of learning, his theory of connectionism. Whereas previous theories had emphasized practice or repetition, Thorndike gave equal consideration to the effects of reward or punishment, success or failure, and satisfaction or annoyance on the learner. Building on the idea of the reflex arc, which said that the brain and neural tissues were connected with the total behavior of the organism, he eliminated the idea that the mind was a separate entity, placing it in the total response of the learner to his environment. Moreover, Thorndike discarded the earlier views that man is either sinful or good and that he is completely modifiable. Human nature, Thorndike maintained, was simply a mass of "original tendencies" that could be exploited for either good or evil, depending on what learning took place.[4]

Thorndike's laws of learning provided the basic principles that led to his particular technology of instruction. We describe here only his three primary laws:

1. **The law of exercise or repetition.** The more often a stimulus-induced response is repeated, the longer it will be retained.

2. **The law of effect.** The law of effect states the pleasure-pain principle: A response is strengthened if followed by pleasure and weakened if followed by displeasure.

3. **The law of readiness.** Thorndike assumed that, because of the structure of the nervous system, certain conduction units, in a given situation, are more predisposed to conduct than others.[5]

Fig. 3.1. Photograph of Edward L. Thorndike (1874-1949)
(Courtesy of Wesleyan University Press.)

Thorndike based these laws on the stimulus-response hypothesis: that a neural bond would be established between the stimulus and the response when a particular stimulus produced a satisfying response within a given environment.[6] Learning took place when these bonds formed into patterns of behavior.

Thorndike's Technology of Instruction

According to the connectionist concept, the instructional task of the teacher is guided by two broad rules: (1) to put together what should go together, and (2) to reward the expression of desirable connections and create discomfort for the expression of undesirable connections.[7] In his classic three-volume work, *Educational Psychology*, Thorndike formulated the basic principles underlying his technology of instruction: (1) self-activity, (2) interest (motivation), (3) preparation and mental set, (4) individualization, and (5) socialization. To implement these principles, a teacher needed to steer learners' activity in the desired direction, without ignoring their interests and individual responses to stimulation. Since the nature of the learning response, according to Thorndike, depended on past experience and mental set, the stimuli presented had to be adapted to the experience and mental set of the particular learners. To establish desirable connections, learners' individual differences had to be taken into consideration in the design of situations and in the use of instructional media. Finally, every response had social implications, so all learning responses had to be developed in natural social settings.

Thorndike's studies on the design of instructional media, the organization of instruction, individual differences, and methods of evaluation were both extensive and original. For example, he anticipated programmed instruction when he wrote, in 1912:

> If, by a miracle of mechanical ingenuity, a book could be so arranged that only to him who had done what was directed on page one would page two become visible, and so on, much that now requires personal instruction could be managed by print. Books to be given out in loose sheets, a page or so at a time, and books arranged so that the student only suffers if he misuses them, should be worked in many subjects. [8]

He commented further on the misuse of textbooks:

> On the whole, the improvement of printed directions, statements of facts, exercise books and the like is as important as the improvement of the powers of teachers themselves to diagnose the condition of pupils and to guide their activities by personal means. Great economies are possible by printed aids, and personal comment and question should be saved to do what only it can do. A human being should not be wasted in doing what forty sheets of paper or two phonographs can do.... The best teacher uses books and appliances as well as his own insight, sympathy, and magnetism. [9]

Thorndike's impressive demonstration of empirical-inductive means in the development of a science and technology of instruction unquestionably marked him as the first modern instructional technologist. Nevertheless, by the time many educators began to believe in the imminence of a science of instruction, Thorndike's influence was eclipsed by that of the great educational philosopher John Dewey. Thorndike was criticized by Dewey and by prominent members of the Progressive Education Movement in America for his frequent use of such terms as *habit, repression,* and *systematic practice*, and for his conservative social ideas. [10] Perhaps part of the waning influence of Thorndike's ideas, near the first quarter of this century, can be attributed to the fact that his psychology of learning seemed less adequate than the new, emerging systems of behaviorism [11] and Gestalt psychology.

Thorndike's contribution to modern educational technology cannot be overestimated. He began systematic laboratory investigation of animal learning; produced the first scientific learning theory; made a comprehensive analysis of human learning; performed extensive scientific studies of mental tests, scales of achievement, and textbooks; pioneered in the application of quantitative measures to certain sociopsychological problems; and invented new techniques in the field of lexicography. Today his influence can be seen in the views of B. F. Skinner of Harvard University. [12] Indeed, Thorndike is the historical starting point for any study or analysis of modern educational technology.

Theories of Instruction According to Dewey and Kilpatrick

John Dewey's importance in educational technology stems primarily from his vast influence on American education and, particularly, from his analysis of thinking in reflective, problem-solving terms. Dewey studied with G. Stanley Hall at Johns Hopkins University, where he received his doctorate.[13] He then taught at the universities of Michigan, Minnesota, and Chicago, before joining the Columbia University faculty in 1904. More than anyone, Dewey was responsible for the application of pragmatism to education, the notion that education was life. However, Dewey's ideas were frequently misinterpreted, and taken to excess by many of his followers in the Progressive Education movement.

Dewey's Psychology of Learning

A comprehensive analysis of John Dewey's psychology of learning has yet to be accomplished; only a few of the most significant ideas underlying his view of instruction are presented here.

In contrast to Thorndike, Dewey believed that stimulus and response were not to be sharply distinguished, but rather should be seen as organically related. In a short paper that is now regarded as a psychological classic,[14] he attacked the widely held reflex arc concept, contending that learning involved interaction, or two-way action between the learner and his environment.[15] In his view, the environment supplied cues and problems, and the human nervous system functioned to interpret the cues so problems could be evaluated and satisfactory solutions found. Moreover, Dewey explained that the experiences of learners within their environments become the materials out of which they make meanings and upon which they base goals and actions.

Dewey's Experimental Laboratory School

In 1896, while at the University of Chicago, Dewey decided to establish a Laboratory School for the purpose of testing his educational theories and their sociological implications. Beginning with 16 pupils and 2 teachers, it grew by 1902 to 140 children, 23 teachers, and 10 assistants. Dewey served as director; his wife was principal; Ella Flagg Young, who became Chicago's first woman superintendent of schools, was supervisor of instruction. The Laboratory School closed in 1903, and the next year Dewey left Chicago to teach philosophy at Columbia University.

During its seven years the Laboratory School became the most interesting experimental endeavor in American education. An observer found none of the conventional arrangements, routines, or activities. Desks and benches were not arranged in rows; the traditional teacher's desk with bell and ruler was missing; drills and recitations were never heard. Subject matter was not clearly separated. Some children might be busily engaged with books; others, with pen and paper; and some might be painting or using hammers. The teacher could usually be found mingling with the children, offering guidance as the pupils proceeded in their activities.

From the time Dewey established this experimental school he was hailed as the guiding light of the Progressive Education movement. But, as Dewey himself observed, the school was overweighted on the individualistic side so that he might obtain data. More important, Dewey sought to substitute a new curriculum that was better planned, better designed, and more effectively organized than the conventional curriculum, which he pointedly criticized. Although his instructional approaches at the school were clearly effective, he did not consider his innovations as final, but only as the first step in developing a science of instruction.

He was, however, destined for disappointment; a quarter of a century later he declared progressive education a failure because it had too hastily destroyed the traditional instructional pattern without replacing it with something better.[16]

Fig. 3.2. Portrait of John Dewey (Courtesy of Special Collections, Morris Library, Southern Illinois University-Carbondale.)

The Reflective Method of Instruction

Dewey's lasting contribution to a technology of instruction was probably his conception of instruction in terms of scientific method (defined in its broadest sense). To him, all worthwhile thinking was reflection, or the "active, persistent, and careful consideration of any belief or supposed form of knowledge in the light of the grounds that support it and the further conclusions to which it tends." The essence of this reflective method was contained in his little book *How We Think* (1910), which described reflection as a psychological process made up of the following steps:

1. The learner sensed and recognized a problem. Preferably, he became aware of some goal and felt blocked by an intervening obstacle, so that he felt a need to restore continuity.

2. After having sensed a problem or felt a discrepancy in known data, he would formulate hypotheses for the purpose of providing tentative answers or generalizations that might offer possible solutions.

3. Once the problematic situation had been surveyed, deductive observations had been checked against present knowledge, or experiments had been designed to test hypotheses, steps could be taken to restore the continuity of the learner's activity: His goal could be more adequately visualized.

4. The learner would test hypotheses and attempt to verify the consequences of the logical implications.

5. Finally, the learner would draw conclusions. He might accept, modify, or reject his hypotheses or decide that the available evidence did not provide a basis for action, for making an unqualified statement, or for taking a firm position.

Dewey did not mean to imply that reflection was a rigid, mechanical process. All the steps were closely interrelated and a learner did not necessarily go through them consecutively. A learner might move back and forth, from problem to hypotheses to evidence to conclusions, in varying order. Thus, Dewey's instructional approach resembled that of a scientific investigation in which hypotheses could be formulated and tested.

Many so-called followers of Dewey never understood the full implications of his theory of instruction, either because they found his writing difficult to understand or because they tended to ignore his insistence that the reflective approach be the center of the instructional process. Dewey believed the primary goal of instruction was the improvement of intelligence, and he attacked much of the formalism inherent in both the mental discipline theory and the connectionism of Thorndike. Dewey gave teachers a philosophical, theoretical-deductive psychology of learning that made empirical inquiry unnecessary for most educators who accepted his ideas. And although he urged inquiry and experimental investigation, his philosophy tended to block educational research. Thus, until Dewey's hypothesis is tested against predictions made from it, it cannot meet the basic criterion of a scientific technology of instruction.[17] Nevertheless, his theory continues to hold important implications for current instructional design.

Kilpatrick: The Popularizer of Dewey

The man who probably had most to do with popularizing Dewey's educational ideas was William Heard Kilpatrick (1871-1965). After graduating from Mercer University in Macon, Georgia, Kilpatrick taught for a time in the public schools before returning to Mercer, first as a teacher of mathematics, later as vice-president, and then as acting president. In 1906 he resigned, and the following year became a graduate student and Dewey disciple at Columbia University. After completing his doctoral dissertation in 1912, he joined Teachers College as a full-time faculty member, an association that lasted throughout his professional life.

Kilpatrick was simplifying and clarifying Dewey's complex thinking and writing, as well as adding his own interpretations. He became known as "the million-dollar professor," because his estimated 35,000 students (mostly classroom teachers and school administrators) had paid a total of more than a million dollars in fees to Columbia University. Kilpatrick was, in fact, a compelling teacher who was extraordinarily successful in acquiring his own disciples. Although acclaimed as the great interpreter of Dewey, it seems clear that Kilpatrick ended by transforming Dewey's ideas into something quite different than Dewey had originally intended.

Kilpatrick's Project Method

Some of the theoretical differences between Dewey and Kilpatrick come clearly into focus when Kilpatrick's project method is examined. In his effort to present a purposeful approach to instruction, Kilpatrick developed the project method in the spring of 1918.[18] It was also his purpose to reconcile Thorndike's connectionism with Dewey's theory of instruction. By emphasizing purposeful activity that was in harmony with the learner's goals, he sought to take full account of Thorndike's law of effect; by locating this activity in a social environment, he believed he could introduce an ethical outcome, since moral character was, for him, anchored in the welfare of the group. Kilpatrick reorganized the curriculum as a succession of projects suitable to the interests of each stage of learners. He summarized the role of the teacher as follows: The teacher helps (1) initiate the activity; (2) plan how to carry the activity forward; (3) execute the plan; (4) evaluate progress; (5) think up new leads; (6) formulate the new leads by writing them down for later reference; (7) keep the pupils critical of their thinking enroute to the solution; (8) look back over the whole process to pick up and recapitulate important kinds of learning, as well as to draw lessons for the future.

Within this particular technology of instruction, Dewey's problem-solving method became only one special type of project. Other types of projects such as building a boat, presenting a play, or developing a skill might be less scientific, or not scientific at all. The other steps of conventional instructional method—presentation, eliciting the trial response, correcting the trial response, and eliciting the test response—were also part of the Kilpatrick approach, in which each assumed a distinctive form. Rather than presenting an instructional task, the teacher assisted the learner in defining it. The object was not to learn something from a book but to meet a need or resolve a problem. Trial responses and their corrections were automatically resolved during the planning and execution process. The test response constituted the results of the activity and the degree to which that activity had achieved a desired goal.[19]

Comparative Analysis of Dewey and Kilpatrick

On the surface, the Dewey problem-solving method and the Kilpatrick project method seemed to have been cast from the same theoretical mold. There were, however, basic differences. Dewey considered problem solving central to the instructional process and was deeply concerned with the interests and purposes of the learner. He also proposed a new body of content, beginning with the learner's experiences and culminating with structured subject matter. Kilpatrick, on the other hand, attacked subject matter that was fixed in advance and emphasized a child-centered approach that Dewey himself had rejected, first in his *The Child and the Curriculum* (1902) and later in his *Experience and Education* (1938). Moreover, Kilpatrick's influential *Foundations of Method* (1926) unequivocally stated a Thorndikean, connectionist psychology, which Dewey had consistently opposed. For example, one of the slogans popularized by Kilpatrick and other progressives, "Children learn by doing," distinctly implies a connectionist psychology of learning. Finally, Kilpatrick seemed to assume the validity of Rousseau's permissivism, which was incompatible with Dewey's views.

The Montessori Method

An important pioneer in nourishing a science of instruction was the remarkable Italian educator Maria Montessori (1870-1952), the first woman to receive a medical degree from the University of Rome.[20] Her dominating interest in the development and welfare of children soon diverted her from medicine to education, and she was placed in charge of a state school for defectives, a position she held from 1899 to 1901. During this period, Montessori began to develop techniques for teaching mentally deficient children, based on the methods and materials of Edouard Seguin (1812-1880).[21]

Fig. 3.3. Maria Montessori giving a lesson (Courtesy of Association Montessori Internationale.)

In 1901, Montessori resigned to reenter the University of Rome for courses in experimental psychology and anthropology, hoping to obtain a scientific foundation on which to build the science of instruction she wished to develop for normal children. By 1907, she was ready to apply her theories to the instruction of culturally deprived children in the first of the *Case dei Bambini*, or Children's Houses, which she established in a low-cost housing development in a Roman slum.[22] Montessori trained a resident teacher for each school, selected the instructional materials, and devised techniques derived partly from Seguin, partly from Froebel, and partly from her own experience with teaching mental defectives. She continued this work with extraordinary success until 1911.

When Montessori published her *Scientific Pedagogy as Applied to Child Education in the Children's Houses* in 1909, people came from all over the world to observe her schools. She devoted herself to two principal activities: acquainting teachers and educational leaders outside of Italy with her methods, and working out applications of those methods to older children.[23] Many prominent Americans became intensely interested in her work, including such diverse personalities as Alexander Graham Bell, psychologist Dorothy Canfield Fisher (better known for her novels), Arnold Gesell, Howard C. Warren, and Lightner Witmer.[24] S. S. McClure, publisher of the muckraking *McClure's Magazine*, helped communicate Montessori's methods to the public, generating an interest that exploded into a social movement.[25]

By 1917, however, American interest had already subsided. This was partly due to a false tension that developed between educational progressivism and Montessori. For example, the basic criticism of Montessori, as offered by William Heard Kilpatrick, centered on her failure to provide for "self-directing adaptation to a novel environment."[26] Also, as Joseph Hunt pointed out in his introduction to *The Montessori Method*, she collided with several of the more firmly held psychological beliefs relative to "fixed intelligence" and the "unimportance of early experience."[27]

A second explosion of American interest occurred during the mid-1950s, partly because many of her instructional practices seemed justified in the light of new contributions to learning theory. One of the decisive catalysts in the revival of the Montessori movement was the work of the American Montessori Society, founded in 1956 by Nancy McCormick Rambusch in Greenwich, Connecticut.[28] A third revival of American interest occurred in the early 1990s.

Basic Concepts of the Montessori Method

Montessori's genius lay in her ability to anticipate what a learner was attempting to do in his informational interaction with his environment, and then to develop a plan that provided relevant experiences. Her technology of instruction possessed three characteristics: adaptation of schoolwork to the individuality of each learner; provision for freedom in which the teacher did not dominate the learner nor did the learner become overly dependent on the teacher; and emphasis on sensory discrimination, perhaps the most distinguishing feature of the system.

Two of the basic principles of the Montessori method—respect for the learner's individuality and encouragement of his freedom—determined not only the psychological climate and physical arrangement of the classroom, but also the relation of teacher and learner, the instructional media, and the nature of instructional procedures. For example, she used small, light chairs and tables that the children could rearrange as they chose. Each learner selected from a central room those materials he wished to use, took them to a place that suited him, and proceeded to work in his own way. There was no group instruction, although the children sometimes played group games or did their work together on their own initiative. A teacher was always present to observe and guide. If a learner failed to complete an exercise, he received no penalty; his failure indicated that he was not yet ready for the work, and the teacher would suggest some other exercise. Whenever possible, the instructional materials used by the children were self-corrective, so that learners could discover their own mistakes and become progressively more independent.[29]

To reinforce the idea that freedom implies independence, small children in the Montessori schools were taught how to dress themselves, keep themselves clean, dust the room, care for school equipment, and help serve lunch. The youngest began with exercises in buttoning, hooking, and lacing pieces of cloth together. Later they learned to walk quietly, to move their chairs without noise, and to be able to handle increasingly delicate objects. At first, the younger children were helped by the older children, but they were encouraged to decline aid as soon as possible.

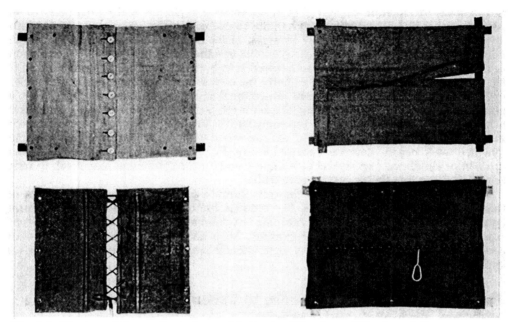

Fig. 3.4. Montessori frames for lacing and buttoning (Courtesy of the Association Montessori Informationale.)

Montessori emphasized the senses, individually and in association with one another, working particularly with visual, muscular, tactile, and auditory sensations. Through sight, sound, and touch, the children learned to distinguish shapes, sizes, weights, textures, colors, and pitch. They were also trained to observe and care for plants, birds, and animals. Thus the Montessori technology of instruction was a blend of three somewhat divergent elements: the two fundamental tenets of learner individuality and freedom, and the specific technique of sensory training.

Contributions of Montessori

Montessori's stated theories often diverged sharply from their implementation. In general, her theories were derivative, whereas her practices stemmed from her own clinical observation and special insights. As a consequence, her instructional procedures often either contradicted her theoretical principles, or at least had no apparent relation to them. Thus Montessori often did the right things for the wrong theoretical reasons. However, she considered her system completely scientific. And despite the fact that she never employed techniques of measurement, statistical design, or analysis, many of her concepts suggest that she built a sounder system of instruction than her critics realized. For example, Montessori's emphasis on sensory learning, based as it was on her careful observation of mentally retarded children, was closer to reality than the theories of critics who held such learning in contempt. Recent evidence appears to indicate that the role of the eyes and the ears, and perhaps the tactile organs, may be much more important in the organism's development than was thought possible.[30]

Another example from recent data seems to provide an important psychological basis for Montessori's notion that children have a spontaneous interest in learning and that motivation is inherent within a human's interaction with the environment.[31] In accordance with this idea, Montessori attempted to grade didactic materials and match them to standards the learner had already developed in the course of his past experience. What is more, by having children aged from three to seven years together, she provided the younger children with a graded series of models to imitate and the older children with an opportunity to learn by teaching. Thus Montessori succeeded in breaking the lockstep process and provided an opportunity for the learner to make his own selection of materials and models.[32]

Of particular relevance to current educational problems of cultural deprivation was Montessori's contention that the young learner is characterized by self-creating energies that can be sustained and enhanced by the imaginative and controlled use of environmental materials. Her "prepared environment," so successful with the Italian slum children among whom her work began, deserves renewed study. For example, it is well known that the restriction of childhood experiences to a narrow and drab environment may result in serious psychological damage that is often irremediable.

Modern educational technology suggests many extensions of Montessori's idea of a prepared environment. For example, her didactic materials could be expanded through programmed instruction or optimum learning environments could be devised for particular groups of learners. What is more important, Montessori has provided an instructional approach that, when supplemented by experimental research, can provide the basis for a scientific technology of instruction.

Individualized Instruction According to Burk, Washburne, Parkhurst, and Morrison

Prior to 1800, instruction in American schools was predominantly individual. The introduction of blackboards, slates, and steel pens brought about innovations in methods of instruction. The monitorial method, as used in the Lancasterian schools, was a shift from an individual to a more systematic group instruction approach. With the evolution of the graded school, graded instructional materials, and even graded teachers in the middle of the nineteenth century came the advent of a lockstep educational machine that has changed little since those days.

However, beginning in the 1880s, there arose what has been an almost continuous interest in individualizing instruction. One of the first attempts to break the lockstep of graded instruction came with the general introduction of the laboratory method about 1885. Each student was encouraged to initiate individual experimental procedures; the laboratory was the core of his learning experience. Moreover, a number of individualized instructional materials such as stereographs, scientific apparatus, construction materials, hand tools, study prints, self-checking devices, and diagnostic tests were utilized.

Burk's System of Individualized Instruction

Frederic Burk (1862-1924) developed one of the first systems of individual instruction, at the San Francisco State Normal School in 1912.[33] He and his faculty rewrote courses of study to permit learners to advance at their own rate with a minimum of teacher direction. Self-instruction bulletins in arithmetic, geography, grammar, history, language, and phonics were written, published, and distributed throughout the United States and foreign countries. Over 100,000 bulletins were sold, without any advertising, or profit to the authors. However, in 1917 publication was abruptly halted when the California Attorney General ruled that the power to publish textbooks or printed instructional materials rested entirely with the state board of education. As a result, the fruitful work begun by Burk was curtailed. It remained for two of his associates, Carleton W. Washburne and Helen Parkhurst, to develop two of the most outstanding and distinctive plans of individual instruction.

Washburne's Winnetka Plan

The Winnetka Plan was developed by Carleton W. Washburne (1890-1968) when he was appointed superintendent of the Winnetka, Illinois, public schools in 1919. The plan provided self-instructional and self-corrective practice materials (workbooks), a simple record-keeping system in which each pupil's progress was noted, and prepared materials appropriate to each pupil's particular project and assignment. Thus, the twofold task of the faculty was to analyze course content into specific objectives and develop a plan of instruction that would enable learners to master each objective at their own rate.

The Winnetka Plan not only allowed learners to proceed at different rates, but also recognized that learners proceed at different rates in different subjects. Each learner was given diagnostic tests to determine what goals and tasks he should undertake. When the learner thought he had accomplished his goals, he took a self-test to see whether he was ready to be tested by the teacher, and also to see whether he was prepared to undertake new goals and tasks.[34]

Parkhurst's Dalton Plan

The Dalton Plan, first developed by Helen Parkhurst (1887-1973) in 1919 in an ungraded school for crippled children, was adopted by the Dalton, Massachusetts, high school in 1920. Its principal features were: differentiation of assignments for different ability levels, self-instructional practice materials, and assistance with individual study difficulties. Under this plan, the teacher made a contract with each student concerning assignments. The student was free to budget his time in order to complete every phase of the contract.[35]

Group activities in both the Winnetka and the Dalton plans were not neglected, but the emphasis was on individualized instruction. The Winnetka Plan emphasized group activities more than did the Dalton Plan, devoting approximately half of each morning and afternoon to such activities as plays, music, student government, and open forums. In both plans, classrooms became laboratories or conference rooms, and teachers became consultants or guides.[36]

The Morrison Plan

Another instructional proposal, highly influential from about 1925-1935, was that of Henry Clinton Morrison (1871-1945), former director of the University of Chicago High School. His system provided a sequence of units and guide sheets for lesson assignments.[37] The classroom was viewed as a laboratory where units and assignments were differentiated for learners of varying ability. Morrison's (1931) formula for mastery was, "Pretest, teach, test the result, adapt procedure, teach and test again to the point of actual learning."[38]

For science-type units or those designed to develop understanding, Morrison devised a five-step procedure reminiscent of Herbart's four-step plan: exploration, presentation, assimilation, organization, recitation. Exploration was a test to determine how much each learner already knew or how much understanding he possessed. Presentation usually involved a lecture, which provided an overview or summary of the unit as a whole and explained the principle to be learned. Assimilation represented the achievement of unit understanding. Once the learner had passed a mastery test, he reached the organization phase, which Morrison referred to as the time when the learner provided a written outline discussing the logical arguments that supported the basic understanding or principle embodied in the unit. Recitation was practically the reverse of the first step, presentation: now the learner orally presented a summary version of the principle learned in the unit.

Morrison's plan called for individualized instruction, but unlike Washburne's Winnetka Plan, class members began and ended each unit together. Moreover, learners tended to remain together through all the steps with the exception of step three, assimilation, when each was on his own. To inform each learner what was expected of him, a guide sheet (worksheet) was provided. The teacher maintained close supervision as the learners worked, reading their notebooks, conversing with them, or conducting group discussions.

Analysis of Individualized Instructional Plans

The significance of these individualized instructional plans lay in their attempts to provide for individual differences in learning and, at the same time, to teach for specific objectives. A study of the current programmed instruction approach reveals that early individualized instruction plans anticipated much of what has been called today's major breakthrough in education.[39]

At this point, it seems relevant to note that the phrase *science of education* was expanded by Washburne and others (such as Bobbitt and Charters) to mean not only basing a technology of instruction on scientific principles, but also employing statistical analysis of the activities people most frequently perform or the kinds of information or words most frequently used, as a basis for selecting curriculum content.[40]

These individualized instructional plans made an outstanding contribution to educational technology by breaking the lockstep method of learner progress and substituting mastery learning for partial learning. They opposed the concept of a normal distribution curve and the notion that only a small percentage of learners should complete the period of study with a thorough mastery of the subject. Individualized instruction enabled learners to progress at their own rate but required that they reach an approved level of achievement as a requisite for advancement.

Another contribution of these particular methods to a technology of instruction was their emphasis on careful organization of assignments. Organizing materials on an individual basis often led to a deeper appreciation of the nature of learning and the realization that much could be eliminated from courses formerly considered essential. Moreover, the teachers in these programs found that they had to analyze their own instructional materials more carefully than when they had employed traditional procedures. Thus individualized instruction led to a technology for organizing the curriculum as well as to a technology of instruction.

Lewin's Field Theory and a Science of Instruction

The series of experimental studies directed by Kurt Lewin (1890-1947) at the University of Berlin in the late 1920s were models of theoretical creativity combined with brilliant experimentation. Although Lewin was associated with an active center of Gestalt psychology at Berlin, his theories had little formal relationship to those of the orthodox Gestaltists.[41] Lewin's early work on motivational problems led to an interest in personality organization and also in a wide variety of problems in social psychology. This culminated in his development of the group dynamics movement and action research (i.e., research directed at producing social changes). Lewin also concerned himself with the problem of constructing scientific principles of learning as the basis for a science of instruction. In all these diverse areas, he took the same fundamental approach: He emphasized the psychological over the simple, environmental factors.

A native of Germany, Lewin received his doctorate at the University of Berlin, where he later became a professor of psychology and philosophy. He came to the United States in 1932 and taught at the universities of Stanford, Cornell, and Iowa. In 1944, he was named director of the Research Center for Group Dynamics at the Massachusetts Institute of Technology, where he remained until his untimely death in 1947.

Lewin's Theoretical Approach

It is not necessary to review the substance of Lewin's field psychology, since excellent expositions are readily available.[42] A primary concern is, rather, to point to Lewin's general theoretical orientation so that the reader may have a clearer understanding of the constructs that supported his theory of learning.

Although Lewin began his scientific career as an associationist, he soon became convinced that the associationist concept of learning had to be radically revised. Moreover, he also diverged from the views of the major Gestalt psychologists, saying: "Psychology cannot try to explain everything with a single construct, such as association, instinct, or Gestalt. A variety of constructs has to be used. These should be interrelated, however, in a logically precise manner."[43]

To Lewin, scientific method included not only the processes of observing and classifying data, but also those of formulating and testing hypotheses. He stressed the importance of theory by stating that "a science without theory is blind because it lacks that element which alone is able to organize facts and give direction to research."[44] He was also convinced that, in order to understand and predict learner behavior, he had to focus on careful, full descriptions of particular, learner-environmental instructional situations.

To portray his conceptualization of psychological processes, Lewin chose topological geometry as the best mathematical model, because he felt it adequately represented concepts that were broad enough to be applicable to all kinds of behavior and, at the same time, were specific enough to apply to a specific person in a concrete situation.[45] Since topology lacked directive concepts, Lewin invented a new hodological (from the Greek *hodos*, translated as path) space geometry, which he used to represent certain dynamic factors in psychological relationships.

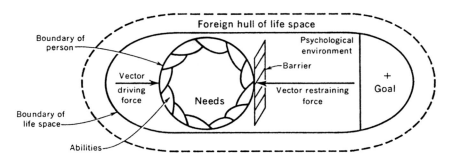

Fig. 3.5. Life space of an individual according to Lewin.

Lewin formulated three key constructs—life space, topology, and vector. He defined life space as the whole of one's psychological reality, or the total pattern of factors that affect behavior at any one time. He also viewed life space as a dynamic series of events in which a person and his environment are in simultaneous, mutual interaction and are mutually interdependent. Lewin used topological concepts to represent the structure of a life space in order to define the range of possible perceptions and actions. He accomplished this by explaining the functional parts of a life space in terms of regions and boundaries, and indicated that, when an individual structures or makes sense of his life space, he divides it into regions. For example, if the region "eating" is located in a person's life space, the person is either eating or thinking about eating.

Lewin used the vector concept to represent direction and strength as two of the three properties of a force. The third property was its point of application. Thus Lewin saw vectors symbolizing the tendencies of the life space to change or to resist change. For example, both driving and restraining forces may arise from the needs and abilities of a particular learner, from the actions of another person, or from the impersonal aspects of an instructional situation. Lewin's guiding formula, based on a summary of his work, could be written

$$B = f(P, E)$$

Behavior depends on the interaction of the Person and the Environment within a psychological field, or life space.

Lewin's Cognitive-field Theory of Learning

Lewin's cognitive-field theory often is called merely "field theory." However, "cognitive field-theory" is more truly descriptive, since the theory describes how a learner comes to know (from the Latin verb *cognoscere*, which means to know) or gains insights into himself and his environment and how, using his insights or cognitions, he acts in relation to his environment.

Learning, to Lewin, was perceived as problem solving—seeking perceptions to restructure the cognitive field, acting to overcome barriers, and incorporating understandings (or insights and ways of behaving) into a newly reorganized life space. Within this process, he distinguished four kinds of change, namely: change in cognitive structure (knowledge); change in motivation (learning to like or dislike); change into group belongingness or ideology; and gain in voluntary control and dexterity of musculature.

Implications for a Technology of Instruction

Within a field approach to educational technology, the teacher's unique function is to implement the development of useful insights, helping students respond more intelligently and more effectively in differing situations. To accomplish this, a technology of instruction built around the field concept must provide for analysis of the instructional situation as a whole. According to Lewin:

> A teacher will never succeed in giving proper guidance to a child if he does not learn to understand the psychological world in which the individual child lives. To describe a situation "objectively" in psychology actually means to describe the situation as a totality of those facts, and of only those facts, which make up the field of the individual. To substitute for that world of the individual the world of the teacher, of the physicist, or of anybody else is to be, not objective, but wrong.[46]

The Lewin field theory of learning can be used as a starting point for the technical analysis of instruction design. One approach is to ask what characteristics could be used in a scientific technology of instruction to symbolically, as well as functionally, represent the following three interrelated aspects of the instructional situation: (1) the teacher-communicator and his production and/or manipulation of sign-symbol material with the intent of cognitively structuring the field for learners with respect to their specific needs and demands; (2) the learner-communicant, who perceives or cognitively structures specific sign-symbol material in terms of his present pattern of needs, expectancies, and demands; and (3) the nature of the instructional message as part of an organized, planned stimulus field in which sign-symbol materials are produced and used with the intent of structuring the cognitive-perceptual fields of both the teacher and the learner via single or multimedia channels.

Thus, the central task of the teacher or the instructional designer in the Lewinian theoretical context is essentially creative, because it involves the unique potentials of signs and symbols, the structuring of content, and a particular relationship with each learner in terms of how he perceives the instructional situation and what he wants in it.

Contributions of Lewin

Lewin made historic contributions to the development of psychology, in the areas of child psychology and social psychology, exemplified by his early research on behavior in experimentally manipulated social climates.[47] For example, leadership techniques were experimentally varied in boys' clubs (laissez-faire, democratic, autocratic), and various behaviors were correlated with the different social climates that resulted. These studies not only opened an important new area of social research but continue to hold significant implications for a technology of instruction.

Lewin's contributions to psychological theory were of great scope and originality. He developed concepts and experimental techniques, such as level of aspiration, that have significantly influenced modern educational technology.

A Technology of Instruction According to Skinner

In essence, B. F. Skinner's (1904-1990) psychology, operant conditioning or behaviorism, was a modern extension of the earlier stimulus-response psychologies—Thorndike's connectionism and Watson's behaviorism. Thorndike dealt with both physical and mental elements but was always mechanistic. Watson, too, was mechanistic, but he limited his study to the behavior of biological organisms. Skinner, as did both Thorndike and Watson, assumed that man is neutral and passive and that all behavior can be described in mechanistic terms.

A professor at Harvard University starting in 1947, Skinner was influenced by the research of Pavlov and Watson while attending Harvard as a graduate student in biology. Following several years of postdoctoral fellowships, he taught at the University of Minnesota and at Indiana University before returning to Harvard to join the faculty. Skinner displayed great breadth of interest and ingenuity in his work.[48] He concerned himself with an analysis of verbal learning, "missile-guiding pigeons," teaching machines, and the control of behavior by scheduled reinforcement.

Skinner's goal was a science of behavior in which the basic order of nature can be discovered, including human nature, for the purpose of achieving predictability and control of human behavior. To Skinner, a science of instruction had to be based on operant reinforcement in which sets of learner acts are reinforced, or strengthened, to increase the probability of reoccurrence. In this process, it was essential that teachers use properly timed and spaced schedules of reinforcement.

Fig. 3.6. Photograph of B. F. Skinner (Courtesy of B. F. Skinner.)

Skinner's System of Operant Conditioning

Skinner's thesis has been that, since an organism tends to repeat actions that are reinforced, it can be led to do much what the experimenter or the teacher wishes. For example, Skinner taught rats to use a marble to obtain food from a vending machine, pigeons to play a modified game of tennis, and dogs to operate the pedal of a refuse can in order to retrieve a bone. He concentrated his study on lower animals because their behavior is simpler, their environments are more easily controlled, and techniques for observation can be less complicated.[49]

On the basis of his many animal experiments, Skinner developed his psychological theory of operant conditioning. However, he considered his methodological approach strictly atheoretical, because he long felt that the state of knowledge in psychology inadequate to justify elaborate, formal theorizing, particularly physiological speculations. He also insisted on a thorough analysis of the behavior of a single organism, rather than that of large groups of subjects.

In operant conditioning, the important stimulus is the one immediately following a response, not the one preceding it. Any emitted response that leads to reinforcement is thereby strengthened. According to this viewpoint, it is not the specific response that is strengthened but rather the general tendency to make the response. The law of operant conditioning states that if the occurrence of an operant is followed by presentation of a reinforcing stimulus, the strength probability is increased.

In instructional terms, this concept implies that the key to successful instruction is to analyze the effect of reinforcement and then design techniques and set up specific, reinforcing sequences in which a response is followed by a reinforcing stimulus. Operant conditioning occurs, for example, when a child is taught reading by being reinforced with "right" or "wrong" according to his response to appropriate visual stimuli. Implicit in operant conditioning is the conviction that "when all relevant variables have been arranged, an organism will or will not respond. If it does not, it cannot. If it can, it will."[50]

A Technology of Instruction Based on Operant Conditioning

Skinner was convinced that operant conditioning, which is very fruitful when applied to animals, held great possibilities for more complex instruction. He felt that achieving efficient control over human learning requires instrumental aid and, therefore, that steps should be taken to rectify the shortcomings of traditional instructional practice by developing a scientific technology of instruction.

For example, Skinner criticized conventional instruction as being dominated by aversion stimulation and as lacking a planned program of serial reinforcement. Thus, according to Skinner, a learner is usually trying to escape or keep away from something; there is an excessive time lapse between behavior and reinforcement; or desirable behavior may not be reinforced at all. Skinner contended that a test given near the end of a week is too far removed from the behaviors the learners emitted (sent out) while studying the subject matter earlier that week. Instead, reinforcement should immediately follow the behavior.

According to Skinner, in order to develop a technology of instruction based on operant conditioning, certain specific questions need to be answered: (1) What behavior is to be established? (2) What reinforcers are available? (3) What responses are available? (4) How can reinforcements be most efficiently scheduled?[51] The teacher is the builder and architect of behaviors; he must establish specific learner objectives and define them in terms of desired behaviors. Skinner contended, however, that a teacher is not an effective reinforcing mechanism and that mechanical and electrical devices must be used for efficient control of learning.

To schedule reinforcements efficiently, Skinner made them contingent on the desired behavior. Skinner said:

> The whole process of becoming competent in any field must be divided into a very large number of very small steps, and reinforcement must be contingent upon the accomplishment of each step.... By making each successive step as small as possible, the frequency of reinforcement can be raised to a maximum, while the possible aversive consequences of being wrong are reduced to a minimum.[52]

This is the purpose of programmed instruction, according to the Skinnerian concept. In Skinner's view, teaching machines encourage learners to take an "active" role in the instructional process because they must develop the answers before they can be reinforced. In building a case for teaching machines, Skinner stated, "The effect upon each student is surprisingly like that of a private tutor."[53]

Influence of Skinner

Skinner's influence guided the mainstream of developments in programmed instruction during the late fifties and early sixties. Historically, the term *program* as applied to a sequence of instruction presented by a teaching machine derived from his 1954 and 1958 papers.[54] In some respects, Skinner represents a renewal of Watsonian behaviorism. Like Watson, he too attracted many young experimenters eager to make behavior study an exact science. Such Skinnerians resent the orthodox restrictions of the American Psychological Association's journals (particularly the unwritten regulations concerning sample size and statistical tests), and so established their own, the *Journal of the Experimental Analysis of Behavior.*[55]

Piagetian Approach to Instructional Design

Jean Piaget (1896-1980), born in Neuchatel, Switzerland, began his work in the field of biology, but eventually became the foremost developmental psychologist of the twentieth century.[56] From 1920 until his death in 1980, Piaget (at the University of Geneva) and his associates at the Institute J. J. Rousseau in Geneva, Switzerland studied many aspects of children's intellectual development, including perception, imagery, play, language, memory, reasoning, problem solving, and awareness of as well as conceptions of causality, quantity, space, time, distance, movement, speed, number, probability, geometry, and morality.[57] What most intrigued Piaget was epistemology, the branch of philosophy that focuses on the nature of knowledge.[58] But most important, from the point of view of educational technology, was his formulation of models of cognition, which provided guidelines for a fresh, fruitful approach to the problems of instructional design.

Fig. 3.7. Photograph of Jean Piaget (Courtesy of the Foundation Archives Jean Piaget, Université de Genéve.)

This discussion of Piaget's theory will first introduce some of his basic concepts, then review his models of cognitive development, and finally suggest some implications of his theory and research for educational technology. Rather than comprehensively elucidate Piaget's theory, the discussion will explain its basic elements for a general purpose understanding of his contributions.

Tests of Various Types of Conservation

	Start with:	Then:	Ask the child:	Preoperational children usually answer:
CONSERVATION OF LIQUIDS 	Two equal glasses of liquid.	Pour one into a taller, thinner glass.	Which glass contains more?	The taller one.
CONSERVATION OF NUMBER	Two equal lines of checkers.	Lengthen the spaces between one line.	Which line has more checkers?	The longer one.
CONSERVATION OF MATTER 	Two equal balls of clay.	Squeeze one ball into a long, thin shape.	Which piece has more clay?	The long one.
CONSERVATION OF LENGTH	Two sticks of equal length.	Move one stick.	Which stick is longer?	The one that is farther to the right.
CONSERVATION OF VOLUME	Two glasses of water with equal balls of clay inside.	Change the shape of one ball.	Which piece of clay will displace more water?	The long one.
CONSERVATION OF AREA 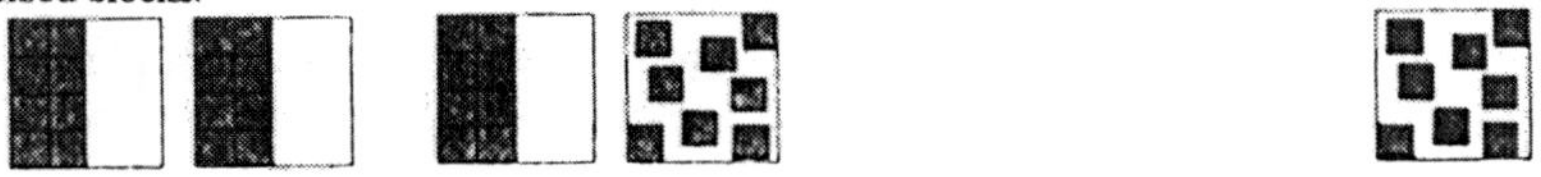	Two identical pieces of cardboard on which are placed the same number of equally-sized blocks.	Rearrange blocks on one piece of cardboard.	Which has more cardboard covered up?	The one with the blocks not touching.

Fig. 3.8. Piaget's conservation tests (From Kathleen Stassen Berger, *The Developing Person through the Lifespan.* New York: Worth Publishers, 1983, 224. Used with permission of the publisher.)

Basic Concepts

According to Piaget, cognition developed not through maturation or learning alone, but through the continuous interaction between learner and environment. As the learner continues to cope with his environment, his cognitive processes become more and more complex.

One of the basic notions underlying Piaget's theory was the *scheme*, a complex concept involving both overt motor-behavior patterns and internalized thought processes.[59] It includes simple, predictable responses at the reflex level and also a complex cognitive structure involving broad understandings. Piaget asserted that every scheme has certain unitary properties and that all the actions involved in it are parts of a single scheme.

To Piaget, the scheme represents the structure that adapts and adaptation is the cognitive striving of the learner to achieve equilibrium or stability between himself and his environment. Equilibrium depends on two interrelated processes: *assimilation* and *accommodation*. Assimilation is the process of change through which the learner becomes able to cope with situations that are initially too difficult for him. Accommodation is the process whereby the learner adjusts to new environmental conditions and incorporates new elements into his scheme. For example, an infant may be unable to pick up small objects, although he may be able to pick up slightly larger ones. In order to adapt to the demands of his environment, the infant's grasping scheme must *accommodate* to the demands of the small objects. Once the ability to pick up these small objects has been acquired, the grasping scheme can *assimilate* such behavior. Thus, the processes of accommodation and assimilation are always mutually interactive.

Piaget's basic question was: Under what laws does cognition develop and change? He answered this question by formulating chronologically successive models, or phases, that represent cognitive development as inherent, unalterable, and ordered in time. Each model reflects a range of behavioral patterns that occur in a definite sequence within approximate age spans. Whether or not the learner would realize his potential or whether the learner's rate of progression varies were separate questions.

What was important, according to Piaget, was the order of these phases. While Piaget set down approximate ages for each phase, he did not contend that these were absolutely fixed. He simply held that the order would not vary from one learner to another. Each phase of development carries possibilities for new ways of processing and representing information. However, unless each of these abilities is sufficiently stimulated as it emerges, it will not develop fully and will therefore not adequately prepare the learner for the demands of the next phase.[60]

Piaget's theory encompassed the development of cognition from the infant's first sucking, looking, and grasping to the adolescent's ability to manipulate logical propositions in a symbolic fashion. The learner simultaneously moves along two dimensions. Along one dimension, he moves from a completely subjective view of the world to one that is increasingly objective. On another dimension, the learner moves from the concrete world of things present to a world of things possible.

Cognitive Models

Piaget represented cognitive development with four chronologically successive models: (1) sensory-motor, (2) preoperational, (3) concrete operations, and (4) formal operations. In his attempts to characterize these models, Piaget made sophisticated use of logic and mathematics. An extended discussion of these models, however, is not justified for our purposes. The general attributes of the four models of cognition will be looked at in their developmental order.

Phase 1 of cognitive development, the sensory-motor, lasts from birth until approximately eighteen months to two years. The child perceives and acts, but does not have internal representations of the world. However, he develops the beginnings of internalized schemata, if not actual concepts of space, time, matter, and causality. Related to causality is the concept of probability; Piaget pointed out that the infant comes to recognize the likelihood that the footsteps he hears approaching are those of his mother. With respect to the concepts of space and matter, the large concept that develops during this phase is that of permanence. The infant first believes that an object no longer exists when it disappears from sight. But at some time during the first year, the infant comes to realize that an object can continue to exist even if he does not see it; thus the infant develops a notion of permanence.

The next development phase involves continuity in space-time. Piaget repeatedly hid a toy at point A while the child observed. The child learned to look at A and found the object there. Piaget then moved the object to point B and, with the child watching, hid it there. The child began his search, not at point B, but at A. If the object was moved to point C, the infant again began at A, went to B, and then to C. This cannot be explained by sensory experience alone. On the basis of earlier experience, the child had stored information about where to find the object; he needed additional interactions to learn differently.

Piaget held that the fundamental categories of cognition are developed in the sensory-motor phase of development. The conception of causality begins then as well as the development of prehension (grasping) and what Piaget calls primary, secondary, and tertiary circular reflexes. Behavior begins to manifest the directionality that suggests purpose. Finally, the sensory-motor phase ends with the first signs of imagery, or the beginnings of the symbolic processes. In Piaget's view, the clearest signs that a child has begun to represent absent objects to himself are a particular kind of imitation and a particular kind of representational play. Piaget believed imagery makes language possible, and therefore asserted that language begins to become important to the infant at about eighteen months.

Phase 2 in cognition development is the preoperational, which extends roughly until six or seven years of age. The child's thinking during this period is distinguished by what it lacks, namely, logical operations and, particularly, reversibility. The child cannot reverse a thought process and therefore knows the world only as he sees it; he knows no alternatives. Further, he sees his physical and social worlds only as he has previously experienced them. This leads to his assumption that everyone thinks as he does and understands him without any particular effort on his part to communicate.

In one of Piaget's tests, "Cows in the Field," the child is presented with two pieces of green cardboard that represent fields of grass. A cow is placed in each field, and the child is asked if each cow will have the same amount to eat. Then a barn (a small model) is placed on each field, to which the six-year-old may say, "The barn takes up some room and each side has a barn so the grass is the same." Barns are added one at a time to each field; but in one field the barns are lined up in a horizontal row with their sides touching, whereas in the other field the barns are scattered. The child continues to assert equality while the barns are equal in number, but only up to a certain point. Beyond that point (which may be as many as ten barns), unoccupied space in the fields begins to look different; one field looks as if there were a great deal more grass. The child in the preoperational phase falters; he is judging in terms of perceptions, and so he now says that one cow has more to eat than the other. Or he may say that one cow can eat all around the edges of the barns, while the other cow cannot. Because he cannot perform certain mental operations on the data before him, he is misled by his perceptions.

Piaget saw in play and imitation during this phase the emergence of symbolic schemes, or internal schemes that make symbolic behavior possible. There are two types of symbolic schemes, the verbal and the nonverbal. Verbal schemes become objective, fitted to cultural norms, and, through language, serve as a medium of social communication. Nonverbal schemes remain idiosyncratic, subjective, and appear in fantasies, dreams, and play.

From two years until eleven or twelve, the child is working out a conception of the world. Piaget found that a child during this period does not distinguish as adults do concerning mental, physical, and social reality. For a time he believes everything that moves is alive. Moral law and physical law are not clearly distinguished. The child's theory is that everything was originally made or created, the creators being his parents, early men, or gods. The child's parents are the source of everything and are simultaneously omniscient, omnipotent, and omnipresent. In the child's eyes, as Freud argued in *The Future of an Illusion* (1927), they are God.

The preoperational child's perceptions, play, and language clearly reveal his egocentrism. He is not aware of other points of view nor does he recognize that he has a point of view. The child is unable to explain something clearly to another person because he assumes that the listener already understands everything.

When the child is old enough to begin school, his language is largely the verbalization of his mental processes. Much as he once employed motor apparatus to act out his thinking, he now uses speech. However, he can think of only one idea at a time, and his perceptions and interpretations remain largely egocentric and at variance with the thinking of adults. He also lacks the ability to combine related objects into classes and thus establish a hierarchy of classification. He may say that a rose is, indeed, a flower, and then identify certain other flowers by name. However, if one asks, "If all the roses in the world were to die, would there be any flowers?" one is likely to get a negative answer. For the child, a rose is a rose, but at the same time comprises the complete class of flowers. He is not capable of understanding the ascending nature of a hierarchy—he cannot combine subclasses into a supraclass of one of the subclasses and still have something left.

A child in this phase also uses appropriate language without fully understanding its meaning. For example, the child in the early years of this phase may know his right arm from his left, but he has no notion of the *concepts* of right and left. Further, the child can think only in terms of an ongoing event. All experiences are judged by their final results. A toy car that arrives first in a race is the "fastest," regardless of whether it only traveled half as far as the other cars did. His reasoning proceeds directly from premise to conclusion. It is typical for a child in this phase to see the world in terms of opposing absolutes—something is either the best or the worst.

In phase 2, language serves a threefold purpose: first, it is an important tool of intuitive thought to reflect on an event and project it into the future; second, it serves as a vehicle of egocentric communication; and third, it is a means of understanding and adapting to the external environment.

Phase 3 begins, at about six or seven years of age, with the emergence of logical operations, which Piaget call *groupment*. For example, the child becomes able to mentally reverse a process and see an event from different perspectives. Piaget's tests for demonstrating whether or not a child has achieved this level are well known. One of them involves a ball of clay that is rolled into a ball, flattened, or broken into small pieces. As the clay's appearance changes, the child is asked whether he thinks the amount of clay has changed.

The child may use an identity operation to arrive at a logical conclusion. Thus, one test involves establishing an identity between two amounts of liquid and then testing to see whether the child retains that identity relationship when he sees one vessel of liquid poured into another vessel of different shape.

The child also learns to combine subclasses into a supraclass and to separate supraclasses into their components. Thus he knows that if all the roses in the world died, there would be no roses left, but there would still be other flowers. Although the child has long been aware of objects belonging together, it is only in this phase that he begins to be able to hold a large category constant while he manipulates subcategories. For example, he recognizes that a general class such as animals can be subdivided into land animals and sea animals.

Finally, there is the operation of associativity. In arithmetic, this means that $3 + (4 + 2)$ achieves the same result as $(3 + 4) + 2$. In other words, the child learns that the same goal can be reached by different paths, and is able to manipulate data in various ways to test his hypotheses. However, he is not yet able to think abstractly about a problem, but can only work out the relationships of concrete variables.

At approximately eleven or twelve years of age, or in *Phase 4*, Piaget again found changes occurring in the child's cognitive processes. Between the ages of eleven and fifteen, thought becomes decreasingly tied to the concrete; the adolescent becomes more and more capable of abstract reasoning and cognition begins to rely more on symbolism and the use of propositions. He can also logically combine such propositions. For example, he can compare by conjunction—"Both A and B make a difference"—or by disjunction—"It's got to be this or that." He understands implication—"If it's this, then that happens"—and incompatibility—"When this happens, then that doesn't." Thus, his thinking becomes fixed on possibilities rather than on specific objects or events.

The ability to reason supplies the youth with new methods of understanding his physical world and his social relationships. One of these new tools is logical deduction, which allows him to bring together apparently contradictory and unrelated wholes into logical relationships. This becomes a new means of generalization and differentiation that opens up new possibilities in dealing effectively with abstractions.

Around fourteen or fifteen, the youth usually achieves maturity in cognitive thought. Then he can depend solely on symbolism for operational thought; he thinks by using symbols to formulate hypotheses and structure a wide variety of combinations of events as they might occur. Simultaneously, he attempts to prove empirically which possibilities could materialize. Meanwhile, language continues to develop more fully, encouraging cognitive thought and behavior.

Near the end of the formal operations phase, Piaget saw the adolescent achieving equilibrium through his ability to tie together propositional operations into structured patterns of relationships and systems that eventually form a single unit. Piaget concluded that "the structured 'whole,' considered as the form of equilibrium of the subject's operational behavior, is therefore of fundamental psychological importance."[61] At this juncture, Piaget's analysis of cognitive development ended. Although he did not specifically say so, Piaget implied that the individual has reached cognitive maturity at the end of this phase.[62]

Some Implications for Instructional Design

This section examines the broad significance of Piaget's theory of cognitive development for instruction and attempts to extract some guiding principles for instructional design from Piaget's research and other Piaget-relevant studies.

The primary implication of Piaget's theory and research is that they provide a scientific basis for a technology of instruction. Thus, a Piagetian instructional design makes it possible for a teacher-communicator to predict the cognitive mode and range of a learner's understanding, while it also serves as a frame of reference for synchronizing instruction with individual development.

The real significance of Piaget's system is that it suggests a new approach to the old problem of readiness, or developmental capacity, through instructional design, a problem that has faced the educational profession at least since Comenius. Until Piaget developed his theory, two views of cognitive development dominated instructional design and the selection of content.

Probably the oldest view is based on the notion of the progressive emergence of inherent abilities: The learner cannot learn something until he has reached the appropriate stage of maturity for its achievement.[63] According to this view, learning depends entirely on the maturation of the learner; it is believed that maturation takes place within the organism and is governed by its own laws and conditions, quite apart from environmental influences. In its extreme this view holds that cognitive development occurs independent of instruction and that teaching children reading, writing, and counting before they are eight years old is, at best, a waste of time, and might actually be harmful.

A second traditional view rules out stages of development and considers any cognitive change the direct result of a change in the quantity of synaptic connections. The clearest statement of this position was given by Thorndike; it is also found in associative or behavioristic psychology that is based on the theory of the conditioned responses a learner acquires. Thus, according to this view, cognitive change occurs when the right stimuli are provided at the proper time.

In contrast to these two traditional views, Piaget's theory suggested that cognitive development is a product of organism-environment interaction. He considered neither maturation nor learning, by itself, to be sufficient for cognitive change. Both are necessary factors in the cognitive growth of the learner, but cognitive growth and change consists in the interaction of these two factors. Moreover, this interaction process implies that the learner's cognitive development depends upon his opportunities to have and think about new experiences. Also, what a learner incorporates into his cognitive processes or what stimulates him to reorganize or reclassify information is, in part, dependent on the cognitions he already possesses. Concrete or abstract cognitions do not emerge automatically, but rather are the product of a series of encounters with things and ideas.

In summary, the Piagetian view considers the following factors vital to cognitive development: first, certain stages of maturation; second, the results of experience with the environment; third, the results of explicit and implicit instruction of the learner within the society; and fourth, the process of equilibration, a kind of catalytic motion generated whenever the learner's cognitive system begins to contain self-contradictions or doubt.[64]

Piaget's views of cognitive development clearly differed considerably from the two established traditional views. The basic implication of Piaget's theory is the possibility of developing a technology of instruction that can be based on an individual rate of cognitive development.

Match between Information and Cognitive Structure

The first implication concerns the match between information and cognitive structure, an implication that Piaget himself suggested but never quite formulated. This poorly understood factor appears to be of prime importance for instructional design and educational practice. It has been pointed out that cognitive conflict, or discrepancy between the learner's cognitive structure and his environmental encounters, may or may not promote cognitive growth. We know, for example, that it is useless to expect a four-year-old learner (in Piaget's preconceptual phase) to see that an increase in length is compensated for by a decrease in thickness or that a particular bead can be counted as both a brown and a wooden bead.[65] Discrepancies that are too large may cause emotional disturbance whereas lesser discrepancies may be a positive challenge. Unfortunately, although a true understanding of this relationship is essential to an effective science and technology of instruction, it is still largely a process of trial and error.

Concrete Operations Precede Symbolic

The second implication of Piaget's system is that the young learner must initially be led, with concrete materials, to perform cognitive operations that he will later handle through symbols alone. As actions are repeated and varied, they become interrelated and internalized conceptual patterns are formed.

Piaget's investigations showed that from the time the learner begins elementary school until he reaches the more advanced stages of learning, he moves toward the process of abstracting the forms of cognitive operations from the instructional content he encounters.

Teachers long before Piaget, of course, understood the importance of using concrete materials, especially in the instruction of young children. However, many have continued to emphasize the concrete rather than the symbolic long after the learner entered the phase of formal operations, when he could begin to deal verbally with concepts and no longer required concrete materials. In fact, there is research that seems to indicate that presenting a learner with a wealth of stimuli that approximate reality is not necessarily the most effective way to facilitate cognitive change. What is more, excesses of realism may actually interfere with the transmission of information.

Thus, the teachers instructing the learner in the early stages of the concrete operational phase (the early elementary school years) might begin by having the child directly manipulate concrete materials, move to pictorial representation later in this phase (approximately nine to eleven years of age), and finally shift to cognitive anticipation and retrospection of earlier operations for the learner in the formal operations phase (approximately eleven to fifteen years of age). In the formal operations phase, the learner is able to manipulate symbols in various ways to accomplish what he could previously accomplish only with things. He is capable of thinking abstractly and of systematically using the kinds of formal methods characteristic of scientists, mathematicians, and philosophers. The learner's failure to think systematically and to perform symbolic operations may be due to the teacher's failure to get him to reflect on his actions, something he must do in order to generalize symbolic operations beyond their instructional context. It appears that considerable improvement in the educational program could be realized, at both the elementary and secondary levels, if instruction in logical operations could be appropriately geared to the developmental phase of each learner.

A Frame of Reference for Instructional Design

The third implication of Piaget's system is the need to liberate the learner from his egocentrism through group interaction with his peers, and also the importance of the process of equilibration in cognitive development. The development of organized belief systems, or groupment as Piaget described it, becomes a necessity as part of a whole, coherent system which sustains the individual's ego. However, as the learner in a group situation confronts other learners with different belief systems, doubt and conflict may arise. The challenge of a belief may throw his whole system into disarray and imbalance. Equilibrium is re-established either by explaining away the evidence and saving the belief or by modifying or discarding the belief itself. Thus, the cognitions of the learner are organized into a coherent, harmonious system that functions as a whole.

Piaget's theory of equilibration suggests a frame of reference for a group-oriented instructional design. Current instructional approaches in this direction are reflected in what has come to be known as the discovery method, which has been characterized by such words as conflict, surprise, doubt, contradiction, dissonance, and incongruity. The object is to encourage a learner to independently find information required to solve a vexing problem, rather than relying largely on the teacher for information and help. The first stage of this problem-solving process is what Dewey termed the *felt difficulty*.[66]

The present state of our knowledge calls for caution in judging the ultimate value of the discovery method and, above all, for intensive research on the psychological processes involved. Nevertheless, the notion that a learner can profitably search for his own answers is supported by Piaget's research and fits with recent experimental and theoretical work on problems of motivation. In fact, experimental analysis of motivation is just beginning; when research has progressed further, we may find that the essential base for a science and technology of instruction rests not on independent discovery, but on such factors as curiosity and conflict. Moreover, the current version of discovery learning does not incorporate conflicts that occur in the symbolic domain; not all the significant problems the learner faces have to do with concrete situations. For example, the learner should be helped to examine, reflectively, issues in various areas of American culture. Reflective problem-solving instruction might be drawn from conflicting propositions in such areas as minority group relations, social classes, religion, morality, and national beliefs.[67]

Assessing Cognitive Development

The fourth implication of Piaget's system is that it may make possible a psychometrics that can be anchored to cognitive-field theory. Such tests may be a better predictor of cognitive functioning than those now available. For example, conventional test scores often fluctuate radically and show poor predictive validity because of the considerable variability of the quality of the learner's interaction with his environment, which the tests do not assess.

Piaget's method of assessing cognitive development involved clinical observations of children, devising practical tasks, and asking precise questions about events taking place or about their own actions. Piaget wrote:

> This study of the child's actions brought me to the conception of logic based on operations—an operation being considered as internalized action which becomes reversible, that is to say, can be carried out in both directions, and links up with others. In the sphere of intelligence, operations always constitute whole structures rather like the Gestalt in the sphere of perception; the structures being, however, larger, more mobile and essentially reversible and capable of coordination.[68]

In contrast to Piaget's method, American psychologists usually present a problem to the learner that he could not have learned outside of the laboratory. The learner may be required to memorize a list of nonsense syllables or to acquire some type of conditioned response. Some procedures may even be adapted from methods used with animals. The serious danger in this strategy is that these methods are not representative of the cognitive operations a child can perform. Thus, the acquisition of such cognitive operations as language, number, and quantity may involve cognitive processes that have no relation to classical problems of the psychological laboratory, such as discrimination learning, serial learning, and conditioning.

There is little question that Piaget's unique contributions to the study of cognition hold great potential for the development of new testing instruments. Although the psychometrization of Piaget's cognitive tasks is itself just beginning, it promises a new approach in the years ahead.

Need for Revised Teacher Education Programs

The fifth implication of Piaget's system relates to the need for new teacher insights. As Piaget suggested, cognitive change occurs within a relatively narrow range of moderate uncertainty. Or, in other words, the learner can learn only in the range of the knowable unknown. This implies that the teacher must be aware of and sensitive to each learner's competence, and possess some understanding of each learner's ability to accept and use uncertainty. Barring unforeseen advances in educational technology, only the teacher can move fast enough to modify uncertainty effectively, to vary the learning conditions of the classroom in order to assure useful uncertainty for most learners, and to support the development of reflective problem solving in each learner.

Obviously, before this situation can be realized, the teacher will have to be the product of a radically different kind of teacher education than that offered currently, and will have to work in a totally different school from the one we know today.

Conclusion: The Absence of a Synthesis in Theories of Instruction

From the foregoing survey of selected instructional theories and methods, it should be clear that almost every significant system of instruction, from the time of Comenius to Piaget, has left a residue of theory and technique in current educational technology. It is also clear that a scientific technology of instruction has developed at a painfully slow rate and, simultaneously, that there is a general lack of agreement upon concepts of educational technology. Nor have these concepts been synthesized into theories of instruction that could be tested empirically. What is needed are theories of instruction that *prescribe* what the teacher should do to improve learning, theories of learning that *describe* what the learner does, and theories of communication that explain the interaction between teacher and learner.

Notes

[1] Sometimes called the father of educational measurements, Thorndike cannot be credited with initiating the movement in the United States. This happened in 1895, when J. M. Rice, editor of *The Forum*, undertook a ten-month study to show teacher effectiveness in teaching spelling. He tested nearly 33,000 children with this aim: "I endeavor to prove that the first step toward placing elementary schools on a scientific basis must necessarily lie in determining what results may reasonably be expected at the end of a given period of instruction" (J. M. Rice, "The Futility of the Spelling Grind," *The Forum* 23 (March-August 1887, 163). Rice was a physician who, after a brief medical practice, left for a two-year visit to Europe where he studied pedagogy and psychology at the universities of Jena and Leipzig. Upon his return to the United States, he began to devote his efforts to educational reform, through publication and by undertaking research studies of instructional practices. Professional educators of the time paid scant attention to his work, and little reference to him is found in the educational literature of the period. Yet most of the reforms for which he worked have been implemented in modern educational practices.

[2] See Edward L. Thorndike and R. S. Woodworth, "The Influence of Improvement in One Mental Function upon the Efficiency of Other Functions," *Psychological Review* 8 (May 1901), 247-61; (July 1901), 384-95; (November 1901), 553-64. For a refutation of G. Stanley Hall's recapitulation theory, see Edward L. Thorndike, *Educational Psychology*. Vol. 1, *The Original Nature of Man*. New York: Teachers College Press, Columbia University, 1913.

[3] Both James and Cattell significantly influenced Thorndike. Thorndike commented in an autobiographical piece that he had "no memory of having heard or seen the word psychology" until his junior year at Wesleyan University (1893-1894). During his first year at Harvard, Thorndike dropped literature in favor of psychology as his doctoral subject, as a result of a psychology course with James. Although James was not an experimentalist, he started to conduct informal psychological experiments about 1875 and contributed to the growth and development of psychology through his ability to synthesize psychological principles. His definitive work in psychology was the famous, two-volume *Principles of Psychology* (1890).

Cattell probably influenced Thorndike to an even greater extent through his pioneering work in promoting mental tests and his interest in individuals' differences. As a result of work with Wilhelm Wundt (founder of the first psychological laboratory) at the University of Leipzig, Cattell founded a psychological laboratory at Columbia in 1891.

[4] Thorndike, *Educational Psychology*. Vol. 1, *Original Nature of Man*, chapter 17, 270-312.

[5] In later writings, Thorndike disavowed his law of exercise and modified his law of effect. However, through implication, he continued to emphasize repetition in learning, and though he shifted the emphasis to pleasure in his law of effect, the pain aspect was not completely discarded.

[6]Thorndike developed the most complete system of psychology as yet developed along associationist lines. Since associationism has its roots in philosophy, its history extends back to Aristotle. Associationism as a doctrine was developed by British empiricists during the seventeenth and eighteenth centuries. For John Locke (1632-1704), ideas were the units of a mind, and associations consisted of combinations of ideas. David Hartley (1705-1757) developed Locke's concepts still further and established associationism as a systematic doctrine. Such men as James Mill (1773-1836), John Stuart Mill (1806-1873), and Herbert Spencer (1820-1903) also postulated associationist positions. The experimental work of Hermann Ebbinghaus (1850-1909), Ivan P. Pavlov (1849-1936), and Vladimir M. Bekterev (1857-1927) during the nineteenth century replaced the association of ideas with association of stimuli and responses. This shift was related to the transition of psychology into an empirical and natural science in its own right.

[7]Edward L. Thorndike, *Educational Psychology.* Vol. 2, *The Psychology of Learning.* New York: Teachers College Press, Columbia University, 1913, 4.

[8]Edward L. Thorndike, *Education.* New York: Macmillan, 1912, 164-66.

[9]Ibid., 167.

[10]Many of Thorndike's major concepts were counter to the prevailing social and intellectual ideas in early twentieth-century America. For a comprehensive account of the social implications of Thorndike's ideas, see Merle Curti, *The Social Ideas of American Educators*, Paterson, N.J.: Littlefield, Adams, 1961, 323-24.

[11]John B. Watson (1878-1958) published *Behavior* (1914) and championed a new school of psychology that came to be known as behaviorism. Watson claimed that environment (stimuli or conditioning) forms the organism and, therefore, that any child could be reared to become anything from a thief to a professional. The behavioristic theory of learning, a logical extreme of Thorndike's connectionism, assumed that learning was simply a result of what happened to the learner.

[12]B. F. Skinner's system of instruction is discussed later in this chapter.

[13]Hall received, in 1878, the first American doctorate in psychology under William James at Harvard. He then went to Germany, where he did two years of postdoctorate work under Wilhelm Wundt at Leipzig. In 1883, he founded the first psychological laboratory in the United States, at Johns Hopkins. Hall developed a number of new areas in psychology, proceeding from child psychology — where he popularized the questionnaire as a research tool — through adolescent psychology to the psychology of old age. He was also one of the leaders in developing the field of educational psychology.

[14]For Dewey's criticism of reflex arc psychology, see "The Reflex Arc Concept in Psychology," *Psychological Review* 3, 4 (July 1896), 357-70.

[15]Dewey anticipated this Gestalt-field viewpoint twenty years before it was first formulated.

[16]The published records of the Dewey Laboratory School are voluminous. See especially the nine monographs published monthly through 1900 as *The Elementary School Record* and successive issues of *The Elementary School Teacher* for 1901 and 1902. The entire June 1903 issue of *The Elementary School Teacher* was devoted to the Laboratory School. Also, for firsthand accounts of the school, see Katherine Camp Mayhew and Anna Camp Edwards, *The Dewey School.* New York: Appleton-Century, 1936.

[17]This is not a criticism of Dewey's theoretical model in itself, but only of the failure to test it and to use the empirical method to revise it.

[18]Franklin Ernest Heald (1870-1943), specialist in agricultural education (1914-1918) in the U.S. Department of Agriculture, first used the term *project* in connection with vocational agricultural education.

[19]See William H. Kilpatrick, *Foundations of Method.* New York: Macmillan, 1926.

[20]Maria Montessori was born at Chiaravalle, in the province of Ancona. Her father, Allessandro Montessori, was descended from a noble family of Bologna; her mother was a niece of Antonio Stoppani, noted philosopher-scientist-priest.

[21]Educational technology owes much to the French educator Seguin for his ingenious work with idiots. Sequin is one of the forgotten men of education, although he had a great influence on the training and testing of children of low ability. Even today, one finds evidence of his work in kindergartens and first-grade classrooms. Although Seguin did not organize the special tests he devised for mental defectives, as did Alfred Binet, his were the first modern tests for the measurement of intelligence. The student of today meets his name mainly in reference to the Seguin Formboard, which is one of the tests in the third year of the Binet Scale.

[22]Montessori worked with children as young as two and one-half years at a time when American educators were discussing the relevance of her ideas for four- and five-year-olds in American public school kindergartens.

[23]Montessori established her first training course for teachers in Rome in 1913. This training program was attended by seventy American teachers. She ultimately set up similar programs or served as a consultant in England, Spain, Holland, India, and the United States. She did not, however, succeed to any extent in realizing her goal of applying her methods to older children.

[24]Arnold Gesell was director of the Yale University Clinic of Child Psychology and pioneering investigator in the scientific study of child behavior. Howard C. Warren was president of the American Psychological Association (1912). Lightner Witmer founded the first psychological clinic at the University of Pennsylvania (1914).

[25]S. S. McClure offered to build an institution for Montessori in the United States in 1913, but she rejected his offer.

[26]See William Heard Kilpatrick, *The Montessori System Examined.* Boston: Houghton Mifflin, 1914, 10.

[27]See Joseph McVicker Hunt, Introduction, in Maria Montessori, *The Montessori Method.* New York: Schocken, 1964, xi-xxxix.

[28]Largely through the influence of the American Montessori Society, Montessori schools have been organized throughout the United States. The current Montessori movement revives its historical danger of becoming a cult, which could restrict innovation and experimental research much as did the cult that developed around Dewey despite his own intentions.

[29]One of Montessori's exercises consisted of a series of wooden blocks with ten holes of different diameters and ten wooden cylinders that exactly fitted the holes. Since a child could not put a cylinder into a hole too small or too large for it without having a cylinder left at the end of the exercise, the materials automatically informed him of his errors. This can probably be considered the first "teaching machine." Maria Montessori, *The Montessori Method* (translated by A. E. George). Philadelphia: J. B. Lippincott, 1912.

[30]See O. K. Moore, *Automated Responsive Environments*, film, parts 1 and 2. Hamden, Conn.: Basic Education, 1960.

[31]See, for example, Joseph McVicker Hunt, "Motivation Inherent in Information Processing and Action," in O. J. Harvey, ed., *Motivation and Social Interaction: Cognitive Determinants.* New York: Ronald Press, 1963, chapter 3, 35-94.

[32]According to current knowledge about the proper matching of materials to learners, probably the learner is the only one who can make an appropriate selection.

[33]A member of Burk's faculty, Mary Ward, deserves the credit for initiating the Burk program. After trying an informal experiment using self-instructional materials with a small group of students, she explained to Burk what she had done and the successful results. Burk was impressed with her approach and proposed that every teacher-supervisor begin to prepare self-instructional bulletins for his classes. At first, these bulletins were used with existing textbooks, but in time they became complete in themselves.

[34]For a comprehensive report on the Winnetka Plan, see Carleton W. Washburne and Sidney P. Marland, *Winnetka: The History and Significance of an Educational Experiment*, Englewood Cliffs, N.J.: Prentice-Hall, 1963. The Winnetka Plan has continued as established by Washburne; meanwhile, other schools in various sections of the United States have introduced a compromise between the Winnetka Plan and traditional practice.

[35]See H. H. Parkhurst, *Education on the Dalton Plan*, London: G. Bell & Sons, 1922. In this book, Helen Parkhurst refers to her earlier association with Maria Montessori.

[36]The Dalton Plan has generally been discontinued: too many pupils accepted the freedom but neglected their responsibility. However, the New York City Dalton School still uses the plan.

[37]Although the term *unit* was employed prior to Morrison, it was Morrison who apparently inaugurated its widespread use. Today the term is so standard in educational terminology that it is not often realized how recent is its origin. What is more, its use today does not usually follow the Morrison pattern, but more frequently refers to long-term assignments of two to three weeks or more, in contrast to daily lesson assignments.

[38]See Henry C. Morrison, *The Practice of Teaching in the Secondary School*. Chicago: University of Chicago Press, 1931, 81.

[39]Preston W. Search (1853-1932) organized an individualized instructional program as early as 1877 at West Liberty, Ohio. When he became superintendent of the Pueblo, Colorado, public schools in 1888, Search introduced his then fully developed plan, which practically dispensed with home study and recitations. Instead, the school day became a working period or a kind of laboratory where pupils mastered their assignments as rapidly as their differing abilities permitted. Although there were inadequate instruments or hardware for recording or checking pupil progress, the results were startling. Some pupils completed their work in half the normal time. However, this method was discontinued after Search left to become superintendent of schools in Los Angeles, where he was unsuccessful in establishing his plan. See P. W. Search, *An Ideal School*. New York: Appleton & Company, 1901.

[40]Franklin Bobbitt (1876-1952), professor of education at the University of Chicago, proposed an "activity analysis" of the broad range of human experience into major fields, in order to arrive at an effective curriculum and sound instructional objectives. See Franklin Bobbitt, *How to Make a Curriculum*, Boston: Houghton Mifflin, 1924. W. W. Charters (1875-1956), another pioneer in activity or job analysis, contended that educational aims were far too general to be effectively translated into teaching directives. By careful analysis he broke the broad aims down into their constituent parts. This approach met opposition from educational philosophers, especially Boyd H. Bode (1873-1953), who claimed that science was not equipped to determine educational aims.

[41]Max Wertheimer (1880-1943), Kurt Koffka (1886-1941), and Wolfgang Kohler (1887-1967), who had been together as research students at the University of Berlin, founded the Gestalt school of psychology about 1912, while working together at the Psychological Institute in Frankfurt-am-Main. They began by criticizing the analytical methods of connectionism and associationism, contending that learning does not arise from a specific response to a specific stimulus, but rather as the individual sees the overall pattern (or Gestalt) in a situation and changes his behavior accordingly. Thus the learner responds as a whole organism and not automatically, or mechanically, through specific reflexes.

[42]For example, see Ernest R. Hilgard, *Theories of Learning*, 2d ed. New York: Appleton-Century-Crofts, 1956.

[43]Kurt Lewin, "Formalization and Progress in Psychology," *University of Iowa Studies in Child Welfare* 16, 3 (February 1940), 16.

[44]Kurt Lewin, *Principles of Topological Psychology.* New York: McGraw-Hill, 1936, 4.

[45]Topology is a nonmetrical geometry that encompasses concepts such as inside, outside, and boundary but has no dealings with length, breadth, or thickness. No distances are defined; rather, topology is concerned with the relative position of the geometric figures being considered. Topologically, things may be next to, inside, or outside one another. Size or shape has no significance in a topological figure. It may be helpful to think of a topological plane as a perfectly elastic sheet of rubber that may be stretched, twisted, pulled, and bent, but whose relationships to other objects remain the same. See H. Arnold Bradford, *Intuitive Concepts in Elementary Topology.* Englewood Cliffs, N.J.: Prentice-Hall, 1962, 24.

[46]See Kurt Lewin, *Field Theory in Social Science.* New York: Harper & Row, 1951, 62.

[47]For example, three of the present emphases within motivational theory have direct connections with Lewin's "level of aspiration." One of these is the achievement motivation concept of McClelland and his associates; another is cognitive dissonance, associated with Festinger; the third is cognitive balance, a theory developed by Heider.

[48]His accomplishments include a novel on a utopian theme, *Walden Two* (1948), and the invention of an automated baby-tending device, which has been commercially marketed.

[49]For his animal studies, Skinner invented the Skinner box, a simple form of puzzle box that contained a rat, a lever, and a device for delivering a pellet of food each time the rat pressed the lever. Recording devices were set outside the box to record the rat's responses during the experimenter's absence.

[50]B. F. Skinner, *Science and Human Behavior.* New York: Macmillan, 1953, 112.

[51]Ibid., 152-53.

[52]Ibid., 153.

[53]B. F. Skinner, "Teaching Machines," *Science* 128 (October 24, 1958), 971.

[54]B. F. Skinner, "The Science of Learning and the Art of Teaching," *Harvard Educational Review* 24, 2 (Spring 1954), 86-97; "Teaching Machines," 969-77.

[55]A complete discussion of behaviorism and educational technology can be found in chapter 10 of this book.

[56]See Hans G. Furth, *Piaget and Knowledge.* Englewood Cliffs, N.J.: Prentice-Hall, 1969.

[57]The pioneering studies of the 1920s were reported in such books as *The Child's Conception of the World* (1926), *The Child's Conception of Physical Causality* (1927), and *Judgement and Reasoning in the Child* (1928). In the 1930s there were studies of infancy, especially the books *The Construction of Reality in the Child* (1937) and *The Origin of Intelligence in Children* (1936). The studies of the 1940s and 1950s typically began with a systematic comparative analysis of adult and child conceptions of number, measurement, geometry, velocity, the law of floating bodies, chance, logical groupings, and the like.

[58]See Sarah F. Campbell, ed., *Piaget Sampler.* New York: John Wiley & Sons, 1976. This is a good introduction to Jean Piaget through his own words.

[59]Jean Piaget, *Psychology of Intelligence.* New York: Harcourt, Brace and World, 1950.

[60]The inclusion of the concept of a phase or stage in Piaget's theory has produced considerable criticism. Many critics do not understand that Piaget used *stage* in a statistical sense, to denote the

probability that a certain percentage of children at a particular age will be functioning intellectually in a certain way. To other critics, *stage* implies a discontinuity in development rather than a continuous process, and they reject the notion of discontinuity. However, many critics fail to recognize that Piaget did not view the process as discontinuous; in fact, in analyzing protocols of test responses he made provision for a transition from one stage to another.

[61] Jean Piaget, *Logic and Psychology*. New York: Basic Books, 1957, 45.

[62] The reader with some knowledge of symbolic logic will understand more fully the Piaget model of adolescent thinking, for Piaget used the language and symbols of logic. See B. Inhelder and Jean Piaget, *The Growth of Logical Thinking from Childhood to Adolescence*. New York: Basic Books, 1958.

[63] This viewpoint is usually associated with such men as Jean-Jacques Rousseau, G. Stanley Hall, and Arnold Gesell.

[64] It should be clear that Piaget's view of the interaction process did not differ essentially from views traditionally held by cognitive-field psychologists (e.g., Kurt Lewin). Nevertheless, it is important to note that Piaget's monumental investigations provided increased scientific support for this view and generated some important principles for instructional design.

[65] See J. Piaget et al., *The Child's Conception of Geometry*. New York: Basic Books, 1960.

[66] See J. Dewey, *How We Think*. New York: D. C. Heath, 1910.

[67] See H. Gordon Hullfish and Philip G. Smith, *Reflective Thinking*. New York: Dodd, Mead, 1963.

[68] Jean Piaget, *The Construction of Reality in the Child*. New York: Basic Books, 1954, 32.

Select Bibliography

Bobbitt, Franklin. *How to Make a Curriculum*. Boston: Houghton Mifflin, 1924.

Bradford, H. Arnold. *Intuitive Concepts in Elementary Topology*. Englewood Cliffs, N.J.: Prentice-Hall, 1962.

Cremin, Lawrence A. *The Transformation of the School*. New York: Knopf, 1961.

Curti, Merle. *The Social Ideas of American Educators*. Paterson, N.J.: Pageant Books, 1959.

Dewey, John. *Democracy and Education*. New York: Macmillan, 1916.

_____. *How We Think*. Boston: Heath, 1933.

James, William. *Pragmatism: A New Name for Old Ways of Thinking*. New York: Longmans, 1907.

_____. *Principles of Psychology* (vols. 1-2). New York: Holt, 1890.

_____. *Talks to Teachers on Psychology*. New York: Holt, 1899.

Kilpatrick, William H. *The Montessori System Examined*. Boston: Houghton Mifflin, 1914.

Lewin, Kurt. *Field Theory in Social Science*. New York: Harper & Row, 1951.

Mayhew, Katherine C., and Anna Camp Edwards. *The Dewey School*. New York: Appleton-Century, 1936.

Montessori, Maria. *The Montessori Method*, tr. A. E. George. Philadelphia: J. B. Lippincott, 1912.

Morrison, Henry C. *The Practice of Teaching in the Secondary School*. Chicago: University of Chicago Press, 1931.

Parkhurst, H. H. *Education on the Dalton Plan.* London: G. Bell & Sons, 1922.

Piaget, Jean. *Psychology and Epistemology.* New York: Grossman, 1971.

Piaget, Jean, and Bärbel Inhelder. *The Psychology of the Child.* New York: Basic Books, 1969.

Search, P. W. *An Ideal School.* New York: Appleton & Company, 1901.

Skinner, B. F. *Science and Human Behavior.* New York: Macmillan, 1953.

_____. *The Technology of Teaching.* New York: Appleton-Century-Crofts, 1968.

Sully, James. *Teacher's Handbook of Psychology.* New York: Appleton, 1886.

Thorndike, Edward L. *Educational Psychology*: Vol. 1. *The Original Nature of Man*; Vol. 2. *The Psychology of Learning.* New York: Teachers College Press, Columbia University, 1913.

Washburne, Carleton W., and Sidney P. Marland. *Winnetka: The History and Significance of an Educational Experiment.* Englewood Cliffs, N.J.: Prentice-Hall, 1963.

4

Evolution of the Educational Film: 1900–1950

Aside from providing a short review of the technical history of the film, this chapter shows the historical relationship of the educational film to mainstream theatrical films and identifies the people who shaped the form and content of the first educational films as well as the agencies that set the patterns for production and distribution. The evolution of the educational film is intimately related to the larger history of educational technology, and that relationship will be shown in this chapter.

A Brief History of the Technical Development of Film

Although many accounts of the technical development of the film have been published, it may be helpful to provide a brief historical background at this juncture so that the reader may gain a broader perspective of the educational film.

Some sixty-five years before Christ, the Roman poet Lucretius noted in his *Rerum Natura* the persistence of vision—the capacity of the retina of the eye to retain the impression of an object for a fraction of a second after its disappearance. About two hundred years later, the Greek astronomer Ptolemy experimentally proved its existence when he revolved a spot of color to form an apparently continuous circle. The wish for pictorial reality was further illustrated in Leonardo da Vinci's *Trattato della Pitture*.[1]

Mankind's first picture without substance, neither a drawing nor a shadow but an apparition in full color and moving, was what was to become known as the *camera obscura* (see figure 4.1). It may have been observed first in a cave or a dark chamber when a slit between stones or a knothole in a door let in the rays of light. These produced on the wall opposite the opening a live image, upside down, of whatever happened to be outside. Giovanni Baptista Della Porta is often erroneously credited with the invention of the camera obscura mainly because he popularized it and described it in his book *Magia Naturalis* published in 1560. The camera obscura demonstrated the principles of photography and foreshadowed its potentialities.

Fig. 4.1. *Camera obscura.*

In 1646, a German Jesuit named Athanasius Kircher published *Ars Magna Lucis*, in which he gave the first recorded description of his *Magin Cataoprica*, or magic lantern. In an early premiere of the magic lantern, before an assembly of nobles he projected crude hand-painted images of devils, demons, and skeletons on the wall of a dark room, using the light of a smoky lamp. In this same book he also described a revolving glass cylinder device that probably contributed to the later invention of the zoetrope.

About 1824, Peter Mark Roget, the author of the famous *Thesaurus of English Words and Phrases*, was stimulated to experiment with the idea of creating motion in pictures when he caught a chance glimpse of a passing baker's cart through the slits of his venetian blind. He had the visual impression that each distinct, fleeting image of the cart and horse was arrested in successive phases of motion. This led to the first scientific investigation into the phenomenon of illusory motion.[2]

Fig. 4.2. Magic lantern, Germany circa 1890.

The work of Roget inspired others to experiment with motion. Joseph Plateau of Ghent, Belgium, invented a twirling disc device called the phenakistiscope (see figure 4.3); William Horner of Bristol invented a zoetrope, or "wheel of life" toy;[3] and Franz Uchatius of Austria invented a new device that wedded the magic lantern with the zoetrope.

By 1860, photography had progressed to the extent that short exposures could be taken, but it could not yet be done quickly enough to record objects in motion. In 1861, Coleman Sellers of Philadelphia invented the kinematoscope. This machine consisted of various pictures arranged around an axis, much like the paddles of a water wheel. The pictures were viewed through a device like the eyepiece of a stereopticon and were turned by a knob.[4]

A complete anticipation of the modern motion picture was embodied in a patent application by Louis Arthur Ducros du Hauron in France in 1864. In 1870, the Sellers method of photographing posed phases of motion was applied to a projecting zoetropic device by Henry Renno Heyl of the Franklin Institute of Philadelphia. This device, known as the phasmatrope, was the culmination of the contributions of Plateau, Stampfer, Uchatius, and Daguerre.[5] And, simultaneously, the motion picture had been attained and was complete in every detail except that it was still necessary for the camera to acquire the ability of making the basic record negatives at the speed of reality.

The next evolutionary step in the development of the motion picture occurred in California. Governor Leland Stanford made a $25,000 bet that a horse in a gallop would have all four feet off the ground at once. To prove it, he had a photographer by the name of Eadweard Muybridge take instantaneous photographs of his horses, using a battery of

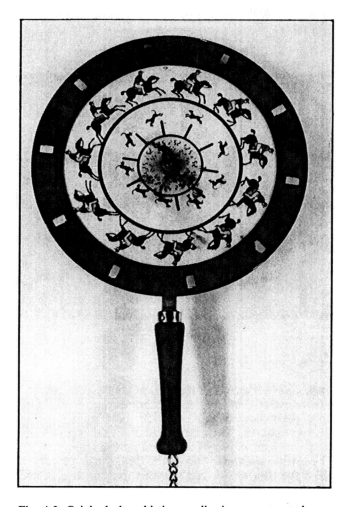

Fig. 4.3. Original phenakistiscope disc in reconstructed wheel.

twenty-four cameras to record the movement against a slanting board fence that had been covered with rock salt to reflect as much sun as possible.[6]

When drawings of Muybridge's results were published in American, French, and English scientific journals, it was clear that Stanford's assumption was correct. All of the horse's feet were off the ground during the gallop; but surprisingly, they were in mid-air only when the feet were bunched together.

Jules-Etienne Marey, a French physiologist who had been experimenting in problems of locomotion, wrote Muybridge for details, and soon began to use his own technique. Instead of a series of cameras, Marey used only one and recorded on a single plate successive phases of motion. Meanwhile, Muybridge's sudden fame brought an invitation from the University of Pennsylvania to further pursue his work in motion photography. During his stay, from 1883 to 1885, Muybridge launched into an extensive study of animal and human locomotion, which was published in 1887 and consisted of over seven hundred large photogravure plates that filled eleven volumes.

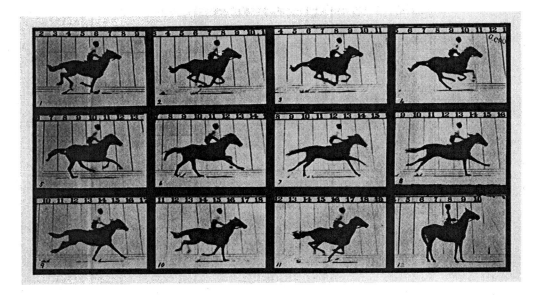

Fig. 4.4. Proof of a bet.

On October 6, 1889, the first model of the Edison kinetoscope, the parent of the modern motion picture, was demonstrated at the Edison laboratories in West Orange, New Jersey.[7] The kinetoscope was a peep-show device in which the film ran continuously between a magnifying lens and a light source. The machine had a total capacity of about fifty feet of film; the film was about one inch wide and presented sixteen frames, or about forty-eight exposures, a second. The Edison standard sizes of the film, the image, and the arrangement of sprocket holes by which the film was driven into this first machine, remain the world standards today.

After its invention, the kinetoscope was pushed into an inauspicious corner because it no longer stimulated Edison. However, by the winter of 1894, a demand had arisen for a machine that combined the kinetoscope's moving film with the magic lantern, so that the picture might be freed from the peep-show. The earliest projectors were theatrical machines adopted for booth projection in auditoriums, but because of their size and cost, these projectors were later supplemented by portable and semi-portable types that cost less, available under proper fire protection for classroom use in 35mm. Also, at the same time a number of motion picture projectors appeared, some for 28mm, others for 23mm, and still others for 16mm or less.

With the invention of the Vitascope, Thomas Armat and C. Francis Jenkins made an important contribution to the development of the modern motion picture projector. Their first public exhibition, on June 6, 1894, was historic not only because it was the first showing of motion pictures, but also because it was the first showing of colored films.[8] The commercial career of the motion picture on the screen began with the presentation of the Vitascope in a showing at Koster and Bial's Music Hall, in Herald Square, New York, the night of April 23, 1896.[9]

A number of other makes and models of motion picture projectors were developed during the early part of the twentieth century, including the Panoptikon, Animatograph,

Cinematograph, Mutoscope, Biograph, Edengraph, and Power Cameragraph. Simultaneously, home and school projectors began to be produced and marketed. The most popular were the Optiscope, the DeVry "E" Model, the Victor Animatograph, and the Edison Home Kinetoscope. (See figures 4.5-4.7 for illustrations of various early film projectors.)

Fig. 4.5. *Bell & Howell "Filmo"* 16mm silent motion picture projector.

(Text continues on page 96.)

Fig. 4.6. First 16mm projector—1923 model of the Victor Cine Projector.

Fig. 4.7. Reprint of an advertisement from *Visual Education* (November 1921).

Through the years, many technical film improvements have been made. The Marey Institute in France developed the first slow-motion, ultra-rapid, x-ray, time-lapse, and microphotography. Other technical accomplishments include 16mm reversal film, sound amplification, animated cartoons, the development of sound and color films, and three-dimensional films.

Beginnings of the Educational Film

Even though the inventors and pioneers of the motion picture considered it primarily an educational medium, the majority of the early films were theatrical in nature. Anything that gave the illusion of movement on the screen qualified as proper entertainment. For example, such early films as Edison's tooth extraction (with benefit of laughing gas) in 1893 or the ten negatives of scenes of the municipal schools of France may have been put in some educational classification, but they were generally considered strictly entertainment. However, many alert people were beginning to realize the educational potential of the film.

The first discernible trend toward a separation of the theatrical and non-theatrical films occurred in 1910. At this time motion pictures began to show definite indications of a new, potential entertainment industry as well as of non-theatrical uses. Several movements were producing these changes. Arthur Krows says this specialization of the film was brought about by:

> ... an accumulation of many minor happenings, such as the desire of the factory owner to see his own achievements on the screen, the wish of the local cameraman to augment his income, the hope of the minister to regain the wandering attention of his flock, the more convenient and cheaper supply of film stock, and other conditions....[10]

Consequently, the earliest forerunners of the educational film were the newsreel, the travelogue, and the scientific motion picture. Non-theatrical films in these early days were usually discarded films that were rented from a showman who carried his machine and screen with him and operated the projector himself. Nevertheless, by 1902 Charles Urban of London had exhibited some of the first educational films, and films with slow-motion, microscopic, and undersea views were beginning to be produced. These films included such subjects as the growth of plants and the emergence of the butterfly from the chrysalis. By 1904, Pathe had begun to produce travelogues with rich, stencilled colors. Also in 1904, at the Marey Institute in Paris, Marey and his associates filmed the flight of insects, the locomotion of animals in water, the digestive process of small animals, and the heart in action. Probably the first outstanding adventure motion pictures ever filmed were the *African Hunt Pictures* made on the Paul J. Rainey 1911 expedition.[11]

The period after 1910 resulted in a definite development of the non-theatrical film. News events and foreign expeditions began to be filmed and travel films were used on lyceum circuits. Moreover, industrial, religious, governmental, and educational agencies were awakening to the possibilities of the film.

Thomas Edison was one of the first to produce films for classroom showings. Early in 1911, he released a series of historical films that covered important phases of the American Revolution. The first was released in July 1911 and was entitled *The Minute Men*. A few years later Edison produced another series, on natural and physical science. These films, released in 1914, included *Cabbage Butterfly, Cecropia Moth, Life History of the Silkworm, Magnetism*, and *Microscopic Pond Life*. And as early as 1908, F. Percy Smith had begun to make his magnified picture studies of the housefly, and also made two short subjects, *The Birth of a Flower* and *The Germination of Plants*, by means of time-lapse photography.[12]

However, most of the films used for educational purposes were theatrical films. George Kleine had this to say about the selections contained in his 1910 educational film catalog:

> In a sense, all subjects are educational, but in classifying a mass of motion picture films for educational purposes the line must be drawn about a reasonable area.
>
> A dramatic or comic tale in motion pictures, laid in some foreign country, is educational in so far as it shows the manners, customs and environment of the people....
>
> The word "educational" is here used in a wide sense and does not indicate that these films are intended for school or college use exclusively. They are intended rather for the education of the adult as well as the youth, for the exhibition before miscellaneous audiences, as well as for more restricted use.[13]

Frank Freeman in 1923, classified and offered as a working basis the following four types of educational films: (1) the dramatic, either fictional or historical; (2) the anthropological or sociological, differing from the dramatic in that it is not primarily based on a narrative or story; (3) the industrial or commercial, which shows the processes of modern industry and commerce; and (4) the scientific, which may be classified into subgroups corresponding to the individual sciences, such as earth science, nature study, etc.[14]

By the early twenties there were many who supported a distinct line of demarcation between the entertainment and the educational motion picture. Their motives varied. Producers, distributors, and exhibitors of theatrical films wanted to protect box-office receipts and had calculated that a potentially powerful source of competition could be eliminated if "educationals" were seen as dull illustrated lectures. Meanwhile, educators fell in with this unflattering concept of educational films because of a fear of the effects theatrical films would have on children and because of their own traditional aversion to "entertainment" in the classroom.

It was obvious that more and more films that were originally produced for theatrical purposes possessed educational value as well. For example, very few educators could deny that such documentary films as Pare Lorentz's *The River* or Robert Flaherty's *Nanook of the North* or *Man of Aran* could contribute to understanding and influence attitudes and perceptions. The rigid classification of films as either educational or entertaining has proved detrimental to the development of a broad, realistic concept of the educational film.

Most films used for instructional purposes prior to World War I were salvaged old theatrical, industrial, government, or welfare films. An early evaluation of these films was made by M. J. Cohen.

> In some quarters there is an impression that right now we are ready to go ahead with the motion picture as a means of imparting knowledge to those seeking an education. Many schools have already installed motion picture machines and have found them more than valuable along certain lines.
>
> This impression that we are ready to supply just what the schools need in the way of educational pictures, either supplying or supplementing the textbook, is quite general and absolutely erroneous. It is true that we have an array of educational releases which when properly marshalled in a catalogue, appear quite imposing, but it is also true that not one of these pictures represents a systematic effort to supply a definite series of pictures for a definite purpose.[15]

In 1922, W. M. Gregory identified and evaluated sources of so-called educational films.

> Present sources of educational films are: Old commercial films that have been junked and are now reworked into so-called educational pictures.

Advertising films giving an interesting but one-sided story of a particular product.

Government films consisting of: war-propaganda films, distinctly out of date; excellent agricultural films, and a few health films.

Welfare films of large corporations; suitable in only a few cases for general educational purposes.

Health films; some special health films too technical and too costly for general use in schools; a large group of films produced from junk and of no value.

Educational films for schools—comprising stories, technical subjects, travel, geography, history, language, and hygiene. The group of films especially prepared for school use is very small. Most of the so-called educational film consists of material that has been stripped from cast-off commercial film and retitled, and is being offered now for school purposes. Much of the film is shown in schools because of the novelty of the motion picture. In the effort to keep pace with the commercial exhibitor the schools frequently have disregarded quality.

Experienced and skilled educators have given the film material but comparatively little attention. The material has been too often accepted without protest if it is low priced.[16]

First Educational Film Catalog

Shortly after the turn of the century, there were a number of individuals in both the United States and Europe who envisaged the use of motion pictures in education. In a 1907 pamphlet titled *The Cinematograph in Science, Education, and Matters of State*, Charles Urban, working in England, stated that he had "spent the past five years in equipping a qualified staff to provide animated films depicting various manifestations, transformations, and phenomena of nature." By August 1909, Urban had control of enough educational film footage to publish the second edition of a catalog of educational films titled *Urbanora*. Not finding a ready market for his films in England or on the Continent, Urban moved to the United States and continued his activities in New York City.

The first educational film catalog to appear in the United States was the *Catalogue of Educational Motion Pictures*, published by George Kleine in New York in 1910. This catalog contained 330 pages and listed 1,065 titles classified under 30 main topics. It also had a foreword by the anthropologist Frederick K. Starr of the University of Chicago; a quoted statement from P. Chambers, Secretary of the Zoological Society of London, England; and a letter from Thomas A. Edison to Kleine, dated December 20, 1909. Edison became so enthused over the educational possibilities of the motion picture that he was quoted in the New York *Dramatic Mirror*'s issue of July 9, 1913, with the statement, "Books will soon be obsolete in the schools. Scholars will soon be instructed through the eye. It is possible to teach every branch of human knowledge with the motion picture. Our school system will be completely changed in ten years." The enthusiasm of men like Edison for the instructional value of the motion picture served to motivate many individuals, businessmen and educators alike, to enter the budding field of visual education.

First School Use of Educational Films

In 1910, George Kleine undertook the promotion of a school film service, and with this objective, screened selected films at a meeting of the New York City Board of Education. However, despite the impressive presentation, Kleine's plan was not accepted because of a lack of inexpensive, portable motion picture projection equipment. Later the same year, the public schools of Rochester, New York, became the first to adopt films for regular instructional use.[17]

Early Commercial Enterprises

When the realization grew that educational films were different in form and objective from theatrical or industrial, public relations, religious or political films, schools became potential markets for projection equipment and for the rental and purchase of films for instructional purposes. As a consequence, a number of commercial organizations were established during the first two decades of this century for the purpose of manufacturing low-priced nonprofessional equipment, producing "educationals," and serving as film distribution centers. An additional impetus to this development was brought about by the special demand for training films during World War I.

Herman DeVry Company

One of the earliest commercial concerns that catered to the needs of users of educational films was founded in Chicago in 1900 by Herman DeVry. By 1913, DeVry had begun to manufacture his famous E Model, DeVry suitcase, 35mm projectors. Subsequently, this company built up large collections of films and slides and was among the first to offer short reels for school use.

Bell and Howell Company

The Bell and Howell Company came into being in Chicago on New Year's Day, 1907, when Don J. Bell, a young inventor, formed a partnership with Albert S. Howell. This company began by specializing in projectors and cameras. Later it added a library of over one thousand 16mm silent films and some two hundred 16mm sound-on-film motion pictures. Branch film libraries were established in many parts of the country; users of the Bell and Howell educational film library were supplied with a projector, a screen, and an operator.

Victor Animatograph Company

This company was founded by Alexander F. Victor, a former Swedish magician, with Samuel G. Rose, in Davenport, Iowa, in 1910. A year before, Victor had invented the Animatograph, the first portable projector that combined a camera with sound-on-disc. Following this achievement, Victor and his associates continued to make a number of technical contributions. In 1912, the company produced the first portable lantern-slide projector and made smaller, lighter slides. Other achievements were the first 16mm projector, the first spring-driven 16mm projector, and the first spring-driven 16mm cameras (which dispensed with a tripod). Victor was prominent among those who first proposed 16mm film as the standard for educational films.

Charles Urban Company

Although the Charles Urban Company was not strictly an American company, it did exert an important influence on the development of educational films in this country. Urban had experimented with educational film production in England as early as 1896, and founded the Kinemacolor Company in 1911. He later came to America to help develop an educational film production company known as the Urban-Kineto Corporation, in Lowville, New York.[18]

Kleine Optical Company

Urban's American distributor was George Kleine, who developed the first catalog of educational films and attempted to promote their use in the schools. He also made such film classics as *Julius Caesar* and *Quo Vadis* available to schools at low rentals and was the first to distribute films through the college and university extension divisions on a profit-sharing arrangement. Through the Kleine Optical Company, which had been organized in the late nineteenth century by his father, Kleine also sold portable 35mm projectors.

The Edison Film Library

In 1911, a notable educational film effort began: The Edison Company began a series of educational films, known as Edison's Library, on history and on natural and physical science.

The early Edison educational-film production attempts at West Orange, New Jersey, were brought to an abrupt end by two disastrous fires, in April and December of 1914, that destroyed much of the Edison Library of negatives and discouraged the continued manufacture of the Edison Kinetoscope home projector. The negatives that were not destroyed were subsequently scattered and lost. However, some of the Edison films were being distributed by the Kleine Optical Company as late as 1929. Edison did much to promote the use of films in schools, but his efforts were misunderstood and he was distinctly ahead of his time.

Educational Films Corporation

This company was formed in New York City in 1915 by Earle W. Hammons. After a period of experimentation, George A. Skinner provided some needed financial support and became president. Skinner had a more advanced understanding of the role of educational films than most of the producers at this time.[19] He wanted to make films specifically for the schools and objected to the term *educational* as it was applied to the typical films of the day. Hammons disagreed with him, believing that theatrical films possessed sufficient educational content; he later purchased Skinner's interest in the company and developed a cooperative exchange system with the Hudson Bay Company of London.

The Pathescope Company of America, Inc.

Willard B. Cook was the organizer and chief executive of the Pathescope Company, which was organized in 1912. Cook built cameras and projectors as well as an extensive library of "educational" films. He also used off-standard 28mm safety film. By 1919, he had distributing centers in the principal cities and was able to offer more than 1,500 reels of film to his subscribers. He also issued a 245-page catalog edited by A. S. Balsom, who was Director of Visual Instruction at Newark, New Jersey.

The pathescope approach anticipated the successful attempt of George Eastman to standardize the narrow width production of 16mm film. However, since Cook was dependent on Eastman for film, he was left wanting when Eastman went to standardized 16mm films, cameras, and projectors.[20]

The Bureau of Commercial Economics

This company, which had no official connection with the federal government, was founded in 1913 by Francis Holley. Supported by endowments and subscriptions, the company created a lending library of some 3,000 films and distributed these on a free, worldwide basis to those subscribers who agreed not to charge admission. By 1921, the Bureau was affiliated with over a hundred universities and colleges and its film and projector service reached around the world.[21]

Bray Pictures Corporation

John R. Bray was the president of several companies that all embraced his name. The Bray Company was incorporated in 1916. Bray primarily produced comic or cartoon films, but he was interested in educational films and his company established a large library of "educational" subjects on 35mm and 16mm film, and a few sound-on-film. Even though Bray was a pioneer inventor, his original Brayco slide film projector "was never a commercial success."[22]

Educational Motion Pictures Bureau, Inc.

This company, organized in 1914, was the first producing company to issue teaching syllabi with their educational films. The old Edison studio and many of the Edison films were purchased with notes, but the company eventually went into bankruptcy because it lacked both capital and planning, as well as being far advanced for the times.[23]

The Atlas Motion Picture Corporation

This company was formed in Detroit, Michigan, in 1916 and financially backed by Henry Ford. With its large laboratory and extensive equipment, it was soon releasing *The Ford Educational Weekly*. In the summer of 1919, a committee of educators, headed by William H. Dudley of the University of Wisconsin, was invited to the Ford plant to edit fifty-one Ford films for instructional use. In 1920 *The Ford Educational Library* was announced as ready for distribution. It is interesting to note that "each film had a complete synopsis or syllabus containing: the title and subtitles, the instructional aim, data suitable to aid the teacher, definite questions for presenting the lesson, problems, questions, and a list of references."[25] The advertising, however, was unsuccessful, and even created some antagonism toward the Ford Motor Company and the educators who had served on the selection committee.

The Society for Visual Education, Inc.

Somewhat in the tradition of a medieval guild, Harley L. Clarke, a utilities magnate, together with Forest Ray Moulton, professor of astronomy at the University of Chicago, founded the Society for Visual Education in November 1919. The officers of the company were Rolin D. Salisbury, president; H. L. Clarke, vice-president; F. R. Moulton, secretary; and Frank A. Vanderlip, chairman, board of directors. Its objective was to produce instructors' films specifically for school use.

Both Salisbury and Moulton were professors at the University of Chicago and other directors on the board were associated with such educational institutions as the universities of Harvard, Columbia, and Michigan. There was also a general advisory board of sixty-four members and a host of committees with rosters of eight to fourteen members each. The men and women comprising the board represented the leading educators of the country.[25]

Although the Society for Visual Education began with $400,000 and the best educational consultants available, failure followed less than three years after its founding. George Skinner observed that the society "lacked competent producers."[26] The society produced the first extensive library of films for school use, but its 110 productions lacked both appeal and technical excellence.[27] The films were not "systematically built to supplement existing courses of study" nor were educators serving on the various committees that were consulted regarding the films' educational merits or demerits. The situation was made more untenable by Clarke's reportedly unethical business practices and by tasteless advertising that antagonized many who had supported the society.[28]

Although the society had begun industrial production and had become affiliated with the Acme Motion Picture Projector Company in bringing out the Acme suitcase projector, by 1923 it was clearly not meeting with financial success. That same year, Clarke sold the society to Marie Witham, a member of the staff.

Witham fared far better and continued the society on a smaller scale. In October 1923, the society manufactured a slide-film projector known as the Picturol. This led to the production and distribution of slide-films and slide-film projection equipment. At the same time, the society started and has since maintained the most complete library of slide-films in the world.

Chronicles of America Photoplays

As the result of the publishing success of a series of histories known as the *Chronicles of Canada* and the *Chronicles of America*, the Canadian firm of Glasgow and Brook became interested in 1918 in the possibility of producing an educational film series based on their publications. Accordingly, a material survey was made, a budget prepared, and theatrical continuity writers began writing the first scenarios. The plan called for five sequences of eight units each, covering the history of America from Columbus through Woodrow Wilson.

By 1920, Glasgow and Brook was ready to form the Chronicles of America Picture Corporation. George Parmly Day, head of the Yale University Press and treasurer of Yale University, was made president.[29] Robert Glasgow became vice-president; Arthur E. Krows, secretary; and Arthur Brook, treasurer.

Just as film production was to start, a series of unexpected difficulties arose. First, plans were disrupted because of the death of Glasgow. Then a distinguished committee of historians, who had been appointed by the Council of Yale University, began to dispute the various historical and technical details in the scenarios that had been written by theatrical writers. In order to resolve this impasse, Brook gave production authority to the historians. They eventually succeeded in putting out a series of films known as the *Chronicles of America Photoplays*.

Only forty-seven of the one hundred reels originally planned were ever completed. The initial plan had called for the lease of the complete series to schools on a ninety-nine-year basis for $20,000, but few sets were actually leased because of the fifty-three missing reels. Attempts were made to release the series for theatrical film distribution so that some of the large financial investment could be recovered. However, their lack of dramatic appeal and their factual, academic approach caused them to be rejected.[30] McClusky gives this appraisal of the *Chronicles of America Photoplays*:

1. The first big effort to produce a systematic series of films on one subject.

2. The first time "educators" were, in an official capacity, working with "producers."

3. Planning failed, however, to bring historical experts, teachers, and producers together at the outset.

4. Theatrical continuity writers did not win approval from historians.... This cost $50,000.

5. The historians then took charge but failed to produce pictures which made a hit with teachers of American history in elementary and secondary schools.

6. By the time this was discovered, the money was exhausted and the series was only half completed.

7. Theatrical showings failed to reap box office returns because the films were as dead as the historical detail which characterized them.

8. A grand opportunity was wasted because of poor management and lack of harmony in the organization.

9. Had the Yale University Press done some proving-ground work, sought the advice of experienced visual educators, teachers, and educational psychologists, this failure might have been avoided. Cost was too high and the episodes took too long to show.[31]

Eastman Teaching Films

The Eastman Kodak Company formed Eastman Teaching Pictures, Inc., in 1928, with Thomas E. Finegan, former deputy commissioner of education for New York State and superintendent of public instruction for the state of Pennsylvania, as president. The enterprise was capitalized at $1 million and designed as an elaborate research-demonstration project under the direction of Ben D. Wood of Columbia University and Frank N. Freeman of the University of Chicago.[32]

The first Eastman Teaching Films were made in the subject areas of geography, general science, and health. Ultimately, some 250 silent educational films (most one reel in length) were produced, containing much material taken directly from the negatives of industrial films that had been given to Eastman Kodak.

The impact of the educational sound film, the depression of the thirties, and the deaths of George Eastman and Thomas E. Finegan combined to bring an abrupt halt to the Eastman Kodak Company's film production activity in 1932. No attempt was made to replace Finegan, but W. H. Maddock was made sales manager of Eastman Teaching Films, and the sale of films continued. In 1944, the Eastman Kodak Company finally gave the University of Chicago its entire stock of film negatives.

Electrical Research Products, Inc.

The introduction of the educational sound film provided a new impetus for the development of commercial enterprises.[33] The most important of these was Electrical Research Products, Inc. (better known as ERPI and pronounced "urpi").[34]

ERPI was organized as a subsidiary of the Western Electric Company, the manufacturing division of the American Telephone and Telegraph Company. At first ERPI confined itself to supplying Western Electric sound systems to theaters throughout the country; inevitably the attention of the company turned toward non-theatrical possibilities. Since sound equipment had been in such demand in the theaters, it seemed logical to ERPI that the schools' requirements would be equally urgent. Consequently, ERPI fitted sound-on-disc attachments into approved 35mm silent models, such as the Holmes and Super-DeVry projectors, and proceeded to establish an elaborate sales organization. ERPI leaders also became convinced that the non-theatrical field would need encouragement and support, so a non-theatrical film producing unit was formed as a model for others to follow.

ERPI's first film explained how sound was put on film. Called *Finding His Voice*, it became one of the most popular short subjects of all time and was screened in all important theaters. Max Fleisher did the cartoon, which showed how the silent motion picture, symbolized by a caricature figure, attempted to become articulate. Carlyle Ellis did the narration.[35]

In January 1929, the non-theatrical division of ERPI, known as the educational department, was formed with Colonel Frederick L. Devereux as president. Devereux had been an executive for many years in the American Telephone and Telegraph Company, but he was a complete stranger to the non-theatrical film field. Howard Gale Stokes was chosen to assist him.

Shortly after the organization of ERPI, it had been announced that the company would specialize in the manufacture and sale of portable sound projectors for non-theatrical use. To provide guidance for this venture, a committee of educators was chosen by Devereux, including N. L. Engelhardt, Paul Mort, and Alexander J. Stoddard. Ironically enough, none of these men had experience in motion picture production. Varney C. Arnspiger was selected as the director of educational research. Other research associates were Melvin Brodshaug, Edgar Stover, Howard Gray, Max R. Brunstetter, Laura Krieger Eads, and James A. Brill.

One of the educational committee's first efforts was producing a demonstration educational sound film. The scheme was to use excerpts from a series of diverse shots to illustrate a talk by Harry Dexter Kitson of Teachers College, Columbia University. The result, in two reels, was entitled *First Experimental Demonstration of Educational Talking Pictures*. The ERPI demonstration film was first publicly exhibited on July 23, 1929, at Macy Hall, Teachers College, Columbia University, to a gathering of 200 members of the Columbia faculty.

During the early months of 1929, William Lewin of Newark, New Jersey, urged Devereux to make a survey of the school market. When the plan was approved, Lewin embarked on a nation-wide tour to show the demonstration film and distribute questionnaires regarding the advantages and disadvantages of the new medium, the comparative value of the various parts of the film, and the improvements that might be made. Upon his return, he recommended to ERPI that there be a close correlation between textbooks and film production.[36] He further suggested that ERPI purchase the motion picture rights to textbooks. However, Devereux rejected these recommendations.

The next important undertaking of the ERPI educational division was a four-reel sound film on civics entitled *Our Government at Work*, which was produced by Fox Films.

Following this, a number of films were produced with the guidance of specialists, particularly in music, science, and teacher education.

Robert Hutchins, then president of the University of Chicago, was a major influence in the continued production of films by ERPI. Hutchins had long contended that film production should be associated with an outstanding university, free to enter any subject-matter field where a contribution to education could be made. In 1932, therefore, ERPI entered into a contract with the University of Chicago to produce a series of educational sound films under the direction of the university faculty.

A new source of support came to ERPI in 1936 when William M. Benton became vice-president of the University of Chicago. Benton made a detailed analysis of the instructional possibilities of the film medium and recommended expanded production of educational films. From 1936 on, Benton worked for an ever-closer relationship between the university and ERPI. In 1943, the university acquired the Encyclopaedia Britannica Films and later purchased the ERPI films, with the aid of money furnished by Benton. Thus, ERPI Classroom Films, Inc., became Encyclopaedia Britannica Films.

An evaluation of ERPI by McClusky follows:

ERPI's production has been second and third rate with the exception of the University of Chicago films. Much of ERPI's production has been salvaged from U.F.A. and other sources. ERPI has spent large sums (reputed to have been seven million dollars) for advertising and sales efforts, but few sales resulted. The total gross volume during the first ten years did not exceed $200,000. ERPI's educational talent (except that secured through the Chicago tie-up) has consisted largely of young graduate students taken from Teachers College, Columbia University. The only thing that ERPI can point to with pride is its contract with the University of Chicago. Even there, the production cost of from $8,000 to $10,000 per reel is too high. What does an ex-American Telephone and Telegraph Company Accountant [Devereux] know about the needs of American education anyway?[37]

Fox Films Corporation

Some theatrical film producers have attempted to establish educational film departments, but these efforts have tended to be rather transitory.

Fox Films Corporation was a case history of an early educational film production effort by a theatrical film producer. William Fox opened an educational division in 1922 under the direction of Herbert Hancock, former head of Fox News. By 1926, the first films for school use had been produced. Part of the Fox plan was to install a sound projector in every classroom and every church. However, by 1930 Fox had become so deeply indebted that he sold his voting shares to Harley Clarke, one of the co-founders of the Society for Visual Education.

Once again Clarke dreamed of making educational films. Early in 1931, a group of school superintendents succeeded in interesting him in producing films that would correlate with the school curriculum at the junior high level. The first, known as The Movietone School Series, were made in May 1931. Ten films were ready for release by July, and a public demonstration was held in Washington, D.C. Despite this auspicious beginning, however, Fox Films Corporation ceased educational film production a few years later.[38]

Other Early Enterprises

The aforementioned were a few of the more prominent early companies associated with the production or distribution of educational films. Others that deserve mention include the Educational Motion Pictures Bureau, Inc., F. S. Wythe Pictures Corporation, Rowland Rogers Productions, the University Film Foundation (founded at Harvard University in 1927), and the Jamison Handy Company.

Era of Crisis for the Educational Film

The advent of the sound film in the late 1920s introduced a critical period in educational film history.[39] Just as educators were becoming convinced of the educational merits of the silent film, the advocates of the sound film realized they had to fight the battle all over. The first educational sound films brought mixed reactions. Some educators repudiated the old silent films; others rejected the new sound films; still others refrained from either open approval or disapproval until they became convinced that the addition of sound was not just another technical novelty. Many hesitated to accept the sound film because they feared their silent equipment would become useless.

Aside from the sound crisis, in the late 1920s and the early 1930s commercial educational film enterprises were failing at an alarming rate. Although the depression contributed to their decimation, it could not account for all the failures. Ironically, too, commercial educational film producers seemed to be failing just when research findings were emphasizing the particular usefulness of the film as a medium of instruction. Unless a permanent corporation could be established to produce acceptable educational films and also show a financial profit, the development of educational technology would be hampered. Obviously, no commercial educational producer could achieve success without national support, and that support could not be attained until the users of educational films were convinced that no "special interests" were invading the classroom.

In 1937, David H. Stevens of the Rockefeller Foundation asked F. Dean McClusky to investigate the causes of the failure of commercial educational film producers so that remedial steps might be taken. According to the McClusky study, there had been a general lack of coordination between educational and commercial interests due to the following reasons.

1. Educators have failed to make their problems articulate to the commercial producers, and both educators and business men developed the notion that entertainment, commercialism, and education do not mix.

2. Commercial interests have failed to grasp or to study the nature of instruction and the complexity of educational institutions.

3. Business men dominated by the quick profit motive lost sight of the necessity of gaining the confidence and backing of professional leadership in education.

4. Educational leaders have been critical of the bad taste, stupidity and low moral tone of theatrical motion pictures. As a result, those in whom the control of education rested developed a feeling of opposition to motion pictures in general. They regarded with suspicion all plans and all enterprises which had as their aim the introduction of motion pictures into schools. While leading educators have recognized the potential value of motion pictures in education, they have quietly and continuously opposed all attempts to introduce into broad classroom use motion pictures which smacked of commercialism, low moral tone, propaganda or controversial issues.

The unsatisfactory pictures were found to be so numerous that the good ones suffered from being too frequently found in bad company.

5. The stupidity which has characterized the advertising, propaganda, and sales methods of companies producing and distributing so-called "educational" motion pictures created strong opposition in educational circles to school films, good or bad. Some of this propaganda created a fear in teachers that motion pictures would supplant them and mechanize instruction. The notion expressed in this propaganda that films would be used to supplant textbooks aroused not only the opposition of teachers to visual education, but also the antagonism of the authors and publishers of books.

6. Non-theatrical exhibitors and distributors met vigorous opposition from theatrical distributors and exhibitors who feared that school and church competition would hurt the theatrical box office receipts.

7. Low financial returns to producers and distributors of motion pictures in the non-theatrical field have been caused to some extent by the competition of "free" films and "subsidized" distributors such as state universities and museums.

8. Heads of educational institutions have devoted little time, energy or thought to the organization, supervision and administration of visual education. This resulted in a lack of leadership and guidance needed by sincere producers and distributors of "educational" motion pictures, and by pioneering teachers using this new medium of instruction.

9. The mechanical problems involved in the use of motion pictures in classrooms have been a strong inhibitory factor. Before the safety standard 16mm film was perfected, the fire hazard was great, and laws prohibited the use of films in classrooms unless equipped with fire proof booths. Many teachers have been timid about operating the machines. Many, also, would not take the trouble to order films, set up the projector, etc. even when such were available for use.

10. Commercial interests and educators alike have failed to develop definite, agreed upon policies with respect to production and use of motion pictures in education. The resultant confusion was matched only by that created by producers and distributors of visual material who were competing with each other in their efforts to capture the school market. Slides and stereographs, silent films, sound films, models, and charts have each been sold for the most part by competing companies. This competition between different types of visual materials confused school boards and executives.

11. Many of the failures of commercial efforts in the non-theatrical field have been traced directly to poor management due to incompetent executives, or unsound business methods or questionable business ethics, or to excessive overhead and/or lack of planning.[40]

McClusky then suggested the following remedies:

1. The production of motion pictures for schools can be successfully accomplished only by independent companies working in conjunction with educators—not by theatrical producers or by any others with whom the production and distribution of motion pictures is a side line or medium for propaganda or purely a commercial enterprise.

2. In order that coordination between educators and commercial interests may be made effective—

   a. Educational leadership would be obtained through advisory boards, or committees, each member of which would retain his or her professional standing and position.

   b. These educational advisors would blueprint needs, conduct research, and validate materials.

   c. They would operate in a non-profit framework.

3. The cooperating commercial producers would manufacture the productions outlined by the educational advisory groups and market only those materials which they had validated.

   a. The commercial producers would operate at a profit, but the service motive would be dominant.

   b. The object of the commercial producers would be to market materials for instruction independent of special interests.[41]

In 1932, Will H. Hays, president of the Motion Picture Producers and Distributors of America, attempted to deal with the competition problem. He called a private conference for the officials of ERPI, Eastman Teaching Films Division, and the representatives of twelve other educational film producers to effect a merger of their film efforts. None of the participants came to an agreement.[42]

Early College and University Educational Film Production

A number of colleges and universities were engaged in some form of educational film production as early as the 1910s.[43] One of the first attempts at providing complete film coverage of a subject came in 1921 and 1922 with Yale University's *Chronicles of America Photoplays* (discussed earlier in this chapter).

In the early 1930s, another prominent production effort was made at Arnold Gesell's Clinic of Child Development at Yale University. And in 1932, the University of Minnesota established the General College under the leadership of Dean Malcolm McLean. In order to implement the General College program, a Visual Education Service, under the direction of Robert A. Kissack, was organized to collect and classify sources of visual materials, develop a servicing program, and produce educational films.

Early Production of Government Educational Films

The federal government was the first to use motion pictures for instructional purposes. Educational films have been made by the government:

1. To obtain on film a record of a government activity (Signal Corps—war films).

2. To furnish a visual demonstration of techniques (Soil Conservation Service—*Sowing Mustard for Erosion Control*).

3. To teach specific steps on a particular job (Signal Corps—training films).

4. To obtain a measure of public cooperation or participation in a public "action" program (Social Security, Federal Housing Administration, etc.).

5. To inform the public or as a public relations vehicle for a bureau or its activities (National Park Service, Forest Service Films).

6. To dramatize and document in a cause-and-effect fashion great social and economic problems, with pictorial evidence of what the government was doing about such problems (*The Plow That Broke the Plains* and *The River*).[44]

For most of the first half of this century, the United States government consistently used the motion picture as a medium of information and education. Mercey considered the government's pioneering efforts to have been the Bureau of Reclamation film-making of 1911-1912.[45] For example, it was then that the Reclamation Service exhibited its first films showing the work of the bureau in reclaiming arid lands. Meanwhile, the Department of Agriculture made educational films surreptitiously from 1908 until 1912, using films in many diverse ways. A county agent could use a film to demonstrate methods requiring a full day if offered as live instruction. For example, opposition to cattle-tick eradication was fought by showing "The Charge of the Tick-Brigade" supplemented by "Making the South Tick Free." Agents offered help in hog cholera eradication by the use of the film "Control of Hog Cholera." By the dawn of the 1930s, educational film production had become established in the federal government.

Fig. 4.8. An early camera crew of the U.S. Department of Agriculture (Courtesy of U.S. Department of Agriculture.)

Fig. 4.9. Howard Greene of the Motion Picture Service of the U.S. Department of Agriculture—inventor of the first time-lapse mechanism for filming. "Studies in Plant Growth" was an early film made with this mechanism. (Courtesy of U.S. Department of Agriculture.)

Fig. 4.10. First motion picture studio of the U.S. Department of Agriculture (Courtesy of U.S. Department of Agriculture.)

Early Educational Film Distribution Agencies

From 1910 to 1940, a number of educational film distribution agencies came into existence. Distribution agencies were organized, for example, in state departments of education,[46] in college and university extension divisions, in local and state museums,[47] in public and school libraries,[48] and in state and federal governments.[49] In addition, a number of cooperative and commercial rental libraries were organized throughout the country. There were also a number of national organizations with their own film distribution networks that promoted the effective use of educational films, such as the YMCA Motion Picture Bureau, founded in 1914. Other important agencies, all established during the 1930s, were the American Institute of Cinematography, the American Film Center, the International Film Center, the Association of School Film Libraries, and the Psychological Cinema Register.[50]

Educational Film Libraries in
City School Systems

The Chicago Bureau of Visual Instruction established the first educational film library in a city school system in 1917. Newark, New Jersey, founded its visual instruction department and film library in 1918; Detroit and Kansas City in 1919; and Los Angeles, Buffalo, and New York City in 1920. The year 1922 marked the beginning of four more film libraries, in Atlanta, Pittsburgh, Berkeley, and Sacramento.[51]

Educational Film Libraries in
Extension Divisions

The U.S. Bureau of Education Motion Picture Department provided an important impetus to the growth of educational film libraries in extension divisions of colleges and universities, state departments of education, normal schools, and museums when it began distributing war films to these divisions in 1919. Each extension division received an average of 113 reels and agreed to act as a distributor to its local area. What is more, national advertisers soon followed this example by placing hundreds of reels of advertising film in extension depositories. By 1941, over thirty film libraries had been established in various extension divisions.

The earliest unique development in a state department of education extension division occurred in North Carolina. In 1916, the North Carolina Bureau of Commercial Service, which later became a division of the state department of education, was organized. The following year, the North Carolina legislature appropriated $25,000 to the bureau for work "designed to improve social and educational conditions" in rural communities through the distribution and showing of motion pictures selected by the Department of Public Instruction. The program also included the organization of complete, portable operating units for ten community circuits. In applying for this service, a community simply agreed to pay two-thirds of the cost, with the remaining third paid by the state. To raise their share of the expenses, most communities charged a small attendance fee at monthly meetings. Eventually over 400 community meetings were held each month, with a total average attendance of 45,000. Ellis and Thronborough reported that "people often walked for either eight or ten miles to attend a meeting."[52] There was obviously a hunger for information, which was not easily available in those days. Such an effort was considered a slight expenditure considering the knowledge they would gain.

Extension divisions distributed films to all who did not intend to use them for personal profit. The only charge was either a small service fee or the cost of transportation. This development soon began to adversely affect non-theatrical commercial enterprises, which depended on educational film rentals. To successfully compete with extension divisions, they had to reduce film rental fees so low that their profit margins were critically narrowed. Thus an era of hostility began between non-theatrical producers and distributors and extension divisions that operated film libraries.

College and university extension division leaders soon realized that operating a film library on a free basis was not satisfactory and that continued reliance on advertisers for films could not be condoned if certain educational objectives were to be achieved. By 1923, the movement to select only educational films and operate on a sound financial basis, led by W. H. Dudley of the University of Wisconsin, had become so widespread that practically all state bureaus were charging service and rental fees.

Excerpting of Theatrical Films for Instructional Purposes

Although the National Education Association Judd Committee had first recommended the excerpting of theatrical films for instructional use in 1923, the first large-scale, systematic excerpting of theatrical films did not take place until 1936.[53] The reason for this long delay was that the Motion Picture Producers and Distributors of America had repeatedly refused to approve the release of theatrical films because they feared excerpting would destroy the motion picture industry.

Committee for the Study of Social Values in Motion Pictures

The first small-scale excerpting of theatrical films came about as the result of the organization of a Committee for the Study of Social Values in Motion Pictures in September 1927 by the Payne Fund.[54] A sum of $65,800 was allocated to underwrite a two-year period of activity, including a survey of the motion picture field by William H. Short of the Motion Picture Research Council and a series of studies by leading social scientists.

By June 1928, Short's study had been completed and was printed for the private use of Payne Fund members in a 400-page volume entitled *A Generation of Motion Pictures*. This preliminary study was next placed in the hands of people selected for their knowledge of education and social science as well as of the history and problems of the motion picture industry. In addition, a conference was organized "to secure factual data regarding motion pictures on the basis of which a national policy, socially constructive in character, may be formulated."[55] As a result, twenty-one studies were proposed, twelve of which served as a basis for the subsequent Payne Fund studies of motion pictures.[56]

In 1929, the motion picture industry, in order to disarm some of its critics, finally permitted the Committee for the Study of Social Values in Motion Pictures to excerpt portions of theatrical films. A 35mm silent film series entitled *Secrets of Success*, dramatizing certain moral issues, was created and distributed by the committee to schools, churches, and other organizations for character education.[57] This series failed after a few years, largely because of opposition from the motion picture industry, limited projection equipment, and chaotic distribution.

Commission on Human Relations

The Committee for the Study of Social Values in Motion Pictures of the Payne Fund secured a grant of $75,000 from the Rockefeller Foundation in 1936 for the Progressive Education Association, so that its work on the excerpting of theatrical films might be continued.[58] A Commission on Human Relations of the Payne Fund was established under the chairmanship of Alice V. Keliher in July 1936, which led to the first large-scale excerpting. By 1938, sixty excerpts known as *The Human Relations Series* had been prepared and had begun to be used experimentally in a number of schools to help adolescents solve their personal problems and develop a better understanding of human relations.[59]

Advisory Committee on the Use of
Motion Pictures in Education

In 1934, Will H. Hays of the Motion Picture Producers and Distributors of America called in a number of consultants to discuss a plan whereby the motion picture industry could contribute to the use of theatrical films in the schools. As a result of this meeting, Hays sent Mark A. May, director of the Institute of Human Relations at Yale University, to Hollywood to further explore the possibilities of excerpting theatrical films, with the advice that he avoid using two words—"16mm" and "education." May cautiously probed Hollywood producers without discussing his mission and on his return prepared a memorandum recommending the release of theatrical films for school use. Reluctantly the major producers, with the exception of Metro-Goldwyn-Mayer, agreed to go along with May's recommendation, despite protests from countless exhibitors.

The advisory committee, supported by the Rockefeller Foundation and the Motion Picture Producers and Distributors of America, called in some 50 educators to review 1,800 theatrical shorts, from which 360 were selected and put on 16mm film for distribution to schools.[60] Moreover, film descriptions were prepared and catalogs printed. The advisory committee was incorporated in the state of New York in 1939 as a nonprofit membership corporation under the name of Teaching Film Custodians, Inc.[61]

An Emerging Technology for Instructional
Application of Films

A clear distinction between the film as an entertainment and informational medium and as a medium of instruction was first made early in this century, although educational films were usually considered aids to teaching rather than self-contained sequences of instruction.

One of the first descriptive technologies for the instructional use of the film came about when the F. S. Wythe Pictures Corporation of San Francisco produced a series of civics films in 1918, entitled *Citizens in the Making: A Film Text Composed of Thirty Lessons*. A *Manual of Civics Film Text* by C. A. Stebbins, published by the Wythe Company, contained suggestions to teachers for the use of this "film textbook."

During the 1920s, the first books were written describing a methodology for the film in the classroom, and the first courses were established for teachers concerning the use of the educational film. By the late 1920s, a definitive methodology had been developed. For example, Weber adapted Johann Herbart's "instructional step" plan by dividing his methodology for film use into six steps:

1. preparation, or discussing the synopsis of the film in light of the learner's previous experience;

2. presentation, or presenting the film when learners' "curiosity is at high pitch and their minds sharpened for the central message of the film";

3. informal discussion and assignments consisting of readings, problems, or projects;

4. supplementary showings, either running the film again without interruption or, preferably, showing it in parts, followed by more informal discussion;

5. formal recitation, or assimilating the film's concepts through generalization and application, with the teacher having a carefully prepared lesson plan structured as to aim, content, and procedure; and

6. check-up, or oral or written review quizzes or a list of test items in the form of an essay, report, or project.[62]

Much of the theorizing behind the methodology of film use was based on the concept that the pictorial is inevitably "real," "concrete," and "meaningful"; that is, the film medium not only brought visual reality but added concreteness through the quality of motion.

Although the term *visual instruction* has been used since the beginning of this century to refer to a variety of visual instructional media, it is not surprising that the educational film intensified its use and provided a great impetus to the development of the visual instruction movement in American education.

The Educational Film during World Wars I and II

Unlike in the public schools, widespread use of the educational film had become firmly established in the armed forces before World War II.[63] During World War I, the War and Navy Departments had organized film divisions for the twofold purpose of supplying informational films to the public and of instructing officers and men in the science of war. At the beginning of World War I, a Committee on Public Information was created to disseminate information concerning the war activities of the government.

When World War II began, the use of educational films was made a part of the official policy of the War Department. The effect of this policy was that the armed forces produced more than six times the number of films than had ever been produced before for educational purposes. Moreover, the demand for training millions of industrial workers as rapidly and effectively as possible brought about a historic production of educational films for training purposes.[63]

Educational Film Production in the Postwar Years

Even after World War II, most educational films were stilted, pedantic, and talkative. Low budgets and a narrow margin of profit handicapped the production of a sufficient number of good educational films.

Commercial Educational Film Production

Before World War II, ERPI Classroom Films, Eastman Classroom Films, and Films Incorporated were the leading producers of educational films. ERPI had entered educational film production because it wanted to sell its equipment; the Eastman Kodak Company had envisioned a profitable commercial venture. Neither company, however, enjoyed overwhelming success. Eastman Kodak produced silent films just before the advent of sound and ERPI encountered the depression and the lethargy of educators. During World War II and in the postwar years, many old and new companies increased the production of educational films, including Coronet, Vocational Guidance Films, Young America, McGraw-Hill Book Company, United World Films, Films Incorporated, Simmel-Misery and others.

By the 1950s, Encyclopaedia Britannica Films led world production and distribution of educational films. This was made possible by the purchase of the ERPI library of 200 films from Western Electric on December 3, 1943, and also by the acquisition of 250 silent films from Eastman Teaching Films on April 12, 1944.

Another notable development occurred in 1946 when Universal Pictures Company established United World Films, Inc., in cooperation with the British companies of J. Arthur Rank. The new company purchased Bell and Howell Film's sound film library of 6,000 short subjects and features as well as the Castle Films producing company. By the end of 1946, United World Films had begun worldwide production and distribution of 16mm educational films.

The McGraw-Hill Book Company made a notable contribution to educational films with its so-called textfilm. The textfilms, first produced in 1947, were designed to supplement widely used textbooks by extending the pictorial scope of the subject, rather than by duplicating any material in the texts. Along with textfilms, McGraw-Hill provided supplementary filmstrips and instructor's manuals that included suggestions for integrating these three types of teaching materials. Since the textfilm idea proved to be successful, Encyclopaedia Britannica Films also began to produce textfilms for more than 300 of the most widely used textbooks published by 20 American textbook publishers.

University-Produced Educational Films

In the postwar era, colleges and universities became increasingly active in producing educational films. One of the most active university production centers in the world was at the University of Chicago, made possible by the donation of films by Encyclopaedia Britannica Films and by generous grants from the Carnegie Foundation for the Advancement of Teaching. Production units were also organized at the University of Southern California, Ohio State University, the University of Wisconsin, Pennsylvania State College, New York University, the University of Indiana, the University of Minnesota, Iowa State University, the University of Michigan, Boston University, and Syracuse University.[64]

Postwar Distribution of Educational Films

One of the persistent problems associated with educational films has been distribution. By 1950, more than 287 educational film libraries offered more than 6,000 titles for educational use. These libraries were a part of city, county, state, college, and university institutions. In addition, governmental, museum, public library, and private organizations developed educational film libraries throughout the country.

Two of the largest educational film libraries in the United States by 1950 were the University of Wisconsin's Department of Visual Instruction, with over 7,000 films, and the Department of Visual Instruction of the University of California, with over 10,000 educational films.[65]

Teaching Films Survey

In the spring of 1945, a group of publishers met at Princeton, New Jersey, to discuss the advisability of making a formal survey of educational films and motion picture production.[66] The main sources of data were questionnaire replies from school superintendents, audiovisual directors, principals, and elementary and secondary school teachers from 424 of the largest public school systems in the country. Also, 137 personal interviews were held with audiovisual directors in major cities, motion picture producers, projector manufacturers, film distributors, heads of film lending libraries, and other key persons in the field. A cooperative experiment in educational film production was also undertaken with Teaching Film Custodians; three completed films entitled *Osmosis, The Seasons,* and *Borrowing in Subtraction* resulted.

The following conclusions were made:

1. The only market for film designed solely for school use is today only a rather small market, with most of the business concentrated among a few customers—a small number of very large school systems in the biggest cities, and a small number of film-lending libraries.

2. This market will probably double in size (but not in total expenditures for films) by sometime in the early 1950s; but the increase will come mainly in the elementary schools. Further growth in the high schools seems likely to be relatively small during the next five to ten years.

3. There is a lack of enough good films for the schools to use. This lack is commonly interpreted as need, but it does not appear to have crystallized into strong and widespread demand for specific films on specific topics. Such demand as now exists is generally rather vague and ill-defined.

4. Only a relatively small portion of the visible opportunity to produce and sell new motion pictures, in the market now existing and likely to exist in the next few years, appears to center on types of motion pictures that the textbook publishers are most obviously qualified to produce. In most subject areas, especially in elementary schools, the preference of the teachers is dominantly concentrated on background films and social attitude films.

5. Much of the present lack of enough good films can be met only by continuing output of "by-product" films and subsidized films and offers no profitable opportunity for commercial producers of school films.

6. The total opportunity for profitable commercial production of school films is not as yet big enough to provide room for more than a few producers. The day when it will be big enough must lie some years distant.[67]

Concluding Comments

Clearly, the educational film has provided an impetus to American educational technology. However, even today, the film has not reached its full potential as a medium of instruction. As Worth says, "Film-making could become one of the important tools by which we allow and help the child as well as the adult to develop skill in building cognitive structures and in structuring reality in a creative, communicative way." He says further that "although we can teach through film, we must begin to understand how the structure of the film itself and the visual modes in general structure our ways of organizing experience."[68]

Although the term *visual education* has been used since the beginning of this century to refer to a variety of instructional media, the evolution of the educational film has played a vital role in the development of the visual instruction movement. Chapter 5 is a historical survey of this important facet of educational technology.

Notes

[1]The principal reference for much of the material concerning the technical history of the film has been: Terry Ramsaye, *A Million and One Nights.* New York: Simon and Schuster, 1926.

[2]Wheatstone, the inventor of the stereoscope, announced almost simultaneously that "a series of brief illuminations made it possible for a moving object to seem immobile." Lancelot Hogben, *From Cave Painting to Comic Strip.* New York: Chanticleer Press, 1949, 253.

[3]In the zootrope or zoetrope, a band of pictures was mounted inside a revolving drum and viewed through slots in the outside of the drum. The band was detachable and could be changed at will. When twelve or more phase drawings were arranged in order and when the disc was rotated in front of a mirror, the reflected image viewed through the slots was seen as continuous motion.

[4]The name "kinematoscope" was the first use of the Greek root for motion, and is a direct ancestor of the word cinema.

[5]Simon Ritter von Stampfer of Vienna designed a device similar to the one developed by Plateau. Jacques Mande Daguerre, a French painter, invented a diorama, which anticipated motion pictures, in 1826.

[6]Edward James Muggerridge took on the strange name of Eadweard Muybridge in the belief that it was the Anglo-Saxon original of his name. Muybridge was recommended to Governor Stanford because of his fame as photographer of Yosemite Valley and Alaska. Muybridge failed in his first try to photograph Governor Stanford's horses and then a personal incident delayed his work for three years: Muybridge was accused of murdering his wife's lover, but a two-day trial brought an acquittal on a temporary insanity plea. For the next three years, Muybridge lived in the hinterland ranch property of Leland Stanford, and in 1877, again returned to his experiment. This time, John D. Isaacs, an engineer of the Central Pacific Railway, worked out a system of electrical contacts with wire stretched across Stanford's race track so that instantaneous photographs could be taken whether or not any object touched the ground. When the photographic equipment was complete, Isaacs returned to his railroad job and Muybridge stayed to operate the device and to enjoy all the subsequent fame and prestige that grew out of this invention. Ramsaye states that "one of the greatest myths in the history of motion pictures has been the repeated credit given to Muybridge for fathering the motion picture." See Ramsaye, *Million and One Nights*, 21.

[7]After Thomas Edison had completed the phonograph in 1877, he began to attack the problem of motion pictures. His first motion picture machine recorded spirals of tiny pictures on a cylinder, in the pattern of a phonograph groove. The pictures were given an intermittent motion and were viewed under a microscope. Edison soon abandoned this method because of the problem of magnification. He then conceived the idea of images being handled on a tape or belt. Experimental films were made by drying collodion varnish that was coated with photographic emulsion on glass and then stripping it off into sheets. This material was unsatisfactory because of its fragility. In August 1899, George Eastman, who was making similar material for the purposes of "roller photography," began the manufacture of photographic film with a flexible nitro-cellulose base. Edison heard of this material, purchased a sample fifty-foot strip, and found that his problems were solved.

[8]Don Carlos Ellis and Laura Thornborough, *Motion Pictures in Education.* New York: Thomas Y. Crowell, 1923, 11. The subject of the film was a butterfly dance and each frame had been patiently colored by hand.

[9]Lewis Jacobs, *The Rise of the American Film: A Critical History*. New York: Harcourt, Brace, 1939, 1-2.

[10]Arthur E. Krows, "Motion Pictures—Not for Theaters," *The Educational Screen* 17 (October 1938), 249.

[11]Arthur E. Krows, "Motion Pictures—Not for Theaters," *The Educational Screen* 18 (January 1939), 51.

[12]Ibid.

[13]George Kleine, *Catalogue of Educational Motion Pictures*. New York: George Kleine Company, 1910, 1.

[14]Frank N. Freeman, "Requirements of Education with Reference to Motion Pictures," *The School Review* 31 (May 1923), 340-50.

[15]M. J. Cohen, "The Evolution of the Motion Picture." Unpublished manuscript, 1918, 1.

[16]W. M. Gregory, "Problems Concerning the Educational Motion Picture," *Moving Picture Age* 5 (January 1922), 20.

[17]Although educational institutions were beginning to realize the value of films, the fire-hazard problem succeeded in hampering the diffusion of the educational film. For example, in 1910, the Boston schools barred all films in the schools because of the fire menace. The first fireproof booth for projecting motion pictures, built as an integral part of a school, was constructed in Vanderlip Hall at the Scarborough School in New York State in 1916.

[18]Urban developed the Kinemacolor process, which involved revolving discs of red and green filters through which black-and-white film was projected at double speed. The mechanical complexity of the process and patent difficulties hampered its acceptance. Urban encountered his greatest failure on the lyceum circuits because the theaters did not have the necessary special equipment.

[19]Skinner supervised and produced two outstanding early educational films, titled *The Valley of the Ten Thousand Smokes* and *Unhooking the Hook Worm*.

[20]F. Dean McClusky, *Motion Pictures for the Schools*. Unpublished report presented to the Rockefeller Foundation, 1937, 5.

[21]Ibid., 8.

[22]Ibid., 6.

[23]Ibid., 7.

[24]Ibid., 9.

[25]Many of the educators on the board of the Society of Visual Education had the impression that the company was a nonprofit organization and, as a consequence, allowed their names to be used. However, many also invested their money in this venture.

[26]George A. Skinner, "A Short History of the Educational Motion Picture Organizations Which Have Been Projected during the Past Twenty-five Years." Unpublished manuscript, undated, 2.

[27]One of the first films of this series, often credited as the first true educational motion picture, was *The Story of the Monarch Butterfly*.

[28]A pioneering activity of the Society for Visual Education was the magazine *Visual Education*. This was an elaborate monthly house organ that first appeared in January 1920, with Nelson L. Greene as its editor. The journal was later co-edited by W. C. Bagley and F. R. Moulton. The December 1924 issue

announced the merger of *Visual Education* with *The Educational Screen*. In 1926, the society reentered the publishing field when it issued an annual *Visual Review*. This periodical was first edited by Marie Witham.

[29]Arthur E. Krows, secretary of the Chronicles of America Picture Corporation, reveals that George Parmly Day succeeded in securing the financial support of the Harkness family, which was reputedly worth about $2 million. See Arthur E. Krows, "Motion Pictures—Not for Theaters," *The Educational Screen* 21 (March 1942), 104-6.

[30]Daniel C. Knowlton and J. Warren Tilton conducted a study of the *Chronicles of America Photoplays* to determine their effectiveness as an aid in seventh-grade history instruction. See D. C. Knowlton and J. W. Tilton, *Motion Pictures in History Teaching*. New Haven, Conn.: Yale University Press, 1929.

[31]McClusky, *Motion Pictures*, 15-16.

[32]See Ben D. Wood and Frank N. Freeman, *Motion Pictures in the Classroom*. Boston: Houghton Mifflin, 1929.

[33]New companies organized during the thirties included Castle Films, Films Incorporated, Academic Films Corporation, Vocational Guidance Films, Knowledge Builders, Garrison Films, and the William H. Dudley Visual Education Service. Dudley, a former director of the Bureau of Visual Instruction of the University of Wisconsin, founded his company primarily for the distribution of educational slides and films. A circuit plan of distribution was used and schools were organized on a commercial basis. By 1937, more than four thousand schools were on his circuit service. Each school paid $50 per year for the service and received 120 reels of film and a projector.

[34]Henceforth, Electrical Research Products, Inc., will be referred to as ERPI.

[35]Bell Laboratories engineers first studied the possibilities of educational sound films for ERPI and concluded that moving graphs and charts would make effective educational films. The problem was next handed to the Carpenter-Goldman Laboratories, which had made some of the first animated films for ERPI's parent company, Western Electric.

[36]This was the forerunner of the McGraw-Hill Book Company Text-Films, which were developed in 1947.

[37]McClusky, *Motion Pictures*, 25.

[38]Ellis and Thornborough quoted an undisclosed theatrical film producer who had produced educational films as saying: "The non-theatrical exhibitor is usually a poor businessman, he is unreliable, far from a steady customer, he does not know what he wants, yet he is dissatisfied with what has been produced, or else he wants us to produce a film according to his ideas to meet the needs of no other user of educational films. In addition, his equipment is often poor, he damages films far more than does his theatrical neighbor, and yet he is willing to pay less than a fifth of the price the theatrical exhibitor expects to pay. It is because the non-theatrical exhibitor wants everything for nothing or practically nothing that we have abandoned, at least for the present, the non-theatrical field." See Ellis and Thornborough, *Motion Pictures in Education*, 23.

[39]Sound films have existed since before the close of the nineteenth century. One of Edison's first efforts, after the invention of the Kinetoscope, was to combine his phonograph with film. Leon Gaumont supervised a demonstration of a sound film in New York City in 1913 for which a French patent had been granted him in 1901. Other early variations of the sound film were Whitman's Cameraphone (1904), Powers's Fotofone (1910), and Greenbaum's Synchronoscope (1908). In 1923, Lee De Forest gave a public showing of the Phonofilm in New York City. The first "all talkie," known as *Oil Films on Water*, was exhibited by the Bell Telephone Laboratories at the Philadelphia sesquicentennial exposition in 1926. The first public sound program was presented by Warner Brothers at the Knickerbocker Theater in New York City on August 7, 1926. The first educational sound film was produced by Don Carlos Ellis for the Western Electric and Manufacturing Company in 1929. This film was titled *Dynamic America*.

[40]McClusky, *Motion Pictures*, 25.

[41]Ibid., 26.

[42]George A. Skinner had implanted the merger idea in Hays's mind. F. Dean McClusky wrote *Visual Instruction: Its Values and Needs* in 1932 with a merger in mind. These men's ideas influenced the merger and they attended the Hays merger conference.

[43]These included the universities of Yale, Chicago, Illinois, Indiana, Iowa, Oklahoma, Michigan, Nebraska, Wisconsin, Utah, and Harvard, and the Massachusetts Institute of Technology.

[44]Arch Mercey, "Streamlining Adult Films." Lecture given at the National Council for Social Studies, Pittsburgh, Pa., November 26, 1938. (Mimeographed abstract.)

[45]In 1912, Jim Wilson, then secretary of agriculture, recognized the motion picture as an important educational medium and officially established the Motion Picture Service. This effort began with W. S. Clime, George R. Goergens, and Andre Boetcher, who were regularly assigned to the production of educational films. In 1917, Congress formally recognized this work by appropriating $10,000 for educational film production. At this same time, Don Carlos Ellis was placed in charge of the department's film production.

[46]The Ohio State Department of Education established its Central Slide and Film Exchange in 1926.

[47]The Museum of Modern Art and the American Museum of Natural History of New York City were among the first museums to distribute educational films.

[48]The first experiment in public library film distribution was made by the Kalamazoo, Michigan, Public Library in 1929.

[49]Such federal agencies as the Department of Agriculture, Department of the Interior, Bureau of Mines, and the Office of Education were early government distributors of educational films.

[50]The Association of School Film Libraries, founded in August 1938 by the Rockefeller Foundation, made one of the first attempts to decentralize the distribution of educational films, but it succeeded in bringing nothing but frustration to its members. The Psychological Cinema Register was founded in 1938 by Adelbert Ford of Lehigh University to develop a film library in the field of psychology.

[51]In 1923, the Berkeley public school system distinguished itself by being the first to publish a graded list of films. Most of the early educational film catalogs listed the available films according to subjects and titles, rather than making any attempt to supply graded lists. See *Visual Instruction*, Course of Study Monographs no. 7. Berkeley, Calif.: Curriculum Committee on Visual Education, The Berkeley Public Schools, 1923.

[52]Ellis and Thornborough, *Motion Pictures in Education*, 29.

[53]See chapter 8 of this book for details of the Judd Committee activities.

[54]Dean Howard M. LeSourd of Boston University was chairman of the Committee for the Study of Social Values in Motion Pictures.

[55]*The Payne Fund Annual Report* (1928), 5.

[56]As a result of the Payne Fund studies by the Committee for the Study of Social Values in Motion Pictures, the Committee on Educational Research was organized under the direction of W. W. Charters of Ohio State University. The Payne Fund studies evolved out of the work of the Committee on Educational Research.

[57]Hugh Harshorne and Mark A. May had found in their 1928 *Studies in Deceit* that verbal learning of moral codes did not seem to have much effect on behavior. As a result of these studies, May became interested in finding some type of instruction that would produce what he called an "emotional

punch." It occurred to May, probably as a result of the earlier Judd Committee recommendation, that live situations in the form of filmic stories would be more effective. After using the *Secrets of Success* series for character education, he found a more systematic approach was necessary.

[58]When the motion picture industry finally permitted the Committee for the Study of Social Values in Motion Pictures to excerpt theatrical films, the first major bulwark had been penetrated. In 1936, Paramount Studios became the first theatrical film producer to release film classics to the schools. Eric Haight of Films Incorporated, a non-theatrical film producer and distributor, deserves much credit for persuading Paramount to consent to this release. As a result of Paramount's action, other studios later joined in this move.

[59]To achieve the objective of the commission, a number of provocative films were used. These included a film called *Fury*, which centered on the behavior of a mob in a lynching; the film *A Devil Is a Sissy*, which revealed the problems faced by a boy who moves from one community to another; and *An Educating Father*, a film centering on the dispute between father and son over the choice of the son's vocation. Participants in the human relations experiment included two New York City high schools, Benjamin Franklin and Washington Irving; two New York City private schools, Dalton and Lincoln; and the following: Bronxville Public Schools, New York; Freehold Public Schools, New Jersey; Cambridge School, Massachusetts; Stephens Junior College, Missouri; University High School, Oakland, California; Francis W. Parker School, Chicago; North Shore Country Day School, Winnetka, Illinois; Western Military Academy, Illinois; Shaker Heights Public School, Cleveland; Oak Lane Country Day School, Philadelphia; George School, Pennsylvania; and the Denver public high schools, Colorado. Adult and parent groups in Vermont also took part in this experiment. See *The Human Relations Series of Films*. New York: Commission on Human Relations, Progressive Education Association, 1939.

[60]Somewhat related to this development was the rise of the motion picture appreciation movement in the 1930s. Although this movement was generated to a large extent by the Payne Fund studies, the increased accessibility of theatrical films for school use had an important influence. William Lewin and Max J. Herzberg of the Newark, New Jersey, Public Schools were early leaders in this movement. The basic object was to establish courses designed to analyze and discuss theatrical motion pictures for the purpose of influencing the attitudes and behavior of adolescents. See William Lewin, *Photoplay Appreciation in American High Schools*. New York: Appleton-Century, 1934.

[61]The first officers of Teaching Film Custodians, Inc., were Mark A. May, chairman and director of research; Carl E. Milliken, general business and financial manager; and Roger Albright, director of educational services. When Teaching Film Custodians was first established, contracts were negotiated with the motion picture industry that provided for three-year contracts to schools. The films were to be used only during school hours and not for entertainment. No admission was to be charged, nor were the films to be used for fund raising by school organizations. A number of other restrictive clauses were also included. In effect, the service of the Teaching Film Custodians was not satisfactory for many reasons. Prominent among these was the fact that films were often loaned to certain schools while others were arbitrarily excluded.

[62]Adapted from Joseph J. Weber, *Visual Aids in Education*. Valparaiso, Ind.: Valparaiso University, 1930, 47-50. (Mimeographed.)

[63]See chapter 6 of this book for the history of the educational film during World War II.

[64]By 1951, this development had become significant enough to warrant the formation of a professional group known as the College and University Film Producers Association.

[65]In August 1951, the Library of Congress inaugurated the first printing and distribution of catalog cards for motion pictures and filmstrips.

[66]These publishers were Harcourt, Brace & Co.; Harper and Brothers; Henry Holt and Co.; Houghton Mifflin Co.; the Macmillan Co.; Scott, Foresman and Co.; and Scholastic Magazines.

[67]*A Report to Educators on Teaching Films Survey*. New York: Harcourt, Brace; Harper and Brothers; Henry Holt; Houghton Mifflin; Macmillan; Scott, Foresman; and Scholastic Magazines, 1948, 96.

[68]Sol Worth, "The Uses of Film in Education and Communication," in David R. Olson, ed., *Media and Symbols: The Forms of Expression, Communication, and Education*, Part I, Seventy-third yearbook of the National Society for the Study of Education. Chicago: University of Chicago Press, 1974, 302.

Select Bibliography

Bollman, Gladys, and Henry Bollman. *Motion Pictures for Community Needs.* New York: Henry Holt, 1922.

Buchanan, Andrew. *The Film in Education.* London: Phoenix House, 1951.

Ceram, C. W. *Archaeology of the Cinema.* London: Thames and Hudson, 1965.

Ellis, Don C., and Laura Thornborough. *Motion Pictures in Education.* New York: Thomas Y. Crowell, 1923.

Gregory, W. M. "Problems Concerning the Educational Motion Picture." *Moving Picture Age*, vol. 5, no. 1 (January 1922): 20.

Jacobs, Lewis. *The Rise of the American Film: A Critical History.* New York: Harcourt, Brace, 1939.

Knowlton, Daniel C., and J. Warren Tilton. *Motion Pictures in History Teaching.* New Haven, Conn.: Yale University Press, 1929.

Krows, Arthur E. "Motion Pictures—Not for Theaters." *The Educational Screen*, vol. 21 (March 1942): 104-6.

Ramsaye, Terry. *A Million and One Nights.* New York: Simon and Schuster, 1926.

Saettler, Paul. *History of Instructional Technology*, vol. 2: *The Technical Development of the New Media.* Washington, D.C.: NEA Technological Development Project, 1961.

5

The Rise and Decline of the Visual Instruction Movement: 1900-1950

Many mistakenly proclaim or assume that the American visual instruction movement began sometime in the early 1920s, but it can actually be traced back to the first decade of this century and even earlier. In fact, the abstract-concrete theoretical rationale that was the foundation of the visual instruction movement appeared as early as 1886. Although the term *visual education* did not evolve until about 1906, many developments and trends were already crystallizing into a distinctly new movement in American education. The technological progress achieved by the invention of a practical stereoscope, a perfected process of photography, and the invention of the motion picture projector aided immeasurably in the birth of the visual instruction movement.

It is not clear who first used the terms *visual education* and *visual instruction*. Rather, it is safe to assume that they developed quite spontaneously. Many began to see inherent instructional value in new media that were becoming available. These people comprised two groups: One was composed of social workers and a few imaginative educators; the other consisted of commercial producers and distributors of such new visual media as stereographs, lantern slides, maps, models, slidefilms, and motion picture films, who envisioned an extended market for their wares. It is easy to see why the commercial promoters soon christened this new movement "visual education." The name was formally declared in 1906, when the Keystone View Company of Meadville, Pennsylvania, published *Visual Education*, a teacher's guide to Keystone's "600 Set" of stereographs and lantern slides.

Adult Education Movement: Forerunner of Visual Instruction

The adult education movement became an important aspect of American intellectual life and established the mold of academic respectability for the visual instruction movement. In the United States the early forms of adult education were the New England town meeting, the lyceum, the Chautauqua Institution, community public libraries, extension education, commercial or proprietary schools, and the Young Men's and Women's Christian Associations. The latter four, established in the last quarter of the nineteenth century, still continue; the former have largely disappeared.

A direct forerunner of the visual instruction movement was the American lyceum founded by Josiah Holbrook in the villages of Massachusetts in 1826. On these early lyceum circuits, the lantern slide became the most popular medium of instruction. When the Chautauqua Institution, founded by John Heyl Vincent and Louis Miller in 1874, became a dominant movement in American life, the lantern slide was again used extensively for educational purposes.

There was also a group of itinerant lecturers who saw the possibilities of making still pictures for use in travel lectures. One of the first to launch travel lectures accompanied by lantern slides, which brought him immediate success and fame, was John L. Stoddard, in the 1880s.

Elias Burton Holmes, as a boy of nine in 1880, was spellbound by Stoddard's oratory and his black-and-white slides. As a result, Holmes was determined to become another Stoddard. When he took a world tour with his grandmother, Holmes prepared a complete visual account of his journey in the form of illustrated colored slides. He made his first professional appearance in 1893. Later, in 1897, he became the first to present travel lantern slides in kodachrome. By 1900, Holmes had become famous and successful. He began to make contracts with commercial houses so they could sell prints of still photographs he had taken, and sold theatrical rights for motion picture studios. To add to these achievements, Holmes published his travel lectures in fifteen volumes and established his own film-processing laboratory and lantern-slide factory in Chicago.

Holmes made two significant contributions to the visual education movement. First, he was undoubtedly one of the most important figures in the popularization of illustrated lectures and, second, he created the largest and most valuable early source of films that could be successfully used in the classroom. When this author called these contributions to Holmes's attention in an interview several years ago, Holmes, with a wry smile, denied that he had had educational objectives. He went on to say that he had actually been financially harmed because his travel films were popular in the schools and had been called "educational."[1]

Other pioneers in the adult education movement who were aware of the educational potential of lantern slides and motion pictures included Lyman H. Howe, Frederick T. Burlingham, Dwight L. Elmendorf, Ernest M. Newman, and C. J. Hite. In 1900, Howe obtained every suitable film he could find and pieced them all together to create a complete evening's educational experience. Hite, in 1906, organized the C. J. Hite Motion Picture Company to supply the growing demand for films on the lyceum circuits. Although these men were not the only lecturers who projected lantern slides and films, their realization of the potential educational value of lantern slides and films was a significant contribution to the early development of the visual instruction movement.

Impact of the Early School Museum Movement

From the earliest days of the American museum, there has been a concerted effort to cooperate with the public schools. Rather than serving merely as storage houses, museums have also played an instructional role. This role influenced the selection and presentation of museum exhibits. There were period rooms, dioramas, and habitat groups that showed a single item—a painting, a model, or a zoological specimen—as part of its environment, creating a display quite distinct from a loose collection of objects. The increasing fulfillment of this instructional function was acknowledged as early as 1880, when, at the opening of the new building of the Metropolitan Museum of Art in New York City, museums were declared to be social instruments for the educational progress of the masses.

Fig. 5.1. Portrait of Burton Holmes (Courtesy of Burton Holmes.)

Of major importance in the museum movement was the development of new methods of instruction. Specimens and object collections were made an integral part of the instructional process. Functioning tools or machines illustrated essential principles of mechanics, and concrete objects—models, drawings, and stuffed animals—provided firsthand experiences.

Guided tours, lectures, and cooperative instructional programs with the public schools were organized by many museums. Temporary loans of collections or single specimens were made to libraries, schools, associations, individuals, or even other museums.

Early Museum Instructional Programs

In 1878, the Davenport (Iowa) Academy of Sciences arranged a cooperative instructional program with the Davenport Public Schools. In 1904, the school board of Davenport paid half of the curator's salary, for his educational work. In the same year, the science teachers of Buffalo, New York, were encouraged to use the collections and rooms of the Buffalo Society of Natural Sciences. The Buffalo museum also prepared lantern slides and specimens for educators' use.[2]

The Children's Museum was established in 1899 as a branch of the Central Museum of the Brooklyn Institute of Arts and Sciences "to form an attractive resort for children, with influences tending to refine their tastes and elevate their interests; to create an attractive center of daily assistance to pupils and teachers in connection with school work; and to offer new subjects of thought for pursuit in leisure hours."[3] Anna Billings Gallup, the first curator of this museum, described the original plan as including (1) the preparation of collections that children could enjoy, understand, and use; (2) an arrangement of material pleasing to the eye and expressive of fundamental truth; (3) briefly descriptive display labels expressed in simple language and printed in clear, readable type; and (4) a system of instruction that children would voluntarily employ.[4] The Brooklyn Children's Museum led to the establishment of a similar children's museum at the Smithsonian Institution in Washington, D.C., in 1900.

Museums of Arts and Sciences

Art museums and museums of science contributed to educational technology early on by developing a number of instructional programs in cooperation with public schools, colleges, and universities. The Fogg Art Museum of Cambridge, Massachusetts, began working very closely with Harvard University in the early 1900s. The Field Museum of Natural History in Chicago began a system of museum service to the Chicago Public Schools in 1911. This system was based on the assumption that city-born boys and girls are complete strangers to the natural world. Therefore, nature study collections were emphasized and resided with each Chicago school for a year. The schedule was arranged so that each school could have five deliveries of three cases of natural objects—objects common to the fields of zoology, botany, and geology.[5]

American Museum of Natural History

An outstanding example of museum instruction rendered to the public schools is provided by the American Museum of Natural History of New York City. From its inception in 1869, the guiding motto of this museum has been, "For the people, for education, for science." In 1880 Albert S. Bickmore inaugurated his illustrated lectures for teachers, and in 1904 nature-study collections were first distributed to the schools. Some of the museum's most useful services have been the distribution of lantern slides, films, filmstrips, study prints, and the establishment of outdoor museums for schoolchildren in Adirondack State Park (New York).

Within the museum, mammals, birds, reptiles, amphibians, and fishes were mounted or modeled in lifelike attitudes and grouped as in nature. Each exhibit was shown in a pictorial setting that realistically reproduced its natural environment. Actual specimens, including real trees, bushes, and rocks, were included in the terrestrial group displays; all exhibits were supplemented by explanatory labels and well-written pictorial handbooks.

Philadelphia Commercial Museum

Edward Brooks, school superintendent of Philadelphia, following the 1893 Chicago Columbian Exposition, conceived the idea of a new and expanded museum service for the schools.

During my visit last summer at the World's Fair I was naturally impressed with the great benefits accruing to teachers in having the opportunity of seeing and studying representative school work. In reflecting upon the matter I formed the purpose of establishing on a small scale a Pedagogical Museum for the use of teachers of Philadelphia. My plan was to take some of the best of our own work as a nucleus and combine with it some of the best representative work from several other leading cities of the country, and place the whole in one of our unoccupied or partially occupied school buildings for the observation and study of our teachers. This purpose was presented to a special committee of the Board having charge of the educational exhibit, and was cordially approved by them. Soon after making this arrangement I learned that Dr. Wm. P. Wilson, who was representing the Park Commission at Chicago, in securing material for an Economic Museum, had conceived the idea of a large and complete educational museum, and had entered into negotiations with the authorities having charge of the educational exhibits of various foreign countries with a view of securing them for Philadelphia. Realizing the immense value to Philadelphia of such a collection of educational material I immediately directed my representatives at Chicago to turn over all the material, of which they had obtained the promise, to Dr. Wilson, and also sent two other representatives to Chicago to aid in the selection of such other material as might be desirable.[6]

The aforementioned Dr. Wilson finally secured the entire German exhibit of instructional charts and models, as well as the educational exhibits of Japan, Brazil, Russia, Egypt, Costa Rica, Guatemala, New South Wales, France, and Canada. The Argentine Republic donated 200 photographs of plans of school buildings. The Japanese exhibit, which cost some $15,000 and included 1,000 costumes and valuable statistical maps and charts, filled three freight cars.[7]

The collection was housed in two of the old Philadelphia Centennial (1876) buildings and organized into what became known as the Philadelphia Commercial Museum. Beginning in 1900, this museum

prepared and presented free of cost to the schools in Pennsylvania 250 collections. Each set contained several hundred specimens of imported commercial products, and from 100 to 200 photographs. These collections were distributed not as a loan, but as a gift so that the specimens were always available. The collections proved to be of great service, furnishing object lessons of much value in the study of geography and commerce.[8]

In 1925/26, Philadelphia public school teachers were appointed to the museum staff for the purpose of conducting a systematic instructional program. Attendance for this first year of formal classes was 49,323. By 1926, the total of visits by pupils from the Philadelphia Public Schools had passed 90,000.

The circular that announced the lectures and classes of 1924/25 is of particular interest because of its reference to visual instruction.

Museums are the most potent factors of visual education. Exhibits properly displayed stimulate interest in the subject matter of textbooks and tend to a liberal education.

The aim of any museum should be education, not a storehouse of inanimate objects alone, but really a collection of labels illustrated by specimens, for the sole purpose of explaining visually those things, and especially the simple things with which we are brought in daily contact.[9]

In 1905, the Pennsylvania State legislature recognized the educational value of the Philadelphia Commercial Museum by appropriating $25,000 for its work, and has since supported the museum with annual grants.[10]

St. Louis Educational Museum

In 1905, the St. Louis Educational Museum became the first administrative unit for instructional media in a public school system. Much of the impetus for this development came from former United States commissioner of education William Torrey Harris. In 1875, when Harris was superintendent of the St. Louis Public Schools, he stated in his annual report that, "every lesson should be given in such a way as to draw out the perceptive powers of the pupil by leading him to reflect on what he sees or to analyze the object before him."[11]

Fig. 5.2. "Bring the World to the Child," symbol of the St. Louis Educational Museum (Courtesy of St. Louis Public Schools.)

The first opportunity to implement this so-called original-instruction concept of education did not come until 1904, when the city of St. Louis played host to the Louisiana Purchase Exposition. As the direct consequence of organizing and managing a public schools exhibit, Carl G. Rathmann, then assistant superintendent of the St. Louis Public Schools, became aware of the instructional potential of these exhibits.

Fig. 5.3. First display room and workshop in Wyman School Building (Courtesy of St. Louis Public Schools.)

On September 13, 1904, the St. Louis Board of Education first authorized Rathmann to purchase appropriate instructional materials; the school museum dream subsequently became a reality.[12] The first art objects and models were soon supplemented by extensive collections donated by national museums and countries around the world. Amelia Meissner, the daughter of a famous horticulturist, was ready to "bring the world to the child." She organized the museum's materials and became its first curator.[13]

On April 11, 1905, the museum opened in an old school building. A short time later, a horse and wagon were acquired to make weekly deliveries of instructional materials to the St. Louis schools. After the horse and wagon were retired by the Educational Museum, the first delivery truck with hard rubber tires was obtained. In the 1905/06 school year, about five thousand deliveries were made, thus effectively supplementing museum visits by students and their teachers. This service was such an essential part of the museum's function that its collections were designed to supplement rather than supplant the course of study. There was even a catalog arranged in terms of the course of study.

Fig. 5.4. The first horse-drawn delivery wagon of the St. Louis Educational Museum, put into operation in 1905 (Courtesy of St. Louis Public Schools.)

The museum collections were listed in the teachers' catalog as follows:

(1) food products; (2) materials for clothing; (3) other natural products; (4) industrial products; (5) articles and models illustrating the life and occupations of the different peoples of the world; (6) plants and models and charts of plants; (7) the animal world; (8) minerals, rocks, and ores; (9) apparatus for illustration of physics and physical geography; (10) charts, colored pictures, maps, and objects illustrating history; (11) collections of art objects and models used by classes in drawing; and (12) photographs, stereoscopic pictures, and lantern slides to accompany the preceding groups.[14]

In 1927, a tornado completely wrecked the museum building and destroyed the bulk of the material. This could have been the final chapter in the history of the St. Louis Educational Museum, but for the courageous effort made to restore it. Materials that could be salvaged were moved to a bowling alley. Although the electricity was out, the restoration process proceeded at once by candlelight. In the meantime, Carl Rathmann began a

Fig. 5.5. First delivery truck (Courtesy St. Louis Public Schools.)

nation-wide tour, appealing for aid. Museums and other organizations throughout the country responded quickly by supplying numerous materials that replaced much of what had been lost. The St. Louis Educational Museum, which changed its name to the Division of Audio-Visual Education in 1943, has remained an integral part of the St. Louis public school system.

Fig. 5.6. The St. Louis Educational Museum Exhibit at the San Francisco Panama Pacific Industrial Exposition (Courtesy St. Louis Public Schools.)

Reading Public Museum and Art Gallery

The Reading (Pennsylvania) Public Museum was established in 1908 as only the second museum designed solely to provide instructional materials to the schools. Credit for its founding belongs largely to a Reading public school teacher, Levi W. Mengel. Although the idea for such a museum had occurred to Mengel, he observed firsthand the practicality of a school museum when he visited the 1904 St. Louis Louisiana Purchase Exposition.

When Mengel returned to Reading, he secured permission from school superintendent Charles S. Foos to procure materials from the St. Louis Exposition that could be useful in teaching. By the end of the fair, Mengel had been promised enough material to begin organizing a museum. However, when it came time to transport the collection to Reading, it was found that the foreign exhibits could not be moved until cleared through United States Customs. Meanwhile, the Philadelphia Commercial Museum was also attempting to obtain the release of material it had been promised by exhibitors at the same exposition. Since customs clearance would take months, Superintendent Foos appealed to Dr. William P. Wilson, director of the Philadelphia Commercial Museum, for help. The Philadelphia Museum agreed to clear the material and then transport it to the Reading Public Schools.

Eventually, in 1905, the Reading Public Schools received nearly two thousand items from the exhibits of Japan, China, India, Ceylon, the Philippines, and the Central and South American republics. The bulk of the material was stored in Reading High School until it could be organized and arranged. In 1907, the Reading Board of Education passed a resolution approving organization of these materials and reserved the third floor of the old high school building for a museum. After the considerable work of cleaning, labeling, and arranging—done after school hours, at night, and on holidays—the museum opened in 1908 to teachers and pupils of all grades.

During the 1909/11 school year, illustrated lectures for schoolchildren were established. At first lantern-slide sets were borrowed from the Philadelphia Commercial Museum, but within a few years a resident slide library had been built. In 1913, the Reading Board of Education authorized the addition of an art gallery; the museum thus became the Reading Public Museum and Art Gallery.

In 1924, the Reading School Board requested a loan for additional school buildings that included a provision for a modern museum building. After a campaign in which even the children took part, the loan referendum passed. However, a bitter controversy over the new location of the museum ended in stalemate. Fortunately, a botanical garden was offered as a home for the museum, thus resolving the question. The modern building of the Reading Public Museum and Art Gallery, set amid the beauty of a park filled with flowers and birds, makes this school museum one of the most impressive in the country.

Cleveland Educational Museum

The third school museum in the country was established by the Cleveland Public Schools in 1909. The influence of the St. Louis Educational Museum is evident from the following statement made by J. M. H. Frederick, former superintendent of the Cleveland Public Schools: "The schools of St. Louis are supplied with illustrative material from an educational museum which has more than 22,000 cases of materials. Educational authorities of this country have fully approved the St. Louis plan of providing the teacher and pupils with illustrative materials."[15] The first curator of the Cleveland Educational Museum was W. M. Gregory. Following the St. Louis pattern, collections of instructional materials were sent to the teacher as requested.

Fig. 5.7. Exhibit of bird mounts distributed by the Cleveland Educational Museum in 1909 (Courtesy of Cleveland Public Schools.)

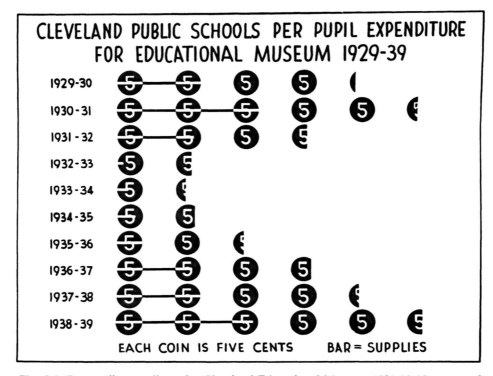

Fig. 5.8. Per pupil expenditure for Cleveland Educational Museum 1929-39 (Courtesy of Cleveland Public Schools.)

The First Visual Instruction
Departments or Bureaus

As early as 1886, the education department of the state of New York had begun, through legislative appropriations, to encourage the concept of visual education. These appropriations totaled as much as $50,000, a considerable sum at that time.[16] In 1904, New York State organized the first so-called visual instruction department.[17] This department distributed collections of lantern slides to the schools and, in the process, built the largest collection of lantern slides then in existence.

The University of Texas began a bureau of visual instruction in 1910, and by 1914, visual instruction departments had been established at the University of Wisconsin, the University of Indiana, Iowa State College, the State University of Iowa, and the University of Kansas. By 1920, six more visual instruction departments had been formed.

The increase of these university extension visual instruction departments or bureaus was due in large part to the need to organize accumulated collections of lantern slides, stereopticons, and colored postal cards into one central agency, which could then distribute these materials to those who needed them. Another contributing factor was the development of the 35mm silent motion picture. Dudley observed in 1915 that:

> one does not need to be a seer or even a prophet, but simply an ordinary observer
> of the trends of events to perceive that the movement throughout the country for
> clean, pure, uplifting films is gathering force, and will soon sweep from one

end of the land to the other. Powerful organizations, some commercial, but many civic, are now springing up all over the United States—organizations whose sole purpose is to promote the use of educational film.[18]

Early Visual Instruction in
City School Systems

An important early aspect of the visual instruction movement was its development in city school systems. The organization of visual instruction did not occur solely in cities with established visual instruction departments, but was also evident in school systems that had no such department. Indeed, every school that possessed even a set of slides or stereographs could be considered a part of the movement to visualize instruction.

The development of visual instruction in city school systems progressed in three distinct phases: (1) the school museum movement, (2) the organization of slide libraries, and (3) the establishment of educational film libraries. Concrete examples of each step can be seen in the various school systems.

Phases 1 and 3 have been discussed; a treatment of phase 2, the organization of slide libraries, follows. Examples of this phase can be seen in the establishment of slide libraries in the cities of Philadelphia, Detroit, and Chicago. (See chart on page 136.)

One of the more intriguing histories is that of the Chicago slide library. In 1895, a group of ten enthusiastic principals organized a projection club entirely independent of the board of education. Each principal personally contributed $25 to a slide fund that was used to purchase slides and projection machines. This small group of educators not only distributed slide sets among their respective schools and within the community, but they purchased additional sets and kept their collection in good repair. The Chicago Projection Club eventually became so popular that nearly half of the Chicago schools were members. In 1917, the complete collection of some 8,000 slides was given to the Chicago Board of Education with the proviso that "it be built up, its use fostered, and its advantages extended" to all schools in the system.[19]

Early Visual Education Bureaus in City Schools

City	Date bureau established	Name of director	Title of person in charge
St. Louis	1905	Amelia Meissner	Curator, Educational Museum
Reading	1908	Levi W. Mengel	Director, Reading Public Museum and Art Gallery
Cleveland	1909	W. M. Gregory	Director, Educational Museum
Philadelphia	1915(?)	Ada F. Liveright	Librarian, Pedagogical Library
Chicago	1917	Dudley C. Hays	Director, Bureau of Visual Instruction
Newark	1918	A. S. Balcom	Ass't Supt. of Schools in Charge of Visual Instruction
Detroit	1919	B. A. Barnes°	Supervisor of Visual Instruction
Detroit	1919†	Julia Gilmore	Curator, Children's Museum
Kansas City	1919	Rupert Peters	Director, Division of Visual Instruction
Los Angeles	1920‡	A. Loretta Clark	Acting Director, Visual Education Dept.
New York	1920	E. L. Crandall	Director of Public Lectures and Visual Instruction
Atlanta	1922	E. R. Enlow	Supervisor of Visual Instruction
Pittsburgh	1922	John Hollinger	Director of Dept. of Visual Instruction and Nature Study
Berkeley	1922	Anna V. Dorris	Director of Visual Instruction
Sacramento	1922	O. G. Cummings	Director of Visual Instruction
Buffalo	1920§	Carlos Cummings	Director of Visual Instruction
Buffalo	1923	Orrin L. Pease	Supervisor of Visual Instruction
Oakland	1923	H. O. Welty¶	Department of Visual Instruction

° Appointed for 1923–24.
† Children's Museum under general direction of the supervisor of visual instruction.
‡ Organized as a separate department, 1923; formerly division of the City School Library.
§ Buffalo Society of Natural Sciences, Department of Visual Instruction, subsidized in part by city for service to public schools.
¶ Chairman of committee which organized department, started operations September, 1923.
SOURCE: F. Dean McClusky, "The Administration of Visual Education: A National Survey." Unpublished report made to the NEA, 1923, p. 11.

Early National Survey of Visual Instruction

The most complete and reliable source of data concerning the early administrative history of visual instruction is the unpublished national survey conducted by F. Dean McClusky in 1923 for the NEA.[20] McClusky reported on such subjects as salaries of visual instruction personnel; value, types, and amounts of materials and equipment; visual instruction department budgets; distribution methods; and film and utilization procedures used in the schools.[21]

Cost of Visual Instruction

The cost of visual instruction in fourteen city school systems in 1923 was summarized by McClusky as follows:

1. The total sum expended for visual education was $73,218.80. This is approximately .15 of one percent of all school expenditures.

2. The value of equipment and materials in the possession of the departments is estimated as $371,872.00.

3. The largest total expenditure reported by a city is $91,004.24 (Los Angeles). The smallest is $2,190.00 (Sacramento). The average is $24,881.25. The city with the largest budget for visual instruction is Chicago. The budget is $30,400.00.

4. One finds by analyzing the visual education budgets; that 37.30 percent was spent for salaries; that 15.40 percent was spent for equipment such as projectors, stereopticons, etc.; that 14.70 percent went for film rentals; that 6.76 percent was spent for the purpose of films; and so on down to the .39 percent spent for the purchase of miscellaneous materials.

5. The sum spent for the rental and purchase of moving pictures is surprisingly small, being about $48,660.49.[22]

Types and Amount of Visual Materials and Equipment

McClusky reported the following types and amounts of visual material and equipment used in city departments of visual instruction in 1923:

1. There were 686 projectors of all types in the sixteen cities most active in visual instruction in 1922-23. Portable or semi-portable projectors were also common.

2. Eleven city departments have established libraries consisting of 1,755 reels of film of which 36.18 percent were loaned to the departments by industrial firms, government bureaus, and state bureaus. Many of the remaining 63.82 percent classified as "owned" were donated to the departments.

3. Fifteen city departments either rent or borrow film for distribution. In 1922-23, 3,852 reels were rented and 317 were borrowed on the short loan basis.

4. There were 1,642 stereopticons in the cities surveyed, of which 7.67 percent are owned by the departments of visual instruction. The number of stereopticons is 2.4 times the number of projectors.

5. Fourteen city departments are building libraries of slides totaling 236,884. These range in size from Chicago which boasts 85,000 to Buffalo with 337 slides. Many thousands of slides are also the property of individual schools within the cities.

6. The total number of stereographs owned by departments is 63,601 and by individual schools is 268,072. Three departments, Los Angeles, Buffalo, and St. Louis, are circulating a large number of stereographs.

7. Seven departments have collections of exhibits for circulatory purposes. The size of these collections ranges from 1,500 "groups" (St. Louis) to 14 "cases" (Kansas City).

8. The chief stock in trade of the city departments is the slide which is followed in order by the moving picture projector, stereopticon, stereograph, film, picture exhibit, graphic booklet, chart, costume doll, set of apparatus, and model.

9. In many cities, exhibits, pictures, charts and models are circulated by public museums and libraries.[23]

Fig. 5.9. Portrait of F. Dean McClusky (Courtesy F. Dean McClusky.)

Interestingly, the McClusky survey showed that a large percentage of the schools in 1923 were using slides, stereographs, pictures, and exhibits rather than films. Slides were the most widely used visual media.

Distribution Methods

One of the principal problems of bureaus of visual instruction concerned distribution. Two methods were commonly used: the "circuit" and the "special-order" methods, each differing in purpose and operation. Both were often used by the same department.

In the circuit method, a film is passed from school to school until it has been to each school on an established circuit. This type of service was so regular that schools could depend on receiving specific films or visual materials at regular intervals throughout the school year. The principal advocates of the circuit method were Iowa State College and the University of Wisconsin. In 1922/23, Iowa State College served sixty-six schools. Churches, farm bureaus, and others received slide service on eleven circuits during the same academic year. W. H. Dudley, director of the University of Wisconsin Bureau of Visual Instruction, expressed the opinion that the circuit plan could be carried on quite successfully if there were a "systematic and constructive effort to have a yearly program worked out in advance and if the users are instructed and educated in the proper use of slides and films before they are received."[24] In the year 1919/20, through thirteen circuits the visual instruction service of the University of Wisconsin was extended to some 275 Wisconsin communities; more than 20,000 slides and 1,000 reels of film were distributed.

The cities of Atlanta, Detroit, Kansas City, Newark, New York, and Sacramento used the circuit method of distribution in 1923. New York, Atlanta, and Sacramento rented their films, while the cities of Detroit, Kansas City, and Newark purchased films in addition to renting and borrowing. Films were initially selected by the director of the visual instruction department in each city, but in New York, a committee of teachers and commercial producers also previewed each film. Generally, films were booked for a circuit at the beginning of each school semester, but Atlanta booked its films a month in advance and Detroit booked its films for the circuit at the first of each week. Some cities sent printed or mimeographed outlines and lecture notes with visual material, either a few days in advance or along with the materials.

The special-order method of distribution was relatively simple in contrast to the circuit method. A teacher or principal contacted the school system's visual instruction department and reserved a film for a specific day and time. Usually, the visual instruction department transported the film to and from the school. Four distinct approaches characterized the special-order method. First, "the film may be purchased outright by the department and placed at the disposal of the schools"; second, "the film may be borrowed by the department for a year or longer from the government bureaus and national manufacturing concerns and distributed to the schools which desire to make use of such materials"; third, "the departments may rent or lease for a period of time reels which are listed along with those already available at the department"; and, fourth, "the departments may act as a broker by ordering films for schools from exchanges, university bureaus, and other distribution agencies."[25]

Some cities, such as Kansas City and Los Angeles, employed all four practices.

Nondepartmentalized Visual Instruction

The systematization of visual instruction also took place in city school systems without formal visual instruction departments. McClusky found three types of organizations that had evolved in such schools. The first approximated a visual department, with a visual education committee composed of teachers and administrators that concerned itself with the problems and administration of visual instruction in the school system. Typical examples of this type were the school systems of Dayton, Indianapolis, Providence, and San Francisco. For example, the Dayton (Ohio) Board of Education authorized the superintendent to appoint a committee of three elementary school principals and two supervisors to administer the visual instruction program.

A second type of organization was identical with the first, in that a committee was placed in control. However, the committee members were representatives of a group of teachers and principals interested in visual education, rather than official representatives of the superintendent or of the board of education. Examples of this type were the school systems of Portland, Seattle, and Tacoma.

The third type of organization was confined to the individual school, where responsibility for visual instruction rested entirely with the principal or teachers of the school, independent of the city visual instruction department.[26]

Theoretical Rationale for the Visual Instruction Movement

From the earliest days of the visual instruction movement the predominant theoretical rationale justifying the visual approach to instruction was based on the concept that visual materials would serve as an antidote for verbalism. The traditional rationale has identified devices, machines or media, use of particular senses (primarily vision), and characteristics of instructional aids or teaching materials on the basis of their levels of concreteness or abstractness. One of the earliest concrete-abstract continuums designed to serve as a guide to instruction appeared in 1886. It stated:

> The objects of thought used in teaching are the *real object*, which is the material object in relation with the senses, or the mental object distinctly in consciousness; the *model*, which represents, in the solid, the form, color, size, and relative position of the parts of the object; the *picture*, which imperfectly represents on a surface the appearance of the object in position, form, color, and relative position of parts; the *diagram*, which represents on a surface the sectional view of the object; the *experiment*, which shows the action and effects of physical forces; *language*, as an object of thought, in the formation of words ... and the *book*, how to read and use books.[27]

Further, all ideas must be acquired primarily "from the object which is associated with spoken and written words, which thus becomes the signs of ideas and the medium for the interchange of thought."

William G. Bagley, professor of education at Teachers College, Columbia University, wrote an introductory section, "Concreteness in Education" for the first edition of *Visual Education*. Bagley stated that "the most effective kind of education is that in which the learner is brought face to face with actual concrete situations," and that the approach to reality is "more closely realized by pictures projected through the stereopticon, by moving pictures, and by stereographs." And the stereograph, he proclaimed, "is superior to the ordinary projected picture" in terms of concreteness.[28]

John Adams, in 1910, wrote *Exposition and Illustration in Teaching*, which included the following "order of merit" concerning concreteness: "(1) the real object, for which anything else is a more or less inefficient substitute; (2) a model of the real object; (3) a diagram dealing with some of the aspects of the object; and (4) a mere verbal description of the object."[29] Adams went on to explain that "too frequently the above general order of merit is carried over to the purely illustrative field (and there is) an unwarranted glorification of objects."[30]

In 1928, Weber observed that "we can acquire visual experience from situations that are as concrete as reality and as abstract as the scheme of typical visual aids which follows: (1) actual reality, as we find it on a school journey; (2) pseudo-reality, as exemplified by artificial models and exhibits; (3) pictorial realism, as depicted in drawings and photographs; (4) pictorial symbolism—similes, metaphors, and plain language."[31]

Fig. 5.10. Early stereographs.

Fig. 5.11. Early stereopticon (1900-1912).

Fig. 5.12. An early field trip (Courtesy of St. Louis Public Schools.)

Hoban et al. expressed the concrete-abstract rationale in their popular book, *Visualizing the Curriculum*. Their stated purpose was to eliminate verbalism from school instruction by giving priority to visual aids. The levels of experience from concrete to abstract were listed as follows: "(1) objects; (2) models; (3) films; (4) stereographs; (5) slides; (6) flat pictures; (7) maps; (8) maps; (9) diagrams; and (10) words."[32] Hoban et al. considered the school journey the most effective method of visual instruction for three reasons: "(1) because it brings the pupils into direct contact with a functional situation in which the elements being studied are perceived in their various relationships as they exist; (2) because it provides experience in all elements of concreteness—it is the most real and the most concrete of the visual techniques; and (3) because it is the most accessible and often the least expensive of the techniques of visual instruction."[33] On the other hand, they considered graphic materials the most abstract of visual aids.[34]

Many other leaders in the visual instruction movement developed similar concrete-abstract continuums. Edgar Dale developed his own concrete-abstract continuum called the "Cone of Experience." He began with the learner as participant in the direct experience and then showed how the learner moved to increasingly abstract levels of experience. Dale asserted that learners could make valuable use of more abstract instructional activities drawing on reservoirs of their more concrete experiences. Dale's "Cone of Experience" was one of the most influential in the decade after World War II.

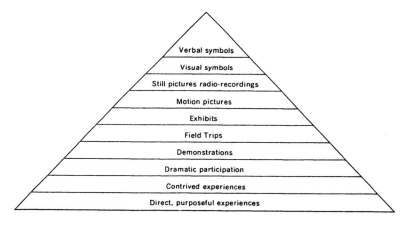

Fig. 5.13. Dale's "Cone of Experience."

A Decade of Growth

An intense period of growth in the visual instruction movement occurred during the decade 1918-1928. During this ten-year period, these events took place:

The first formal credit courses in visual instruction were offered for teachers at the college and university level.

The first visual instruction professional organizations were founded at local and national levels.

The first visual instruction professional journals appeared.

The first systematic research studies of visual instruction were reported.

The first administrative units of visual instruction were organized in public schools, colleges, universities, and state departments of education.

A sound basis for the visual instruction movement was established when the U.S. Bureau of Education donated hundreds of reels of surplus war film to thirty-three university extension divisions throughout the United States.

Professionalization of Visual Instruction: Development of National Organizations

Beginning in 1919, five national visual instruction organizations were established. Two were short-lived; one lost its national status; one served the visual instruction field for twelve years; and one continues to provide leadership in the visual instruction movement.

First National Visual Instruction Organizations

The first two national organizations formed in the emerging visual instruction field lasted less than a year. They were the National Academy for Visual Instruction, incorporated in Washington, D.C., in October 1919, and the American Educational Motion Picture Association, which began operations in New York City, also in October 1919. The American Educational Motion Picture Association was formed to study school requirements for the classroom use of motion pictures. Allen S. Williams was president and A. D. V. Storey was executive secretary.

The National Academy of Visual Instruction

This organization (not to be confused with the National Academy *for* Visual Instruction mentioned in the preceding paragraph) was the result of a conference of some forty educators held during the annual meeting of the Department of Superintendence of the NEA, at Cleveland, Ohio, in February 1920. A committee of nine was appointed to organize a national association. On April 7, 1920, this committee met at the University of Michigan and drew up a constitution and bylaws, adopted a name, and elected temporary officers. The first annual meeting of the National Academy of Visual Instruction was held in Madison, Wisconsin, July 14-16, 1920.[36] In the opening address, William H. Dudley, chief of the bureau of visual instruction at the University of Wisconsin, addressed the historic importance of this meeting:

> It is for us to prepare the field, to plant our standards, to set the pace. We must establish fundamental principles, must work out specific and constructive programs of procedure, must study the needs of the schools and other educational groups and point out definite ways to meet such needs. We must recognize, however, that basic educational principles and policies are already firmly established, that ends to be accomplished are clearly defined, and that hence we are not to attempt ends, but rather to introduce devices that will lead more directly to ends already in view.[37]

The stated purpose of this organization was to promote nonflammable film, distribute suitable reels of educational film, organize state associations, improve subject matter, establish standards, and conduct tests.[38] The organization merged with the NEA Department of Visual Instruction in 1932.

The Visual Instruction Association of America

Two years after the national academy was established, the Visual Instruction Association of America was organized at Boston, Massachusetts, on July 6, 1922.[39] It had its beginnings in the New York City Visual Instruction Association first organized in 1920 to assist the New York City public schools in their experimental use of instructional films.

The particular contribution of the association to the budding visual instruction movement was its initiation of visual instruction demonstration centers at educational conferences throughout the country. The association, in cooperation with the NEA, sponsored the first national visual instruction demonstrations as well as the first national commercial exhibits of visual instructional materials. The association further distinguished itself by accepting, as full voting members, representatives of commercial companies that served the visual instruction field.[40]

When Ernest Crandall, president and guiding force, retired in the late 1920s, the association reverted to its original status as the New York City Visual Instruction Association. In 1931 the association became a part of the National Academy of Visual Instruction and changed its name to the Metropolitan New York Branch of the Academy. When the academy merged with the NEA Department of Visual Instruction in 1932, the Metropolitan New York Branch joined in the merger.

NEA Department of Visual Instruction

The NEA Department of Visual Instruction (DVI) was established on July 6, 1923, at the Oakland, California, NEA summer convention. Two factors contributed to the development of the DVI: (1) the suggestion to create such a department within the NEA by Dudley Grant Hayes, president of the National Academy of Visual Instruction, and A. W. Abrams, head of the New York State Division of Visual Instruction, at the NEA Boston convention in 1922; and (2) the creation of the Judd Committee. Since the ramifications of the Judd Committee were rather extensive, it is considered in some detail in the next section.

There had been a long-felt need for an organization such as the DVI. Nelson Greene, editor of *Educational Screen*, commented:

> Some thousands of earnest educators, to be sure, have been working along these lines for years, but against fearful odds. The wise action of the NEA will give a strong additional impulse and incentive to their work. In the minds of many other thousands, visual education will now cease to be a "fad" — as they were afraid it might be — because the fiat of the great Association has been set upon it. The visual movement now has its credentials, with the official vise upon them. With such credentials it will travel fast and far.[41]

The Judd Committee: The First Formal Assessment of the Visual Instruction Movement

The so-called Judd Committee was an important early influence on the professional organization of the visual instruction movement. Its investigations also provided the first formal assessment of the movement.

Will H. Hays, president of the newly formed Motion Picture Producers and Distributors of America (MPPDA), appeared before the general assembly of the 1922 NEA summer convention in Boston, pledging the resources of the motion picture industry in support of visual instruction.[42] Following the convention, Will Owens, NEA president, appointed a committee, chaired by Charles H. Judd of the University of Chicago, to cooperate with the MPPDA.[43] The committee immediately received a grant of $5,000 from the Hays office.

Subcommittees Formed

Upon receipt of the MPPDA grant, two subcommittees were appointed. The first, headed by Ernest Crandall of the New York City schools, and president of the Visual Instruction Association of America, reviewed old theatrical films to determine their educational value.[44] The second subcommittee, chaired by F. Dean McClusky of the University of Illinois, made a nation-wide survey of the administration of visual instruction.[45]

The Judd Committee Summary Report

After the subcommittees had reported back in June 1923, a report was presented to the NEA at its Oakland convention in July 1923 and to the Hays office. Among other things, the Judd report recommended that a clearinghouse of visual instruction information be formed.[46] The direct result was the establishment of the NEA's Department of Visual Instruction (DVI).

The Judd report also revealed that visual instruction was receiving inadequate financial support, that educators were forced to rely almost entirely on national advertisers for their films—the films could not be obtained free of charge, and educators had no means of knowing how it was done elsewhere—and that educators had no information exchange on current methods or on how their own work could be organized and administered effectively.

The prevailing theme was the lack of uniform practices in the administration of visual instruction. Some cities used the circuit method of distribution, while others followed the special-order system. Some school systems provided delivery service; in others, the teachers had to pick up their own materials and equipment. In most school systems, only some of the schools secured their films directly from the visual instruction administrative agency; others preferred to make their own arrangements with film exchanges and industrial firms, and purchased and operated their own equipment. In some cities and some university and college extension divisions, films were sent free of charge; in others, there was a rental fee. In some cases, schoolchildren themselves contributed to help defray film costs. When it came to projectors, some schools used trained projectionists, others taught their teachers projector operation, and still others had older students operate the projectors.

The Judd report also pointed out the fire hazards of film projection and recommended that "the use of inflammable films should be restricted to licensed persons and exhibition places fully equipped with fire protective devices."[47]

The report goes on to say that there were

> few films in existence which were created with the definite purpose of using them as adjuncts in the teaching of specific lessons in the conventional subjects.... Also, the schools showed a considerable number of recreational and amusement films, and in a good many cases, these were pretty frankly employed as a sort of sugar-coating to make the diet of advertising films somewhat more palatable.[48]

The Judd Committee reached the conclusion that

> Much work needs to be done in educational experimentation and research having for its purpose the discovery and development of the best methods for using motion pictures in teaching.... Second, ... a clearing-house for information is greatly needed.[49]

The Judd Committee and Commercialism

Charles H. Judd asked that the Judd Committee be disbanded and a new committee appointed. Because of experiences with commercial organizations, Judd recommended

> that this new committee be specifically instructed not to attempt to organize any plan of picture censorship and that the Committee be instructed not to give its approval directly or indirectly to any projecting apparatus or any film or any plan for the preparation of scenarios or films. The experience of the year has shown the unqualified wisdom of the restrictions here recommended. The present committee has been literally besieged by promoters of all kinds of plans for the production of projectors and particular films.[50]

Despite this recommendation, the Judd Committee was continued; Thomas E. Finegan, superintendent of public instruction in Pennsylvania, became chairman when Judd withdrew in 1923. Beginning in the fall of 1926, Frank Cody, superintendent of schools in Detroit, served as chairman until the committee was dissolved in 1927.

During the period from 1923 to 1927, the Visual Education Committee, as it was often referred to after Judd left, was financed by the Hays office and literally built its own empire by paralleling or dominating the work of the DVI. A 1924 committee report made by chairman Finegan announced that five subcommittees had been appointed: "(1) on legislation; (2) on designation of communities doing excellent work in visual education; (3) on courses of study; (4) on gathering materials relative to administrative methods in current use, etc.; (5) on cooperation and research."[51] The roster of these committees listed thirteen names, of which nine were leaders in the DVI, the National Academy of Visual Instruction, or the Visual Instruction Association of America. What is more, the committee had begun to work very closely with the Eastman Kodak Company in planning the Eastman experiments with 16mm instructional films; chairman Finegan became director of the Eastman Teaching Films Division in September 1926!

National Visual Instruction Organizations Merge

Probably the most significant event in the early history of the visual instruction movement was the merging of the three national visual education organizations in February 1932.[52] Nelson Greene, editor of *The Educational Screen*, called it "the greatest step forward to date in the advance of the visual instruction movement."[53] Since 1923, these organizations had been working parallel to each other, with much duplication and overlap of activities. Many wondered why three organizations existed and why some people were members of all three.

Early Barriers to Merger

Although the three surviving organizations all had the same general motivation, there were fundamental differences separating them. One basic policy conflict centered in commercial versus professional interests. In the National Academy of Visual Instruction, individuals with commercial affiliation were not permitted to vote or hold office. In the Visual Instruction Association of America, on the other hand, active membership was open to educators and commercial persons alike. This basic controversy was camouflaged by the argument that the academy was dominated by representatives of college and university extension divisions from the midwestern region of the United States. Although it was true that the academy leadership was centered in the Midwest and that all of its officers were associated with extension divisions, three of the seven-member executive committee were from city school systems.

When the Visual Instruction Association of America was first proposed in March 1922, its effect on the national academy was instantaneous. At the third annual convention in Lexington, Kentucky (April 18-20), the academy took five significant steps to meet the competition of the new organization backed by commercial interests. First, it became an affiliate of the NEA Department of Superintendence and, beginning in February 1923, held all annual meetings concurrently with those of the Department of Superintendence. Second, it elected a new slate of officers representing the East, the Midwest, large cities, universities, and even museums. Third, the academy's newly elected president, Dudley Grant Hayes, director of visual education in the Chicago schools, with Alfred Abrams, head of the division of visual education of the New York State Department of Education, began negotiations with the NEA to establish a department of visual instruction.[54] Fourth, the national academy reinforced its policy of excluding individuals with commercial connections from voting membership. Fifth, it recommended that a full-time secretariat be established. Meanwhile, J. W. Shepherd of the University of Oklahoma called for unity.

> The National Academy is already in the field. It has the definite backing of a large share of those most active.... It stands pledged by its constitution to high ideals and lofty purposes. Its policies are still in the making and can be readily shaped to reach worthy ends. The organization, therefore, should be not only given an opportunity to prove its merit but it should also be given the definite support of all interests.[55]

The Merger Movement

The merger idea first took definitive form when F. Dean McClusky was president of the national academy in 1930/31. McClusky was particularly qualified to provide the national leadership to bring about a merger because of his long experience in the visual instruction movement, and because of his rather unique professional standing at that time. In addition to being president of the national academy, he was first vice-president of the DVI, a member of the executive committee for the Visual Instruction Association of America, and director of the Scarborough School, New York, where he had the backing of Frank A. Vanderlip, an ardent supporter of visual instruction.

McClusky was aided by Charles Roach of Los Angeles; William H. Dudley of the University of Wisconsin, founder of the academy; William Gregory of Cleveland; John Hollinger of Pittsburgh; Abraham Krasker of Boston; and Ellsworth Dent of the University of Kansas, secretary of the academy. Nelson Greene, editor of *The Educational Screen*, also enthusiastically supported the proposed merger. McClusky first determined the status of the Visual Instruction Association. This was clear when the association voted to change its name to the Metropolitan New York Branch of the National Academy of Visual Instruction and make the necessary changes in its constitution and bylaws.

The national academy's position thus strengthened, a committee consisting of McClusky and Grace Fisher Ramsey went to the NEA to negotiate a merger of the academy and the DVI. Negotiations were successful, and the DVI voted at its Los Angeles 1931 summer convention to merge with the academy. The final step was taken by the membership of the academy at its twelfth and final convention, held on February 23-24, 1932, in the National Press Club, Washington, D.C. There it voted to merge with the DVI. Simultaneously, a vote was cast to merge the publications of the two organizations—the *Visual Instruction News* and *The Educational Screen*.

First Officers

The first president of the new DVI was Charles F. Hoban, Sr., director of the Pennsylvania State Library and Museum and director of visual education for the state of Pennsylvania. McClusky was elected first vice-president; W. W. Whittinghill, second vice-president; and Ellsworth Dent, secretary-treasurer. Members of the first executive committee included Grace Fisher Ramsey, William H. Dudley, John A. Hollinger, Abraham Krasker, A. S. Balcom, and Daniel Knowlton.[56]

Teacher Education in Visual Instruction

The expansion of the visual instruction movement brought with it the demand for formal teacher education. F. Dean McClusky, Joseph J. Weber, W. M. Gregory, and A. G. Balcom were particularly vocal about this aspect. McClusky aptly stated in 1923 that "the movement for visual education will progress in direct ratio to the number of teachers who are trained in the technique of visual instruction."[57] He said further that "textbooks and syllabi must be prepared ... courses of study must be introduced into normal schools ... teachers must be given an opportunity to learn the advantages and disadvantages of visual instruction through formal and informal instruction."[58]

Weber observed that the visual instruction movement rested upon a number of facts:

> The sense of vision plays an important role in the educative process; the exclusive use of language in education dulls interest and tends to verbalism; the perfection of photography has extended the material environment of the learners; experimental education has revealed evidence that visual aids vitalize the curriculum and thus effect marked economies in the learning process.
>
> *These considerations justify the formulation of visual aids courses in normal schools, colleges, and universities*, at least temporarily until the transition from the old to the new methodology is complete.[59]

In the meantime, courses in visual instruction began to be offered in scattered areas of the country.

First Teacher Education Courses

Probably the first official credit course in visual instruction was given at the University of Minnesota in 1918 by Albert M. Field.[60] Other early visual instruction courses were offered at the University of Kansas and North Carolina State Teachers College in the fall of 1921. Joseph J. Weber developed one of the first comprehensive courses in visual instruction at the University of Kansas; the same course was given at the University of Texas and the University of Arkansas during the summers of 1923 and 1925, respectively.

The Dorris Survey

Anna V. Dorris of San Francisco State College made a survey in 1922 to determine what provisions were being made for teacher education in visual instruction. A questionnaire was sent to 171 normal schools (30 replied) and to 114 colleges and universities (37 replied). Four of the normal schools offered summer session courses; the Michigan Normal School offered one non-credit course. One university taught "graphs"; another gave a course on photography and slide making. Seventeen of the thirty-seven colleges and universities said they operated film distribution centers. Only four normal schools reported such service.[61]

The McClusky National Survey of 1923

As mentioned previously, F. Dean McClusky conducted a nation-wide survey of visual instruction administrative practices as part of the investigations made by the Judd Committee of the NEA. In the process of making this survey, McClusky and his assistants uncovered much valuable data concerning teacher education. In general, two types of instruction prevailed. One was "training in service" and the other was "training in preparation for service."[62] The survey observed that much training in service had been concerned with the technique of handling visual equipment, rather than with the technique of instruction.[63]

In 1922/23, some twenty-one educational institutions offered courses in visual instruction, most in the summer session; conferences of visual instruction teachers were held at the universities of Missouri and Utah. In addition, the state department of education in Michigan gave a series of short, informal courses in the normal schools of the state, with these objectives: to familiarize teachers with the theory and techniques of using films in teaching, to explain the sources and care of films, and to teach how to operate and care for a motion picture projector. Individual instruction in the operation of projectors was given on request, and all teachers in the immediate area of the school were invited to attend discussions and conferences on the weekends.

Various problems confronted the visual instruction administrator in 1923. In his survey, McClusky stated these problems in the form of the following recommendations:

a. A clearing house for information needs to be established. Every department and bureau has acquired much experience of value which should become the common knowledge of all.

b. Educational institutions and city school systems should materially increase the financial support of bureaus of visual education, thus placing them on a sound and respectable economic basis.

c. Departments of visual instruction should secure funds and time for carrying forward experiments and surveys in the field.

d. The training of teachers in the use and value of visual instruction should be promoted by leaders of the movement.

e. The administrative status of directors of visual instruction needs to be clearly defined. Their work should be so organized that the utmost co-operation is made possible between them and other school officials.

f. Directors of visual instruction should draw up a uniform set of record and report forms, thus enabling each one to interpret intelligently the statistics gathered by another.

g. Educational experts should assist in the creation of all visual aids, and not postpone co-operation until the materials are ready for distribution.

h. All activities of visual instruction should look toward the mental development of the individual child in the school or classroom.

i. Bureaus of visual instruction should avoid dependence on free film and other donations to build up their collections.

j. Departments of visual instruction in city school systems need to take stock at regular intervals of their own equipment and that of individual schools within their jurisdiction.

k. Methods of selecting visual materials for school use need to be systematically analyzed, and a more scientific procedure evolved.

l. Catalogues need to be carefully graded and systematically arranged to correlate with the course of study.

m. Rules and regulations covering service should not be too involved or numerous. Periodic changes should be avoided.

n. Lesson aids and descriptive notes accompanying visual materials should stimulate the teacher to make self active preparation for the lesson.

o. In cities where visual instruction is organized, an attempt should be made by school authorities to direct the work along systematically planned lines. Much needless expense will thus be saved.

p. City and state bureaus should make systematic studies of the materials in circulation in terms of their use by patrons.

q. Adequate housing, storage and transportation facilities should be furnished to every bureau.

r. Bureaus of visual instruction should be encouraged to study and to provide good wholesome entertainment films for school use.

s. Those state institutions and city school systems which contemplate the organization of visual instruction in a separate department should build institutions based on pioneers in the field.[64]

The National Academy of Visual Instruction Survey

In 1924, the National Academy of Visual Instruction made a survey that indicated that twenty-three educational institutions were offering elective courses in visual instruction. In three institutions, they were correspondence courses; the majority were offered in summer. The survey also found that some teacher education in visual instruction was offered at teacher institutes in Berkeley, Detroit, Newark, and Kansas City.[65]

The Balcom Survey

In his 1924 survey of normal schools and colleges, A. S. Balcom found that about half of the eighty-two institutions that responded gave any training in the teaching value of the slide, and less than half offered stereopticon training. Less than half reported that films were used, a still smaller number (twelve) gave instruction on classroom use of the film, and only five offered instruction in the operation of a motion picture projector.[66]

Later Surveys

A survey of college courses in February 1925 showed that the technical aspects of photography and the mechanics of projection were emphasized; visual instruction courses were generally elective rather than required.[67]

In 1926, a committee on teacher education recommended to the DVI that a laboratory course be established for student teachers and teachers in service. The committee's report also pointed out that several teacher institutions were offering courses in visual instruction and that the University of Wisconsin had created a professorship in visual instruction.[68]

In 1936, W. Gayle Starnes's comprehensive study showed a significant increase in visual instruction courses since Anna V. Dorris's 1922 survey of visual instruction courses. Starnes also detailed the extreme differences in course content, materials used, and credit offered.[69] A survey made in 1940 by the U.S. Office of Education showed that 114 colleges and universities, 12 percent of the 933 institutions whose catalogs were examined, offered a total of 140 courses, usually in the department of education.[70] An NEA questionnaire was sent out this same year to 150 educational institutions offering courses for prospective secondary school teachers. Of the seventy-six returns, forty-two colleges offered a total of ninety-two courses. All these surveys revealed a need for teacher education in the use of visual materials.[71]

Classification of Visual Instruction Courses

Visual Instruction courses varying from two to three hours of credit have been given during the academic year, in summer sessions, or by extension. Their number has been increasing since 1921. In 1937, a significant increase occurred when thirty-seven new courses were initiated. Courses in visual instruction have included short courses, workshops, correspondence courses, and off-campus courses. Short courses or workshops were held for those teachers unable to attend a regular course; correspondence courses, first offered in 1924, were not extensively available; and off-campus courses were generally conducted in large cities during a regular semester.[72]

Organization of Visual Instruction Courses

There were generally two types of visual instruction courses: a core or basic course and an integrated approach that exploited available visual materials. Dale et al. listed the three most common points of view in regard to visual instruction:

> (1) It is an essential part of practically every field of education, and the best possible preparation of teachers to make use of visual materials is to observe and use them in their functional relationships in each course. (2) Special courses are necessary in order to effect the necessary learning involved in the full scope of visual education. (3) A combination or compromise between the two positions is the best solution.[73]

Some early visual instruction programs illustrating these various types of organization were those of Fresno State College, New Jersey's four-year teachers' colleges, Bucknell University, San Francisco State College, and the Winnetka (Illinois) Public Schools. At Fresno State College, where an integrated plan was in effect, W. F. Tidyman stated: "In defense of the integrated plan, it may be said that it squares with our currently accepted philosophy of learning in integrated, lifelike situations, and that the tendency in the administration of teachers' colleges is to reduce the number of highly specialized professional courses, rather than to increase them."[74]

New Jersey's curriculum illustrated the compromise position that used every department of the college in offering a basic course. This plan, developed in 1937, offered a course in visual instruction in the third year that organized, supplemented, and systematized the more incidental factual material of visual education that was supposed to be obtained in other courses. For example, courses in geography supposedly used maps, excursions, slides, still pictures, and models; courses in English employed motion picture appreciation in the study of literature and developed discrimination and appreciation of the art of the motion picture; courses in the physical sciences included the study of the mechanics of projection or photography; courses in psychology dealt with perception and learning.[75]

The San Francisco State College plan offered a full-credit course to teachers in 1923 to encourage the wider use of visual materials. By the time they had completed these courses, the teachers had assembled their own collections of mounted pictures, exhibits, charts, and graphs.[76] Another aspect of visual instruction was apparent in the Winnetka Public Schools, which, through their department of education, took part in the film service offered by the state university. Students enrolled in the Graduate Teachers College of Winnetka did most of their work in the Winnetka schools using visual materials furnished by the visual instruction department.[77]

Scope and Content of Visual Instruction Courses

The scope of visual instructional courses has theoretically been quite broad. Dale et al. thought courses should include:

> orientation both historically and philosophically; acquaintance with all types of visual aids, from the excursion to the sound motion picture, both as to their writing, slide making and the like; knowledge of sources of both free and commercial materials; criteria for selection; technical and mechanical problems in the use, care, and repair of apparatus and equipment; methods of use in various school fields and on the several educational levels, including psychology and techniques; application of the theatrical motion picture to education; and problems of supervision and administration.[78]

Probably the first outline of a course in visual instruction was prepared by Albert Field of the University of Minnesota in 1918.[79] Other early visual instruction course outlines were prepared by B. A. Aughinbaugh, Anna V. Dorris, William M. Gregory, H. A. Henderson, J. Raymond Hutchinson, F. Dean McClusky et al., C. J. Primm, and J. J. Weber.[80] Many other suggested courses of study have appeared in various educational journals. The state of Pennsylvania offered its core course in mimeographed form in 1935 for the use of instructors in the state's normal schools.[81] Some of the courses dealt with specific aspects of visual instruction: A course at the American Museum of Natural History in New York City in 1930 concerned itself only with the mechanics of visual instruction.[82]

In 1932, a committee appointed by the DVI presented the report "Proposed Core Course in Visual Instruction." This report stated that:

> Visual instruction has become an integral part of the school curriculum. Visual instruction teachers and school administrators no longer need argue for a visual-sensory aids program. It is an accepted reality. The problem now is to determine those common elements of the course and perfect suitable techniques for carrying out the program.... The merged organizations of visual education contemplate carrying out the far-reaching resolution set forth at the Los Angeles Meeting of the Department of Visual Instruction.[83]

(Text continues on page 159.)

Table 5.1.
Outline of San Francisco State Teachers College Early Visual Instruction Course.

I.   The scope of visual education
   1.   Why the need for improving our methods?
      a.   Post-war situation
      b.   Need for conserving time
      c.   Need of greater efficiency
      d.   Provide for individual differences
      e.   Make learning a living experience

II.   The use of visual instruction outside the schools
   1.   Commercial and industrial institutions
   2.   Government
   3.   Natural and medical sciences
   4.   Missionaries
   5.   Athletes

III.   Reasons underlying the success of visual education
   1.   History of object and visual learning
   2.   Psychological reasons
   3.   Experimental tests
   4.   Relation of visual instruction to progress and retardation

IV.   What other states and education institutions are accomplishing in visual education
   1.   State boards
   2.   Universities
   3.   Normal schools
   4.   City schools

V.   Practical pedagogical methods of procedure for the use of visual aids in classroom teaching
   1.   Concrete demonstrations of uses of materials
      a.   The preview to introduce a topic to be studied
      b.   For concrete information during the study period, to enrich the text, solve problems or explain some difficulty (the project lesson made a living experience)
      c.   The review

VI.   The larger use of visual aids in teaching
   1.   Flat pictures; demonstration of materials
      a.   Where they may or may not be used to the best advantage in teaching
      b.   Sources of materials and how to get collections
   2.   Exhibits and excursions
      a.   Demonstration of their uses to enrich all subjects of the curriculum
      b.   Laboratory work
   3.   Charts, maps, globes, and graphs
      a.   Special uses of the graphs as a means of teaching

Source: F. Dean McClusky, "The Administration of Visual Education: A National Survey." Unpublished report presented to the NEA, 1923, pp. 202-3. Course described was given by Anna V. Dorris.

    4. The use of the stereograph to enrich all subjects
    5. How to operate a stereopticon lantern and the use of slides in classroom instruction
       a. Demonstrations of different materials
       b. The making of slides-laboratory work
    6. The moving picture as a means of teaching
       a. Best methods for its use
       b. Materials available for classroom teachers
       c. Classification of materials according to subjects
       d. How to operate a portable moving picture machine

VII. The place of the museum in visual education
    1. How to start a distributing center

VIII. How to equip a school for visual education
    1. Ways and means of earning money for individual schools

IX. After-school entertainments
    1. How to manage entertainments
    2. How to secure materials
    3. Suggestions for programs

Table 5.2.

Outline of Kansas University Early Visual Instruction Course

I. The psychology of visual aids
    1. Primary sources of knowledge
    2. Visual sensation, perception, and imagery
    3. Comprehension, retention, etc.
    4. Standards for evaluating visual aids
    5. The word-picture balance
    6. Emotional effects
    7. Moral value, etc.

II. Types and their sources
    1. Diagrams
    2. Sketches
    3. Photographs
    4. Stereographs
    5. Lantern slides
    6. Moving pictures
    7. Models
    8. Museum exhibits; and where to get these

III. Administrative problems
    1. Booking
    2. Renting

Source: F. Dean McClusky, "The Administration of Visual Education: A National Survey." Unpublished report presented to the NEA, 1923, 199. Course given in 1922 summer session by Joseph J. Weber.

Table 5.2. *(continued)*

    III. Administrative problems *(continued)*
        3. Purchasing
        4. Circulating visual aids

    IV. General and special methods
        1. General methods, and
        2. Methods in the various school subjects

    V. Picture projection technique
        1. Learning to operate projectors, and so on

Table 5.3. Outline of Cleveland School of Education and Western Reserve University Early Visual Instruction Course

    I. Fundamental principles of visual education

    II. Visual aids
        1. Types:
            a. Diagrams and charts
            b. Pictures
            c. Stereographs
            d. Lantern slides
            e. Motion pictures
            f. Museums exhibits
                (1) Natural history museum
                (2) Art museum
                (3) Historical museum
        2. Sources of visual aids:
            a. Museums
            b. Commercial firms
            c. Industrial concerns
            d. United States Government departments
            e. State extension divisions

    III. Types of exhibits and classroom methods

    IV. Simple and complete exhibits for illustrative uses

    V. Pictures, photographs, and stereographs

    VI. Charts, graphs, and diagrams

    VII. Lantern slides for classroom use and lesson plans

Source: F. Dean McClusky, "The Administration of Visual Education: A National Survey." Unpublished report presented to the NEA, 1923, 198. Course was taught in 1922 summer session by William M. Gregory and William E. Krieger. Two semester hours of credit were granted for completion.

   VIII.   Moving pictures: Selection, methods of use, sources

    IX.   School lectures and regular classroom instruction

     X.   Museums and special instruction

    XI.   Museum loan exhibits

   XII.   Field lessons: Studies of industrial plants and civic institutions; field lessons in geography and nature study

  XIII.   Measuring the results of visual education

  XIV.   Program of visual instruction by subjects and grades

---

Table 5.4. Core Course Offered by State of Pennsylvania in 1935

     I.   Name of course: Visual-sensory aids in education (Core Course) 3 hours per week, 3 semester hours credit

    II.   General description of the course
This course is based upon the philosophy that sensory experiences and mental activities parallel each other in the learning process. Visual and other sensory aids, therefore, should hold a major place in the teaching of practically all subjects and on all levels of learning. To be a well balanced course, and of the greatest value to prospective teachers and the teachers in service, it should give training in and an effective technique for the use of all types of visual-sensory aids. This core course should be mandatory on the part of every person preparing to teach in the public schools. The course is designed for the preparation of teachers of the various subjects, and should contain those elements common to practically every subject.

  III.   Objectives
1. To learn the meaning of the common terms used in visual-sensory education (Give the student a concrete and meaningful vocabulary)
2. The development of skill in selecting suitable teaching aids from those available for the teaching of a specific subject
3. The development of a projection technique which will assure an efficient use of all the essential projectors in classroom work
4. To provide the prospective teacher with a body of knowledge as well as a direct acquaintance with the useful sources of information which will be helpful in the teaching of the various subjects of the curriculum.
5. To give training in the organization of the visual-sensory aids for the various subjects so that the aids may be on hand, available, and usable in the classroom.

Source: *A Summary of the Techniques of Visual-Sensory Aids for Teachers in Service and Teachers in Training.* Harrisburg, Pa.: Commonwealth of Pennsylvania, 1935.

Table 5.4. *(continued)*

III. Objectives *(continued)*
  6. The development of a proper technique for the efficient use of all the teaching aids
  7. To acquaint the prospective teacher with the value of research in determining educational materials and methods
  8. To acquaint the prospective teacher with the psychological aspects underlying visual-sensory aids
  9. To acquaint the prospective teacher, or the teacher in service, with minimum standards for visual-sensory equipment and standards for evaluating the various visual-sensory aids

IV. Method
The lecture-demonstration, discussion, and laboratory method will be used throughout the course. Certain phases of the work can be best presented by the instructor in lecture-demonstration form. Other phases of the work lend themselves to other methods of instruction. Projects suitable for the various grades will be worked out by the group. Emphasis will be placed upon suitable methods of presentation and ways of further stimulating the interest of the student. The student will be taught how and when to use visual and other sensory aids. Maps, specimens, objects, models, the blackboard, projectors, slides, films, field trips, etc., will constitute the materials of the course.

V. Outline of the course
  1. Research-summary of research investigation in visual instruction
  2. Historical background
  3. Psychological aspects and verbalism
  4. Projectors and projection techniques
       Still and motion picture projectors; housing, care techniques
  5. The school journey
       Organizing, conducting, checking results
  6. Museum procedure
  7. Pictorial materials
       Standards for evaluating, mounting, and filing flats
       Housing and care of stereographs
       Making lantern slides
       Mending films and film-strips
       Housing and care of slides and films
       Techniques for all
  8. Object-specimen-model
       Assembling, housing, care, sources
  9. Photography
       Still and motion picture techniques
       Developing films and making prints
       Standards and sources
  10. Blackboard and bulletin board techniques
  11. Administrating and budgeting visual materials
  12. Radio-vision
       Apparatus, procedure, and programs
  13. Bibliography

IV.   Brief bibliography
   1.   Cameron, J. R. "Motion Picture Projection"
   2.   Dorris, Anna V. "Visual Instruction in the Public Schools"
   3.   "Educational Screen" (a magazine)
   4.   Freeman, Frank N. "Visual Education"
   5.   Johnson, William H. "Fundamentals in Visual Instruction"
   6.   Merton, Elds. "Visual Instruction"
   7.   Routzahn, E. G. "A.B.C. of Exhibit Planning"
   8.   Pa. Dept. Public Instruction: "The School Journey Bulletin"; "The Object-Specimen-Model Bulletin"
   9.   Weber, J. J. "Picture Values in Education"
   10.   Wood and Freeman. "Motion Pictures in the Classroom"

The aforementioned resolution of the Los Angeles meeting of the DVI read:

> Resolved, that the Department of Visual Instruction of the National Education Association earnestly recommend that a course in visual and other sensory aids in teaching be established and that teacher-training institutions in every state be required to organize and offer such courses beginning with the scholastic year of 1931-1932.[84]

State Departments of Education

Almost since the beginning of the visual instruction movement, state agencies have established separate visual instruction divisions. These divisions have provided leadership and financial support by serving as lending libraries, publishing visual instruction materials, providing pre-service and in-service training, and obtaining certification laws for visual instruction.

On October 10, 1934, the Pennsylvania State Council of Education passed the following resolution:

> Resolved that all applicants for permanent teaching certificates on and after September 1, 1935, shall be required to present evidence of having completed an approved course in visual and sensory techniques.[85]

Thus, Pennsylvania was the first state to require a course in visual instruction for a teacher's credential. Later, in 1937, the state of New Jersey required that a course in visual instruction be added to the curriculum of the four-year teachers' colleges. A syllabus, *Visual Aids in Education*, was written by the New Jersey State Committee for the Improvement of Visual Instruction, for use in New Jersey colleges of education.[86]

A number of state departments of education have offered in-service training to teachers and administrators, most frequently through conferences and institutes. Such programs allowed teachers to examine various types of visual equipment, observe classroom visual demonstrations, and listen to lectures and panel discussions on various aspects of visual education.

State departments of education have also provided many helpful published visual materials, including visual bulletins, catalogs of available visual materials, and lists of visual materials to supplement courses of study.

As well, state departments of education have assisted individual schools in organizing their own in-service education programs in visual instruction. Some state divisions have offered a school visitation service, sending visual instruction consultants to those schools that encountered special problems.

University Extension Divisions

University extension divisions have distributed visual materials for educational purposes for a number of years. Traditionally, they have also assisted their own institutions with pre-service teacher education in visual instruction, by supplying materials and equipment and by making their staff members available to teach visual instruction courses. Extension divisions have offered short courses, correspondence courses, and off-campus courses; sponsored and conducted conferences and institutes; and published various materials for in-service teacher education in visual instruction.

Four-year Institutions

The primary agency for teacher education in visual instruction has been the four-year institutions. Their practices have varied widely and many have been handicapped by a lack of suitable equipment. Many others, however, have expanded, offering short courses and correspondence courses, conducting conferences and institutes, assisting schools in organizing in-service teacher education, offering a school visitation service, and establishing film libraries.

Early Teacher Education Conferences

State departments of education, university extension divisions, and four-year institutions have conducted a number of teacher education conferences and institutes in visual instruction. Two early, significant conferences on teacher education were initiated by the ACE Committee on Motion Pictures in Education.

A conference on Teacher Training in Visual Instruction convened on November 5, 1936, at the University of Wisconsin in Milwaukee, with a number of prominent visual instruction leaders present.[87] Questions discussed included the following:

1. Should there be a general course in visual instruction required for every teacher in training, as in the state of Pennsylvania?

2. Should this be given as a separate course, or should a series of units be taught in such fields as science, school administration, etc.?

3. If such courses are to be required, do we have now the personnel to teach them? If not, how can this situation be remedied?

4. What should be the content of a general course in visual instruction?

5. How much credit should be given or required for a teacher-training course?

6. To what extent can the material of such a course be individualized to let teachers work out their material in the fields in which they expect to teach?

7. Should teachers of special subjects, such as science, mathematics, art, etc., also be required to give units of instruction on visual aids? How should this be set up?

8. What degree of skill do we wish in operating the various types of equipment?

9. How can we most expeditiously develop these skills?

10. What shall be the nature and extent of the in-service training of teachers in the use of visual aids?

11. Is one of the most important problems in the entire field that of getting the college instructors of teachers in training to use visual aids in their work?

12. To what extent are national, state, regional, and local film libraries a factor in the establishment of adequate teacher training courses?

13. What can groups such as this one do to promote the introduction of courses in visual instruction in the teacher training institutions?

14. What reference materials, especially for reading, are desirable for a course in visual instruction?

15. What is the minimum equipment that should be available for giving such a course?[88]

An interesting outcome of these discussions was a statement of minimum equipment for a course in visual instruction.

On January 18, 1937, a second conference was sponsored by the ACE at Columbia University in New York City. As at the preceding meeting, the problems of teacher preparation in visual instruction were discussed. These discussions clarified many points and gave additional impetus to the organization of other conferences and institutes by various educational agencies.[89]

Early Visual Instruction Journals

One of the most important landmarks in the visual instruction movement was the founding of journals devoted exclusively to visual instruction. By April 1921, four publications had been established: *Moving Picture Age, Educational Film Magazine, Visual Education,* and *The Screen.*

Reel and Slide and *Moving Picture Age*

Reel and Slide was the first journal devoted to visual instruction. This pioneering periodical, which appeared in March 1918, was "a monthly magazine to make the screen a greater power in education and business."[90] It was edited by Lynne S. Metcalfe and published by the Reel Publishing Company of New York. In October 1919, the name was changed to *Moving Picture Age* when a group of educators was persuaded to join the governing board.

Moving Picture Age achieved a reputation for genuine service to the visual instruction movement. It became the official organ of the National Academy of Visual Instruction and published the first annual annotated catalog of instructional or non-theatrical films. Entitled

1001 Films, this catalog was a forerunner of *The Bluebook of 16mm Films* (later *The Bluebook of Audio-Visual Materials*) subsequently published by *The Educational Screen*.

Moving Picture Age began its existence with flexible policies. The early issues of "The Only Independent Magazine in the Field of Visual Instruction" indicate that subscribers were expected to accept as authoritative the editorial contributions, some of which had a commercial bias. However, these same issues also had financially disinterested contributors.

In accordance with the publishers' wishes, the editorial policies of the magazine were revamped in 1921, when Milton Ford Baldwin became editor and a distinguished group of contributing editors, most of them educators, was enlisted.[91] The magazine drew considerable criticism when it ruled against accepting contributions from persons with a financial interest in any commercial enterprise in visual instruction. This, of course, was a complete reversal of the policy previously in force.

Finally, in December 1922, *Moving Picture Age* merged with the newly established *The Educational Screen* when it became clear that it was "in no sense a perfect servant of the field of visual instruction."[92] The final, nostalgic editorial of *Moving Picture Age* read:

> From time to time we have recognized flaws in the magazine's attempts to serve; and just before the amalgamation of publications was broached we had laid plans for the strengthening and broadening of the assistance rendered by the *Moving Picture Age*. And yet, although not setting itself up as a model in any sense, this publication has at least aspired to be dependable, honest, and practical: the subscriber has seen it appear without fail twelve times a year, while other publications have withered and died; he has seen it take issue editorially upon matters that needed frank treatment, when the more comfortable method would have been to overlook the subject; he has seen it emphasize the practical needs of the man in the field and pay but secondary attention to the theory of visual instruction, on the basis that both were valuable but the first always imperative.[93]

The Screen

"A Journal of Motion Pictures for Business, School and Church," *The Screen* was established in January 1920 by the Aldan Publishing Company of New York. The first editor was Albert H. Gross; the associate editor was Ruth Madlon.[94] In the spring of 1922, *The Screen* stopped publication.

Educational Film Magazine

This journal was also established in the early 1920s in New York City. Its first editor was Dolph Eastman. After a brief duration, it ceased publication in the spring of 1922.

Visual Education

In January 1920, the Society for Visual Education, a new organization for producing and distributing visual aids, began publishing *Visual Education*. This monthly house organ, "A Magazine Devoted to the Cause of American Education," brought together an extraordinary amount of useful information concerning educational films. The executive viewpoint of Harley Clarke and the educational one of Forest Ray Moulton set the policy and tone. Nelson L. Greene was the first editor; later editors were W. C. Bagley and F. R. Moulton.[95]

The broad policy of utilizing all avenues to expand and develop visual instruction meant that columns often publicized competing enterprises. Also, authoritative articles about new developments were featured, uses of non-theatrical films illustrated and described, and discussions of new instructional films included. Subscribers were encouraged to make the magazine a medium for the exchange of pertinent ideas in the visual instruction field. Although *Visual Education* was a commercial house organ, it rarely fell below its high educational standards.

The December 1924 issue announced the merger with *The Educational Screen*. The editors made the following comment:

> The Society for Visual Education, formed its foundation more than five years ago, has served education by the dissemination of information regarding all visual aids and practices throughout the early stages of the development of the visual field, in addition to the pursuit of its other essential activities—the production and distribution of visual aids. The sale of the magazine has been arranged in order that the time and energy of the Society for Visual Education can be devoted more specifically to the activities of production and distribution.[96]

Visual Review

In 1926, the Society for Visual Education reentered publishing with *Visual Review*. This periodical, first edited by Marie Witham, later discontinued publication.[97]

The Educational Screen

Late in 1921, *The Educational Screen* was established in Chicago under the leadership of Herbert E. Slaught of the University of Chicago. The directorate was composed of educators "from university professors to grade school principals—and of business executives and experts in the publishing field who have been connected with established publications."[98]

A short time later, Nelson L. Greene, former professor of languages and literature and the first editor of *Visual Education*, was selected as first editor of *The Educational Screen*.

The first issue of the magazine appeared in January 1922, with the slogan "The Independent Magazine Devoted to the New Influence in National Education."[99] The editorial proclaimed:

> The Educational Screen is not the official organ of anything or anybody. It is published to give American education, and every American who believes education important, the thing that they have needed ever since the so-called "visual movement" started—namely, a magazine devoted to the educational cause and to no other; a magazine distinctly intellectual and critical, rather than commercial and propagandist; a magazine written and produced exclusively by those whose scholarly training, experience, and reputation qualify them to discuss educational matters.[100]

The purpose of *The Educational Screen* was stated as follows:

> This magazine intends to get at the truth about visual education—in all its phases and its broadest aspects—and serve it up in a form palatable to thinking Americans.
> We shall endeavor to supply for you the best in theory, opinion, and experience that the country affords....

We shall wade through the welter of "literature" provoked by the movies ... and offer a digest of all that is worth your attention.

We shall present a monthly survey of really significant visual activities along educational lines which will keep you constantly in touch with everything that points toward progress in this undeveloped and more or less unknown field.

We shall develop at the earliest possible moment a technical department....

We shall become the one impartial and authoritative source of information on the new field....

We shall aim at something unique in regard to the theatrical "movie."[101]

Fig. 5.14. Cover of Volume 1 of *The Educational Screen*.

The Educational Screen, which became the first official organ of the DVI, made many notable contributions to the visual instruction movement.[102] Beginning with the November 1922 issue, it devoted a portion of its space to the Visual Instruction Association of America. At the end of 1922, *The Educational Screen* absorbed *Moving Picture Age*; in its second year, several other visual education magazines were discontinued; at the close of the third, it announced the purchase of *Visual Education*. *The Educational Screen* was the only visual instruction magazine by 1925. The last acquisition made it possible for *The Educational Screen* to expand its pages and add to its departments. Simultaneously, it began to publish visual instruction books and pamphlets, continuing publication of *1001 Films*, which had been started by *Moving Picture Age* in 1920. In 1932, *The Educational Screen* acquired *Visual Instruction News*. Its name was changed in 1956 to *Educational Screen and Audiovisual Guide* as a result of another merger.

The Educational Screen published one of the first comprehensive catalogs of films available for school use.[103] They were also first to print a systematic summary of research as a guide to the utilization of visual materials, as well as the first to give critical appraisals of the theatrical film.

Visual Instruction News

In January 1927, the bureau of visual instruction at the University of Kansas began to publish *Visual Instruction News* under the sponsorship of the National Academy of Visual Instruction. Ellsworth C. Dent was its first and only editor; Dorothea Bowen was his assistant. The quarterly periodical continued until the National Academy of Visual Instruction merged with the DVI in 1932. The April 1932 issue was the first combined publication of *Visual Instruction News* and *The Educational Screen*.

Film and Radio Guide

In 1935, William Lewin became founding editor of *Film and Radio Guide*. A few years previously he had begun to implement a 1923 Judd Committee recommendation by publishing illustrated guides to theatrical motion picture appreciation, because he believed outstanding theatrical films could be used in the classroom. The *Film and Radio Guide* (later the *Audio-Visual Guide*) extended these efforts.

On the periodical's twentieth anniversary, McClusky listed its contributions to the visual instruction movement:

First, it fostered closer cooperation between the theatrical motion picture industry and schools by publishing its guides....

Second, it has published bibliographies and unit outlines which have been both practical and helpful to teachers and professionals in the visual field.

Third, *Audio-Visual Guide*, following World War II, originated and promoted the establishment of pilot programs and visual demonstration centers in secondary schools throughout the United States.[104]

In 1956, the *Audio-Visual Guide* merged with *The Educational Screen*.

Early Visual Instruction Textbooks and Guides

The first modern visual instruction monograph, or guide, was *Visual Education*, published in 1906 by the Keystone View Company. With the exception of two important bulletins printed by the U.S. Bureau of Education, no significant visual instruction publications appeared between 1906 and 1919. In 1915, the bureau published Carl G. Rathmann's account, *The Educational Museum of the St. Louis Public Schools*, and in 1919, it distributed F. W. Reynolds and Carl Anderson's *Motion Pictures and Motion Picture Equipment*.

During the 1920s, a number of significant visual instruction books were published. The first handbook concerning the purely mechanical aspects of visual instruction was Austin C. Lescarboura's *The Cinema Handbook* (1921). Gladys and Henry Bollman wrote the first full-sized book devoted to visual instruction and included information about visual materials for educational, religious, and social work in their *Motion Pictures for Community Needs* (1922). Don Carlos Ellis and Laura Thornborough's *Motion Pictures in Education* (1923) covered the history, principles, use, and sources of visual materials, with an emphasis upon motion pictures. In 1924, *Visual Education* (unrelated to the 1906 Keystone View Company monograph) was published. Although this book was primarily a research report of the University of Chicago's experimental studies of the motion picture, the introductory section contains some helpful material on classroom use of the film. Other important visual instruction books published in the 1920s included: A. P. Hollis's *Motion Pictures for Instruction* (1926), William H. Johnson's *Fundamentals in Visual Education* (1927), and Anna V. Dorris's *Visual Instruction in the Public Schools* (1928).[105]

Visual instruction books began to be published at an increased rate in the 1930s. F. Dean McClusky's *Visual Instruction—Its Value and Its Needs* (1932) analyzed the status of visual instruction; W. W. Charters's *Motion Pictures and Youth* (1933) summarized the twelve Payne Fund studies; and F. L. Devereux et al. discussed the many aspects of the sound film in the classroom in *The Educational Talking Picture* (1933). In 1934, the NEA Department of Elementary School Principals published *Aids to Teaching in the Elementary School*; Ellsworth Dent's *Audio-Visual Handbook* (1934) and Cline M. Koon's report *Motion Pictures in Education in the United States* (1934) were also issued. In 1937, three notable visual instruction books were published: M. R. Brunstetter, *How to Use the Educational Sound Film*; Edgar Dale et al., *Motion Pictures in Education*; and C. F. Hoban et al., *Visualizing the Curriculum*.[106] Three other important visual instruction books published during the 1930s were Elizabeth Laine's *Motion Pictures and Radio* (1938), Grace F. Ramsey's *Educational Work in Museums of the United States* (1938), and H. C. Atyeo's *The Excursion as a Teaching Technique* (1939).[107] In 1936, the H. W. Wilson Company published the first comprehensive catalog of educational films—the *Educational Film Catalog* (changed to *Educational Film Guide* in 1945).

In the early 1940s, Harry C. McKown and Alvin B. Roberts wrote *Audio-Visual Aids to Instruction* (1940) and Charles F. Hoban, Jr., prepared *Focus on Learning* (1942) for the ACE Committee on Motion Pictures in Education.

Visual Education during World War II

The visual instruction movement reached its maturity during World War II. Prior to 1940, visual materials were still generally neglected, often considered an expensive luxury or fad. When the war demanded rapid, effective training for both the armed forces and industry, visual materials began to be intensively utilized.

The widespread use of visual materials during World War II was largely due to the leadership of a few men in both the armed forces and the public schools. These men, with imagination and foresight, worked to influence these two large, conservative groups, which were indifferent, unimaginative, and either skeptical or fully complacent toward their methods of training. The use of visual materials in the armed forces was aided by the impressive backlog of basic procedures and research data that had been compiled by civilian educators.

With the talents of educators, artists, publication specialists, advertising experts, and motion picture personnel combined in the armed forces, a wide array of effective visual materials were produced, including graphics, demonstrations, mockups, breadboards, projected aids, films, and "realistic" training.

The story of the impact of the visual instruction movement during World War II can be found in chapter 6 of this book, "A Case Study of Educational Technology during the War Years."

Decline of the Visual Instruction Movement

Following World War II, a brief period of expansion began in the visual instruction movement, but, simultaneously and ironically, its distinct identity as a movement in American education was eroded by changing perceptions of its traditional function and its role in the instructional process.[108] In the late 1940s, leaders of the movement became increasingly uneasy about the adequacy of the visual instruction label with reference to new media. There was also a growing dissatisfaction with the traditional conceptual rationale that supported their practices. In the meantime, the DVI, official sponsor of the visual instruction movement, became the Department of Audiovisual Instruction (DAVI) in 1947. Although this name change was not immediately reflected in a new theoretical orientation, it did signify a changing of perspective. Dale et al. at the time stated: "Audiovisual materials and devices should not be classified as 'eye' and 'ear' experiences. They are modern technological means of providing rich, concrete experiences for students."[109] Increasingly, the terminology was changing from *visual* or *audiovisual materials* to *instructional media*; visual or audiovisual specialists were beginning to be called media specialists; and visual instruction departments were becoming instructional media centers. It was also apparent that the visual instruction movement was tending toward convergence with the broad mainstream of educational technology.

By the late 1940s, the communications orientation began to influence a new conceptual framework. It was during this period that departments of communications, graduate communications programs, and communications centers were being developed. Communications research had accelerated during World War II when studies were demanded on the effects of communications upon military personnel, on adjustment to military life, and on attitudes toward military leaders, enemy propaganda, and civilian morale. After the war, the momentum of these studies stimulated the development of communications theory and research.

The concrete-abstract continuums of visual instruction began to be replaced with a number of communications models of the instructional process.[110]

By the early 1950s, *audiovisual instruction* had begun to be replaced by *audiovisual communications*.[111] Emphasis began to shift from the "things" of the instructional situation to the complete communications process involved in transmitting information from a source (a teacher) to a receiver (the learner).

In 1953, the DAVI sponsored the founding of the *AV Communication Review*, a publication that signaled a historic change in the traditional theoretical orientation of the visual instruction movement in American education. Although *audiovisual* was still not discarded, Finn observed at the time that "the adoption of the term communication by the leadership of the audiovisual movement has had and will have a much more profound effect on the thinking and direction of the field than is yet realized by most practitioners."[112]

By 1963, the DAVI defined audiovisual communications as "that branch of educational theory and practice concerned primarily with the design and use of messages which control the learning process." Thus, it became clear in the early 1960s that the visual instruction movement had been definitely replaced by new theory and models; it was now part of the historical past.

Concluding Assessment

McClusky made an excellent assessment of the visual instruction movement several years ago that is well worth quoting.

> The coming of the machine age and the realization that all who went to school could not enter white-collar jobs implemented the growing demand for more practical curricula and more functional methodologies. A wholesome distrust of "book learning," as such, was to be found in many quarters. However, educators in general were slow to adopt new techniques of communication as they became available at the close of the nineteenth century. Evolving slowly were ideas on how best to use new media, such as the museum exhibit, the photograph, the projected still picture, and the motion picture, in instruction.
>
> There were pioneers, of course, who experimented with the new media, and they made history. But the impact of their efforts on the broad stream of instruction caused little more than a ripple on the surface. Education is conservative. It takes time to bring about widespread changes in content and methodology. It was twenty-three years after the establishment of the first unit for the administration of visual media in public schools that the first comprehensive book on the use of the new media in schools was published. In fact, the early label "visual education" came into widespread use and acceptance more than a decade after the first educational museums were established at St. Louis (1905), Reading (1908), and Cleveland (1909), and more than twenty-five years after New York State began to collect and distribute lantern slides for the public schools.
>
> One factor which characterized general overall thinking about the use of the new media in education, at top policy-making levels, was specialization in the production and administration of instructional media. At the outset, following the turn of the century, commercial interests producing media for school purposes centered on one or two media. Many companies still do. Certain companies made blackboards, others produced slides, some produced motion pictures, others concentrated on maps and models, one centered on sets of slides and stereographs, others produced slidefilms, and some specialized in recordings.
>
> Parallel with specialization by producers of media there was specialization in the administration of instructional media. For example, New York State's Division of Visual Education collected and distributed lantern slides only. The St. Louis Educational Museum concentrated on exhibits. The University of California's Department of Visual Education in University Extension distributed motion pictures only. In a number of universities, the department of visual instruction was in charge of the distribution of motion pictures and another department was charged with education by radio. During the 1930s, there was at one time a national association of visual educationists, a national association of educators specializing in school excursions, and a national association of those in charge of education by radio. As time went on, there were those who administered

audiovisual materials under one central unit and who tried to develop a rationale for the value and place of each device in instruction.

The commercial interests competed with each other for the school's dollar and in so doing sold their wares under the overall label "visual education." All this fragmentation was confusing to teachers and administrators. To some, visual education meant the motion picture, and to others, visual education centered in the museum. The competition was between things rather than ideas.[113]

Relationship of the Visual Instruction Movement to Educational Technology

Having completely examined the visual instruction movement, it is appropriate to point out the relationship of visual instruction to the concept of educational technology.

First of all, a rarely made historical distinction needs to be drawn between the visual instruction movement, whose traditional primary concern has been the use of specific media, and a technology of instruction, which is primarily oriented toward psychological principles and empirical data based on the total teaching-learning process. Chapters 2 and 3 of this book reflect much of the history of educational technology, which reaches back to the era of the Elder Sophists. On the other hand, the visual instruction movement was a relatively late development, not coming until this century, and emerged as a small, specialized movement almost completely separated from the mainstream of educational technology. References to the visual instruction movement rarely appear in histories of educational practice or in books devoted to the psychology of learning. For example, in Cremin's definitive history of American education, the term *visual instruction* does not appear at all.[114]

Although the visual instruction movement has been little affected by learning theory, communication theory, or by theories of group process, social change, innovation, and diffusion, it does have a research tradition. Chapter 8 shows that this tradition has been confined largely to studies of the effectiveness of conventional procedures as compared to that of selected types of so-called visual or audiovisual media. Despite the paucity of significant differences produced by this pattern of research, it has been the one area where the visual instruction movement and educational technology were never separate.

The discontinuity of the visual instruction movement with the discipline of educational technology can probably best be illustrated by developments in programmed instruction. For example, Montessori began developing programmed instructional devices during the first decade of this century, just about the same time that the visual instruction movement began. About a decade later, Sidney Pressey and others began their experiments in programmed instruction. Yet, for four decades or more, there was no connection between these two developments! Also, it is clear from the historical development of the visual movement that it has generally ignored psychological theory, stressing group presentation of materials without explicit regard for individual differences in learning ability. Educational technology, on the contrary (as reflected in the programmed approach), is increasingly dependent on theory and empirical data.

Notes

[1]Burton Holmes, interview with the author, July 26, 1951.

[2]American Association of Museums, *Proceedings of the American Association of Museums* 2. Pittsburgh, Pa.: The Association, 1908, 65.

[3]American Association of Museums, *Proceedings of the American Association of Museums* 3. Pittsburgh, Pa.: The Association, 1908, 75.

[4]Anna Billings Gallup, "The Work of a Children's Museum," *Proceedings of the American Association of Museums* 1. Pittsburgh, Pa.: The Association, 1907, 144.

[5]Charles E. Skinner, "Museums and Visual Education," *The Educational Screen* 3 (October 1924), 308.

[6]*Annual Reports of Superintendents of Philadelphia Public Schools*, Philadelphia, Pa.: Philadelphia Public Schools, 1894, 90.

[7]The complete collection required fifteen freight cars. The Pennsylvania Railroad supplied the cars free of charge.

[8]Charles R. Toothacker, *The Educational Work of the Commercial Museum of Philadelphia*. U.S. Bureau of Education, Bulletin 13, Washington, D.C.: GPO, 1920, 16.

[9]*Circular Announcement of Commercial Museum Classes*, 1924/25.

[10]See James G. Sigman, "Origin and Development of Visual Education in the Philadelphia Public Schools." Ph.D. dissertation, Temple University, 1933.

[11]William T. Harris, *Twenty-first Annual Report of the Board of Directors of the St. Louis Public Schools* (1875), 164.

[12]*Minutes of the St. Louis Board of Education*, September 13, 1904.

[13]Amelia Meissner's organizational skill was illustrated in her preparations and direction of the St. Louis Public Schools Exhibit at the 1915 Panama Pacific Exposition in San Francisco. Her work was so well received that she was requested to remain six months longer in order to help organize the San Francisco Public Schools' visual instruction department.

[14]Carl G. Rathmann, *Educational Museum of St. Louis Public Schools*. U.S. Bureau of Education, Bulletin 48, Washington, D.C.: GPO, 1915, 11.

[15]J. M. H. Frederick, *Annual Report of J. M. H. Frederick, Superintendent, for the School Year 1914-15, to the Board of Education*. Cleveland, Ohio: Board of Education, January 24, 1916, 62.

[16]Alfred W. Abrams, "Visual Instruction as Encouraged by the New York State Education Department," *Moving Picture Age* (February 1922), 5.

[17]*Second Annual Report of the New York State Education Department*. Albany, N.Y., 1906, 488-89.

[18]William H. Dudley, "Cooperation in Visual Instruction," *Proceedings of the First National University Extension Conference*. Madison: University of Wisconsin Press, March 1915, 244-51.

[19]Dudley Grant Hayes and William McAndrew, *Visual Instruction: The Inception, Development and Present Status of Visual Instruction in the Chicago Public Schools* (monograph). Chicago: Chicago Board of Education, 1924, 5-6.

[20]F. Dean McClusky, *The Administration of Visual Education: A National Survey*. Unpublished report presented to the NEA Committee on Visual Education and Cooperation with the Motion Picture Producers, November 1924.

[21]Personnel of city departments of visual instruction ranged from "one to twelve with a median of five" in 1923 (ibid., 43).

[22]Ibid., 43-44.

[23]Ibid., 44-46.

[24]William H. Dudley, *Organization for Visual Instruction*. U.S. Bureau of Education, Bulletin 7, Washington, D.C.: GPO, 1921, 11.

[25]McClusky, "National Survey," 54-55.

[26]Ibid., 80-85.

[27]*Proceedings of the National Education Association*, "Reports of Committees and Discussions," Washington, D.C.: NEA, 1886, 274.

[28]William C. Bagley, "Concreteness in Education," *Visual Education*. Meadville, Pa.: Keystone View Co., 1906, ix-x.

[29]John Adams, *Exposition and Illustration in Teaching*. New York: Macmillan, 1910, 319.

[30]Ibid.

[31]Joseph J. Weber, "Picture Values in Education," *The Educational Screen*, 1928, 126.

[32]Charles F. Hoban et al., *Visualizing the Curriculum*. New York: Dryden Press, 1937, 23.

[33]Ibid., 29.

[34]Ibid.

[35]Edgar Dale, *Audiovisual Methods in Teaching*. New York: Dryden Press, 1946.

[36]The first officers elected at the first meeting of the National Academy of Visual Instruction were: president: F. W. Reynolds, University of Utah; vice-president: G. E. Condra, University of Nebraska; secretary: J. V. Ankeney, University of Missouri; treasurer: Charles Roach, Iowa State College.

[37]*Proceedings of the First Annual Meeting of the National Academy of Visual Instruction*, 43. Meeting held July 14-16, 1920, in Madison, Wis.

[38]*Moving Picture Age*, "The National Academy of Visual Instruction," 4 (October 1921), 43.

[39]The first president of the Visual Instruction Association was Ernest L. Crandall, director of lectures and visual instruction of the New York City Public Schools. In addition to Crandall, members of the association included Rita Hochheimer, assistant to Crandall; A. G. Balcom, assistant superintendent of the Newark, New Jersey, Public Schools; George Zehrung, director of the YMCA Motion Picture Bureau; Rowland Rogers, Columbia University; Illsley Boone; Don Carlos Ellis of the U.S. Department of Agriculture; Clyde Fisher, American Museum of Natural History; John H. Finley, and George D. Strayer, both of Columbia University.

[40]A complete exhibition and demonstration of slides, films, stereographs, posters, maps, charts, stereopticons, portable and standard projectors, optical instruments, and slidefilm projectors was held. The Visual Instruction Association of America provided conference rooms as well as a specially equipped projection room. Visual Instruction Association of America, "Visual Instruction Association of America: Its Origin and Achievements," *Visual Instruction Handbook* 1 (June 1924), 39-41.

[41]Nelson L. Greene, "The New Department of the NEA," *The Educational Screen* 2 (September 1923), 317.

[42]In 1922, the motion picture industry selected Will H. Hays, a member of President Harding's cabinet and an elder in the Presbyterian church, to head the newly formed MPPDA in Washington, D.C. Although the purpose of the organization was to create a favorable public image of motion pictures, the public gradually realized that it had been duped; Hollywood productions did not reflect the image Hays was attempting to build. After some five years of parrying criticism and dissatisfaction, Hays found the way out through the formulation of a morals code. At this juncture, he selected two assistants on the basis of the influence they wielded in other fields: Carl E. Miliken, who had served two terms as governor of Maine and had been, for three years, a federal officer charged with prohibition enforcement in New England; and Colonel Jason S. Joy, former executive secretary of the American Red Cross. Miliken was put in charge of New York studio relations work; Joy was sent to Hollywood for the same purpose. In 1929, Mrs. Thomas G. Winter, former national president of the General Federation of Women's Clubs, was added to the Hays staff. For another three years the motion picture industry used the Hays office as a smoke screen behind which it continued to do as it pleased. When it became apparent that further negotiations with the Hays office were useless, a well-knit Catholic force developed the Legion of Decency, an organized attack upon the motion picture industry at the box-office level. For the first time, the motion picture producers became seriously concerned and made policy adjustments that the public had been led to believe were made some twelve years previously. As a result, a real censorship power became centered in the Hays office, with Joseph I. Breen as censor, and the long-promised cleanup became a reality. (Ruth A. Inglis, *Freedom of the Movies*. Chicago: University of Chicago Press, 1947).

[43]The Judd Committee was officially known as the Committee on Visual Education and Cooperation with the Motion Picture Producers and Distributors of America. The original members were Judd, Leonard Ayres of Cleveland, Elizabeth Breckenridge of Louisville, Kentucky, Ernest Crandall of New York City, Susan Dorsey of Los Angeles, Elizabeth Hall of Minneapolis, and Payson Smith of Boston.

[44]The Crandall subcommittee was the first to investigate the possibility of excerpting theatrical films for educational use. Excerpting was first made possible on a large scale when the Progressive Education Association established the Commission on Human Relations in 1936. Hugh Hartshorne and Mark A. May, in 1928, also did some excerpting of theatrical films for educational use in connection with their *Studies in Deceit*. See chapter 8 of this history for further details.

[45]McClusky was assisted by A. Loretta Clark of the Los Angeles Public Schools and Charles Roach of the Extension Division of the University of Iowa.

[46]Charles H. Judd, *Report of the Committee on Visual Education and Cooperation with the Motion Picture Producers and Distributors, Inc., to the National Education Association*. Washington, D.C.: NEA, 1923.

[47]Judd, *Report of Committee on Visual Education*, 3-4. The Scarborough School of Scarborough-on-Hudson, New York, first provided a permanent, fireproof projection booth and established permanently equipped facilities for projecting silent and sound films.

[48]Ibid., 8.

[49]Ibid., 8.

[50]Ibid., 5.

[51]F. Dean McClusky, "The Coalition of 1932," *Audiovisual Instruction* 7 (September 1962), 502-6.

[52]The three national visual instruction organizations in existence in 1932 were the DVI, the National Academy of Visual Instruction, and the Visual Instruction Association of America.

[53]"Editorial," *The Educational Screen* 11 (March 1932), 66.

[54]McClusky observes that "it must seem strange that the Academy having tried unsuccessfully to bring about unity in the profession would now deliberately take steps to create another rival professional organization" (McClusky, "The Coalition," 505). This was due, as McClusky says, to the strong desire for official professional status and recognition.

[55] J. W. Shepherd, "Are More Organizations Needed?" *The Educational Screen* 1 (April 1922), 107-8.

[56] The author of this history is deeply indebted to F. Dean McClusky for supplying unpublished data concerning the merger.

[57] F. Dean McClusky, "The Administration of Visual Education: A National Survey." Unpublished report presented to the NEA, November 1924, 193.

[58] Ibid.

[59] Joseph J. Weber, "Picture Values in Education," *The Educational Screen* 7 (1928), 131.

[60] The University of Minnesota visual instruction course description reads as follows: "Designed to prepare persons for presenting materials by means of slides, films, charts, etc. Students assisted in assembling materials for their own use and in acquiring skill and technique in preparation and operation of various mediums."

[61] Beginning with the summer quarter of 1918, the first course in "graphic methods" was offered at Stanford University by J. Harold Williams. The description of the course in the university announcement read as follows: "188. *Graphic Methods of Presenting Facts.* This course is designed to give practice in graphic methods which are serviceable in the popular portrayal of statistical data. In addition to graphic presentation, some attention will be given to a consideration of the merits of various tabular publicity. There are no prerequisites for the course, but a knowledge of lettering is desirable. Intended primarily to show prospective school officers how best to display statistical facts" (J. Harold Williams, *Graphic Methods in Education.* Boston: Houghton Mifflin, 1924, v-vi).

[62] In Newark, McClusky found that the director of visual instruction "spent several weeks during the spring of 1923 instructing teachers in the use of stereopticons." At Kansas City, "the director of visual instruction held a number of informal teacher conferences dealing with the use of visual aids." He found that Los Angeles had begun to give "training in the use of motion picture projectors at the bureau" (McClusky, "A National Survey," 153).

[63] McClusky found that five city normal schools, located in Chicago, Cleveland, Detroit, San Francisco, and St. Louis, offered courses in visual education. The instructors of these courses were usually the city visual education directors or coordinates. Ibid.

[64] Ibid., 181-84.

[65] F. Dean McClusky, "Finding the Facts of Visual Education, II: Growth Through Teacher Training," *The Educational Screen* 4 (April-May 1925), 203-5, 272-76.

[66] *Addresses and Proceedings of the 62nd Annual Meeting of the National Education Association,* Washington, D.C., June 29-July 4, 1924, vol. 62, 971-74.

[67] William H. Gregory, "A Teachers' Training Course in Visual Aids," *The Educational Screen* 4 (February 1925), 88-90.

[68] J. V. Ankeney, "Report of Committee on Teacher Training in Visual Instruction," *The Educational Screen* 5 (October 1926), 489-91.

[69] See W. Gayle Starnes, *The Present Status of Teacher Training in the Use of Visual Aids.* Lexington: University of Kentucky, 1936.

[70] Katherine M. Cook and Florence E. Reynolds, *Opportunities for the Preparation of Teachers in the Use of Visual Aids in Instruction.* U.S. Office of Education, Federal Security Agency, Pamphlet no. 89, 1940.

[71] E. Winifred Crawford, "A Study of the Status of Visual Education Courses in Teacher-training Institutions," *Journal of Secondary Education* 9 (May 1940), 161-70.

[72]Robert Eulette de Kieffer, "The Status of Teacher-training in Audio-visual Education in the Forty-eight States." Ph.D. dissertation, State University of Iowa, 1948.

[73]Edgar Dale et al., *Motion Pictures in Education.* New York: Wilson Company, 1937, 371.

[74]Quoted in John S. Carroll, *Teacher Education and Visual Education for the Modern School.* San Diego: Office of Superintendent of Schools, 1948, 23.

[75]Dale et al., *Motion Pictures in Education,* 372.

[76]Anna V. Dorris, *Visual Instruction in the Public Schools.* Boston: Ginn and Company, 1928, 377-79.

[77]Carroll, *Teacher Education,* 25-26.

[78]Dale et al., *Motion Pictures in Education,* 371-72.

[79]*University of Minnesota Course Catalog,* 1918.

[80]See B. A. Aughinbaugh, "Outline for Course in Visual Instruction," *The Educational Screen* 8 (December 1929), 307-8; Gregory, "Teachers' Training Course," 88-90; H. A. Henderson, "What Should a Course in Visual Instruction Include?" *The Educational Screen* 2 (June 1923), 186; J. Raymond Hutchinson, "Fundamentals of Visual Instruction Include?" *School Executive* 55 (January 1936), 186-88; F. Dean McClusky et al., *Visual Instruction: Syllabus of a Proposed Textbook for Use in Teacher-Training Schools.* Meadville, Pa.: Keystone View Company, 1932. (Mimeographed.)

[81]*A Summary of the Techniques of Visual-Sensory Aids for Teachers in Service and Teachers in Training.* Harrisburg, Pa.: Commonwealth of Pennsylvania, 1935.

[82]Dale et al., *Motion Pictures in Education,* 456.

[83]*Proceedings of the 70th Annual Meeting of the National Education Association,* Atlantic City, N.J., June 25-July 1, 1932, vol. 70, 790.

[84]*Proceedings of the 69th Annual Meeting of the National Education Association,* Los Angeles, Calif., June 27-July 3, 1931, vol. 69, 963.

[85]"Certification of Secondary School Teachers of Academic Subjects," section 4, *Permanent College Certificate,* Department of Public Instruction, Harrisburg, Pa.

[86]C. W. Leman, *Visual Aids in Education.* Ann Arbor, Mich.: State Teachers College and Edwards Brothers, 1941, 75.

[87]*A Conference on Teacher Training in Visual Instruction.* Washington, D.C.: ACE, 1936.

[88]Ibid., 2-3.

[89]*Teacher Training in Modern Teaching Aids.* Report of conference sponsored jointly by Teachers College of Columbia University and the ACE, held at Teachers College, Columbia University, New York City, January 18, 1937.

[90]Lynn S. Metcalfe, "Editorial," *Reel and Slide,* 1 (March 1918).

[91]Contributing editors of *Moving Picture Age* were J. V. Ankeney, associate professor of visual education, College of Agriculture Experiment Station, University of Missouri; A. G. Balcom, assistant superintendent of schools, Newark, New Jersey; Mrs. Woodallen Chapman, chairman, motion picture committee, General Federation of Women's Clubs, New York City; A. Loretto Clark, Visual Education Division, Los Angeles city schools; William H. Dudley, chief of Bureau of Visual Instruction, University of Wisconsin; James N. Emery, supervising principal, Pawtucket, Rhode Island; W. M. Gregory, curator, Educational Museum, Cleveland, Ohio; Samuel Guard, director of information, American Farm Bureau Federation, Chicago; Austin C. Lescarboura, managing editor, *Scientific*

American, New York City; F. Dean McClusky, instructor in education, University of Illinois; Charles Roach, Visual Instruction Service, Iowa State College of Agriculture; Rowland Rogers, chairman, curriculum committee, Visual Instruction Association of New York; Roy L. Smith, Simpson Methodist Church, Minneapolis, Minnesota; and J. J. Weber, associate professor of education, University of Kansas. *Moving Picture Age* 4 (January 1921), 3.

[92]Milton F. Baldwin, "Editorial," *Moving Picture Age* 5 (December 1922), 6-7.

[93]Ibid., 7.

[94]*The Screen* 1 (January 1920), 1.

[95]*Visual Education* 1 (January 1920). Moulton was the co-founder and secretary of the Society for Visual Education and was also connected with the University of Chicago. Bagley was professor of education, Teachers College, Columbia University.

[96]*Visual Education* 5 (1924), 419.

[97]"Editorial," *The Educational Screen* 1 (January 1922), 8.

[98]Ibid., 8.

[99]In 1925, the slogan of *The Educational Screen* was changed to "The Only Magazine Devoted to the New Influence in National Education," when it became the only magazine devoted exclusively to visual education [*The Educational Screen* 4 (January 1925)].

[100]*The Educational Screen* 1 (January 1922), 8.

[101]Ibid., 5-6.

[102]*The Educational Screen* made a notable contribution to the visual instruction movement by opening its pages to professional organizations that could not afford the luxury of a publication. The Visual Instruction Association of America, the National Academy of Visual Instruction, the Better Films Committee of the National Congress of Mothers and Parent-Teachers Associations, and the Film Council of America all enjoyed this privilege. Following the merger of the Visual Instruction Association of America and the DVI in 1932, the DVI arranged for space in the magazine to be devoted to official news, notes, and proceedings of the organization. The DVI's first "News and Notes" appeared in the May 1932 issue. This arrangement continued until June 1955, when the DVI decided to publish its own journal. No cost to the DVI was ever involved. For a comprehensive history of *The Educational Screen*, see F. Dean McClusky, "What Was AV Journalism in 1922," *The Educational Screen and Audiovisual Guide* (January 1962), 18-20.

[103]*The Bluebook of Non-Theatrical Films* was first published in 1925.

[104]F. Dean McClusky, "On the Occasion of Audio-Visual Guide's Twentieth Anniversary," *Audio-Visual Guide* 21 (April 1955), 5.

[105]Dorris's was the first comprehensive textbook in visual instruction and the first concerning integration of visual materials with the school curriculum.

[106]*Motion Pictures in Education* was the first comprehensive summary of the literature of motion pictures and related aspects of visual instruction. *Visualizing the Curriculum* was probably the most important visual education textbook written during the 1930s because of its systematic treatment of the relation between the concrete materials of teaching and the learning process.

[107]Atyeo's *The Excursion as a Teaching Technique* gives one of the most complete historical accounts of the excursion, or field trip. He notes that the adaptation of the excursion idea in the United States was stimulated by scholars who had received their training in German universities in the late 1890s and early 1920s. Van Liew is credited as being the first important influence in stimulating American interest in the field trip. C. F. Hoban, Sr. was mainly responsible for the endorsement of the excursion method

by the Pennsylvania Department of Education in 1927. National recognition was first given to the field trip at a conference of the Association of Childhood Education in 1931. With the emergence of the "new education," field trips were adopted in many experimental schools throughout the United States. The development of the European youth hostel plan, school surveys, school camping, and other community service projects stemmed from the early school excursion movement.

[108]State leadership in advancing the use of visual media increased steadily after World War II, with the growth of teacher education requirements and the budgeting of considerable sums for the purchase of visual materials. Another impressive index of postwar growth is expenditures for visual materials by city school systems. This period, however, did not last long and by 1950, a leveling-out had begun. There was also growth in graduate programs in visual and/or audio-visual education and a greater concern with professional certification for audio-visual personnel.

[109]Edgar Dale et al., "Research on Audio-Visual Materials," *AV Materials of Instruction*, Part I, 48th yearbook of the National Society for the Study of Education. Chicago: University of Chicago Press, 1949, 253.

[110]See chapter 9 of this book for a history of communication and educational technology.

[111]See chapter 9 of this book for the historical relationship between the communications movement and educational technology.

[112]James D. Finn, "Directions in AV Communication Research," *AV Communication Review* 2 (Spring 1954), 83.

[113]See Paul Saettler, *A History of Instructional Technology*. New York: McGraw-Hill, 1968, 78-80.

[114]See Lawrence A. Cremin, *The Transformation of the School*. New York: Knopf, 1961.

Select Bibliography

Adams, John. *Exposition and Illustration in Teaching*. New York: Macmillan, 1910.

Atyeo, H. C. *The Excursion as a Teaching Technique*. New York: Teachers College Press, Columbia University, 1939.

Bode, Carl. *The American Lyceum: Town Meeting of the Mind*. New York: Oxford Press, 1956.

Brown, H. Emmett, and Joy Bird. *Motion Pictures and Lantern Slides for Elementary Visual Education*. New York: Teachers College Press, Columbia University, 1931.

Brunstetter, M. R. *How to Use the Educational Sound Film*. Chicago: University of Chicago Press, 1937.

Dale, Edgar. *Audiovisual Methods in Teaching*, rev. ed. New York: Dryden Press, 1954.

Dale, Edgar, and Lloyd Ramseyer. *Teaching with Motion Pictures: A Handbook of Administrative Practice*. Series 2, vol. 1, no. 2. Washington, D.C.: AEC, April 1937.

Dale, Edgar, et al. *Motion Pictures in Education: A Summary of the Literature*. New York: Wilson Company, 1937.

Dale, Edgar, et al. "Research on Audio-Visual Materials," in *AV Materials of Instruction*. 48th Yearbook, Part 1, National Society for the Study of Education. Chicago: University of Chicago Press, 1949.

Dorris, Anna V. *Visual Instruction in the Public Schools*. Boston: Ginn and Company, 1928.

Dudley, William H. *Organization for Visual Instruction*. U.S. Bureau of Education Bulletin 7. Washington, D.C.: GPO, 1921.

Dunn, Fannie W., ed. *Materials of Instruction.* 8th Yearbook of the Department of Supervisors and Directors of Instruction of the NEA. New York: Teachers College Press, Columbia University, 1935.

Finn, James D. "A Look at the Future of AV Communication." *AV Communication Review* vol. 3, no. 4 (Fall 1955): 244-56.

_____. "Professionalizing the Audiovisual Field." *AV Communication Review* vol. 3, no. 4 (Fall 1955): 6-17.

Grattan, C. Hartley, ed. *American Ideas about Adult Education.* New York: Teachers College Press, Columbia University, 1959.

Hamilton, G. E. *The Stereograph in Education.* Meadville, Pa.: Keystone View Co., 1935.

Hayes, Cecil B. *The American Lyceum: Its History and Contribution to Education.* U.S. Office of Education Bulletin 12. Washington, D.C.: GPO, 1932.

Hoban, Charles F., et al. *Visual Education and the School Journey.* Educational Monographs, vol. 1, no. 6. Harrisburg, Pa.: Commonwealth of Pennsylvania, Department of Public Instruction, 1930.

_____. *Visualizing the Curriculum.* New York: Dryden Press, 1937.

Johnson, William H. *Fundamentals in Visual Instruction.* Chicago: The Educational Screen, 1927.

Knowlton, Daniel C., and J. Warren Tilton. *Motion Pictures in History Teaching.* New Haven, Conn.: Yale University Press, 1929.

McClusky, F. Dean. *Audio-Visual Teaching Techniques.* Dubuque, Iowa: W. C. Brown Co., 1949.

_____. *The A-V Bibliography.* Dubuque, Iowa: W. C. Brown Co., 1950.

_____. "The Coalition of 1932." *Audiovisual Instruction* vol. 7, no. 7 (September 1962): 502-6.

_____. *Visual Instruction: Its Value and Its Needs.* Report to Will H. Hays, President, Motion Picture Producers and Distributors of America, Inc., February 2, 1932. New York: Mancall Publishing, 1932.

McClusky, F. Dean, and James S. Kinder, eds. *The Audio-Visual Reader.* Dubuque, Iowa: W. C. Brown Co., 1954.

Ramsey, Grace Fisher. *Educational Work in Museums of the United States.* New York: H. W. Wilson Co., 1938.

Rathmann, Carl G. *Educational Museum of St. Louis Public Schools.* U.S. Bureau of Education Bulletin 48. Washington, D.C.: GPO, 1915.

Toothacker, Charles R. *The Educational Work of the Commercial Museum of Philadelphia.* U.S. Bureau of Education Bulletin 13. Washington, D.C.: GPO, 1920.

Visual Education. Meadville, Pa.: Keystone View Co., 1908.

Weber, Joseph J. *Visual Aids in Education.* Valparaiso, Ind.: Valparaiso University, 1930.

Wittlin, Alma S. *The Museum: Its History and Its Task in Education.* London: Routledge and Kegan Paul, 1949.

6

A Case Study of Educational Technology during the World War II Years: 1940–1946

The development of educational technology in American schools slowed during the war years due to lack of equipment, materials, and instructional specialists. Conversely, a period of expansion began in the industrial and military sectors, brought about by four important developments: (1) the establishment of training programs that produced unprecedented demands for an effective technology of instruction; (2) the application of a technology of instruction based on prewar scientific research; (3) the emergence of an official military policy that encouraged production of a wide variety of instructional materials, instructional media, and new instructional approaches; and (4) the allocation of almost unlimited financial resources (at least $100 million) to implement this technology of instruction. In a vast industrial and military proving ground, old concepts of learning were tested, and new instructional procedures and patterns emerged that held historic implications for the development of educational technology in American education.

Industrial Training

World War II brought an unprecedented need to train millions of industrial workers as rapidly and effectively as possible. The U.S. Office of Education, led by Commissioner John W. Studebaker, assumed the major burden of meeting this challenge.

Division of Visual Aids for War Training

The U.S. Office of Education, which had an established interest in training films, requested funds for film production in the fiscal budget of 1940/41. This was initially refused, but when the international situation worsened, President Franklin D. Roosevelt supported the request.

In January 1941, the Office of Education formed the Division of Visual Aids for War Training with Floyde E. Brooker as director. Brooker was chosen because he had served for many years as associate director of the ACE's research studies in the area of educational technology and had valuable experience in educational film production. Brooker's first task was to promote training films, informing congressmen, government officials, vocational instructors, and laymen concerning the films' function and use. Brooker heard arguments for and against various types of instructional media, and observed that "men who started out by asking what motion picture stars would be used ended with a new appreciation of an entirely different kind of motion picture."[1]

Between January and June 1941, the staff of the Division of Visual Aids for War Training increased from one to three, working space was secured, preliminary plans were made, and synopses of the first twenty proposed films were written. By October 1942, the staff had increased to nine and contracts were being awarded to producers throughout the country. In the spring of 1943, the division received $2 million to further expand the staff and produce additional materials. Regional offices were established in Los Angeles, Chicago, and New York City to handle productions in their respective sections of the country. By January 1944, the new productions were beginning to appear in schools and training centers. By June 1, 1945, most of the productions had been completed.

First Office of Education Training Films

By June 5, 1941, the first film was completed and delivered to the U.S. Office of Education, where a hopeful, tense group sat down to find out whether or not films could speed training. Brooker recorded this experience as follows:

> The projection was in a huge auditorium with a projector in the last stages of usefulness. The curtains at the windows, billowing open with every puff of air, admitted beans of bright sunlight. The sound drizzled through a sound system that provided its own static. The room was far too light — when curtains billowed, the dim picture disappeared. No audience ever sat more tensely than the four individuals who were almost lost in the middle of the auditorium. The picture ended ... and almost at once the argument started. It's confusing ... it goes too fast ... the job is too technical ... it's not confusing to shop students ... it's a step by step explanation ... the picture would be clear if the curtains would not billow open ... the film is made for trainees who have already seen the machine.
>
> The suggestion was made that the film be shown again. There was no rewind equipment so two of the individuals improvised by putting the 35-mm reels on pencils to do the job of rewinding. The second showing was started. Brief splashes of light continued to wash the picture off the screen ... and usually at key points of explanation. This time it became clear that the individuals experienced in shop work viewed the picture in one way, and those inexperienced in shop work viewed it another. Some thought it too elementary while the others thought it too technical; some thought it went too slowly, the others were certain it went too fast. Finally, it was decided to await the coming of the second and third pictures before arriving at any decision. It was also decided that vocational shop instructors were really the ones to make the decision.[2]

By July 2, 1941, more training films had been completed. These were viewed by President Roosevelt, the Bureau of the Budget, officials of the Federal Security Agency, the Navy Department, and a number of war agencies then being formed. They were also shown to a committee of congressmen. The reactions were mixed; some were unexpected. Some thought the skills being taught were very simple and could not understand why training programs were even necessary. Others thought the jobs so difficult that no training films could solve the problem. However, training films gradually gained the favor of key government officials, including President Roosevelt, when selected groups of these films began to be used in vocational and industrial training centers in Hartford, Boston, Worcester, Springfield, New York City, Buffalo, Detroit, Cleveland, Chicago, Cincinnati, Philadelphia, Baltimore, Camden, Paterson, Newark, and Washington, D.C. All who used the films felt they were an effective training aid.

Film Production

Two basic production plans were considered: (1) establishing a complete, independent production unit, and (2) using existing facilities and the experienced personnel of commercial producers. It was decided that the Division of Visual Aids for War Training would administer and supervise the work rather than actually produce it, including planning, research, policy making, administration of fiscal and contractual obligations, and supervision of all aspects of production and distribution.

The division first determined the subject areas where the training need was most critical. Once an area was approved, subject-matter specialists conducted preliminary research to decide on the specific aspects to be filmed. Then a visual aids specialist and a technical specialist co-wrote a content outline or synopsis. Once the synopsis had been approved by the division, the film was produced.

In order to make the film most useful to both experienced and inexperienced teachers, a *visual aids unit* was created, consisting of the motion picture, a correlating silent filmstrip, and an instructors' manual. The filmstrip was a planned review of the motion picture; the manual gave instructions for the use of the film and the filmstrip. The basic purpose of the training film was to present those aspects of a subject that could be shown most effectively with film. Each film in a series was essentially a lesson, designed to teach a specific task.

In the initial production of these training series, two problems arose. First, the educators had to fight the entire motion picture industry because of disagreements over the educational and theatrical cutting of a film. Second, the verbal tradition, which emphasizes words over pictures, handicapped the making of training films. It was finally concluded that "the film maker must first commit himself to a specific picture," and "the training film maker cannot exercise complete control of his content."[3] In other words, training film production was a cooperative process.

A number of production principles evolved as a result of this experience, in relation to film audience, content, and form. Three basic assumptions were made regarding the film audience: (1) the trainee would want to learn the job, (2) the trainee would see each film several times, and (3) each motion picture, as part of a visual aids unit, would be accompanied by a silent filmstrip and an instructors' manual. It was also assumed that the films would convey information, principles, and attitudes in terms of the performance of specific jobs. The object was to develop films for self-identification whereby the learner would be invited, as it were, to live the experience shown in the film.

It was decided that the films would be organized around visual content. This automatically limited the content of a single film, which made it easier to develop an instructional sequence. Since film length was thus determined by content or concepts rather than by the size of reels, the Office of Education's 16mm productions ran from 275 to 1,150 feet, averaging close to 650 feet per title.

Two important contributions to educational technology came out of the experience of the division: the development of the "operator's viewpoint" and the "first-person commentary" principles in film production. The first requirement was that the viewpoint of the camera always be that of the operator's own eyes. Quite often, this ran contrary to accepted production techniques and caused some difficulty. However, this technique allowed the audience to see the operation as if they were actually doing the job. This reversed the usual procedure, which showed a demonstration from a position opposite the demonstrator.

Another result of this technique was the introduction of more camera movement and the elimination of camera angles that presented familiar material in an unfamiliar way.

The first-person commentary technique was designed to keep the commentary closely related to the content of every scene. It was decided that the particular role of commentary was to name the objects shown, to indicate the degree of generalization applied to the content of the picture, and to prevent the camera from having to tell the entire story. Also, verbalism was avoided as much as possible in the writing of the commentary. Sound effects were used as needed to develop a complete sense of familiarity with the job. With a few minor exceptions, music was not used. Color films were not produced because of the difficulty of obtaining color during the war and because it was thought that color would not add to the reality of the presentation.

Brooker described some of the many problems associated with wartime film production as follows:

> Training film production required machine tools, jigs, cutters, blueprints, castings, work pieces, and skilled operators at the very time in our history when these were the most scarce. Arbors were made by the operator working all night to turn one the right size; dividing heads were secured by rushing with a motorcycle to borrow one from a shop where the operator on the night shift was ill, and his part of the picture was shot between midnight and dawn. Raw stock was on priority, and when for instance, a horse kicked over a can of unexposed film, difficulties arose that were hard to explain. Telegrams requesting the loan of machine tools went unanswered, and shipbuilding jobs, partially photographed on the day shift, were completed by the night shift and when the camera crews returned — the work was gone.[4]

Despite the difficulties, between January 1941 and June 1945, the Division of Visual Aids for War Training produced 457 visual aids units — 457 sound motion pictures, 432 silent filmstrips, and 457 instructors' manuals.

Developing Patterns of Distribution

In order to achieve the widest possible use of the training films, a plan had to be developed that would meet the following basic objectives:

1. Distribution had to be based on sales. The films were to be available at a nominal cost to every individual, school, or agency who could use them.

2. Distribution system had to pay for itself — no funds had been appropriated for this purpose. Later Congress specified that sales of the films should also bring return to Government which would amortize the production cost of the films.

3. It was necessary to have facilities for previewing the pictures before purchases.

4. It was desirable to work out a plan which would use existing facilities for distribution rather than to create a large organization within the Government.[5]

These requirements were stated in a bid invitation sent to all commercial distributors. Ultimately, the success of this plan proved its efficiency.

Evaluation and Conclusions

The characteristics of the training films of the Division of Visual Aids for War Training were given as follows:

1. The films were produced in the instructional tradition. In this sense of the term they are instructional films furthering instructional objectives in terms of generally accepted educational philosophy and psychology.

2. The films produced were planned to further many different objectives by using a wide variety of methods. Films were produced to provide orientation, introduce ideal work patterns, present the factors of judgment, develop the acquisition of facts and information, and to serve as a basis and a source of motivation for discussion, as well as to develop physical, mental, and social skills.

3. These films, according to current terminology, are referred to as training films, but it would be a mistake to consider them as being alike, as serving only skill objectives, and as being limited in usefulness to only training programs. It might be more accurate if the collective term used in speaking of the entire body of productions was "instructional films."

4. The production program was a pioneering one. The development of the visual aids unit, the production of films in an integrated series, the production of films to further physical skills acquisition, and others ... were activities never before undertaken to the same extent tried by this program.

5. The program was also experimental. The use of stream-of-consciousness commentary in the problems of pattern making, the intimate type of commentary in the films on aircraft maintenance, the pattern of organization followed in the nursing films, the introductions used in the elementary wood working series ... all these factors, and others, are experimental. To provide experimental ideas with concrete form is to make available the raw material requisite for further research and study.[6]

Training films were evaluated by collecting the judgments of directors in the training program, by conducting informal spot surveys, and by the records of the film used by training groups. A summary of the observations of training directors was stated as follows:

1. The use of the films speeded up training without any loss of effectiveness. The estimates on this point ranged from 10 percent to "a film doing in 20 minutes what it would take two weeks under the usual system to do." There was general agreement, however, that the acceleration of the training with films did not lead to any loss in effectiveness.

2. The use of films made the class work more interesting and resulted in less absenteeism. All the training directors were asked to report on this point and they agreed that this was true.

3. Films made for the university and college level were at times useful on lower grade levels. Reports have come in of films such as the "Slide Rule" being used effectively and successfully on the lower high school levels.[7]

The general conclusions reached by the division staff follow.

1. Training films will work. They can be used effectively to train more people, more quickly, and in more subject matter. As training films, they have not as yet really been tried. Their present success is based on only a partial use. Films were designed to expedite the development of a physical skill; most of them were actually used to provide orientation, to provide facts and information, and to explain principles of operation.

2. It can be said that we know much about the production of an effective training film — or that we know little about the production of an effective training film. Both can be said with equal validity. In comparison with what we would like to know, the second half of the statement seems the more true and the more important. The use of pictorial forms of communication is so new that we do not yet have the facts needed to produce the most effective possible training film. Stated another way — we do not as yet know or fully comprehend the logic, grammar, or rhetoric of this form of communication. The fact that it has proven so effective, with partial use and with the present imperfect state of our understanding, should serve to indicate undeveloped possibilities and to stimulate more research and study.

3. The field of visual aids is new, the tools it uses are powerful, but the general lack of understanding of the field is so pervasive that there are inherent dangers requiring the most serious consideration. Films are not general panaceas, they will not solve all instructional problems; they are not "good" per se, they are "good" only as the producers make them so and as the instructors use them. There is danger that over-optimism may cause an over-expansion that is as dangerous as it is unnecessary.

4. New patterns of production will have to be developed before the true and unhampered production of instructional films can take place. It is quite likely that today's accepted division of labor may have to be reconsidered and that new divisions of labor may have to be developed. It also is more than likely that production more fully integrated will develop producers specializing in the production of a single type of instructional film. This specialization cannot come, however, until the market can support it.

5. There is, at the present time, a serious need for professional training courses in the field of visual education. The production of an effective training film requires thorough knowledge and competency in the broad field of education, film production, and the technical aspects of the film content. It is probably impossible to secure all three of these in the same individual. It is desirable, however, to keep the smallest possible number of individuals who must work closely together in order to produce an effective film. It follows that it is most desirable that a broad understanding of education and of film techniques be combined in the person responsible for instructional film production. The need for the development of such individuals is a growing one. It becomes increasingly doubtful that a background of skill and competency in film production alone is enough to insure the production of an effective instructional film.

6. Instructional films can be produced in great numbers, but this should not be confused with mass production or with assembly line production. They will turn out to be good or bad according to whether some individual becomes definitely and

personally interested in them. They are artistic forms, and, as such, must result from the "loving care" of some one individual.

7. Along with the need for better and more complete knowledge of the production of films and the film media of communication, there goes the need for a better understanding of the manner in which students learn from films. There is some indication that a kind of almost unconscious learning takes place when students view a film. This leads the students to believe that they know more than they do, and paradoxically leads them to actually know in practice more than they think they know or can verbally express. These are only first guesses, but certainly there is serious need for additional and more definite information on this point.[8]

Development of Military Training

The armed services had recognized prior to World War II that educational technology held important implications for military training. During World War I, both army and navy had introduced training films and had begun to establish instructional procedures for such media as slides, filmstrips, and models. The urgent and rapid expansion of military training due to World War II created a new demand for training materials.

The dominant influence in the character of military training programs was exerted by civilian educators. For a number of years, educators had been conducting experimental research on instructional media and had developed a technology of instruction. In the armed services these same educators came into contact with artists, communication specialists, advertising people, and theatrical and motion picture personnel. These specialized groups combined to develop a military technology of instruction. At the same time, military direction provided stability and continuity in the training program.

The entire war experience was summed up by Hoban as follows:

In developing films for these important educational purposes, the Army applied to educational films the dramatic techniques hitherto used only in entertainment films. These techniques resulted in films which were emotionally possessive as well as intellectually stimulating, and, as a consequence, Army films penetrated deeper into the recesses of the human mind than do school films which coldly present a series of related facts without relating these facts to the backgrounds, interests, motives, and actions of the people to whom they are shown. Behind the developments in Army films was a broad concept of the dynamics of human behavior, an empirical understanding of the reasons why people behave as they do, and a positive approach to the direction and control of human behavior. In the past, schools and colleges have been primarily concerned with what people know, assuming that what they know will influence what they do. The Army, on the other hand, was responsible for what men do as well as what they know, and to make this responsibility even greater, for what men do under conditions which frequently call for supreme sacrifice of life or body. Its films, therefore, dealt not only with *what men must know* but also *what men must do*, and *why they must do it*.[9]

Early Surveys of Training Needs

Surveys by both the navy and army at the beginning of the war revealed that the utilization of instructional media was unsatisfactory. What is more, instructional equipment was generally lacking or was obsolete. Instructors were often inexperienced and frequently failed to use what visual media they possessed at the appropriate times or in effective ways. A survey conducted in 1941 by Lt. Colonel Darryl Zanuck for the army disclosed a widespread lack of understanding of the proper function of educational films. One result of this survey was the establishment of a visual aids section in the Office of the Chief Signal Officer to develop an effective utilization program for films, filmstrips, and other instructional media.[10]

A similar problem was experienced in early navy training. A 1942 survey revealed that about one-fourth of the navy instructors did not use films at all and about one-half used them inadequately. About 97 percent of the officers interviewed expressed a need for training in the use of instructional media. The navy survey itself covered seven points: (1) present film utilization, (2) film needs, (3) film distribution, (4) cataloging, (5) continuing services, (6) film production, and (7) special problems, such as administrative location within the navy. The recommendations called for:

1. A greatly expanded program of training film production.

2. Increased funds and personnel for Training Film Unit.

3. The establishment of Bureau film liaison officers.

4. Development of additional film distribution centers.

5. The development of a production manual.

6. Study by appropriate bureaus of the subjects suggested during the survey for new films.

7. The production of morale films.

8. A study of the use of training films in the Fleet.

9. Procurement and distribution of several thousand 16-mm motion picture projectors and an equal number of 35-mm film strip projectors.[11]

The results of these recommendations can be seen from the following actions:

1. Request from the Bureau of Naval Personnel to all Training Activities to study their curricula in order to devise ways to employ visual media to the maximum extent.[12]

2. Request from the Chief of Naval Personnel to the Chiefs of the various bureaus for similar action, and for the appointment of training film liaison officers.[13]

3. Request from the Chief of Naval Personnel to Chief of Bureau of Ships for procurement of fifty-five hundred 16-mm motion picture projectors for delivery to Naval Training Activities.[14]

4. Request from the Chief of Naval Personnel to Commandants of the First, Fifth, Ninth, Eleventh, Twelfth, and Thirteenth Naval Districts for the establishment of Training Aids Libraries for service to the forces afloat and to the training activities of the districts concerned.[15]

5. Initiation of a program of audio-visual aids utilization to forces afloat.[16]

6. Organization by the Bureau of Naval Personnel of a Navy-wide program of audio-visual aids utilization, and assignment of a staff of officers to carry on the program.[17]

The survey created considerable interest in training films throughout navy training establishments and provided many officers with information on the proper methods of requesting the production of new films. Also, it gave a solid foundation of fact to the expanded film production program. Without question, the survey was one of the most important events in the Training Film Branch.[18]

Both the army and navy surveys led to the decentralization of film libraries and the establishment of central and sub-libraries at camps and bases. In turn, the creation of libraries highlighted the need for training aids officers. As training programs developed in both the army and the navy, training aids officers were secured to serve as coordinators of audio-visual materials. In special schools, the training aids officer cooperated with other staff administrators in developing specific objectives in each course.

Instructional Media Used in the Armed Forces

The instructional media used in armed services training programs during World War II included projected, graphic, sound, three-dimensional and "realistic" aids supplemented by manuals, guides, handbooks, bulletins, and other literature. Much of the printed material was aimed at the instructor. It was not to be used in the classroom itself nor was the textbook to be a substitute for lesson planning.

Graphics used included charts, graphs, posters, maps, cartoons, and schematic drawings. Graphic portfolios or "transvision" booklets illustrated a sequence of related equipment or processes. The United States Armed Forces Institute (USAFI) used a graphic chart kit—a set of colored charts used as instructional media—in twenty-three basic courses. Photography was used effectively by the navy to develop such graphic presentation sets as "Heaving a Line" (showing the actual heaving of a line in various stages), and its Self-Teaching Recognition Tests (juxtaposition of similar but distinguishable silhouettes for identification training).

Devices and demonstrations of various kinds were also used in the armed services. Synthetic trainers helped develop specific skills and discrimination. Some of these trainers achieved almost perfect simulation of the real situation. One type of Link trainer, for example, provided a cadet pilot with a moving view of the earth over which he was passing, accompanied by the realistic sound of aircraft engines. Mockups simulated many types of equipment operation. Also, various types of models and "breadboards" showed the operation and layout of equipment. A miniature model, for example, was functionally complete in showing a port installation. Other areas of combat operations were also realistically simulated. The Army Engineering Corps at Fort Elvis, Virginia, trained in a "tropic" building, where men working in high temperature in a high-humidity room were taught installation and maintenance of air-conditioning equipment. Many schools in various branches had exhibit rooms where displays of all types of equipment and some of the conditions of their use were shown by the use of sand tables. Models, mockups, breadboards, and other such devices became standard instructional equipment in military classrooms.[19]

Projected visual media of all types were used in military training programs during this period. Films and filmstrips were shown extensively. The *Catalog of Training Films for the Navy, Marine Corps, and Coast Guard* listed approximately nine thousand films available in 1945. The Army Air Force's *Training Film and Film Strip Catalog* listed several thousand films. The army film *Military Training* (TF7-295) was probably the best filmic expression of why, how, and what was taught by the army. Produced in 1941, it was used to disseminate the army's philosophy and methods of teaching. The navy later produced *Film Tactics* and *Methods of Teaching* for instructor training. In all these instructor training films, emphasis was upon teaching methods rather than content. Films varied from simple animations to highly technical expositions.

In some cases, slides were used for instruction. An unusual still projection device was the navy's visual aid projector. The visual aid projector, with transparencies and accessories, projected charts, drawings, photographs, and miniature models, with animation of the projected image by means of pointing, writing, or marking on the transparent plates of the device. "Vectograph" equipment provided three-dimensional presentations of photographs and drawings through the use of polaroid viewers. Stereoscopic illustration was also introduced through the use of stereographs in lantern slide projectors.

Many self-instructional devices and materials were also developed. Graphic aids and posters were displayed everywhere. Systematic programs created poster series on fire prevention, security, first aid, and venereal disease. Large-scale war maps were printed weekly by the thousands as a joint army-navy service for troops at home and abroad. Cartoon series — simple lessons illustrating the right and wrong ways of doing things — were often employed. A cartoon character called Little Dilbert was "engaged" by the navy to teach simple lessons. Cartoon characters such as Superman helped train illiterates to read and write. By 1944, the navy had developed a series of training aids through which a sailor might practice code, test himself on his knowledge of navy flags or his ability to recognize ships and aircraft, or check his prowess in free gunnery. Some of these devices were types of teaching machines whereby the individual could test himself as he developed a particular skill.

Auditory devices were used in several aspects of service training. The Morse code was taught with recordings and recorders. Disc recordings were used to teach air-traffic or communications procedures, to provide "cockpit checkouts" for pilots, and to test pilot or crew reactions in a variety of emergencies. Recordings were also effectively employed to simulate sounds of equipment, actual combat noises, and other sounds of military life.

Undoubtedly, the most important use of recordings during World War II was the teaching of foreign languages. This was, in effect, the beginning of the modern language laboratory. Language lessons were recorded on a series of records and provided with playback equipment and supplementary print materials. The army specialized training program known as area studies covered several foreign countries and offered an integrated study of the language, customs, geography, and culture of each for the enlightenment of prospective army officers. Primary stress was put on modern European languages, but oriental languages were also taught at particular schools. For example, Chinese was offered to army officers and enlisted men at the Chinese Language School of Yale University using dictation machines (sound scribers). The navy's oriental language program consisted of the entire first book of the Japanese course on approximately sixty-two recordings. Students were provided with playback equipment and tape recordings so they could play the records in their rooms and hear their own speech. The oriental language school at Boulder, Colorado, had its own radio station that broadcasted a half-hour program of news each evening, which students were required to hear and report on the following morning. Sound recordings were produced in forty languages in the navy language laboratories, together with accompanying texts containing the romanized transcriptions, and translations. These intensive language training programs provided the principal impetus for the development of language laboratories in the postwar years.[20]

Instructional Materials Produced in the
Armed Forces

Since there was a scarcity of adequate equipment and instructional materials in the early days of World War II, military schools and instructors improvised a number of training devices. As a result, there was little uniformity in army instructional materials until the Training Aids Division of the Army Ground Forces was established in September 1943. In each branch of the army, an officer was placed in charge of training devices, graphics, film library, and publications. Specialized training organizations included the Infantry School at Fort Benning, the Engineers School at Fort Belvoir, and the Ordnance School at the Aberdeen Proving Ground. Key schools, including those at Fort Lee, Fort Sill, and Fort Monmouth, developed specialized facilities and methods for their particular arm of the service and demonstrated training devices, graphics, films, and filmstrips. Hundreds of Army Air Force schools made their own contributions.

The navy had similar schools, among which the Great Lakes School at Great Lakes, Illinois, and the ordnance and fire control school at Anacostia, D.C., were especially important. The destroyer base at San Diego, California, under the command of Captain Byron McCandless, made the first extensive use of military instructional technology in the navy.

Out of the training aids centers emerged some production units. The Training Aids Division, located at various times in Washington, D.C., Orlando, Florida, and New York City, was the Army Air Force's main production agency. However, the actual production of standard training devices and films was accomplished by various Army Air Force agencies and commercial firms. Training equipment was designed by the Training Equipment Branch of the Engineering Division. Air force training films were first produced by the Signal Corps, but in 1942 a separate training-film production unit was established at Wright Field. Simultaneously, commercial film studios in Hollywood began to produce orientation, morale, and enlistment films for the Army Air Force. A Hollywood unit later took over the function of the training-film unit at Wright Field, and thereafter the Hollywood Eighteenth Base Unit and a New York Fifth Base Unit operated under the Army Air Force Headquarters Office of Motion Pictures. The central agency for the production of training materials in the navy was the Bureau of Aeronautics.

The Training Aids Development Center was established in New York City in 1942 by the Bureau of Naval Personnel. Three major departments were developed in this agency: an engineering department to produce mockups, models, and other three-dimensional aids; and engineering illustration department to produce technical charts and cross-sectional illustrations; and a graphics department to develop charts and posters.[21]

The production of complex navy training materials was the chief function of the Bureau of Aeronautics. A division of special devices developed a number of synthetic devices for training in the estimation of ranges, in airborne gunnery (both fixed and flexible), and in the recognition of friendly and enemy planes. For example, a pursuit trainer was designed, "with the fleeing enemy plane projected on a screen ahead, on which is also projected a background of clouds. As the pilot manipulates his controls, the objects on the screen rotate and move as they may be seen to do if he carried out the same maneuvers in actual flight."[22]

In another type of trainer produced by the Bell Laboratories for the Navy Special Devices Division, a fuselage with all standard equipment was provided, except that no one could "see out." The controls and indicators were all connected electronically to a control panel operated by an instructor. The general effect was that the bomber crew manned their plane, took off, maneuvered, cruised, patrolled, navigated, and eventually returned and landed; and in so doing they operated all equipment just as they would in actual flight.

The army's expanding program of photographic functions and operations within the Signal Corps brought about the establishment of the Army Pictorial Service in mid-1942. By late 1942, the Army Pictorial Service had formed the Photographic Equipment Branch to review requirements for various projection devices and other pictorial equipment. Signal

Corps projector specifications were practically nonexistent at that time, but with the establishment of the Pictorial Engineering and Research Laboratory (PEARL) in early 1943, the army standardization of projectors and other pictorial materials was begun. It was also the responsibility of the laboratory to investigate, design, and develop new types of photographic equipment. This was the nucleus of the Photographic Branch of Squire Signal Laboratory (SCEL), Fort Monmouth, New Jersey.

At the beginning of the war, the chief signal officer was assigned the responsibility for providing visual training aids, which included: the production and distribution of training films; combat photography for both military and historical purposes; maintaining the morale of troops by presenting theatrical motion pictures; and photographic laboratory development and research, as well as all aspects of ground and aerial photography. These responsibilities were discharged through three widely separated and inadequately housed facilities: the photographic laboratories at the Army War College in Washington and two training-film production laboratories, one at Fort Monmouth and the other at Wright Field. Each had a specialized function. The Signal Corps Photographic Laboratory at the Army War College was the still photography center; the Training Film Production Laboratory at Wright Field produced training films exclusively for the Army Air Force; photographic training was conducted formally at Fort Monmouth.

There had been a long debate over whether the Signal Corps should purchase the Paramount studio at Astoria, Long Island, which was on the market. For months, Colonel Melvin E. Gillette, commander of the Signal Corps Training Film Production Laboratory at Fort Monmouth, had urged the purchase of this studio because it would provide an up-to-date plant where all training-film production, processing, and distribution could be centered, leaving the Signal Corps Photographic Laboratory at Washington free to concentrate on still photography. In February 1942, the purchase of the Paramount studio was finally authorized and in May 1942, the modest Fort Monmouth Training Film Production Laboratory moved to Long Island. The courses in still photography were also transferred there and consolidated with the motion picture courses to form the Training Division of the new Signal Corps Photographic Center. Once established, the photographic center outgrew its quarters several times before the war ended.

The photographic center made a significant contribution to educational technology by establishing new techniques and uses for training films. Motion picture training at Astoria began with an eight-week course that was later lengthened to twelve and, finally, to seventeen weeks. Training was highly practical. A student was given a short period of instruction in the mechanical details of photographic equipment and then moved directly to producing a film. After learning story coverage, he made a series of phantom shots out-of-doors on a controlled problem, under close supervision. Then he was given a live film to shoot. The next phase of his training included the coverage of simple daily assignments around New York City, instruction on 16mm film and color film, and more complicated assignments in editing and working on press arrangements. Little theory or training literature was involved until late in the war. Throughout the learning period, particular attention was given to actual field conditions that might be encountered. Hasty fortifications were built after long marches over difficult terrain, overnight bivouacs trained students how to use and protect their equipment under adverse weather conditions, and practice shooting of films was done from moving vehicles.

The Signal Corps Photographic Center at Astoria, together with its Washington, D.C., Culver City, and Burbank, California, units made an impressive record in wartime training-film production. By July 1942, it had ten training-film units in the field, four teams making film bulletins, one team filming scenes for the Special Services Branch, and one making propaganda pictures for the Bureau of Public Relations. Selective Service provided first-class professional photographers, actors, scriptwriters, and laboratory technicians. As a result, training films produced by the Signal Corps Photographic Center became increasingly professional and effective.

The chief of staff, General George C. Marshall, was so enthusiastic about the films that he was eager to extend their use to include troop orientation. Early in 1942, Colonel Schlosberg of the Army Pictorial Service was asked to find a qualified person in the motion picture industry to direct a series of orientation films. Frank Capra agreed to undertake the work, and was commissioned as a major in the Signal Corps. By the end of April 1942, Hollywood writers under Capra's guidance had completed a series of scripts based on the Signal Corps Bureau of Public Relations lectures. In June 1942, a special unit of men drawn from the various technical fields began producing a series of orientation films entitled *Why We Fight*. Altogether, Capra produced seventeen excellent, highly successful feature films, at the rate of one about every two months, during the approximately three-year assignment.

Most of the difficulties that beset the army's training-film program occurred during the first eighteen months of the war. The demand for material was too great and too sudden. Also, recruits from the commercial field were new to army procedures and to the production of films as training aids. Instructors and educational advisors, on the other hand, knew the effectiveness of visual aids but were not familiar with the techniques needed to produce them effectively. Regular army officers knew what they wanted their men to know and to do, but they were not aware of the limitations and the capabilities of films. Nevertheless, a substantial production record was achieved. During the fiscal year 1943, approximately 135,000 16mm prints and 24,000 35mm prints were made available to film libraries in the United States and overseas. There were 200,000 bookings of forty-four subjects filmed for the Corps of Engineers alone. Some 655,600 still photographs were distributed for technical and publicity use. More than 16,000 16mm projectors were procured from several commercial manufacturers.[23]

During the war years, the United States Army Air Force produced more than four hundred training films and over six hundred filmstrips. Films were produced by the Army Air Force First Motion Picture Unit, Culver City, California. Filmstrips were developed in five filmstrip preparation units located in different sections of the country. In addition to films and filmstrips, a number of training devices were designed to teach perceptual motor skills—flying an aircraft, operating a radar set and interpreting scope presentations, firing at a rapidly moving target, and recognizing friendly and enemy aircraft. Also, films and filmstrips helped solve many new operational problems. For example, stereovision was used to interpret aerial photographs; high-speed photography was employed to slow down explosive action for study; and operational events were recorded on film.

The United States Coast Guard also produced a number of training films and filmstrips, as well as many other materials. Early in its training program, the coast guard discovered that the process could be considerably accelerated by (1) using integrated kits of motion pictures and discussional slide films; (2) correlating "show-how" filmstrips with "practice-how" training aids; (3) including class examinations with discussional filmstrips; and (4) packaging related films together.[24]

Distribution of Instructional Methods

At the beginning of the war, instructional materials were distributed directly from agencies in the War and Navy departments. However, it soon became obvious that central distribution was too inefficient to meet increasing demands. A survey made by the navy in September 1942, revealed that the distribution of films had increased from two thousand prints in January 1942, to approximately fifty thousand in August 1942. As a consequence, distribution was decentralized in both the navy and the army.

In the army, the old Visual Aids Section of the Signal Corps was abolished and a new section formed, the Film Distribution and Utilization Branch. Distribution agencies were established in the navy in both the Bureau of Aeronautics (later under the Chief of Naval Operations) and the Bureau of Naval Personnel, each of which submitted lists to the

Training Film Unit for initial distribution of films. The coast guard and the marine corps also made use of the Training Film Unit. The army, navy, and their aviation forces established film library systems in selected areas nearest to the classroom that needed them.[25]

Hoban's description of the distribution system of the armed services follows:

> It was characteristic of the film distribution systems of the various branches of the armed services that each was organized in a *network* which covered the entire country, and that this network was duplicated in each overseas theater where American troops or naval units were deployed. In the military and naval distribution systems there was for each, one central agency charged with supply of all films, equipment, and projectors. In each theater of operation, service command, or naval district, a similar agency gave direct service to installations within the command area, and on all large posts there was a local agency which supplied all military or naval units with film service. Thus, one central film supply agency served a Central Film Library in each theater, service command, or naval district, and these, in turn, served the film libraries of local posts, camps, or stations. The film library or training-aids section on the post served the local consumer — the instructor and the troops. Under this system, any training officer could obtain any film he needed through the service chain stemming out of one central agency of supply. In the case of the Army, this central supply agency was the Signal Corps Photographic Center, Long Island City, New York.[26]

Utilization of Instructional Materials

Cumulative data show that during some of the most intensive thirty-day training periods, more than 200,000 prints of 16mm training films — almost a quarter of a million projections — were shown to military personnel.

The success of the various training aids programs was largely due to the standardization of the curricula and the publicizing of the training materials available. The use of instructional media was tremendous. It has been estimated that over four million film showings were made before Army Ground and Service Force audiences in the continental United States from July 1, 1943, to June 30, 1945. Four surveys by the Utilization and Evaluation Section of the Training Aids Division, Bureau of Naval Personnel, indicated that graphics, devices, and films were widely used in training. However, these reports also emphasized the need for better planning of training so that preparation for films and follow-up discussions could take place. The last two surveys reported personal evaluations of films and filmstrips by instructors. These reports showed that navy schools made wide use of all types of instructional media, although not always with great effectiveness.

The four educational objectives of the United States Army in the use of motion pictures were summarized by Hoban as follows:

1. Orientation in the moral purposes for which the war was fought, the nature of our allies and our enemies, and the importance of the part played by various components of the Army.

2. Understanding of and habituation in self-control and proper conduct of the individual soldier.

3. Information on current material development and military progress on all fronts.

4. Instruction in basic technical subjects and skills.[27]

Among the many attempts to test the effectiveness of educational technology was a study by the United States Army Air Force of the filmstrip as an instructional medium. This revealed that:

1. A large percentage of training aids officers and instructors indicated confidence in filmstrips as a major aid in teaching.

2. Practically all instructors and training aids officers indicated a real desire to use filmstrips more extensively in training.

3. Instructors were making only a partial use of available strips, primarily because of improper practices in selection and integration of filmstrips into courses of instruction.

4. Instructors and training aids officers lacked training and experience in the use of visual aids and in teaching.

5. Techniques and practices in selection and integration of filmstrips into the curriculum fell short as judged by generally accepted practices and criteria.

6. The nonuse and/or disuse of filmstrips was caused primarily by shortcomings and defects in application of filmstrips to training problems.[28]

Other research demonstrated that a film may have definite effects on attitudes. One test group of soldiers saw the film *Battle for Britain*, while a second group did not. Among those who had not seen the film, only 46 percent believed that Britain would have been conquered had it not been for determined resistance, whereas 70 percent of those who had seen the film expressed such a belief. Still another study made by the Psychological Test Film Unit of the Army Air Force compared learning derived from (a) a training film, (b) studying a well-illustrated manual, and (c) an organized lecture using nineteen lantern slides. Both the superior and inferior portions of the film group did significantly better than the other two groups.

In 1945, the Training Aids Division of the Bureau of Naval Personnel surveyed instructors about 159 motion pictures and 45 filmstrips. The opinions of these instructors were summarized as follows:

1. Navy instructors think training films constitute an effective part of the training program.

2. Motion pictures are considered more valuable in training than filmstrips in the specific instructional units under consideration.

3. Training films are reasonably well adapted to the curriculum in which they are being used.

4. Films can be successfully used to present highly technical subjects in a clear and understandable manner.

5. Navy instructors believe that men learn more, remember longer, and show more interest in learning when training films are used than when more traditional methods are employed.

6. Films tend to standardize training, shorten training time, and make instruction more practical.

7. Instructors generally think the present length of training films is satisfactory, but more think they should be longer than think they should be shorter.

8. Instructors think that slightly more humor, drama, and combat scenes should be included in both films and filmstrips.[29]

Educational technology came of age during World War II. As Brooker said, "In the long run the period of World War II will mark the crossover from regarding films as an educational luxury to regarding them as a necessity."[30] Training devices became the major medium of instruction. When questioned about the lack of research concerning the effectiveness of training aids, officers usually gave lack of time and personnel as reasons and often stated that techniques known in educational technology prior to the war served to guide their efforts. For example, many officers reported that the Motion Picture Project of the ACE, completed just before the war, profoundly affected the navy program, both in terms of broad concepts of use and in providing experienced key personnel.[31]

Wartime Problems

A look at the armed services' war experiences, in retrospect, reveals a series of problems in bold relief. As film production increased, the services' production facilities across the country were used to capacity and serious bottlenecks developed. The consequent delays evoked the criticism that "it takes too long!" The lack of trained personnel also impeded production. There was a constant shortage of artists, writers, cutters, editors, photographers, and other specialists. The most serious consequence of inadequately trained personnel was the effect on the technical and educational quality of the films.

The army produced its own films in its own studios; the navy, on the other hand, had most of its work done on contract. However, both found that they had to resort to both methods for certain films.

There is a great deal of material in the files of the various armed services concerning their wartime training activities in relation to production, distribution, and utilization, but no detailed study has yet been made of this data. Regardless of this knowledge gap, Goldner's evaluation is clearly accurate:

> The armed services—Army, Army Air Force, Navy, Marine Corps, Coast Guard—all, made records that will stand. Their patterns of operation, their standards and criteria, and their personnel and facilities had to be developed rapidly to meet highly specialized needs of a pressing and varied nature and under conditions never before experienced. The training needs out of which the training film programs emerged, and which they were organized to meet, were greater in number, more complex, and more urgent than any that had been encountered in the history of the country.[32]

Implications for Educational Technology

The war effort brought the first significant convergence of the visual instruction tributary with the mainstream of educational technology. Also, as a result of the war experience, educators generally grew in sensitivity to scientific theories of learning being applied to practical problems of instruction. Moreover, the function and role of the media/communications specialist became more sophisticated within the total context of educational technology.

Notes

[1]Floyde E. Brooker, *Training Films for Industry*. U.S. Office of Education, Federal Security Agency, Bulletin 13, Washington, D.C.: GPO, 1946, 2.

[2]Ibid., 2-3.

[3]Ibid., 24.

[4]Ibid., 5.

[5]Ibid., 19.

[6]Ibid., 84.

[7]Ibid., 84.

[8]Ibid., 86-87.

[9]Charles F. Hoban, Jr., *Movies That Teach*. New York: Dryden Press, 1946, 21-22.

[10]U.S. Department, Office of the Chief Signal Officer, Special Activities Branch, "Training Films in the Second World War" (November 1944), Historical Division, War Department Special Staff, 106-8.

[11]See U.S. Navy Bureau of Aeronautics, *Audio-Visual Instruction Survey Report*, section 2. Unpublished report, 1942, 10-12.

[12]BuPers ltr. P-243-EK, S85-1/PII-1 (2350), dated December 2, 1942, to All Training Activities. Unpublished manuscript.

[13]BuPers ltr. P-243-EK, S85-1/PII-1 (992), dated December 1, 1942, to BuAer. Unpublished manuscript.

[14]BuPers ltr. P-243-JLG, S85-1/PII-1 (2372), prep. December 3, 1942, to BuAer. Unpublished manuscript.

[15]BuPers ltr. P-243-ED, P/II-2/ND5 (24), dated December 3, 1942, to Commandant, Fifth N.D. Unpublished manuscript.

[16]BuPers ltr. P-243-EK, prep. December 2, 1942, to Cominch. Unpublished manuscript.

[17]Ibid.

[18]Ibid. *Audio-Visual Instruction Survey Report*, 8.

[19]Breadboards clarified mechanical operations and theories. Instruction on electrical equipment frequently employed breadboards. The circuits of a particular service radio might be laid out, part by part, on one large board. Circuits could be traced, the function of each part discussed, and the results of Thompson and D. R. Harris, *The Signal Corps: The Outcome*, Washington, D.C.: GPO.

failure of parts demonstrated. The combined use of graphics, models, mockups, breadboards, and films was common in mobile training units in the army and the navy.

[20]Recordings were also used to cover the full scope of a teaching unit, in the selection and testing of personnel, for practice drills, for explanations and demonstrations, and for creating vicarious experiences in dramatic form.

[21]The War Services Program of the Works Progress Administration, a development of the WPA Federal Art Project, had offered its help to the armed services. However, the training materials produced were not given wide application. It became obvious that the design and development of training aids by this organization could make an important contribution if there were a wider distribution of materials. To accomplish this, the navy requested the WPA's cooperation on a national scale, in making known all training aids previously developed and undertaking the development of specific aids for the Bureau of Naval Personnel. See William Exton, Jr., *Audiovisual Aids to Instruction*. New York: McGraw-Hill, 1947, 18-19.

[22]Ibid., 321.

[23]For a complete history of the United States Signal Corps Photographic Center training-film activities during World War II, see George R. Thomspon et al., *The Signal Corps: The Test*. Department of the Army, Office of the Chief of Military History. Washington, D.C.: GPO, 1957. See also George R. Thompson and D. R. Harris, *The Signal Corps: The Outcome*.

[24]Exton, *Audiovisual Aids to Instruction*, 82-88.

[25]The Educational Film Library Association (EFLA) was formed in Chicago, March 17-18, 1943, for the purpose of reviewing the arrangements established by government agencies for the free distribution of their films. It was recognized by all present that unless educational institutions and agencies were given an opportunity to qualify as depositories, they would not be able to meet requests for government war films from school and adult groups. The first officers of EFLA were: L. C. Larson, chairman; Bruce A. Findlay, vice-chairman; and R. Russell Munn, secretary. Donald Slesinger, then director of the American Film Center, served as acting administrative director. EFLA provided the impetus for the organization of the Sixteen Millimeter Advisory Committee, formed in November 1943 to protect the interests of educators.

[26]Hoban, *Movies That Teach*, 111-12.

[27]Ibid., 22-23.

[28]John R. Miles and Charles R. Spain, *Audio-Visual Aids in the Armed Services*. Washington, D.C.: ACE, 1947, 63.

[29]Ibid., 73-74.

[30]Floyde E. Brooker, "Communication in the Modern World," *Audio-Visual Materials of Instruction*, Part I, 48th yearbook of the National Society for the Study of Education. Chicago: University of Chicago Press, 1949, 17.

[31]See chapter 8 of this history for a discussion of the Motion Picture Project.

[32]Orville Goldner, "Films in the Armed Services," in Godfrey M. Elliott, ed., *Film and Education*. New York: Philosophical Library, 1948, 395.

Select Bibliography

Brooker, Floyde E. *Training Films for Industry*. U.S. Office of Education, Federal Security Agency, Bulletin 13. Washington, D.C.: GPO, 1946.

Business Screen. *A Report on the Training Film Program of the United States Navy*, vol. 6, no. 5 (June 1945): 18-120; and *A Report on Activities of Army Pictorial Service, Signal Corps*, vol. 7, no. 1 (January 1946): 15-97. Chicago: Business Screen Magazines, Inc.

Exton, William, Jr. *Audiovisual Aids to Instruction.* New York: McGraw-Hill, 1947.

Flynt, Ralph C. M. "Use of Training Aids by Army and Navy." *Higher Education* vol. 2 (September 1945): 1-3.

Gibson, James J., ed. *Motion Picture Testing and Research.* AAF Aviation Psychology Program Research Report no. 7. Washington, D.C.: GPO, 1947.

Hoban, Charles F., Jr. *Movies That Teach.* New York: Dryden Press, 1946.

Miles, John R., and Charles R. Spain. *Audio-Visual Aids in the Armed Services.* Washington, D.C.: ACE, 1947.

Thompson, George R., and D. R. Harris. *The Signal Corps: The Outcome.* Washington, D.C.: GPO, 1966.

Thompson, George R., et al. *The Signal Corps: The Test.* Department of the Army, Office of the Chief of Military History. Washington, D.C.: GPO, 1957.

7

Emergence of Educational Radio: 1921–1950

Another tradition of educational technology has been the use of radio as an educational instructional tool. Although experiments in educational broadcasting began in the mid-1920s, there is still little empirical data concerning effective instructional use of radio.

The growth of educational radio occurred primarily from 1925 to 1935. During this period formal courses in radio education were established at colleges and universities; professional conferences, institutes, and organizations concerned with radio education were formed; systematic radio research projects were launched; and the U.S. Office of Education organized a radio section designed to meet the growing professional needs of radio education.

By the late 1930s, the growth period of radio education had already begun to decline. With the advent of World War II, professional activity in educational radio came to a standstill and has failed to appreciably revive. Today it is easier to find a television set than a radio receiver in most schools. Very few authentic "schools of the air" still exist, and even school systems that operate their own radio station often fail to use it properly or integrate its programming with the school curriculum.

Early Schools of the Air

A number of public school systems pioneered in extensive instructional use of radio. This was especially true in the cities of Cleveland, Chicago, Detroit, Portland, Des Moines, Buffalo, and Rochester. For example, in Rochester, a rather unique arrangement correlated public school curriculum with the schedules of the Rochester Civic Music Association, the Rochester Public Library, and the Rochester Museum of Arts and Sciences.

In the early years of radio many institutions of higher learning set up their own stations and established schools of the air. Notable schools of the air were founded at the universities of Wisconsin, Kansas, Michigan, and Minnesota, and at Oregon State College. These first years of university broadcasting were generally ineffective because many a professor repeated his classroom lecture before the microphone without realizing that a good lecturer was not necessarily an effective broadcaster. Moreover, they did not realize that radio technique was not easy to master and that much research and experimentation would be needed before radio could be used as an effective medium of instruction.

The Ohio School of the Air:
A Case Study

The Ohio School of the Air was organized under what appeared to be the most favorable conditions. Financial support was provided by the state, and cooperation and aid were received from the Payne Fund (see chapter 8), Ohio State University, Station WLW of Cincinnati, and numerous civic-minded people. Despite this auspicious beginning, however, the Ohio School of the Air was disbanded less than one decade after it had been established.

The story of the origin of the Ohio School of the Air can best be told in the words of Ben H. Darrow, its founder:

> After varied and interesting experiences in country life institute work, and with the agricultural extension of Maryland State College, I found myself in 1924 in charge of children's programs at Station WLS, Chicago. I became intensely interested in educational broadcasting then, but left WLS to promote a patent....
>
> More and more there grew upon me the idea of a National School of the Air. I was convinced that the radio might become a tremendous agency for public-school education. The idea presupposed three big "ifs." IF educators could be induced officially to sponsor the project. IF a radio station might be persuaded to broadcast educational programs free of charge, and IF financial support could be secured to pay the cost of administration, a school of the air could be established.
>
> From one end of the country to the other I traveled, speaking to enlist the aid of organizations and individuals to help me put my idea across. Finally, late in 1927, the Payne Study and Experiment Fund of New York became sufficiently interested to put me on its staff to investigate and develop the possibilities of broadcasting for schools on a national scale, under the guidance of organized educational authorities.[1]

In October 1928, the Payne Fund offered Darrow financial assistance to establish a school of the air if he could obtain official educational sponsorship. Darrow approached J. L. Clifton, superintendent of public instruction for the state of Ohio, and received his support. Prior to this, Darrow had secured radio facilities on WAIU, Columbus, Ohio. However, when the time for broadcasting came, the WAIU transmitter was destroyed by fire. WTAM, Cleveland, agreed to provide broadcast time but would not pay the telephone-line charges from Columbus to Cleveland. Darrow's problem was finally solved when free use of WLW, Cincinnati, was offered. This acquisition not only assured satisfactory reception for the school broadcasts but also extended the broadcast range from Canada to the Gulf states and from the Atlantic Ocean to the western plains.

Darrow now began to consider the program content of his broadcasts.

> During November and December (1928) many feverish days and nights were spent in determining the curriculum, listing and enlisting radio teachers, determining the number of broadcasts and the length of each feature, providing for shifting of classes, the time of day, the formation of the first draft of the program, the choice of theme and signature for the hour, the issuance of lesson leaflets, the writing of press releases, the gathering of lesson materials, preparation of manuscripts, and finally, the rehearsals for the first broadcast.[2]

The Ohio School of the Air finally made its debut on January 7, 1929, with this weekly broadcast schedule:

Weekly Schedule

Monday: Story plays and rhythmics and health talks,
                alternating.
             Current events.
             History dramalogs.

Tuesday: Special features, question and answer periods.
             Art appreciation.
             Civil government, by those who govern.

Wednesday: Stories for younger pupils.
             Stories for intermediate grades.
             Stories for upper grades.

Thursday: Dramatization of literature for high schools.
             Geography.

Friday: No program in deference to the Damrosch lessons
             in music.[3]

This schedule was flexible enough to include outstanding public events. On January 14, 1929, for instance, the Ohio gubernatorial inauguration ceremonies were broadcasted followed on March 4, 1929, by a broadcast of the presidential inauguration. This first year of the Ohio School of the Air also featured broadcasts of the Ohio Senate and House sessions.

In spite of these achievements, Darrow did not carry out one part of his experiment: No adequate provision was made for lesson leaflets during the first months. However, some advance programs and mimeographed lesson materials entitled *Guide Book to the Radio Journeys of the School of the Air* were sent to schools.

The first year of this school of the air proved to Darrow "that schools, colleges, libraries, magazines, schools of drama, theaters, and the radio stations could furnish broadcasting teachers of worth—that schools could and would equip to hear the broadcasts—that teachers and pupils received added benefits from the introduction of radio."[4]

The second year allowed more time to prepare lessons with an expanded staff. Cline M. Koon was made assistant director, Gwendolyn Jenkins became the dramatic coach, and Ruth Carter made contacts with listeners. A teachers' manual called the *Ohio School of the Air Courier* was prepared and issued monthly to teachers using the broadcasts.

One of the many notable events in the history of the Ohio School of the Air occurred on January 19, 1931, when a temporary studio was established in the NEA headquarters in Washington, D.C. As a result, a whole series of outstanding educational programs were produced.

Other accomplishments from 1929 to 1931 were:

The staff had become more nearly adequate. The lesson materials had reached schools on time—nearly ten thousand copies of a 266-page *Courier*.

The audience had grown several fold and was still growing ... research had functioned.

The first broadcasts ever made from the NEA Headquarters had presented, for the first time by radio, a President's Cabinet as speakers. A series of Living

Writers and Adventurers had set a new high in classroom appeal. The first Radio Institute (statewide) and the first National Radio Institute had been held. The first Parent-Teachers meetings had been held by radio. It had been a golden age— but what was to come?[5]

The answer soon became evident. In January 1931, the Ohio legislature reduced funding for the Ohio School of the Air so far that it seemed impossible to continue. But by selling radio lesson plans, renting (instead of buying) scripts, discontinuing the rental of telephone lines, and aided by a small grant from the National Committee on Education by Radio, the Ohio School of the Air managed to survive until 1937 when legislative funding ended.[6]

Despite its discontinuance, the Ohio School of the Air made three significant contributions to educational technology: It provided a model and impetus for similar schools of the air; it demonstrated that radio could be an effective instructional technique; and it produced a wealth of research data concerning radio instruction.

RCA Educational Hour

One of the first national schools of the air began on October 26, 1928, sponsored by the National Broadcasting Company (NBC).[7]

Forty-eight half-hour music appreciation lessons were arranged for four grade groups ranging from third to twelfth. Walter Damrosch, conductor of the New York Symphony Orchestra, organized these lessons, assisted by eminent music educators. A seventy-page *Teacher's Manual*, containing a schedule of broadcasts for the school year, was sent free to all teachers using the broadcasts. The manual also contained a list of guide questions for each lesson as well as lists of available phonograph records of musical selections to be played. A symphony orchestra demonstrated the lessons as they were taught, to supplement rather than supplant local instruction in music appreciation.

This was the most ambitious music education program ever undertaken. Widespread publicity, the finest broadcasting facilities available, and one of the country's greatest musical organizations combined to make the effort unsurpassed in educational broadcasting. The program produced an overwhelming response from listeners. More than fifty thousand letters were received the first year, and polls indicated an audience of more than three million.

The RCA Educational Hour continued until Damrosch retired in 1942. As nothing before, these broadcasts showed the value of a national school of the air and awakened many educators to the potential of radio.

The American School of the Air

The second national school of the air was launched over the Columbia Broadcasting System (CBS) on February 4, 1930. A year previously, CBS had announced that it would proceed with educational broadcasts as soon as it had received the report of the Advisory Committee on Education by Radio. In the meantime, the Griggsby-Grunow Company of Chicago decided to sponsor such a series and employed Ray Erlandson, a former school principal and educational director of the NEA. Erlandson, with program men of CBS, planned a series to be broadcast Tuesday and Thursday afternoons to the intermediate and junior high school grades. Alice Keith, formerly of the Cleveland schools, was appointed broadcasting director. Furthermore, Miss Keith organized an advisory faculty headed by William C. Bagley of Teachers College, Columbia University, and an advisory committee consisting of such people as Secretary of the Interior Ray Lyman Wilbur, Commissioner of Education William J. Cooper, Frank Cody, Willis Sutton, Angelo Patri, and twenty-nine others.

The American School of the Air continued under commercial sponsorship until May 1930. In the fall of 1930, CBS took over the program until it was terminated in 1940.[8]

The World Radio University

The idea for an international school of the air was first conceived by Walter Lemmon, a young radio engineer, when he was assigned to Woodrow Wilson's peace ship, the *George Washington*. He had been impressed by the lack of communication between delegates during their tedious peace conversations, and realized that something would have to be done if people of contrasting cultures were to be brought together in mutual understanding.

In 1935, Lemmon built an experimental 20,000-watt shortwave transmitter on the South Shore near Boston, Massachusetts. This station, known as W1XAL, began to broadcast a series of radio courses in literature, music, economics, languages, aviation, astronomy, and electronics in 1937, in cooperation with the Massachusetts Institute of Technology, Mount Holyoke College, Boston University, Harvard University, Brown University, Tufts College, and Wellesley College. In 1938, a basic English course was beamed to Latin American countries, and by the following year the World Radio University was speaking directly to thirty-one countries in twenty-four languages.[9]

By 1939, the call letters were changed from W1XAL to WRUL. With the arrival of World War II, broadcasting increased considerably. When children were transported to the United States from their bombed homes in England, they were brought to the microphone so that they might speak to their parents. The *Christian Science Monitor* prepared a daily news broadcast especially for people in occupied areas. College professors gave suggestions on how to live on limited diets and how to repair failing radio sets. By 1942, letters to the station smuggled out of occupied countries were being received at the rate of 20,000 per year.

After the war, WRUL reestablished its extensive educational broadcasting. In 1948, WRUL opened a new station in Washington, D.C., so that international broadcasting might proceed directly from the nation's capital. Over the years, this short-wave station has demonstrated the broad possibilities of international educational broadcasting.

Educational Stations

Educational stations were the real pioneers of radio education. Ohio State University began to broadcast weather reports and other information as early as 1912; the University of Wisconsin station began broadcasting in 1916; and the State University of Iowa began operating its station in 1919. These early stations were not "educational stations" in the true sense, but were actually experimental stations built by electrical engineering or physics departments.

First Educational Stations

The radio division of the U.S. Department of Commerce began licensing both commercial and educational stations in 1921. The first educational license was issued to the Latter Day Saints' University of Salt Lake City, Utah, on an unlisted day and month in 1921.[10] On January 13, 1922, two more educational broadcast licenses were issued — to the University of Wisconsin and the University of Minnesota.[11] Shortly after, a number of other educational institutions applied for and received licenses.

Programming of these early educational stations reflected the pedantry of the typical classroom. White said: "To a student of educational radio, prowling through yellowed scripts, it seems almost incredible that teachers who presumably hoped to reach men's minds elected to attempt it with anesthetics. Surely, secrets of audience psychology readily mastered by semi-literate movie stars and dance-band leaders are not hidden from the academicians."[12]

Microphones were set up in classrooms in order to pick up a lecture as a professor gave it. Extension divisions conducted radio courses, but these too often lacked mass appeal. Aside from the dull educational programs, there undoubtedly were many that gained more widespread interest. Campus bands, orchestras, and dramatic productions were also presented on the college and university stations.

Some administrators believed that individuals who listened to educational programs on the campus station would be motivated to enroll in courses. Others saw the station as an excellent publicity tool. Generally, very few saw any great potential in radio education. Most of the administrators, as well as many faculty members, were not overly enthusiastic about radio; many others were indifferent and even antagonistic. A vivid example was given by Levering Tyson. While doing extension work at Columbia University, Tyson read one morning the story of the KDKA broadcast of the Harding-Cox election returns. So overwhelmed was he with the idea that this new medium would be ideal for his work in extension education that he immediately wanted to use it.

> I did not even finish my bacon and eggs that morning but hurried over to the University. At five minutes after nine I walked into President Butler's anteroom. Of course he was not there, but I waited and at a quarter to eleven he walked in. I told him what I had read, and my enthusiasm had not been dimmed at all by my long wait. In effect he said, "Tyson, don't bother about that. There are gadgets turning up every week in this country, and this won't amount to anything." I argued but did not get to first base, and I finally left his office downcast.[13]

Tyson's story illustrates the indifference and even condescension of many educators toward radio in its early days. Conceptions of radio as a plaything that had little or no relevance to instruction were commonplace. Despite these prevailing attitudes, a few persuasive educators believed radio could be an effective instructional tool. If these educators had not insisted on their point of view, educational technology might have lost the educational radio station.

Federal Regulation and Educational Broadcasting

In response to the expanding uses of radio, Herbert Hoover—then secretary of commerce—called four historic Hoover Conferences to discuss the problems of the control and support of American radio. In the fourth and last conference, held in Washington in November 1925, Hoover voiced a decision that would determine the future of radio broadcasting in the United States:

> The decision that we should not imitate some of our foreign colleagues with governmentally controlled broadcasting supported by a tax upon the listener has secured for us a far greater variety of programs and excellence in service free of cost to the listener. This decision has avoided the pitfalls of political, religious, and social conflicts in the use of free speech in this medium.[14]

Educator Levering Tyson, who attended this conference, stated that "we in America decided then that we were going to have a commercialized radio."[15] If Secretary Hoover and the attendees of the four national conferences were generally convinced that the surest way to retain freedom of the air was through commercial radio, their stand directly affected the development of educational broadcasting. Educational stations simply could not compete financially or maintain the same production standards. This may have been when the United States sold its cultural birthright.

A large measure of blame for the existing system of American broadcasting can undoubtedly be attributed to the Federal Radio Commission. This regulatory agency (created in 1927), by repeatedly ostracizing educational stations, made it technically possible for an increase in the number and power of commercial stations. Frequently, the commission rationalized its preference by contending that educational stations produced inferior programs. Ironically, this criterion was never applied to commercial stations. It soon became apparent that either a sweeping reorganization was needed within the commission itself or a new regulatory agency was needed that would be efficient and just.

In July 1934, acting on the recommendation of President Franklin Roosevelt, Congress passed the Communications Act, which assigned the following specific task to the re-created commission:

> The Commission shall study the proposal that Congress by statute allocate fixed percentages of radio broadcasting facilities to particular types or kinds of nonprofit radio programs, or to persons identified with particular types or kinds of nonprofit activities, and shall report to Congress, not later than February 1, 1935, its recommendations altogether with its reasons for the same.[16]

As the hearings got underway, it was clear that the battle between commercial broadcasters and educators was about to be restaged. It also became obvious that advocates of a definite allocation of frequencies for education as well as some government control had not convinced the Federal Communications Commission (FCC) of their case. This was partly because the group was divided. The moderate faction, represented by the National Advisory Council on Radio in Education, urged working with existing commercial facilities because they felt that education was not yet prepared to use additional facilities. This view was also taken by the U.S. Office of Education. At the other end of the spectrum was an extreme fringe of educators who advocated taxing commercial stations to fund the construction of a chain of government- and state-owned stations and also advocated control of commercial program content.

The commercial broadcasters, on the other hand, were united. They countered educators' accusations by indicating a complete willingness to cooperate. The networks maintained that allocating frequencies for educational broadcasting would only disrupt a successful system of broadcasting that had just begun to function well. One pointed argument was that the educators themselves could not agree as to what type of broadcasting system was desirable. Finally, the commercial broadcasters pleaded for cooperation from educators.

The educators had clearly failed to make a united case. As a result, the FCC recommended to Congress that the existing system be continued. It also proposed a national conference to make plans for cooperative efforts by educators and commercial broadcasters.

White made an excellent analysis of the government's role in educational broadcasting:

> The Federal Communications Commission found itself caught in the spiral of precedent: in the beginning the commercial people had got the best frequencies, the most power; ever since, when a noncommercial station had applied for a share of favors thus pre-empted, the pre-emptors could cite not only the law of possession but also the inevitable fact that they "served a wider area." Having for so long tolerated the situation, the educators discovered belatedly that the Federal Communications Commission was bound to accept them at their own estimate....
>
> The Commission sought to cover its sins of omission by reporting to the Congress that "it would appear that the interests of the nonprofit organizations

may be better served by the use of existing facilities." Pontius Pilate could not have done better.

As a palliative to the death sentence they thus passed on the educators, the Federal Communications Commission added that "it is our firm intention to assist the nonprofit organizations to obtain the fullest opportunities for expression." Not until 1945, when it set aside twenty FM channels for educational broadcasting, did the Federal Communications Commission lift more than an occasional hesitant finger to implement that pledge.[17]

Decline of Educational Stations

Educational stations had hardly completed their first burst of growth before their decline began. The advent of stringent federal regulation, the rise of national commercial networks, and their use of inexperienced faculties were the chief factors promoting their failure.

Some educational stations made an attempt to develop creative instructional programming, but these efforts were rare. Other educators tried to get their institutions to finance formal radio courses of instruction; some even went so far as to suggest college credits for courses; but these men were labeled by many of their colleagues as "radicals" or "fanatics."[18]

The cause or causes of the decline of educational stations is a subject of considerable controversy. An extensive analysis by Frost revealed some thirty-nine causes underlying the loss of educational licenses.[19] The majority were ostensibly lost because of financial reasons. Some educators complained that the licensing authority was antagonistic or that commercial interests attempted to eliminate them, but Frost's study gave little credence to these accusations. However, there is another consideration, commonly overlooked in studies of causal factors. Financial failure may have been only a partial cause. Since the licensing authority had accepted the philosophy of commercial radio, no place was left for educational stations, which had to withdraw when costly commercial standards were applied to their operations. Regardless of the explanations offered, it is clear that educators were generally apathetic toward educational broadcasting.

FM Channels for Educational Broadcasting

The FCC first allocated a portion of the FM band for educational stations in 1938. In 1941, the FCC again reserved educational channels, this time on the FM band between 42 and 43 megacycles. The third allocation of educational channels came in 1945 when the FCC changed the FM band. Throughout this period commercial radio was complacent: the off-the-band AM frequencies were commercially worthless; the short-lived FM change could not be stopped; and finally the opening of one hundred FM channels created more space than commercial interests could occupy.

The first educational FM station (WBOE) was established by the Cleveland Public Schools in 1938, but World War II forced a freeze on FM before significant educational broadcasting could develop. The assignment of channels for educational broadcasting in 1945 stimulated the interest of educators, and by December of that year more than forty institutions had applied for an educational FM station. In order to encourage educators to take advantage of educational channels, the FCC made it possible (in 1948) to build low-power ten-watt stations.

A number of states developed plans for educational FM networks, but most did not materialize. The states of Indiana, Minnesota, Texas, Wisconsin, and New York have succeeded in developing comprehensive educational FM networks. The Empire State FM School of the Air (formed in 1949) comprises the world's largest educational FM network. However, the "usual result has been a spark of interest, a meeting of a few interested school men, a map showing possible station locations, and then general apathy."[20]

Preliminary Committee on Educational Broadcasting

The Preliminary Committee on Educational Broadcasting was among the first of many organizations that were established to meet the need of (1) clarifying objectives; (2) exchanging relevant information; and (3) fortifying and ensuring the progress of instructional radio. Its organization was largely due to Ben H. Darrow's efforts to convince educators of the need for a national school of the air.

The Preliminary Committee on Educational Broadcasting was first forced to investigate the feasibility of a national school of the air, at the NEA Department of Superintendence meeting in Boston in 1927. The results of a survey (sponsored by the Payne Fund) made by the committee were announced in spring of 1928. The majority of respondents indicated that they wanted a national school of the air.[21]

Advisory Committee on Education by Radio

In May 1929, the Preliminary Committee on Educational Broadcasting requested that Secretary of the Interior Ray Lyman Wilbur appoint a committee to investigate instructional radio. Accordingly, he convened the so-called Wilbur Conference on May 24, 1929, in Washington, D.C. The first meeting was an emotionally charged discussion reflecting the fear of commercial domination. The educators felt they should control educational broadcasting, but conceded that little was known about instructional radio. It was decided that a survey should be taken and that Secretary Wilbur should appoint a committee composed of educators and commercial broadcasters, as well as other interested persons.[22] On June 6, 1929, Wilbur appointed the Advisory Committee on Education by Radio; supporting grants came from the Payne Fund and the Carnegie Corporation.

The advisory committee completed its task in four meetings. The first meeting was held in Chicago, June 13, 1929, under the chairmanship of U.S. Commissioner of Education William J. Cooper. The second was held October 18 at Pittsburgh, Pennsylvania; and the third and fourth, on November 6 and December 30 in Washington, D.C.

The first complete report of the survey results was submitted at the final meeting. H. R. Shipherd of the fact-finding subcommittee made a forty-seven-page report that immediately drew the ire of the commercial broadcasters. His most controversial recommendation was that a National University for National Radio Education be established. Shipherd was followed by Armstrong Perry (1930), also of the fact-finding subcommittee, who stressed three points:

(1) That educators interested in educational broadcasting have come to a realization that the key to the situation lies with those who have facilities to broadcast; (2) That this makes the control of radio channels the most important problem of the many which this new institution brings to the front; (3) That educators, as a result, generally feel that some air channels should be reserved exclusively for educational purposes.[23]

Both Shipherd and Perry plainly indicated that the activity of both the commercial stations and the FCC did not provide sufficiently for educational broadcasting. Perry expressed the opinion

> that the educators of the country must either arrive at a consensus of opinion, formulate a plan of action and secure the assistance of the Federal Government, or see the broadcasting facilities of the country come so firmly under the control of commercial groups that education by radio would be directed by business men instead of by professional educators.[24]

Shipherd summarized the lack of cooperation between educators and commercial broadcasters.

> General lack of co-operation between the two groups appears: as in (a) widespread distrust among educators of commercial motives and "propaganda"; (b) the belief among educational stations that they are given the inferior positions on the broadcasting spectrum and in the allocation of hours; (c) the tendency among commercial stations to reduce educational programs to shorter and poorer periods as their time becomes more salable; (d) the practice among the commercial stations of offering educational programs to cultivate general good will and create publicity, rather than to build up a sound educational method and research with the help and guidance of educational experts.[25]

The representatives of the commercial networks obviously did not share these views, although they appeared willing to accord education a more distinguished role. Warren H. Pierce, educational director of CBS, stated that the broadcasting companies were "willing to give ample time for educational programs and would attempt to exercise no censorship whatever."[26] John Elwood, vice-president of NBC, concurred, saying that "both companies had been giving much time to educational subjects and that one of the companies estimated that approximately 22 percent of its time on the air is now given over to programs of an educational nature."[27]

The most significant result of the advisory committee's work was the series of recommendations that came out of the fact-finding subcommittee survey. These recommendations, in part, were as follows:

1. That there be established in the Office of Education, Department of the Interior, a section devoted to education by radio....

2. That the funds necessary for financing such a section in the Office of Education be provided in the regular budget for the Department of the Interior.

3. That there be set up in connection with this unit an Advisory Committee representing educational institutions, commercial broadcasters, and the general public.

4. That an effort be made to secure from interested persons or foundations an amount of money sufficient to bring to the microphone, for a period of two to three years, a high grade program in certain formal school subjects and to check carefully the results obtained.

5. That the Secretary bring to the attention of the Federal Radio Commission the importance of the educational interests in broadcasting.[28]

When funding was exhausted in 1930, the advisory committee disbanded. Meanwhile, an atmosphere of distrust still existed between educators and commercial broadcasters, which became evident when the two major commercial networks (NBC and CBS) openly opposed the recommendations of the fact-finding subcommittee.

And there was a growing rift among the educators themselves. One group had worked with the networks in developing educational programs and believed that the needs of education would be best served by not disturbing the status quo. Another group felt that, unless remedial legislation was secured, the educators would be driven from the field by commercial broadcasters. Some commercial stations had been granted the use of wavelengths previously assigned to educational stations; it appeared to many educators that such gradual encroachment would eventually eliminate the educator from radio. The schism led ultimately to the establishment of the National Advisory Council on Radio in Education, representing the first group, and the National Committee on Education by Radio, representing the latter group.

National Advisory Council on Radio in Education (NACRE)

This council grew out of an idea advanced by the American Association for Adult Education (AAAE) soon after the passage of the Radio Act of 1927, but nothing was done to promote it until the presidential campaign of 1928 had concluded. It appeared that Herbert Hoover, the new president, and Ray Lyman Wilbur, his secretary of the interior, were both favorably disposed toward the proposals for radio education being advanced by the AAAE. William J. Cooper, commissioner of education, also joined in the early discussions.

Wilbur appointed a committee to investigate how radio affected education, and the Carnegie Corporation agreed to underwrite a survey of instructional broadcasting by the AAAE. In its effort to bring together top people, the Carnegie staff enlisted the interest and support of the Rockefeller Foundation, as well as such leaders in commercial radio as Owen D. Young, the acting chief of the General Electric Company and a member of the board of NBC. The federal government was then approached through General Saltzman, chairman of the Federal Radio Commission (now the FCC).

These groups agreed to create an experimental organization that combined the interests of the government, commercial broadcasters, educational agencies, and prominent citizens interested in educational broadcasting. The National Advisory Council on Radio in Education (NACRE) was composed of forty members and began to function on July 1, 1930. Operating funds for a three-year period were granted by the Rockefeller and Carnegie foundations.

The goals of the council were to further the "development of the art of radio broadcasting in American education" and to make an "analysis of the problems faced by those in the educational world, or in the broadcasting industry, or elsewhere, who are engaged in or are sympathetic to educational broadcasting." The council also undertook "to assemble and interpret the content of broadcast programs and information concerning the practices and experience of broadcasting stations in conducting or developing educational features as part of such programs" and "to stimulate and suggest problems and projects for research or experiment with a view to increasing the effectiveness of broadcasting in education." Another objective of the council was publishing "the opportunities for education in the utilization of broadcasting as such opportunities are discovered." In summary, the council would make every effort "to mobilize the best educational thought of the country to devise, develop and present suitable programs, to be brought into fruitful contact with the most appropriate facilities."[29]

Commercialism and Radio Education

The council had hardly gotten underway before a major split occurred in the radio educator ranks. Commissioner of Education Cooper sponsored a new organization with an entirely different policy, the National Committee on Education by Radio (NCER), which is discussed more fully in the next section of this chapter. Briefly, the NCER, intent on changing the American system of broadcasting to more closely resemble the British system, proposed that 15 percent of the total broadcasting frequencies be set aside for educational service. This antagonized commercial broadcasters, who hastened to fight the proposal, as described by Tyson:

> The upshot was that industry people as a whole were forced to take the attitude, "well if these people are asking for a fight, we will give it to them." Of course, the result was foreordained. The allocation of channels was never made and from that point on, the commercial boys rode high, wide, and handsome. We have now reaped the result, what with singing commercials and all the other obnoxious features which detract from the real job that, in my opinion, radio broadcasting might have accomplished.[30]

The booklet *Four Years of Network Broadcasting* contains a thorough indictment of commercial broadcasters in regard to their treatment of educational broadcasters. This minority report by the members of the NACRE's Committee on Civic Education by Radio is the most complete actual case history of the conflict between educational and commercial broadcasting. Their report described

> a conflict between the commercial interests of the National Broadcasting Company and the educational uses of the radio which threatens to become almost fatal to the latter. Educational broadcasting has become the poor relation of commercial broadcasting, and the pauperization of the latter has increased in direct proportion to the growing affluence of the former.
>
> It is well to remember at this time that the Federal Radio Act of 1927 required that broadcasting be conducted in the public interest, convenience, and necessity. Also, it might be recalled that NBC was formed originally without any idea that its operations were to show a profit, but to present a well-rounded program service to the American public.[31]

With their objective of establishing a cooperative working relationship with commercial broadcasters thus shattered by the NCER, the NACRE turned to other activities such as experimentation, demonstration, research, and conferences. An extensive library was created and monographs were published covering every aspect of radio instruction. Annual assemblies were held to provide a meeting ground for all those interested in educational broadcasting.[32]

The most notable work of the NACRE was its series of educational broadcasts on the radio networks of NBC. These broadcasts established a pattern for outstanding educational broadcasting, and included programs in the fields of history, government, law, art, medicine, economics, and labor. However, the programs were mostly like lectures and, as a result, often did not compete effectively with commercial programs. The *You and Your Government* series broadcast in 1935/36 probably enjoyed the most favorable reception.

The NACRE discontinued its operations in 1938 when the Rockefeller Foundation withdrew its funds.

National Committee on Education
by Radio (NCER)

The organization of the NACRE did not satisfy many educators, who felt that the move was not an adequate solution to the existing situation. Among the dissenters were presidents of many state universities, representatives of state departments of education, heads of important national educational associations, and directors of educational radio stations. Although these educational leaders realized that cooperation with commercial interests was desirable, they were apprehensive of the steady decline of educational stations and disturbed by the aggressive nature of radio advertising. Furthermore, they held little or no hope for the eventual cooperation and goodwill of commercial broadcasters.

Some educators reasoned that radio grants should be made in the public interest, just as land grants were made to colleges by the various states. They felt they had to organize on their own to achieve their real objectives; this conviction became so strong that educational broadcasters asked the commissioner of education to call a national conference to determine ways and means for self-preservation.

Commissioner William Cooper called the Conference on Radio and Education at Chicago on October 13, 1930. After much discussion, the conference was adjourned with the following resolutions:

1. The appointment of a committee to represent "the Association of College and University Broadcasting Stations, the Land-Grant College Association, the National University Extension Association, the National Association of State University Presidents, the National Education Association, the National Catholic Educational Association, the Jesuit Education Association, the National Advisory Council on Radio in Education, the Payne Fund, and other similar groups." Commissioner Cooper was to appoint this committee.

2. The protecting and promoting of broadcasting originating in educational institutions.

3. The promotion of broadcasting by educational institutions.

4. Legislation by Congress "which will permanently and exclusively assign to educational institutions and government educational agencies a minimum of fifteen (15) per cent of all radio broadcasting channels which are or may become available to the United States."

5. The calling of "an organization meeting of this committee at the earliest possible moment."[33]

Commissioner Cooper immediately appointed the requested committee and asked Joy Elmer Morgan of the NEA to act as temporary chairman. Shortly after, the Payne Fund supplied a small grant. On December 30, 1930, the new committee held its first meeting at Washington, D.C., and designated itself the NCER. The committee's members were the accredited representatives of nine educational organizations.[34]

Before the second meeting on February 28, 1931, Joy Elmer Morgan had been elected chairman for one year; headquarters had been temporarily established at the Hotel Martinique in Washington, later to be moved to the NEA headquarters; and a bulletin, *Education by Radio*, had been published. Also in early February, a service bureau, housed in the National Press Building and directed by Armstrong Perry and Horace L. Lohnes, was created. By April, the NCER had chosen Tracy F. Tyler to be its research director and secretary.

The objectives of the NCER were:

> to foster research and experimentation in the field of education by radio; to safeguard and serve the interests of broadcasting stations associated with educational institutions, to encourage their further development, and to promote the coordination of the existing facilities for educational broadcasting; to inform the members of the organizations represented on the Committee, educational journals, the general public, and the state and national governments as to the growing possibilities of radio as an instrument for improving the individual and national life; to develop plans and create agencies for the broadcasting of nationwide educational programs; to bring about legislation which would permanently and exclusively assign to educational institutions and to government educational agencies a minimum of fifteen percent of all radio broadcasting channels available to the United States.[35]

The NCER and Commercial Broadcasters

The NCER immediately launched a vituperative assault against the growing domination of commercial broadcasters in radio. Through its bulletin, *Education by Radio*, an endless cannonade was hurled at the "monopolistic" commercial broadcasters.

This rebellion began with a reaffirmation of Herbert Hoover's words on monopoly: "The question of monopoly in radio communication must be squarely met. It is not conceivable that the American people will allow this new-born system of communication to fall into the power of any individual, group, or combination."[36]

Since educational radio had already lost considerable ground, the first task of the NCER was to maintain remaining radio channels. An immediate attempt was made to claim or recover a fair share of broadcasting frequencies for education. The first decisive step came in the form of legislation.

On January 8, 1931, Senator Simeon D. Fess of Ohio, with the NCER's support, introduced a bill that would reserve 15 percent of radio broadcasting channels for educational stations. Although little was done to push the bill (which remained buried in committee from January 1931 until Congress began to consider the Communications Act of 1934), its introduction produced a vociferous defense and stimulated new aggression from commercial broadcasters; it also drove a decisive wedge between the two disputing groups of educators by interrupting a planned program of cooperation between the NACRE and the commercial networks (NBC and CBS).

Congress finally passed the new Communications Act in 1934, which was the crucial year in the attempt to secure educational reservations. The organizers and chief protagonists of the Fess bill were Catholic organizations and some of the groups associated with the NCER.[37]

It was almost inevitable that the Fess bill would be defeated. Not even all the groups who were members of the NCER gave the bill their active support; the NACRE took no position whatsoever. As a consequence, the Fess bill never reported out of committee and lost whatever consideration it may have had in Congress.[38]

Special Services for Educational Broadcasters

The original objectives of the NCER were to aid, protect, and give counsel to educational broadcasters. The first formal undertaking in this direction was made with the establishment of a service bureau on February 2, 1931. Its function was to provide "a representative on the ground in Washington for stations which are not able to spend large sums for travel."[39] It also provided legal aid and attempted to help educators preserve what they already possessed. The service bureau also meticulously examined all Federal Radio Commission reports in order to determine potential commercial threats to educational stations.

In addition, the NCER began an educational script service that was the first of its kind, setting a historical precedent for the script service later inaugurated by the U.S. Office of Education.

Probably the most important single activity of the NCER was the dissemination of information through its bulletin *Education by Radio*. Early in 1931, the NCER published the program schedules of educational stations, reported on the use of instructional radio in school systems throughout the country, and provided the results of important surveys in radio education.

Research in radio instruction was also an important function of the NCER. Probably the most extensive sponsored research was Tracy Tyler's *An Appraisal of Radio Broadcasting in the Land-grant Colleges and State Universities* (1933).[40]

NCER Sponsors National Educational Radio Conference

By the spring of 1934, the NCER had been in existence for three years, during which time radio and other facets of American life were being subjected to scrutiny by educators regarding their cultural contribution to society.

It was therefore apropos that the NCER sponsored on May 7-8, 1934, in Washington, D.C., "The First National Conference on the Use of Radio as a Cultural Agency." The general trends of the addresses, discussions, and committee reports reflected views antagonistic to commercial broadcasters and in favor of some measure of government control of radio broadcasting. Probably the single most important result of this conference was a committee report, "Fundamental Principles Which Should Underlie American Radio Policy," that advocated government control.[41]

A System of Educational Broadcasting

After an extensive survey of the civic and cultural possibilities of radio, Arthur G. Crane developed "A Plan for an American System of Radio Broadcasting to Serve the Welfare of the American People."[42] The plan, presented to the FCC on May 15, 1935, proposed a system of public councils—state, regional, and national—to develop public-service broadcasting. The federal government would construct and operate stations to broadcast the programs developed by the various councils. The objectives of such councils would be:

(1)   to aid educational and civic organizations in the region in mobilizing and coordinating their broadcasting resources and to raise the quality and number of their presentations;

(2)   to demonstrate and emphasize the value of radio as an instrument of democracy;

(3)   to give the listening audience in the region a wider range of choice in serious broadcasts, including programs distinctive to the area.[43]

Crane was primarily responsible for developing this concept, although the NCER had germinated the idea. It had always been the NCER's belief that "the American states should play an organized part in cultural broadcasting and ... the federal government should make some positive contribution to education on the air."[44]

Early Radio Councils

The first development of a radio council based on the Crane plan began in New Mexico in the fall of 1935, but it never materialized because of lack of funds. Early in 1936, there was considerable enthusiasm for a similar council, but, here again, there were no positive results for a variety of reasons.

The first council developed according to the NCER plan was the Rocky Mountain Radio Council. The council itself grew out of "the recognition of need on the part of three distinct groups: the owners of commercial radio stations in the area; the educational and civic organizations of the two states of Colorado and Wyoming; and radio listeners."[45]

The first organization meeting of the council was held on January 29, 1938. The executive committee selected Robert B. Hudson, former director of the Adult Education Council of Denver, and Charles Anderson, of the staff of Station KOA, Denver, as staff members. A short time later, these men received Rockefeller Foundation fellowships for radio training in New York City.

Although financial, technical, and personnel problems hampered the early development of the Rocky Mountain Council, it began active broadcasting on December 23, 1939.[46] During its initial test period from December 23, 1939, to July 31, 1940, the council produced 222 educational radio programs. Council members engaged their own scriptwriters, actors, and production directors. In addition, a transcription library service was established at the University of Colorado, and transcripts of these broadcasts were made available to schools and civic groups in the Rocky Mountain region. With the advent of World War II, the Rocky Mountain Radio Council was discontinued because of lack of funds.[47]

Contributions of NCER

Many changes occurred from the time the NCER was founded in 1930 to the time it was dissolved in 1941, most significantly in the attitudes of commercial broadcasters, the FCC, and educators themselves toward educational radio.

The shift in attitude of the commercial broadcasters could be seen in the networks' temporary installation of education departments (now all disbanded), their adoption of a broadcasters' code, and the large sums they spent on cultural and educational programs. On the other hand, the FCC became more vigilant and aggressive in relation to questionable programming and monopolistic practices. Also, it eventually succeeded in setting aside definite channels for educational broadcasting.

Educators likewise altered their approach to educational radio. Radio research became an established activity. Colleges and universities began incorporating radio courses so that teachers would be able to use radio more effectively in their instructional procedures. Moreover, public and private schools began to make wider use of radio and many began to apply for their own FM licenses. Another important outgrowth was the organization of the Association for Education by Radio, a group composed of educators who were actually doing educational broadcasting or actively using radio in their classrooms.

These developments ran parallel with many of the accomplishments of the NCER itself. Their own evaluation was stated in the final report:

Glancing back to 1930 and the objectives of the National Committee as outlined by its organizers, one sees that the Committee has completed the cycle of its activities. It is gratifying to have had the opportunity to play a part in the development of this great medium and to have contributed to the advancement of the American way of life. It is now ready to turn its activities over to the newer groups, groups which did not exist at the time of its founding in 1930.

The National Committee on Education by Radio can look back on the eleven years of its history with both pride and humility. It has made mistakes; in some cases it has created animosities; it has at time lost hard-fought battles for the rights of education. But the story of the Committee—from a total point of view—is one of progress and accomplishment.[48]

Educational Radio Activities of the U.S. Office of Education

The U.S. Office of Education was one of the first national organizations to promote the use of radio instruction. John J. Tigert, commissioner of education, clearly indicated his interest in the use of radio for instructional purposes as early as 1924.

Establishment of Radio Section

In accordance with a recommendation of the Advisory Committee established in 1929 under the chairmanship of Commissioner of Education William J. Cooper, congressional approval established a Radio Section and staff in the Office of Education on July 1, 1931. Cline M. Koon, assistant director of the Ohio School of the Air, was made the first senior radio specialist.

The purposes of the Radio Section were stated as follows:

1. Organize and maintain an informational service for all who are interested in the field of education by radio.

2. Keep the educational and governmental interests of the country posted and alive to the importance of this new educational device.

3. Initiate and assist with research studies of radio as an educational agency in regularly organized schools and for adult students.

4. Attempt to prevent conflicts and duplication of effort between various educational broadcasting interests.

5. On invitation of state departments of education, institutions of learning and national broadcasting chains, assist in setting up and evaluating broadcast programs of educational material.[49]

Through the years, the U.S. Office of Education Radio Section has issued a radio manual, bibliographies, glossaries, a newsletter, extensive catalogs of scripts and transcripts, and numerous pamphlets on radio instruction.

Radio Education Project

A major instructional radio research project of the U.S. Office of Education began in 1935 when Commissioner John W. Studebaker proposed to the Department of the Interior that an educational radio project be established by a grant from emergency relief funds. Following a conference with President Franklin D. Roosevelt, an allocation of $75,000 was made to the Office of Education on December 20, 1935, to create a Radio Education Project. The purpose as stated by President Roosevelt was:

To present high-grade radio programs over radio facilities offered free to the Office of Education by commercial radio corporations for public service programs in accordance with the provisions of the basic law governing radio wavelengths, using talent-actors, singers, directors and playwrights in the ranks of those on relief.[50]

William D. Boutwell of the regular Office of Education staff was named director of the project by Commissioner Studebaker. The project formally began when a small group met at the National Press Club in Washington, D.C., on December 16, 1935. Among them were Major Silas M. Ransopher, assistant educational director of the Civilian Conservation Corps (CCC); Guy McKinney, director of information for the CCC; Ray Hoyt, editor of *Happy Days*; Shannon Allen, production director of stations WRC and WMAL; and Philip Cohen, educational advisor of a CCC camp in Pennsylvania.

The original staff was composed of CCC advisors and commercial broadcasters who set up an organization with the following units: a script division for writing programs; a production division in charge of programs; an audience preparation division; a business division for the work of answering listeners' mail, keeping accounts of time, and ordering supplies; a personnel division; and an educational radio script exchange division.

When Commissioner Studebaker proposed the formation of an advisory committee, to include representatives of both of the major radio networks, NBC named Franklin Dunham and CBS chose Edward R. Murrow. Studebaker selected Ned Dearborn, dean of the general education division of New York University, and Sidonie Gruenberg of the Child Study Association of America as additional members of this committee.

In February 1936, sixteen program ideas were presented to the advisory committee. Dunham and Murrow each selected three proposals and the Office of Education Script Division then began to prepare scripts. For NBC, the Office of Education created *Answer Me This*, a social science question-and-answer program, and *Have You Heard*, a natural science program on the "wise-person-and-stooge" pattern. For CBS, the script division prepared a safety education program called *Safety Musketeers*. Early in March, the advisory committee heard and approved samples of these programs. *Answer Me This* went on the air on March 16, 1936, over the NBC network, followed three days later by *Have You Heard*. *Safety Musketeers* made its debut on CBS early in May 1936. Other programs presented were *Treasures Next Door, The World Is Yours, Let Freedom Ring,* and *Brave New World*.

Public response to these programs was impressive. During the first year, more than 366,000 letters were received. When offers of supplementary material were made, the volume of mail almost doubled. The Office of Education, by experimentation with various approaches to the problem of adapting education to radio, found some limitations in the medium and learned many effective broadcasting techniques. Significantly, it became obvious that radio had greater possibilities for the stimulation of learning than it had for systematic teaching. Indeed, the Radio Project made such an important contribution to the understanding and use of educational radio that it was allocated an additional $130,000 in October 1936, so that it could continue for another school year. In spite of a splendid record of achievement, the Radio Project was cut off from further funds by Congress in 1940, and all active radio production by the Office of Education ceased. It has since concentrated on the development of a script, transcript, and information exchange.

Early in 1936, Commissioner of Education John Studebaker, on the recommendation of Radio Project director William D. Boutwell, had decided that training in educational radio might be provided by the establishment of a center where teachers and students could obtain experience by writing and producing programs. New York University had planned for radio instruction as early as May 1934, when the division of adult education was established. By 1936, deliberations were underway for the creation of a radio workshop at New York University. Eventually, this radio workshop was made possible by a cooperative arrangement between the U.S. Office of Education and the division of general education of New York University; Boutwell and the division of general education joined forces to set it up. The first session of the workshop was conducted during the summer of 1936; the second, in January and February 1937; the third, during April and May 1937; and the fourth, in July and August 1937.

This radio workshop, which also received the cooperation of the educational director of NBC, the director of talks of CBS, and of many other New York City stations, was different in many respects from all similar attempts. First, "it afforded opportunity for a study not of one or two stations but of a dozen, and these included the central plants of the three national networks."[51] Also, the instructors, the visiting lecturers, and the student's opportunities for practice were outstanding. Workshop students had the opportunity to attend rehearsals and broadcasts of the five Office of Education programs then on the air. The composition of the classes was unique in that only teachers, or students who expected to be teachers and intended to make broadcasting a part of their educational activities, were admitted.

The success of this workshop set the pattern for the many others. An alumni association and a Radio Laboratory Club were formed, and the term *workshop* came into common usage.

Institute for Education by Radio-Television

The Institute for Education by Radio-Television (formerly the Institute for Education by Radio) was organized at Ohio State University in 1930 as a direct consequence of an earlier institute held in the state house of representatives at Columbus, Ohio, on November 22-23, 1929. This early radio institute, sponsored by the Ohio Department of Education, was attended by the superintendents and teachers who were participating in the Ohio School of the Air.

Such radio instruction pioneers as J. L. Clifton, Ben H. Darrow, W. W. Charters, and Edgar Dale were among those taking part. Clifton stated that the purpose was to discuss freely the ramifications of the many problems in educational broadcasting. Darrow presented a brief history of educational broadcasting and Charters analyzed the work of the Federal Radio Commission as it pertained to educational radio. Dale led a discussion on the use and effectiveness of radio instruction.

Cline M. Koon, assistant director of the Ohio School of the Air, proposed that similar institutes be organized on a national basis. Out of this suggestion came the idea for establishing an annual national institute for educational broadcasting. Charters received a grant from the Payne Fund and thus the Institute for Education by Radio held its first annual meeting at Ohio State University from June 23 to July 3, 1930.

More than one hundred representatives of both commercial and educational broadcasters attended. Every section of the United States and three foreign countries were represented. The sessions themselves consisted of forty-six well-prepared addresses on various phases of educational broadcasting. These proceedings and those of succeeding institutes have been published in annual volumes titled *Education on the Air.*

The objectives of the first Institute for Education by Radio and also of succeeding institutes were: (a) to enable teachers in educational broadcasting to become acquainted with each other, (b) to pool existing information, (c) to make the information available for general use by publishing the proceedings of the institute, and (d) to develop a plan for cooperative fact-finding and research.[52]

The objectives first stated by the founding members of the institute have been realized in many ways. The institute has grown from a group of a few more than one hundred people to one of over a thousand. It has always been a place where workshops and discussions dealing with every problem of educational broadcasting have had free rein. Above all, the institute has been a sounding board in the continual controversy between commercial and educational broadcasters. Simmering resentments and misunderstandings have at times violently erupted at these meetings; the discord between the two groups is evident in the *Education on the Air* yearbooks.

The institute has survived because it is one of the few places where the problems of educational broadcasting can be thoroughly evaluated by all interested parties.

Federal Radio Education Committee

In 1935, the Federal Radio Education Committee (FREC) was established, consisting of forty leading educators and commercial radio representatives. John W. Studebaker, U.S. commissioner of education, served as chairman. Funds were secured from the broadcasting industry and from various foundations. National conferences were held, studies made, reports and newsletters published. However, by the early 1940s, FREC had become only a relic of an idealistic compromise between educators and the radio industry, and it has long since faded away.

National Association of Educational Broadcasters

On November 12, 1925, broadcasters attending the Fourth National Radio Conference in Washington, D.C., adopted a resolution calling for full recognition by the Department of Commerce of the needs of educational broadcasting stations. The resolution also recommended that "adequate, definite and specific provision should be made for these services within the broadcast band of frequencies."[53]

As a consequence, a group of educational broadcasters attending this conference formed the Association of College and University Broadcasting Stations (ACUBS).

The purpose of the organization was stated as follows:

> Believing that radio is in its very nature one of the most important factors in our national and international welfare, we, the representatives of institutions of higher learning, engaged in educational broadcasting, do associate ourselves together to promote, by mutual cooperation and united effort, the dissemination of knowledge to the end that both the technical and educational feature of broadcasting may be extended to all.[54]

The first annual ACUBS convention was held in Columbus, Ohio, on July 1-2, 1930, in conjunction with the Institute for Education by Radio. Plans for better coordination and a more unified organization were made. President Robert Higgy, director of WOSU, Ohio State University, became the first executive secretary and the first regular mimeographed *Bulletin* was sent to ACUBS members.

During the years from 1930 to 1936, the National Association of Educational Broadcasters (new name adopted at the 1934 convention in Columbus, Ohio), or NAEB, was handicapped by the decline of educational stations, limited membership (there were only twenty dues-paying members in 1933), and lack of finances. In the spring of 1936, the first effort was made to develop a permanent headquarters and some type of program exchange. Also during this year, the *Newsletter* became the official publication and was issued more or less regularly by executive secretary Harold Engel.

The late 1930s failed to produce many important changes in educational broadcasting or in the NAEB. Some exchange of programs was made by some of the educational stations and there was some experimentation in rebroadcasting direct pickups from nearby stations. Early in 1938, the FCC reserved twenty-five channels in the ultrahigh (later FM) frequency band for noncommercial, educational broadcasting, but the NAEB *Newsletters* of this period do not reflect any great interest in FM on the part of most educational broadcasters.

During World War II, there was little change in the NAEB. Membership still failed to increase (there were only twenty-three member stations in 1944), but its financial condition improved somewhat. Plans for a permanent headquarters were again considered in 1945 but not realized until 1951. Largely through the efforts of Wilbur Schramm of the University of

Illinois, the NAEB received a grant in 1951 from the Kellogg Foundation for the establishment of a permanent NAEB headquarters at the University of Illinois and of an NAEB tape network.[55] The grant also provided funds to allow the NAEB to hold annual seminars for the training of educational broadcasters and to conduct radio instruction research.[56]

As a result of a merger with the Association for Education by Radio-Television in 1956, the NAEB became the major national radio education organization. The NAEB continued to provide leadership in educational radio but, unfortunately, the NAEB ceased to function in November 1981 because of a lack of funds and a $360,000 deficit.[57]

First National Conferences on Educational Broadcasting

The first national conferences on educational broadcasting were sponsored by the U.S. Office of Education and the radio industry. The first conference was held in Washington, D.C., December 10-12, 1936. George Z. Zook, President of the AEC, opened the first conference with these words:

> Education is concerned with the transmission of knowledge to individuals. Any modern device, therefore, which reaches such a large proportion of our population so speedily and so effectively as does radio will inevitably affect educational practice vitally.

> This is the fundamental reason for this conference. It is a fact that, notwithstanding considerable attention to the new situation created by the advent of radio, possible uses of this new medium for educational purposes have not been at all adequately explored or fully considered.[58]

The first national conference was considered so successful that a second one was scheduled for the following year. The second national conference was held in Chicago November 29-30, and December 1, 1937. The specific objectives of this conference were stated as follows:

> To provide a national forum where interests concerned with education by radio can come together to exchange ideas and experiences.

> To examine and appraise the situation in American broadcasting as a background for the consideration of its present and future public service.

> To examine and appraise the listeners' interest in programs that come under the general classification of public service broadcasting.

> To examine the present and potential resources of education through radio.

> To examine and appraise the interest of organized education in broadcasting.

> To bring to a large and influential audience the findings that may become available from studies and researches in the general field of educational broadcasting.[59]

University Association for Professional Radio Educators

Organized as the University Association for Professional Radio Education in 1947, this group is composed primarily of educational broadcasters from colleges and universities. It has emphasized the exchange of radio instruction information, the establishment of professional standards for courses in radio instruction, and the development of a curriculum for radio courses. Beginning in 1956, the association began publishing a quarterly titled *Journal of Broadcasting*.

Trends in Educational Radio

By the 1980s, publications and research relating to instructional radio had virtually ceased; course offerings in radio instruction were considerably reduced; commercial radio networks had closed their radio education departments and discontinued their school broadcasts; and the once-vigorous leadership of the Radio Section of the U.S. Office of Education and the NAEB had disappeared. It was evident that educational broadcasting was shifting its focus from radio to television. Whether intentional or not, radio instruction had become the stepchild of educational technology.

Notes

[1]Ben H. Darrow, "The Origin and Growth of the Ohio School of the Air." Unpublished manuscript, 1936, 3.

[2]Ibid., 7-8.

[3]Ibid., 8-11.

[4]Ibid., 30.

[5]Ibid., 54.

[6]When the Ohio School of the Air was disbanded, WLW, Cincinnati, continued much of its work in the Nation's School of the Air.

[7]The first experimental broadcast of this program series was held on January 21, 1928, in the New York studios of the National Broadcasting Company. Two more experimental programs were broadcast on February 11 and 17, 1928. These tests proved so satisfactory that it was decided that a regular series should be instituted.

[8]The curriculum of the American School of the Air was changed many times during its existence. In general, the focus was such subjects as literature, science, nature study, music, and the social studies. CBS enlarged the scope in 1940 by changing its name to School of the Air of the Americas and beaming its programs to twenty-two nations in the Western Hemisphere. The American School of the Air was discontinued in 1940. Gilbert Seldes astutely observed: "*The American School of the Air* was for years a morning program, available in classrooms, highly praised by educators and offered as an example of public service by the company. The fatality was that a half-hour of education broke the mood of the daytime serial; sponsors who wanted to buy a block of quarter-hours, letting the audience flow from one to the other, could not tolerate this dam in the stream; and no one wanted to start from scratch after the educational program was over, knowing that the home audience was committed elsewhere" (Gilbert Seldes, *The Great Audience*. New York: Viking, 1950, 123).

⁹W1XAL (changed to WRUL in 1939) was probably the first noncommercial station operated on a listener-subscription basis. Supporting subscribers were organized as the World Wide Broadcasting Foundation.

¹⁰S. E. Frost, Jr., *Education's Own Stations*. Chicago: University of Chicago Press, 1937, 178.

¹¹Ibid., 464.

¹²Llewellyn White, *The American Radio*. Chicago: University of Chicago Press, 1947, 101.

¹³Levering Tyson, "Looking Ahead," in *Education on the Air*. Columbus: Ohio State University Press, 1936, 58.

¹⁴Fourth National Radio Conference, *Proceedings and Recommendations for Regulation of Radio*. Washington, D.C.: GPO, 1926, 3.

¹⁵Tyson, "Looking Ahead," 61.

¹⁶White, *American Radio*, 157.

¹⁷Ibid., 109-10.

¹⁸Levering Tyson, (ed.), *Proceedings of the Third Annual Assembly of The National Advisory Council on Radio in Education*. Chicago: University of Chicago Press, 1933, 4.

¹⁹See S. E. Frost, Jr., *Is American Radio Democratic?* Chicago: University of Chicago Press, 1937.

²⁰William B. Levenson and Edward Stasheff, *Teaching through Radio and Television*. New York: Rinehart, 1952, 523.

²¹*National Survey by the Preliminary Committee on Educational Broadcasting*. Payne Fund, December 1927.

²²The Advisory Committee on Education by Radio consisted of sixteen members: W. W. Charters, J. L. Clifton, Frank Cody, J. H. Finley, H. J. Stonier, G. B. Zehmer, H. R. Shipherd, W. G. Chambers, M. H. Aylesworth, W. S. Paley, J. A. Moyer, Mrs. H. H. Moorhead, Alice Keith, Katherine Ludington, W. J. Cooper, and Ira E. Robinson.

²³*Report of the Advisory Committee on Education by Radio, Appointed by the Secretary of the Interior*. Columbus, Ohio: F. J. Heer Publishing, 1930, 26.

²⁴Ibid., 51.

²⁵Ibid., 36.

²⁶Ibid., 26.

²⁷Ibid., 26.

²⁸*Report of Advisory Committee*, 75-76.

²⁹Levering Tyson, *National Advisory Council on Radio in Education, Inc.* Information Ser. no. 1, Bulletin. New York: NACRE, 1936, 4.

³⁰Levering Tyson, personal letter to author dated October 26, 1951.

³¹*Four Years of Network Broadcasting*, a report by the Committee on Civic Education by Radio of the NACRE and the American Political Science Association. Chicago: University of Chicago Press, 1937, 49-50.

[32]The first annual assembly was held at the New School for Social Research at New York City, May 1931; the second at Buffalo, New York, May 1932; the third at New York City, May 1933; the fourth at Chicago, October 1934; and the fifth and final assembly, held at Columbus, Ohio in May 1935, was a joint session with the sixth Institute for Education by Radio (now Institute for Education by Radio-Television). Reports of all assemblies were published in a series of volumes entitled *Radio and Education*, see Josephine H. MacLatchy (ed.), *Education on the Air*. Yearbook of the Institute for Education by Radio. Columbus: Ohio State University, 1930-1944.

[33]Frank Ernest Hill, *Tune in for Education*. New York: NCER, 1942, 16-17.

[34]The first member-organizations of the NCER were: the NEA, represented by Joy Elmer Morgan, who was editor of the *NEA Journal* and first chairman; the ACE: John Henry MacCracken, Washington, D.C.; the Association of Land-grant Colleges and Universities: H. Umberger, Kansas State College, Manhattan, Kansas; the Jesuit Education Association: Rev. Charles A. Robinson, S.J., St. Louis University, St. Louis, Missouri; the National Association of College and University Broadcasting Stations: Robert C. Higgy, director, Station WEAO, Ohio State University, Columbus, Ohio; the National Association of State University Presidents: Arthur G. Crane, president, University of Wyoming, Laramie, Wyoming; the National Catholic Educational Association: Charles N. Lischka, Washington, D.C.; the National Council of State Superintendents: J. L. Clifton, director of education, Columbus, Ohio; and the National University Extension Association: J. O. Keller, head of engineering extension, Pennsylvania State College, State College, Pennsylvania (The NCER, *Education by Radio* 1 [February 12, 1931], 1).

[35]Ibid.

[36]*Education by Radio* 1 (March 26, 1931), 25.

[37]Catholic interest in educational reservations dated back to the Federal Radio Commission spectrum reallocations decisions which favored general-interest stations over special-point-of-view stations. Religious stations had been hard hit by this policy and one of the hardest hit had been WLWL, owned by the Paulist Fathers in New York City.

[38]New York Congressman Rudd drafted a bill incorporating the suggestion of the Paulist Fathers of New York that 25 percent of the radio channels should be reserved for educational, religious, agricultural, labor, and similar organizations. The congressional committee voted against the bill, but its proposals were embodied in an amendment to the Communications Act of 1934 by Senators Wagner of New York and Hatfield of West Virginia. The Wagner-Hatfield amendment was eventually defeated 42 to 23, and any real prospect for legislative reservations disappeared. However, Sec. 307(c) of the new Communications Act (1934) ordered FCC hearings on the desirability of reservations. During October and November 1934, the FCC heard 135 witnesses. The educators lacked unity; the commercial industry mobilized all its forces and overcame any threat of reservations. On January 22, 1935, the FCC reported to Congress, recommending that: "At this time no fixed percentages of radio broadcast facilities be allocated by statute to particular types or kinds of nonprofit radio programs or to persons identified with particular types or kinds of nonprofit activities" (*FCC Monograph*, no. 11861. Washington, D.C.: GPO, 1935, 5-6).

[39]Hill, *Tune In*, 23.

[40]Tracy F. Tyler, *An Appraisal of Radio Broadcasting in the Land-grant Colleges and State Universities*. Prepared under the direction of the Joint Radio Survey Committee on Education, the NCER, Washington, D.C., 1933.

[41]This committee consisted of the following ten members: Arthur G. Crane of the University of Wyoming; W. G. Chambers, dean of the school of education, Pennsylvania State College; W. W. Charters, director of the bureau of educational research, Ohio State University; Jerome Davis, Yale Divinity School; Harold B. McCarthy, manager, station WHA, Madison, Wisconsin; Walter E. Myer, Civic Education Service, Washington, D.C.; Reverend Charles A. Robinson, S.J., St. Louis University; James Rorty, author, New York City; and Armstrong Perry and Tracy F. Tyler, both of the NCER.

[42]Crane organized a subcommittee consisting of J. O. Keller and Father Charles A. Robinson.

[43]*Education by Radio* 11 (Fourth Quarter 1941), 38.

[44]Hill, *Tune In*, 76.

[45]S. Howard Evans, "The Rocky Mountain Radio Council," *Education by Radio* 10 (Second Quarter 1940), 8.

[46]Robert Hudson, director of the Rocky Mountain Council, became ill shortly after he completed his radio training in New York City. While the board was debating his replacement, he recovered in time to begin his work in the fall of 1939. Another obstacle appeared when, with the rise of war in Europe, the General Education Board was willing to supply only $5,000 instead of providing sufficient support for a five-year experiment. Along with these problems were numerous technical obstacles.

[47]The pioneer radio council was the University Broadcasting Council—composed of the University of Chicago, Northwestern University, De Paul University, the three existing commercial networks (Mutual, NBC, and CBS), and any independent stations that wished to join. Allen Miller conceived the council and obtained the support of the Rockefeller Foundation and the Carnegie Corporation for four years beginning in July 1935, at an annual budget of $55,000. Administrative control of the council was vested in a board of trustees, with each university represented by two members. The broadcasts of the council were unusually successful. Programs developed by the council included *The Northwestern Stand* and *Of Men and Books*. Miller realized that the high performance standards of the council could not be maintained when the yearly contributions were reduced by the withdrawal of the University of Chicago in 1939. By the fall of 1940, the council had been disbanded.

In the late 1930s, so-called consulting councils were organized in several cities. These councils have made audience studies, established production committees, developed study courses in radio, promoted better programs, and established educational programs in program discrimination. One of the earliest consulting councils was the Ohio Civic Broadcasting Committee (1938). The Radio Council on Children's Programs was organized in New York City in 1940. Other notable councils include the Radio Council of Greater Cleveland, the Cedar Rapids Council, the Des Moines Radio Council, the Portland Radio Council, the Radio Council of New Jersey, and the Pioneer Radio Council of Western Massachusetts.

[48]*Education by Radio* 11 (Fourth Quarter 1941), 40.

[49]*The Purpose of the Office of Education in Regard to Education by Radio*, U.S. Department of the Interior, Office of Education, Bulletin 57031, September 1931, 2.

[50]See C. S. Marsh (ed.), *Educational Broadcasting*. Proceedings of the Second National Conference on Educational Broadcasting. Chicago: University of Chicago, 1938, 204.

[51]Frank Ernest Hill, *Listen and Learn*. New York: American Association for Adult Education, 1937, 125.

[52]See Josephine H. MacLatchy (ed.), *Education on the Air*. Fifth Yearbook of the Institute for Education by Radio. Columbus: Ohio State University, 1934, vii-viii.

[53]Copy of resolution included in report of conference by W. I. Griffith.

[54]From original constitution of ACUBS.

[55]The development of the NAEB tape network in 1951 was the outgrowth of the noninterconnected tape network developed by Seymour N. Siegel of Station WNYC, New York City, in 1949.

[56]Much of the postwar development of NAEB can be attributed to the stimulus afforded by the Allerton House conferences of 1949 and 1950 at the University of Illinois. See Robert B. Hudson, "Allerton House 1949, 1950," *Hollywood Quarterly* 5 (Spring 1951), 239.

[57]For a complete history of the NAEB, see Harold E. Hill, *The National Association of Educational Broadcasters: A History*. Urbana, Ill.: The NAEB, 1954.

[58]C. S. Marsh (ed.), *Educational Broadcasting*. Proceedings of the First National Conference on Educational Broadcasting. Chicago: University of Chicago Press, 1937, 4.

[59]Ibid., Marsh, Second National Conference, ii.

Select Bibliography

Atkinson, Carroll. *Public School Broadcasting to the Classroom*. Boston: Meador Publishing, 1942.

_____. *Radio in State and Territorial Educational Departments*. Boston: Meador Publishing, 1942.

Darrow, Ben H. *Radio, the Assistant Teacher*. Columbus, Ohio: R. G. Adams & Co., 1936.

_____. *Radio Trailblazing*. Columbus, Ohio: College Book Co., 1940.

Four Years of Network Broadcasting. Report by the Committee on Civic Education by Radio of the National Advisory Council on Radio in Education and the American Political Science Association. Chicago: University of Chicago Press, 1937.

Frost, S. E., Jr. *Education's Own Stations*. Chicago: University of Chicago Press, 1937.

_____. *Is American Radio Democratic?* Chicago: University of Chicago Press, 1937.

Harrison, Margaret. *Radio in the Classroom*. New York: Prentice-Hall, 1937.

Head, Sydney W., and Christopher H. Sterling. *Broadcasting in America: A Survey of Electronic Media*. Fifth edition. Boston: Houghton Mifflin, 1987.

Hill, Frank Ernest. *Listen and Learn*. New York: George Grady Press, 1937.

Hill, Frank Ernest, and W. E. Williams. *Radio's Listening Groups*. New York: Columbia University Press, 1941.

Laine, Elizabeth. *Motion Pictures and Radio*. New York: Regent's Inquiry, McGraw-Hill, 1939.

Levenson, William B. *Teaching through Radio*. New York: Rinehart, 1945.

MacLatchy, Josephine H., ed. *Education on the Air*. Yearbook of the Institute for Education by Radio. Columbus, Ohio: Ohio State University, 1930-1944.

Marsh, S. C., ed. *Educational Broadcasting*. Proceedings of the First and Second National Conferences on Educational Broadcasting held in Washington, D.C. Chicago: University of Chicago Press, 1936-1937.

Stewart, Irvin, ed. *Local Broadcasts to Schools*. Chicago: University of Chicago Press, 1939.

8

Beginnings of Media Research: 1918–1950

This chapter provides the general background of media research, which has been historically significant in the growth and development of educational technology. Since this development was influenced critically by educational film and radio research during the period 1918-1950, the chapter will focus on these areas.

Early Educational Film Research: Prior to 1934

Although tests of instructional films were reported as early as 1912,[1] the first experimental studies on educational films were those by D. R. Sumstine[2] of the Pittsburgh Public Schools, reported in 1918, and by J. V. Lacy[3] in two New York City schools, reported in 1919. The primary value of these studies was to raise questions and stimulate further research. One notable pioneering experiment was Weber's 1921 study of the comparative effectiveness of several visual aids, including the motion picture.[4] Weber introduced pictorial tests in this study and thus became the first investigator to measure the results of learning using a pictorial medium rather than verbal tests.

Educational film research began in the United States near the end of World War I and has since advanced through a series of major studies subsidized by foundations, institutions of higher learning, and commercial organizations.

Johns Hopkins University Studies

The first large-scale educational film research was undertaken in 1919 when a grant of $6,600 was made by the United States Interdepartmental Social Hygiene Board to the psychological laboratory of Johns Hopkins University "for the purpose of assisting the laboratory in investigating the informational and educative effect upon the public of certain motion pictures used in various campaigns for the control, repression and elimination of venereal diseases."[5] The study was conducted by Karl S. Lashley and John B. Watson under the supervision of an advisory board consisting of Adolph Meyer, S. I. Franz, and R. S. Woodworth.

The film selected was *Fit to Win*, a six-reel, 35mm film prepared from the World War I version, *Fit to Fight*. In the experiment, the film was shown to approximately five thousand people. Results were tested using questionnaires on the informational and emotional effects of the film and through interviews with thirty-five men, from six to eighteen months after the showing. Pretests on venereal disease information were obtained from approximately 425 people, and posttests were obtained from 1,230 people of the various audiences to whom the film was shown. The experimental population included a medical group, an executive and clerical group, a group of literary club women, a mixed audience of male and female youths and adults, and separate groups of male streetcar company employees, merchant sailors, and soldiers.

Results indicated that the film effectively disseminated information on venereal disease, but also indicated that a single film may not be effective in bringing about basic attitude changes.

The Lashley-Watson study is a classic because it anticipated many of the conceptualizations rediscovered or formulated since. For example, the observation by Lashley and Watson that learning from films varies according to audience characteristics has only recently come to be appreciated. Moreover, their analytic study of the variables of film treatment antedate many later theoretical formulations.

The University of Chicago Experiments

The University of Chicago experiments (sometimes called the Freeman-Commonwealth study) was the first major media program supported by an institution outside the mainstream of educational technology.

The origin of the University of Chicago experiments can be traced to a 1920 conversation between Frank N. Freeman, professor of educational psychology at the University of Chicago, and F. Dean McClusky, a graduate student there. Freeman had been impressed by the instructional possibilities of the film and felt that a systematic study should be made to determine its educational potential. He suggested such a study to McClusky as a doctor's thesis. Freeman then approached the Society for Visual Education (a commercial instructional film production company established in Chicago in 1919) with the request that they assist the McClusky study by supplying some of their films. Although the society supplied fourteen films, it soon became apparent that the experiments warranted additional support. Therefore, Freeman contacted the Commonwealth Fund of New York, which, on April 1, 1922, granted $10,000 to the University of Chicago for the McClusky study and a series of additional studies, all of which became known as the Freeman-Commonwealth study.

The University of Chicago experiments were conducted under the direction of Frank N. Freeman in eight school systems, involving over five thousand students, for a period of three years.[6] The final report, *Visual Education*, was published by the University of Chicago Press in 1924. The University of Chicago study "gives no support to the belief that pictures may be substituted for language. It does indicate, however, that they have a definite function to perform. This function is determined by the nature and purpose of the instruction."[7] Moreover, "the relative effectiveness of verbal instruction as contrasted with the various forms of concrete experience ... depends on two major conditions: the nature of the instruction to be given, and the character of the pupils' previous acquaintance with the objects which are dealt with in the instruction."[8] These studies also showed that

> the usefulness of motion pictures would be enhanced if they were so organized as to confine themselves to their peculiar province. Their province seems to be the exhibition of moving objects and particularly to facilitate the analysis of motion. They are outside their province when they show still objects or when they enter the field of abstract verbal discussion. They cannot compete, in these respects, with still pictures and with the teacher.[9]

Thus, it was recommended that "subject matter should not be included in educational films which is not primarily the representation of motion or action" and "it is probably desirable to have motion picture films in small units."[10] Clearly, the University of Chicago experiments contributed some important theoretical insights concerning the function of the educational film. However, these insights were largely ignored and were not rediscovered until almost two decades later (for example, the development of the single-concept film).

The Eastman Experiment

The history of the Eastman experiment began with the establishment of the Judd Committee by the NEA in 1922, whose mission was to collect data on the production and distribution of educational films. The MPPDA granted the Judd Committee $5,000 in 1923 to carry on the investigation under the chairmanship of Charles H. Judd, chairman of the School of Education, University of Chicago.

In the process of this investigation, the Judd Committee applied to a number of film concerns, including the Eastman Kodak Company, for information about educational films. Thus the Eastman Kodak Company became aware of the interest of educators and decided to launch their own investigation of the status of educational films and the probable market for new ones. Much of the data collected by McClusky in his 1923 national survey of visual education for the NEA was used by Eastman, but they also conducted a survey of their own. Simultaneously, Eastman began the production of a few pilot educational films.

The outcome of the Eastman investigation became known in February 1926, when George Eastman wrote the following letter to Will H. Hays, president of the MPPDA:

> For the last three years, the Eastman Kodak Company has been making a survey of the use of motion pictures in teaching as a supplement to textbooks, to find out what has been done and what promise there was of future sound development. Such films were not practicable until an easily operated projector and economical films were available to schools. We believe that these two problems have been solved by the Kodascope and our new standard narrow width film.
>
> The survey led us to the conclusion that very little had been accomplished in producing teaching films suitable for classroom use and that there was little prospect of any organization with the necessary resources attempting to solve the problem. Therefore, after full consideration, *the company has decided to approach the solution of this problem in an experimental way. It proposes to make a number of teaching films closely correlated with selected courses and in accordance with a definite educational plan. These films will be prepared with the advice and assistance of competent educators and will be put into a limited number of representative schools in different cities for trial in their classrooms* [italics mine]. As the work of production goes on, the company will thus have definite information as to whether the right sort of films are being made.
>
> In making this announcement the company wants it to be clearly understood that it will have no apparatus or films for sale to schools during this experimental period, which will take about two years. Any future developments will be determined by the success of these experiments. The company leaves itself free to discontinue this undertaking if at any time it feels that there are unsurmountable obstacles to its success.[11]

In March 1926, George Eastman invited a group of educators to Rochester, New York, to reveal the details of his film production plans and obtain their support.[12] A few months later, in September 1926, Thomas E. Finegan, commissioner of public instruction for

Pennsylvania, was asked by Eastman to become director of the educational film production project.

When Finegan assumed his duties, a few more than twenty films were already underway. Ten were planned on geography, five each on health and general science, one on the life of a New England fisherman, and one to show the effect of iron on the industrial progress of the United States. In addition, more than thirty other educational films were planned for the fall of 1927. To prepare their content, selected teachers came to Rochester during the summer months to serve as consultants and to review each stage of the productions. The technical supervision of these films was done by Herford Tynes Cowling, the well-known producer of travelogues.

By early 1928, the Eastman Kodak Company had produced the first comprehensive series of educational silent films. Eastman Teaching Films was established the same year with Thomas E. Finegan as president and general manager. Finegan remained with Eastman until he died in November 1932.

In February 1928, the experimental phase began. Ben D. Wood, director of the Bureau of Collegiate Educational Research at Columbia University, and Frank N. Freeman of the University of Chicago were asked to serve as co-directors of the Eastman teaching film experiment. The investigation was extensive: It included twelve cities in widely separated areas of the United States, with nearly eleven thousand students and two hundred teachers, in grade levels four to nine.[13] From February to May of 1928, twenty instructional films were integrated into two, twelve-week units in geography and general science. The films and textbooks were designed especially for the experiment. The units of instruction were carefully outlined and taught alike in similar classes; except for one control group of classes, the instruction utilized films. The teachers of the control groups were encouraged to use any other media that seemed appropriate. The relative effectiveness of the two methods of instruction was measured by objective tests. Comprehensive examinations were given to all the students at the beginning and at the end of the experiment.

The general conclusion by members of the Eastman teaching film experiment was that films had enormous educational potential. Wood and Freeman emphasized that

> the casual introduction of films into the curriculum without careful organization is of comparatively little value. Insofar as possible, a classroom film should always be used for some definite and particular purpose. It should be a necessary link in the chain of development of the subject. It should constitute the necessary basis for the understanding, by the pupil, of the phases of the topic which follow, and a clarifying of those that have preceded.[14]

Wood and Freeman concluded, "If we examine the average gains made by the entire group of children in all cities and on topics taken together, we find that the X group excelled the C group by a substantial and significant margin."[15]

An unpublished critique by McClusky made a quite different assessment:

> When I first approached this book [*Motion Pictures in the Classroom* by Ben D. Wood and Frank N. Freeman] it was with the belief that here was a new contribution to visual education. I have a genuine interest in the use of the motion picture in teaching and believe it has value and a place of worth in the educative process. Furthermore, the reviewer believes that the Eastman Kodak Company (has) done a service to education to show a concrete constructive interest in motion pictures for instruction. My first reading of *Motion Pictures in the Classroom* brought a feeling of anxious questioning, this later turned to disappointment....
>
> A mistake has been made to attempt classroom experimentation for a few weeks on a "big" scale and to deal with mass statistics on the assumption that discrepancies in experimental technique may be ironed out in the general results.

As an example of scientific experimentation in teaching this book will find a place as an illustration of how not to do research in education....

I feel that propaganda has no place in visual instruction or in any type of instruction dressed up in the clothes of experimental and statistical procedure. In the future, "research" of this sort should be avoided.[16]

Despite the questionable experimental procedures illustrated by the Eastman experiment, it did provide the impetus for the expanding use of the educational film. For example, much of the initial stimulus of the audiovisual movement in California came from this experiment, with the San Diego County audiovisual agency as a concrete result.

Yale University Studies

At about the same time that the Eastman Kodak Company was producing silent educational films, Yale University was producing a series of silent educational films known as the *Chronicles of America Photoplays*. Beginning in November 1927, and ending in June 1928, Daniel C. Knowlton and J. Warren Tilton, of the Yale faculty, undertook to discover whether these films could aid in the teaching of seventh-grade history. The plan of the experiment involved 15 classes, 521 pupils, and 6 teachers. In teaching the control group, the teachers used textbooks, maps, and other media, with the exception of motion pictures. Objective tests were designed to show (1) the amount of time saved by the use of films; (2) the amount of factual historical knowledge obtained by the pupil; and (3) pupil attitudes toward the subject matter of history. Knowlton and Tilton's experimental design showed rare insight by including test questions that involved a knowledge of time relationships, historical relationships, and the influence of personages on historical events. The design also incorporated a rather rare experimental approach in which the effects of films on class discussion were investigated. Eight classes were selected for observation by three experienced observers who recorded the number of hands raised in response to teaching questions as well as the responses and questions of the pupils themselves. From three to seven months after the experimental instruction had been given in the various courses of study, delayed-recall tests were given.

The general results of this study were as follows:

1. The ten photoplays made a large contribution to the teaching of an enriched course of study, increasing the pupil's learning by about 19 per cent.

2. This contribution was of such magnitude that average children with the aid of photoplays learned as much as bright children did without them.

3. The increase in the total number of pupil participation attributable to the use of the photoplays was 10 per cent.[17]

In closing the account of their investigation, Knowlton and Tilton make this very important point:

The ability of the pupils to grasp and appreciate these relationships was in no small degree determined by the teacher's own interest in them and the emphasis which she attached to them. However inherently effective the photoplays may be—and the evidence submitted here indicates the potentialities of such material—it will only attain its highest degree of effectiveness when accompanied by good teaching, based on the appreciation of the general goal to be attained and of the capacity of this material to contribute to its attainment. The teacher has at her command an instrument which, as these results indicate, will go far toward economizing her time and effort and stimulating her pupils to secure those abiding values inherent in this vital subject.[18]

While the Eastman experiment was extensive, the Knowlton and Tilton investigation was less so. Also, in contrast to the Eastman experiment, Knowlton and Tilton devised more scientific methods for securing their basic data.[19]

Media Research to 1930

Weber summarized the media research completed up to 1930 as follows:

> It should be pointed out that the usefulness of visual aids—films, slides, stereo-graphs, and other realia—is specific: that is, the usefulness of any one visual aid varies with every topic or project. Visual aids are supplementary to actual experience, and both are fundamental to verbal instruction. Visual aids thus provide perceptual foundations where actual experience is lacking and enable verbal instruction to transmute these into conceptual products through the processes of interpretation, integration, and generalization. This truth being self-evident, there is no further need for experimentation of the kind discussed (over 30 experiments conducted during the 1920's).... Future research must progress into areas of specification and application.[20]

Weber went on to name a number of unsolved research problems. He suggested, for example, that research studies should be conducted to determine "the optimum length and content of informational films for the use of classroom teachers."[21] He also suggested that researchers analyze and evaluate the factor of animation in motion pictures and "go into the problem of individual differences as well as into the matter of interrelationships between animation and other psychological factors."[22] In both of these suggestions it is clear that Weber anticipated the current approaches to instruction and also the study of the media characteristics that provide desirable conditions for learning.

Carnegie Foundation Study

One of the first serious attempts to investigate the educational potential of sound films was made by the Harvard Film Foundation and the Harvard Graduate School of Education under the sponsorship of the Carnegie Foundation for the Advancement of Teaching. This study, conducted by P. J. Rulon in 1932, dealt with the contributions of films and textbooks that, except for two films, were specially designed and produced by the Harvard Film Foundation to include specific subject-matter content in order to meet specific instructional objectives.[23]

The results of this study showed a significant increase in informational and conceptual learning when films are used in combination with textbooks.[24]

Payne Fund Studies

The first comprehensive, careful studies that dealt with the effect of theatrical films on the cognitive and affective learning of children were the Payne Fund studies, made during a four-year period (1929-1932). These studies, supervised by W. W. Charters of Ohio State University, were made by professors and their associates from several major institutions of higher learning.[25]

The history of the investigations is brief. In 1928 William H. Short, executive director of the Motion Picture Research Council (which had been formed in 1927 to gather factual evidence against the motion picture industry in order to replace the Hays office), invited a group of behavioral scientists and educators to confer with the council about the possibility of discovering what effect theatrical motion pictures had on children. When these men proposed a research study, Short appealed to the Payne Fund for a grant. He found the foundation receptive because the Payne Fund itself had formed a National Committee for the Study of Social Values in 1927, to secure factual data regarding motion pictures on the basis of which a national policy could be formulated. Thus Short's proposal gave the Payne Fund an opportunity to implement its stated policy with reference to theatrical motion pictures.

The distinctive techniques used in the Payne Fund studies were (1) to analyze a complex social problem and break it down into a series of subordinate problems, (2) to select competent investigators to work on each of the subordinate projects, and (3) to integrate all the findings into a solution of the initial problem.

The approach was to assemble data in answer to a series of questions. For example, the council asked, "What is the amount of knowledge gained and retained from motion pictures by children of various ages and the types of knowledge most likely to be thus gained and retained?"[26] The council also wanted to know "the extent to which motion pictures influence the conduct of children and youth either in desirable or undesirable directions and particularly in regard to patterns of sex behavior."[27] What effect motion pictures had on children's attitudes toward significant social concepts and on their standards and ideals was also a matter of concern. The council wished to know the effect of motion pictures on the emotions and health of children; the number and ages of children who attended motion picture theaters; the frequency with which they attended; and what could be done to teach children to discriminate between good and poor films. The council also raised a number of questions concerning the effect of theatrical films on the standards of American life. Finally, the investigators sought to find data, but could not, to prove that the onset of puberty is or is not affected by motion pictures.

The studies fell into two broad groups: one was to measure the effect of motion pictures, as such, on children and youth; the other was to study theatrical film content and children's attendance at commercial theaters. In measuring the effect of films on children, the studies focused on five areas — information, attitudes, emotions, health, and conduct. By determining the effect of motion pictures in these five areas, it would be possible to measure the influence of theatrical motion pictures on children by ascertaining what they see when they attend the theaters and how often they go.

In reviewing the Payne Fund studies, Charters concluded:

> The motion picture, as such, is a potent medium of education. Children, even of the early age of eight, see half the facts in a picture and remember them for a surprisingly long time. A single exposure to a picture may produce a measurable change in attitude. Emotions are measurably stirred as the scenes of a drama unfold and this excitement may be recorded in deviations from the norm in sleep patterns, by visible gross evidences of bodily movement and by refined internal responses. They constitute patterns of conduct in daydreaming, phantasy, and action.
>
> Second, for children the content of current pictures is not good. There is too much sex and crime and love for a balanced diet for children.
>
> Third, the motion-picture situation is very complicated. It is one among many influences which mold the experience of children. How powerful this is in relation to the influence of the ideals taught in the home, in the school, and in the church, by street life and companions or by community customs, these studies have not canvassed.[28]

The Payne Fund studies are relevant today because many of the theatrical films evaluated, together with similar films, have now been shown repeatedly throughout the United States on television. In view of the massive evidence contained in this twelve-volume report, the contention that little is definitely known about the effects of television viewing on children is not justified, at least not where old Hollywood films are concerned.

Although the Payne Fund studies stimulated a short-lived motion picture appreciation movement in the schools in the mid-1930s, they appear to have had little influence on the use of the theatrical motion picture in formal instruction. These studies were, however, a precursor to modern communication research, constituting the first systematic studies of mass media that were tied to a concrete operational problem.

Motion Picture Project of the American Council on Education (ACE)

Probably the most significant project in educational technology during the 1930s was the Motion Picture Project of the ACE. This project generated insights and theories of instruction that led to instructional techniques that almost totally determined the pattern for the instructional programs of the U.S. Office of Education and the armed forces during World War II.

Background

The concepts underlying the Motion Picture Project were first given expression when U.S. commissioner of education George F. Zook, deeply impressed by the recent findings of the Payne Fund studies, decided there was a need to harness this powerful medium for the purposes of education. Zook knew that, despite the demonstrated power of film in influencing information, attitudes, conduct, and emotions of children and young adults, use of the motion picture had been unorganized and neglected in the nation's schools and in educational agencies. For example, Koon had reported in 1934 that less than 10 percent of the nation's public schools systematically used the motion picture for instruction. What is more, there was no responsible agency to which these schools could turn for accurate information on films, equipment, and allied questions; there was a lack of educationally worthwhile films; a comprehensive distribution system did not exist; and cumbersome, expensive, 35mm silent projectors predominated.[29] It was true that some commercial organizations (Eastman Kodak, for example) and a few educational organizations (Department of Visual Instruction of the NEA) had attempted to solve these problems; but they had failed, either because they misunderstood the needs of educators or because they had not sufficiently equipped themselves for the task, or for both reasons.

During the summer of 1933, the U.S. Office of Education was invited to report to, and participate in, the International Congress on Educational and Instructional Cinematography to be held in Rome in April 1934, under the auspices of the International Institute of Educational Cinematography.[30] Soon after this invitation, Zook called a conference for September 25, 1933, of thirty-five representatives of universities, city school systems, motion picture producers and distributors, equipment manufacturers, educational organizations, and governmental agencies, to consider whether the United States should participate in the congress. It was agreed that the United States should make a report, and Cline M. Koon, senior specialist in radio and visual education of the U.S. Office of Education, was appointed to compile the so-called Rome report.

Due to the intense work done in connection with the Rome report, Zook began to see the need for some type of national cooperative organization that could lead efforts to realize the full educational potential of the motion picture. About this time, Lorraine Noble, a

Hollywood scenario writer and long-time advocate of the educational film who had also been strongly influenced by the Payne Fund studies, conferred with Zook and Koon and volunteered her services for the development of a national educational film institute. By January 1934, Noble had prepared the first outline for the institute.

Also, during March 1934, Cline Koon completed the Rome report, now entitled *Motion Pictures in Education in the United States*, and sent it to the International Institute of Educational Cinematography in Rome. The last two paragraphs of this report are significant:

> (d)   A strong national film institute is needed in the United States.
>
> In comparison with the theatrical motion picture, the non-theatrical picture in the past usually lacked technical excellence, is used comparatively little, and with varying regularity. Many agencies have pioneered in the development of the educational film, but the result in the United States today is chaotic and disorganized. The principal reasons for this condition seem to be the past policy of the Federal Government to leave to private industry and voluntary endeavor many activities that the typical European government would assume, and the educational system of the country which is not centralized in the Federal Government, but, in the main, is left to each of the 48 States. Private industry is dead-locked over the fact that producers cannot afford to make films until a sufficient number of projectors is sold to make the work profitable, and the projector concerns cannot sell their apparatus because there is no comprehensive library of suitable films available for their use.
>
> Commendable efforts are being made in many places to overcome these difficulties, but there is a great need for a national film institution (1) to assemble, edit, classify, publicize, and catalog non-theatrical film material, and to set up a convenient and economical distribution system; and (2) to produce and stimulate the production and effective utilization of educational films. An entire nation seeks enlightenment — courage to look forward and inspiration to work for the new social order wherein every human being would have the chance to enjoy living and working. The education of tomorrow should give a new appreciation of leisure and its usefulness and a new sense of citizenship and cooperation. The vast potentialities of the use of motion pictures in the nation's education are only beginning to be generally recognized.[31]

Shortly after the Koon report was published, Zook persuaded Secretary of State Cordell Hull to appoint an American delegation to the Rome congress. Thus, for the first time in American history, the United States officially participated in an international meeting concerned with educational films.

The American delegation was active at the Rome congress. W. W. Charters (director of the Payne Fund studies), as vice-president of the congress, helped shape its policies and projects; C. F. Hoban, Sr., director, State Museum and Visual Education, Pennsylvania State Department of Public Instruction, and Paul B. Mann, head of the biology department at Evander Childs High School in New York City, made useful contributions concerning the school use of films; Chester A. Linstrom, associate chief, Office of Motion Pictures, U.S. Department of Agriculture, contributed to the discussions on the use of films in agricultural education; Carl E. Milliken, secretary of the MPPDA, assembled and delivered examples of American educational films; and Cline M. Koon served as chairman of the American delegation and spoke at the opening and closing sessions of the congress.

The congress was extremely significant to American educational technology. First of all, it gave the American delegation a tremendous insight into the production, distribution, and use of educational films in European countries. Second, it left the vivid impression that the United States educational establishment was backward in its use of the film medium, both for instructional purposes and for influencing attitudes and behavior. In a letter to Secretary of State Cordell Hull, W. W. Charters gave perhaps the clearest statement of the implications of the congress for educational technology:

> The influence of both recreational and educational films is amazing. In 30 years they have become more influential in distributing ideas, patterns of conduct and the like than printing has been able to achieve in 400 years. Their concreteness, dramatic power and simplicity of presentation make them understandable by the masses to a degree that reading can never attain. This conviction is based upon the research studies of the Payne Fund—and on the accumulated practical experience of European experts assembled at the Cinema Congress in Rome....
>
> That this power may be utilized equally in raising the ideals and culture of a nation or in debasing them is entirely clear. Attitudes toward races may be powerfully directed toward either a better understanding or increased hostility. Fact and error are indiscriminately accepted by audiences....
>
> The European peoples with their canny recognition of realities have caught the vision of the cultural and political possibilities of the motion picture ... in many European countries the educational film, which is indistinctly separated from the recreational film, has become the matter of persistent attention. This interest is widespread among twenty or more nations....
>
> People in the United States have not yet caught the vision of the place of the motion picture in American civilization....
>
> The United States should study authoritatively and in statesmanlike fashion the place of motion pictures in our culture, formulate the factors to be considered and work toward solutions in accordance with the temperament of our people.
>
> To this end I make the proposal that the Office of Education be given the responsibility of assembling persons under governmental auspices and representing the Government, the public, the university, the schools and other appropriate agencies to study the problem in all its bearings, and that to this end it secure preferably from Congress or possibly from a foundation, a modest appropriation to provide for meetings, a collection of necessary data and the publication of conclusions....
>
> The study herein proposed is merely the first step of a historical series.[32]

Zook was also convinced that a study should be made but took no immediate action because he was leaving his position as commissioner of education to assume the presidency of the ACE in June 1934. In this new capacity, he went to work at once on the implications of the Charters report, visiting the British Film Institute in London and conferring with representatives of the Swiss, French, and other European educational film organizations. On his return to the United States, Zook brought before the Problems and Plans Committee of the ACE a project to establish an organization that would act as a national clearinghouse for educational films. In October 1934, Zook was authorized to formulate a proposal for foundation financing that would result in the organization of a film institute. In the meantime, the Payne Fund made a grant to carry on the preliminary work and Zook asked Lorraine Noble to continue her services in connection with this activity.

Within the next few months, Zook had called two conferences with selected educational leaders to consider the establishment and organization of a national film institute.[33] At the first conference, held on December 4-5, 1934, at the ACE in Washington, D.C., the following objectives were framed:

1. To develop a national appreciation of the potential contribution of the motion picture to the cultural life in America.

2. To collect and distribute significant information concerning motion pictures in education, at home and abroad.

3. To stimulate the production and use of motion pictures for educational purposes.

4. To promote the cooperation of all agencies interested in the production and use of motion pictures in education.

5. To initiate and promote research pertaining to motion pictures and allied visual and auditory aids in education.[34]

In addition, a number of tasks were assigned to staff members of the ACE and those of cooperating groups. Among them were the following:

1. A budget was to be prepared for submission to a foundation.

2. A series of conferences with various motion picture industry groups was to be held; one with the equipment industry, another with producers, another with the representative of the motion picture theaters.

3. All of the leading educational associations were to be interviewed.

4. The form or organization, the charter and constitution, were to be worked out.

5. A document describing the proposed institute and its aims was to be prepared.[35]

The entire direction of the project was left in the hands of George F. Zook, with Lorraine Noble as assistant director.

The second conference was held on February 28-March 1, 1935, at the ACE in Washington, D.C. More than one hundred educational organizations had already been contacted by Noble, and all opinions favored the establishment of a film institute. Thus it was decided that immediate steps should be taken for the organization and financing of the institute, and a committee was formed to do so, which consisted of the following: W. W. Charters, Edgar Dale, C. F. Hoban, Sr., Cline M. Koon, Levering Tyson, and George F. Zook, ex officio.[36]

After receiving the approval of the Problems and Plans Committee of the ACE, Zook submitted the first formal proposal for a national educational film institute to the General Education Board of the Rockefeller Foundation in May 1935, to obtain a supporting grant.[37]

Initiation of Studies on the Use of Instructional Film

While the ACE was awaiting the decision of the General Education Board, it decided that the incorporation of the institute should be postponed until the most appropriate form for its organization became clearer. A number of ground-clearing projects were therefore presented to the General Education Board with the suggestion that these be completed before the actual financing and launching of the film institute. A document entitled "Proposed Studies Relating to the Use of Films in Education," calling for five interim projects and a budget of $12,500, was submitted to the General Education Board; a grant was made for these projects in June 1935.[38]

The first of the five interim projects began in the fall of 1935. Interim project no. 1, dealing with sports films, was assigned to Gladys Palmer of Ohio State University.[39] Interim project no. 2 resulted in the publication *Teaching with Motion Pictures: A Handbook of Administrative Practices* by Edgar Dale and Lloyd Ramseyer, in April 1937.[40] Interim project no. 3 was devoted to the preparation of a bibliography of literature in the instructional film field. The digest of this work was published by the H. W. Wilson Company in a volume entitled *Motion Pictures in Education*. Interim project no. 4 resulted in the preparation of a catalog of instructional films, and interim project no. 5 was a survey of audiovisual equipment in the public schools of the United States.

Interim project no. 3 was originally started by Lorraine Noble, with the assistance of Fannie Dunn, Robert A. Kissack, Jr., Charles F. Hoban, Jr., and Alice Keliher. The intent was to build a central library in Washington, D.C., consisting of reference books and annotated literature concerned with instructional films. During the spring and summer of 1936, two lengthy volumes of digests, prepared mainly by Fannie Dunn and Etta Schneider, were issued in experimental form by the ACE. About five hundred sets of these two digests were distributed to educators throughout the country.[41]

Interim project no. 4 was assigned to Lorraine Noble and developed in cooperation with the U.S. Office of Education and the H. W. Wilson Company (a publishing firm). More than eighteen hundred film sources were located and, for the first time, a large body of information on all existing educational films was collected in one place. Moreover, a uniform system of film classification was developed.[42] As a result of this work, the first comprehensive educational film catalog was published in 1936.[43]

Interim project no. 5 was first assigned to Robert A. Kissack, Jr., to be administered from the University of Minnesota, to consider the problems of schools in relation to the purchase and use of various types of audiovisual equipment. However, the project was taken over by Cline M. Koon of the U.S. Office of Education, under the sponsorship of the ACE, when Koon presented a proposal for a national survey of visual instruction in the United States. Questionnaires were sent to 21,000 superintendents of schools throughout the country; approximately 9,000 replies indicated the following equipment was owned by the schools reporting:

17,040 lantern slide projectors
 3,007 stillfilm attachments
 2,733 filmstrip projectors
 2,073 micro-slide projectors
 2,720 opaque projectors
 6,074 16mm silent motion picture projectors
   458 16mm sound motion picture projectors
 3,230 35mm silent motion picture projectors
   335 35mm sound motion picture projectors
11,501 radio receiving sets
   841 centralized radio-sound systems[44]

A direct result of this project was a conference of motion picture projector manufacturers in St. Louis, Missouri, in February 1936, to work out some plan for reducing the price of apparatus. Other by-products of this project were educational film handbooks, film lists, directories, and newsletters.

Inasmuch as the initial application for a grant to support a national film institute had been withdrawn by the ACE a few weeks after it was first submitted to the General Education Board, a new proposal entitled "Proposed First Year Program of the American Film Institute" was presented to the board in March 1936. When the ACE was told that the proposed $60,000 budget could not be approved, a revised proposal was prepared calling for $40,000. However, the General Education Board also rejected the second proposal and provided, instead, $25,000 for completion of the interim projects to the end of June 1937.

In view of the prevailing orientation and activities of the Rockefeller Foundation during the middle and late 1930s, it is difficult to understand why the ACE's request for funding of a national educational film institute was refused. For example, in 1935 the trustees of the Rockefeller Foundation decided to strike out experimentally in new fields, authorizing the officers to develop projects in the general areas of libraries and museums, radio, drama, and the motion picture. The president of the Rockefeller Foundation later said:

> From being aristocratic and exclusive, culture is becoming democratic and inclusive. The conquest of illiteracy, the development of school facilities, the rise of public libraries and museums, the flood of books, the invention of the radio and the moving picture, the surge of new ideas—and above all, perhaps, the extension of leisure, once a privilege of the few—are giving culture in our age a broader base than earlier generations have known.... New interests are in the making—an adventurous reaching out for a fuller life by thousands to whom non-utilitarian values have hitherto been inaccessible.... Any program in the humanities must inevitably take account of this new renaissance of the human spirit.[45]

An exploratory beginning was made in 1935 in radio with a series of grants for worldwide experimentation with educational broadcasting. The grants were given to the World Wide Broadcasting Foundation, which operated a shortwave station in Boston. Another supporting grant was given the same year to a cooperative educational broadcasting experiment (University Broadcasting Council) in Chicago, involving the University of Chicago, Northwestern and De Paul universities, NBC, and CBS. Still another 1935 grant for experimentation along regional lines laid the groundwork for the Rocky Mountain Radio Council, embracing the states of Colorado and Wyoming. And in the motion picture field, the Rockefeller Foundation in 1935 provided assistance to the Museum of Modern Art in New York City for the establishment of a film library, a repository for film literature, and a distribution center.

With this background, there seems to be no obvious reason why the foundation should not have supported a national educational film institute, an organization whose functions seemed perfectly compatible with similar activities then being supported by the General Education Board.

Committee on Motion Pictures in Education

For whatever reasons the General Education Board rejected their proposal, and it was clear to Zook and the ACE that a new approach must be taken. Therefore, Zook formed the Committee on Motion Pictures in Education (CMPE)[46] in 1936 to set about developing a new foundation proposal to define "the functions of motion pictures in general education" and facilitate "the development of general education through the use of motion pictures."[47] In December 1937, the General Education Board awarded $135,000 ($15,000 was added later) for a three-year study on the use of films in general education. Meanwhile, the CMPE chose Charles F. Hoban, Jr., as director of the study, with Floyde E. Brooker as assistant director.

Film Evaluation Centers

When the Motion Picture Project of the ACE was inaugurated, a lack of basic information on available instructional films constituted one of the chief obstacles to effective use of films in the classroom. Under the new CMPE grant from the General Education Board, it was decided that the films listed in the *Educational Film Catalog* (produced by interim project no. 3) be evaluated and that this evaluation be made available to all teachers.

For three years, from 1938 to 1941, the CMPE spent most of its time and effort evaluating educational films in four key evaluation centers throughout the country. Hoban describes this program as follows:

> Four centers cooperated for two years in the extensive study of motion pictures in the curriculum: Tower Hill School, Wilmington, Delaware; and the public schools of Denver, Colorado, and of Santa Barbara, California. Each of these was engaged in the development of curriculum programs. Supplementing these centers during the second year of the evaluation program were the public schools of Minneapolis, Minnesota; Rochester, New York; and Pittsburgh, Pennsylvania; and a group of schools and colleges in the southeastern states, organized through the Division of General Extension of the University System of Georgia.[48]

The first evaluation center was established at Tower Hill School, Wilmington, Delaware, in the spring of 1938. Answers were sought to such questions as the following:

> What is the function of motion pictures in education? What educational objectives can specific films serve? What are the strengths and weaknesses of existing films? Is there one or are there several best ways of using films? Can the same film be used on different grade levels and on the same grade level for different purposes? Are reactions of children on these different levels the same or different?[49]

Answers were obtained from teachers and students on the basis of their experience with the actual use of films in normal school activities. Through arrangements made by the CMPE staff, films were made available by producers and distributors. Moreover, the study was purely descriptive. There was no experimental interruption of regular class activities and only anecdotal data were secured from students and teachers.

Beginning in 1938, a two-year study also began in the Santa Barbara (California) schools.[50] Earlier this same year, the Santa Barbara schools had begun a curriculum-revision program with help from the School of Education at Stanford University. Over two hundred Santa Barbara teachers participated in the film evaluation program. The pattern was similar to that used in the Tower Hill evaluation center. For example, techniques used in film evaluation included teachers' and students' judgments, anecdotal records, stenographic records of class discussions, specimens of creative activities, interest inventories, and paper-and-pencil tests of pupil behavior.

Two departures from the film evaluation approach occurred in Denver and at the University of Minnesota. In Denver, a project was developed under the supervision of Floyde E. Brooker and Eugene Herrington that demonstrated that schools could produce technically satisfactory motion pictures for their own use.[51] At the General College of the University of Minnesota, a series of experimental studies on the influence of educational films in biological and social science revealed that measures of functional information were not significantly different between film and non-film classes. Measures of interest between these groups, however, showed a significant difference, with greater interest in the subject of human biology in the film group than the non-film group.[52]

Results of the CMPE Motion Picture Project

Lorraine Noble, assistant director of the motion picture project during its first years (1934-1937), expressed the following assessment to this author:

The original concept of a national film institute was the dominant motive of the Motion Picture Project when it began in 1934. The film institute was visualized as freewheeling, that it would be equally controlled by the schools, the motion picture industry, and government: *that it would operate without a profit motive and not become the creature of any organization* [italics mine]. When the film institute failed to materialize, a period of boondoggling began, and none of the projects finally undertaken was very vital.[53]

Charles F. Hoban, Jr., director of the project during its final years (1937-1942), focused his assessment on the film evaluation program:

> After three years of experience in the use of panel judgments and of teacher and student judgments based on classroom use, it is the conclusion of the staff of the Motion Picture Project that a combination of the three makes for well-roundedness of evaluation intended to assist the teacher in selecting the film appropriate to a given purpose and in assisting him to prepare for its most effective use. In other words, film evaluations based on teacher and student judgments help the teacher with no previous knowledge of specific films to select those which are most likely to serve the purposes intended.[54]

A number of publications resulted from the final film evaluation phase (1938-1941) of the project. Probably the most important document was a descriptive encyclopedia of educational films titled *Selected Educational Motion Pictures* (1942).[55] This encyclopedia contains essential information on approximately five hundred 16mm films that were judged by educators to be of value in the classroom. About 5,500 teacher judgments and 12,000 student judgments were collected and analyzed in this process. In addition, the previewing of all films included in the encyclopedia and the preparation of their content descriptions were supervised by Blake Cochran, Robert S. Sackett, and Floyde E. Brooker of the project staff, who were assisted by a group of Rockefeller fellows.[56]

Although some of the activities of the motion picture project were not very significant, the project stimulated the classroom use of films and called attention to the need to critically evaluate the relationship of film content to the school curriculum.

In the final analysis, the direction taken by the motion picture project lay solely in the hands of the ACE. In contrast to the Ford Foundation, the Rockefeller Foundation had no specific program for education.[57] It wished to explore the use of films for general education and therefore provided money for R & D (research and development) and for the education of personnel. Responsibility for the merit or lack of merit of these studies rests entirely with those educators involved in the project. Lorraine Noble suggested to this author that the projects, in her opinion, were not very vital because "most educators did not know what they wanted."[58] There is no question, however, that the motion picture project provided a unique training ground for the many future leaders in educational technology who were associated with it.

Some Final Considerations

When the early, unpublished documents of the motion picture project are examined, a number of questions inevitably arise. Why, for example, was the "interim projects" proposal developed within a few days after the ACE had submitted a major proposal for its supposed primary area of interest—the national education film institute? The official reason was that these projects would keep alive the interest already generated in the film institute. But if, in fact, the ACE had developed these interim projects for the purpose of sustaining interest in the film institute, why did they withdraw the film institute proposal as soon as the interim projects grant was made? Did the ACE anticipate rejection of the film institute proposal and wish to avoid this rejection? Or did they propose the interim projects as a face-saving retreat from the film institute plan because they realized they were not ready or able to implement the latter? This would explain why the ACE quickly withdrew its film institute proposal when a grant was made for the interim projects. Then again, why did the council decide to resubmit the film institute proposal almost a year later and did this delay have any influence on the General Education Board's decision to reject it? If the primary goal of the ACE was to establish a film institute, why were no efforts made to approach other foundations? Finally, was there any pressure from the theatrical motion picture industry on either the council or the foundation, or both, that led to the ultimate failure of the film institute proposal, or even doomed it from inception? Certainly there has been abundant evidence over the years that the motion picture industry is antagonistic to the idea of educators producing their own films.

It appears unlikely that satisfactory answers to these questions will be forthcoming. Nevertheless, they continue to generate productive speculations.

Early Radio Education Research: Prior to 1937

The impetus for educational radio research first came from commercial radio. Since radio did not have the convenient audience indexes available to the film (box-office returns) or print (circulation figures) media, commercial radio audience research was undertaken as early as 1927.

Assessment of Early Instructional Radio Research

Foundations have played an important role in educational radio research just as they have in educational film research. Much of the credit goes to John Marshall of the Rockefeller Foundation and to S. Howard Evans of the Payne Fund. Significant contributions have also been made by the Carnegie Corporation and by the Alfred P. Sloan Foundation.

Unfortunately, few early studies of educational radio have actually been published in detail. Many were briefly summarized in the *Education on the Air* yearbooks published by the Institute for Education by Radio at Ohio State University. A number of these studies, constituting work for advanced degrees, have not been published in any form. As a result, many of their instructional implications have not been widely known.

An effort to coordinate radio research investigations was begun in 1931 by the Bureau of Educational Research at Ohio State University, with the help of the Payne Fund, through the publication of a bulletin entitled *Research Studies in Education by Radio—Cooperative Group*. W. W. Charters directed the activities of the bureau and F. M. Lumley directed radio research.

Many of the early radio projects were media comparison studies that presaged the now-familiar pattern of "no significant differences" in educational television research. A few provided more specific data on the effect of radio instruction on the learning process. Radio was usually found to be more effective for those subjects in which aural-verbal skills predominate.

Typical Early Studies

In order to suggest the nature of early educational radio studies, a few typical ones are listed:

1. A survey of the use of radio in adult education was made by the AAAE under the sponsorship of the Carnegie Foundation (1929).[59]

2. Ben H. Darrow and Cline M. Koon of the Ohio School of the Air studied classroom use of the Ohio School of the Air broadcasts (1929).[60]

3. The Department of Rural Education of Teachers College, Columbia University, studied classroom use of radio in one hundred rural schools (1929).[61]

4. John Guy Fowlkes and H. L. Ewbank of the University of Wisconsin studied the effectiveness of radio in teaching music appreciation (1929).[62]

5. H. Cantril and Gordon Allport made a series of studies to determine the extent to which a personality could be judged from the voice; a comparison of listeners' attitudes toward male and female voices; a study of the differences between a radio lecture and a regular lecture; a comparison of the mental processes of an audience listening before a radio with the same audience in the presence of the broadcaster; a study of the conditions influencing the relative effectiveness of visual and auditory presentation; a determination of the most effective conditions for broadcasting; and a study of certain attitudes and preferences of radio listeners (1932).[63]

6. F. M. Lumley and Frank N. Stanton of Ohio State University did some of the first systematic work in radio measurement (1934).[64]

7. Merton E. Carver of Harvard University studied some of the conditions that influence the relative effectiveness of visual and auditory presentations of identical material (1934).[65]

Major Educational Radio Research Projects

When the results of the Payne Fund studies became generally known between 1933 and 1935, the same storm that raged earlier over films now set the airwaves reverberating. There were emotional thunderbursts from women's organizations over children's programs. The result was a repetition of the film experience: The Federal Radio Education Committee of the FCC drew up a research program and submitted it to the Rockefeller Foundation.[66] Out of this effort came the support of the General Education Board in the launching of three major radio projects—the Ohio evaluation of school broadcasts project, the Princeton project (which was the beginning of the Office of Radio Research), and the Wisconsin research project.

Ohio Evaluation of School Broadcasts Project

The evaluation of school broadcasts project was unique in scope and cost. It was "a research and service project engaged in analyzing the educational values of radio in schools and classrooms, and in studying the social and psychological effects of radio listening upon children and young people."[67] The project, started in the fall of 1937 and terminated in the spring of 1943, was directed by I. Keith Tyler of the Bureau of Educational Research of Ohio State University. The associate director was J. Wayne Wrightstone.

The actual work was carried on in centers located in Chicago, Detroit, New York City, and the San Francisco Bay region; in the fall of 1938, the Ohio School of the Air was added. Also, certain advisory centers were located at Rochester, New York; Cleveland, Ohio; Madison, Wisconsin; Zanesville, Ohio; and the Nation's School of the Air at WLW, Cincinnati, Ohio.

After the selection of the centers, the major activities of the project staff during the years 1937-1940 were: meeting with groups of teachers who were using radio in their classrooms; and demonstrating the effective uses of radio for instructional purposes. Two or three such meetings were held each year with teachers of English, music, science, and social studies from the Chicago, Detroit, and New York City areas. Between meetings, the teachers kept diaries of their schools' use of radio and prepared anecdotal records of pupils' behavior while listening to school broadcasts. Members of the project staff analyzed these records and observations and prepared a list of classified objectives and sample evaluation instruments. After these objectives had been critically evaluated by the teachers, they were published as a tentative form of a *Dictionary of Objectives*.[68] These objectives were later classified into the following categories: (1) attitudes and appreciations, (2) interests and self-motivation, (3) critical thinking and discrimination, (4) creative expression, (5) social behavior and personal-social integration, (6) skills and techniques, and (7) informational background. Furthermore, objectives were also stated for each of the four fields of music, social studies, English, and science.[69]

After this preliminary work, which consumed some eight months, the staff began the second phase of the study, directed toward obtaining research evidence regarding school broadcasts. Instruments of evaluation were developed in tentative form and tried out by some of the cooperating teachers. Many more evaluation instruments were developed at summer workshops held in cooperation with the General Education Board and the Progressive Education Association at Bronxville, New York; Denver, Colorado; and Oakland, California. Special fellowships were given by the General Education Board to thirty-seven people who came to these workshops and worked closely with the project staff. In addition, special committees of the workshops prepared a manual on the utilization of broadcasts, a script series of school broadcasts, and outlines for work in radio program discrimination. By the fall of 1938, twenty-one exploratory studies of school broadcasting were in progress.

After the renewal of the original two-year grant in 1939, the results of the preliminary studies were used as a basis for planning more comprehensive research in the remaining three years.

CBS's American School of the Air was subjected to a thorough-going critical analysis during the 1940/41 series by a selected group of teachers and members of the project staff. From these analyses, the conclusions were:

First: Teachers who used the broadcasts in their classrooms sometimes found them extremely valuable in providing educational experiences not otherwise available to their students, in constituting interesting and worth-while curricular materials, in serving as integrative experiences in broad areas of subject matter, in stimulating students to engage in other educational activities, and in furnishing enjoyable classroom listening experiences to students. Of the three series, the "New Horizons" broadcasts were judged to be the most educationally worth-while, and the "Americans at Work" broadcasts the least worth-while.

Second: Even though the broadcasts in general were educationally worth-while experiences to both teachers and students in classrooms, the three series contained various curricula defects and deficiencies, notable in the failure to define purposes sharply, to consider criteria governing the scope of the series and the sequence of the broadcasts, to recognize the major functions of education in American democracy, and to develop accurate printed aids to accompany the broadcasts.

Third: Most of the broadcasts were clear and comprehensible to classroom listeners, but in the three series there were various minor errors in the selection of the content and in the form of presentation which, according to teachers, made the broadcasts at times and in spots extremely difficult for students to understand. By and large, these errors of content and production seemed attributable to a lack of knowledge concerning classroom listening conditions and to a lack of understanding of the social and educational backgrounds of pupils nine to fourteen years of age.

Fourth: Most of the broadcasts were enjoyable classroom listening experiences for students, but in these series there were certain techniques used which made the radio programs less interesting to boys and girls than they might have been. Some of these errors were due to limitations of budget and personnel at the Columbia Broadcasting System, but others were due to a lack of understanding of the social maturity of students in grades four to nine.[70]

Studies in the effectiveness of recordings were also conducted by the project staff. A study made at Cicero, Illinois, showed that student interest in scientific information could be greatly stimulated through the use of recordings.[71] Another study, made at Zanesville, Ohio, revealed that recordings could be used effectively in the creation of desirable interests and attitudes.[72] R. R. Lowdermilk, in utilizing a series of transcripts of *America's Town Meeting of the Air*, found that classroom use of recordings possessed value superior to that of assigned home listening to live broadcasts.[73] Furthermore, a study by Irving Robbins indicated that criteria of discrimination could be evolved and that recordings could be used as a stimulus for the discernment of such criteria.[74]

Perhaps the most significant study of recordings was the joint study conducted by the ACE and the evaluation of school broadcasts project at Ohio State University. More than one thousand educational recordings were collected and listed by Emilie L. Hale for the ACE Committee on Motion Pictures in Education. This report, made in January 1939 and entitled *Study of Recordings for General Education*, was divided into three parts: (a) a survey of the efforts that were being made to produce educational recordings, (b) an account of organizational rulings that affected the release of recordings for classroom use, and (c) a description of the methods used in recording programs, with a statement of comparative costs.[75] In commenting on the status of educational recordings in 1939, Haley remarked:

It is unfortunate that recordings of the various Schools of the Air are not available. In some cases off-the-air recordings are made for reference and study purposes but no permanent recording is being done to date. It is advisable that a thorough analysis should be made of these off-the-air recordings to ascertain the programs that would be suitable for re-recording for general distribution to schools.

The directors of the Schools of the Air, as well as the directors of civic educational broadcast programs, are willing to cooperate in making their programs available for recording if funds were provided.

In a coast-to-coast survey conducted to discover available recordings, great enthusiasm was shown with reference to the acquisition of educational recordings to supplement classroom curricula.

Expressions of interest and cooperation on the part of organizations affecting the recording of educational broadcast programs indicate complete accord towards the proposed project.[76]

Subsequently, these recordings were described and evaluated in *Recordings for School Use: A Catalog of Appraisals.*[77]

Without question, the evaluation of school broadcasts project made a significant contribution to educational broadcasting and educational technology. It provided valuable factual evidence and produced helpful aids to the educational broadcaster in the planning and effective use of educational broadcasts.

Wisconsin Research Project

In 1937, the Rockefeller Foundation also supported a study at the University of Wisconsin to test a number of fundamental assumptions concerning the strengths and limitations of radio as a medium of communication and instruction. The initial phases of this study concentrated on planning radio lessons in all subjects at all grade levels and on establishing research designs involving different combinations of subject matter, educational objectives, and listening groups. The planning of each series of broadcasts was a cooperative effort of classroom teachers, supervisors, administrators, and the staff of the state department of public instruction.

During the 1937-1939 period, the following programs were broadcast over the Wisconsin School of the Air to serve as the basis for comparative studies:

Music: Journeys in Music Land.....................	grades 5 and 6
Nature Study: Afield with Ranger Mac..............	grades 7 and 8
Geography: Neighbors Round the World............	grades 6 and 7
Social Studies: Community Living..................	grades 7 and 8
English: (1) English as You Like It.................	grades 10, 11, 12
(2) Good Books.........................	grades 10, 11, 12
Speech: Good Speech............................	grades 10, 11, 12[78]

In general, the results of these comparative studies showed no significant differences. The comparisons consistently favored the radio groups only in the field of music, and even there the differences were not large enough to be statistically significant.

Probably the most important results of the Wisconsin project were the training in radio research it afforded graduate students and the subsequent research it stimulated in other phases of educational broadcasting.

Princeton Project

The third major radio research project financed by the Rockefeller Foundation began at Princeton University in the fall of 1937 with the establishment of an Office of Radio Research (part of the FREC) headed by Paul F. Lazarsfeld as director, and Frank N. Stanton and Hadley Cantril as associate directors.

The project attempted to answer such questions as: What individuals and social groups listen to radio? How much do they listen and why? In what ways are they affected by radio? Since the radio industry had already studied the size and distribution of this audience as prospective purchasers for products advertised over the air, the Princeton study began where industry left off.

In June 1939, the first progress report summarized the principal findings as follows:

1. For listeners to the serious type of program, content of the program is more important than dramatic effects or personalities of the speakers.

2. People not likely to read for serious content are usually unlikely to listen for serious content.

3. Low-income families who read little are inclined to listen to the radio extensively and to seek the escape that comes with the non-serious content.

4. Higher-income families who have a wide variety of interests and available entertainment find most radio programs, which are commonly written for the listener with average ability and tastes, to be rather boring.[79]

As the project progressed, field headquarters were established in New York City, and the Institute of Public Opinion at Princeton began to publish valuable materials in the field of radio. Eventually, however, it became apparent that the total research program would be considerably expedited if it were transferred to a university located in New York City. Therefore, in the spring of 1940, the project was moved to Columbia University.[80]

The Office of Radio Research at Columbia University extended the scope of research begun at Princeton. By collecting work done in the radio industry and in universities, the office created, in a series of publications, a body of techniques and data about the radio audience that held important educational implications. Its next major publication after *Radio and the Printed Page* was *Radio Research 1941*. In this volume, six studies were reported as representative of the range of problems that were being confronted. These included studies of foreign language broadcasts over local American stations, the popular music industry, the radio symphony, the problems of serious music broadcasting, radio and the press among young people, and the relation of the radio to the farmer.

Although World War II made it technically difficult to continue the publication of the radio research series begun in 1941, radio research expanded during World War II and the activities of the Office of Radio Research directly influenced the creation of the Radio Bureau in the Office of War Information.

Simultaneously, three trends in radio research became apparent: a tendency toward integrating a variety of approaches to the same problem; innovation in research methodology, for example, the development of the Program Analyzer by Paul F. Lazarsfeld and Frank N. Stanton; and the study of technical problems in listener research. Examples can be found in the panel method of interviewing, in the detailed case studies of specific radio programs, and in the content analysis of enemy broadcasts carried through by the Research Project on Totalitarian Communication.

Indeed, it was becoming evident to Lazarsfeld and others that radio research would ultimately merge with the study of other mass media to form the broad field of communications research. One of the first indications of this trend became manifest in the Office of Radio Research publication *Radio Research 1942-1943*.[81] In this book, there was a report on the use of the Program Analyzer in the study of educational films and one on biographies in popular magazines.

In 1944, in recognition of the fact that the office was increasingly conducting research beyond the field of radio, it was reoriented toward the broad field of communications and renamed the Bureau of Applied Social Research. Under the brilliant leadership of Lazarsfeld, this organization continued to contribute to historical advances in the field of communications research.

Status of Educational Radio Research: End of World War II

By the end of World War II, educational radio research was still generally immature, inadequate, and incidental. With the exception of commercial radio surveys and the radio studies sponsored by the Rockefeller Foundation during the late 1930s, no long-range systematic studies had been undertaken in many important, unexplored areas of the teaching-learning process. In most instances, the results of the studies that had been conducted indicated that learning through the medium of radio is more effective than through print, especially among the less educated and the less intelligent. Moreover, the studies dealt largely with the characteristics of radio audiences or the effectiveness of radio as a medium of instruction in some specific subject matter. Although the content of radio broadcasts was analyzed and the relationships of program control and content were explored during World War II, educational radio research had virtually ceased by the close of the war.

United States Army Media Studies during World War II

The major media research programs during World War II were conducted by the army in the use of films. Three series of research studies were undertaken by various army agencies. Two dealt with the effectiveness of films in achieving specific learning outcomes, and the third, with the organizational factors influencing the extent of film use in training situations.[82]

Experiments on Mass Communication

Studies conducted by the Experimental Section, Research Branch, Information and Education Division of the War Department were reported by Hovland et al. in *Experiments on Mass Communication*.[83] This report is of great historical value because it contains a comprehensive discussion of various hypotheses concerning the effectiveness of films, and also contributes hypotheses offering suggestions for additional research.

Film Testing and Research

Another phase of army film research during World War II was undertaken by the Psychological Test Film Unit of the Aviation Psychology Program of the Army Air Force, located at Santa Ana Army Air Base in Santa Ana, California. The research evolved out of the unit's efforts to utilize the film medium for psychological testing and the classification of air crews. In the process of this research, the unit became involved with such problems as the representation of three-dimensional space by pictures, perceptual learning, and problems associated with the projection of films and still pictures.[84]

Major Postwar Military Film Research Programs

The immediate postwar years saw the initiation of two major film research programs by military sponsors. The United States Navy, in collaboration with the United States Army, supported a series of studies by Pennsylvania State University beginning in 1947 and ending in 1955. A counterpart film research program was organized by the United States Air Force from 1950 to 1957. Both of these programs were primarily planned to meet a national emergency in which there would be a serious shortage of time, instructional facilities, and instructors.

Instructional Film Research Program

This project, conducted by the Division of Academic Research and Services at Pennsylvania State University under the direction of C. R. Carpenter, involved over eighty individual research studies resulting in some 155 publications. It was probably the most extensive single program of experimentation dealing with instructional films ever conducted.

The basic experimental approach used in the instructional film research program was to produce special versions of films, incorporating defined variables, and then to compare the effects of these versions on appropriate groups of learners under controlled conditions.

To carry on these experiments, a response system called the classroom communicator was designed and built in the early 1950s to do the following: (1) allow individuals in a classroom to signal their choice from five answers given with a question; (2) record the responses of the individuals so that the data could be collected and analyzed; and (3) inform each individual whether his choice was correct or what the correct response should have been. The classroom communicator was the early prototype of contemporary response systems.

The general conclusions reached in these studies indicated the following:

1. Well-produced films, either used singly or in a series, can be employed as the sole means of teaching some types of performance skills and conveying some kinds of factual data.

2. Postviewing tests will increase learning when students have been told what to look for in the film and that a test on the film content would be given.

3. Students will learn more if they are given study guides for each film used.

4. Note-taking by students during the showing of a film should be discouraged because it distracts them from the film itself.

5. Successive showings of a given film can increase learning.

6. Short films can be spliced end-to-end in a loop and are beneficial in practice or drill situations.

7. Students can watch motion pictures for one hour without reduction in training effectiveness.

8. The effectiveness of film learning should be evaluated by tests.

9. After a film has been shown, its major points should be summarized and discussed lest students form misconceptions.

10. Follow-up activities should be encouraged to provide carryover of generalizations.[85]

Another section of this summary provided these guidelines for instructional film-makers:

1. *Camera angle.* Show a performance on the screen the way the learner would see it if he were doing the job himself.

2. *Rate of development.* Keep the rate of development of a film slow enough to permit the learner to grasp the material as it is shown.

3. *Succinct treatment.* Do not present only the bare essentials or cover subject matter too rapidly.

4. *Introductions.* Present relevant information in the introduction and tell the viewer what he is expected to learn from the film.

5. *Summary.* Summarize important points in the film in a clear, concise manner. Summaries probably do not significantly improve learning unless they are complete enough to serve as repetition and review.

6. *Concentration of ideas.* Present ideas or concepts at a rate appropriate to the ability of the audience.

7. *Commentary.* Don't "pack" the sound track: the number of words (per minute of film) in the commentary has a definite effect on learning.

8. *Special effects.* Avoid the use of special effects as attention-getting devices; it has no positive influence on learning.

9. *Color.* Experimentation has not yet demonstrated any general over-all increase in learning as a result of using color in instructional films.

10. *Music.* Preliminary experimentation suggests that music does not add to the instructional effectiveness of an informational film.[86]

Most of the studies conducted in this film research program were bound together in two volumes (*Instructional Film Research Reports*, vols. 1 and 2) and are available from the Office of Technical Services, U.S. Department of Commerce. In addition, a valuable by-product of this project was a report summarizing more than two hundred educational film studies conducted between 1918 and 1950.[87]

In 1954, the instructional film research program was reorganized and new objectives were formulated. There seemed to be similarities between educational sound films and educational television, so a more integrated research program was initiated. A general agreement was reached with the Fund for the Advancement of Education (subsidiary of the Ford Foundation) that a closed-circuit instructional television research project would be conducted on an exploratory basis during the 1954/55 period by part of the instructional film research program staff in cooperation with the departments of chemistry and psychology of Pennsylvania State University. After the completion of preliminary work during the first year, the fund agreed to continue the television project and the instructional film research program was terminated.

Air Force Film Research Program

During the period 1950/57, the Research and Development Command of the United States Air Force conducted, under the direction of Arthur A. Lumsdaine (former assistant director of the Yale motion picture research project), a series of research studies on educational films as well as other forms of media. From 1950 to 1953, there was a rather intensive focus on educational film research. All of the studies in the air force film research program involved the manipulation of film variables and techniques for eliciting and/or guiding overt responses during a course of instruction. These studies were conducted by a number of individuals at different locations over an extended period of time. Reports on this program have been largely confined to mimeographed reports of limited circulation. The largest collection of the main studies in this program appeared in the book *Student Response in Programmed Instruction.*[88]

It is clear from the available studies that they hold significant implications for the use and design of instructional films and related media. However, it is a puzzling fact that this extensive air force program failed to influence the film production techniques employed while these studies were in progress. Moreover, it is puzzling that the results of the hundred or more studies that flowed from both the army-navy Pennsylvania State University program and the air force program have yet to be implemented in the instructional films produced by the armed forces. One explanation for this paradox may lie in the almost complete separation of researchers from film production personnel that occurred in the joint army-navy studies as well as in the air force studies. Kanner suggests that film production personnel typically resent researchers who attempt to influence the film-making process.[89] In addition, he describes the prevailing perception of film production personnel that "anyone who could make a successful entertainment film could easily adapt to making a training film—a kind of film often described as a minor subspecies where a homely mixture of 'motivation,' humor, and animation could carry the teaching message."[90] It is clear from the history of both of these military studies that there is a need for a close working relationship between research and film production personnel and that some effective methods of dissemination and innovation must be devised whereby the results of media research can be readily put into effect.

Nebraska Film Research Program

The Nebraska Program of Educational Enrichment through the Use of Motion Pictures (sponsored by the Carnegie Corporation and the Motion Picture Association of America through Teaching Film Custodians), was launched in September 1946, under the joint direction of the University of Nebraska and the state department of public instruction.

Background

Nebraska's educational leaders had long recognized the educational deficiencies of small high schools located in villages and towns throughout the state. They were aware that the schools were hampered by poor or nonexistent libraries, inadequate laboratories, and, in some cases, inadequately prepared teachers. Many educators were convinced because of the World War II educational program of the armed forces that films could help solve some of these problems. Thus, in the autumn of 1945, a group of educators toured Nebraska to assess the school situations firsthand and to explore the possibilities of using films to improve the instructional program.[91] The result was that Frank E. Sorenson, who had made the initial trip across Nebraska, completed a proposal entitled "The Nebraska Program of Educational Enrichment, a Four-Year Experimental Study Designed to Develop an Enriched Instructional Program in Nebraska Schools through the Use of Motion Pictures." This was submitted to the Carnegie Corporation of New York in April 1946. After a grant was obtained in May 1946,[92] TFC provided an additional $5,000 for the acquisition of films the first year of the project and supplied, at no charge, films from its own stock.[93]

In July 1946, an administrative committee was organized and Wesley C. Meierhenry, assistant professor of education, University of Nebraska, was selected to be the administrator of the program. In addition, an area film director was appointed to each of four state teachers colleges and to the University of Omaha and the University of Nebraska in order to:

1. Give general direction and supervision to area programs of action designed to develop enriched instructional programs in schools through the use of the motion pictures;

2. Stimulate and assist with studies related to the program;

3. Work cooperatively with his own college and the high schools in developing and evaluating programs of action; and

4. Assist with the production of guides for teachers and pupils, program progress reports, and other essential publications.[94]

Since the Sorenson proposal defined the research study only in broad outline, work on refining the research design continued until the middle of October 1946, with final approval for the recommended design given by the administrative committee in November 1946. The actual experimental phase of this study did not begin until January 1947.

Overview of the Experiment

The Nebraska film program used with Nebraska public school children in grades 9-12 was confined to courses most common in the Nebraska school curriculum. Each of the seventy secondary schools chosen for experimentation was selected jointly by the program administrator and the area directors.

One of the most important tasks was selecting the motion pictures. Two basic criteria were used for selecting films. They were:

1. The motion picture had to show a real potential for enriching the course of activity in which it was to be used.

2. The motion picture had to be of such a nature that its integration into one or more of the courses chosen for experimentation might be readily accomplished.[95]

The general design of the study called for the use of standardized achievement tests and film tests. In addition, an intelligence test was administered and provisions were made for recording, observing, and reporting the experiences that gave evidence of changes in behavior as a result of motion pictures shown.

The main results of this study indicated that the experimental groups generally learned subject matter from the films that they would not have learned otherwise, and also that bright students profited more from films in terms of actual learning.

Motion Picture Association of America Studies

Following World War II, the Motion Picture Association of America (MPAA) supported two important projects in instructional film research: (1) the Commission on Motion Pictures of the ACE and (2) the Yale Motion Picture Research Project.

Background

The Commission on Motion Pictures and the Yale motion picture project grew out of a series of joint conferences and committee meetings of educators and leaders of the motion picture industry held between April 1943 and February 1944. The purpose of these meetings, which were sponsored jointly by the ACE and the MPAA (then the MPPDA), was to explore methods of developing a cooperative program for the production and use of educational films in the postwar period. The first conference, held in Los Angeles, California, on April 5, 1943, was attended by some twenty-five persons, about half from the motion picture industry and half invited by the ACE. The result was the general agreement that some cooperative effort should be undertaken by the motion picture industry and educators in the production of educational films.

The second meeting was also held in Los Angeles, on July 15, 1943. The chairman of the agenda committee, George F. Zook, president of the ACE, presented four questions for discussion:

1. Can major producers, in making feature pictures, include in them certain educational items or points which would teach the vast theatrical audiences?

2. Can the short subjects now distributed by Teaching Film Custodians within the United States be distributed to foreign countries, especially among our English-speaking allies?

3. Can the industry make certain new short subject films based on educational specifications, but also having sufficient entertainment value to repay their production costs by theatrical exhibition?

4. Can the industry afford to make more of the so-called "message" films (for example, *Wilson* and *One Foot in Heaven*)?[96]

In the ensuing discussion, a fifth question was introduced:

5. To what extent can the needs of the schools for new films be met by so-called "industrial," or advertising, films sponsored by private companies?

In response to the first question the producers generally asserted that theater audiences pay primarily to be amused and entertained, rather than to be educated or informed. The answer to the second question was affirmative; the third question was left open for further exploration. In regard to the fourth question, there was agreement that more "message" pictures should be made, but this raised the further question of what the educational leaders could do to stimulate attendance at the showing of such films. Discussion of the fifth question focused on the possibilities of producing industrial films with sufficiently high educational standards. At the close of the meeting it was agreed that a joint committee should be appointed to formulate a plan of cooperation between educators and the motion picture industry. The industry representatives on this committee were N. Peter Rathvon (RKO), chairman; Joseph Hazen (Warner Brothers); and J. Robert Rubin (MGM); representatives from the ACE were George F. Zook, George D. Stoddard, and Mark A. May.

After a series of meetings and discussions the joint committee recommended the following broad, cooperative program:

1. A survey of the needs of the schools for new pictures, particularly in the field of international understanding, and the preparation of curricular materials for filming.

2. The production of certain needed films.

3. The experimental evaluation of existing educational films and of new films as they are produced.

4. Promotion, including the demonstration to schools and colleges of the values and possible uses of teaching films.[97]

It was obvious that this program revived many of the notions embodied in the proposal for a national film institute that had been developed by the ACE as far back as 1934. The ACE, at that time, failed to receive foundation support for a number of obscure reasons, among them the possible intervention of some members of the motion picture industry. Since the council could not expect to secure sufficient financial support for this new program from foundations, there was some hope that the MPAA itself would be willing to underwrite a program that it had helped develop. However, the MPAA indicated that it was not ready to undertake the financing of an educational film institute. Instead the MPAA agreed to recommend that the motion picture industry fund that part of the program that had to do with the selection of film topics and the preparation of educational specifications for these films. The MPAA also made it clear that this would be done through an outright gift to the ACE and that the materials prepared would be made freely available to all member companies of the MPAA. Moreover, the association did not commit to the production of any of the materials prepared by the ACE. The council accepted this offer and appointed a Commission on Motion Pictures in Education, in February 1944, to survey the requirements of schools and develop a series of educational specifications for needed films.

When Eric Johnston became president of MPAA in 1945, a new policy was adopted with reference to educational films. In March 1946, the board of directors of MPAA, on the recommendation of the MPAA's Committee on Educational Matters, appropriated $100,000 for the production of several experimental films to gain information on procedures, processes, and costs of producing effective instructional films.[98] Although only three pilot films were produced, they were historically significant because they essentially anticipated the single-concept film developed in the early 1960s and because they represented the MPAA's first attempt to produce a genuine instructional film. The entire production of these experimental films was under the general management of Arthur L. Mayer of New York City and was coordinated by Roger Albright, director of the newly created Division of Educational Services of the MPAA. Two of the three pilot films, *Seasons* and *Osmosis*, were produced in cooperation with the Macmillan Company and Henry Holt and Company, respectively.[99]

Meanwhile, Mark A. May, chairman and director of research of TFC (a film distribution organization of the MPAA), organized the Yale motion picture research project, secured financing from the MPAA, and served as general director from its beginning in 1946 to its end in 1954.[100] Its stated purpose was to discover, through controlled experimental studies, methods of improving the teaching effectiveness of educational films.[101] Thus, the industry had come full circle from similar objectives first stated in 1934 as part of the ACE's national film institute proposal. However, there were two important differences: First, there was adequate financial support to conduct such experimentation and, second, there was wholehearted psychological support and cooperation from the motion picture industry.

Commission on Motion Pictures (CMP)[102]

The commission's main tasks were (1) to study the needs of schools for teaching films, particularly for pictures that would help meet the opportunities and challenges presented by problems of the postwar period, (2) to write educational specifications for the production of needed films and to select and organize content materials, and (3) when possible and feasible, to prepare film treatments and scripts.[103]

The CMP, basing its assessment of film needs to a large extent on the Seaton survey of teacher opinion concerning films, selected five general areas of instruction—geography, problems of democracy, mathematics, music, and art.[104] Plans for 141 films in these areas were prepared, but the CMP actually released to producers the materials for a total of only 117 films. Work on preliminary treatments for films in problems of democracy for senior high schools was carried on by a committee under the general chairmanship of George S. Counts of Teachers College, Columbia University. Late in 1946, the CMP employed George F. Kneller as general editor of the series.[105] On the basis of criticisms received from readers, the CMP finally selected fifteen treatments and released them to producers.

About a year before the commission was organized, Clark University president W. W. Atwood and F. Dean McClusky, headmaster of the Scarborough School in Scarborough-on-Hudson, New York, had received a grant of $10,000 from RKO Pictures to develop an outline for a series of films on global geography. Their completed outline, entitled *Widening Our Horizons*, was first presented in a CMP meeting in April 1944, by N. Peter Rathvon, president of RKO. Following a series of meetings, discussions, and outline revisions, a committee consisting of Atwood, McClusky, and Gardner L. Hart, director of the CMP, was appointed to select ten key topics in the outline and write detailed specifications for the production of these films, including scripts. This decision, however, raised a question of policy as to the function of the commission. Prior to this the CMP had not engaged in the writing of shooting scripts, confining itself to the preparation of educational specifications and an outline of film content. Some members felt that script-writing should be left to commercial producers. Nevertheless, with Atwood insisting that the film materials could and should be carried to the script stage, the CMP agreed to engage a scriptwriter and authorized Atwood to find a producer for the series. A contract was made with Louis de Rochemont Associates for the production of thirty-six films and Atwood was engaged as an educational consultant.

In getting the mathematics film treatments started, Gardner Hart first consulted W. D. Reeve of Teachers College, Columbia University, who was then editing a yearbook prepared by the Multi-Sensory Aids Committee of the National Council of Teachers of Mathematics. Reeve recommended that this committee would be especially well qualified to plan for needed films in mathematics, and his suggestion was accepted by the CMP. Harold L. Walton, general research associate for the commission, was placed in charge of the development of the mathematics material; educational specifications were developed for seven films on algebra and nine on geometry.

The work of the CMP in the field of art grew out of an exchange of letters among Stanley A. Czurles, director of art education at New York State College for Teachers, Buffalo; Mark A. May, the CMP's chairman; and Gardner L. Hart, its director. Czurles volunteered to prepare a report for the commission entitled *Outline for Motion Pictures to Teach the Basic Skills and Techniques in Art*, which was presented to a CMP meeting in October 1945. As a result of this presentation, the commission established an art committee to develop plans for art films and appointed one of their members, superintendent A. L. Threlkeld of the Montclair, New Jersey, Public Schools, as chairman. The materials prepared and released by the art committee included educational specifications for twenty-one films on art.[106]

The commission then set up a music committee at its meeting in March 1947. Since this was the last committee to be organized, the group benefited from the problems encountered by other committees, particularly in determining the format of the materials to be developed. The committee worked in cooperation with the Music Research Council of the Music Educators National Conference, which was headed by William Sur of Michigan State College. The materials prepared by the music committee were unique; they included two special reports covering the fields of music reading and music listening, in addition to specifications for a number of different music films. Plans were developed for a series of fifteen films on music.[107]

The work of the CMP has been variously evaluated. There is no question that it represented a significant cooperative endeavor between educators and the motion picture industry. Unfortunately, however, much of the commission's work has yet to prove useful. With the one single exception of the geography series, sponsored at the initiative of Rathvon of RKO before the commission was even organized, none of the CMP's film treatments have been produced to date. Since the original, comprehensive, mimeographed film treatments and outlines for these 117 films are in the sole possession and control of the MPAA, it is unlikely that the work of the commission will ever come to fruition.

Yale Motion Picture Research Project

The financial support for this project, beginning in 1946 and ending in 1954, came from TFC, a film distribution organization affiliated with the MPAA. The initial grant was for the purpose of experimentally evaluating certain pilot teaching films that were being produced under the sponsorship of the MPAA. However, the project was soon expanded to include exploratory experimental studies of problems associated with instructional film production and utilization.[108] Thus the project came to be focused on two broad objectives: First, to discover principles of effective production and utilization of educational films, and second, to explore the instructional potential and limitations of existing types of films and to find out why teachers were not using more films and graphic presentations in the classroom. The series of studies conducted compared the effects of alternate ways of utilizing a finished film product and measured the learning of factual information, the acquisition of skills, and the modification of interests, attitudes, and opinions. However, these studies were generally devoid of theoretical orientation and uneven in methodology. TFC developed the film materials used to test experimental variables, but as far as can be determined, these films were completely unaffected by theory or by the findings of past film research. The common attitude of the MPAA was that successful entertainment films could be edited, modified, and transformed into effective educational films. Since the researchers in the project had little or no control over the basic structure of the films produced for this experiment, they could hardly be expected to test complex experimental variables in any systematic or penetrating fashion. It is regrettable that this lengthy project did not produce results that could have significantly influenced the production and utilization of educational films.[109]

Concluding Comments

By the end of World War II, it was evident that a new phase of media research was at hand, a phase characterized by increasing scientific sophistication in the development of research designs and in the use of experimental procedures. Chapter 15 discusses the intensification of media research during the period from 1950 to 1980.

Notes

[1]One of the first tests was made at the Brooklyn Teachers Association. Films used were screenings of diverse theatrical subjects.

[2]David R. Sumstine, "A Comparative Study of Visual Instruction in the High School," *School and Society* 7 (February 1918), 235-38.

[3]J. V. Lacy, "The Relative Value of Motion Pictures as an Educational Agency," *Teachers College Record* 20 (November 1919), 452-65.

[4]Joseph J. Weber, "Comparative Effectiveness of Some Visual Aids in Seventh Grade Instruction," *Educational Screen* 1 (1922). For a report of Weber's 1921 study see Joseph J. Weber, *Picture Values in Education.* Chicago: Educational Screen, 1928.

[5]K. S. Lashley and J. B. Watson, *A Psychological Study of Motion Pictures in Relation to Venereal Disease Campaigns.* Washington, D.C.: U.S. Interdepartmental Social Hygiene Board, 1922, 3.

[6]The investigators were F. Dean McClusky, H. W. James, E. H. Reeder, A. P. Hollis, Caroline Hoefer, Edna Keith, Howard Y. McClusky, E. C. Rolfe, Lena A. Shaw, D. E. Walker, Nina J. Beglinger, and Jean A. Thomas.

[7]Frank N. Freeman, *Visual Education.* Chicago: University of Chicago Press, 1924, 79.

[8]Ibid., 69.

[9]Ibid., 77-78.

[10]Ibid., 79.

[11]George Eastman, personal letter to Will H. Hays, February 17, 1926.

[12]Those who attended the Eastman meeting were Thomas E. Finegan of Harrisburg, Pennsylvania; John H. Finely, of the *New York Times*, and member of the board of directors of Harmon's Religious Film Foundation; Payson Smith, Massachusetts commissioner of education; Mary Pennell, Columbia University; Otis Caldwell, principal of Lincoln School of Teachers College, Columbia University, and member of the board of directors of the Society for Visual Education; William A. McAndrew, superintendent of Chicago Public Schools; Howard Burge, principal of Fredonia New York State Normal School; and from Rochester, Herbert S. West, superintendent of schools, Charles E. Finch, director of vocational schools, and Mabel Simpson, supervisor of primary grades.

[13]The cities participating in the Eastman teaching film experiment were the following: Newton, Massachusetts; Rochester, New York; New York City, New York; Winston-Salem, North Carolina; Atlanta, Georgia; Detroit, Michigan; Chicago, Illinois; Lincoln, Nebraska; Kansas City, Missouri; Denver, Colorado; Oakland, California; and San Diego, California.

[14]Ben D. Wood and Frank N. Freeman, *Motion Pictures in the Classroom.* Boston: Houghton Mifflin, 1929, 223.

[15]Ibid., 214-15.

[16]F. Dean McClusky, "An Experiment with School Films." Unpublished manuscript, 1929, 15.

[17]D. C. Knowlton and J. W. Tilton, *Motion Pictures in History Teaching.* New Haven, Conn.: Yale University Press, 1929, 90.

[18]Ibid., 91.

[19]Yale University sponsored another study based on the *Chronicles of America Photoplays*, in 1938, that proved to be a valuable supplement to the Knowlton and Tilton studies. See H. A. Wise, *Motion Pictures as an Aid in Teaching American History*. New Haven, Conn.: Yale University Press, 1939.

[20]J. J. Weber, *Visual Aids in Education*. Valparaiso, Ind.: Valparaiso University, 1930, 195.

[21]Ibid., 209.

[22]Ibid., 199.

[23]P. J. Rulon, *The Sound Motion Picture in Science Teaching*. Cambridge, Mass.: Harvard University Press, 1933.

[24]Other notable studies of the instructional sound film made during the early 1930s include the following: V. C. Arnspiger, *Measuring the Effectiveness of Sound Pictures as Teaching Aids*, Teachers College Contributions to Education, no. 565, New York: Teachers College Press, Columbia University, 1933; and C. C. Clard, *Sound Pictures as an Aid in Classroom Teachings*, Ph.D. dissertation, New York University, 1932.

[25]Members of the Committee on Educational Research were: L. L. Thurstone, Frank N. Freeman, R. E. Park, Herbert Blumer, and Philip M. Hauser, all of the University of Chicago; George D. Stoddard, C. A. Ruckmick, P. W. Holaday, and Wendell Dysinger of the University of Iowa; Mark A. May and Frank K. Shuttleworth of Yale University; Frederick M. Thrasher and Paul G. Cressey of New York University; Charles C. Peters of Pennsylvania State College; Ben D. Wood of Columbia University; and Samuel Renshaw, Edgar Dale, and W. W. Charters of Ohio State University.

[26]W. W. Charters, *Motion Pictures and Youth*. New York: Macmillan, 1935, vi.

[27]Ibid.

[28]Ibid., 60-61.

[29]Cline M. Koon, *Motion Pictures in Education in the United States*. U.S. Department of the Interior, Bulletin 130. Washington, D.C.: GPO, 1934, 43.

[30]The International Institute of Educational Cinematography was founded in 1928 in Rome, Italy, by the Committee on Intellectual Cooperation of the League of Nations. Its principal activity was the publication of a periodical, *International Review of Educational Cinematography*, later called the *Intercine*.

[31]Koon, *Motion Pictures in Education*, 43-44.

[32]Quoted in ibid., 7-9.

[33]Persons attending this first conference were: Chancellor S. P. Capen, University of Buffalo, Buffalo, New York; William P. Farnsworth, National Recovery Act Administrator, Washington, D.C.; Superintendent Vierling Kersey, California State Department of Education, Sacramento, California; Superintendent C. H. Lake, Cleveland Public Schools, Cleveland, Ohio; B. F. Langsworthy, president, National Congress of Parents and Teachers; Cline M. Koon, U.S. Office of Education; Lorraine Noble, ACE; Henry B. Ward, American Association for the Advancement of Science; W. W. Charters, professor of education, Ohio State University; and George F. Zook, president, ACE.

[34]*Minutes of Conference to Consider Establishment of a National Film Institute*, Washington, D.C., December 4-5, 1934.

[35]Ibid.

[36]*Minutes of Second Conference to Consider Establishment of a National Film Institute*, Washington, D.C., February 28-March 1, 1935.

[37]One of the first proposals for a national educational film institute was probably made by George A. Skinner in his 1925 schoolmaster plan. His plan called for (1) a thorough piece of research into the social value of the motion picture; (2) a noncommercial, independent clearinghouse for the gathering and disseminating of information concerning the social and educational use of the motion picture; and (3) a commercial company operated solely for the production and distribution of the teaching film.

[38]An interim committee, consisting of George F. Zook, Edgar Dale, Cline M. Koon, Robert A. Kissack, Jr., and Lorraine Noble, was formed in July 1935, for the purpose of supervising the studies under this grant.

[39]Gladys E. Palmer, "A Motion Picture Survey in the Field of Sports for College Women," *The Research Quarterly of the American Association for Health, Physical Education, and Recreation* 7 (March 1936), 166-67.

[40]Edgar Dale and Lloyd L. Ramseyer, *Teaching with Motion Pictures: A Handbook of Administrative Practices*. Washington, D.C.: ACE Studies, ser. 2, vol. 4, no. 2, April 1937.

[41]The H. W. Wilson Company published the digests in 1937.

[42]Credit for the development of the first uniform educational film classification system goes to the following: E. Winifred Crawford, director of visual instruction, Montclair, New Jersey; Marion Evans, director of the visual instruction center, San Diego, California; and Annette Glick, director of the audiovisual department, Los Angeles, California.

[43]The first issue of the *Educational Film Catalog* was published in May 1936, with credit given to the ACE and the U.S. Office of Education, by the H. W. Wilson Company. The first volume, set up on a Dewey basis, listed 1,175 educational films. The first supplement to the catalog was published in January 1937. The name of the catalog was changed to *Educational Film Guide* in 1945.

[44]Cline M. Koon and Allen W. Noble, *National Visual Education Directory*. Washington, D.C.: ACE, 1936, 9.

[45]R. B. Fosdick, *The Story of the Rockefeller Foundation*. New York: Harper & Row, 1952, 45.

[46]Members of this committee were: Ben G. Graham, chairman; W. W. Charters; Frank N. Freeman; Mrs. B. F. Langworthy; Mark A. May; J. C. Wardlaw; and George F. Zook, ex officio.

[47]Charles F. Hoban, Jr., *Focus on Learning*. Washington, D.C.: ACE, 1942, p. v.

[48]Ibid., 2.

[49]The Staff of Tower Hill School, Wilmington, Del., *A School Uses Motion Pictures*. Washington, D.C.: ACE Studies, ser. 2, vol. 4, no. 3, September 1940, 10.

[50]Much of the credit for the selection of Santa Barbara as a film evaluation center belongs to Francis W. Noel, audiovisual director of the Santa Barbara schools during this period. When, on an eastern tour, Noel learned about Charles F. Hoban, Jr.'s, plans to make an inspection trip West, he invited Hoban to Santa Barbara to observe its curriculum-revision program and consider it as a possible film evaluation center. Although Hoban had been considering Los Angeles and San Diego, he accepted Noel's invitation. Noel alerted Santa Barbara superintendent Curtis Warren and they set about preparing the "right" activities for each classroom along the path designated for Hoban's observation. However, Noel's plans went slightly awry when Hoban inadvertently strolled off the planned path and entered the wrong room! Then it happened that a first-year teacher had even better activities in progress than those that had been planned. Hoban was so impressed that he remained in this classroom and never completed the tour planned for him (Francis W. Noel, interview with the author, March 15, 1952).

[51]Floyde E. Brooker and Eugene Herrington, *Students Make Motion Pictures*. Washington, D.C.: ACE Studies, ser. 2, vol. 5, no. 7, 1941.

[52]Reports of the Minnesota experiments were prepared in manuscript form by C. I. Potthoff, L. C. Larson, and D. O. Patterson (1940); E. C. Wilson, L. C. Larson, and F. Lord (1940). Unpublished. Project was under Robert Kissack.

[53]Lorraine Noble, interview with the author, April 12, 1952.

[54]Hoban, *Focus on Learning*, 146.

[55]This publication is the historical antecedent of the *Educational Media Index*, which was begun in 1964 by the Educational Media Council.

[56]Rockefeller fellows involved included: James D. Finn, Colorado College of Education; William H. Bowen, Jr., and James W. Brown, Virginia Board of Education; and Abram VanderMeer, Laboratory School, University of Chicago.

[57]The Ford Foundation's usual policy is to develop a program and then set out to implement it with grants.

[58]Lorraine Noble, interview with the author, April 12, 1952.

[59]Frank E. Hill, *Listen and Learn*. New York: AAAE, 1937, 36-37.

[60]B. H. Darrow, *Radio Trailblazing*. Columbus, Ohio: College Book Company, 1940, 39-40.

[61]Margaret Harrison, *Radio in Rural Schools*. Address given before Department of Rural Education of the Department of Superintendents at Atlantic City, February 26, 1930. (Mimeographed.)

[62]John Guy Fowlkes and H. L. Ewbank, "The Radio in Wisconsin Rural Schools," *Elementary School Journal* 30 (May 1930), 642-43.

[63]Hadley Cantril and Gordon W. Allport, *The Psychology of Radio*. New York: Harper and Brothers, 1935.

[64]F. M. Lumley, *Measurement in Radio*. Columbus: Ohio State University Press, 1934.

[65]Merton E. Carver, "A Study of Conditions Influencing the Relative Effectiveness of Visual and Auditory Presentation." Ph.D. dissertation, Harvard University, 1934.

[66]The Federal Radio Education Committee was created in 1935 by the FCC to eliminate controversy and misunderstandings between industry and educators and to promote cooperative undertakings in educational broadcasting.

[67]Norman Woelfel and I. Keith Tyler, *Radio and the School*. Tarrytown-on-Hudson, N.Y.: World Book Company, 1945, iii.

[68]*Tentative Report on Objectives*, Bulletin 1, Evaluation of School Broadcasts, Ohio State University, Columbus, Ohio, 1938.

[69]Ibid., 33.

[70]*Network School Broadcasts: Some Conclusions and Recommendations*, Bulletin 35, Evaluation of School Broadcasts, Ohio State University, Columbus, Ohio, 1941.

[71]See *Auditory Aids and the Teaching of Science: Two Experimental Studies*, Bulletin 57, Evaluation of School Broadcasts, Ohio State University, Columbus, Ohio, 1942.

[72]Ibid.

[73]*A Study of America's Town Meeting of the Air*, Bulletin 46, Evaluation of School Broadcasts, Ohio State University, Columbus, Ohio, 1942.

[74]Irving Robbins, *Teaching Radio Program Discrimination*, Bulletin 56, Evaluation of School Broadcasts, Ohio State University, Columbus, Ohio, 1942.

[75]*Study of Recordings for General Education*, Motion Picture Project, ACE, January 1939, i.

[76]Ibid.

[77]J. Robert Miles, *Recordings for School Use: A Catalog of Appraisals*. Tarrytown-on-Hudson, N.Y.: World Book Company, 1942.

[78]*Radio in the Classroom*, report of the Wisconsin Research Project in School Broadcasting. Madison: University of Wisconsin Press, 1942, 4.

[79]Paul F. Lazarsfeld, *Radio and the Printed Page*. New York: Duell, Sloan & Pearce, 1940, vii.

[80]Out of the Princeton project grew another project that had wide-reaching implications. In 1940, the Princeton School of Public and International Affairs, with the help of the Rockefeller Foundation, began to record and analyze shortwave broadcasts dealing with the war and beamed to America from Europe. At the same time, a similar station located at Stanford University in California, also with the assistance of the Rockefeller Foundation, began to monitor shortwave broadcasts from across the Pacific. Some of this broadcasting was news; much of it was propaganda. The results of the analysis in both institutions were made available in the form of bulletins and sent to students of communications and international affairs. When the United States entered the war, the FCC established at Washington the Foreign Broadcasting Monitoring Service, using the basic methods developed at Princeton and Stanford.

[81]Paul F. Lazarsfeld and Frank N. Stanton, *Radio Research 1942-1943*. New York: Duell, Sloan & Pearce, 1944.

[82]The third series of army film research studies was conducted at the Signal Corps Photographic Center and dealt with patterns of film supply, print utilization, and film library administration. Results of these studies were incorporated in a report by C. F. Hoban, Jr., *Movies That Teach*. New York: Dryden Press, 1946.

[83]C. I. Hovland et al., *Experiments on Mass Communication*. Princeton, N.J.: Princeton University Press, 1949.

[84]The work of the Psychological Test Film Unit was directed by J. J. Gibson. The report of the work of this unit can be found in AAF Aviation Psychology Program Research Report no. 7, entitled *Motion Picture Testing and Research*. Washington, D.C.: GPO, 1947.

[85]C. R. Carpenter and L. P. Greenhill, *Instructional Film Research Reports* 2. Technical Report 269-7-61, MAVEXPS P1543, Port Washington, N.Y.: Special Devices Center, 1956.

[86]Ibid.

[87]See C. F. Hoban, Jr., and E. B. Van Ormer, *Instructional Film Research 1918-1950*. Technical Report SDC 269-7-19, Port Washington, N.Y.: U.S. Naval Training Devices Center, December 1950.

[88]A. A. Lumsdaine, ed., *Student Response in Programmed Instruction*. Washington, D.C.: National Academy of Sciences, National Research Council, 1961.

[89]J. H. Kanner, "The Development and Role of Teaching Aids in the Armed Forces," in *New Teaching Aids for the American Classroom*. Stanford, Calif.: Institute for Communication Research, 1960, 123-24.

[90]Ibid., 124.

[91]The team was composed of Frank E. Sorenson, professor of secondary education, University of Nebraska; David B. McCulley, director of the department of audiovisual instruction, University of Nebraska; and Roger Albright, educational director of Teaching Film Custodians.

[92]Grants totaling $53,900 were made to the Nebraska film program over a four-year period.

[93]TFC provided $10,857.44 over the four years to apply toward the cost of loaned prints from other distributors or producers.

[94]Wesley C. Meierhenry, *Enriching Curriculum through Motion Pictures*. Lincoln: University of Nebraska Press, 1952, 28.

[95]Ibid., 41.

[96]Mark A. May, *Planning Films for Schools: The Final Report of the Commission on Motion Pictures*. Washington, D.C.: ACE, 1949, 5.

[97]Ibid., 6-7.

[98]The members of the Committee on Educational Matters were N. Peter Rathvon, J. Robert Rubin, and Joseph Hazen, the same men who had represented the motion picture industry on the joint committee of the MPAA and the ACE in 1943.

[99]The script of *Seasons* was written by Philip Knowlton, elementary school textbooks editor for Macmillan. The script of *Osmosis* was written with the technical advice of Milton Hopkins, science editor for Henry Holt and Company.

[100]Mark A. May was a professor of educational psychology and director of the Institute of Human Relations at Yale University.

[101]Mark A. May, "Educational Projects," *The Educational Screen* (April 1947), 201.

[102]The original members of the Commission on Motion Pictures, appointed by the ACE in February 1944, were: Edmund E. Day, president, Cornell University; Monsignor George Johnson, director, Department of Education, National Catholic Welfare Conference; Willard E. Givens, executive secretary, NEA; George S. Counts, director, Division of the Foundations of Education, Teachers College, Columbia University; Mark A. May, director, Institute of Human Relations, Yale University, chairman; and George F. Zook, president, ACE, ex officio. George N. Shuster, president, Hunter College, replaced Monsignor Johnson when he died in May 1944. Four more members were added later: A. L. Threlkeld, superintendent of schools, Montclair, New Jersey; W. W. Atwood, president, Clark University; Mary D. Barnes, principal, William Livingston School, Elizabeth, New Jersey; and Frank N. Freeman, dean, School of Education, University of California. Edmund E. Day resigned in 1947 because of other commitments.

[103]May, *Planning Films for Schools*, 1.

[104]See Helen Hardt Seaton, *A Measure for Audio-Visual Programs in Schools*. Washington, D.C.: ACE, 1944.

[105]Kneller found that it was difficult to find individuals who had a talent for dramatic writing and could at the same time stay within the bounds of historical accuracy. The result was that not all the research material collected and organized was put into the form of film treatments.

[106]The members of the CMP staff assigned to this project were Gardner Hart, R. S. Hadsell, and H. L. Walton.

[107]R. S. Hadsell and H. L. Walton were the commission staff members assigned to this project.

[108]This project was carried out under the general direction of Mark A. May, director of the motion picture research project and of the Institute of Human Relations, Yale University. Other staff members included: Arthur A. Lumsdaine, associate director from 1946 to 1949; R. S. Hadsell, assistant director from 1950 to 1954 and director of the Commission on Motion Pictures in Education during the years 1948 to 1950; Arthur I. Gladstone, member of the staff for the year 1948/49; John J. Howell, part-time member of the staff while a graduate student in the department of education at Yale University from 1950 to 1954; Mary C. Arnold, secretary, research assistant, and office manager of the project from 1946 to 1949; Gardner Hart, director of the Commission on Motion Pictures in Education from 1945 to 1948 and staff member of the project from 1946 to 1948; Edna Kauffman, part-time staff member from 1947 to 1949; and J. J. Wulff, a part-time member of the staff while a graduate student in psychology at Yale University. The testing program was conducted in the public schools of New Haven, West Haven, East Haven, and Hamden, Connecticut; in St. Louis, Missouri; and in New York City.

[109]For a complete report of the Yale motion picture project, see Mark A. May et al., *Learning from Films*. New Haven, Conn.: Yale University Press, 1958.

Select Bibliography

Arnspiger, V. C. *Measuring the Effectiveness of Sound Pictures as Teaching Aids.* Teachers College Contributions to Education no. 565. New York: Teachers College Press, Columbia University, 1933.

Brooker, Floyde E., and Eugene Herrington. *Students Make Motion Pictures.* Washington, D.C.: ACE Studies, ser. 2, no. 7, 1941.

Cantril, Hadley, and Gordon W. Allport. *The Psychology of Radio.* New York: Harper and Brothers, 1935.

Carpenter, C. R., and L. P. Greenhill. *Instructional Film Research Reports*, vols. 1 & 2. Technical Report SDC 269-7-61. Port Washington, N.Y.: U.S. Naval Training Devices Center, 1956.

Charters, W. W. *Motion Pictures and Youth.* New York: Macmillan, 1935.

Dale, Edgar, et al. *Motion Pictures in Education: A Summary of the Literature.* New York: Wilson Company, 1937.

Devereaux, Frederick L. *The Educational Talking Picture.* Chicago: University of Chicago Press, 1933.

Freeman, Frank N. *Visual Education.* Chicago: University of Chicago Press, 1924.

Gibson, James J. *Motion Picture Testing and Research.* AAF Aviation Psychology Program, Research Report 7. Washington, D.C.: GPO, 1947.

Hoban, Charles F., Jr. *Movies That Teach.* New York: Dryden Press, 1946.

Hoban, Charles F., Jr., and E. B. Van Ormer. *Instructional Film Research 1918-1950.* Technical Report SDC 269-7-19. Port Washington, N.Y.: U.S. Naval Training Devices Center, December 1950.

Hovland, Carl I., et al. *Experiments on Mass Communication.* Princeton, N.J.: Princeton University Press, 1949.

Knowlton, Daniel C., and J. Warren Tilton. *Motion Pictures in History Teaching.* New Haven, Conn.: Yale University Press, 1929.

Lashley, K. S., and J. B. Watson. *A Psychological Study of Motion Pictures in Relation to Venereal Disease Campaigns.* Washington, D.C.: U.S. Interdepartmental Social Hygiene Board, 1922.

Lazarsfeld, Paul F. *Radio and the Printed Page.* New York: Duell, Sloan & Pearce, 1940.

Lazarsfeld, Paul F., and Frank Stanton. *Radio Research 1941.* New York: Duell, Sloan & Pearce, 1942.

_____. *Radio Research 1942-1943*. New York: Duell, Sloan & Pearce, 1944.

Lumley, F. M. *Measurement in Radio*. Columbus: Ohio State University Press, 1934.

Lumsdaine, A. A., ed. *Student Response in Programmed Instruction*. Washington, D.C.: National Academy of Sciences, National Research Council, 1961.

McClusky, F. Dean. "Comparisons of Different Methods of Visual Instruction," in Frank N. Freeman, ed., *Visual Education*. Chicago: University of Chicago Press, 1924.

_____. "The Content of Educational Films," in ibid.

May, Mark A., et al. *Learning from Films*. New Haven, Conn.: Yale University Press, 1958.

Meierhenry, Wesley C. *Enriching the Curriculum through Motion Pictures*. Lincoln: University of Nebraska Press, 1952.

Radio in the Classroom. Report of the Wisconsin Research Project in School Broadcasting. Madison: University of Wisconsin Press, 1942.

Weber, Joseph J. *Picture Values in Education*. Chicago: *The Educational Screen*, 1922.

Wood, Ben D., and Frank N. Freeman. *Motion Pictures in the Classroom*. Boston: Houghton Mifflin, 1929.

Part III

Growth of Theoretical Thought and Practice: From Mid-Century to 1980

Part three contains seven chapters that explore different theoretical orientations and practices in educational technology that have developed since the middle of this century. Chapter 9 is a historical overview of the relationship of communication and educational technology. Chapter 10 describes the historical impact of behaviorism on educational technology. Chapter 11 explores the practical implications of cognitive science for educational technology. Chapter 12 describes the history and process of instructional design and the systems approach to instruction. Chapter 13 is a historical account of the development of educational broadcasting, continuing the history begun in chapter 7. Chapter 14 describes the emergence of the information society and its historical relationship to educational technology. Chapter 15 examines the history of the bureaucratic and political aspects of research and development under the sponsorship of the federal government and continues with the history of research in educational technology as begun in chapter 8.

9

Communication and Educational Technology: 1950-1980

This chapter shows the relationship between communication and educational technology. Although the communication movement began in the United States in the 1920s, it had little influence on the theories and practices of educational technology until the 1950s. Even today, education remains the one sector of our society in which the potential of the communications revolution has not been fully utilized or even completely understood.

Finding ways to enhance the educational experience is the prime task of educational technology, but it is exactly this area that is threatened because teachers and schools no longer are the sole dispensers of knowledge. Gerbner has observed that the formal educational enterprise exists in a cultural climate largely dominated by a "hidden curriculum" whereby the media "manufacture the shared symbolic environment, create and cultivate large heterogeneous publics, define the agenda of public discourse, and represent all other institutions in the vivid imagery of fact and fiction designed for mass publics."[1]

On the theoretical level, educational technology is seriously hampered by the absence of a theory of the structure of symbols and their effects or function relating to the mediation of cognitive processes. For example, it is still not clear how the structure of information in film differs from that in pictorial representation or in language. In Bruner's words, "media cannot be chosen in terms of their ability to convey certain kinds of content, but must also be chosen in terms of their ability to develop the processing skills that make up such an important part of human intelligence."[2]

This chapter shows the historical relationship between communication and educational technology by: (1) tracing the development of communication theory; (2) reviewing the development of selected communication models; (3) providing a historical background of communication research; (4) identifying the first communication centers in institutions of higher learning; and (5) showing the convergence of communication and educational technology during the 1950-1980 period.

Development of Communication Theory

The roots of the communication concept lie deep in the past. In essence, a theoretical analysis of communication has emerged in some form whenever social scientists sought to describe the broad dimensions of society. As a consequence, contributions to a theory of communication have flowed from specialists in such fields as philosophy, sociology, anthropology, political science, and psychology. Most significant, the changes that have brought about an industrial, urban, and secular society since the beginning of the nineteenth century have forced all thinking men to evolve a conceptualization of the communication process.

This section focuses on some of the primary sources of modern communication theory. A number of other published works provide more extensive treatments of the various theoretical domains of communication theory.[3] However, it appears hopeless to delineate reasonable limits for communication study: Reusch has listed more than forty disciplines or fields of communication.[4]

Symbolic Interactionism

Symbolic interactionism, a theoretical viewpoint primarily from the field of sociology, provides one of the broadest views of communication and contains a core of primary concepts about communication and society. This perspective is rooted in the ideas of George Herbert Mead, the social psychology of Charles Horton Cooley, and the views of such American pragmatists as William James, Charles Peirce, and John Dewey. Mead's principal ideas were enunciated in the early 1920s in his popular Social Psychology course at the University of Chicago.[5] Mead's view is that individuals are actors rather than reactors and that "the social act involves a three-part relationship: an initial gesture from one individual, a response to that gesture from another (covertly or overtly), and a result of the act, which is perceived or imagined by both parties."[6] In essence, for the symbolic interactionist, all human behavior is communication. The influence of Mead's course can be seen in the fact that such communication "fathers" as Harold Lasswell, Douglas Waples, Charles W. Morris, and Herbert Blumer were his students.[7]

Beginnings of Mass Communication Theory

Mass communication theory began as media developed, a result of the increasing need to understand how media functioned in the mass society and what influences they might have on individuals. Golding and Murdock have suggested that the first communication research had roots in "the theory of mass society."[8] Lowery and DeFleur also point to the term *mass*, as used in *mass society*, as the intellectual source of the concepts of mass media and mass communication.[9]

This view of mass society focused on the effects of media and produced most mass communication theory. During the late 1920s and early 1930s, scholars developed an interest in mass media research and began to systematically study the impact communication content had upon particular kinds of people. Theories such as the "uniform influences," "hypodermic," and "magic bullet" theories of media effects became dominant. All reflected a reductionist, cause-effect approach that still persists. As DeFleur concluded in his study of modern theories of mass communication:

> The all-consuming question that has dominated research and the development of contemporary theory in the study of mass media can be summed up in simple terms—namely, "what has been their effect?"[10]

Although "magic bullet"-type theories were repudiated in some quarters by mid-century because the reported effects of mass communication did not always conform to the assumptions made, the cause-effect orientation remained dominant. In the 1960s and 1970s, some theorists shifted to a uses-and-gratification theory, or the ways that individuals use media for their own needs. This caused some other behavioral scientists to modify their belief that media cause direct effects and adopt a "limited effects" perspective. However, by the late 1970s, it became evident that the dominant theoretical paradigm was once again the S-R (stimulus-response) model.

Communication Models

This section extends the discussion of the development of communication theory by reviewing the most important models that emerged between 1950 and 1980 to describe the communication process.[11]

The 1950s proved to be particularly fertile in the development of conceptual modes of communication. According to Johnson and Klare, it was the mathematician Claude Shannon who provided the stimulus to social scientists to formulate new communication models.[12] Although the model developed by Shannon and his co-worker Warren Weaver applies more specifically to telephone and broadcasting technology, it has been important in the reformulation of communication theory.[13] This model describes communication as a linear, one-way process that includes such components as information source, transmitter, signal, and receiver. The one dysfunctional factor is entropy or noise which may make it difficult for the receiver to determine what the message of the source may be if many messages are sent simultaneously.

Another influential communication model was developed by the American political scientist Harold D. Lasswell. His model classically stated that communication is:

Who
Says What
In Which Channel
To Whom
With What Effect?

Lasswell went on to explain that those who study the *who* are operating within the field of *control analysis*, and those concerned with the *says what* are engaging in *content analysis*. On the other hand, specialists who concentrate upon the mass communications media are doing *media analysis*. If research focuses on the persons reached by these media, then it is *audience analysis*. Finally, the impact of these media upon audiences is referred to as *effect analysis*.[14]

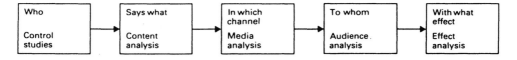

Fig. 9.1. The Lasswell Formula with corresponding fields of communication research.

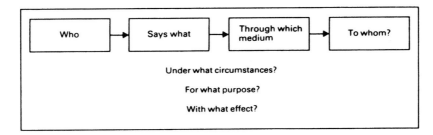

Fig. 9.2. Braddock's extension of the Laswell Formula.

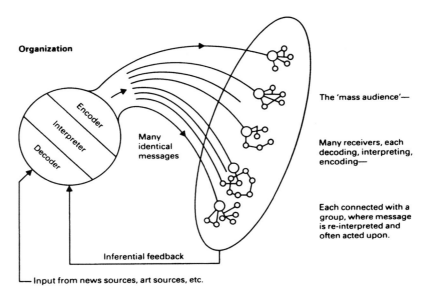

Fig. 9.3. Schramm's mass communication model.

The sender-channel-message-receiver models were increasingly modified during the 1950s as social scientists became more sophisticated and incorporated a number of other important aspects of communication. Feedback was included as an essential component as well as selective perception, interpretation, and retention of messages.

Communication Models of the 1950s

The 1950s were a particularly active era for developing communication models. One prevailing hypothesis stated that human beings strive to keep their thinking and behavior logically consistent. Whenever their concept of consistency is threatened or disturbed, they try to change their ideas, attitudes, or behavior to restore balance. Newcomb's social psychological model, formulated in 1953 (often called the ABX model), looks at relationships between participants and objects and how these relationships affect and are affected by communication.[15] The model takes the form of a triangle, the points of which represent individuals A and B and an object in their common environment, X. Discrepancies between

A and B in their orientation toward X stimulate communication and this communication tends to restore balance. Festinger's theory of cognitive dissonance held that decisions, choices, and new information can create a feeling of inconsistency or dissonance, thereby motivating a person to seek information to support his choice.[16]

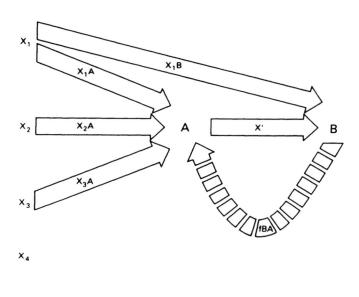

Fig. 9.4. ABX model.

Westley and MacLean adapted Newcomb's ABX model in 1957, adding the channel C, which stands for mass communicator.[17] This component acts as the "gatekeeper" for the transmission of messages between A and B. Thus, A stands for a source in society and B for a member of the society. The channel has the impartial task of interpreting the needs of B and satisfying them by transforming meaning into a shared symbol system and transmitting messages to B through a medium or channel.

In 1954, Wilbur Schramm and C. E. Osgood built a model on the Shannon-Weaver formulation with some variations.[18] First, the Osgood-Schramm model is circular rather than linear; second, whereas Shannon's model is essentially directed to the channels mediating between the senders and receivers, Schramm and Osgood focus on the behavior of the senders and receivers.

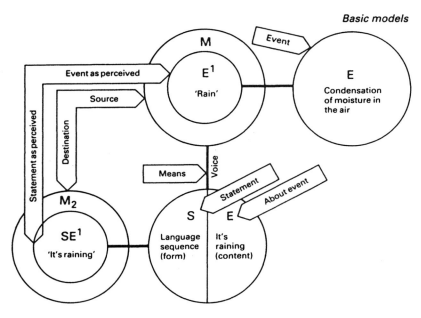

Fig. 9.5. Gerbner's model.

The communications specialist George Gerbner developed a model in 1956 that was almost Lasswellian:

1. Someone
2. perceives an event
3. and reacts
4. in a situation
5. through some means
6. to make available materials
7. in some form
8. and context
9. conveying content
10. with some consequence[19]

Katz and Lazarsfeld's two-step flow model of mass media and personal influence emerged from the study of the effects of mass communication in the presidential election of 1940.[20] After assessing the research results, Katz and Lazarsfeld developed the concept of a two-step flow of communication and the idea of "opinion leaders." After more research and a theoretical reevaluation, a revised model was developed in 1955. McQuail and Windahl have observed that, according to this model, "mass media do not operate in a social vacuum but have an input into a very complex web of social relationships and compete with other sources of ideas, knowledge, and power."[21]

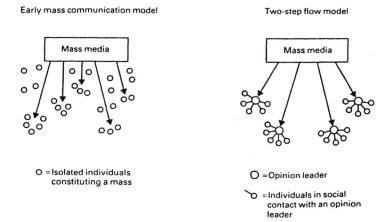

Fig. 9.6. Two-step flow model of media influence compared with traditional model of mass communication (after Katz and Lazarsfeld 1955).

Communication models implied that communication took place in a social vacuum and that influence from the total social context was not significant, until the emergence of the Riley and Riley model in 1959.[22] The Rileys presented a so-called working model of communication and pointed to the important roles played by primary groups and reference groups. Primary groups are distinguished by their degree of intimacy, while a reference group is a group by which a person may define his attitudes, values, and behavior. As a communicator or a receiver, a person is influenced by the primary group. The communicator and the receiver are part of two larger structures that are interrelated by feedback mechanisms. For example, a learner may be tied to one peer group (primary group) that is part of the class and the school as a whole (a larger social structure). The primary group is influenced in its attitudes and behavior partly by each other and partly by the larger social structure which may also influence the learner directly. Mendelssohn observed that the Rileys can be considered the originators of "the new look in mass communication" in that they "focus on the mediating role of other psychological factors in influencing the impacts that the mass media can produce on individuals and groups."[23]

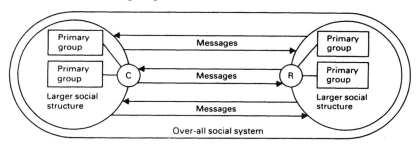

C = Communicator   R = Receiver

Fig. 9.7. Riley and Riley model.

Communication Models of the 1960s and 1970s

In 1960, David K. Berlo popularized the source-message-channel-receiver (SMCR) model of communication in his influential textbook *The Process of Communication.*[24] Written expressly for students of communication, his SMCR model included many of the factors that could affect how sources and receivers create and react to messages. He also included elements that related to the topic, organization, and language of messages.

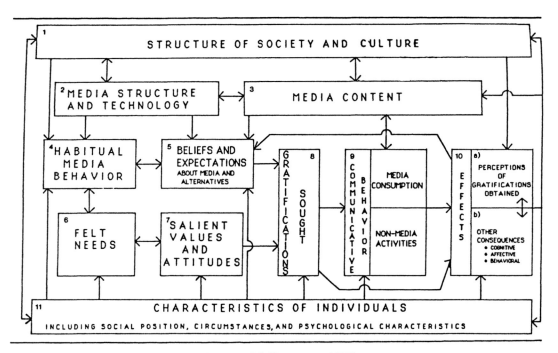

Fig. 9.8. Rosengren's media gratifications model (Rosengren 1974)

One of the most important applications of mass communication and research has focused on the process of innovation-diffusion. One of the more interesting models related to diffusion was developed by Rogers and Shoemaker in 1973.[25] Their model assumes that there are at least four distinct steps in an innovation-diffusion process: knowledge, persuasion, decision, and confirmation. Diffusion of innovation may involve different communication sources and different functions.

Another model that received considerable attention in the 1970s is the so-called agenda-setting paradigm.[26] American researchers Malcolm McCombs and Donald Shaw stated their hypothesis as follows:

> Audiences not only learn about public issues and other matters through the media, they also learn how much importance to attach to an issue or topic from the emphasis the mass media place upon it.[27]

Comstock et al. developed a psychological model in 1978 in their attempt to find an organizing framework for research out of a broad and varied collection of data concerning the effects of television.[28] This model was tested in relation to research concerning aggression, erotic arousal, political socialization, and social behavior of children and adolescents.

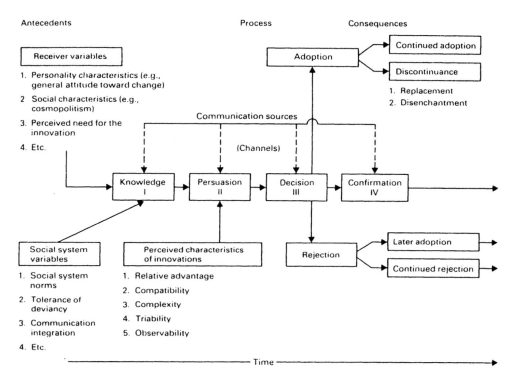

Fig. 9.9. Rogers and Shoemaker's paradigm of the innovation-decision process, indicating the four steps of knowledge, persuasion, decision, and confirmation (Rogers and Shoemaker 1973).

Ball-Rokeach and DeFleur developed a dependency model of mass communication effects in 1976.[29] This model focuses on those who depend on mass media for their knowledge and perspective of what is occurring in their own society. Their degree of dependency will relate to the extent that the society is subject to change, conflict, or instability and also to the extent that the mass media serve distinctive or primary information functions. This model essentially illustrated the interrelationships between societal systems, media systems, and audiences.

In the 1960s and 1970s, media research into media uses and gratifications began to appear. Katz et al. described the underlying logic of such investigations as follows: "They are concerned with (1) the social and psychological origins of (2) needs, which generate (3) expectations of (4) the mass media or other sources, which leads to (5) differential patterns of media exposure (or engagement in other activities), resulting in (6) need gratification and (7) other consequences, perhaps mostly unintended ones."[30] In essence, the uses-and-gratifications approach to mass communication research posed the questions, "What do people do with the mass media?" "How do the mass media satisfy our needs and our wants?" "How can we use the media for our purposes and goals?"

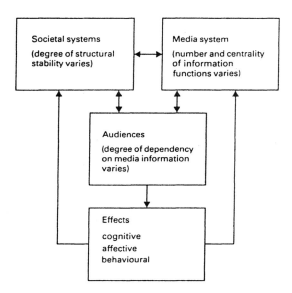

Fig. 9.10. Ball-Rokeach and DeFleur's dependency
model (Ball-Rokeach and DeFleur 1976).

A number of uses-and-gratifications models were developed in the 1960s and 1970s, but Rosengren's model of 1974 (see figure 9.8) seems most complete in discussing all the relevant elements of this media approach.[31] The needs of the individual is a starting point, with a reference to Maslow's hierarchy of needs. In another section of the model, Rosengren introduces the concept of problems, which are created by the interaction of needs, individual characteristics, and the social context. On the individual level, perceived problems and their solutions may provide motivation for action. Action may take the form of media consumption or be manifested in other behavior. The result of action may be either gratification or non-gratification. Finally, the model deals with effects. However, rather than following the traditional concept of effects intended by the communicator, this model focuses on the effects more or less consciously intended by the consumer.

During the 1960s and 1970s, there was a shift from an emphasis on understanding the entire communication process toward considering specific aspects of this process. Such aspects as social, cultural, and ideological effects as well as the social and psychological bases of audience choice and response became relevant factors in communication models. Other conceptual advances made during the twenty-year period from 1960 to 1980 included a change from a conception of direct and general effects on an audience toward a recognition of the mediating role played by personal contacts in transmitting and validating media information and ideas. Another conceptual shift was related to the increasing attention that was given to the structure of media systems and to indirect and long-term effects over direct, short-term effects. Still another change was a greater emphasis on the audience as initiator and interpreter of communication. Also, more attention was given to latent meaning and the sources of communication rather than merely to its effects.

Despite the proliferation of communication models during the thirty-year period from 1950 to 1980, it was clearly unrealistic to expect the formulation of a definitive, all-embracing communication model in the years ahead. Nevertheless, it was also apparent that communication models would continue to play an important role in clarifying new ideas and theories and stimulating research activity.

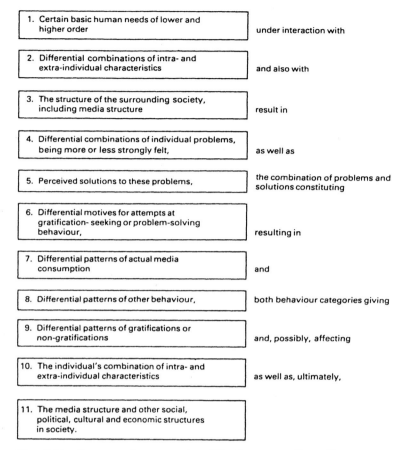

Fig. 9.11. Rosengren's uses-and-gratifications paradigm (Rosengren 1974).

McLuhan's Theories

Marshall McLuhan's controversial writings in mass communications created a stir in the early 1960s. Although McLuhan published for many years, writing such books as *The Mechanical Bride* (1951) and *The Gutenberg Galaxy* (1962), it was not until he wrote *Understanding Media* in 1964 that he came to public attention. According to McLuhan's main thesis, "the medium is the message," and the medium is "hot" or it is "cool."[32] His basic hypothesis is that people adapt to their environment through a certain balance of the senses and that the primary medium of the age determines a particular sensory ratio. McLuhan sees every medium as an extension of some human faculty with the media of communication exaggerating this or that particular sense. In his words, "The wheel is an extension of the foot. The book is an extension of the eye.... Clothing, an extension of the skin.... Electric circuitry, an extension of the central nervous system."[33]

McLuhan's distinction between hot and cool media are the most confusing and, probably, the most controversial in his writing. Hot media require little or no effort because the perceiver has no need to become involved by filling in incomplete data. Hot media, because they supply everything, create a dulling sensation. Cool media, on the other hand, require extensive participation from the perceiver. Film, for example, is considered a hot medium because the screen image is complete in every detail, while television is considered cool because it provides the viewer with only a sketch through the illumination of tiny dots.

During the last years of his life, McLuhan changed some of his earlier ideas. He became less certain, for example, in ascribing a causal link between media and personal perception. Where he once saw the human being as a passive responder to media, he came to believe that individuals are active creators of their own environments. Despite his tendency to overstate and his inability to provide scientific evidence for his provocative pronouncements, he did stimulate creative thought about the mass media of communication in the mid-1960s and the early 1970s.

Mediums and Instruments of Communication

Definitions do not make a theory of communication, but different definitions of media do reflect contrasting theoretical orientations. For example, Gordon contends that media (or, preferably, mediums) are not properly understood and are commonly confused with devices or instruments of communication. According to Gordon, there are only three mediums of communication and they have no relation to the history of mechanics or science. From a logical point of view they are "discrete, highly differentiated conduits for the transfer of thought and feeling."[34] And from the psychological viewpoint, they are qualities of mind. The true mediums, then, are narrative, picture, and re-creation or re-enactment. Gordon views all three as complementary in human communications.

On the other hand, what are usually called media Gordon considers instruments or technological devices of supply. They merely limit what may be transmitted in the conduits, but have no value or form by themselves. As Gordon says,

> we have for at least half a century, fallen into the habit of regarding our attractive technology—movie projectors, television receivers, revolving stages, etc.—not only as mediums but as messages. In the first place they are not mediums, and in the second place, they are not messages. They are ... extremely effective devices which serve as instruments by which mediums of communication of three sorts (narrative, picture, and impersonation) may be distributed to wide audiences.[35]

Thayer states that media should refer to all of the means—"all of the devices, technologies, etc.—utilized for acquiring, storing, transporting, or displaying messages. The human ear is a medium as are all human languages. The microscope and the telescope are media. A piece of parchment, like the wall of an inhabited cave ... is also a medium."[36]

Background of Communication Theory and Research

In the early 1930s, a small group of men began to realize the necessity of blending the diverse elements that had emerged in the various areas of the humanities and the social sciences. In 1931, the Social Science Research Council (organized in 1923 to correlate and stimulate research in the social sciences), under the leadership of David Stevens (professor of English at the University of Chicago and vice-president of the General Education Board of the Rockefeller Foundation), appointed an interdisciplinary committee for the study of communication. An important result of this committee's work was the publication of the first comprehensive, annotated bibliography of professional literature related to communication and mass media.[37]

In 1938, John Marshall of the Rockefeller Foundation organized a monthly seminar group, the purpose of which was twofold: first, to provide an integrated, philosophical approach to communication and, second, to construct a systematic pattern of communication research methodology.[38]

An important early contribution to communication theory and research came from the political scientists. Other fields or disciplines might have been expected to provide this impetus, but they failed to do so for a number of reasons. Schools of journalism, business, and advertising did not provide the early interdisciplinary leadership because they were essentially trade schools on the periphery of academic scholarship. Schools of education had devised instructional approaches that had implications for communication research, but they never achieved a working relationship with the social science or humanities departments. Such fields as law, divinity, medicine, literature, history, linguistics, music, architecture, or any of the creative arts also might have given the initial stimulus to the communications movement, but they lacked the broad perspectives being developed by the political scientists.

The advent of readership and audience surveys, public opinion polls, and propaganda studies in the 1920s and 1930s resulted in the development of mass media research activity in institutions of higher learning, and thus foreshadowed the later emergence of the university communication research center. Probably the Payne Fund studies, conducted by investigators from a number of universities between 1929 and 1933, provided the first important impetus to communication research. In 1933, George Gallup (who developed one of the first systematic techniques of public polling in 1928) conducted the first experimental readership survey while teaching psychology at Iowa State University. In 1937, Clyde Miller of Teachers College, Columbia University, and associates from other universities began the first systematic propaganda research with the establishment of the Institute for Propaganda Analysis in New York City. Other significant influences on the development of communication research during the 1930s came from the work of Paul F. Lazarsfeld and others at Princeton and later Columbia University (Office of Radio Research), and from Gordon Allport and Hadley Cantril in their studies of the psychology of radio at the Harvard Psychological Laboratory.[39] Moreover, studies of why and how people read and how reading affects people first began at the University of Chicago Library School in 1930 with the work of Douglas Waples and others.[40] Later, Kurt Lewin and his associates at the University of Iowa studied individual behavior under group pressures in a variety of experimental settings.[41] Additional valuable sources of hypotheses for communication research have flowed from psychotherapy, advertising, semantic theory, and from the analysis of communication problems in industry.

Communication studies stimulated by World War II brought a significant impetus to communication research. From pioneering studies by Carl I. Hovland and others for the research branch of the War Department's Information and Education Division came the widely accepted concepts of the psychological processes of communication and persuasion.[42] Samuel A. Stouffer, as research director for the information and education branch of the army during World War II, organized several hundred attitude surveys among soldiers all over the world.[43] Robert K. Merton studied the effects of a World War II bond drive conducted as a marathon radio appeal by Kate Smith and provided one of the classic studies of the communication process in his monograph *Mass Persuasion*.[44]

The momentum of World War II studies stimulated communications research in the postwar years. A major influence on communication research came from cybernetics scholars like Norbert Wiener and John Neuman, and from communications mathematicians like Claude Shannon and Warren Weaver.[45] Vital theoretical contributions to communications research were also made by Ernest Cassirer, Colin Cherry, George Gerbner, Elihu Katz and Paul F. Lazarsfeld, Susanne K. Langer, Harold Lasswell, Marshall McLuhan, George A. Miller, Jurgen Ruesch and Gregory Bateson, Wilbur Schramm, and Joseph Klapper.[46]

Despite these impressive contributions to communication research, by the end of the 1970s, there was still no integrated, generally accepted theory of communication. There is no question that newly developing communication technologies will demand new approaches in communication research.

Beginnings of Communication Study in the United States

The first systematic study of communication in the United States took place in institutes established in the early 1930s for public opinion polling, radio audience surveys, and commercial consumer studies.[47] Some institutes such as the Bureau of Applied Social Research at Columbia University were established to conduct social research. After World War II, more institutes grew largely out of government wartime use of empirical research. For example, Carl Hovland, fresh from his experience as chief psychologist and director of experimental studies for the U.S. War Department, founded the Yale University program in Communication and Attitude Change, and Sam Stouffer, who had worked with Hovland during the war, became head of the Institute of Social Relations at Harvard University. Simultaneously, some universities saw a need to develop institutes of communication in the late 1940s. Much of the impetus for this movement came from departments of journalism, speech, broadcasting, and film. As more teachers with research experience joined these departments, the concept of communication study began to develop. At the universities of Minnesota and Wisconsin, for example, the departments of journalism and mass communication were organized.

It was Wilbur Schramm, more than anyone else, who conceived that communication should become a separate field. As a consequence, Schramm founded the first Institute of Communication Research at the University of Illinois in 1947. This institute is of historic importance for two reasons: first, it marked the formal beginning of mass communication research in higher education; second, it served as the first major point of convergence of related disciplines.

Within the next decade, several other institutes were founded. Their curricula blended such traditional areas as cinema, radio, television, journalism, and speech. Supporting areas might include psychology, social psychology, social science, English, library science, and educational technology. Graduate work for advanced degrees followed. Research was published in new journals and communication yearbooks and communication conventions were held.

By the late 1970s, however, communication institutes and the communication sciences had entered an era of transition and uncertainty. Because of the extraordinary impact of new communication technologies, it appeared likely that new changes would take place. Schramm has predicted a reintegration of the social sciences that may make it doubtful whether communication institutes will become permanent components of university structure. He observed that there was "a phase of academic evolution which will confirm the importance of communication study, and greatly enrich studies of the media and other communication," but "as the social disciplines come to value their exclusivity less and a broader base of theory more, is it too much to anticipate that communication theory and research, along with social psychology, sociology, anthropology, political science, and others might not be absorbed into a more broadly conceived disciplinary study of human society?"[48]

Convergence of Communication and Educational Technology

The convergence of communication and educational technology did not occur until the 1950s despite the significant implications of communication theory and research. McQuail has noted, for example, that "the case of education is an interesting one where we can see at first sight a set of circumstances favorable to the application of mass media, or the technologies of mass media, to existing purposes, yet in practice rather little use made of them."[49] Aside from the usual resistance of educational institutions and teachers to new ways or means of communicating, the primary reason that educational technology did not incorporate communication within its conceptual framework to any great degree is that behaviorism began to exert its influence in the early 1960s, just about the time that communication was beginning to have some impact on educational technology. Regardless of this deflection of its potential impact, some convergence of communication and educational technology did take place in the thirty-year period between 1950 and 1980.

The Founding of the *Audio-Visual Communication Review*

The first significant convergence of communication and educational technology took place in 1953 with the publication of the *Audio-Visual Communication Review* (later *A V Communication Review*).[50] It was launched with the purpose of bringing "to all persons interested in any aspect of human communication ... professional information and thinking at the highest possible levels" and "to provide a means through which specialists in communication may publish the results of research studies, theoretical constructions and critical analyses of the problems of the field" and "to bring to bear through publication of pertinent materials, the broad thinking of such associated disciplines as sociology, social psychology and social anthropology on the problems of communication in modern society."[51] The first editor, William H. Allen, and James D. Finn, as a member of the editorial board, wrote the first charter.

The early issues of the *A V Communication Review* emphasized the nature of communication. For example, Finn stressed the communication concept when he stated that:

> The adoption of the term communications by the leadership of the audiovisual movement has had and will have a much more profound effect on the thinking and direction of the field than is yet realized by most practitioners. For the concept of communication or communications, as the case may be, is a seminal, organizing concept in all of the social sciences similar in scope and effect to the concept of field theory that swept through physics and biology into psychology and philosophy.[52]

This author at the time concluded that:

> audiovisual specialists will of necessity find it more expedient to erect a broader conceptual framework if they are to utilize the theoretical contributions of communication theorists. Perhaps some term such as "Educational Communication" will ultimately be required to describe the communication activities, both verbal and non-verbal, which have a particular application to the classroom.[53]

After 1960, only a handful of articles in the *Audio-Visual Communication Review* dealt with communication and educational technology. In 1972, an article by Mielke expressed the view that "it appears that both fields (mass communication and educational technology) have progressed beyond a fixation on hardware to the utility of media in meeting communication objectives within a systems approach."[54] However, Mielke observed that behaviorism was dominating educational technology and that the early interest in communication was being superseded by concerns with instructional development and aptitude-treatment interaction as well as by a focus on programmed instruction and systems approaches to instruction.[55]

Although it was apparent in the 1970s that communication was not being integrated within the conceptual pattern of educational technology, the *AV Communication Review* was changed to *Educational Communications and Technology* in 1978, and in effect, recognized that communication was still part of the conceptual frame for educational technology. After Torkelson's appraisal of the twenty-five years of *AV Communication Review* in 1977, he said:

> I think we're still uncertain as to whether we are first and foremost educational communication specialists, and secondarily, and uniquely, technologists, when the latter role is placed in the perspective of other relevant specialties in and outside of education. If one adds up the emphasis in the articles that have dealt with the breadth, complexities, and interdisciplinary nature of human communication, one might argue for specialization in educational communications as the generic area of study for the field. If one accepts this context, technological processes are subsidiary to the study of human communication, in the sense of being processes for examining and delimiting human communication problems. Who among professional educators worth their salt could not be called an educational technologist? If this be so, do our present terms and labels reflect our true uniqueness among other professionals in education? How particularized should we become as an applied professional field?[56]

From Audiovisual Instruction to Audiovisual Communication

The year 1963 marked a historic turning point in the audiovisual instruction movement with the publication of the monograph *The Changing Role of the AudioVisual Process in Education: A Definition and a Glossary of Related Terms.*[57] This document signaled an official new definition that changed audiovisual instruction to audiovisual communications. But rather than just a name change, this was also a major theoretical change. Thus, from an emphasis on audiovisual materials as aids in providing concrete experience came a new emphasis on the total process of communication. The new definition stated that "audiovisual communications is that branch of educational theory and practice concerned primarily with the design and use of messages which control the learning process." It was stated further that audiovisual communications undertakes:

> (a) the study of the unique and relative strengths of both pictorial and non-representational messages which may be employed in the learning process for any purpose; and (b) the structuring and systematizing of messages by men and instruments in an educational environment. These undertakings include the planning, selection, management and utilization of both components and entire instructional systems.[58]

It is clearly stated in this monograph that learning theory and communication theory provide the basic conceptual framework for educational technology. Moreover, it is clear that the traditional media view of educational technology with the prevailing product concept had been discarded and replaced with the process concept of the behavioral sciences view. Therefore, the terms *materials* and *machines* were no longer considered to be useful distinctions; *messages* and *media-instrumentation* were the new terms.

To implement this new definition, a communication model was developed to show the relationships between communication and educational technology (see figure 9.12). The model synthesizes communication and learning theory concepts, emphasizing the idea of feedback. The sender-receiver element was identified as the learning-communicant system. The term *communicant* was chosen to suggest the dual functions of reception and response.

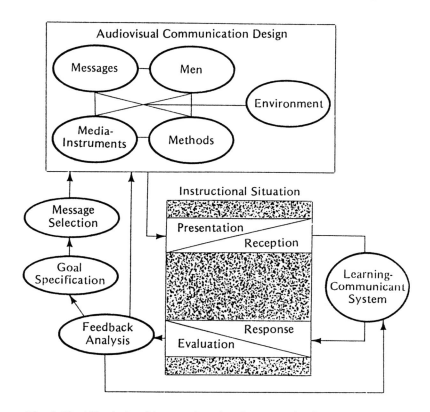

Fig. 9.12. AV relationships to educational-communication process.

This redefinition not only emphasized the complete process of communication, but, in addition, included a systems approach to instruction. Thus, message selection was considered as "one way of stating aspects of curriculum design" and the inclusion of people in the system is specifically related to the presentation element of the larger model.[59] Moreover, it was stated that "consideration of any of the design system elements requires close and continuing attention to the learner-communicant who is the intended receiver of the presentation."[60] Also, "attention must be given to responses made by the learning-communicant, to verify that the presentation was actually linked to the learning-communicant and, if possible, to verify the nature and amount of the linkage achieved."[61] Finally, if the primary goal of the system is considered to be an appropriate response of the learning-communicant, then "goal specification is the original task of the educational system, and message selection is based upon goal specification."[62]

Although this definition contained much of the systems approach concept, it did not integrate the complete systems theoretical framework because all necessary elements were not included. Meanwhile, there was a growing confusion with the use of such terms as *audiovisual communications, educational communications,* and *instructional technology.* Although the professional journal of the field still retained the term *educational communications* in its title, it was clear by the middle 1960s that communication theory and design in instructional application was becoming less influential and that behaviorist concepts were beginning to dominate in educational technology. The definitive withdrawal and severance of its ties with communications theory and practice was symbolized in 1989 when the title of the professional journal of the field was changed from *Educational Communications and Technology* to *Educational Technology Research and Development (ETR&D).*[63] Whether this vital part of educational technology will ever be recovered and incorporated into its theory and practice remains a question for the future.[64]

The next chapter examines the impact of behaviorism on the theoretical and applied aspects of educational technology.

Notes

[1]George Gerbner, "Teacher Image in Mass Culture: Symbolic Functions of the 'Hidden Curriculum'," in David R. Olson, ed., *Media and Symbols: The Forms of Expression, Communication, and Education,* Part I, 73rd yearbook of the National Society for the Study of Education. Chicago: University of Chicago Press, 1974, 470-71.

[2]Ibid., 17.

[3]See, for example, Ernest G. Bormann, *Communication Theory.* New York: Holt, Reinhart and Winston, 1980; and Melvin L. DeFleur and Sandra Ball-Rokeach, *Theories of Mass Communication.* New York: Longman, 1982.

[4]Jurgen Ruesch, "Clinical Science and Communication Theory," in Floyd W. Matson and Ashley Montagu, eds., *The Human Dialogue.* New York: Free Press, 1967, 58.

[5]Mead's primary work is *Mind, Self and Society,* Chicago: University of Chicago Press, 1934.

[6]Stephen W. Littlejohn, *Theories of Human Communication,* 2d ed. Belmont, Calif.: Wadworth Publishing, 1983, 47. Sociologists such as Manfred Kuhn and others in the Iowa School of symbolic interactionism, such as Carl Couch, pursued the basic ideas of Mead and attempted to develop their own variations. Herbert Blumer, the foremost spokesman of Mead, coined the term *symbolic interactionism* and developed a unified view. However, some accused Blumer of misinterpreting Mead. In the 1960s and 1970s, interactionism brought about renewed controversy over the "proper" interpretation of Mead.

[7]Harold Lasswell made World War II propaganda studies, developed "content analysis" in various communications areas and formulated an influential communication model; Douglas Waples distinguished himself in reading research; Charles W. Morris developed an approach to language analysis that scholars in a number of disciplines have used to clarify the foundations of the field; and Herbert Blumer coined the term *symbolic interactionism* and furthered the interactionist perspectives of Mead.

[8]Peter Golding and G. Murdock, "Theories of Communication and Theories of Society," *Communication Research* 5 (December 1977), 339-56.

[9]Shearon Lowery and Melvin L. DeFleur, *Milestones in Mass Communication Research.* New York: Longman, 1983, 3-4.

[10]Melvin L. DeFleur, *Theories of Mass Communication*, 2d ed. New York: David McKay, 1970, 118.

[11]A basic source for this section was Dennis McQuail and Sven Windahl, *Communication Models*. New York: Longman, 1981.

[12]F. C. Johnson and G. R. Klare, "General Models of Communication Research: A Survey of a Decade," *Journal of Communication* 11 (1961), 13-26.

[13]Claude Shannon and Warren Weaver, *The Mathematical Theory of Communication*. Urbana: University of Illinois Press, 1949.

[14]Harold D. Lasswell, "The Structure and Function of Communication in Society," in Lyman Bryson, ed., *The Communication of Ideas*. New York: Harper and Brothers, 1948, 37-51.

[15]T. Newcomb, "An Approach to the Study of Communicative Acts," *Psychological Review* 60 (November 1953), 393-404.

[16]L. A. Festinger, *A Theory of Cognitive Dissonance*. New York: Row and Peterson, 1957.

[17]B. H. Westley and M. MacLean, "A Conceptual Model for Communication Research," *AV Communication Review* 3 (1955), 3-12.

[18]McQuail and Windahl, *Communication Models*, 14-15.

[19]George Gerbner, "Toward a General Model of Communication," *AV Communication Review* 4 (1956), 171-99.

[20]E. Katz and Paul Lazarsfeld, *Personal Influence*. Glencoe, Ill.: Free Press, 1955.

[21]McQuail and Windahl, *Communication Models*, 50.

[22]J. W. Riley and M. W. Riley, "Mass Communication and the Social System," in R. K. Merton et al., eds., *Sociology Today*. New York: Basic Books, 1959.

[23]H. Mendelssohn, "Sociological Perspectives on the Study of Mass Communication," in L. A. Dexter and D. M. White, eds., *People, Society and Mass Communication*. New York: Free Press, 1963.

[24]See David K. Berlo, *The Process of Communication*. New York: Holt, Rinehart and Winston, 1960.

[25]E. M. Rogers and F. Shoemaker, *Communication of Innovations*. Glencoe, Ill.: Free Press, 1973.

[26]M. E. McCombs and D. L. Shaw, "The Agenda Setting Function of Mass Media," *Public Opinion Quarterly* 36 (1972), 176-87.

[27]M. E. McCombs and D. L. Shaw, "Structuring the Unseen Environment," *Journal of Communication* 26 (Spring 1976), 18-22.

[28]G. Comstock et al., *Television and Human Behavior*. New York: Columbia University Press, 1978.

[29]S. Ball-Rokeach and Melvin L. DeFleur, "A Dependency Model of Mass Media Effects," *Communication Research* 3 (1976), 3-21.

[30]E. Katz et al., "Utilization of Mass Communication by the Individual," in J. G. Blumer and E. Katz, eds., *The Uses of Mass Communications*. Beverly Hills, Calif.: Sage Publications, 1974.

[31]Karl E. Rosengren, "Uses and Gratifications: A Paradigm Outlined," in Jay G. Blumer and E. Katz, eds., *The Uses of Mass Communications*. Beverly Hills, Calif.: Sage Publications, 1974.

[32]See Marshall McLuhan, *Understanding Media*. New York: McGraw-Hill, 1964.

[33]Marshall McLuhan and Quentin Fiore, *The Medium Is the Message*. New York: Bantam, 1967.

[34]George N. Gordon, *The Languages of Communication*. New York: Hastings House, 1969.

[35]Ibid., 158.

[36]Lee Thayer, "On the Mass Media and Mass Communication: Notes toward a Theory," in Richard W. Budd and Brent D. Ruben, eds., *Beyond Media: New Approaches to Mass Communication*. Rochelle Park, N.J.: Hayden Book Co., 1979, 58-59.

[37]See Bruce Lannes Smith et al., *Propaganda and Promotional Activities: An Annotated Bibliography*. Minneapolis: University of Minnesota Press, 1935.

[38]The regular participants of this seminar were as follows: Lyman Bryson of Teachers College, Columbia University; Douglas Waples, University of Chicago Library School; Harold Lasswell, University of Chicago; I. A. Richards, Cambridge University; and Charles Siepmann, BBC director of program planning, who had been invited by the Rockefeller Foundation to come to the United States to study the status of educational radio.

[39]Hadley Cantril and Gordon W. Allport, *The Psychology of Radio*. New York: Harper and Brothers, 1935.

[40]Douglas Waples and Ralph Tyler, *What People Want to Read About*. Chicago: University of Chicago Press, 1931.

[41]Kurt Lewin, "Behavior and Development as a Function of the Total Situation," in L. Carmichael, ed., *Manual of Child Psychology*. New York: John Wiley, 1946.

[42]Carl I. Hovland et al., *Experiments on Mass Communications*, vol. 3. Princeton, N.J.: Princeton University Press, 1949.

[43]Samuel A. Stouffer et al., *The American Soldier*, vol. 3. Princeton, N.J.: Princeton University Press, 1949.

[44]Robert K. Merton, *Mass Persuasion*. New York: Harper & Row, 1946.

[45]See Norbert Wiener, *Cybernetics*, New York: John Wiley, 1948; Claude E. Shannon and Warren Weaver, *The Mathematical Theory of Communication*, Urbana: University of Illinois Press, 1949.

[46]Joseph T. Klapper made a comprehensive examination of the mass media research literature in 1950 to find answers to these questions: Do the mass media raise or lower popular taste, and how? What are the comparative effects of books and each of the other media, including face-to-face discourse, and of multiple-media operations? What is the function and effect of "escapist" communication (best sellers, soap operas, etc.)? How is persuasion with regard to important civic attitudes carried on with greatest likelihood of effectiveness? In 1960, Klapper brought his earlier memorandum up to date and summed up twenty years of theory and research that reflects a field theory of behavior. Rather than regarding mass communication as a cause of audience effects, his approach emphasizes the total communication situation, including such decisive factors as perception, cognition, attitudes, group values, and personal influence. See Joseph T. Klapper, *The Effects of Mass Communication*. New York: Free Press, 1960. For information about other contributions, see Ernest Cassirer, *The Philosophy of Symbolic Forms*, New Haven, Conn.: Yale University Press, 1953; Colin Cherry, *On Human Communication*, New York: John Wiley, 1957; George Gerbner, "Toward a General Model of Communication," *AV Communication Review* 4 (Summer 1956), 171-99; Elihu Katz and Paul F. Lazarsfeld, *Personal Influence*, New York: Free Press, 1955; Susanne K. Langer, *Philosophy in a New Key*, New York: New American Library of World Literature, 1948; Harold Lasswell, "The Structure and Function of Communication in Society," in Wilbur Schramm, ed., *Mass Communications*, 2d ed., Urbana: University of Illinois Press, 1960, 117; Marshall McLuhan, *Understanding Media*, New York: McGraw-Hill, 1964; George A. Miller, *Language and Communication*, New York: McGraw-Hill, 1951; Jurgen Ruesch and Gregory Bateson, *Communication: The Social Matrix of Psychiatry*, New York: W. W. Norton, 1951; Wilbur

Schramm, *The Process and Effects of Mass Communications*, Urbana: University of Illinois Press, 1954.

[47]See Wilbur Schramm, "The Beginnings of Communication Study in the United States," in Everett M. Rogers and Frances Balle, eds., *The Media Revolution in America and Western Europe*. Norwood, N.J.: Ablex, 1985, 200-11. Schramm gives credit to the following four men as "fathers" of communication studies: Kurt Lewin, the social psychologist; Paul Lazarsfeld, the sociologist; Harold Lasswell, the political scientist; and Carl Hovland, the experimental psychologist.

[48]Ibid., 210-11.

[49]Denis McQuail, "The Influence and Effects of Mass Media," in Morris Janowitz and Paul Hirsch, eds., *Reader in Public Opinion and Mass Communication*, 3d ed. New York: Free Press, 1981, 278.

[50]James D. Finn deserves much of the credit for the founding of *Audio-Visual Communication Review*. When Finn became chairman of the DAVI Committee on Professional Education in 1951, he began to work actively to establish a journal of theory and research in educational technology. He first obtained a meeting with C. J. VerHalen, Jr., and Harry Simonson, publisher and editor, respectively, of *Film World*, to discuss the possibilities of subsidizing a new quarterly publication. VerHalen agreed to subsidize such a publication without influencing its content but expressed the desire that it assume a broad communications perspective. When Finn transmitted this generous offer to the DAVI, it was received coldly because some wished to avoid a commercial tie and also because of some power struggles going on in DAVI at the time. A previous experience with *The Educational Screen* had not been particularly satisfactory because the DAVI Research Committee had some difficulty getting adequate research coverage, which was then the official outlet for DAVI. When the VerHalen offer was turned down, a decision was made to proceed with the publication of *Teaching Tools* with James D. Finn and William H. Allen as co-editors. Two years later, DAVI did launch *AV Communication Review* with William H. Allen as its first editor. William Allen stated to this author in a letter dated July 1, 1961, that he was certain that *AV Communication Review* would never have started—at least at that time—if *The Educational Screen* had been willing to devote even one page per issue to research.

[51]"Editorial Policy and Charter," *AV Communication Review* 1 (Spring 1953), 67-69.

[52]James D. Finn, "Directions in AV Communication Research," *Audio-Visual Communication Review* 2 (Spring 1954), 83.

[53]Paul Saettler, "Conceptual Legacy of Audio-Visual Communication," *Audio-Visual Communication Review* 3 (Fall 1955), 280.

[54]Keith W. Mielke, "Renewing the Link between Communications and Educational Technology," *AV Communication Review* 20 (Winter 1972), 394.

[55]Ibid.

[56]Gerald M. Torkelson, "AVCR-One Quarter Century: Evolution of Theory and Research," *AV Communication Review* 25 (Winter 1977), 333.

[57]Donald P. Ely, ed., *The Changing Role of the AudioVisual Process in Education: A Definition and a Glossary of Related Terms* (January-February 1963), Supplement 6.

[58]Ibid., 19.

[59]Ibid., 19.

[60]Ibid., 26.

[61]Ibid., 26.

[62]Ibid., 26.

[63]*Educational Technology Research and Development* (*ETR&D*) began in 1989 as a result of a merger between *Educational Communications and Technology Journal* and the *Journal of Instructional Development*. These journals, in turn, were preceded by *AV Communication Review*.

[64]It is interesting to note that the Association of Educational Communications and Technology (AECT) still continues to retain "communications" in its title.

Select Bibliography

Berger, Charles R., and Steven H. Chaffee, eds. *Handbook of Communication Science*. Beverly Hills, Calif.: Sage Publications, 1987.

Berelson, Bernard, and M. Janowitz. *Reader in Public Opinion and Communication*, 2d ed. New York: Free Press, 1966.

Berlo, David K. *The Process of Communication*. New York: Holt, Rinehart & Winston, 1960.

Blumer, Herbert. *Movies and Conduct*. New York: Macmillan, 1933.

Charters, W. W. *Motion Pictures and Youth*. New York: Macmillan, 1933.

Cherry, Colin. *On Human Communication*. New York: John Wiley, 1957.

Communication Yearbook. New Brunswick, N.J.: Transaction Books, 1977 (annual).

DeFleur, Melvin L., and Sandra Ball-Rokeach. *Theories of Mass Communication*. New York: Longman, 1982.

Dewey, John. *Human Nature and Conduct*. New York: Holt, Rinehart & Winston, 1922.

Doob, Leonard W. *Propaganda*. New York: Henry Holt & Co., 1935.

Gerbner, George. "Toward a General Model of Communication." *AV Communication Review* 4 (Summer 1956): 171-99.

Gordon, George N. *The Languages of Communication*. New York: Hastings House, 1969.

Hovland, Carl I., et al. *Communication and Persuasion*. New Haven, Conn.: Yale University Press, 1953.

_____. *Experiments on Mass Communication*. Princeton, N.J.: Princeton University Press, 1949.

Innis, H. *The Bias of Communication*. Toronto: University of Toronto Press, 1951.

Johnson, F. C., and G. R. Klare. "General Models of Communication Research: A Survey of the Development of a Decade." *Journal of Communication* 11, 1961: 13-26.

Katz, Elihu, and Paul F. Lazarsfeld. *Personal Influence*. New York: Free Press, 1955.

Klapper, Joseph T. *The Effects of Mass Communication*. New York: Free Press, 1960.

Lasswell, Harold D., et al. *Language of Politics*. New York: Stewart, 1949.

Lazarsfeld, Paul F., et al. *The People's Choice*. New York: Duell, Sloan & Pearce, 1944.

Lowery, Shearon, and Melvin L. DeFleur. *Milestones in Mass Communication Research*. New York: Longman, 1983.

McLuhan, Marshall. *Understanding Media*. New York: New American Library, 1965.

McLuhan, Marshall, and Eric McLuhan. *Laws of Media*. Toronto: University of Toronto Press, 1988.

McQuail, Denis, and Sven Windahl. *Communication Models for the Study of Mass Communications*. London: Longman, 1981.

_____. *Mass Communication Theory: An Introduction*. Newbury Park, Calif.: Sage Publications, 1984.

Manis, J. G., and B. N. Meltzer, eds. *Symbolic Interaction*, 2d ed. Boston: Allyn & Bacon, 1972.

Mead, George H. *Mind, Self and Society*. Chicago: University of Chicago Press, 1934.

Rosengren, Karl E. *The Uses of Mass Communications*. Beverly Hills, Calif.: Sage Publications, 1974.

Schramm, Wilbur L., and D. F. Roberts. *The Process and Effects of Mass Communications*, rev. ed. Urbana: University of Illinois Press, 1971.

Shannon, Claude, and Warren Weaver. *The Mathematical Theory of Communication*. Urbana: University of Illinois Press, 1949.

Sterling, Christopher H. *The Media Sourcebook: Comparative Reviews and Listings of Textbooks in Mass Communications*. Washington, D.C.: National Association of Educational Broadcasters, 1974.

Westley, Bruce H., and Malcolm S. MacLean, Jr. "A Conceptual Model for Communications Research." *A V Communication Review* 3, 1955: 3-12.

10

Behaviorism and Educational Technology: 1950–1980

This chapter traces the development of behaviorism and its impact on educational technology. Ironically, even though behaviorism developed in the early decades of this century, it did not exert any great influence on educational technology until about the time it's dominance in American psychology was beginning to wane in the 1960s.

Behaviorism began to make an impact on educational technology in the early 1960s, with B. F. Skinner's concepts of reinforcement and with applications in teaching machines and programmed instruction. The traditional theoretical framework of educational technology had emphasized the stimuli or messages to the learner; behaviorism shifted emphasis onto the behavior of the learner and its reinforcement. Thus, the primary purpose of media became reinforcement rather than merely presentation. In fact, in this view, media can be seen as displacing the teacher in many instructional situations. Moreover, the behavioristic impact on educational technology brought with it the beginning of the design movement and the germination of the systems approach to instruction.

To gain a broad perspective, a brief overview of historical behaviorism is provided. The remainder of this chapter is devoted to five areas that demonstrate the impact of behaviorism on educational technology: the behavioral objectives movement; the teaching machine phase; the programmed instruction movement; individualized instructional approaches; and computer-assisted instruction (CAI). A sixth area of impact, the systems approach to instruction, is discussed in chapter 12.

A Brief Historical Overview

Behaviorism has a long heritage extending back to the ancient Greeks. Its more recent antecedents were the doctrine of positivism of nineteenth-century Frenchman Auguste Comte and such Russian physiologists as Ivan Sechenov (1829-1905), Ivan Pavlov (1849-1936), and Vladimir Bekhterev (1857-1927), who provided the basis for American behaviorism some fifty years before it began. Behaviorism as a formal system of psychology was announced by John B. Watson

(1878-1958) in his 1913 *Psychological Review* article, "Psychology as the Behaviorist Views It."[1] However, Roback asserts that "it is little short of a violation of the truth to single him out as the founder" since the rudiments of behavioristic psychology were developed by Max F. Meyer as early as 1911.[2] Nevertheless, there is no question that Watson was the promoter and leader of behavioristic psychology.

Watson proclaimed that human and animal behavior, rather than mind and consciousness studied introspectively, were the only legitimate areas of study for psychologists. Using the work of Pavlov and Sechenov, he held that virtually all of human behavior could be explained as conditioning. Although Watson did not rule out completely the existence of innate behavior patterns, he saw any supposedly innate behavior as mechanical, inborn reflexes. His notions of stimulus and response constituted the fundamental units of analysis and all behavior was ultimately assumed to be reducible to molecular movements of gandular secretions. In essence, his system was a descriptive S-R psychology whose goal was to predict and/or control behavior.

Watsonian behaviorism dominated American experimental psychology from the 1920s to the mid-1930s. However, variations known as neobehaviorism vied for eminence during the 1930s: Edwin Guthrie (1886-1959) emphasized classical conditioning rather than reinforcement; Edward Tolman (1886-1959) stressed the cognitive aspects of learning; and Clark L. Hull (1884-1952) developed a complex, mathematical learning theory based on the idea that learning involves stimulus-response conditioning by repeated need-satisfaction.

The period from 1940 to 1960 is sometimes known as the Hullian era because of Hull's wide influence on a number of theorists. Foremost among these were Kenneth Spence (1907-1967), who was Hull's principal advocate; Neal Miller (1909-), whose research on conflict, motivation, and biofeedback was inspired by Hull; Hobart Mowrer (1907-), who proposed a two-factor theory based on Hull's views; and Albert Bandura (1925-), whose social-learning theory was influenced by Hull's ideas. According to Sigmund Koch, editor of the seven-volume series *Psychology: A Study of Science*, Hull's contributions include "(a) clarifying the role of scientific theory for psychologists; (b) recognizing the complexity of psychological phenomena; (c) providing many useful hypotheses to test; and (d) improving experimental design."[3] However, by the 1950s, most psychologists had lost interest in Hullian theory because it was overly complex and not highly predictable of human behavior.

By the 1960s, B. F. Skinner (1904-1990) was recognized as the leading behaviorist. His theory of operant conditioning, discussed in chapter 3, began to be applied extensively in educational technology and, in particular, in programmed instruction. Skinner also developed systematic methods to modify behavior and determined the types of response patterns associated with different schedules of reinforcement.[4] Specifically, he developed behavior modification techniques for instruction, language learning, and for the treatment of psychotics. Moreover, Skinner made a significant contribution to both psychology and educational technology by developing a simple conceptual system involving mostly descriptive terms, which he consistently used in a variety of instructional and therapeutic settings. As a consequence, in a review of Skinner, Guttman stated: "Skinner has become a symbol; he has become more than himself. Skinner is, as it were, the leading figure in a myth already made in the popular imagination and awaiting a new occupant. He has succeeded to the role of the scientist-hero, the Promethean fire-bringer, the master technologist and instructor of technologists."[5]

By the 1970s it was clear that Skinnerian behaviorism was no longer dominant in American psychology. Roughly in the decade from 1955 to 1965 a quiet revolution in thought had taken place among many research psychologists. Most active researchers began to refer to the new point of view as *cognitive psychology* or *information-processing psychology*. Although behaviorism still influenced animal research and clinical psychology, there was a strong trend in the cognitive direction in most other areas of psychology. Moreover, mentalistic psychology had made a vigorous comeback with studies of mind and consciousness. (Chapter 11 traces this development and explores its present and ultimate implications for educational technology.) The remainder of this chapter focuses on the relationship of behaviorism to educational technology during the 1950-1980 era.

Behavioral Objectives Movement

Although the current behavioral objectives movement in education can be traced to the early decades of this century, its revival in the 1960s reflected the impact of behaviorism. B. F. Skinner viewed a curriculum as the formation of behavioral objectives and described the teacher as one "who arranges the contingencies of reinforcement" whereby the learner is conditioned to perform specified, quantifiable, terminal behaviors.[6] Behavioristic theory also assumes that any behavior that cannot be described in overt, observable terms is unscientific.

Early Antecedents of Behavioral Objectives

The Elder Sophists of ancient Greece, Cicero, Johann Herbart, and Herbert Spencer can be considered early antecedents of behavioral objectives, but it was Franklin Bobbitt (1876-1952) who first developed the modern concept, in 1918 in his book *The Curriculum*.[7] Bobbitt maintained that it was the task of the curriculum maker to define the major fields of adult experience and analyze them into hundreds of specific aims. In a later book, Bobbitt gave a further elaboration and described an extensive plan of activity analysis from which such objectives could be extracted.[8] The specific activities, similar to job specifications in industry, comprised the content of the various subject areas and in no way conflicted with the traditional subject-matter organization of the curriculum. This method was also highly compatible with behaviorism.

Another pioneer in curriculum construction, W. W. Charters (1875-1956), formulated principles stating how to get from aims to curriculum content.[9] His strategy was to take major objectives and break them down into subgroups of minor objectives until one could determine what activities were to be performed. It is important to note that Bobbitt and Charters did not agree concerning the source of objectives. Whereas Charters advocated that the philosopher establish the aim and the analyst provide only the technique for integrating the aim into the curriculum, Bobbitt's approach was to "discover" curriculum objectives by scientific analysis. In other words, Bobbitt insisted that one can determine what people should do by identifying the things they do, while Charters viewed activity analysis as a means of implementing previously selected objectives. Bobbitt's approach prevailed and became the new concept of curriculum development.

Ralph Tyler also used behavioral description in curriculum construction, beginning in 1929 at the University of Ohio. Tyler stated the educational objectives of a course in behavioral terms and then designed carefully developed tests to determine whether these behaviors had been achieved. In 1949, Tyler carried the concept of educational objectives farther in his historic publication *Basic Principles of Curriculum and Instruction*.[10] In what came to be known as the Tyler rationale, he posed the following questions:

1. What educational purposes should the school seek to attain?

2. What educational experiences can be provided that are likely to attain these purposes?

3. How can these educational experiences be effectively organized?

4. How can we determine whether these purposes are being attained?[11]

Essentially, Tyler's questions represent the four-step sequence of (1) identifying objectives, (2) selecting the means to attain these objectives, (3) organizing these means, and (4) evaluating the outcomes. Tyler's conception of educational objectives is consistent with the experimentalist view of the learner as an autonomous, thinking individual and in conflict with the behavioristic conception of the learner as a response system, but his definition of education "as a process of changing the behavior patterns of people" is behavioristic.[12] And, as a consequence, Tyler's rationale has been used extensively by behaviorists.

Taxonomic Approaches to Objectives

The development of taxonomic analyses of learning behaviors has been closely associated with the behavioral objectives movement. This effort had its beginning at the 1948 convention of the American Psychological Association, when those interested in test development and construction expressed a need for standardized terminology regarding human behavioral characteristics. Benjamin Bloom and his colleagues at Chicago and Michigan began to put together a theoretical framework to meet this need. The original plans called for a complete taxonomy in three domains—cognitive, attitudinal (or affective), and psychomotor.

The first taxonomy, based on the cognitive domain, appeared in 1956.[13] Based on a hierarchy of simple to complex, it included: (a) knowledge, (b) comprehension, (c) application, (d) analysis, (e) synthesis, and (f) evaluation. The second taxonomy, on the affective domain, appeared in 1964 and applied a similar analysis to the affective domain under five categories: (a) receiving, or attending to, (b) responding, (c) valuing, (d) organization, (e) characterization by a value or value complex.[14] A third taxonomy, on the psychomotor domain, was published by Harrow in 1972.[15] These taxonomies have proved useful as guides for specifying educational objectives.

Another taxonomy was developed by Robert Gagnè in 1972, which comprised the five categories of verbal information, intellectual skill, cognitive strategy, attitude, and motor skill. The last two of these categories, attitude and motor skill, are similar to Bloom's affective and psychomotor domains. Gagnè proposed that the cognitive domain should incorporate the three major categories of verbal information, intellectual skill, and cognitive strategy. The basic assumption is that the mental processing required for learning and retention of verbal information is different from that demanded for the learning and retention of intellectual skills, and that similar differences can be found among all five categories of learned capabilities.[16]

Mastery Learning

The use of instruction objectives as a basis for evaluation gave rise in the late 1970s to what has come to be known as mastery learning. The ideas, research, and classroom procedures of Benjamin Bloom and James H. Block, among others, have created a modern version of the mastery learning developed by Henry C. Morrison in the 1930s (see chapter 3). However, the current approach is tied to a behaviorism that emphasizes cognitive, affective, and psychomotor objectives.

Mastery learning suggests that units of learning can be mastered by almost all students. In this view, effective evaluation requires a specific, operationally defined concept of mastery, or the need for a set of instructional objectives. Bloom states that "most students become very similar with regard to learning ability, rate of learning, and motivation for further learning."[17] According to Bloom, "Some of the apparent weakness of the schools may be due to lack of clear-cut objectives for education and their implementation by carefully developed instructional materials and procedures."[18]

Bloom's mastery plan is primarily appropriate for hierarchical or sequential subject matter and inappropriate for higher levels of organizing and communicating ideas, divergent thinking, creativity, and such developmental objectives as self-expression and sensitivity to social problems. Since mastery learning is viewed as a total educational program, objectives that do not fit the system are simply eliminated.

The Military and Industrial Approach to Behavioral Objectives

In the late 1950s, there was a shift from educational to instructional objectives and finally to behavioral or performance objectives in educational terminology. This shift was due primarily to the entry into education of a number of people who came from military and industrial psychology.[19] The military and industrial approach to behavioral objectives brought a return to the industrial model the school exhibited during the so-called efficiency period in American education, from about 1903 to 1925.[20] Education was once again confused with training. The military/industrial approach to teaching and learning prepared teachers in the same manner that training was typically used in military/industrial situations where behavioral objectives were written descriptions of specific, terminal behaviors that were manifested in terms of observable, measurable behavior.

The publication of Robert Mager's brief book *Preparing Instructional Objectives* in 1962 stimulated the first widespread interest in and use of behavioral objectives among educators.[21] Simultaneously, an avalanche of instructional and curricular packages on "behavioral" objectives flowed from publishers. Mager, who had a background in military/industrial psychology, produced a classic set of instructions for writing objectives. His model is still used, for the most part, in other approaches to the writing of objectives. For Mager, an objective is simply "a description of a pattern of behavior (performance) we want the learner to be able to demonstrate."[22] He proposed using three components in writing such descriptions:

(1) identify the action the learner will be taking when he has achieved the objective (e.g., to write, to speak);

(2) describe the relevant conditions under which the learner will be acting (e.g., without the use of references);

(3) specify how well the learner must perform the action (e.g., 100 percent correct).[23]

According to Mager, objectives should be stated in performance terms: what the learner will be doing when he has achieved the specified goal. Words such as "understanding," "insight," "appreciation," and "interest" refer to qualities that cannot be observed directly; therefore, such words are not sufficiently precise or clear. For many behaviorists, one of the major problems of educational objectives is that they are educationally meaningless because they cannot be observed or measured. Ideally, behavioral outcomes should identify appropriate situations to observe measurable performance and specify the criteria to establish a standard level of success. These behavioral outcomes have also been referred to as criterion-referenced behavioral objectives. Behaviorists such as McAshan and Popham argue that criterion-referenced measures are superior to standardized tests, which are norm-reference.[24] Norm-reference measures compare students, while criterion-referenced tests are used to assess student competences.

Robert Gagnè and Leslie Briggs, who also had backgrounds in military/industrial psychology, proposed an alternative to Mager's model for performance objectives in 1974. Their model had five components: (1) action, (2) object, (3) situation, (4) tools and constraints, and (5) capability to be learned.[25] Kibler and Bassett have pointed out three major differences between the Mager model and the Gagnè-Briggs model. First,

> Gagnè and Briggs distinguish between (a) verbs which identify an observable action the learner is performing, and (b) verbs which identify the learned capability which may be inferred from the action, while Mager does not. Second, the component of "objective of performance" is included in the Gagnè-Briggs Model, but not as a separate component in the Mager Model. Third, while the performance standard is included in Mager's objectives, Gagnè and Briggs suggest that it not be included in performance objectives, but that the standard be decided after the test over the objective has been prepared.[26]

Gagnè has stated that

> possibly the most fundamental reason of all for the central importance of defining educational objectives is that such definition makes possible the basic distinction between content and method. It is the defining of objectives that brings an essential clarity into the area of curriculum design and enables both educational planners and researchers to bring their practical knowledge to bear on the matter. As an example of the kind of clarification which results by defining content as "descriptions of the expected capabilities of students," the following may be noted. Once objectives have been defined, there is no step in curriculum design that can legitimately be entitled "selecting content."[27]

In this view, the behavioral objective is designed to predict what the student will be able to do and, in effect, also to determine the curriculum.

By the late 1960s, many teachers had begun to write and use behavioral objectives, and they became the new doctrine of education. However, some educators rejected behavioral objectives and there was intense criticism from some sectors of the scholarly community. For example, Tanner and Tanner observed that "the most damaging result of breaking down the curriculum into minute particles is that it must, of necessity, lead away from an understanding of the unity of all knowledge."[28] Eisner challenged the assumption that the "prespecification of goals is the rational way in which one must always proceed in curriculum planning." This assumption, he said,

> is rooted in the kind of rationality that has guided much of Western technology. The mean-ends model of thinking has for so long dominated our thinking that we have come to believe that not to have clearly defined purposes for our activities is to court irrationality or, at least, to be professionally irresponsible. Yet, life in classrooms, like that outside of them, is seldom neat or linear.[29]

Accountability Movement

In the late 1960s and 1970s, the behavioral objectives movement revived efforts to apply scientific management to education, with calls for "educational engineering," "accountability," and "performance contracting." This movement embodied a complex of concepts flowing from politics, economics, and behaviorism. The high priest of the movement, Leon Lessinger, a former U.S. associate commissioner of education, urged that the schools be made accountable "in the same way that planning ... and performance warranties determine industrial production and its worth to consumers, so should we be able to engineer, organize, refine, and manage the educational system to prepare students to contribute to the most complex and exciting country on earth."[30] In another place, he stated:

what we need is data for all children that shows the educational gain produced by specific sequence of teaching.

Once the output of schools is measured in proven learning ... the next step is to relate learning to its cost.... We simply keep accounts of the cost of a specific teaching sequence and measure the change in performance against a standardized evaluation given before and after it.[31]

This simplistic model of education defines instruction and determines its effectiveness in terms of behavioral objectives and their specifications.

A comparable so-called efficiency movement had arisen in early twentieth-century America in response to the same political and economic factors present in the 1960s. Because of growing interest in a new system of industrial management known as scientific management and the fact that American schools were considered grossly mismanaged, Franklin Bobbitt, a member of the faculty in educational administration at the University of Chicago, proposed in 1912 that education utilize this new technology to reform the schools. The following year, Bobbitt elaborated his ideas in the Twelfth Yearbook of the National Society for the Study of Education. He asserted that "education is a shaping process as much as the manufacture of steel rails" and that education must follow the example of industry and focus on the product.[32] The process begins by developing standards and scales of measurement, but it is worth noting how these standards are to be developed:

A school system can no more find standards of performance within itself than a steel plant can find the proper height or weight per yard for steel rails from the activities within the plant.... In the case of the instructions of our general society to its agent, the school, specifications must be equally definite.

The commercial world can best say what it needs in the case of its stenographers and accountants. A machine shop can best say what is needed in the workers that come to it.[33]

This statement precisely describes the idea of accountability, competency-based education, or performance-based education. As Callahan commented in his classic book *Education and the Cult of Efficiency*, "doubtless many educators who had devoted years of study and thought to the aims and purposes of education were surprised to learn that they had misunderstood their function. They were to be mechanics, not philosophers."[34]

What is more, the practice of scientific management gave educators a sense of security and protection from public criticism. For example, Callahan quotes one superintendent as follows:

One may easily trace an analogy between these fundamentals of the science of industrial management and the organization of a public school system. For example: (1) the state as employer must cooperate with the teacher as employee, for the latter does not always understand the science of education; (2) the state provides experts who supervise the teacher and suggest the processes that are most efficacious and economical; (3) the task system obtains in the school as well as in the shop, each grade being a measured quantity of work to be accomplished in a given term; (4) every teacher who accomplishes the task receives a bonus, not in money, but in the form of a rating which may have money value; (5) those who are unable to do the work are eliminated, either through the device of a temporary license or of a temporary employment; (6) the differential rate is applied to the teacher, quantity and quality of service being considered in the rating; (7) the result ought to be a maximum output at a low relative cost, since every repeater costs as much as a new pupil; (8) the teacher thus receives better wages, but only after demonstrated fitness for high position; (9) hence we ought to have the most desirable combination of an educational system—relative cheapness of operation and high salaries.[35]

Such a statement appears consonant with the current accountability movement even though it was uttered in the early twentieth century. The prevailing view during the so-called efficiency period (1903-1925) saw society as the consumer of the school's products and children as the raw material to be processed according to the consumer's specifications. Although such modern terminology as quality control and cost-benefit analysis was not used, early twentieth-century attitudes and conceptions were not distinctly different from those of the present.

The current accountability movement is not only interwoven with economics and behavioristic concepts, but is bound with politics as well.[36] The majority of the states has mandated competency-based (CBE) or performance-based education (PBE) and legislated accountability, planning-programming-budgeting-systems (PPBS), assessment, and other data-based educational management systems. The major component of accountability has involved the doctrine of behavioral objectives that casts educational results in terms of quantifiable performance. Behavioristic theory also dictates that any behavior that cannot be translated into overt, observable behavioral objectives be dismissed as unscientific.[37]

Performance Contracting

Between 1969 and 1972, education and government turned to business and industry for solutions to educational problems. Performance contracts were negotiated between government and private corporations for the development of learning systems to improve pupil performance in reading and arithmetic as measured by standardized achievement tests.

Beginning in 1969/70, the Office of Economic Opportunity (OEO) sponsored twenty projects involving a total of 120,000 students and costing more than $6 million. Other projects were supported with federal money from Title I of the Elementary and Secondary-Education Act (see chapter 15). Some of the largest companies in the country were brought in, including Westinghouse, General Electric, Brunswick, Burroughs, RCA, Sylvania, Philco-Ford, and Northern Natural Gas.[38]

By the summer of 1972, performance contracting had virtually come to an end because it had failed to produce the results that were promised.[39] Although this was disappointing, it was hardly unexpected. As Tanner comments, "What remains a puzzle is why educators continue to believe that business can do everything better—including education. Equally puzzling is why scant attention is given to the dangers posed to a free society by such intervention."[40]

Teaching Machines and Programmed Instruction Movement

A major impact of behaviorism on educational technology can be seen in the development of teaching machines and programmed instruction during the 1960s. Although the concept of programmed instruction could be traced back to the Elder Sophists of ancient Greece and to such early educators as Comenius, Herbart, and Montessori,[41] the recent impulse was generated by B. F. Skinner in the spring of 1954, at a conference on current trends in psychology at the University of Pittsburgh. Skinner gave an address titled "The Science of Learning and the Art of Teaching" and demonstrated a machine to teach spelling and arithmetic.[42] In a later article in *Science* in 1958, he described the need for teaching machines and provided a historical comparison of his machine and techniques with the devices that had been used in the 1920s by Sidney L. Pressey.[43] He also separated teaching machines and programmed instruction from their experimental laboratory foundations and introduced the revival of such concepts as individualized instruction, the systematic development and evaluation of instructional materials, and changes in testing and evaluation practices.

Somehow this new approach to instruction became known as a "teaching machine revolution." Although Skinner had consistently used the term *teaching machine*, he had also attempted to point out that the really vital aspect of this approach was not the machine per se, but rather the arrangements of the materials so that the student could make correct responses and receive reinforcement when correct responses were made. Nevertheless, the teaching machine drew primary attention and more machines than programs were produced during the first years of the movement.

By the early 1960s it was recognized that the program rather than the machine was the most important component of this instructional approach. Therefore, the movement now came to be known as programmed instruction. Interest in programmed instruction accelerated rapidly. A number of textbooks on programmed instruction appeared, courses in programmed instruction began to be offered in colleges and universities throughout the country, and teaching machines of various types were sold to schools, industry, and the military. Soon programmed textbooks on a variety of subjects were published and, simultaneously, began to replace machines because they were more economical to produce and were considered just as effective. The National Society for Programmed Instruction (NSPI) was formed and the NEA Department of Audiovisual Instruction (DAVI) published a historic source book entitled *Teaching Machines and Programmed Learning*.[44]

Early Contributions of Pressey

Sidney L. Pressey, a psychologist at Ohio State University, exhibited a device that anticipated the modern teaching machine at the 1925 meetings of the American Psychological Association. This device had four multiple-choice questions and answers in a window and four keys. If the student thought the second answer was correct, he pressed the second key; if he was right, the next question was turned up. If he was not correct, the initial question remained in the window, and the learner persisted until he found the right answer. Meanwhile, a record of all attempts was kept automatically.

There were two unique features of this early device that have not been repeated. First, a simple mechanical arrangement made it possible to lift a lever that reversed the action and transformed the machine into a self-scoring, record-keeping, testing device. Second, a simple attachment made possible the placing of a reward dial set for any desired goal-score that, if attained, automatically gave the learner a candy lozenge.[45] Thus Pressey's device both taught and tested by providing immediate feedback to the learner.

Pressey's former student J. C. Peterson devised "chemosheets" in which the learner checked his answer with a swab. Wrong answers turned red and correct ones turned blue.[46] Pressey later devised a punchboard device and a selective-review apparatus using cards.[47] Later, he urged what he called adjunct auto-instruction, which called for a whole array of instructional media—textbooks, films, television, etc.—to be used in conjunction with programmed instruction.

Pressey developed a number of other devices and conducted many experiments with auto-instruction during the 1920s and the early 1930s, but their impact on educational technology was almost inconsequential. Although he discontinued this first phase of his work in 1932 because of lack of funds (most of his work was financed with his own money), he remained confident that automated instruction would eventually generate an "industrial revolution" in education.[48] Except for sporadic developments (mainly during World War II), Pressey's work was virtually forgotten until B. F. Skinner stimulated a new surge of interest in programmed instruction in the mid-1950s.

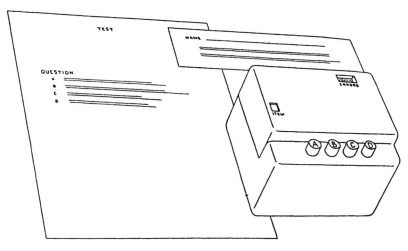

Fig. 10.1. Pressey multiple-choice machine.

Programmed Instruction during World War II

Several military training devices constructed in the 1940s and 1950s were developed to teach by individualized self-instruction. These devices, called phase checks, both taught and tested. Each step of a skill, such as the disassembly-assembly of a piece of equipment, was organized on the assumption that constructed responses with immediate automatic feedback had special value in learning. This was a linear program in which the learner's problem was to complete the steps involved in learning a manual skill or to accomplish certain terminal behaviors.[49] Thus the basic concepts of contemporary programmed instruction were anticipated.

Crowder's Intrinsic Programming

Norman A. Crowder developed a programmed instruction approach somewhat similar to Pressey's in the 1950s when he was associated with the United States Air Force and engaged in training troubleshooters to find malfunctions in electronic equipment. Crowder's intrinsic, or branching, style of programming, as represented in Tutortexts, or "scrambled textbooks," consists of steps that contain a limited amount of information, usually less than a page, and a multiple-choice question presented at the same time (see figure 10.5 on p. 302). After reading the text, the learner chooses whichever answer he thinks is correct and then proceeds to the step indicated by his choice. If an incorrect answer is given, the learner is directed to information designed to overcome the cause of his error and is then returned to the step where the error occurred. Thus the Crowder program simulated a tutor by presenting material, testing the learner, and providing corrective instruction or advancement to new information based on the learner's performance.[50]

Skinner: Father of the Programmed
Instruction Movement

Skinner's programming approach was based almost exclusively on work he and his colleagues had done in animal laboratory research. As to the applicability of this research, he pointed out that

> the advances which have recently been made in our control of the learning process suggest a thorough revision of classroom practices, and fortunately, they tell us how revision can be brought about. This is not, of course, the first time that the results of an experimental science have been brought to bear upon the practical problems of education. The modern classroom does not, however, offer much evidence that research in the field of learning has been respected or used.[51]

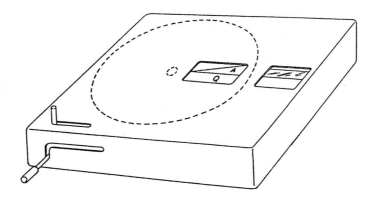

Fig. 10.2. Skinner teaching machine and program disk for the machine.

Skinnerian programmed instruction is based on operant conditioning, in which the learner's responses are "shaped" to pronounce and to write responses correctly and whereby his behavior is brought under various types of stimulus control. Thus, a relatively small unit of information, called a *frame*, is presented to the learner as a *stimulus*. The learner is then required to make a *response* by completing a statement or answering a question. Through *feedback* he is informed as to the correctness of his response and is *reinforced*. The learner is presented with a second frame and the stimulus-response-reinforcement cycle is repeated until a series of hundreds or thousands of frames has presented a complete *program* in a logical sequence of information.

Effective Skinnerian programming requires instructional sequences so simple that the learner hardly ever makes an error. If the learner makes too many errors—more than 5 to 10 percent—the program is considered in need of revision.

During the decade following the introduction of Skinnerian programs, a majority of those produced were Skinnerian or variations. Yet research had already questioned the theoretical validity of Skinnerian programs, despite extravagant claims for the method. Nevertheless, Skinner revived programmed instruction and set the stage for a closer relationship between the behavioral sciences and educational technology.

Early Use of Programmed Instruction

American schools were generally slow to adopt programmed instruction. In 1962 and again in 1963, the Center for Programmed Instruction, at the request of the U.S. Office of Education, conducted surveys to determine patterns of programmed instruction use in schools throughout the country.[52] Each survey year, the most responses were received from school administrators who considered themselves nonusers of programmed materials. It was reported, however, that nonusers were usually familiar with some of the terminology and indicated that they had seen programmed instructional materials of some kind or had read some of the basic literature.[53] Within those schools using programs in 1962, teachers and curriculum coordinators played the dominant role in initiating programmed instruction; by the 1960s, the principal had replaced the curriculum coordinator as an innovator.

Although the most common use of programmed materials indicated by these surveys was within large school systems, programs were tried in most cases with individuals or small groups of students, rather than with entire classes. There also appeared to be more frequent use of programmed materials in junior high schools than in either senior high or elementary schools. The most programs used were in the area of mathematics (60 percent), followed by English (21 percent), foreign language (4 percent), science (3 percent), and social science (3 percent). Teacher evaluations of programs (four out of five programs were commercially produced) were generally favorable, with only about 5 percent negative.[54]

First School Use of Programmed Instruction

Aside from the early experiments of Pressey and others in the 1920s and 1930s,[55] programmed instruction was first employed in higher education on a regular basis as part of courses in behavioral psychology taught by B. F. Skinner and James G. Holland at Harvard University in 1957.[56] The second pioneering use of programmed instruction in higher education occurred in 1958 when Evans et al. of the University of Pittsburgh printed programs in a unique book format designed to simulate certain characteristics of a teaching machine.[57]

The first sustained use of programmed instruction in a public elementary school began in 1957 at the Mystic School in Winchester, Massachusetts, when Douglas Porter conducted, under the sponsorship of the U.S. Office of Education, a year-long experiment in teaching spelling to second- and third-graders.[58] The first use of programmed instruction in a secondary school started in 1959 when Eigen and Komoski conducted an experiment in teaching modern mathematics (see figure 10.3, page 298).[59]

A Case Study: Denver, Colorado

The public school system of Denver, Colorado, was among the first large-city systems to investigate programmed instruction. It was through superintendent Kenneth Oberholtzer's personal interest that, in 1960, Denver became the first school system to free teachers from classroom duties to be trained as programmers.

The pioneer in the Denver development was Jerry E. Reed, a supervising teacher of English who, in the spring of 1960, was sent to Collegiate School in New York City to learn about programmed instruction.[60] Reed spent three weeks at the Collegiate School and then returned to Denver to begin preparing programmed materials for English courses. Six other English teachers were also relieved of classroom duties and assigned to work with Reed. Together they produced 2,800 frames, covering sixteen units of work, during the summer of 1960. When the teachers went back to their classes in the fall, their programs still needed testing and editing. However, just about this time a decision was made to try English 2600, a

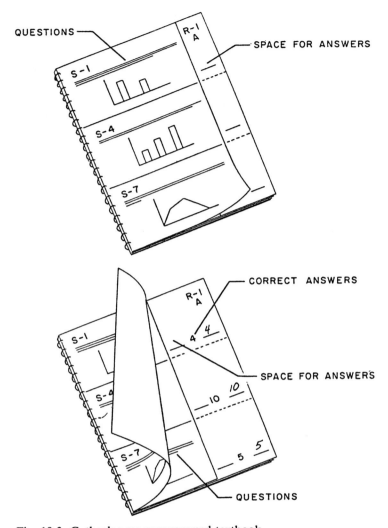

Fig. 10.3. Cutback-page programmed textbook.

new commercial program that covered almost the same ground and was aimed at the same tenth-grade level as the Denver teacher-made units.

In trying out English 2600, Denver was assisted by a research team from the Stanford University Institute for Communication Research, which was engaged with the Denver schools in an educational television project. A research design was made and the English 2600 program was tested during the school year of 1960/61.

The results of this experiment showed substantial learning in all ability groups. The program proved to be more effective with accelerated classes but the accelerated students were also the ones who complained most, because they were bored by the repetition. Regular classes did about as well with the program as with class practice. On the other hand, low achievers who did *not* use the program scored higher than those who did.

This experiment showed that English 2600 did not meet Denver's needs for low-ability students. As a result, attention was shifted back to the 2,800 frames prepared by the Denver teachers, and in the summer of 1961 Reed recruited the best student writers from the previous year for additional work on the English programs. They revised portions and developed short booklets to implement the "lay reader system" of teaching English composition. Under this system, developed by Paul Diederich of the Educational Testing Service and pioneered in the Denver schools, the student's written work was first checked by a lay reader to identify specific, key errors. Each type of error was recorded on an error grid (an ingenious device that provides the English instructor with a profile of his students and the kinds of errors they make). With the error grid serving as a diagnostic tool, the student was assigned to a series of programmed units to remedy the types of errors revealed in his or her written work.

In Denver's second major experiment with programmed instruction, Del Barcus, a young teacher of Spanish, was assigned to construct a sixth-grade Spanish program. This was also part of the Denver-Stanford research project testing the use of programmed materials in combination with instructional television in the teaching of Spanish. One aspect of this experiment was to use television to facilitate the transition from the wholly audio-lingual method of language teaching to a combination of speaking-listening and reading-writing. Since there was no program in existence to meet these needs, Barcus began developing a program designed to teach word recognition, reading, and writing. He worked from 1960-1962 before he had developed and thoroughly tested his program.

Denver had learned from its experience with the English programs about the effective introduction of programmed instruction. Thus, when it came time to implement the Spanish program, teachers were paid to come to a series of Saturday morning workshops where they had an opportunity to try parts of the program and discuss its use. The value of these workshops cannot be underestimated because they contributed in large part to the ultimate success of the Spanish program.

The results of the Spanish program experiment, which involved more than six thousand students, showed that when the new program was used for part of the classroom time, the amount of learning was substantially increased. In other words, programmed instruction plus classroom teaching was more effective than either alone. The experiment also indicated that the more enthusiastic the teacher was about programmed instruction, the better work the students did, even though they worked independently. Another significant finding was that there appears to be an optimum time to introduce certain types of programs to particular learners. For example, many of the sixth-grade students who used the Spanish program in the first semester could not take full advantage of it because they were not yet proficient enough in listening and speaking. When the program was not introduced until the second semester, it proved to be more effective.

The success of the Spanish program created a new climate for programmed instruction in the Denver schools and generated great enthusiasm among the teachers as well as the administration. Teachers began to ask for programs, and some took steps toward preparing their own. In 1963, Del Barcus became a supervising teacher with primary responsibility for programmed instruction in Denver.

The early programmed instruction experiences of Denver did not produce dramatic instructional innovations, with perhaps one exception: the creation of a teaching team consisting of a master television teacher, a classroom teacher, and cooperative parents, whereby Spanish was taught to elementary children.

The most significant lesson learned in Denver was that it is a difficult, time-consuming task to introduce programmed instruction. This appears to be true whether the school system prepares its own programs or selects commercial programs.[61]

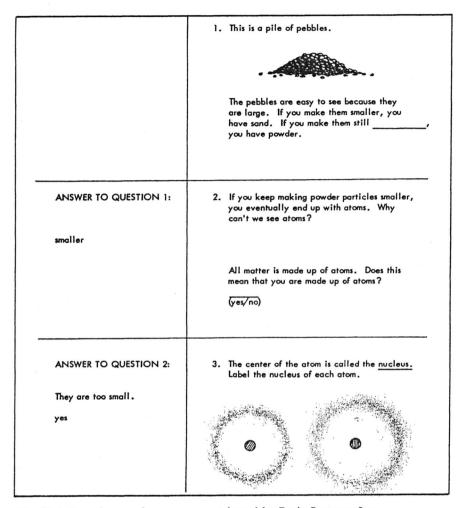

Fig. 10.4. Sample page from a program issued by Basic Systems, Inc.

A Case Study: Manhasset, Long Island, New York

Early in 1960, the Manhasset Junior High School administration enthusiastically supported the use of programmed instruction and began to make plans for an experimental study. After three months of preliminary study, the experiment began in January 1961, with the same English 2600 program used in Denver. For the experiment, one seventh-grade class and two eighth-grade classes would be taught solely by the English 2600 program, while all other classes in these grades would continue to be taught by the usual methods. Grammar was taught to the experimental group in three half-hour class periods per week and the students were given minimum assistance by monitoring teachers. Teachers in the other classes taught grammar, as before, as part of a ninety-minute English-social studies block period.

The experimental groups in grades seven and eight made significantly higher grades. However, Herbert and Foshay found it difficult to interpret the findings and observed that "the text used was the one designed to test the material of the English 2600 program, and no clear evidence exists that the content taught in the other classes was comparable."[62] Although the experimental design was far from adequate, the conclusions drawn from observations convinced the administration and the eighth-grade teachers that it would be worthwhile to continue the program. The seventh-grade teachers, on the other hand, decided against using English 2600 during the subsequent year because they felt it was far beyond the scope and depth of what was customarily taught in grade seven.

The second-year results led teachers to examine a number of assumptions they had held about teaching and to organize new instructional patterns.[63] For example, the teachers developed an informal team-teaching structure that enabled them to become involved in joint planning, teaching, and evaluation of the program. In addition, they began to hold individual conferences once or twice a week for each student, established a class in remedial grammar, and developed a system of grouping students homogeneously in relation to speed and accuracy in English grammar.[64]

The Manhasset experience did not provide the model that Denver did for introducing programmed instruction. In this respect, it was somewhat disappointing. Also, the use of only one regular program and the lack of precise experimental data deprived the project of the scope and depth one might have expected from an administration that had so strongly supported the concept of programmed instruction. Although some worthwhile instructional innovations were introduced, they were by no means foreseen by the Manhasset administration when programmed instruction was first initiated in 1960.

Comparative Analysis of the Denver and Manhasset Case Histories

The case histories of Denver and Manhasset are only two illustrations of the early American school use of programmed instruction. Other early experiments were conducted in such diverse places as Roanoke, Virginia (1960),[65] Provo, Utah (1961),[66] and Pittsburgh, Pennsylvania (1962).[67] However, it is apparent from a study of these other case histories that certain themes of the Denver and Manhasset cases tend to be representative of many of the early school histories of programmed instruction.

The Denver and Manhasset cases indicate that while programmed instruction may introduce a more flexible instructional pattern, it can also generate new problems. Since programs are more difficult to adapt to curriculum changes than textbooks, a change in the curriculum could easily make a program obsolete, or a program could hamper or obstruct a desirable curriculum change. In the case of the Manhasset district, for example, when it discontinued the Encyclopaedia Britannica Films elementary algebra program TEMAC to change to new mathematics, the TEMAC teaching became obsolete since the machines could not be adapted to the new subject matter.

The Denver and Manhasset cases also illustrate different attitudes toward individualized instruction. In Denver, the teacher-made programs were designed, from the first, to be teacher aids; the goal was to keep the students together rather than encourage divergent rates of progress. In Manhasset, some efforts were made to individualize the study of English grammar in the eighth grade. On the other hand, Denver chose to discard the English 2600 program in favor of individualizing instruction, while Manhasset considered the same program an ideal way to free the teacher for individualized instruction.

In both the Denver and Manhasset cases, it is clear that teacher attitudes proved to be a critical factor in the success of programmed instruction. For example, in Denver it was found that students did better when the teacher's attitude was favorable toward programmed instruction. This was quite obvious in the cases of the Denver teachers of Spanish and the eighth-grade teachers in Manhasset. It even held true when all the teacher did was keep order!

Finally, the Denver and Manhasset cases support the need for structuring the learning environment to bring about optimal learning conditions. The Manhasset teachers, for example, who initially attempted to use the grammar program for individual instruction soon found that they would have to make extensive modifications in existing classroom structure and organization and that they would need to adopt new teacher roles before individualized instruction could be accomplished.

129
[from page 125]

YOUR ANSWER: In ordinary arithmetic, it is not always true that, if a, b, and c are numbers, $a(b + c) = ab + ac$.

Well, let's get at it this way. Suppose you were selling magazine subscriptions. For every subscription you sold you earned 50 cents. On Monday you sold two subscriptions; on Wednesday you sold three subscriptions; on Saturday you sold one subscription.

Now, there are two ways of figuring up how much money you made. You can either (1) figure the amount of money you earned each day and then add these daily amounts to give you the total for the week, or (2) keep track of the number of subscriptions you sold each day and then figure your earnings at the end of the week by multiplying the total number of subscriptions sold by 50 cents.

(1) Monday: 2 subscriptions @ 50¢ = 2 × .50 = $1.00
    Wednesday: 3 subscriptions @ 50¢ = 3 × .50 = 1.50
    Saturday: 1 subscription @ 50¢ = 1 × .50 = .50
                                    Total weekly earnings: $3.00

(2) Monday: 2 subscriptions
    Wednesday: 3 subscriptions
    Saturday: 1 subscription
    Weekly total: 6 subscriptions

    Weekly earnings: 6 subscriptions @ 50¢ = 6 × .50 = $3.00

So you see, if two or more numbers are to be multiplied by the same number, they can be either multiplied individually and then added together or added together first and then multiplied; it makes no difference in the result.
Now return to page 125 and choose the correct answer.

125
[from page 123]

YOUR ANSWER: If $y = 3(5 + 4)$, $y = 27$.

You are correct. The 3 multiplies the entire quantity inside the parentheses. So if

$$y = 3(5 + 4),$$
$$y = 3(9) = 27.$$

Now, we would get the same result in this case if, instead of adding the two numbers inside the parentheses and then multiplying by 3, we first multiplied each number inside the parentheses by 3 and then added the products together.

$$y = 3(5 + 4)$$
$$y = 3(5) + 3(4)$$
$$y = 15 + 12 = 27$$

In ordinary arithmetic is it always true that, if a, b, and c are numbers,

$$a(b + c) = ab + ac?$$

Yes. page 121

No. page 129

Fig. 10.5. This is the way an algebra course looks in the Crowder scrambled book, the Tutor Text called "Adventures in Algebra."

The Machine-Program Dichotomy

Two opposed schools of thought arose in the programmed instruction movement that could be characterized as the machine-program dichotomy. The early machine viewpoint emphasized the use of machines and the problems of developing highly sophisticated instrumentation to automate the instructional process. This view focused on identifying decisive machine functions and specifying the manner in which these functions were to be accomplished, rather than on methods of programming or implementation of learning theory.

The program (and current) school of thought emphasizes instead the development of programs based on an analysis of learning and the goals of instruction. The predominant concept of this orientation is that programmed instruction should be based on learning theory. What is more, this view holds that programmed instruction should provide a means for more complex experimental designs to better understand teacher-learner interactions, so that more effective instructional strategies may be developed.

This conceptual dichotomy has cut deeper than might be assumed and was further exacerbated by competing commercial interests in the development of machines and programs. For example, the Finn-Perrin survey of 1962 revealed that an almost equal number of companies were occupied either with producing machines or developing programmed instruction and that both sides were prone to make exaggerated advertising claims without adequate program testing.[68] In most cases, commercial producers supported almost no research on programming nor did they make any serious attempt to introduce programming innovations. As a result, programs tended to congeal into stereotyped forms just at a time when more flexible approaches might have been expected.

Another facet of the machine-program dichotomy was the prevailing conception that programs (software) were more important than machines (hardware). Also, machines and programs were perceived as having separate, distinct functions. The simple nature of most teaching machines made it appear as if the program was the essential item and the device was merely a dispensing mechanism. This arbitrary division of functions appeared questionable in the light of the development of more sophisticated computer-based instructional systems.

Decline of Programmed Instruction

By the late 1960s the decline of the programmed instruction movement was already evident. The high expectations and extravagant claims had led to disappointing outcomes. Robert Glaser observed in 1965 that "teaching machines and programmed learning" are heard less and less, and one hears more about 'behavioral science research relevant to education' and 'educational and teaching technology.' "[69] In 1964, B. F. Skinner expressed concern about the decline of programmed instruction when he said, "unfortunately, much of the technology has lost contact with its basic science. Teaching machines are widely misunderstood."[70]

There were a number of problems associated with the programmed instruction movement. Research studies conducted on its effectiveness showed that differences in achievement did not consistently or substantially favor programmed instruction over conventional instruction.[71] Also, many of the requirements originally based on theoretical grounds were not supported in practice. For example, the need for the student to make an overt response,[72] the need for carefully sequenced frames,[73] and the need for continuous and high rates of positive reinforcement were not demonstrated.[74] Nor was it found necessary for all the students to go through the same set of frames in a linear sequence.[75] But, even more devastating, students frequently found the materials boring and often found ingenious ways to circumvent the program, including the destruction of their teaching machines! And some students were unable to pass tests even after successfully completing a program.

Literally thousands of programs began to flood the market and the skills of programmers seldom matched their exaggerated claims. Many publishers were deluded into thinking that a book with "frames" is a program and that almost anyone could produce an acceptable program. However, as their storage bins began to fill with unsold programs, it became obvious that serious retrenchment was necessary. By the early 1970s, most publishers had left the programmed text business and the output of programmed materials had shrunk dramatically.

Although the programmed instruction movement did not last very long, it did have important effects on educational technology. It revived the early ideas of individualizing instruction and influenced a number of programs for individualized instruction in the 1960s and 1970s. Programmed instruction also fostered the growth of sounder technology in the development of instructional materials and in the evaluation of instruction on the basis of behavioral objectives rather than on the instructional techniques used. Finally, the programmed instruction movement set the technological stage for the development of computer-assisted instruction and the systems approach to instruction.

Individualized Approaches to Instruction

As described in chapter 3, the roots of individualized instruction go back to practices early in this century, but in the 1960s, the notion of adapting to individual differences revived when a series of approaches developed that reflected behavioristic concepts. Aside from programmed instruction, these approaches included Keller's personalized system of instruction, individually prescribed instruction (IPI), the program for learning according to needs (PLAN), and individually guided education (IGE).

The Keller Plan

F. S. Keller, a behavioral psychologist and a colleague of Skinner's, described his plan for a "personalized" course in psychology in 1963. In 1968, he amplified the Keller plan in the first issue of the *Journal of Applied Behavior Analysis.*[76] Although his technique grew out of Skinnerian concepts, he did not include the use of teaching machines or programmed materials. His basic plan included the following five features:

(1) The go-at-your-own-pace feature, which permits a student to move through the course at a speed commensurate with his ability and other demands upon his time.

(2) The unit-perfection requirement for advance, which lets the student go ahead to new material only after demonstrating mastery of that which preceded.

(3) The use of lectures and demonstrations as vehicles of motivation, rather than sources of critical information.

(4) The related stress upon the written word in teacher-student communications.

(5) The use of proctors, which permits repeated testing, immediate scoring, almost unavoidable tutoring, and a marked enhancement of the personal-social aspect of the educational process.[77]

Within four years of its introduction the Keller personalized system of instruction (PSI) had been used in 877 courses in psychology alone.[78] By the mid-1970s, it was estimated that more than 2,000 college courses had been organized around the Keller plan. A review of published studies showed that final-examination performance in Keller plan courses usually exceeds or equals performance in lecture-type courses.[79] However, the Keller plan does have its critics. Jaynes, for example, states:

> What is learned by the Keller Method is also much more than the material: It is an attitude of subservience and dependence that comes with the removal of the material from the interpersonal community in which it is real. And I suggest that the learned subservience will last long after the material is forgotten.[80]

Although students have liked the self-pacing that frees them to study when and where they please, Berliner found that students had to study between 20 and 40 percent more and that greater than normal dropout rates sometimes occur.[81]

Individually Prescribed Instruction (IPI)

Individually prescribed instruction was first developed by the Learning Research and Development Center of the University of Pittsburgh in 1964. Many of the concepts were derived from programmed instruction. Units were prepared, particular behavioral objectives were specified, and instructional sequences were planned. In the fall of 1964, IPI was initiated at the Oakleaf Elementary School in a suburb of Pittsburgh. IPI procedures and materials were used in grades K-6 for reading, mathematics, and science.[82]

Based on a pretest, the teacher prescribed the appropriate unit for each student. When the student finished the unit, he was given a posttest. After the results were examined by the teacher, the student was either allowed to proceed to the next unit (if he showed mastery of the material) or given further work and retested until mastery had been achieved.

Throughout the developmental process, IPI materials and procedures were continuously evaluated in terms of their effectiveness in achieving behavioral objectives. As a result, changes were introduced almost annually for the first five years of the project. Moreover, curricular areas were expanded and tryout areas involved a national network of over 375 schools in more than forty states.

In the late 1970s, government funding for IPI was discontinued, and Research for Better Schools, the regional laboratory that had been involved in field testing and disseminating the system, also terminated its activity in this area. Since that time, use of IPI has waned.

Some critics of IPI held that its reading or mathematics materials were too complicated and required too much paperwork, and also that it was too expensive. One critic indicated that students had too little human contact and tended to become dehumanized.[83] Also, the so-called "new" teacher tasks of diagnosis and prescription were not considered synonymous with teaching, but merely precursors to good teaching.[84]

Program for Learning in Accordance with Needs (PLAN)

PLAN was another individualized approach that encompassed language arts, mathematics, science, and social studies in grades 1-12. It developed in 1967 under the sponsorship of the American Institutes for Research (AIR), Westinghouse Learning Corporation, and fourteen school districts from various regions of the United States. John C. Flanagan of AIR headed the project.

PLAN was organized so each school that participated could select sets of behavioral objectives from approximately 6,000 that were part of the system. About five objectives made up each instructional module, which required about two weeks of instructional time. Each module contained teaching-learning units that listed objectives, materials to be used, and alternative methods to achieve objectives. These alternatives took such forms as a textbook, filmstrip, programmed materials, or lectures. If mastery of the objectives was demonstrated by tests, students moved on to another unit. If the objectives were not mastered, the student was given remedial activities and retested. A record of each student's progress was kept by a computer.[85]

By the mid-1970s, more than 65,000 elementary and secondary school students in more than 100 schools in 19 states were participating in PLAN, but, by the late 1970s, PLAN had become outdated and its use eventually discontinued because the sponsors were not willing to spend the large sums of money required for the updating and incorporating of new instructional materials in the system.

Individually Guided Education (IGE)

The origin of the IGE system dates back to 1965 when Herbert Klausmeier served as principal investigator of a project undertaken by the Wisconsin Research and Development Center. The IGE approach was similar to that of other individualized instructional programs. Teachers and assistants assessed the entry skills of students, identified the behavioral objectives, and planned an instructional program designed to attain those objectives. The plan also provided for training teachers and testing instructional innovations. Team teaching was employed, nongraded classes were organized, and cross-age tutoring was used.[86]

In 1971, the U.S. Office of Education provided funds for a large-scale implementation of IGE. During the next two years, more than five hundred elementary schools in nine states utilized the system, and by 1976 there were approximately three thousand elementary and middle schools using some form of IGE. In the late 1970s, however, government funding ceased and since that time, schools using IGE have progressively decreased.

Decline of Individualized Instruction

By the mid-1970s, individualized instruction was waning. There were a number of reasons for this decline. First, many of the schools that had adopted individualized programs had not implemented them properly nor had they made any substantial changes in their regular instructional practices. When comparative evaluations were made of so-called innovative programs and traditional programs, the results were equivocal.[87]

Whenever significant changes are made in traditional practices, these changes must be concerned with the total social, political, and economic contexts if they are to succeed. Without the support of the community and the entire teaching staff, sustained innovation is unlikely.

Computer-Assisted Instruction (CAI)

Computer-assisted instruction (CAI) first began to be used in education and training in the 1950s. Much of the early work in CAI was done at IBM, where researchers developed the first Coursewriter language and the 1500 system.[88] Other pioneers included Gordon Pask, with adaptive machines in 1953,[89] and O. M. Moore's 1960 computer-based "autotelic responsive environment" system for teaching nursery school children to read.[90]

CAI began its ascent just about the time the programmed instruction movement as exemplified in teaching machines and programmed texts reached its nadir. The sudden, vigorous growth of CAI occurred in the mid-1960s when millions of dollars began to flow from federal funding for research and development in schools, colleges, universities, and industrial laboratories. Computer companies visualized a new, lucrative educational market and merged with publishing companies. However, by the late 1960s, CAI had already begun to fade.

Despite the decline of CAI, the federal government, through the National Science Foundation (NSF), decided to determine whether CAI could be made effective and available to as many teachers and schools as possible. This was the viewpoint behind the $10 million grant made in 1971 to two private companies, Control Data Corporation (CDC) and Mitre Corporation, with the idea that the two companies would compete with each other and that at least one viable CAI national system would emerge. These were the PLATO and TICCIT projects.[91] These projects illustrated two different approaches to CAI, which will be described in this section.

Regardless of the efforts to prove its effectiveness, it was clear by the mid-1970s that CAI had not succeeded. Federal aid began to dwindle, the new educational market that had been optimistically projected had not developed, and computer companies had retrenched, withdrawn from the field, or gone out of business.

A number of reasons for the failure of CAI can be given. CAI had been oversold and had not delivered on its promises. Moreover, the usual problems associated with educational innovation had not been fully understood nor had the antagonism from some quarters been expected. The technical problems had not been appreciated or foreseen. Since time-shared computing was the prevailing technology of the 1960s, the goal was to utilize the computer to serve as many people as possible, but this approach confined the computer to computer-assisted instruction with reference to the traditional curriculum, rather than generating a completely new learning environment. Also, wide use of the BASIC programming language propounded the myth that the algebraic, non-intuitive language would be ideally suited for teaching children programming and for developing programs, which it was never intended to do. These problems were further aggravated by the lack of quality software, which often had to be supplemented by teachers who did not possess sufficient expertise. Finally, a major impediment that continually blocked the progress of CAI was cost.

Early CAI Projects and Theoretical Orientation

Practically all the money that has been spent on CAI by the federal government and by foundations was spent on CAI projects with a behaviorist viewpoint. Some institutions establishing CAI projects include the University of Texas, Florida State University, the University of Wisconsin, Harvard University, University of California at Santa Barbara and Irvine, Dartmouth College, MIT, the University of Pittsburgh, and a number of public schools including Chicago, Los Angeles, and Philadelphia public schools.

The bulk of the CAI projects during the 1960s and 1970s were directly descended from Skinnerian teaching machines and reflected a behaviorist orientation. The typical CAI presentation modes known as *drill-and-practice* and *tutorial* were characterized by a strong degree of author control rather than learner control. The student was asked to make simple responses, fill in the blanks, choose among a restricted set of alternatives, or supply a missing word or phrase. If the response was wrong, the machine would assume control, flash the word "wrong," and generate another problem. If the response was correct, additional material would be presented. The function of the computer was to present increasingly difficult material and provide reinforcement for correct responses. The program was very much in control and the student had little flexibility.

Stanford University CAI

The development of CAI at Stanford University was one of the first major research and development projects and has been one of the largest and most enduring programs in the field. The Institute for Mathematical Studies in the Social Sciences at Stanford University, under the direction of Richard Atkinson and Patrick Suppes, developed some of the earlier applications of CAI at both the elementary school and university levels in collaboration with IBM. The project has been funded at various stages by the Carnegie Foundation, the NSF, and the U.S. Office of Education.[92]

A drill-and-practice system began in 1963 in elementary mathematics and reading. From a small beginning of computer drill for forty-one fourth-grade children in one school in 1965, the system expanded so that by 1968 almost three thousand students were receiving computerized instruction in reading, arithmetic, spelling, logic, and elementary Russian in seven California schools and in such distant areas as Mississippi and Kentucky.[93]

The original 1500 Tutorial System for reading instruction had a student terminal consisting of a screen on which images could be projected from frames randomly accessed under computer control, a cathode ray tube (CRT) on which material could be presented, a light pen that made it possible for the student to respond by merely touching a part of the television screen, a typewriter keyboard, a set of earphones, and a microphone.

Suppes, a behaviorist, sees behavior as a collection of discrete stimulus-response units that, as Solomon observed, involves teaching children by

> presenting them with exercises (stimuli) and reinforcing their responses. Telling the children they are "correct" and presenting a new exercise, telling them they are wrong, telling them the correct response, and then re-representing the exercise. The teacher's job (assumed by the computer) is to present increasingly harder exercises, each building on the previous experience of the children and leading finally to knowing the specified body of information.[94]

In this behaviorist view, feedback is considered important only after correct responses, and individualization involves the pace that an individual student takes to work through the program material. Individualization, historically, meant students' receiving material that was different from that received by any other student.

In 1967, the Computer Curriculum Corporation (CCC) was founded by Patrick Suppes, Richard Atkinson, and William Estes to develop CAI drill-and-practice materials in mathematics, reading, and language arts. The CCC materials, used with low income and minority students, have proven to be helpful in improving scores on such standardized tests as the Stanford Achievement Test (SAT) or the Comprehensive Test of Basic Skills. Evaluative studies conducted between 1971 and 1977 indicate a pattern whereby the students showed a grade placement improvement of 1 to 1.5 years at the end of their CAI program in mathematics and about 0.6 year in reading or language arts. A study of the effects of CCC materials in the Los Angeles schools from 1976 to 1980 showed that students made significant gains in computational skills, but the reading and language arts did not show similar improvement.[95]

CCC has continually improved and expanded the capability of its systems. For example, in 1980, they introduced a digital speech system that has been used to teach English as a second language to native speakers of Spanish, Japanese, and Chinese. Also, in 1984, CCC introduced its own computer system based on a 68000 processor using the UNIX operating system. The terminals used in this system provide minimal graphics and a range of courses from the teaching of programming languages such as BASIC and PASCAL to a computer literacy course and a logic course for junior high school students. The materials produced by CCC continue to be evaluated and improved.

The PLATO Project

The second example of the tutorial and drill-and-practice modes of CAI is the PLATO (Programmed Logic for Automatic Teaching Operation) project at the University of Illinois. One of the earliest university CAI efforts, the PLATO project began in 1960 with these goals: "First, to investigate the potential role of the computer in the instructional process; second, to design an economically and educationally viable system incorporating the most valuable approaches to teaching and learning developed in the investigation."[96]

The principal emphasis of PLATO was to develop a comprehensive system of hardware and software. During the first years of the project, Illinois progressed through the original PLATO system to PLATO II, III, and IV. The NSF-funded PLATO IV went into operation in 1972 featuring a terminal that consisted of a keyboard and a transparent display panel, which enabled the student to communicate with the program by touching a screen rather than typing. PLATO IV began with around 950 terminals located at about 140 sites and about 8,000 hours of instructional material contributed by over 3,000 authors. Other devices such as random access audio and slide selectors, music synthesizers, film projectors, and laboratory apparatus may be added to the terminal.

A basic instruction programming language, TUTOR, was developed for use in a variety of university disciplines. For example, there are TUTOR commands to gather data and perform statistical analysis. The TUTOR language is easy, but the resulting program is typically an unsophisticated drill-and-practice or tutorial with the possibility of elementary branching.

There has not been a major focus on evaluating the effectiveness of individual courses in PLATO. The data that have been collected do not provide any compelling statistical evidence that PLATO has had either a negative or positive effect on student achievement. Although the principal investigators have focused on producing low-cost, viable hardware and software, evaluations have not dealt with either the technical aspects or the cost of PLATO implementation.

One of the persistent goals of PLATO has been the extension of the system so that every school in America would have at least one PLATO terminal. Since the technological ground rules have changed, it is no longer true that larger systems are necessarily more economic. With this in mind, plans for PLATO V focus on such services as mail delivery and information retrieval rather than being solely devoted to CAI. Since it is no longer economically feasible for many educational institutions to use PLATO IV, a microcomputer-based version or Micro PLATO has been introduced that can be linked to a mainframe PLATO system. Ultimately, the lasting value of the original PLATO concept will be tested by the quality of its teaching programs.[97]

The TICCIT Project

A third major project that reflected the tutorial and drill-and-practice modes of presentation was the TICCIT (Time-Shared, Interactive, Computer-Controlled Information Television) project.

The TICCIT system was conceived by the Mitre Corporation in 1969 and plans were made to utilize 128 television terminals with digital graphics capability for CAI in elementary schools. In the late 1970s, the focus shifted to providing CAI for mathematics and English at community colleges. Mitre was to design and develop hardware and software and a related contract was given to what became the Institute for Computer Uses in Education at Brigham Young University. NSF also provided for an evaluation of the TICCIT project by the independent Educational Testing Service.

The objective was to demonstrate that CAI could provide more effective instruction at lower cost than traditional instruction in community colleges. TICCIT was designed to be a primary source of instruction of what was called "mainline CAI." Material was produced by a team composed of an instructional psychologist, a subject-matter expert, an instructional design technician, an evaluation technician, and a packaging specialist.

TICCIT placed great emphasis on learner control. The student was presented with displays on a television screen to which he responded on a typical typewriter keyboard that was augmented by a series of learner-control keys. The keys consisted of rule, example, practice, and help keys by which a student could access various types of displays for a given segment or content topic. For each lesson the student was shown a map that indicated all the topics to be covered by a particular lesson. The student could then select the topics he wished to pursue or any displays he would like presented. The student could also skip topics if he chose to do so. Thus, the student had control in the sense of determining the sequence of materials to be presented. Nevertheless, the mode was still essentially a tutorial that was predetermined by the programmer.[98]

The final evaluation of TICCIT has never been published in full, but Alderman has given a summary and conclusions statement.[99] The main conclusion was that TICCIT had a significant positive effect on student achievement in both mathematics and English composition and that students who completed TICCIT courses generally achieved higher posttest scores than similar students in lecture-discussion classes. There was some concern about the number of students who did not complete TICCIT courses. Jones attributed the low completion rates to a low instructor involvement in monitoring student progress.[100] Also, there was no evidence that the learner-control approach and the advisor programs improved learning strategies and responsibility. Interestingly, the faculty response to TICCIT was less than enthusiastic. For example, one of the college project directors wrote that the initial presentation to the faculty was a "total disaster" and turned faculty away with its hard sell and tactless humor.

Clearly, the NSF-funded projects PLATO and TICCIT can be considered failures by their own criterion, namely, that of achieving commercial profitability. Their emphasis on technological hardware was misplaced and they did not solve the basic problem of producing effective instructional software.

Parts of TICCIT are still in use at two community colleges, Phoenix College in Arizona and Northern Virginia Community College in Alexandria, Virginia. Little is heard today of TICCIT. Since 1976, TICCIT has been marketed by Hazeltine Corporation and is in use at a number of military training sites.

The Changing Status of Computer-Based Instruction

Technical and psychological changes in the late 1970s transformed the role of the computer in education. By 1980, CAI could no longer be considered a simple derivative of the teaching machine or of the behavioristic programmed instruction that was popular during the 1960s and early 1970s.

From a technical viewpoint, the development of the microcomputer in 1977 simplified the delivery of CAI materials, but it is not clear whether the emphasis will shift once again to devices over concepts. Meanwhile, the development of cognitive psychology holds many important implications for future educational use of the computer. For example, Solomon describes the vision of the future as follows:

> children will use the computer as an expressive medium. They will communicate in a number of ways: by speech, by typewriter, by touch, by body movement. They will talk to the computer about a number of things from a wide assortment of computer-controlled responsive toys, animated graphic images, interactive stories represented on videodiscs, images generated by the computer on the fly, and including historical data on a wide range of subjects, interactive science labs. The student will be in control, either writing programs to probe different

environments or choosing knowledge-based programs to interact with. The computer will become an instrument of communication in written word as well as spoken; it becomes a flexible, interactive encyclopedia.[101]

The next chapter continues with the historical development of the computer in education and shows the relationship of the cognitive sciences to its future development.

Conclusions

Programmed instruction, the various individualized instructional systems, and CAI provided a valuable testing ground for a behavioristically oriented educational technology. However, by the late 1970s, modern cognitive psychology was becoming the dominant theoretical orientation in psychological science. The impact of the Skinnerian behavioristic approach still dominated educational technology, but behaviors of human performance being studied in the context of cognitive psychology suggested new approaches to educational technology.

Notes

[1]John B. Watson, "Psychology as the Behaviorist Views It," *Psychological Review* 20 (March 1913), 158-77.

[2]A. A. Roback, *History of American Psychology,* revised ed. New York: Collier Books, 1964, 265. Besides Max F. Meyer, others who developed earlier variations of behaviorism were Walter S. Hunter, Albert P. Weiss, Karl S. Lashley, Edwin B. Holt, James Rush, and Z. Y. Kuo.

[3]Sigmund Koch, "Clark L. Hull," in William K. Estes et al., eds., *Modern Learning Theory.* New York: Appleton-Century-Crofts, 1954.

[4]Skinner was greatly influenced by Thorndike's law of effect. Before Thorndike's work, psychologists had relied exclusively on stimuli that precede responses as the primary influence on behavior. Thorndike's research with the law of effect had shown that stimuli that follow the response could also have a very important influence on behavior.

[5]Norman Guttman, "On Skinner and Hull: A Reminiscence and Projection," *American Psychologist* 32 (May 1977), 321-22.

[6]B. F. Skinner, *The Technology of Teaching.* New York: Appleton-Century-Crofts, 1968, 249-56.

[7]Franklin Bobbitt, *The Curriculum.* Boston: Houghton Mifflin, 1918.

[8]Franklin Bobbitt, *How to Make a Curriculum.* Boston: Houghton Mifflin, 1924.

[9]W. W. Charters, *Curriculum Construction.* Boston: Houghton Mifflin, 1924.

[10]R. W. Tyler, *Basic Principles of Curriculum and Instruction.* Chicago: University of Chicago Press, 1949.

[11]Ibid., 1.

[12]Ibid., 5-6.

[13]B. S. Bloom, ed., et al., *Taxonomy of Educational Objectives — The Classification of Educational Goals. Handbook I: Cognitive Domain.* New York: David McKay, 1956.

[14]D. R. Krathwohl et al., *Taxonomy of Educational Objectives—The Classification of Educational Goals. Handbook II: Affective Domain*. New York: David McKay, 1964.

[15]A. J. Harrow, *A Taxonomy of the Psychomotor Domain*. New York: David McKay, 1972.

[16]See Robert M. Gagnè, "Domain of Learning," *Interchange* 3 (1972), 1-8.

[17]Benjamin S. Bloom, *Human Characteristics and School Learning*. New York: McGraw-Hill, 1976, 213.

[18]Ibid., 213.

[19]There are too many of these people to mention who came to education from the training laboratories of the military, industry, and foundation "think tanks." Many examples of their work can be found in Gagnè's *Psychological Principles in Systems Development*. New York: Holt, Rinehart and Winston, 1962.

[20]See Raymond Callahan, *Education and the Cult of Efficiency*. Chicago: University of Chicago Press, 1962.

[21]Robert Mager, who had been a staff member of the Army Human Research Unit at Fort Bliss, Texas, came to Varian Associates, a California electronics company, to assist in designing some procedures for specifying objectives. The result was *Preparing Objectives for Programmed Instruction* (1961). The following year he published *Preparing Instructional Objectives*, Palo Alto, Calif.: Fearon Publishers, 1962.

[22]Ibid., 3.

[23]Ibid., 3.

[24]See H. H. McAshan, *Competency-Based Education and Behavioral Objectives*. Englewood Cliffs, N.J.: Educational Technology Publications, 1979, 133; and W. James Popham, "Crumbling Conceptions of Educational Testing," in *Educational Evaluation: Recent Progress, Future Needs*. Minneapolis, Minn.: Research and Evaluation Center, 1981, 32.

[25]See R. M. Gagnè and L. J. Briggs, *Principles of Instructional Design*. New York: Holt, Rinehart and Winston, 1974.

[26]Robert J. Kibler and Ronald E. Bassett, "Writing Performance Objectives," in L. J. Briggs, ed., *Instructional Design*. Englewood Cliffs, N.J.: Educational Technology Publications, 1977, 72-73.

[27]Robert Gagnè, "Curriculum Research and the Promotion of Learning," in Ralph Tyler et al., eds., *Perspectives of Curriculum Evaluation*. AERA Monograph 1. Chicago: Rand McNally, 1967, 21-22.

[28]Daniel Tanner and Laurel N. Tanner, *Curriculum Development,* 2d ed. New York: Macmillan, 1980, 337.

[29]Elliot W. Eisner, *The Educational Imagination*, 2d ed. New York: Macmillan, 1985, 116.

[30]Leon Lessinger, "Accountability for Results," in Leon Lessinger and Ralph Tyler, eds., *Accountability in Education*. Worthington, Ohio: Charles A. Jones Publishing, 1971, 14.

[31]Leon Lessinger, *Every Kid a Winner: Accountability in Education*. Palo Alto, Calif.: Science Research Associates, 1970, 3.

[32]Franklin Bobbitt, "The Supervision of City Schools: Some General Principles of Management Applied to the Problems of City-School Systems," *12th Yearbook of the National Society for the Study of Education*, Part I. Bloomington, Ill.: National Society for the Study of Education, 1913, 11.

[33]Ibid., 83.

[34]Raymond E. Callahan, *Education and the Cult of Efficiency.* Chicago: University of Chicago Press, 1962, 84.

[35]Ibid., 103-4.

[36]Aside from reducing educational costs, accountability was also designed to combat the rising collective power of teachers and to prevent them from achieving any degree of self-management. As a result, teacher unions became involved in the politics of accountability.

[37]For an excellent analysis of the accountability movement, see Arthur E. Wise, *Legislated Learning.* Berkeley, Calif.: University of California Press, 1979.

[38]Some other private companies involved in performance contracts included Behavioral Research Labs, Learning Research Associates, Macmillan Educational Services, Educational Development Laboratories, Harcourt Brace Jovanovich, Quality Education Development, Dorsett Educational Systems, Alpha Learning Systems, Learning Foundations, Plan Education Centers, Singer/Graphflex, Thiokol Chemical Corporation, and Education Solutions. Most of these companies were formed primarily to take advantage of the influx of federal dollars to the schools by way of performance contracts. Other companies had been dealing with the government in such areas as defense and space exploration. In one performance contract conducted by Dorsett Educational Systems in Texarkana, Arkansas, it was discovered that a programmer had fed reading, math, and vocabulary exercises from the Iowa tests into the software used in Texarkana's rapid learning centers. One internal evaluator estimated that 30 to 60 percent of the questions on the achievement tests administered were invalidated as a result. In other words, they were accused of "teaching to the test." Exactly what occurred remains a matter of dispute and may never be resolved short of legal action. Charles Blaschke, president of Education Turnkey Systems, Inc. helped design the Texarkana project in 1969. He had learned of performance contracts while serving in the military where such contracts were sometimes used. For further details on performance contracting, see Roald F. Campbell and James E. Lorion, *Performance Contracting in School Systems.* Columbus, Ohio: Charles E. Merrill, 1972; James Meckleburger, *Performance Contracting.* Worthington, Ohio: Charles A. Jones Publishing, 1972; and Edward M. Gramlich and Patricia P. Koshel, *Educational Performance Contracting: An Evaluation of an Experiment.* Washington, D.C.: Brookings Institution, 1975.

[39]See P. Carpenter-Huffman et al., *Change in Education.* Cambridge, Mass.: Ballinger Publishing, 1974.

[40]See Daniel Tanner, "Performance Contracting: Contrivance of the Industrial-Governmental-Educational Complex," *Intellect* 101 (March 1973), 361-65.

[41]This author considers Maria Montessori one of the true pioneers of modern programmed instruction. She was probably the first to make a systematic attempt to implement a psychological theory of learning with a mechanism. She began using her so-called didactic devices with young children in Rome in 1907. For example, one of her devices consisted of a block of wood with ten holes of different diameters and ten wooden cylinders to fit the holes. This device was dependent on the activity of the young learner for its use. It was necessarily self-corrective with immediate feedback since (1) a learner could not put a cylinder into too small a hole, and (2) if he put one into too large a hole, he would have, at the end of the sequence, a cylinder left over that would not go into the only remaining hole. Maria Montessori was given a patent in 1914 by the United States Patent Office for a device that trained the sense of touch (Patent No. 1103369). See Maria Montessori, *The Montessori Method* (translated by A. E. George). Philadelphia: J. B. Lippincott, 1912.

[42]B. F. Skinner, "The Science of Learning and the Art of Teaching," *Harvard Educational Review* 24 (Spring 1954), 86-97.

[43]B. F. Skinner, "Teaching Machines," *Science* 128 (October 1958), 969-77.

[44]A. A. Lumsdaine and Robert Glaser, eds., *Teaching Machines and Programmed Learning.* Washington, D.C.: DAVI, 1960. A second source book, *Teaching Machines and Programmed Learning, II*, was published by the DAVI in 1965, with Robert Glaser as editor.

[45]Sidney L. Pressey, "Autoinstruction: Perspectives, Problems, Potentials," in E. R. Hilgard, ed., *Theories of Learning and Instruction*, Part I, 63rd yearbook of the National Society for the Study of Education. Chicago: University of Chicago Press, 1964, 355-56.

[46]Ibid.

[47]With Pressey's punchboard device, the student punched his pencil through a cover paper. His pencil went deepest when he found the right answer.

[48]Sidney L. Pressey, "A Third and Fourth Contribution Toward the Coming 'Industrial Revolution' in Education," *School and Society* 36 (November 1932), 668-72.

[49]H. B. English invented a device used in 1918 to help train soldiers to squeeze a rifle trigger. It provided visual feedback through the use of a manometer, which revealed to the soldier a change in the height of a liquid column. If he squeezed the trigger smoothly or spasmodically, the mercury column would rise correspondingly and provide visual feedback. See H. B. English, "How Psychology Can Facilitate Military Training: A Concrete Example," *Journal of Applied Psychology* 26 (February 1942), 3-7.

[50]N. A. Crowder, "Automatic Tutoring by Intrinsic Programming," in Arthur A. Lumsdaine and Robert Glaser, eds., *Teaching Machines and Programmed Learning: A Source Book*. Washington, D.C.: DAVI, 1960, 286-98.

[51]B. F. Skinner, "The Science of Learning and the Art of Teaching," in A. A. Lumsdaine and Robert Glaser, eds., *Teaching Machines and Programmed Learning*. Washington, D.C.: DAVI, 1960, 107.

[52]*The Use of Programmed Instruction in U.S. Schools*. Washington, D.C.: Center for Programmed Instruction, 1965.

[53]Two journals devoted exclusively to programmed instruction were the *Journal of Programed Instruction* and *Programed Instruction of Educational Technology*, published by The Center for Programed Instruction of Educational Technology, Teachers College, Columbia University, New York City.

[54]*Programed Instruction in U.S. Schools*.

[55]James K. Little used Pressey's devices as part of the regular class procedure throughout a course in educational psychology in 1934. See James K. Little, "Results of Use of Machines for Testing and for Drill upon Learning in Educational Psychology," *Journal of Experimental Education* 3 (September 1934), 59-65.

[56]James G. Holland, "A Teaching Machine Program in Psychology," in E. Galanter, ed., *Automatic Teaching: The State of the Art*. New York: John Wiley, 1959, 69-84.

[57]J. L. Evans et al., "An Investigation of 'Teaching Machine' Variables Using Learning Programs in Symbolic Logic," *Journal of Educational Research* 55 (June-July 1926), 433-50.

[58]Douglas Porter, *An Application of Reinforcement Principles to Classroom Teaching*. Cambridge, Mass.: Graduate School of Education, Harvard University, May 1961.

[59]L. D. Eigen and P. K. Komoski, *Research Summary No. 1 of the Collegiate School Automated Teaching Project*. New York: Center for Programmed Instruction, 1960.

[60]The decision to send Reed to New York City was made on the basis that he was not attracted to programmed instruction. The rationale was that if Reed became enthusiastic about the method, then other English teachers also might be expected to accept it.

[61]See Wilbur Schramm, ed., *Four Cases of Programed Instruction*. New York: Fund for the Advancement of Education, 1964, 30-40.

[62]Ibid., John Herbert and Arthur W. Foshay, "Programed Instruction in the Manhasset Junior High School," 20.

[63]It had been anticipated that the brighter students would be the first to finish the program, but in practice, it was the students of low ability who were first to leave the large program group, since they found the program beyond their capacity and desired individual help.

[64]Schramm, *Four Cases*, 18-27.

[65]E. Rushton, *The Roanoke Story*. Chicago: Encyclopaedia Britannica, 1963.

[66]Schramm, *Four Cases*, 66-94.

[67]R. Glaser et al., *Programmed Instruction in the Intact Classroom*. Pittsburgh: Learning Research and Development Center, University of Pittsburgh, 1963.

[68]James D. Finn and Donald G. Perrin, *Teaching Machines and Programed Learning, 1962: A Survey of the Industry*. Washington, D.C.: NEA Technological Development Project, 1962.

[69]Robert Glaser, ed., *Teaching Machines and Programed Learning, II*. Washington, D.C.: DAVI, 1965, vii.

[70]B. F. Skinner, "Review Lecture: The Technology of Teaching," *Proceedings of the Royal Society* 162 (July 1965), 427-43.

[71]J. A. Kulik, "Individualized Systems of Instruction," in H. E. Mitzel, ed., *Encyclopedia of Educational Research*, 5th ed. New York: Macmillan, 1982, 851-58.

[72]J. D. Krumboltz, "The Nature and Importance of the Required Response in Programmed Instruction," *American Educational Research Journal* 1 (November 1964), 203-9.

[73]J. L. Brown, "Effects of Logical and Scrambled Sequence in Mathematical Materials on Learning with Programmed Instruction Materials," *Journal of Educational Psychology* 61 (February 1970), 41-45.

[74]S. C. Lublin, "Reinforcement Schedules, Scholastic Aptitude, Autonomy Need, and Achievement in a Programmed Course," *Journal of Educational Psychology* 56 (December 1965), 295-302.

[75]As the programmed instruction movement gained momentum, alternatives to Skinnerian linear programs were developed. Examples include Gilbert's mathematics, Homme and Glaser's "rules" system, and Gropper's behavioristic strategies. Gilbert's model, for example, provided a method known as backward chaining that involved the following sequence: "First, show them where things are going — the consequences of performance; next, provide the mediating generalizations they need; and finally, teach the discrimination skills" (Thomas F. Gilbert, *Human Competence*, New York: McGraw-Hill, 1978, 267). One of the best instructional grammars of programming principles published in the 1960s was Susan Markle's *Good Frames and Bad*, 2d ed., New York: John Wiley, 1969.

[76]F. S. Keller, "Goodbye Teacher ...," reprinted in J. Hartley and I. K. Davies, eds., *Contributions to an Educational Technology*. London: Kogan Page, 1978. Keller first developed his method with psychologists J. Gilmour Sherman of Columbia University and Rodolfo Azzi and Carolina Martuscelli Bori of the University of Sao Paulo, Brazil.

[77]Ibid., 83.

[78]See J. A. Hess, Jr., *Bibliography on PSI*. Harrisburg, Va.: PSI Clearinghouse, Eastern Mennonite College, 1972.

[79]J. A. Kulik et al., "The Keller Plan in Science Teaching," *Science* 183 (February 1974), 379-83.

[80]J. Jaynes, "Hello Teacher ...," *Contemporary Psychology* 20 (July 1975), 629-31.

[81]See N. L. Gage and David C. Berliner, *Educational Psychology*. Chicago: Rand McNally, 1975, 577.

[82]C. M. Lindvall and J. O. Bolvin, "Programmed Instruction in the Schools: An Application of Programming Principles in Individually Prescribed Instruction," in P. C. Lange, ed., *Programmed Instruction*, Part II, 66th yearbook of the National Society for Study of Education. Chicago: University of Chicago Press, 1967, 217-54.

[83]Vera Ohanian, "Educational Technology: A Critique," *Elementary School Journal* 71 (January 1971), 182-97.

[84]Ibid.

[85]J. C. Flanagan, "The PLAN System for Individualizing Instruction," *Measurement in Education* 2 (April 1971), 1-8.

[86]See H. J. Klausmeier, "IGE: An Alternative Form of Schooling," in H. Talmage, ed., *Systems of Individualized Education*. Berkeley, Calif.: McCutchan, 1975.

[87]D. F. Walker and Jon Schaffarzick, "Comparing Curricula," *Review of Educational Research* 44 (Winter 1974), 83-111.

[88]L. A. Pagliaro, "The History and Development of CAI: 1926-1981," *Alberta Journal of Educational Research* 29 (March 1983), 75-84.

[89]See Brian N. Lewis and Gordon Pask, "The Theory and Practice of Adaptive Teaching Systems," in Robert Glaser, ed., *Teaching Machines and Programed Learning, II*. Washington, D.C.: DAVI, 1965, 242.

[90]O. K. Moore, "Autolectic Response Environments and Exceptional Children," *Special Children in Century 21*. Seattle, Wash.: Special Child Publications, 1964.

[91]Pagliaro, "History and Development," 78.

[92]P. Suppes, "Computer-Assisted Instruction at Stanford," *Technical Report* 174, Stanford, Calif.: Stanford University, Institute for Mathematical Studies in the Social Sciences, 1971; See Patrick Suppes et al., *Computer-assisted Instruction: Stanford's 1965-66 Arithmetic Program*. New York: Academic Press, 1968; Patrick Suppes et al., *Computer-assisted Instruction at Stanford, 1966-68, Models and Evaluations of the Arithmetic Program*. New York: Academic Press, 1972; Patrick Suppes, ed., *University-level Computer-assisted Instruction at Stanford, 1968-1980*. Stanford, Calif.: Institute for Mathematical Studies in the Social Sciences, Stanford University, 1981.

[93]Ibid.

[94]Cynthia Solomon, *Computer Environments for Children*. Cambridge, Mass.: MIT Press, 1986, 8.

[95]M. Ragosta et al., *Computer-Assisted Instruction and Compensatory Education: The ETS/LAUSD Study, Executive Summary and Policy Implications*. Princeton, N.J.: Educational Testing Service, 1982.

[96]Karl L. Zinn, *An Evaluative Review of Uses of Computers in Instruction, Project CLUE*. Ann Arbor, Mich.: University of Michigan Press, 1970, 40.

[97]C. Victor Bunderson and Gerald W. Faust, "Programmed and Computer-Assisted Instruction," in N. L. Gage, ed., *The Psychology of Teaching Methods*, Part I, 75th yearbook of the National Society for the Study of Education. Chicago: University of Chicago Press, 1976, 70-72.

[98]Ibid., 72-77.

[99]D. L. Alderman, "Evaluation of the TICCIT Computer-Assisted Instructional System in the Community College," *SIGCUE Bulletin* 13 (October 1979), 5-17.

[100]M. C. Jones, "Concerning the Evaluation of TICCIT Computer-Based English Composition and Mathematics Instruction." Paper presented at 1978 AEDS Annual Convention, Washington, D.C.

[101]Solomon, *Computer Environments*, 144.

Select Bibliography

Bloom, B. S., et al., eds. *Taxonomy of Educational Objectives — The Classification of Educational Goals. Handbook I: Cognitive Domain.* New York: David McKay, 1956.

Bobbitt, Franklin. *How to Make a Curriculum.* Boston: Houghton Mifflin, 1924.

Bobbitt, Franklin, et al. *Handbook on Formative and Summative Evaluation of Student Learning.* New York: McGraw-Hill, 1971.

Briggs, Leslie J., et al. *Instructional Media: A Procedure for the Design of Multi-Media Instruction: A Critical Review of Research and Suggestions for Future Research.* Pittsburgh: American Institutes for Research, 1967.

Charters, W. W. *Curriculum Construction.* Boston: Houghton Mifflin, 1918.

Gagnè, Robert M. *The Conditions of Learning.* New York: Holt, Rinehart & Winston, 1970.

Gagnè, Robert M., and Leslie J. Briggs. *Principles of Instructional Design.* New York: Holt, Rinehart & Winston, 1974.

Gagnè, Robert M., and Leslie J. Briggs, eds. *Instructional Technology: Foundations.* Hillsdale, N.J.: Erlbaum, 1987.

Glaser, Robert, ed. *Teaching Machines and Programed Learning, II: Data and Directions.* Washington, D.C.: DAVI, 1965.

Koch, Sigmund, ed. *Psychology: A Study of a Science.* New York: McGraw-Hill, 1959.

Leahey, Thomas H. *A History of Psychology,* 2d ed. Englewood Cliffs, N.J.: Prentice-Hall, 1987.

Lumsdaine, Arthur A., and Robert Glaser, eds. *Teaching Machines and Programmed Learning.* Washington, D.C.: DAVI, 1960.

McAshan, H. H. *Competency-Based Education and Behavioral Objectives.* Englewood Cliffs, N.J.: Educational Technology Publications, 1979.

Mager, Robert. *Preparing Instructional Objectives.* Palo Alto, Calif.: Fearon Publishers, 1962.

Skinner, B. F. *The Behavior of Organisms.* New York: Appleton-Century-Crofts, 1938.

——. *Science and Human Behavior.* New York: Macmillan, 1948.

——. *Verbal Behavior.* New York: Appleton-Century-Crofts, 1957.

——. *The Technology of Teaching.* New York: Appleton-Century-Crofts, 1968.

——. *Contingencies of Reinforcement.* New York: Appleton-Century-Crofts, 1969.

Tyler, R. W. *Basic Principles of Curriculum and Instruction.* Chicago: University of Chicago Press, 1949.

Watson, John. *Psychology from the Standpoint of a Behaviorist.* 2d ed. Philadelphia: J. B. Lippincott, 1924.

——. *The Ways of Behaviorism.* New York: Harper & Row, 1928.

Wise, Arthur E. *Legislated Learning.* Berkeley and Los Angeles: University of California Press, 1979.

Wolman, Benjamin B. *Contemporary Theories and Systems in Psychology.* New York: Harper & Row, 1960.

11

Cognitive Science and Educational Technology: 1950–1980

Beginning roughly in the decade 1955-1965, a quiet revolution began to take place in psychological thought and research that promises to have a significant impact on educational technology. What came to be known as the "cognitive revolution" represented a radical shift in the prevailing behavioristic perspective of the psychology community. With this theoretical shift, the emphasis changed from procedures for manipulating instructional materials to procedures for facilitating learner processing and interaction.

Kuhn's often quoted seminal monograph on the nature of scientific development argued that new knowledge does not always emerge by slow increments, but may erupt in sudden "paradigm shifts" or "scientific revolutions."[1] These shifts, Kuhn claims, may occur in great scientific revolutions such as those associated with Copernicus, Darwin, or Einstein or they may occur less spectacularly in small scientific groups.

Cognitive psychology, now commonly referred to as cognitive science, emphasizes knowing rather than responding, stresses mental structure or organization, and views the individual as active, constructive, and problem solving rather than as a passive recipient of environmental stimulation. As Neisser declared in 1967:

> A new field called cognitive psychology has come into being. It studies perception, memory, attention, pattern recognition, problem solving, the psychology of language, cognitive development, and a host of other problems.[2]

We have noted elsewhere in this book that the impact of behaviorism on educational technology began to manifest itself in the 1950s, just when its dominance in psychology began to wane. However, by the late 1970s, the influence of cognitive science began to be felt in educational technology, as reflected in a large number of publications that explored the application of the cognitive view of learning to the problems of instructional design.[3] Atkinson, for example, observed in 1976,

> we need theories that tell us how knowledge is represented in memory, how information is retrieved from that

knowledge structure, how new information is added to the structure by self-generative processes. The development of such theories is under way, and increasingly work in cognitive psychology is moving in that direction.[4]

Glaser stated "that cognitive psychologists are now preparing to study the problems of the acquisition and utilization of the intellectual skills of everyday life."[5] Meanwhile, instead of speaking of reinforcement, some educators were beginning to emphasize the importance and role that certain types of information could serve in facilitating the cognitive processes of the learner.

It was clear in the late 1970s that educational technology was on the threshold of a new theoretical orientation. However, much work needed to be done to bring about a transition from theory to a scientific approach to instructional design. Resnick summarized the situation well when he said:

> First, there is a shift toward studying more and more complex forms of cognitive behavior. This means that many of the tasks and processes of interest to cognitive psychologists are ones that can form part of a school's curriculum. Psychological work on such tasks is naturally relevant to instruction. Second ... is a growing interest in the role of knowledge in human behavior. Much effort is now directed at finding ways to represent the structure of knowledge and at discovering the ways in which knowledge is used in various kinds of learning.... Finally, today's assumptions about the nature of learning and thinking are interactionist. We assume that learning occurs as a result of mental constructions of the learner. These constructions respond to information and stimuli in the environment, but they do not copy or mirror them. This means that instruction must be designed not to put knowledge into learners' heads but to put learners in positions that allow them to construct well-structured knowledge.[6] (Reproduced, with permission, from the *Annual Review of Psychology*.)

The essential task of educational technology, therefore, is to focus on how learners use their knowledge and constructions to understand what they are taught. There is also a need to appraise or anticipate what cognitive structures or understandings learners bring to the instructional situation. Instructional design must be formed in terms of these preconceptions and the functions they exercise in the learners' fully comprehending what is to be taught.

This chapter begins with a historical overview of cognitive psychology and cognitive science and then focuses on cognitive theory and research that has instructional implications for educational technology. At this time, cognitive educational technology is essentially a descriptive science, rather than a prescriptive science that can provide guidance in the processes of teaching. However, with an impressive growth of research in such areas as memory, thought, and language, a cognitive-oriented educational technology promises the eventual development of a cognitively based instructional design theory.

A Brief Historical Overview

Interest in human cognition can be traced back to the ancient Greeks. For example, Plato and Aristotle speculated on memory and thought and discussed the nature and origin of knowledge. Throughout the centuries, philosophers have discussed human cognition, but some, such as Immanuel Kant, had serious doubts about a scientific study of the human mind.[7] In the nineteenth century, the groundwork of a science of psychology began to be laid by such men as Hermann von Helmholtz,[8] Gustav Fechner,[9] and F. C. Donders,[10] who demonstrated that psychological investigations could yield experimental results in a laboratory. Meanwhile, Franz Brentano, a priest-philosopher, declared that the true subject matter of psychology are the mental acts of seeing, sensing, imaging, or hearing.[11]

The Founding of Psychology and Wilhelm Wundt

Although psychological thinking and research was well underway by the latter part of the nineteenth century, Wilhelm Wundt (1832-1920) founded psychology as a science when he established the first psychological laboratory in 1879 in Leipzig, Germany.[12] Wundt never gave a name to his school of psychology, but it dealt with many of the basic mental phenomena that cognitive psychologists are now rediscovering. His system, often confused with E. B. Titchener's system called *structuralism*, was the scientific study of the human consciousness by means of a method known as introspection.[13] To Wundt, the ordinary act of introspection was untrustworthy because it applied to only some kind of unique experience that had already passed. The kind of introspection Wundt advocated involved a number of objective procedures related to measures of reaction time, emotional states, and other variables. During his years at Leipzig, Wundt worked endlessly to develop what later came to be known as Ganzheit or "holistic" psychology. He supervised many doctoral dissertations, wrote many volumes, founded the psychological journal *Philosophische Studien*, and trained most of the leading researchers around the turn of the century, many of whom were American.

The programs of Wundt and the Leipzig school initially had an important impact on American scholars, mainly through E. B. Titchener, an Englishman, who had been a student of Wundt and then came to America. Titchener later abandoned many of the Wundtian essentials of introspection and built his own psychology on the premise that the mind was made up of sensations and nothing else. Meanwhile, Oswald Külpe (1862-1915), a professor at Würzburg, became involved in a bitter controversy with Wundt and Titchener over "imageless thought" and criticized the Wundtian investigation. In Külpe's own investigations he used a free type of introspection to determine what occurred in a simple thought problem, and found that the response might come somewhat automatically without any intervening images. Therefore, such mental acts as attending, recognizing, willing, and comparing came to be considered a legitimate domain of psychology and, in essence, anticipated many of the concerns of modern cognitive scientists.[14]

Aside from Külpe, many figures of American scientific psychology became disenchanted with Wundt and Titchener, including the distinguished American psychologist William James. Moreover, a new behavioristic movement in psychology was forming in the early 1900s that disputed Wundt's Ganzheit psychology as well as Titchener's structuralism. In 1913, John Watson argued that mind and other mentalistic notions had no place in science. Behaviorism became the primary force in psychology by 1920 and retained its dominance for at least thirty years.

The Beginning of the Cognitive Revolution

The beginning of the cognitive revolution in American psychology was clearly evident by the early 1950s. During the pre- and post-World War II years the influence of Gestalt psychology was reflected in the work of Max Wertheimer, Wolfgang Kohler, and Kurt Koffka. Other scholars in the Gestalt tradition were Kurt Lewin (see chapter 3), Abraham Luchins, and Karl Duncker. As the Gestaltists were concerning themselves with constructive aspects of thinking and holistic solutions, Frederic Bartlett's investigations were indicating that the typical human memory system involves the development of distinctive cognitive structures, or schemas, that have been formed by environmental encounters.[15] Also, such persons as Jerome Bruner, James and Eleanor Gibson, Harry Helson, Adelbert Ames, and

Egon Brunswick were attempting to identify the various effects of past experiences on perception or what was called the "new look" in perception.[16]

Aside from these developments, however, there were four primary influences in the emergence of modern cognitive psychology: first, the development of the information processing approach that grew out of information theory and, particularly, the work of Norbert Wiener, Claude E. Shannon (see chapter 9), and George Miller; second, the impact of the computer, which provided an effective way to simulate human behavior and gave rise to a new subfield called artificial intelligence; third, in the field of linguistics, there was a dramatic shift from behaviorist theories of language toward an analysis of the structures underlying comprehension and production of utterance;[17] fourth, the theory and research of Jean Piaget (see chapter 3) had a profound influence on cognitive developmental psychology and, in effect, launched a whole new field of psychology.

Gardner, in his definitive history of cognitive science, states that "psychologist George Miller sets September 11, 1956 as the official birthdate of cognitive science." This date, he says, "focuses on the Symposium on Information Theory held at the Massachusetts Institute of Technology on 10-11 September 1956 and attended by many leading figures in the communication and human sciences." Two featured papers on the second day were seminal. The first, presented by Allen Newell and Herbert Simon, described the "Logic Theory Machine," which was the first complete proof of a theorem that solved problems in imitation of humans by heuristic search on a computer. The second paper, by the linguist Noam Chomsky, was "Three Models of Language," one of the first analyses of the formal properties of transformational grammars. On that same day, George Miller delivered his famous paper, "The Magical Number Seven, Plus or Minus Two," giving an information processing account of the limited capacity of short-term memory.[18]

In this same historical year of 1956, Bruner et al., in their *A Study of Thinking*, introduced strategies as mediating constructs in cognitive theory.[19] Meanwhile, in the summer of 1956, a group of young scholars, trained in mathematics and logic and interested in the problem-solving potential of computers, met at Dartmouth College. During this summer institute, such men as John McCarthy, Marvin Minsky, Allen Newell, and Herbert Simon reviewed "ideas for programs that would solve problems, recognize patterns, play games, and reason logically."[20]

The developments of the 1950s led to increased growth in the cognitive psychology movement in the 1960s. Jerome Bruner and George Miller founded the Harvard Center for Cognitive Studies in 1960, where scholars could meet and exchange ideas on the newest thinking in cognitive psychology. George Miller—together with his colleagues Karl Pribram, a neuroscientist, and Eugene Galanter, a mathematically oriented psychologist—published in 1960 a book entitled *Plans and the Structure of Behavior*.[21] This book proved to be a landmark because it was the first detailed attempt to discover whether the cybernetic ideas have any relevance for psychology. As Gardner says, "the authors sounded the death knell for standard behaviorism with its discredited reflex area and, instead called for a cybernetic approach to behavior in terms of actions, feedback loops, and readjustments of action in the light of feedback."[22]

The work that legitimized the rise of cognitive science was Ulric Neisser's *Cognitive Psychology*, published in 1967.[23] Neisser stated: "A generation ago, a book like this one would have needed at least a chapter of self-defense against the behaviorist position. Today happily, the climate of opinion has changed, and little or no defense is necessary."[24] Following Neisser's work was the beginning of a new journal, *Cognitive Psychology*, in 1970.

Emergence of Cognitive Science

In the 1970s, individuals, interests, and disciplines coalesced into a field that became known as cognitive science. The journal *Cognitive Science* was founded in 1977, and in 1979 a Society of Cognitive Science was formed at La Jolla, California. However, there was no consensus concerning a research paradigm and no general agreement on a definition of cognitive science.

In order to fill this conceptual void, Gardner proposed that cognitive science be confined to efforts to explain human knowledge and that it contain the following five features:

> First of all, there is the belief that, in talking about human cognitive activities, it is necessary to speak about mental representations and to posit a level of analysis wholly separate from the biological or neurological, on the one hand, and the sociological or cultural, on the other.
>
> Second, there is a faith that central to any understanding of the human mind is the electronic computer. Not only are computers indispensable for carrying out studies of various sorts, but, more crucially, the computer also serves as the most viable model of how the human mind functions.
>
> The third feature of cognitive science is the deliberate decision to de-emphasize certain factors which may be important for cognitive functioning but whose inclusion at this point would unnecessarily complicate the cognitive-scientific enterprise. These factors include the influence of affective factors or emotions, the contribution of historical and cultural factors, and the role of the background context in which particular actions or thoughts occur.
>
> As a fourth feature, cognitive scientists harbor the faith that much is to be gained from interdisciplinary studies. At present most cognitive scientists are drawn from the ranks of specific disciplines—in particular, philosophy, psychology, artificial intelligence, linguistics, anthropology, and neuroscience ... some day the boundaries between these disciplines may become attenuated or perhaps disappear altogether, yielding a single, unified cognitive science.
>
> A fifth and somewhat more controversial feature is the claim that a key ingredient in contemporary cognitive science is the agenda of issues ... it is virtually unthinkable that cognitive science could exist, let alone in its current form, had there not been a philosophical tradition dating back to the time of the Greeks.[25]

Toward a Cognitive Approach to Educational Technology

The cognitive view of educational technology is described in the first chapter of this book. Clearly, the impact of cognitive science has brought about a distinctly new approach to educational technology and has shifted the emphasis from a strictly behavioristic view with its emphasis on external behavior to a concern with internal mental processes and their enhancement in learning and instruction.

Although the theories and techniques of cognitive science are still not highly developed for practical application in educational technology, fruitful implications can be drawn from theory and research to develop a broader-based scientific approach to a science of human cognition. Significant developments have already taken place in the discovery of intellectual components in the fields of reading, mathematics, science, and problem solving.

In the remainder of this chapter, the key assumptions of cognitive science are described as well as selected research data. It is beyond the scope of this book to review the extensive volume of published literature on human cognition or to cover all areas of cognitive science. The purpose here is rather to provide a general introduction to cognitive psychology and to focus on aspects that are particularly relevant for a cognitive science-oriented educational technology.

Human Information Processing

Human information processing was initially influenced by concepts and data flowing from communications engineering and information theory, linguistics, and computer science. The modern computer provided a program analogy of receiving, storing, and retrieving information as well as solving problems for human mental functions. Computers, as Neisser pointed out, provided psychologists with the assurance that cognitive processes were as real as the muscular and glandular responses of human behavior.[26]

Human information processing has often been described as a theory, but as Mandler has correctly stated, "information processing is not a theory; it is at best a way of talking about certain interesting phenomena."[27] Human information processing suggests that humans are processors of information received through sense receptors and that each human processes in his own distinctive fashion. In this continuous process of receiving and transforming information, humans generate cognitive structures to be either stored in memory or used to activate such behaviors as understanding, producing language, and solving problems.

Early Models of Memory

Throughout the 1950s, 1960s, and 1970s, several information processing models were developed by cognitive psychologists. At first, these models simply replaced the stimulus and response units of behavioristic psychology with input and output. The early processing models were simple box models that postulated undefined stages. As cognitive psychology developed, interest shifted to the content of the boxes and the internal mechanisms—the representation of knowledge and the processes involved—were emphasized. These models all separated the act of knowing into the component processes by which knowledge is (1) coded or represented, (2) stored, (3) retrieved or accessed, and (4) incorporated or integrated with previously stored information.

Atkinson-Shiffrin Model

The most influential model of memory was that of Atkinson and Shiffrin.[28] This model viewed memory as having three distinct stores: the sensory registers (including iconic and echoic memories) or the short-term sensory store (STSS), the short-term memory store (STM), and the long-term memory store (LTM). According to this model, information is processed and held in the sensory registers and then entered into STM. The information remains temporarily in STM, with the length of stay a function of the control processes. While information remains in STM, other information related to it in LTM may be activated and brought into STM.

Information in STSS decays rapidly (within one second) and would be irrevocably lost if some of it were not transferred to STM. However, STM has a small capacity and information decays within five to eighteen seconds. One of the characteristics of STM is a rehearsal buffer, which is viewed as being partially under an individual's control, but with a fixed processing capacity. Since STM has a limited capacity, information not rehearsed or directly transferred to LTM is lost. LTM, where our knowledge of the world resides, has unlimited capacity.

Some aspects of the Atkinson-Shiffrin model were anticipated by the Broadbent model (see discussion later in this chapter) of 1958, and more specifically by Waugh and Norman, but it was generally accepted and became known as the "modal" information-processing model.[29] Although this model set the pattern for theoretical interpretations, many details are still to be resolved. It is not clear at this writing how a number of issues that have arisen will be settled, but a historical account of these discussions is beyond the scope of this book.

Sensory Memory

The processing of information by the human memory system begins when the physical signals (visual, acoustical, or tactile) are received by the sensory registers in the eyes, ears, and skin. These signals are retained briefly in sensory memory, either at the receptor level or in the brain. Neisser has called the visual input an *icon*, the auditory memory an *echo*, and the third type of signal retention the *tactile* or the *haptic*. Sensory memory has a high capacity for information but decays rapidly; if it is not quickly converted to a more durable form, it will be forgotten.

Pattern Recognition

An important part of information processing is the identification of selected physical signals. This process, known as pattern recognition, can be initiated while information is in sensory memory. Pattern recognition was once thought to occur according to the template matching theory, which held that incoming stimuli matched "templates" already in a person's memory. However, in the current view template matching is believed to occur through feature analysis. Two important processes that may function together or separately are *data driven processing*,[30] and *event driven* and *bottom-up processing*.[31] An example of pattern recognition is the tick of a clock, which is identified as it is processed. Another process involved in pattern recognition is *conceptually driven* or *top-down processing*, which is guided by motives, goals, and context. Some of these processes are considered *automatic* while others are referred to as *deliberate* processes because they require conscious control.

Visual and Auditory Studies

In the 1960s several influential experiments were conducted on visual sensory registers. George Sperling, then at the Bell Telephone Laboratories, was able to show by a tachistoscopic study that there was more sensory information available following brief exposure to a visual stimulus than the person could report, because the very act of reporting destroyed the brief memory of some of the material that had entered into the STM store.[32] Sperling's experiment helped ignite interest in the structure of the early information processing system.

Darwin et al. investigated echoic memory storage in a manner resembling Sperling's work.[33] The results were similar except for one interesting difference. They found that the temporal duration of echoic storage is generally longer than that of iconic storage. Moreover, preliminary research results on tactile memory were consistent in that they indicated the existence of a sensory register slightly longer in duration than the iconic sensory register.

Short-Term Memory

Once sensory information is encoded it is available in STM, sometimes called working memory (WM). To date there has been no general agreement on how encoding of STM is accomplished or what form it takes. While it was earlier believed that the major difference between STM and LTM was that information loss in STM was due to trace decay and information loss in LTM was due to interference, it is now generally agreed that simple trace decay involves only a small portion of STM loss and that both STM and LTM loss is primarily ascribed to interference.

Rehearsal

Evidence suggests that STM is very limited and that we can hold active in STM only a small number of items of information at any given time. For example, Miller has argued that STM appears to be able to hold only about seven items, or seven "chunks" of information.[34] To retain viable information in STM, we must rehearse. Rehearsal has two primary functions: first, it can be used to *maintain* information over time and, second, it can be utilized to convert or *elaborate* information in STM. Evidence suggests that the greater the amount of rehearsal, the greater the long-term retention.

The Cherry-Broadbent Attention Theories

A generation of *attention* theories began in the early 1950s with Colin Cherry's "cocktail party" experiments and Donald Broadbent's filter theory. Cherry, a British psychologist, devised a shadowing technique that would capture the important characteristics of a cocktail party problem in a controlled laboratory setting. His first experiment involved presenting the subject with two or more simultaneous messages and instructing him to shadow, or repeat aloud, one of these while ignoring the other. Cherry found that subjects were unable to report much of what went into the opposite (unattended) ear and that they could report only gross characteristics of the signal such as speech or music, but not changes in content or tongue.[35]

Broadbent, also a British psychologist, refined the Cherry procedure by requiring subjects to listen to two different messages presented simultaneously via earphones, one message to the right ear and one to the left. Subjects were asked to listen to lists of six digits presented binaurally, three digits to one ear and, simultaneously, three different digits to the other ear. Broadbent found that the persons who achieved the highest scores with least difficulty were those who reported all the digits presented to one ear first, and then all the digits presented to the other ear.[36]

The significant result of the Cherry-Broadbent experiments was Broadbent's proposed sensory filter theory. This theory, which used the metaphor of a funnel that allowed information to be processed from only one channel at a time, was probably the first information processing theory of human cognition and one of the first to describe cognitive functioning with a flowchart.

The work of Cherry and Broadbent established the importance of theory and stimulated much experimentation. However, experimental results that appeared soon after Broadbent's theory was published demonstrated that it was inadequate. For example, Moray's tests contradicted Broadbent's contention that the filter does not respond to meaning, but only to gross physical features. Moray showed that information from an unattended channel is usually inaccessible, but sometimes seeps into consciousness.[37] Later, Treisman argued that the filter serves not as a simple "all or none" switch, but rather as a means of attenuating irrelevant or unattended messages. According to Treisman's attenuation model, only a limited amount of the information that impinges on our senses is recognized and sent to STM.[38] Other theorists, such as Deutsch and Deutsch[39] and Norman,[40] assumed that the filter operates only after the meaning of the sensory input has been processed in LTM. In other words, their late-selection filter models suggested that all information is recognized, but that the human organism is limited in its ability to organize a response and must select some portion of the total information received.

Long-Term Memory

The three primary characteristics of LTM are: (1) information is relatively permanent, (2) information is stored in an organized and meaningful manner, and (3) its capacity is unlimited. Unlike STSS, LTM does not fade with time, but items may be lost if new information blocks or interferes with retrieval of old information. Later access and recall largely depends on the form in which information is stored and its relationship to prior representations or knowledge of the world.

Information in LTM takes a variety of forms. Tulving made a useful distinction between two classes of memories, the *semantic* and the *episodic*. He stated:

> Episodic memory receives and stores information about temporally dated episodes or events and temporal-spatial relations among these events.... Semantic memory is the memory necessary for the use of language. It is a mental thesaurus, organized knowledge a person possesses about words and other verbal symbols, their meaning and referents, about relations among them, and about rules, formulas, and algorithms for the manipulation of these symbols, concepts, and relations.[41]

Two major views on the form of stored information have been proposed. One suggests that information can be stored in both verbal and visual form, and the other holds that information is stored in verbal form only. The so-called dual-code or duplex model will be examined first and then some of the verbal models.

The Dual-Code Model

An influential model known as the dual-code model was proposed by Paivio in 1971. In 1986, he offered this perspective: "The most general assumption in dual coding theory is that there are two classes of phenomena handled cognitively by separate subsystems, one specialized for the representation and processing of information concerning nonverbal objects and events, the other specialized for dealing with language."[42]

The dual-code theory has been applied to many memory phenomena. Interestingly, pictures are more likely to be remembered than concrete words (such as dog, house, women, etc.) and concrete words are more likely to be remembered than abstract words (such as truth, soul, etc.). Paivio assumed that pictures are more likely to be stored in both verbal and visual codes whereas abstract words will typically be stored only in the verbal code. This model also suggests that the processing of verbal stimuli occurs serially, while the visual processing of concrete stimuli seems to occur all at one time.

Levels of Processing

Because of a theoretical debate concerning the duplex theory an alternative model known as "depth of processing" was developed by Craik and Lockhart as an attack against the distinction between STS and LTS.[43] They suggested that memory should simply be viewed as an integral part of the whole information processing system. Their depth of processing approach was that stimuli can be processed at different levels within that system. For stimuli that are analyzed on a superficial basis, such as sensory analyses and pattern recognition, the memory traces are transient. The traces of deeper, more meaningful processing are more permanent. Memory depends on the nature of the code and the type of analysis, not on the structural properties of particular memory stores.

Although this model proved useful in looking at general processing characteristics in relation to memory, it has encountered difficulties. Baddeley has observed that the levels of processing notion "has not proved to be a concept that is easy to develop. The problem of measuring depth of processing has not been solved, while the simple distinction between maintenance and elaborative rehearsal has proved oversimplified" and the model "has led to the problem of short-term and working memory being at best neglected and at worse denied."[44]

Verbal Network Models

Three general types of verbal models have been proposed. The current semantic network models were preceded by earlier paradigms: clustering models and propositional models. Clustering models illustrate words grouped in memory in particular clusters. For example, when words in a list are organized by language or category (e.g., names of animals) or both.

Propositional models identify propositions rather than isolated words as components of memory structure. For example, in a model called HAM (human associative memory) developed by Anderson and Bower (1973), a proposition consists of four types of associations: (1) context-fact; (2) location-time; (3) subject-predicate; and (4) relation-object.[45]

The currently accepted models are not restricted to propositions and are diagrammed in the form of nodes and their connecting links. The links represent meaningful connections between the nodes.

Semantic Network Models

One of the first semantic network models was developed by Collins and Quillian in 1969.[46] This model assumed that memory could be represented as a network of associations between words and their underlying concepts. Their first model used nodes to represent concepts arranged hierarchically. Another key assumption was cognitive economy. For example, we know that canaries can fly, that robins can fly, etc., thus, it would be cognitively wasteful to have information about being able to fly stored with each bird name. As a consequence, they proposed that properties common to virtually all birds are stored at only one bird node, or that information is stored as far up the hierarchy as possible to minimize the storage of information.

Other semantic network models, proposed in the 1970s, include: (1) the "production systems" developed by Newell and Simon,[47] (2) the "active structural networks" developed by Norman and Rumelhart,[48] and (3) the propositional network devised by Anderson.[49]

Declarative and Procedural Knowledge

Although an earlier distinction had been made between declarative and procedural knowledge by the philosopher Ryle,[50] J. R. Anderson also made this distinction in his cognitive theory in 1976.[51] Declarative knowledge is knowledge that something is the case, whereas procedural knowledge is knowledge of how to do something. It is asserted that both are stored in LTM and applied to symbols in STM in order to generate actions or behaviors. Declarative knowledge varies a great deal and is relatively static, while procedural knowledge is more dynamic and involves transforming information rather than simple recall. For example, if one knows that the weather advisory telephone number is 381-8566, you can apply many processes to it, such as dialing it, relating it to someone else, or adding it to your list of important phone numbers. Thus declarative knowledge is simply a way of referring to static, relatively stable representations. Procedural knowledge is highly dynamic in that knowing how to dial telephone numbers can be quite different from knowing a fact. We may know how to dial a telephone number, but many could not give a factual account of how it is done or how we may do it. These two forms of knowledge also differ in the speed with which they are activated. Once procedural knowledge is well learned, information is decoded rapidly and automatically. On the other hand, declarative knowledge activation is slower and more conscious.

Schemas, Frames, and Scripts

The propositional or semantic network models describe the representation of knowledge more specifically. Another form of knowledge representation characterized by larger organizations of knowledge are schemas, sometimes called frames or scripts. The term *schema* was first defined by Bartlett as "an active organization of past reactions which must always be supposed to be operating in any well-adapted organic response."[52] Rumelhart and Ortony describe schemas as data structures that represent the generic concepts underlying objects, events, and actions.[53]

Piaget and the Cognitive Approach to Education

Piaget's theory of cognitive development is discussed in chapter 3. Although major aspects of his theory were formed in the 1920s, Piaget's impact was not felt in the United States until the 1960s, when sufficient English translations of his more important books first became available and American psychology was ripe for a change. An early impetus was provided by the participation of Piaget's chief collaborator, Barbel Inhelder, in the historic 1959 Woods Hole conference chaired by Jerome Bruner. As a result, Bruner described how Piagetian theory could resolve the psychological issues raised in the movement for curriculum reform begun in the mid-1950s. Further interest was generated when Elkind[54] replicated many of the early Geneva experiments and Flavell[55] prepared the first comprehensive guide to Piagetian literature. Hunt[56] pointed out the relevance of Piagetian theory to the psychology of mental testing and individual differences.

Educational Applications of Piaget

Despite the fact that Piaget has had little to say about education directly, his theory has offered a new approach to the understanding of complex cognitive skills. In the curriculum reform of the 1960s, Piaget's early work was applied to mathematics, science, and early childhood curricula. Piaget expressed some educational principles in early essays, but the most substantial Piagetian concepts were enunciated by H. Aebli, a student of Piaget and an experienced schoolteacher, in a doctoral thesis.[57] From these sources, two general techniques can be abstracted. One is concerned with how to teach and the other is concerned with what to teach. The first technique consists of creating a free, problem-solving situation whereby the learner selects a task and is free to do what he likes to complete it. The teacher may intervene by asking appropriate questions so the student can develop hypotheses and test them. The second technique involves a constructive analysis wherein a class of tasks and activities are chosen and their cognitive demands are analyzed.

Modifications of Piaget's Theory

The work of Case, Siegler, and Klahr demonstrates how information processing can be used to modify Piaget's theory of cognitive development. Case, building on the work of Simon[58] and Pascal-Leone,[59] proposed that information processing strategies can be described using computer simulation models.[60] In Piaget's theory, the level of cognitive development is reflected in how many mental operations can be used in an integrated fashion, whereas in Case's theory, developmental level is manifested in the child's level of working memory, or how many pieces of information the child can hold in active memory at one time.

Siegler and Klahr, like Case, each proposed that cognitive development is the ability to perform increasingly sophisticated Piagetian tasks in terms of information processing strategies by children. For example, Siegler used the balance beam problem, used originally by Piaget and Inhelder to study the development of scientific reasoning in formal operations. The child is shown a balance beam with four equally spaced pegs on either side of the fulcrum. While the beam is held in place, weights are placed on pegs on each side of the fulcrum. The child predicts which side of the beam will go down.[61]

Klahr asked children to solve a variation of the Tower of Hanoi, or disk, problem. Klahr developed a monkey can problem wherein the children are told that the cans are monkeys and the pegs are trees. The large can represented the daddy, the medium can the mommy, and the small can the baby. The monkeys are able to jump from tree to tree (peg to peg), but the smaller can may never be put on top of a larger can. One configuration is given on the experimenter's side and the child moves the monkeys so that they will be in the same configuration as on the experimenter's side. In connection with this task, Klahr developed computer simulation models at six levels of difficulty so that he might describe different levels of performance among the children attempting this task.[62]

Bruner's Cognitive Approaches to Instruction

The work of Jerome Bruner was significantly influenced by cognitive psychology. Probably the best known and most often cited concept-learning experiment was conducted by Bruner et al. and published in their classic monograph *A Study of Thinking*.[63] Against this background of laboratory experiments, Bruner began to examine the cognitive processes of children and how they mentally represented the concepts they were learning.

Less than a year following the launch of *Sputnik I*, a conference composed predominantly of scientists, mathematicians, and psychologists was convened at Woods Hole on Cape Cod in Massachusetts by the National Academy of Sciences to explore the possibilities for improving science education in elementary and secondary schools. Several national curriculum projects had already been established under NSF funding, but they were still in a preliminary stage and were not tied to any particular theoretical rationale.

The Process of Education

The chairman of the Woods Hole Conference, Jerome Bruner, wrote a book entitled *The Process of Education* that became a manifesto for curriculum reform in elementary and secondary schools during the following decade.[64] Bruner stated that the "curriculum of a subject should be determined by the most fundamental understanding that can be achieved of the underlying principles that give structure to that subject."[65] His notion of structure concerned applying the fundamental principles, ideas, and generalizations that represent disciplinary knowledge. To make these principals central to the school curriculum, Bruner suggested that leading scholars in each discipline be involved in developing curricula for the schools.

Basic to Bruner's disciplines orientation was the idea that "any subject can be taught in some effectively honest form to any child at any stage of development."[66] Thus, Bruner shaped Piaget's developmental stage theory to make it fit his thesis that the child is a miniature scholar. Related to Bruner's view of the child is his idea of the "spiral curriculum." This approach suggests that one can start with fundamental notions about a topic and expand into more details and more abstract descriptions. As Bruner states, "a curriculum as it develops should revisit these basic ideas repeatedly, building upon them until the student has grasped the full formal apparatus that goes with them."[67] One spiral curriculum developed by Bruner is the social studies curriculum "Man: A Course of Study."

In the last section of *The Process of Education*, Bruner views the various "automatizing devices," or teaching machines, as key instruments to improve instruction. He declares that "the art of programming a machine is, of course, an extension of the art of teaching," and "a program for a teaching machine is as personal as a book."[68]

Inquiry-Discovery Method

One of the most promising premises that came out of the Woods Hole Conference suggested that learning should be a process of discovery or inquiry. Through this process, a learner could gain an understanding of the significance and connectedness of what is learned rather than merely memorizing facts by rote. This approach is equated with induction: The implication is that discovery cannot occur deductively. However, proponents of the inductive model have failed to recognize that inquiry-discovery depends on both inductive and deductive processes. As Dewey noted,

> The inductive movement is toward discovery of a binding principle: the deductive toward its testing-confirming, refuting, modifying it on the basis of its capacity to interpret isolated details into a unified experience. So far as we conduct each of these processes in the light of the other, we get valid discovery, or verified critical thinking.[69]

Assessing Woods Hole

Tanner and Tanner pungently assessed the Woods Hole Conference:

> The failure of Bruner and the members of the Woods Hole Conference to recognize the essential conflict between the inquiry-discovery rationale and the operant-conditioning rationale of programmed instruction remains a mystery. Although the early progress reports of some of the national curriculum-reform projects indicated that consideration was being given to developing programmed

materials, it became evident to scholars working on these projects that pro-grammed instruction is not compatible with the processes of scientific investiga-tion. Consequently, efforts to develop programmed instructional materials for the leading curriculum-reform projects were abandoned in favor of textbooks supplemented by a variety of resource materials, such as laboratory units, cartridge films, slides, teachers' resource books, and paperbacks.[70]

Eleven years after *The Process of Education* was published, Bruner acknowledged some of the weaknesses of the disciplines orientation and called for a movement away from academic formalism to a focus on social problems.

Theory of Cognitive Development

Bruner's work provided a major supplement of Piaget's theory of cognitive develop-ment. As discussed in chapter 3, Piaget's theory proposed four main periods of cognitive growth (i.e., sensorimotor, preoperational, concrete operations, and formal operations). In-stead of four periods, Bruner identified three modes of representation: the enactive, iconic, and symbolic modes. These representations are systems of rules or generalizations by which an individual copes with his environment.

The *enactive* mode is highly manipulative and represents past events by making appro-priate motor responses. For example, a child enactively knows how to ride a bike or tie a knot.

Iconic representation is based on internal imagery, Bruner's expression for perceptual organization. Iconic representation depends upon visual or other sensory organization along with the use of summarizing images that are representative of larger "chunks" of the environment.

Symbolic representation is when the child engages in such symbolic activities as language and mathematics. The symbolic mode of representation is evidenced by a person's ability to solve problems and think creatively.

Ausubel's Subsumption Principles and Advance Organizers

David P. Ausubel was also influenced by cognitive psychology. He stressed the central importance of cognitive processes in the planning of instruction and developed an elaborate theory in terms of the formation of cognitive structures for the solution of real-life problems.

Ausubel proposed his principle of subsumption as a basic theoretical rationale of how one increases and reorganizes one's reservoir of knowledge. Since cognitive structure tends to be hierarchically organized according to level of abstraction, Ausubel maintained that once subsuming ideas are adequately established in cognitive structure, they

> have maximally specific and direct relevance for subsequent learning tasks; possess enough explanatory power to render otherwise arbitrary factual detail potentially meaningful; possess sufficient inherent stability to provide the firmest type of anchorage for newly-learned detailed meanings; and organize related new facts around a common theme, thereby integrating the component elements of new knowledge both with each other and with existing knowledge.[71]

A unique aspect of Ausubel's instructional design theory involves what he calls *advance organizers*. The underlying rationale of advance organizers flows from early Gestalt psychology, which expressed the idea that a complex of information can best be learned by understanding how it fits together, how each part relates to the other parts, and how it is organized. Ausubel would provide special introductory statements to organize the many concepts to be read so that they could subsume and serve as an anchoring framework for the information to be learned.

Ausubel describes two types of advance organizers: expository and comparative. Expository organizers, for the most part, explain new material and usually consist of general concepts, whereas comparative organizers are used with more familiar material.

Ausubel sees learning in terms of information processing and his approach tends to be deductive, which means that instruction proceeds from general ideas to specific information. He calls this "progressive differentiation." He also developed the idea of "integrative reconciliation," which suggests that the teacher should develop new concepts closely related to ideas that have been presented previously. In accordance with these principles, textbooks and instructional materials should be organized so that information proceeds from general organizing concepts to more specific information.[72]

Cognitive Learning Strategies

The cognitive concept of educational technology focuses on the learner as an active participant in the teaching-learning process. This view essentially says that effective learning depends largely on what the learner knows and on the active cognitive processing that takes place during instruction. This section reviews the cognitive learning strategies that have developed in recent years and, in particular, documents the historical change in approach that has taken place in terms of the teacher's role in the classroom. Traditionally, the products of learning, or what the learner should know or be able to do as a result of learning, have been emphasized with little or no regard for developing techniques or strategies that learners can use to accomplish learning. Cognitive learning strategies, instead of viewing learners as passive recorders of the stimuli that the teacher presents, view learning as an active process that occurs within the learner. The outcome of learning, in this view, will depend on how information is presented and on how the learner processes that information.

A number of earlier learning strategies evolved out of research on problem solving and artificial intelligence. In more recent years, computers have been used to model short-term memory processes. A program of research in learning strategies was initiated by the Defense Advanced Research Projects Agency (DARPA) in 1976. Much of the research and findings of this project has been reported by O'Neil.[73] The periodic volume *Advances in Instructional Psychology* also serves as a valuable source of research and proposals for learning strategies.[74] Weinstein and Mayer listed eight categories of learning strategies as follows:

Rehearsal strategies for basic learning tasks—such as repeating the names of items in an ordered list.

Rehearsal strategies for complex learning tasks—such as copying, underlining or shadowing the material presented in class.

Elaboration strategies for basic learning tasks—such as forming a mental image or sentence relating the items in each pair for a paired-associate list of words.

Elaboration strategies for complex tasks—such as paraphrasing, summarizing, or describing how new information relates to existing knowledge.

Organizational strategies for basic learning tasks—such as grouping or ordering to-be-learned items from a list or a section of prose.

Organizational strategies for complex tasks—such as outlining a passage or creating a hierarchy.

Comprehension monitoring strategies—such as checking for comprehension failures.

Affective strategies—such as being alert and relaxed, to help overcome test anxiety.[75]

The encoding process, another important part of the teaching-learning process from the cognitive perspective, was analyzed by Cook and Mayer into the following four main components:

Selection—The learner actively pays attention to some of the information that is impinging on the sense receptors, and transfers this information into working memory (or active consciousness).

Acquisition—The learner actively transfers the information from working memory into long-term memory for permanent storage.

Construction—The learner actively builds connections between ideas in the information that have reached working memory. This building of internal connections involves the development of a coherent outline organization or schema that holds the information together.

Integration—The learner actively searches for prior knowledge in long-term memory and transfers this knowledge to working memory. The learner may then build external connections between the incoming information and prior knowledge.[76]

Problem-Solving Programs

Problem-solving strategies are procedures that can improve the search for a solution for a wide range of problems. Much of the process of problem solving is still not completely understood and much research remains to be done. Two major areas of current research are computer simulations of problem-solving processes and specific investigations in instructional situations. Computer programs have been developed that solve algebra word problems and logic, play chess, and diagnose medical problems.

The landmark effort in problem-solving programs was the General Problem Solver, a computer simulation of problem solving developed by Newell et al. in 1957.[77] Their intent was to design a core set of processes that could be used to solve a variety of problems in a number of subject-matter areas. These processes, briefly summarized, are (1) represent the problem, the given, and legal operators; (2) establish goals and subgoals and begin solving for the subgoals; and (3) use means-ends analysis to assess progress and redefine subgoals if necessary.

Resnick and Glaser developed a different model of problem solving in 1976.[78] The three general steps in their model are (1) problem detection, (2) feature scanning, and (3) goal analysis. The Resnick and Glaser model is specifically designed for invention problems, when the learner must reconstruct a situation to find a solution.

Cognitive Engineering

Cognitive science has generated a renewed interest in teaching problem solving. Norman, for example, has called for the establishment of a discipline of "cognitive engineering" for the design of problem-solving courses. He stated that "we need to develop the general principles of how to learn, how to remember, how to solve problems, to develop applied courses, and then to establish the place of these methods in an academic curriculum."[79] Likewise, Lochhead has called for "cognitive processes instruction."[80]

These ideas are not novel, but they do reflect a growing trend toward building a stronger connection between psychology and educational technology. Simon states that "effective professional education calls for attention to both subject-matter knowledge and general skills."[81] He suggests that problem solving could be taught within the context of a specific subject and that general strategies should be developed for setting goals and representing problems. There is also the future promise of "computer coaches" that allow a student to proceed to solve a problem with the computer providing relevant information about possible strategies and guiding the student concerning the use of selected strategies.

Simulation, Artificial Intelligence, and Computer-Based Instruction

The discussion of CAI in chapter 10 indicated that the early years were dominated by behavioristic conceptions of design and approach. Although artificial intelligence, like cognitive science, had its origins in the 1950s, the cognitive orientation was not widely applied to instruction until the 1970s.

Historical Orientation

In 1956, Allan Newell and Herbert A. Simon published a description of the "Logic Theorist," the first computer program that solved problems by simulating human behavior through a process of heuristic search.[82] The next development occurred in 1957 when Newell et al. produced the General Problem Solver (referred to in the previous section of this chapter).

An early controversy concerned the proper distinction between simulation and artificial intelligence. When the objective is to develop a computer program that imitates the human processes of thinking and problem solving, then the program is a simulation. If, however, the goal is to prepare a program that solves a problem efficiently without analogies to human behavior, then the program is artificial intelligence. The difference rests in the objectives of the program designer.

Artificial Intelligence and CAI

Carbonell and his colleagues started a trend toward incorporating more human-tutoring characteristics into CAI systems with their SCHOLAR program, a system for teaching facts about South American geography.[83] SCHOLAR is a generative system, in that it constructs questions and responses from the information it has stored and does not have these pre-specified. The basic intent was to produce a computer-based Socratic tutor, whereby a student's answers could be diagnosed and an intelligent response made to any unexpected questions the student might ask about geography. The components of this system are the *domain expertise* concerning the knowledge it is programmed to impart, a *student model* that reflects what the student knows or does not know at any particular time, and a set of *tutoring strategies* that specify how planned information is to be presented to the learner.

SCHOLAR was the first attempt to develop a tutorial system that simulated the way human teachers teach. It was organized as a data structure in the form of a semantic network. Each node is systematically related to other elements of the network and denotes some concept. In SCHOLAR, two purposes are served: to direct tutorial actions and respond to questions.

Beginning in 1976, E. A. Feigenbaum and his associates in the heuristic programming project at Stanford University have developed artificial intelligence programs in a number of areas. One program called PUFF diagnoses medical patients for possible pulmonary disorders. Another program named MYCIN has important implications for educational technology.[84] MYCIN attempts to diagnose blood infections and prescribe appropriate treatment. The program provides a large number of rules that suggest possible actions in terms of medical symptoms and a disease. The most impressive project of Feigenbaum's group is DENDRAL and its complement, META-DENDRAL.[85] DENDRAL is a program that enables a skilled chemist to make an accurate guess about the molecular structure of an unknown compound. A later development, META-DENDRAL is designed to make up its own molecular fragmentation rules to attempt to explain sets of basic data.

In 1979, the MYCIN program was developed as a teaching program called GUIDON.[86] The aim of GUIDON was to determine whether the expertise of the MYCIN system could be transferred to a student through a tutorial dialogue concerning a case diagnosis. During a GUIDON tutorial, the student is given general information about a case and then attempts to make a diagnosis on the basis of relevant questions. GUIDON compares the student's questions with those that would be posed by MYCIN in similar cases.

Another intelligent CAI program is SOPHIE, developed by J. S. Brown et al., which teaches problem-solving skills to engineers.[87] This program focuses on troubleshooting in defective electronic equipment. Still another example of a troubleshooting program is BUGGY, also developed by Brown and Burton, which helps teachers diagnose the causes of a student's errors in doing arithmetic problems.[88]

The intelligent tutoring programs described in this section are still in an embryonic stage, but they hold important educational implications for the future. Perhaps, their most immediate practical value lies in their use to illustrate the function of heuristics in human teaching situations.

The problem solving and intelligent CAI movement is closely associated with the LOGO project. LOGO is the programming language devised at Bolt Beranek and Newman Company, Cambridge, Massachusetts, in 1967 and subsequently developed by the Artificial Intelligence Laboratory at MIT. According to Seymour Papert, the theory underlying this approach is based on Piaget's concepts of children's thinking. The origins and theoretical viewpoint of Papert provide a strong contrast to behavioristic CAI approaches. Papert and his associates at MIT opposed CAI activities that reinforced the educational status quo rather than introducing major changes in the education system. Instead, they advocated "more radical experiments in the global re-design of learning environments."[89]

The LOGO computer language was developed to make it easy for young children, age ten or eleven, to learn to program a computer. To help them understand how LOGO worked, a pen-holding robot called the turtle was used to draw on sheets of paper, which has come to be known as turtle graphics. The children learned how to write computer programs at an early stage in their development of mathematical, logical, and problem-solving skills.[90] Moreover, as O'Shea and Self state:

> The learning is individualized, for each student creates programs uniquely his own. Developing programs is a highly motivating activity since there is a continual (if sometimes illusory) feeling of making progress. Errors come to be seen by the student as sources of enlightenment not causes for despair. The student

regularly experiences the "aha-phenomenon," for it is not too much of an exaggeration to regard his program as his own scientific theory to be developed by exploring cause-and-effect questions. Children enjoy it, and if LOGO activities are play so much the better.[91]

Papert's LOGO system is a model of what more sophisticated CAI learning environments may involve. The real problem, however, is how Papert's ideas can be effectively communicated to professional educators so as to utilize the computer within a humanistic tradition. As a result, Papert has called for the establishment of university centers that will conduct innovative experiments and develop model teaching programs.

Still another CAI system was developed by Robert B. Davis, a mathematics educator and a developer of "new math" curricula for elementary schools. Basing his teaching strategy on computational metaphors and techniques provided from the cognitive sciences, Davis began developing materials for grades 4-6 for use in the PLATO computer system. Davis's goal was to broaden the content of elementary mathematics and encourage children's mathematical development through "discovery" and, consequently, to create a repertoire of paradigm-teaching strategies.[92]

The Sharing Jumping Beans lesson is one example of several that illustrate Davis's paradigm-teaching strategy. Instead of breaking up candy bars, children are asked to share a box of jumping beans among the figures appearing on a PLATO screen. The number of figures can vary from two to five. Children interact by touching the graphics screen in different locations.

Problems in CAI

This review of CAI programs is not intended to be exhaustive, but rather to provide a sampling of CAI programs that have been developed in recent years. There are many problems associated with CAI that need to be solved if such programs are to be used effectively in the future. As O'Shea and Self have pointed out, there are four sources of difficulty, namely, "the reaction of the people involved; the poorly-designed materials; technical matters, such as cost and reliability; evaluation, that is, in actually deciding whether what has been done was worth doing."[93]

Since teachers are basically conservative and do not desire to see themselves displaced, they tend to resist computer use. Moreover, they do not want their normal routines disrupted nor do they have the incentive to keep up with swiftly changing developments in computers.

Perhaps, the most serious problem concerns the poor quality of most commercially produced CAI materials. This situation has been further accentuated by the advent of microcomputers because their limited memory capacity necessarily provides for only small teaching programs. A related problem is a need for good documentation of computer programs.

Those who advocate the use of CAI have been most vulnerable with regard to the cost. Since the cost depends on the particular type of CAI involved and on the computing resources needed to sustain it, the cost factor becomes very complex. Cost factors associated with instructional materials are frequently overlooked.

Evaluation has sometimes been difficult because much of CAI has not reflected traditional modes of instruction and has added new skills or knowledge. Papert's work, for example, does not fit standard evaluation methods and, in fact, even raises some questions about the nature of evaluation. Since Papert's approach emphasizes changing education in a significant fashion, Pea, in his study of Papert's LOGO system, concluded that he had perhaps asked the wrong questions.[94] According to Papert, Pea's study was not merely an example of poorly formed questions, but also showed a tendency toward *technocentrism*, or focusing on a technical object such as computers or LOGO.[95]

The Future Decades

The increasing availability of microcomputers possesses a great potential, but it remains to be seen whether computers will significantly transform education. It is likely that microcomputers will continue to be incompatible with existing educational systems until the end of this century. Unfortunately, microcomputer developments are bringing back an emphasis on the devices rather than on the process of educational technology. In other words, more sophisticated equipment does not automatically lead to more effective learning environments. Although there have been astonishing developments in computer hardware, there has been an equally amazing lag in the development of innovative software or good programming.

An effective theory of instruction that can provide a source of prescriptive principles and guide the design and development of instructional materials and techniques is still needed. There is an optimistic hope that cognitive science may eventually hold some potential for the realization of this goal.

Notes

[1]See T. S. Kuhn, *The Structure of Scientific Revolutions*, Vol. 2, No. 2. Chicago: University of Chicago Press, 1962.

[2]Ulric Neisser, *Cognitive Psychology.* New York: Appleton-Century-Crofts, 1967.

[3]See, for example, David Klahr, *Cognition and Instruction*, Hillsdale, N.J.: Lawrence Erlbaum, 1977; Alan M. Lesgold et al., eds., *Cognitive Psychology and Instruction*, New York: Plenum Press, 1978; and M. C. Wittrock, "The Cognitive Movement in Instruction," *Educational Psychologist* 13 (1978), 15-30.

[4]Richard C. Atkinson, "Adaptive Instructional Systems: Some Attempts to Optimize the Learning Process," in David Klahr, ed., *Cognition and Instruction.* Hillsdale, N.J.: Lawrence Erlbaum, 1976, 82.

[5]Robert Glaser, "The Contributions of B. F. Skinner to Education and Some Counter Influences," in Patrick Suppes, ed., *Impact of Research on Education: Some Case Studies.* Washington, D.C.: National Academy of Education, 1978, 257.

[6]L. B. Resnick, "Instructional Psychology," *Annual Review of Psychology* 32 (1981), 660.

[7]See I. Kant, *Critique of Pure Reason* (translated by N. Kemp Smith). New York: Random House, 1958. (Original work published in 1781.)

[8]There are numerous biographies of Helmholtz. A convenient short account is that by J. Beck, "Hermann von Helmholtz," in *International Encyclopedia of the Social Sciences*, Vol. 6. New York: Macmillan, Free Press, 1968, 345-50.

[9]See G. T. Fechner, *Elements of Psychophysics*, Vol. 1 (E. G. Boring and D. H. Howes, eds.; H. E. Adler, trans.). New York: Holt, Rinehart and Winston, 1966. (Original work published in 1851.)

[10]See S. Sternberg, "The Discovery of Processing Stages: Extensions of Donder's Method," *Acta Psychological* 30 (1969), 276-315.

[11]See F. Brentano, *Psychology from an Empirical Standpoint* (translated by A. C. Rancurello). New York: Humanities Press, 1973. (Original work published in 1874.)

[12]Biographical sources on Wundt were limited until recently. Two collections of studies reflecting the rediscovery of Wundt are: W. C. Bringmann and R. D. Tweney, eds., *Wundt Studies: A Centennial*

Collection, Toronto: Hogrefe, 1980; and R. Rieber, ed., *Wilhelm Wundt and the Making of a Scientific Psychology*, New York: Plenum Press, 1980.

[13]See E. B. Titchener, *An Outline of Psychology*. New York: Macmillan, 1896.

[14]G. Mandler and J. M. Mandler, *Thinking: From Association to Gestalt*. New York: John Wiley, 1964, 143.

[15]F. C. Bartlett, *Remembering*. Cambridge: Cambridge University Press, 1932.

[16]See Ernest R. Hilgard, *Psychology in America*. New York: Harcourt Brace Jovanovich, 1987, 161-63.

[17]The rise of cognitive psychology with its renewed interest in thinking, problem solving, and creativity brought with it new theories and new tools to the problems of language and thought. The cognitive era in psycholinguistics began in the United States in the early 1950s when psycholinguists and linguists discovered their common interests and popularized the term *psycholinguistics*. A historic attack on B. F. Skinner's theory is expressed in the book *Verbal Behavior* (1957) by Noam Chomsky, a linguist at MIT in 1959. Chomsky represented what was called the transformational generative grammar and devastated the behaviorist position in his critique, exerting an important influence on cognitive psychology.

[18]Howard Gardner, *The Mind's New Science*. New York: Basic Books, 1985, 28.

[19]See J. S. Bruner et al., *A Study of Thinking*. New York: John Wiley, 1956.

[20]Gardner, *New Science*, 138-40.

[21]G. A. Miller et al., *Plans and the Structure of Behavior*. New York: John Wiley, 1956.

[22]Gardner, *New Science*, 32-33.

[23]Ulric Neisser, *Cognitive Psychology*. New York: Appleton-Century-Crofts, 1967.

[24]Ibid., 6-7.

[25]Gardner, *New Science*, 6-7.

[26]Ulric Neisser, *Cognition and Reality*. San Francisco: Freeman, 1976.

[27]George Mandler, *Cognitive Psychology*. Hillsdale, N.J.: Lawrence Erlbaum, 1985, 90.

[28]R. C. Atkinson and R. M. Shiffrin, "Human Memory: A Proposed System and Its Control Processes," in K. W. Spence and J. T. Spence, eds., *The Psychology of Learning and Motivation*, Vol. 2. New York: Academic Press, 1968.

[29]N. C. Waugh and D. A. Norman, "Primary Memory," *Psychological Review* 72 (March 1965), 89-104.

[30]P. H. Lindsay and D. A. Norman, *Human Information Processing: An Introduction to Psychology*. New York: Academic Press, 1972.

[31]J. R. Anderson, *Cognitive Psychology and Its Implications*, 2d ed. New York: Freeman, 1985.

[32]G. Sperling, "The Information Available in Brief Visual Presentations," *Psychological Monographs* 74, Whole No. 498, 1960.

[33]C. J. Darwin et al., "An Auditory Analogue of the Sperling Partial Report Procedure: Evidence for Brief Auditory Storage," *Cognitive Psychology* 3 (April 1972), 255-67.

[34]G. A. Miller, "The Magical Number Seven Plus or Minus Two: Some Limits on Our Capacity for Processing Information," *Psychological Review* 63 (March 1956), 81-97.

[35]E. C. Cherry, "Some Experiments on the Recognition of Speech, with One and with Two Ears," *Journal of the Acoustical Society of America* 25 (1953), 975-79.

[36]D. E. Broadbent, *Perception and Communication*. London: Pergamon, 1958.

[37]N. Moray, "Attention in Dichotic Listening: Affective Cues and the Influence of Instructions," *Quarterly Journal of Experimental Psychology* 11 (1959), 56-60.

[38]A. M. Treisman, "Contextual Cues in Selective Listening," *Quarterly Journal of Experimental Psychology* 12 (1960), 242-48.

[39]J. A. Deutsch and D. Deutsch, "Attention: Some Theoretical Considerations," *Psychological Review* 70 (January 1963), 80-90.

[40]D. A. Norman, "Memory While Shadowing," *Quarterly Journal of Experimental Psychology* 21 (1969), 85-93.

[41]E. Tulving, "Episodic and Semantic Memory," in E. Tulving and W. Donaldson, eds., *Organization of Memory*. New York: Academic Press, 1972, 386.

[42]A. Paivio, *Imagery and Verbal Processes*. New York: Holt, Rinehart and Winston, 1971; A. Paivio, *Mental Representations: A Dual Coding Approach*. New York: Oxford University Press, 1986, 53.

[43]F. I. M. Craik and R. S. Lockhart, "Levels of Processing: A Framework for Memory Research," *Journal of Verbal Learning and Verbal Behavior* 11 (1972), 671-84. The theoretical debate between the dual-coding and propositional views is important and interesting if one wishes to pursue it. The best beginning is Z. W. Pylyshyn, "What the Mind's Eye Tells the Mind's Brain: A Critique of Mental Imagery," *Psychological Bulletin* 80 (July 1973), 1-24.

[44]Alan Baddeley, *Working Memory*. Oxford: Clarendon, 1986, 28-29.

[45]J. R. Anderson and G. H. Bower, *Human Associative Memory*. Washington, D.C.: V. H. Winston, 1973.

[46]A. M. Collins and M. R. Quillian, "Retrieval Time from Semantic Memory," *Journal of Verbal Learning and Verbal Behavior* 8 (April 1969), 240-47.

[47]A. Newell and H. A. Simon, *Human Problem Solving*. Englewood Cliffs, N.J.: Prentice-Hall, 1972. This book contains a historical addendum on the development of cognitive psychology before and after World War II and traces the information-processing developments during the critical years 1954-1958.

[48]D. A. Norman and D. E. Rumelhart, *Explorations in Cognition*. San Francisco: Freeman, 1975.

[49]J. R. Anderson, *Language, Memory and Thought*. Hillsdale, N.J.: Lawrence Erlbaum, 1976.

[50]See G. Ryle, *The Concept of Mind*. New York: Barnes and Noble, 1949.

[51]Anderson, *Language, Memory*.

[52]Bartlett, *Remembering*, 201.

[53]D. E. Rumelhart and A. Ortony, "The Representation of Knowledge in Memory," in R. C. Anderson et al., eds., *Schooling and the Acquisition of Knowledge*. Hillsdale, N.J.: Lawrence Erlbaum, 1977, 99-136.

[54]See, for example, D. Elkind, "The Development of Quantitative Thinking: A Systematic Replication of Piaget's Studies," *Journal of Genetic Psychology* 98 (March 1961), 37-46.

[55]J. H. Flavell, *The Developmental Psychology of Jean Piaget*. Princeton, N.J.: Van Nostrand, 1963.

[56]J. McV. Hunt, *Intelligence and Experience*. New York: Ronald Press, 1961.

[57]See H. Aebli, *Didactique Psychologie*. Neuchatel: Delacheux et Niestle, 1951. This book is almost unknown in the United States. Many of the ideas that appeared in Piaget's essays first appeared in this book. It is the first treatment by anyone associated with Piaget that later came to be known as "discovery learning."

[58]See H. A. Simon, "An Information Processing Theory of Intellectual Development," in W. Kessen and C. Kohnman, eds., *Thought in the Young Child. Society for Research in Child Development Monographs* 27 (2), 1962, 150-55.

[59]J. A. Pascal-Leone, "A Mathematical Model for the Transition Rule in Piaget's Developmental Stages," *Acta Psychological* 32 (August 1970), 301-45.

[60]R. Case, "Intellectual Development from Birth to Adulthood: A Neo-Piagetian Interpretation," in R. S. Siegler, ed., *Children's Thinking: What Develops?* Hillsdale, N.J.: Lawrence Erlbaum, 1978.

[61]R. S. Siegler, "Three Aspects of Cognitive Development," *Cognitive Psychology* 4 (October 1976), 481-520.

[62]D. Klahr, "Goal Formation, Planning, and Learning by Pre-School Solvers or 'My Socks Are in the Dryer,' " in R. S. Siegler, ed., *Children's Thinking: What Develops?* Hillsdale, N.J.: Lawrence Erlbaum, 1978.

[63]J. S. Bruner et al., *A Study of Thinking*. New York: John Wiley, 1956.

[64]J. S. Bruner, *The Process of Education*. New York: Random House, 1960.

[65]Ibid., 31.

[66]Ibid., 33.

[67]Ibid., 13.

[68]Ibid., 83-84.

[69]John Dewey, *How We Think*. Lexington, Mass.: Heath, 1933, 82.

[70]Daniel Tanner and Laurel N. Tanner, *Curriculum Development*, 2d ed. New York: Macmillan, 1980, 545.

[71]David P. Ausubel, *Educational Psychology*. New York: Holt, Rinehart and Winston, 1968, 52.

[72]Ibid., 153.

[73]See Harold F. O'Neil, Jr., *Learning Strategies*. New York: Academic Press, 1978.

[74]See Robert Glaser, ed., *Advances in Instructional Psychology*, 3 vols. Hillsdale, N.J.: Lawrence Erlbaum, 1978, 1982, 1987.

[75]Claire E. Weinstein and Richard E. Mayer, "The Teaching of Learning Strategies," in Merlin C. Wittrock, ed., *Handbook of Research on Teaching*, 3d ed. New York: Macmillan, 1986, 316-17.

[76]L. K. Cook and R. E. Mayer, "Reading Strategy Training for Meaningful Learning from Prose," in M. Pressley and J. Lewin, eds., *Cognitive Strategy Training*. New York: Springer-Verlag, 1983.

[77]A. Newell et al., "A Report on a General Problem-Solving Program," *Proceedings of the International Conference on Information Processing*. New York: UNESCO, 256-65.

[78]L. Resnick and R. Glaser, "Problem Solving and Intelligence," in L. Resnick and R. Glaser, eds., *The Nature of Intelligence*. Hillsdale, N.J.: Lawrence Erlbaum, 1976, 205-30.

[79]D. A. Norman, "Cognitive Engineering and Education," in D. T. Tuma and F. Reif, eds., *Problem Solving and Education: Issues in Teaching and Research*. Hillsdale, N.J.: Lawrence Erlbaum, 1980, 97.

[80]J. Lochhead and J. Clement, *Cognitive Process Instruction: Research on Teaching Thinking Skills*. Philadelphia: Franklin Institute Press, 1979, 1.

[81]Ibid., Tuma and Reif, 98.

[82]A. Newell and H. A. Simon, "The Logic Theory Machine," *IRE Transactions on Information Theory*. IT-2, 1956, 61-69.

[83]J. R. Carbonell, "AI in CAI: An Artificial Intelligence Approach to Computer-Assisted Instruction," *IEEE Transactions on Man-Machine Systems* 11 (1970), 190-202.

[84]E. H. Shortliffe, *Computer-based Medical Consultations: MYCIN*. New York: American Elsevier, 1976.

[85]E. A. Feigenbaum, "The Art of Artificial Intelligence: Themes and Case Studies of Knowledge Engineering," *Proceedings of the Fifth International Joint Conference on Artificial Intelligence* (STAN-CS-77-621). Stanford, Calif.: Computer Science Dept., Stanford University, 1978.

[86]W. J. Clancey, "Tutoring Rules for Guiding a Case Method Dialogue," *International Journal of Man-Machine Studies* 11 (January 1979), 25-49.

[87]J. S. Brown and R. Burton, "Multiple Representations of Knowledge for Tutorial Reasoning," in D. G. Bobrow and A. Collins, eds., *Representation and Understanding: Studies in Cognitive Science*. New York: Academic Press, 1975, 311-49.

[88]J. S. Brown and R. Burton, "Diagnostic Models for Procedural Bugs in Basic Mathematical Skills," *Cognitive Science* 2 (April/June 1978), 155-92.

[89]S. Papert, "Uses of Technology to Enhance Education," *Artificial Intelligence Memo No. 298*. Cambridge, Mass.: MIT, 1973.

[90]See S. Papert, *Mindstorms: Children, Computers and Powerful Ideas*, New York: Basic Books, 1980. Peter G. Gebhardt has pointed out the parallels in the pedagogy of Maria Montessori and LOGO. See Peter G. Gebhardt-Steele, *The Computer and the Child*. Rockville, Md.: Computer Science Press, 1985.

[91]Tim O'Shea and John Self, *Learning and Teaching with Computers*. Englewood Cliffs, N.J.: Prentice-Hall, 1983, 112-13.

[92]R. B. Davis, *Learning Mathematics: The Cognitive Science Approach to Mathematics Education*. Norwood, N.J.: Ablex, 1984.

[93]Ibid., O'Shea and Self, *Learning and Teaching*, 217-18.

[94]See R. Pea, "Symbol Systems and Thinking Skills: LOGO in Context," *Pre-Proceedings LOGO 84*. Cambridge, Mass.: MIT, 1984, 55-61.

[95]S. Papert, "Computer Criticism vs. Technocentric Thinking," *LOGO 85: Theoretical Papers*. Cambridge, Mass.: MIT, 1985, 53-67.

Select Bibliography

Anderson, J. R. *The Architecture of Cognition*. Cambridge, Mass.: Harvard University Press, 1983.

_____. *Cognitive Psychology and Its Implications*, 2d ed. San Francisco: W. H. Freeman, 1985.

Ausubel, D. P., et al. *Educational Psychology: A Cognitive View*. New York: Holt, Rinehart and Winston, 1978.

Baars, Bernard J. *The Cognitive Revolution in Psychology*. New York: Guilford Press, 1986.

Bartlett, F. C. *Remembering*. Cambridge: Cambridge University Press, 1932.

Berlyne, D. E. *Conflict, Arousal and Curiosity*. New York: McGraw-Hill, 1960.

Bower, G. H. "Cognitive Psychology: An Introduction," in W. K. Estes, ed., *Handbook of Learning and Cognitive Processes*. Vol. I. Introduction to Concepts and Issues. New York: Erlbaum, 1975.

Bowers, C. A. *The Cultural Dimensions of Educational Computing*. New York: Teachers College Press; Columbia University, 1988.

Bruner, J. S., et al. *A Study of Thinking*. New York: John Wiley, 1956.

Chomsky, Norman. *Syntactic Structures*. The Hague: Mouton, 1957.

Feigenbaum, Edward A., and J. Feldman, eds. *Computers and Thought*. New York: McGraw-Hill, 1963.

Gardner, Howard. *The Mind's New Science*. New York: Basic Books, 1985.

Glover, John A., et al. *Cognitive Psychology for Teachers*. New York: Macmillan, 1990.

Lesgold, Alan, and Robert Glaser, eds. *Foundations for a Psychology of Education*. Hillsdale, N.Y.: Erlbaum, 1989.

_____. "Acquiring Expertise," in J. R. Anderson and S. M. Kosslyn, eds., *Tutorials in Learning and Memory*. San Francisco: W. H. Freeman, 1984.

Miller, A., et al. *Plans and the Structure of Behavior*. New York: Henry Holt & Co., 1960.

Neisser, Ulric. *Cognitive Psychology*. New York: Appleton-Century-Crofts, 1967.

_____. *Cognition and Reality: Principles and Implications of Cognitive Psychology*. San Francisco: W. H. Freeman, 1976.

Norman, D. A. *Learning and Memory*. San Francisco: W. H. Freeman, 1982.

12

Development of Instructional Design: 1950-1980

The purpose of this chapter is fourfold: (1) to provide a brief history of instructional design, (2) to explore the historical development of theories and models of instruction; (3) to describe the development of a systems design approach to instruction; and (4) to assess the status of instructional systems design theory.

Brief History of Instructional Design

Systematized models, theories, and methods of instruction can be traced back at least to the Elder Sophists. There is evidence that such early educators as Comenius, Pestalozzi, and Herbart developed instructional systems. In this century, Maria Montessori developed one of the first scientifically based instructional systems and was the first to develop graded instructional materials in accordance with a specific instructional design. Indeed, the survival of her materials over most of this century is testimony to the effectiveness of her instructional design.[1]

Edward L. Thorndike in the early years of this century was the prototype of the application of scientific methods to educational problems, despite the fact that his major concepts were anti-egalitarian.[2] John Dewey played an important role in the great intellectual movement in America at the turn of the century to make science an important force in American life and thought; he was confident that the findings of science would eventually be applied to the practical problems of education. In his presidential address before the American Psychological Association in 1899, Dewey called for the development of "a special linking science" between the theorist and educational practice.[3] Dewey also made a significant contribution to instructional design by developing an innovative problems approach to instruction which is yet to be fully implemented.[4]

While the relationship between psychology and education remained for a time, soon psychology and what became known as educational technology drifted apart. Behaviorism became a laboratory science and did not test its theories under the conditions of real school situations. Psychology increasingly became a natural science rather than a human science; psychologists went into the laboratory to

343

develop experimental techniques in pursuit of theoretical objectives rather than dealing with practical instructional problems. Educational technology, because of this separation, became largely theoretical and focused on hardware or media as aids to teaching rather than on the development of a science of instructional design.

The schism between psychology and educational technology reached its nadir during World War II. After a long separation, psychologists and educational technologists began to work together to develop effective methods of mass instruction and also to develop the principles and procedures for instructional design. After the war, in 1950, the National Society for the Study of Education's yearbook *Learning and Instruction* reflected a new emphasis on the importance of instruction and teaching in the context of learning. By 1964, when the society's yearbook *Theories of Learning and Instruction* focused on the need for theories of instruction of theories of teaching, it was apparent that the early connection between psychology and educational technology had been firmly re-established.[5]

One of the first empirically tested models of instruction evolved from Skinner's behavioristic instructional design and was particularly manifested in programmed instruction. In contrast, Bruner, Ausubel, and others developed instructional models based on cognitive structure. By the late 1950s and 1960s, many recognized the need for instructional theories and took steps to develop such theories. Bruner was the first to propose a "theory of instruction."[6] Earlier, the Association for Supervision and Curriculum Development (ASCD) formed a commission in 1964 "to delineate scientifically based instructional theories from the more intuitively based and somewhat speculative 'theorizing' which had been so characteristic of education previously."[7] This commission made the influential report, *Criteria for Evaluating Theories of Instruction* in 1968.[8]

Task Analysis Approach

Task-analysis instructional theories emerged when laboratory-based learning principles in military and industrial training situations proved to be inadequate or irrelevant for the design of instruction. The pioneering work in task analysis was done by Robert Gagnè and Leslie Briggs. Gagnè suggested that instructional principles and instructional theory could best be developed after the completion of an intensive task analysis of the educational objectives. He identified eight different types of learning and described both the environmental events and the stages of information processing required for each learning category.[9] Briggs used Gagnè's conditions and types of learning as a basis for developing procedures for instructional design.[10]

Robert Glaser also made a notable early contribution to instructional design. He collected much of the relevant work of the 1960s into edited volumes,[11] described the "four components of a psychology of instruction,"[12] and helped in developing the "ruleg" (rule-example) model of instruction.[13] In 1978, Glaser began editing a series of volumes designed to mark the progress and advances in the instructional process.[14]

Another important early contribution to instructional design was the curriculum reform movement of the late 1950s and 1960s. Although the major thrust of the reform followed the mental discipline doctrine, it did stimulate interest in a more systematic approach to instruction and sensitized a need for formulating instructional theories and instructional design. Meanwhile, the new focus on instructional research, associated with the curriculum reform movement, led in 1969 to the coining of a new term, *instructional psychology*. Despite the expectation that instructional psychology might provide data and insights for instructional theory, the literature of the past two decades has shown very little evidence of instructional theory and, as Snellbecker states, there has been "a distinct tendency to compile information about an increasingly large number of areas, with little or no attempt to compress and to synthesize resultant information into coherent interpretative conceptualizations."[15]

The sixties produced most of the major components of the instructional design process. Names associated with this era include Gagnè, Briggs, Glaser, and Mager as well as Carroll, Cronbach, and Scriven. Glaser proposed the idea of criterion-referenced testing (CRT).[16] Glaser emphasized the need of making clear the criterion for successful performance and stressed that test items must measure the behavior described in the objective. Another important component of instructional design which was emphasized in the sixties was evaluation. Previously, evaluation had been equated with research. But this began to change with the use of what Scriven called "formative evaluation" — a term that was used to identify the process of collecting data and information for the purpose of improving instruction.[17] Scriven's work was, in large part, related to the earlier work of Cronbach.[18] The actual implementation of this concept of formative evaluation was primarily influenced by Markle, who used the term "developmental testing" to describe the phases of evaluation that were being used by programmed instruction writers or designers.[19] Markle's work was later reflected in the writings of Baker and Alkin[20] and Dick.[21]

Other historical developments in the sixties include Glaser's Individually Prescribed Instruction (IPI),[22] Keller's Personalized System of Instruction,[23] Bloom's system of mastery learning,[24] and Flanagan's Project PLAN.[25] Moreover, the theoretical models of instruction that were published had important influences on the field. For example, Carroll's Model of School Learning focused on the idea that learning was not the function of any single variable, but involved a complex of interactive factors.[26]

Since the 1960s, a number of instructional models and theories have been proposed, but there is still no sound, comprehensive theory of instruction. Considerable progress has been made, however, and a growing number of professionals are devoting themselves to the development of a viable instructional theory and instructional design. Next is a consideration of some of the more prominent theories of instruction that have emerged.

Instructional Design Theories

This section reviews the major instructional design theories that have evolved during the 1950-1980 period. Not intended to be comprehensive, this review illustrates those theories that have had an important influence on instructional design.

According to Reigeluth, an instructional design theory must include three things: (1) one or more instructional models; (2) a set of conditions under which each model should be used, and (3) the outcomes (desired or actual) for each model under each set of conditions. He says further "a descriptive instructional theory describes the actual outcomes that result from using each model under each set of conditions" while "a prescriptive instructional theory prescribes the models that should be used to achieve desired outcomes under different conditions."[27]

Bruner's Search for a Theory of Instruction

Bruner had proposed some theorems regarding instruction in the early 1960s, but in 1966, in his book *Toward a Theory of Instruction* he specified that a theory of instruction must include the following:

1. Predisposition to learn. A theory of instruction must be concerned with the experiences and contexts that will tend to make the child willing and able to learn when he or she enters school.

2. Structure of knowledge. It must specify the ways in which a body of knowledge should be structured so that it can be most readily grasped by the learner.

3. Sequence. It should specify the most effective sequences in which to present the materials.

4. Reinforcement. It should specify the nature of and pacing of rewards, moving from extrinsic rewards to intrinsic ones.[28]

Bruner elaborated on some of these features, such as individual differences and the differences to be expected with growth, flexibility of sequencing to meet individual differences, and the structural differences required within various fields of knowledge. Although Bruner has been associated with cognitive approaches to instruction, some features of his theory appear behavioristic and reflect more a curriculum theory rather than an instructional theory. Many have been impressed with Bruner's views, but others have found his ideas contradictory and unsupported by empirical evidence.

Gagnè's Hierarchical Task Analysis

Robert M. Gagnè has developed a behavioristic, eclectic approach to instructional design. He emerged from a military background in which he became convinced that the practical tasks of training (in the air force) required a psychological analysis of the component steps a student needs to learn in order to perform some complex skill. Out of this recognition, Gagnè developed his idea of task-skill hierarchies that provide guidance as to sequencing. Moreover, he identified eight distinct types of learning arranged in order of increasing complexity: (1) signal learning, (2) stimulus-response learning, (3) chaining, (4) verbal association, (5) discrimination learning, (6) concept learning, (7) rule learning, and (8) problem solving.

Each variety of learning begins with a different state of the organism and ends with a different capability for performance. Gagnè also stated "that there are eight corresponding kinds of changes in the nervous system which need to be identified and ultimately accounted for."[29] The concept-learning hierarchy implies that all learning is reducible to a mechanistic, S-R, associationist process. Whereas Skinnerian behaviorists emphasize shaping behavior through development of desired responses, Gagnè stresses the organism's selection of stimuli.

Gagnè's concept-learning hierarchies describe the internal conditions of learning. His early work described organized sets of intellectual skills that build from simple to complex, while his later work identified two sets of capabilities that progress from simple to complex, namely, learning hierarchies and procedures. Procedures are organized sets of motor and intellectual skills while learning hierarchies are sets of intellectual skills only. Each capability in a hierarchy is a prerequisite to the next, more complex skill.

Gagnè-Briggs Theory of Instruction

The work on learning hierarchies stimulated Gagnè and Leslie Briggs to develop a theory of instruction. They found it useful, for example, to use the hierarchy concept to sequence a course, a topic within a course, a lesson within a topic, or a component within a lesson.

The five major categories of human capabilities that are outcomes of learning are: (1) verbal information, (2) intellectual skills, (3) cognitive strategies, (4) attitudes, and (5) motor skills.[30]

The Gagnè-Briggs theory proposed that each category requires a different set of conditions for effective learning, and assumed the information-processing model of learning and memory. More specifically, the systems model for instructional design is characterized by three major features: instruction is designed for specific goals and objectives; the development of instruction employs diverse media; and pilot tryouts, materials revision, and field testing of materials constitute an integral part of the design process. In the design model, *formative evaluation* refers to materials tryout with small groups of students to test effectiveness and identify needs for materials revision. *Summative evaluation* evaluates the materials with a typical population and certifies whether or not the objectives achieved are effective for a particular population.

Gagnè and Briggs describe instruction as "a human undertaking whose purpose is to help people learn."[31] Five assumptions support the Gagnè-Briggs concept of instruction design: first, instruction should facilitate the learning of an individual student; second, both intermediate and long-range phases should be planned; third, instruction should be precisely planned; fourth, instruction should be designed using the systems approach; fifth, instruction should be developed from knowledge about how humans learn.[32]

The Gagnè-Briggs theory postulates the information-processing model of learning and memory, as well as the need for reinforcement and feedback. Instruction is defined as a set of events that takes place in approximately the following sequence: (a) gaining attention, (b) informing learner of the objective, (c) stimulating recall of prerequisites, (d) presenting the stimulus material, (e) providing "learning guidance," (f) eliciting the performance, (g) providing feedback, (h) assessing the performance, and (i) enhancing retention and transfer.[33]

The Gagnè-Briggs prescriptive instructional model is distinct because of its use of information-processing theories of learning as well as of the human modeling concept of Bandura.[34] It is also a comprehensive theory that covers a wide range of learning outcomes. However, the model is not easy for a classroom teacher to implement and provides an inadequate basis for reflective teaching and learning. There is also little empirical support for learning hierarchies. White found that Gagnè's intellectual skills are difficult to identify outside of mathematics and that learning hierarchies are most effective in quantitative skills in which the hierarchy contains only a few elements.[35]

Case's Neo-Piagetian Theory of Instruction

Robbie Case's neo-Piagetian theory revolves around the questions of how to optimize the development of children's operational cognitive structures and how to adapt the content of instruction to the cognitive structures that the child already possesses. According to Case, these questions are answered by (1) analyzing the structural underpinnings of the academic discipline that is the content of instruction, (2) assessing the child's current level of functioning in that discipline, and (3) designing instruction so that it is geared to the level of functioning that is assessed. Case proposes that the first step is to identify the goal of the task to be performed and then follow with a series of steps by which the goal might be reached. For example, he suggests that introspection or a protocol analysis might be used. The next step would be to assess a student's current level of functioning.[36]

Instructional design involves a five-phase process. First, a paradigm is established whereby the student may assess the effectiveness of a strategy he uses. This is followed by a scheme that is a potential source of conflict. In the third phase, the learner constructs a higher-order structure to resolve the conflict. Finally, in the fifth phase, the learner consolidates and extends his new structure. Throughout the instruction process, cognitive complexity is minimized in the context of Piagetian maturational variables.[37]

The distinctive feature of this theory, as Case himself states, is that (1) children's current level of functioning cannot simply be assessed in terms of components of skilled performance that are already available, but must be seen as having a distinct organizational structure of its own; and (2) the optimal procedure for dealing with a child's current organizational structure combines elements of Piaget's model of equilibration with Pascal-Leone's model of the performance parameters that affect the equilibration process.

Component Display Theory (CDT)

M. D. Merrill and his collaborators developed a complex prescriptive theory designed to clarify and extend the Gagnè-Briggs theory. Like the Gagnè-Briggs theory, CDT essentially presents specific instructional sequences.

CDT views a specific presentation as a series of discrete displays. Further, all cognitive instruction consists of two modes, either telling or questioning, and these modes can be used with two instructional elements, generalities or examples. The theory lists four primary presentation forms — generality, example, generality practice, and instance practice.

CDT also views learning outcomes in terms of the type of content involved and the task level required of the learner with respect to that content. CDT, unlike other theories, classifies objectives on two dimensions: (1) type of content (facts, concepts, principles, and procedures); and (2) desired level of performance with respect to that content (remember, use, and find). For example, an objective can involve remembering a concept, using a concept, or finding a concept.

CDT includes three types of prescriptions: component specifications, consistency rules, and adequacy rules. Component specifications describe what is required to develop an adequate primary presentation form of the task/content matrix. Consistency rules prescribe optimal combinations of presentation form to achieve learner outcomes. Adequacy rules relate to delivery strategies, including feedback, textual display, and elaboration techniques. CDT also includes specifications for test adequacy, which differs somewhat from presentation adequacy.[38]

CDT provides guidelines to make design decisions for group presentation, but the underlying assumption is that individual learners will control both content and strategy. Learners, for example, are allowed to use their own strategies when sequencing components and determining how much time they will devote to each component.

CDT has been used extensively in instructional design and, in particular, in the design of the TICCIT computer-based learning system. More important, CDT prescriptions have provided research support in both laboratory and field experiments. Although much work still needs to be done to develop CDT, it does offer a highly integrated approach to instructional design.

Elaboration Theory of Instruction

The elaboration theory of instruction described by Reigeluth and associates was designed to extend the CDT to the macro level, that is, to integrate relevant knowledge concerning learning and instruction on the macro level.[39]

The instructional content of Reigeluth's theory is concerned principally with concepts, principles, and procedures. The general theoretical orientation is often represented as a zoom lens approach to instruction. Beginning with a wide-angle view, the detail and complexity of the parts are gradually increased by zooming in on them, but then there is a return to the wide view so that specific details may be integrated into a larger whole.

When instructional sequences are being designed, the presentation of an epitome, or a small number of ideas, is followed by the teaching of an operation, and this, in turn, is followed by a so-called expanded epitome. Once the organizing structure or other supporting structure has been formulated and an epitome abstracted from it, the process of elaboration can be implemented. Thus, there is a cycle of elaborate-synthesize-elaborate-synthesize until instruction is complete.

The elaboration theory is somewhat compatible with Bruner's concept of a "spiral curriculum" and Ausubel's notion of progressive differentiation. The latter two theories also advocate beginning instruction by presenting an overview of the whole, followed by elaboration of the parts that relate to the whole. Although the principles underlying elaboration theory are relatively simple, it still needs to be demonstrated how this approach can easily or effectively be implemented in instructional design.

Structural Learning Theory

Over a long period of time, Scandura has described various aspects of structural learning theory. Scandura has proposed an axiomatic theoretical system that has direct instruction implications. He summarizes his theory as follows: "The present view rejects the idea that overt (and/or potentially overt) stimuli cause behavior. We assume instead that behavior is caused by rules, an underlying construct—in effect, that subjects actually do use rules. Stimuli simply provide the occasion for responding."[40] He also says, "two major assumptions are (1) all behavior is generated by rules, and (2) rules can be devised to account for all kinds of human behavior."[41]

Structural learning theory has particular implications for cognitive processing, for the analysis and assessment of individual learner competence, and for instructional design in terms of problem-solving capability. Scandura's theory is essentially a theory of rule-learning and rule applications. He prescribes teaching the simplest path through a rule first and then proceeding to teach progressively more complex paths until a complete rule has been mastered. Although it can be used for group instruction, his approach is designed for individualized instruction. For example, a major part of his strategy is to make an intensive analysis to determine which paths of which rules each student has or has not mastered and then to teach those paths of those rules the student has not learned.

The particular relevance of Scandura's theory is seen in his work with mathematics, but the scope of his theory does not appear to include other subject areas.

The Algo-Heuristic Theory of Instruction

Different theories and research paradigms have influenced Landa in the development of his algo-heuristic theory of instruction. Much of his early work has been translated from Russian. Essentially, Landa views instruction from a cybernetic viewpoint in which the learner receives feedback concerning his success in achieving a specific goal and uses that feedback to make necessary corrections for future behavior. Thus, instruction is a self-regulating, self-correcting, goal-seeking system.[42]

The primary method that Landa proposes is to bring instruction under learner control by designing explicit procedures for the learner to perform in the process of completing his task. Two general kinds of procedures are advocated: algorithms and heuristics. In Landa's words, "an algorithm is a precise, generally comprehensible prescription for carrying out a defined ... sequence of elementary operations ... in order to solve any problems that belong to a certain class (or type)."[43] Moreover, Landa provides examples of algorithmic instruction in foreign language teaching, geometric problem-solving, and several other instructional areas.

Landa's theory emphasizes the macro strategies of selection and sequencing of instruction. His theory breaks down complex cognitive structures and then, by what he calls a snowball method, instructional sequencing proceeds by the teaching and practicing of each elementary operation separately. When all operations have been taught, they are then practiced together.

Although Landa admits that not all subject-matter tasks can be represented algorithmically, he proclaims the algorithmic-heuristic approach the way to creative thinking.

A Cognitive Theory of Inquiry Teaching

The Collins-Stevens instructional theory focuses on: (1) a set of teacher's goals; (2) a set of strategies for achieving those goals; and (3) a mechanism (or control structure) for deciding which goals to pursue when. The control structure specifies selection and sequencing strategies.[44]

This theory of Socratic tutoring involves a blend of diagnosis and correction strategies. The tutor analyzes the learner's understanding and uses errors as clues to identify misconceptions. The tutor's questions are guided by a number of rules. Twenty-four rules are described, fifteen of which are formulation rules and the remainder, application rules.[45]

This theory is considered especially useful in developing an intelligent CAI system. For example, effectively designed CAI routines can make it possible for students to complete problem-solving exercises in unfamiliar areas of knowledge. Moreover, the process of inquiry can transform learning into problem solving and provide exceptional motivation.

Instructional Systems Design

Instructional systems design is a relatively new concept in educational technology and has, to date, been applied primarily in industrial and military settings. It has become increasingly apparent to progressive educators that education must discard its folklore approach to instruction and move forward to new frontiers if it is to cope adequately with the needs and problems of a swiftly changing technological culture. The approach to education hitherto has been piecemeal; the result, a disconnected, fragmented series of innovations. One answer to this problem is a systems design approach to instruction in which all components of the instructional process are fitted together into a system capable of providing individualized instruction for each learner.

During the 1950s and 1960s, educational technology increasingly focused on language laboratories, teaching machines and programmed instruction, multimedia presentations, and the use of the computer in teaching. Out of this came the systems approach, an effort to design a complete program or develop a course of instruction to meet specific needs and objectives. This movement closely paralleled the military and business worlds. Instructional goals and objectives were precisely defined, various alternatives were analyzed, instructional resources were identified and/or developed, a plan of action was devised, and results were continuously evaluated for possible modification of the program.

Many instructional systems approaches or instructional designs offered flow charts and lists of steps to be followed. One of the clearest early models was developed by Kemp.[46] Banathy,[47] Corrigan,[48] and Gagné[49] also developed early designs for instructional systems. A review of the literature by Andrews and Goodson found sixty descriptions of systems models and identified fourteen tasks accomplished in the systems design process.[50]

A focus on the design of entire instruction systems provides a clear distinction of educational technology in contrast to traditional instruction approaches. Thus, educational technology not only includes problems of instructional design and management of learning, but must also involve development and management of diverse educational systems where instruction and learning can take place.

Finally, a systems approach is a decision-making tool that enables those who manage the system to state their bias in the form of a goal, and to operate the system so that performance will achieve a particular goal. Frequently, the system is viewed as being inhumane or impersonal, but if the purpose of the system is to promote humane interests, the outcome should be an effective and efficient humanized system. It appears obvious that systems can be either inhumane and depersonalized or personalized and humane. They are whatever they were designed to be.

Origin of the Systems Concept

Systems engineering—the invention, design, and integration of an entire assembly of equipment (as distinct from the invention and design of components) geared to the accomplishment of a broad objective—has been a fundamental concept of practical engineering since the beginning of the industrial revolution. One of the most successful applications of the systems concept in the military sphere was the development of the atomic bomb.

In the early 1950s, two significant events took place in systems development. First, the air force formalized the systems concept. Second, within the Air Research and Development Command it drew together those research and development agencies concerned with systems, including their hardware and human components. These developments resulted from the need to improve the predominantly manual air defense control and warning system established over large areas of the United States, Canada, and the peripheral oceans. A radically better air defense control system was required, and in 1953, the intensive development of the first automated electronic system was undertaken by the air force and MIT's Lincoln Laboratory. About five years later, the first elements of the Semi-Automatic Ground Environment system began operations on the East Coast, and within several years the system had been deployed throughout the United States.

During the 1953-1960 period, the systems analyst, programmer, and systems designer emerged, and the term *systems approach* was introduced to combat the prevailing engineer's concept that hardware was the key to a successful system. About 1960, the phrase *total systems approach* came into use to describe the interaction of humans and machines, within the context of an organization, in terms of specific tasks and outcomes. As a result of the pioneering military applications, development of systems technology is accelerating in many industrial, scientific, business, and governmental sectors as well, involving a complex integrated organization of humans and machines, ideas, procedures, and management.

Developments in automation suggest self-contained systems with inputs, outputs, and a mechanism of control. With the introduction of large-scale electronic data processing equipment, computerized information systems have been developed for many applications. Physical distribution systems have received increasing attention from manufacturers and shippers. Concepts of logistics have embraced systems concepts that emphasize the total system of material flow rather than the functions, departments, or institutions involved in the processing. Attention has focused increasingly on massive engineering projects involving weapons systems and space technology systems.

Characteristics of an Instructional System

Systems models have varied widely in the number of steps or stages in systems design, in theoretical base, and in the degree of use. Moreover, a systems model may be used to design a single lesson, a course, or an entire curriculum. The techniques of instructional systems design share certain characteristics. Briggs has described these as follows:

> First of all, a "system" ... is an integrated plan of operation of all components (sub-systems) of a system, designed to solve a problem or meet a need.

> Second, the planning represented by a systems approach implies an analysis of components in logical order, and careful coordination of the total effort among planners.

> Third, the process of planning follows an orderly but flexible sequence.

> Fourth, the design procedures ... are research based, in so far as is possible.

Fifth, the design model calls for empirical testing and improvement of the total instructional plan. Since instructional theory is at an early state of development compared to theory in the physical sciences, heavy reliance must be placed on actual tryout and revision of the instruction....

Sixth, this design model requires comparison of the final version of the instruction with alternate instruction; or in the absence of an alternative, the value of the final form of instruction is to be determined.[51]

Stages in Instructional System Design

Briggs and Wager have described the design process in detail. The following stages are typical and incorporate the tasks found in most systems design models used to develop an entire curriculum:

Stage 1 is analysis of needs, goals and priorities. A group of citizens, educators, and students, by consensus, rank broad goals to be achieved by learners after a period of years, often expressed as "exit goals" from secondary schools.

Stage 2 is analysis of resources and constraints. Resources include time, money, and the capabilities of the people who are to design the system and the capabilities of those who are to operate the system.

Stage 3 is selection of a delivery system. This step defines the major modes of instruction, such as individualized instruction, group instruction, and work-study programs.

Stage 4 is preparation of a curriculum scope and sequence statement. This document lists the year-by-year goals to be achieved for each subject or skill area in the curriculum. It identifies, as separate "courses," yearly subject area goals to be achieved in the curriculum.

Stage 5 is design of the organization of courses. Each course is represented by a course-level instructional curriculum map (ICM), which shows how the unit objectives contribute to the attainment of course objectives.

Stage 6 is design of the organization of course units. A unit-level ICM is drawn up for each major unit in the course. Each such ICM shows the specific objectives for each unit of the course.

Stage 7 is analysis of objectives. Each objective in the unit-level ICM is analyzed into its subordinate elements, which are then classified as either essential or supporting prerequisites. This analysis is aided by the use of defined learning hierarchies for intellectual skills and information processing principles. Their purpose is to make the analysis sufficiently precise in identifying both entering competencies and lesson objectives.

Stage 8 is organization of lessons. Based on the results of the previous stage, objectives for lessons, series of lessons, and parts of lessons are identified.

Stage 9 is designing the lessons. Systems models differ greatly in describing how the strategy of lesson design is conceptualized and carried out. In the model used as a basis for this description of stages in systems design, lessons are designed by (a) identifying lesson objectives, (b) listing the instructional events to be used, (c) writing prescriptions that incorporate the appropriate conditions of learning, and (d) selecting the media of instruction. These choices are recorded on two special forms (Media Analysis Worksheet and Time-Line Plan).

Stage 10 is assessment of learner performance. Assessments may be in the form of written, oral or performance tests, as appropriate to the objectives for the lessons and the course units. When appropriate, end-of-course assessments are also made.

Stage 11 is development of materials. These include instructional materials and media, teachers' guides, and assessment tests.

Stage 12 is empirical tryout and if necessary, revision of the early versions of the instructional materials (formative evaluation).

Stage 13 is summative evaluation of the final form of the course, materials, and curriculum.

Stage 14 is planning teacher preparation and diffusion, when widespread adoption is the goal of the systems design effort.[52]

Status of Instructional Systems Design Theory

The prevailing models of instructional systems design reflect a linear, ends-means view associated with behavioristic concepts. Despite the fact that instructional systems design models like those of Gagnè and Briggs and others have little or no relation to general systems theory, educational technologists, curriculum designers, and others, as Hug and King have aptly stated, "frequently justify their approach to program design in terms of General Systems Theory, when the assumptions and procedures used actually better fit the rubrics associated with instructional design and systems analysis."[53]

General System Theory and Instructional Systems Design

Ludwig von Bertalanffy, the founder of general system theory, states that general system theory "may be considered the science of 'wholeness' or holistic entities which hitherto, under the mechanistic bias, were excluded as unscientific, vitalistic or metaphysical. Within the framework of general system theory, these aspects become scientifically accessible."[54]

Although much theoretical work has been done on biological systems (the living organism), no conceptual framework has been developed that describes how to combine human capabilities with machine capabilities to achieve system goals. The organismic concept of Bertalanffy, however, offers a fruitful biological analogy for general systems theory.[55] The basis of his concept is that a living organism is not a collection of separate elements, but rather is a definite system possessing organization and wholeness. An organism is an open system that remains stable while matter and energy that enter it keep changing (this is called dynamic equilibrium). A central feature of the general systems outlook is its emphasis on the dynamic mutual interaction of subsystems that operate as functional processes. In biological terms, a total organism is a system whose behavior is influenced by a still larger system—the organism-in-its-environment. Life is purposive in the sense that it maintains stability in itself, is self-regulating, and actively explores and manipulates its environment. Life is interactive rather than reactive and organisms exchange energy and information with their environments.

This description of an organismic system adequately fits the instructional setting. The instructional system is a man-made system that dynamically interacts with its environment—teachers, learners, instructional resources, procedures, administrators, school board, parents, local community, government, and many other agencies. Moreover, the instructional system is a system of interrelated parts that work in conjunction with each other to accomplish a number of goals.

The work of Bela Banathy offers an instructional systems design approach at variance with the typical linear designs. For example, he says:

In contrast to the analytical, reductionist, linear-causal orientation of classical scientific thinking, systems philosophy brings forth a reorientation of thought and world view manifested in an expansionist orientation and a dynamic, nonlinear, synthesis-oriented, and holistic mode of thinking. The scientific exploration of the isomorphism of systems and theories of systems in various disciplines has brought forth general theories of systems: a set of interrelated concepts and principles. Systems methodology provides us with a set of paradigms, strategies, methods, and tools that instrumentalize systems thinking and systems theory in design, development, and problem solving for complex systems.[56]

Further, Banathy views instructional systems design as operating in four arenas or spaces:

the *design solution space*, which is embodied in the *knowledge space*, the *contextual space* (which is the environment of design), and the *experience space*. The designer constantly explores these spaces, integrating information and knowledge with emerging images of the design solution. Feedback-feedforward and divergence-convergence are additional attributes of design dynamics.[57]

Instructional systems design models typically focus on producing and validating instructional products or on designing and implementing a particular course or curriculum, rather than concentrating on analyzing the classroom environment or using concepts from general systems theory to gain a better understanding of why and how schools function as they do.

Future Prospects of Instructional Systems Design Theory

The future of instructional design theory is uncertain at this juncture. Although there was vigorous development of instructional design theory and models in the 1960s and the early 1970s, not much progress has been made in recent years. The dwindling of federal support, declining enrollments, and transitional patterns in educational technology have been some of the factors that have slowed the growth of instructional theories. Unfortunately, there is still no sound, comprehensive theory of instruction, and there seems to be a lack of communication between instructional designers and classroom teachers. Even though some theories would warrant further implementation, they have not been codified in a form that educators can easily use in specific instructional situations. Teacher education programs are needed that would make it possible for future teachers and practicing teachers to experiment with alternate theories of instruction in a real school setting. It also remains to be seen whether new computer approaches to instruction will have a significant impact on future instructional design. Some current approaches offer a reasonably optimistic outlook.[58]

Notes

[1]See, for example, Maria Montessori, *The Montessori Method.* New York: Schocken Books, 1964.

[2]For a comprehensive discussion of the social implications of Thorndike's ideas, see Merle Curti, *The Social Ideas of American Educators.* Paterson, N.J.: Pageant Books, 1959, 459-98.

[3]John Dewey, "Psychology and Social Practice," *The Psychological Review* 7 (March 1900), 105-24.

[4]See John Dewey, *How We Think*, 2d ed., Boston: Heath, 1933, 107.

[5]E. R. Hilgard, ed., *Theories of Learning and Instruction*, Part I, 63rd yearbook of the National Society for the Study of Education. Chicago: University of Chicago Press, 1964.

[6]See J. S. Bruner, *Toward a Theory of Instruction,* New York: W. W. Norton, 1966.

[7]Glenn E. Snelbecker, *Learning Theory, Instructional Theory and Psychoeducational Design.* New York: McGraw-Hill, 1974, 141.

[8]The commission was chaired by Ira J. Gordon and included as members Nicolas Fattu, Maria M. Hughes, Grace Lund, E. Brooks Smith, and Robert M. W. Travers.

[9]R. M. Gagnè, *The Conditions of Learning*, 4th ed. New York: Holt, Rinehart and Winston, 1985.

[10]Leslie Briggs, ed., *Instructional Design: Principles and Applications.* Englewood Cliffs, N.J.: Educational Technology Publications, 1977.

[11]See Robert Glaser, ed., *Teaching Machines and Programmed Learning, II*, Washington, D.C.: DAVI, 1965, 771-809.

[12]Robert Glaser, "Components of a Psychology of Instruction: Toward a Science of Design," *Review of Educational Research* 46 (Winter 1976), 1-24.

[13]J. L. Evans et al., "The Ruleg System for the Construction of Programmed Verbal Learning Sequences," *Journal of Educational Research* 55 (June-July 1962), 513-18.

[14]See Robert Glaser, ed., *Advances in Instructional Psychology*, 3 vols. Hillsdale, N.J.: Lawrence Erlbaum, 1978, 1982, 1987.

[15]Glenn E. Snelbecker, "Is Instructional Theory Alive and Well?" in Charles M. Reigeluth, ed., *Instructional-Design Theories and Models.* Hillsdale, N.J.: Lawrence Erlbaum, 1983, 448.

[16]Robert Glaser, "Instructional Technology and the Measurement of Learning Outcomes: Some Question," *American Psychologist* 18 (August 1963), 519-21.

[17]M. Scriven, "The Methodology of Evaluation," in R. Tyler, R. M. Gagnè, and M. Scriven, eds., *Perspectives of Curriculum Evaluation.* Chicago: Rand McNally, 1967, 39-83.

[18]Lee J. Cronbach, "Course Improvement through Evaluation," *Teachers College Record* 64 (May 1963), 672-83.

[19]S. M. Markle, "Empirical Testing of Program," in P. C. Lange, ed., *Programmed Instruction*, 66th yearbook of the National Society for the Study of Education. Chicago: University of Chicago Press, 1967, 104-40.

[20]E. L. Baker and M. C. Alkin, "Formative Evaluation of Instructional Development," *A V Communication Review* 21 (Winter 1973), 389-418.

[21]W. Dick, "Formative Evaluation," in L. J. Briggs, ed., *Instructional Design: Principles and Applications.* Englewood Cliffs, N.J.: Educational Technology Publications, 1977, 311-33.

[22]Robert Glaser and J. Rosner, "Adaptive Environments for Learning: Curriculum Aspects," in H. Talmage, ed., *Systems of Individualized Education*. Berkeley, Ca.: McCutchan, 1975.

[23]F. S. Keller, "Goodbye Teacher," *Journal of Applied Behavioral Analysis* 1 (Spring 1968), 79-89.

[24]B. S. Bloom, "Learning for Mastery," 1, 2, *Evaluation Comment*, 1968.

[25]J. C. Flanagan, "The American Institutes of Research," *American Psychologist* 39 (November 1984), 1272-76.

[26]J. B. Carroll, "A Model of School Learning," *Teachers College Record* 64 (May 1963), 723-33.

[27]Ibid., Reigeluth, 24.

[28]Bruner, *Theory of Instruction*.

[29]Gagnè, *Conditions of Learning*, 62.

[30]R. M. Gagnè, *Essentials of Learning for Instruction*. Hinsdale, Ill.: Dryden Press, 1974, 55.

[31]R. M. Gagnè and L. J. Briggs, *Principles of Instructional Design*, 2d ed. New York: Holt, Rinehart and Winston, 1979, 3.

[32]Ibid., 5.

[33]R. M. Gagnè, "Instructional Programs," in M. H. Marx and M. E. Bunch, eds., *Fundamentals and Applications of Learning*. New York: Macmillan, 1977, 404-28.

[34]According to Bandura, modeling or observational learning is a process whereby a person observes the behaviors of others, forms an idea of the performance and results of the observed behaviors, and uses the idea as coded information to guide his future behaviors. Most of the behaviors that people display have been learned, either deliberately or unintentionally, through modeling. Modeling reduces the hazards of trial and error learning by enabling people to learn from example. See Albert Bandura, *Psychological Modeling: Conflicting Theories*. Chicago: Aldine-Atherton, 1971.

[35]R. A. White, "A Limit to the Application of Learning Hierarchies," *Australian Journal of Education* 17 (1973), 153-56.

[36]Robbie Case, "Piaget and Beyond: Toward a Developmentally Based Theory and Technology of Instruction," in Robert Glaser, ed., *Advances in Instructional Psychology* I. Hillsdale, N.J.: Lawrence Erlbaum, 1978, 204-13.

[37]Ibid., 204-13.

[38]M. David Merrill et al., "Instructional Design in Transition," in Frank H. Farley and Neal J. Gordon, eds., *Psychology and Education: The State of the Union*. Berkeley, Calif.: McCutchan, 1981, 316-20.

[39]Reigeluth, 338-81.

[40]Joseph M. Scandura, *Structural Learning I: Theory and Research*. London: Gordon and Breach, 1973, 15. See Paul F. Merrill, "Task Analysis—An Information Processing Approach," *NSPI Journal* 15 (1976), 7-11 for a cognitive information processing that grew out of the learning hierarchy tradition and that uses the path analysis techniques of Scandura to produce a partial ordering of the different possible paths through an algorithm. Merrill shows how the information processing approach can lead to a revised learning hierarchy.

[41]Ibid., 41.

[42]Lev N. Landa, *Algorithmization in Learning and Instruction*. Englewood Cliffs, N.J.: Educational Technology Publications, 1974.

[43]Ibid., 41.

[44]Reigeluth, 249.

[45]Ibid., 250-78.

[46]Jerrold E. Kemp, *Instructional Design: A Plan for Unit and Course Development*. Belmont, Calif.: Fearon Publishers, 1971.

[47]B. Banathy, *Instructional Systems*. Palo Alto, Calif.: Fearon Publishers, 1968.

[48]G. West Churchman, *The System Approach*. New York: Dell Publishers, 1979.

[49]Gagnè and Briggs, *Instructional Design*.

[50]D. H. Andrews and L. A. Goodson, "A Comparative Analysis of Models of Instructional Design," *Journal of Instructional Development* 3 (Summer 1980), 2-16.

[51]Briggs, *Instructional Design*, 6-8.

[52]L. J. Briggs and W. Wager, *Handbook of Procedures for the Design of Instruction*, 2d ed. Englewood Cliffs, N.J.: Educational Technology Publications, 1981.

[53]William E. Hug and James E. King, "Educational Interpretations of General Systems Theory," in Ronald K. Bass and Charles R. Dills, eds., *Instructional Development: The State of the Art, II*. Dubuque, Iowa: Kendall/Hunt Publishing, 1984, 18.

[54]Ludwig von Bertalanffy, *Robots, Men and Minds*. New York: Braziller, 1967, 70.

[55]See Ludwig von Bertalanffy, *Problems of Life: An Evaluation of Modern Biological Thought*. New York: John Wiley & Sons, 1952.

[56]Bela H. Banathy, "Instructional Systems Design," in Robert M. Gagnè, ed., *Instructional Technology: Foundations*. Hillsdale, N.J.: Lawrence Erlbaum, 1987, 87.

[57]Ibid., 89.

[58]See David H. Jonassen, ed., *Instructional Designs for Microcomputer Courseware*. Hillsdale, N.J.: Lawrence Erlbaum, 1988.

Select Bibliography

Banathy, Bela H. *Instructional Systems*. Belmont, Calif.: Fearon Publishers, 1968.

Block, J. H., ed. *Mastery Learning: Theory and Practice*. New York: Holt, Rinehart and Winston, 1971.

Briggs, Leslie J., ed. *Instructional Design: Principles and Applications*. Englewood Cliffs, N.J.: Educational Technology Publications, 1977.

Briggs, Leslie J., and W. Wager. *Handbook of Procedures for the Design of Instruction*, 2d ed. Englewood Cliffs, N.J.: Educational Technology Publications, 1981.

Dick, Walter, and L. M. Carey. *The Systematic Design of Instruction*, 2d ed. Glenview, Ill.: Scott-Foresman, 1985.

Dick, Walter, and Robert A. Reiser. *Planning Effective Instruction: Teaching ID Skills to Pre-Service Teachers*. Englewood Cliffs, N.J.: Prentice-Hall, 1989.

Farley, Frank H., and Neal J. Gordon, eds. *Psychology and Education: The State of the Union.* I. Hillsdale, N.J: Earlbaum, 1978.

Gagnè, Robert M. *The Conditions of Learning.* New York: Holt, Rinehart and Winston, 1985.

Gagnè, Robert M., and Leslie J. Briggs. *Principles of Instructional Design,* 2d ed. New York: Holt, Rinehart and Winston, 1979.

Galser, Robert, ed. *Advances in Instructional Psychology.* 3 vols. Hillsdale, N.J.: Earlbaum, 1978, 1982, 1987.

Heinich, Robert. *Technology and the Management of Instruction.* Washington, D.C.: AECT, 1970.

Kemp, Jerrold E. *Instructional Design: A Plan for Unit and Course Development.* Belmont, Calif.: Fearon Publishers, 1971.

Landa, Lev N. *Algorithmization in Learning and Instruction.* Englewood Cliffs, N.J.: Educational Technology Publications, 1974.

Reigeluth, C. M., ed. *Instructional-Design Theories and Models: An Overview of Their Current Status.* Hillsdale, N.J.: Earlbaum, 1983.

_____. *Instructional Theories in Action: Lessons Illustrating Selected Theories and Models.* Hillsdale, N.J.: Erlbaum, 1988.

Reiser, Robert A. *Selecting Media for Instruction.* Englewood Cliffs, N.J.: Educational Technology Publications, 1983.

Romiszowski, A. *Designing Instructional Systems.* London: Kogan Page, 1981.

_____. *Producing Instructional Systems.* London: Kogan Page, 1984.

Schank, R. C., and R. P. Abelson. *Scripts, Plans, Goals, and Understanding.* Hillsdale, N.J.: Erlbaum, 1977.

Schmeck, Ronald R., ed. *Learning Strategies and Learning Styles.* New York: Plenum Press, 1988.

Simon, H. A. "Problem Solving and Education," in D. T. Tuma and F. Reif, eds., *Problem Solving and Education: Issues in Teaching and Research.* Hillsdale, N.J.: Earlbaum, 1980.

Snelbecker, Glenn E. *Learning Theory, Instructional Theory, and Instructional Design.* New York: McGraw-Hill, 1974.

Stillings, Neil A., et al. *Cognitive Science: An Introduction.* Cambridge, Mass.: MIT Press, 1987.

Vygotsky, L. S. *Mind and Society: The Development of Higher Psychological Processes,* tr. and ed. M. Cole, V. John-Steiner, S. Scribner, and E. Bouberman. Cambridge, Mass.: Harvard University Press, 1978.

Walbesser, H. H., and T. A. Eisenberg. *A Review of Research on Behavioral Objectives and Learning Hierarchies.* Columbus: Ohio State University Center for Science and Mathematics Education, 1972. ERIC No. ED 059 900.

Wilkinson, Gene L. *Media in Instruction: 60 Years of Research.* Washington, D.C.: AECT, 1980.

Wittrock, Merlin C., and Frank Farley, eds. *The Future of Educational Psychology.* Hillsdale, N.J.: Erlbaum, 1989.

13

Educational Broadcasting and Educational Technology: 1950-1980

As discussed in chapter 7, educational broadcasting and educational technology have had a long relationship. When radio education declined, educational television brought a general expansion of educational technology. This chapter focuses on the development of educational broadcasting from the formative years to the 1950s and 1960s to the transformation years of the 1970s.

Some may use the term *public broadcasting* rather than educational broadcasting, but these two terms carry quite different meanings and have distinctly different educational implications. According to a Carnegie Commission report of 1967, public broadcasting is defined as "all that is of human interest and importance which is not at the moment appropriate or available for support by advertising, and which is not arranged for formal instruction."[1] Moreover, public broadcasting includes public affairs, cultural, and entertainment components.

Educational broadcasting constitutes educational television, educational radio, and other educational telecommunications forms ranging from satellite and microwave systems to closed-circuit cable systems. Instructional television or instructional radio is the component of educational broadcasting directly related to transmitting formal instruction. According to Hawkridge and Robinson, educational broadcasting exhibits four dominant characteristics:

(1) its programs are arranged in series to assist cumulative learning;

(2) they are explicitly planned in consultation with external educational advisors;

(3) they are commonly accompanied by other kinds of learning materials, such as textbooks and study guides; and

(4) there is some attempt made to evaluate use of the broadcasts by teachers and students.[2]

A Historic Opportunity for Educational Broadcasting: The Pivotal Years

Education had long struggled for recognition in its efforts to secure channels for educational broadcasting. Educators had also learned from bitter experience that they needed channels specifically reserved for education if they were to survive and compete successfully with commercial broadcasters. After a lull during World War II, the FCC resumed licensing television stations to commercial broadcasters, but they made no effort to reserve channels for educational stations. Meanwhile, commercial broadcasters were eagerly grasping television licenses and putting stations on the air as rapidly as possible. During 1948 alone, the number of television stations on the air rose from seventeen to forty-one. By the fall of that year the FCC concluded that it must change its rules concerning technical standards and channel assignments and called for a "freeze," suspending all new television station construction until further notice. The unexpected freeze order probably gave educational television its last chance, because it provided the time for educators to organize and submit a formal request for educational channels.

The next development occurred in July 1949 when the FCC issued a *Notice of Further Proposed Rule Making*, which presented a new table of assignments providing for 2,245 stations in 1,400 different communities, but no reservations for any educational television stations. Only one of the seven FCC commissioners dissented from this 1949 *Notice*—Frieda Hennock.[3] She strongly protested this neglect and stressed the need to reserve a portion of the television spectrum for education, even though educators were not organized or well financed and had not developed any operational plans.

On August 26, 1949, U.S. commissioner of education Earl J. McGrath filed a *Notice of Appearance and Comments* that proposed that witnesses representing the U.S. Office of Education should present evidence to show the need for setting aside educational television channels. Although the FCC had scheduled hearings on educational television channels for November 1950, as late as October, educators had done little to prepare. As in years past, in the case of radio education, opinions were divided. The U.S. Office of Education, the NEA, and FCC Commissioner Hennock were demanding educational reservations in VHF. The NAEB had asked for UHF channels only. There was also an issue between "nonprofit" stations for education and "noncommercial" ones.

Commissioner Hennock started the ball rolling for education by inviting a group to her home on October 16, 1950. This meeting proved to be a landmark in educational broadcasting because it marked the beginning of the Joint Committee (later Council) on Educational Television (JCET). In its initial ad hoc stage, it included I. Keith Tyler, who was elected chairman; Belmont Farley of the NEA as secretary-treasurer; and a strategy committee of Robert Hudson, Edgar Fuller, and Stuart Haydon. Richard Hull, NAEB president, presided at the meeting. The JCET was authorized to make a presentation on behalf of the five national organizations whose members were represented at the meeting (the Association of Land-grant Colleges, the Association of State University Presidents, the National Association of State Universities, the National Council of Chief State School Officers, and the NEA).

The immediate problem was to find outstanding educators willing to come to Washington to testify at the FCC hearings in November; money would be needed to defray travel costs. Seymour Siegel, the new president of the NAEB, and George Probst managed this fund raising. Meanwhile, I. Keith Tyler sought help from the ACE and the NEA. Early in November, as a result of a suggestion from Commissioner Hennock, Tyler and Belmont Farley went to New York and retained as committee counsel General Telford Taylor, former general counsel to the FCC and former United States prosecutor at the Nuremburg trials. Subsequently, it was decided that the JCET would ask for at least one VHF channel in every metropolitan area and every major educational center as well as 20 percent of the UHF channels (following the FM precedent).

First FCC Hearings on Educational Television

United States commissioner of education Earl J. McGrath opened the first of a series of FCC hearings on educational television on November 27, 1950, with the following words:

> In its January 16, 1945 report, the Commission guaranteed that the applications of educational institutions for television licenses would be treated "on an equal basis with applications from non-educational applicants." At that time, the Commission felt unready to reserve a television band of educational use because there seemed to be insufficient evidence of an effective interest in the use of television by educational institutions and systems. My purpose in appearing today is to suggest that the conclusion should be re-examined.
>
> The responsibility of government to protect the public interest in all times is a clearly recognized principle, particularly so when a new frontier is being opened. The shameless exploitation of natural resources in the opening of the great west has demonstrated the result of government failure to protect the public interest — likewise the concern of the National Government in protecting and furthering the cause of education goes back to our national beginnings ... in adopting an ordinance which reserved part of the public lands for educational purposes, thereby establishing a precedent.[4]

Testimony was heard from sixty-one people: educators, public officials, prominent members of Congress, university presidents, deans and professors, state and city superintendents of schools, and others interested in educational television. All favored the request for educational reservations. Aside from that of CBS, adverse testimony by commercial interests was restrained.

Monitoring Study of Commercial Television

Concerned by the resistance offered by CBS as well as by the National Association of Broadcasters, Telford Taylor suggested that a log of current commercial programs be presented to the FCC to improve the JCET case. I. Keith Tyler, George Probst, and Richard Hull endorsed this suggestion and enlisted sociologist Donald Horton, of the University of Chicago, and Dallas Smythe, a research specialist from the University of Illinois. Horton and Smythe monitored seven New York City television stations for more than twelve hours a day, with the help of volunteers, from January 4-19, 1951.[5]

The results of this ordeal were eyestrain, recurrent headaches, a low opinion of commercial television, and some incriminating findings. Among the mass of findings was the significant fact that no time was given to educational programs as such; most of the so-called children's programs bore little or no relation to the tastes and needs of children. The monitoring study proved to be a milestone in television research. Similar studies were made in Chicago, Los Angeles, and New York City in subsequent years.

Second FCC Hearings on Educational Television

When the second hearings on educational television were resumed in Washington, D.C., on January 22, 1951, the findings of the monitoring study by the JCET were presented together with the results of a survey of television in the northeastern region of the United States.

Of a total of seventy-six witnesses testifying at the second hearing, seventy-one supported the educators' request. Five witnesses representing commercial television interests opposed the allocation of television channels for education, although admitting that television could be a potentially effective means of instruction.

Assignment of Educational Television Channels

In April 1952, the FCC issued its *Sixth Report and Order*, which reserved 242 television channels (80 VHF and 162 UHF) for educational use. Following this action, a series of important events took place in educational television. A number of states held state-wide conferences to arouse interest in activating these reserved channels. Committees were organized throughout the country to study the financial, programming, and engineering aspects of constructing television stations. Governors and legislatures took steps to investigate the instructional potential of television. Many national foundations became supporters of the educational television movement. The history of educational broadcasting in the United States had entered a new era.

The Allerton House Seminars

While the struggle for educational television reservations were taking place, two historic seminars were held in Allerton Park, Urbana, Illinois, during the summers of 1949 and 1950. These seminars bringing together the leaders in educational broadcasting were cosponsored by the Rockefeller Foundation and the University of Illinois Institute of Communications Research.[6] The primary purpose of these seminars was to discuss the purposes, goals, future, and needs of educational broadcasting in the United States. According to Robert B. Hudson, general chairman of the seminars:

> It seemed that suddenly a great truth had been revealed which had long haunted every man present but which had seldom escaped from deep in his subconscious— the truth that educational radio not only had a job to do, but it was capable of doing it. The sheer relief in getting at this matter was electrifying: the wall of repression, buttressed by years of rationalizations and expediencies, came tumbling down and educational radio, for the first time in its turbulent history, was on the move.[7]

Although the Allerton House seminars were primarily directed toward educational radio, discussions were expanded to include television and facsimile broadcasting as well. The first seminar created a sense of common mission and direction while the second seminar generated a sense of capability for programming.

Largely as a result of the Allerton House seminars, plans were presented at the 1950 NAEB convention for a permanent headquarters for the association's radio-tape network at the University of Illinois in Urbana. Six months later, the Kellogg Foundation provided a $245,000 grant to operate the network for its first five-year period.

The First Educational Television Stations

As early as 1945, Iowa State College (now University) in Ames applied to the FCC for a construction permit, and on February 21, 1950, WOI-TV became the first non-experimental educational station in the world. Richard Hull, the first director of WOI-TV, did not feel that an educational station had to be "noncommercial" and used the term *nonprofit* because this station operated on a commercial channel and carried commercials to help support its broadcasting activities.

The first educational television stations operating on channels reserved for education began in 1953. KUHT, jointly licensed by the University of Houston and the Houston Board of Education, became the first educational noncommercial station on May 12, 1953. The second station, KTHE, licensed to the University of Southern California, went on the air on November 29, 1953, but it went off permanently on September 11, 1954—the only educational station to fail thus far in the history of educational television.[8]

After the inauguration of the first stations in 1953, others followed at an accelerated pace. By mid-1955 sixteen channels had been activated. The first stations were in the major centers where noncommercial TV channels were available in the VHF spectrum. Among them were: WQED Channel 13 in Pittsburgh; KQED Channel 9 in San Francisco; WGBH Channel 2 in Boston; WTTW Channel 11 in Chicago—all on the air by the end of 1955. In other major metropolitan centers, the choice VHF channels already had been committed to commercial interests before the FCC freeze.[9]

Organizational Patterns of ETV Stations

Educational television stations have usually followed three basic organizational patterns. Following is a brief description of each plan, accompanied by a partial list of operating stations in the three categories.

Single-agency station provides that one educational institution is the licensee. The school board, college, or university that holds the license may be responsible for the financial aspects of the operation, but other educational and cultural groups may be members of an advisory board that handles station management and policy and also contributes financial support. Stations organized in this manner include:

Station	Channel	Agency	Location
KUAT	6	University of Arizona	Tucson, Ariz.
KRMA	6	Denver Public Schools, Licensee; Council for Educational Television	Denver, Colo.
WILL	12	University of Illinois	Champaign-Urbana, Ill.
KUON	12	University of Nebraska	Lincoln, Nebr.
WOSU	34	Ohio State University	Columbus, Ohio
WMVS	10	Milwaukee Board of Vocational and Adult Education	Milwaukee, Wis.

Community stations are usually licensed to a single organization such as a nonprofit association organized for this purpose by educational, civic, and cultural interests. The following are stations representative of this setup:

Station	Channel	Agency	Location
WQED	13	Metropolitan Pittsburgh Educational Television Station, Licensee	Pittsburgh, Pa.
WTTW	11	Chicago Educational Television Association, Licensee; Chicago Public Schools, area colleges & universities, and other cultural organizations	Chicago, Ill.
KCTS	9	University of Washington, Licensee; advisory board includes members from university, Seattle Pacific College, public schools, public library, King County School Directors Association	Seattle, Wash.
KETC	9	St. Louis Educational Television Commission, Licensee	St. Louis, Mo.
KQED	9	Bay Area Educational Television Association, Licensee	San Francisco, Calif.

State network stations are activated under a state-wide plan in which a state educational agency or a duly constituted TV authority is the licensee. ETV stations are generally planned as members of a network to be interconnected by microwave relay so that programming originating in one location can be supplied to other station outlets. Some of the stations in operation under this plan are:

Station	Channel	Agency	Location
WAIZ	2	Alabama Educational Television Commission	Andalusia, Ala.
WBIQ	10	Alabama Educational Television Commission	Birmingham, Ala.
WCIQ	7	Alabama Educational Television Commission	Munford, Ala.
KETA	13	Oklahoma Educational Television Authority	Oklahoma City, Okla.
KOED	11	Not licensed to OETA	Tulsa, Okla.
WUFT	5	Florida Educational Television Commission	Gainesville, Fla.
WJCT	7	Florida Educational Television Commission	Jacksonville, Fla.
WTHS	2	Florida Educational Television Commission	Miami, Fla.
WEDU	3	Florida Educational Television Commission	Tampa-St. Petersburg, Fla.[10]

Programming

Early educational programming did not generally keep pace with commercial television in gaining public acceptance. Many citizens were unaware that a local educational television station existed. One major reason for the slow public acceptance of educational television was probably the limited number of hours that educational television stations were on the air. What is more, educational television stations were usually off the air on weekends. Weekday schedules of many of the stations were often irregular. Some stations operated on split schedules, some offered daytime programs rotated with evening programs on alternate days, while others broadcast only in the mornings. Most stations offered regular program schedules during the 7-9 P.M. period, exclusive of weekends.

Programming for educational stations developed on a trial-and-error basis. Many stations began broadcasting without any plans for programs. In the early years of educational television, it was not unusual for stations to carry programs that had been put together a few hours before broadcast time. Staff and budget limitations often restricted the development of creative programming.

Sydney Head suggested that many of the prior assumptions concerning the limitations of commercial television programming as compared to educational television programming were probably fallacious. For example, he said that "commercial television does as good a job in handling controversy as noncommercial television—possibly a better job."[11] He said further "that ETV has created precious little that is genuinely new and exciting while commercial television has done a good deal in this direction."[12] Irving Gitlin, a commercial television producer, said that "unless educational television stations can find some way to produce on a regular basis, dramatic, artistic programs and series which will become a habit for most of television set owners in their communities, they will not get either the money or the loyalty they need."[13]

In the early days of educational television, Hudson pointed out the needed breakthrough in educational television programming as involving:

(1) trained staff personnel in adequate supply; (2) a faculty and performing artists assigned on a rotating basis and observers of the contemporary cultural and political scene; (3) studio and transmission and reception facilities and money with which to operate them in all major localities; (4) a nation-wide interconnected educational television network; and (5) a commitment by educators to use the television instrument as a tool of education.[14]

Personnel

The number of full-time personnel on educational television stations ranged from four to forty-seven with an average of about sixteen. Faced with this constant shortage of trained personnel, station managers usually depended on colleges and universities for free assistance or assigned students to specific station responsibilities. One of the primary problems was obtaining sufficiently trained broadcast engineers. Trained production personnel were drawn principally from the radio, theater, and motion picture fields. Some were graduates of colleges that offered work in radio, television, and films; others came with no particular experience and learned on the job. Television instructors on the faculties of colleges and universities, for the most part, failed to provide effective instruction in television because they, themselves, had not developed the necessary skills. Moreover, they were not always familiar with the theory and research relative to the communication and learning processes that were relevant to their teaching situation.

Financing

One of the most difficult problems of early educational television stations was obtaining adequate financial support. The majority of the stations were controlled by universities, colleges, public school systems, state legislatures, or other tax-supported bodies.

The greatest single source of revenue was the foundation grant. For example, during the decade 1955-1965, the Ford Foundation invested about $70 million in educational television. Another source of money (apart from tax money) was contracts for programs produced locally for national distribution. Another important source was voluntary contributions from the public in the form of member-subscribers.

In the mid-1950s when Station KQED, San Francisco, was threatened with extinction because of financial problems, station manager James Day conceived the idea of the first television auction to raise money. This first auction received national recognition because it was successful, largely due to Kim Novak's bed sheets. The movie actress donated the sheets to KQED's auction as a "gag" item. The sheets were purchased by a tie company, which then donated to the auction a large number of ties made from the sheets; the ties, in turn, became popular items. Auctions have since been held annually by a number of educational television stations. Gross revenues from such auctions have produced almost 3 percent of the total support provided to educational television.[15]

Although the educational television movement was aided by funds made available through the National Defense Act (NDEA) of 1958, the first direct allocation of federal funds was made in 1962 when President John F. Kennedy signed into law the Communications Act, which provided $32 million for the construction of educational television stations. (ETV stations also became eligible to receive donations of United States surplus property.) Despite the various sources of financial support that have developed through the years, adequate financing remains the perennial problem.

Educational Television Networks

Educators have consistently expressed the view that regional and national arrangements were essential for the production and sharing of programs. The first formal proposal for a national educational television network was made in 1952 at the Educational Television Programs Institute held at Pennsylvania State College (now University).[16]

The first state-wide educational television network was developed in Alabama in 1952. The purpose of the network was to raise the standard of instruction throughout the state, a goal most observers agree was successfully achieved. Alabama's first instructional network utilized five television stations, offering classes on the elementary and secondary level to some 158,000 students. Taken all together, at least six hundred schools made use of instructional telecasts in Alabama.

Other states developed state-wide network operations built around the state university system: Maine, Nebraska, New Hampshire, North Carolina, Oregon, Ohio, Pennsylvania, Vermont, Texas, Indiana, Georgia, Tennessee, and Kentucky. In addition, a series of six regional networks were formed.[17] Other stations, in California, Florida, Michigan, Minnesota, New York, North Dakota, Oklahoma, and Washington, were tied together with microwave links.

Emergence of Instructional Television

An important historical distinction must be made between the terms *educational television* and *instructional television*. *Educational television* usually has referred to any type of educational video program presented for any serious purpose, whether to teach something to someone or to develop a broad cultural understanding. *Instructional television* has referred to open- or closed-circuit video programs primarily designed to teach a specific body of subject matter as part of a formal course of study to particular groups of students in school or at home.

The first instructional applications of television occurred between 1932 and 1939 at the State University of Iowa. Following World War II, instructional television was initiated on commercial stations because educational stations were concerned at first with problems of financing, staffing, and developing programs for general adult use. By the mid-1950s, however, instructional television began to receive serious attention from educational broadcasters. By the 1960s almost every course in the public school, college, or university curriculum was being taught somewhere by either open- or closed-circuit television, on educational or commercial stations or in educational institutions.

Instructional Television on Commercial Stations

Some of the pioneer instructional telecasts begun in 1948 on commercial stations included those to the Philadelphia Public Schools by Martha Gable and her associates, the dynamic lectures on Shakespeare by Dr. Frank Baxter in Los Angeles, and the Johns Hopkins *Science Review.*

Probably the most ambitious instructional series broadcast on commercial stations has been NBC's *Continental Classroom*, begun in 1958. These televised courses have been offered for credit by various institutions of higher learning throughout the country, and have attracted large audiences in spite of early morning broadcasts.[18] Also, the programs have been taped, kinescoped, and distributed by NBC in cooperation with educational institutions and foundations.

Instructional Television on Educational Stations

Much of the impetus to instructional television on educational stations can be traced to the pioneer instructional broadcasting experiments in the cities of St. Louis, Pittsburgh, and Chicago, and in the state of Alabama.

The St. Louis Educational Commission and the St. Louis Public Schools made a joint proposal to the Fund for the Advancement of Education in the early 1950s to offer several courses exclusively over television. The pupils were to receive this instruction in groups of up to 150. Accordingly, in the fall of 1955, the St. Louis Public Schools began providing televised instruction over educational station KETC. Courses were offered in ninth-grade grammar and English composition for thirty minutes, five days a week. Lessons in second-grade spelling were telecast for two semesters in the spring and fall of 1956. The results of the St. Louis experiment showed that televised instruction could not be expected to carry the complete instructional burden and that a combination of televised instruction and follow-up instruction by classroom teachers was necessary.[19]

Another pioneer experimental television program series began in Pittsburgh, Pennsylvania, at the time the St. Louis experiment was undertaken. The purpose of the Pittsburgh experiment was to raise the quality of teaching by selecting outstanding teachers and freeing them from other duties to concentrate on the preparation of instructional television programs. Grade school and high school students viewed the resulting telecasts over educational station WQED. Their classes were of conventional size with their regular teachers in attendance; follow-up instruction was provided at the end of the telecasts.

Pittsburgh not only attempted to present superior teachers on television but also tried to offer courses that could not be given under conventional arrangements. For example, conversational French and Russian courses were telecast. In 1956, Harvey E. White of the

University of California developed a new high school physics course and presented it over WQED.[20] Televised instruction was given in fifth-grade arithmetic, reading, and social studies.

From the Pittsburgh experiment it was impossible to conclude which was superior— regular classroom teaching or televised teaching supplemented by classroom activity. The results showed, however, that the effectiveness of televised lessons depended to an important degree on the quality of the follow-up by classroom teachers.[21]

An impressive experiment was undertaken by the Chicago City Junior College in 1956. A final report on its first three years of experimental activity indicated that nine courses were taught each year on WTTW. The courses were purposely varied and included offerings in social science, physical science, literature, biology, English composition, mathematics, modern languages, and business. Students were screened and admitted in the usual way, but instead of attending classes they viewed telecasts at home and kept up with a prepared study guide. Written assignments were submitted and returned by mail. During the experimentation period, a total of about 5,000 students per semester registered, and about 65 percent of the students who enrolled for the television courses completed them. According to evaluations made, it was concluded that junior college courses can be taught as effectively by television as in the classroom.[22]

Closed-circuit Instructional Television

The best known and one of the most elaborate closed-circuit facilities in the United States was built as a result of a grant from the Ford Foundation in Washington County, Maryland, and started operations in 1956. Even before that time, the county board of education had planned the installation of television receivers in new schools to overcome some of the problems confronting them, chiefly, the lack of adequately trained teachers. Of 352 teachers in elementary schools, 97 had no bachelor's degree, and 75 had only emergency teaching certificates.

With the assistance of equipment manufacturers, six studios were provided with vidicon cameras, film projection facilities, and a videotape recorder. This made it possible to produce twenty-five instructional telecasts each day during a school week on such subjects as remedial reading, art, social studies, music, arithmetic, advanced mathematics, general science, United States history, English, French, biology, chemistry, and career guidance. As this closed-circuit system expanded, new courses were added until more than fifty were included in the television program.[23]

The telecasts were transmitted to the schools in Washington County from a television center adjacent to the board of education offices in Hagerstown, Maryland. By 1963, every public school in the county was linked to the television circuit.[24]

Another pioneer closed-circuit instructional television experiment began in 1954, with the aid of Ford Foundation funds, at Pennsylvania State University. Cameras were mounted in ordinary classrooms and connected by coaxial cable to other classrooms, where additional groups of students viewed the lessons. Other courses were offered by television only, and extensive experimentation was done with talk-back systems whereby the student could ask the instructor a question and get an immediate response. The original experiments indicated that the use of television did not seem to reduce the quality of instruction or lower student accomplishment. This experiment also demonstrated that once a closed-circuit system has been installed, a decreased cost of instruction per student can be realized if the system is used effectively.

Midwest Program of Airborne Television Instruction

A novel approach to instructional television is offered by the example of the Midwest Program of Airborne Television Instruction (MPATI), formed in 1959 by a group of Midwestern educators. Much of this project was carried out in conjunction with the Purdue Research Foundation at Purdue University.

First, MPATI recorded, with Ford Foundation funds, a comprehensive series of videotape lessons in various subject-matter areas on the elementary and secondary school levels. Then, through the resources of 15 educational television stations in a 6-state area, 34 courses were televised to approximately 2,000 schools and an estimated 400,000 students. In order to reach schools not served by these stations, MPATI developed a plan to transmit programs from an airplane circling about 23,000 feet over the north-central part of Indiana. Technical problems limited this phase of MPATI's operations, but the feasibility of this method of signal distribution over wide areas was clearly demonstrated.[25]

The first demonstration telecasts began in April 1961; complete programming started in September 1961. The system provided seventy-two half-hour television lessons in a five-hour day by broadcasting five separate programs simultaneously, four days a week, during the school year.

The cost of establishing MPATI exceeded $8 million. It was estimated that the maximum use of this system would demand about $10 million annually. When the Ford Foundation grant was terminated in 1966, MPATI was expected to be sustained largely by member schools in the years ahead, but by 1968 the airplanes came down for the last time. MPATI remained as a production and library organization for another three years. Finally, in 1971 the entire MPATI operation was incorporated into the Great Plains National Instructional Television Library in Lincoln, Nebraska.

Aside from financial problems, MPATI also had a number of technical problems. First, the project could not get the four to six permanent UHF channel assignments it requested from the FCC because, it was reasoned, this would keep other ground-based facilities from developing. Moreover, since MPATI succeeded in stimulating interest in instructional television throughout the six-state region, numerous stations were started. Many used their CCTV systems, and several schools began experimenting with Instructional Television Fixed Service (ITFS). Consequently, by the mid-1960s there was no longer a great need for the flying transmitter, partly because of the stimulus of the MPATI project itself.

Instructional Television in American Samoa

When H. Rex Lee was appointed governor of American Samoa in 1961, he determined almost immediately to attempt to upgrade the school system by means of instructional television. Governor Lee requested $40,000 from Congress for a "feasibility study" to determine whether his idea of using television was a valid one. Congressional approval was given and the governor chose the National Association of Educational Broadcasters (NAEB) to complete the study. Led by Vernon Bronson (executive consultant to NAEB), the study team visited Samoa late in 1961 and gave a report early the following year. Not surprisingly, the NAEB recommended making television the major form of instruction for the first six grades and a regular supplementary medium for the last six.[26]

Twenty-six new elementary schools were constructed and four new high schools were built. A complete modern television facility was built with four production studios and, ultimately, ten broadcast-quality videotape recorders. The instructional television program was inaugurated in October 1964 and television lessons began to be transmitted over six VHF channels.

Approximately thirty television teachers were brought from the U.S. mainland—along with producer-directors and complete production and engineering crews. The programs were designed so that the essence of every subject was taught at every elementary grade level. Most of the native Samoan teachers served to utilize and implement the television instruction. At its peak, the system was broadcasting up to sixty individual lessons per day. By 1974, it had been reduced to forty-five lessons per day. By 1976, the system was using only three broadcast channels and greater emphasis was being placed on community programming.

It was clear by 1980 that instructional television was not alive and well in Samoa. The station was still broadcasting approximately fifty-six hours a week of instructional television; however, practically none of the programming was new, but rather was reruns of old, locally produced programs, some as much as six to ten years old. Most significant, as Schramm et al. pointed out, "telecasts no longer provided the 'core of instruction' as they did when the project was fully operational. Direct instructional broadcasts were now limited to three subjects at the elementary level: oral English along with English sound drill; social studies; and language arts. Beyond that, television's classroom role had been largely reduced to that of a supplemental or enrichment service."[27]

In Samoa television had become more a means of adult entertainment than a medium of instruction. By the early 1970s, the three channels in Samoa were essentially extensions of U.S. commercial networks with some programs from public television, rather than a part of a broad educational program as had been originally planned. Schramm et al. conclude that the failure of instructional television in Samoa teaches several lessons. First, "it is essential for planners to keep in mind that content and method, more than signals, are going to determine whether ETV meets the educational goals set for it."[28] Second, "the Samoan experience demonstrated that television makes an impact on a school system apart from and beyond its contribution to student's learning."[29] One of the most important decisions

> is whether the television teacher or the classroom teacher is going to be in charge of classroom instruction, or how the responsibility is to be divided between them. Samoa went about as far as it is possible to go toward putting television in charge. The substance of the instruction was to be on television; the lesson plans were made in the studio; the classroom teachers were called follow-up teachers and assigned to follow the lesson plans designed to reinforce what was learned from television.[30]

Finally, Schramm et al. listed a series of ifs:

> If more time could have been taken with the original decision.

> If hardware preparation had not been permitted to outrun the planning and preparation of software.

> If there had been time to bring the classroom teachers in.

> If there had been time for a thorough meeting of minds with the community leaders on the goals of education.

> If the decision had been to introduce television one grade at a time, rather than in all subjects and all grades by the beginning of the second year.

> If there had been time to try out and test programs.

If there had been time to find out what changes were taking place in the classroom teachers in the first half-dozen years of the project, particularly in the first two or three years.

If there had been time to consider more carefully what might be the ultimate results of bringing in, with government money, a few American commercial network entertainment programs for evening broadcast.[31]

There were also some positive aspects of the Samoan experiment. Tests have shown that student performance in the elementary grades in the earlier years of the project showed improvement, but, unfortunately, standardized tests were not given at regular intervals during the first half-dozen years of the project. One of the more positive effects of this project could be seen in the Samoan teachers who, after two years of experience with television, were noticeably more confident and had higher aspirations. The Samoan experiment, indeed, illustrates what not to do, but it also provides a model of what might be done in other underdeveloped areas of the world if its mistakes are not repeated.

Development of Instructional Television Libraries

A 1960/61 milestone study undertaken by Jack McBride and W. C. Meierhenry of the University of Nebraska recommended the establishment of pilot regional centers and/or a national center for the distribution of recorded instructional television programs.[32] Subsequently, in early 1962, the National Instructional Television Library (NITL) was created with a Title VII NDEA grant from the U.S. Office of Education. NITL was first administered by the NETRC-NET (National Educational Television and Radio Center) in New York City, then by Indiana University, when it was moved to Bloomington in 1965 and renamed the National Center for School and College Television (NCSCT). At this time it became a project of the Indiana University Foundation. By 1970, it became self-supporting and changed its name to the National Instructional Television Center (NITC). The center continued to assess, duplicate, and distribute programs from various sources. In October 1973, NITC had become international in scope and was changed to the Agency for Instructional Television (AIT). It was established as a nonprofit agency governed by a board of sixteen directors appointed by the U.S. Council of Ministers of Education. The AIT absorbed all the staff and operations of the former NITC and established regional offices in Washington, D.C., Atlanta, Milwaukee, and San Francisco.

While NIT and AIT were developing, other regional and national instructional television production and distribution agencies were established. One of these was the Great Plains National (formerly Regional) Instructional Television Library (GPNITL) at the University of Nebraska. Formed originally as part of the tripartite National Instructional Television Library in 1962, GPNITL is today self-supporting and nationally distributes a variety of programs. In addition, GPNITL has been active in publishing relevant books about instructional television and in cosponsoring professional conferences and other projects with the Nebraska SUN (State University of Nebraska) project. This project was created in the early 1970s to provide televised instruction based on the model of the British Open University.

Pooled programs, cooperative financing, and production of instructional television programs grew rapidly. A number of national, regional, and state agreements were consummated including the videotape library of the ETS (Educational Television Stations) division of the NAEB, Midwest Educational Television, the Southern Educational Communications Association, and the Southwestern Indiana Educational Council. In addition, the Television Subgroup of the Committee on Institutional Cooperation of the Big Ten Universities and the

University of Chicago, the Council on Higher Educational Institutions in New York City, the Texas Educational Microwave Project and the Oregon State Higher Education System were cooperative program exchanges for instructional broadcasting.

Instructional Television Fixed Service (ITFS)

Shortly after the first educational television stations went on the air, it was apparent that single-channel open-circuit broadcasting could not meet all of the needs of education. In July 1963, the FCC established a new class of stations—Instructional Television Fixed Service in the 2,500-2,690 mHz angle of the electromagnetic spectrum. In the ITFS system any single licensee can apply for up to four different channels and also has the potential of making a multichannel service.

The first licensed stations went on the air in late 1964: Mineola (Long Island) and Parma, Ohio, school districts. By the early 1980s more than two hundred different licensees were operating about four hundred channels.

The Educational Television Movement and the Ford Foundation

The greatest single benefactor to the educational television movement was the Ford Foundation. Although one may question many of its educational television projects or doubt the value of much of its sponsored television research, the financial support and the dominant influence of the Ford Foundation expended more than $300 million for the national educational television movement.

The Ford Foundation created two separate funds, the Fund for Adult Education (FAE) and the Fund for the Advancement of Education (TFAE), each to work specifically in one area. The TFAE was concerned with problems and opportunities in formal education from elementary grades through college levels, while the FAE was active in the areas of education that were not part of formal schooling.

The Fund for Adult Education (FAE)

More than any other organization, the FAE provided the unifying impetus in the national education television movement. Although enthusiasts of educational television were scattered throughout the country, most educators and the general public were not awaiting its advent. What had been the dream of a few was caught by the FAE and transformed into an organized reality. Other agencies deserve credit for their contributions to national educational television, but the FAE uniquely mobilized latent forces at the precise historical moment of greatest opportunity.

The FAE was established in April 1951, with Ford Foundation financing, for the following purposes: (1) to create awareness of the major elements and issues of modern culture, (2) to develop concern with them, (3) to develop materials for their study, (4) to instigate activity in learning about them, and (5) to encourage association of adults in such activity. These also became the guiding principles in its vision of how television could serve an educational function.

The FAE was the first to recognize the needs of educational television, secure money for its support, and sustain it until the Fund for the Advancement of Education, in 1954, also became involved.

Early in 1951, Paul G. Hoffman, Robert Hutchins, and Chester Davis, the directorial triumvirate of the Ford Foundation, invited Cyril Scott Fletcher, president of Encyclopaedia Britannica Films, to serve as president of the new Fund for Adult Education. He assumed this position at the founding meeting on April 5, 1951.

The FAE established its first headquarters in Pasadena, California, with other offices in Chicago and New York City. Robert J. Blakely, an Iowa editorial writer, was in charge of the Midwest office; Delbert Clark (followed by John Osman) was in charge of East Coast activities. In mid-1951, Ann Campbell Spinney, an educational radio writer and educational administrator, joined the New York office, and a little later in the year the post of director for the mass media was given to G. H. Griffiths, an educational film producer. Fletcher, Griffiths, and Spinney, along with Robert Hudson, an early consultant, deserve most of the credit for developing national educational television during its formative years.

The FAE's policies on educational television did not develop immediately, although the question of educational broadcasting had been considered from the outset. There had been a request from the Ford Foundation that the FAE take over the problem of developing liberal adult education programs for the mass media. The first approach was a series of experimental programs known as *Omnibus*, produced by a television-radio workshop under the direction of Robert Saudek over a commercial television network. The *Omnibus* idea came from James Young, who had come to the Ford Foundation from the J. Walter Thompson advertising agency, as a mass media consultant. Young intended to develop a higher cultural level in commercial television by obtaining multiple sponsors who would have no control over program content. To Robert Hudson, a pioneer radio educator and also a consultant to the FAE, *Omnibus* was another example of the industry's misunderstanding of the nature of educational broadcasting. Saudek assiduously avoided associating the word *education* with the *Omnibus* programs, holding that it would be the kiss of death. After a few months of these telecasts, the FAE's board decided that *Omnibus* was cultural entertainment rather than educational television and gave the workshop back to the Ford Foundation.

The next question was how far the Ford Foundation was willing to go in providing the FAE with the necessary finances to support educational television. The FAE's funding grant for the mass media had been $3 million, supplemented periodically by such items as the $1.2 million of the television-radio workshop. Finally in 1956 the FAE received a five-year terminal grant of $17.5 million, which did not include the promotion of educational television. When the FAE finally grasped the full scope and meaning of educational television, it became clear that special grants would have to be made.

C. S. Fletcher originally asked the Ford Foundation for $5 million so that the FAE might assist in the construction and maintenance of educational television stations and develop a national program and distribution center. When Fletcher outlined his plans to the foundation trustees, they pointed out that Henry Ford preferred one elaborate model educational television station that would provide an outstanding example to others throughout the country. However, Fletcher himself convinced Ford that the FAE's plans were feasible and won approval. The FAE received $17.5 million (later supplemented by another $4 million) to develop its own policies for educational television.

From the beginning the FAE insisted that it should not hold a monopoly, but that other foundations should be involved in the development of national educational television. The FAE's policy was to provide financial assistance until a qualified group could be organized to administer a grant.

The FAE's first action in regard to educational television was to provide an emergency grant of $90,000 to the Joint Committee on Educational Television through the ACE. The Fund also gave early support to educational film production and to the development of new types of educational television programs by assisting such organizations as the NAEB and pioneer educational television stations. It created a national program center and a national organization to advance educational television. Finally, the FAE provided financial assistance for the development of educational television stations. Before the *Sixth Report and Order* of April 1952, these steps had all been taken and the basic decisions made regarding the future development of educational television.[33]

The Fund for the Advancement of Education (TFAE)[34]

Although this agency, first established in April 1951, was originally not highly concerned with educational television, it eventually became involved with a number of programs dealing with the effectiveness of instructional television. During the period 1954-1963, TFAE supported a variety of instructional approaches of teaching by television at different educational levels. These projects included the transmission of fifth-grade American history lessons by Montclair State College, New Jersey, to nearby schools; state-wide instructional television in Alabama; a major university program at Pennsylvania State University; the state-wide Texas experiment in a series of programs designed for teacher education institutions; the National Program in the Use of Television in the Public Schools, the county-wide, closed-circuit, in-school instructional program in Washington County, Maryland (Hagerstown); the city-wide junior college credit and degree courses in Chicago; the Midwest Program on Airborne Television Instruction; the "Continental Classroom," and many others.[35]

TFAE was formally ended in 1967. A year before, Murphy and Gross made the following judgment:

> After more than a decade of intensive effort and the expenditure of hundreds of millions of dollars, has television made a real impact on American schools and colleges? Has it made a worthwhile contribution to education? The short answer to such a sweeping question would probably have to be 'No.'... In short, TV is still far from fulfilling its obvious promise. Television is *in* education all right, but it is still not *of* education.[36]

There is no doubt, however, that TFAE made a noteworthy contribution by stimulating widespread interest in instructional television. The several projects sponsored by TFAE were of major significance for the future and their instructional television activity significantly influenced the passage of the Educational Television Facilities Act of 1962 and the Public Broadcasting Act of 1967.[37]

Founding of the Educational Television and Radio Center (ETRC)

The Educational Television and Radio Center, created in 1952 by the FAE, became the focal point of early educational television. The ETRC's functions were threefold: (1) to contract for the production of new programs; (2) to acquire completed films from other sources; and (3) to exchange programs among educational television stations. The primary historical heritage of the ETRC came from the experiences and concepts of educational radio of the 1920s and 1930s. It was recognized then that a central program center, for multiple stations not bound by an interconnected network, was indispensable.

A few months after the FCC had made reservations for educational television, the FAE assigned Robert Hudson, professor of the communications division at the University of Illinois, to explore the possibility of establishing a production and exchange center for the development of educational television and radio programs. Hudson wrote a twenty-four page memorandum, "The Educational Radio and Television Program Exchange Center," dated November 15, 1952, that became the working paper in the establishment of the ETRC.

The FAE made an operational grant to the ETRC of over $1 million through 1956, and a programming grant provided that at least $2.5 million be used "in the area of adult education in the liberal arts and sciences."[38]

Shortly after the founding of the center, an organizing committee was formed that consisted of George Stoddard, president of the University of Illinois; Robert Calkins, president of the Brookings Institution of Washington; Harold Lasswell, professor of law at Yale University; and Ralph Lowell, of the Lowell Institute of Boston; and C. Scott Fletcher, serving as president.

Early in 1953 the ETRC was physically located in Ann Arbor, Michigan, with Grant Leenhouts, an educational film producer, as consultant and acting executive. Harry K. Newburn, president of the University of Oregon, was selected as president in June 1953.

Because it was initially believed that theatrical, industrial, or educational film footage would provide needed resources for educational television, a project was established with the Film Council of America to evaluate hundreds of films for possible use on educational stations. It was soon discovered, however, that few films prepared for group viewing could be successfully adapted to the intimate demands of television. Moreover, there were almost insurmountable legal barriers in the clearance of most film material.[39]

The ETRC began its national educational (NET) program service in May 1954, by supplying five hours of programs per week to the four affiliated stations then operating. A large proportion of these early kinescopes was furnished by WOI-TV, Iowa State College. The Extended Services plan developed in 1954 made NET programs available, after the affiliated stations had shown them for broadcast, through educational institutions in cities where no educational television stations existed. In 1955, the NET Film Service, cooperatively planned with Indiana University, inaugurated a service whereby NET films became available for non-broadcast viewing in educational institutions. Meanwhile, regular and larger grants from the Ford Foundation made it possible for the center to implement its activities more effectively.[40]

Historic Changes: ETRC Becomes NETRC

Newburn resigned as president in September 1958. He was succeeded by John W. White, former vice-president of Western Reserve University, where he was instrumental in establishing the first credit telecourses in 1951. More recently, White had been general manager of the educational television station WQED, Pittsburgh. When White took office on October 1, 1958, the Ford Foundation grant had only fifteen months remaining. Within two weeks, White had prepared a plan that included: creating three new vice-presidential positions; establishing a station-relations department; hiring a permanent programming staff; relocating the major part of the center's activities to New York City; investigating the possibility of a Washington office; and actively seeking non-FAE funds. In January 1959, the word *national* was added to the center's title. The same day, the center requested a $5 million, five-year terminal grant from the Ford Foundation.

Within three years, White had tripled the size of the NETRC professional staff. He also established the division of network affairs, which included station relations, distribution, technical affairs, and the NETRC Washington office. Meanwhile, some of the station managers opposed and others defended the center's new policy for separating the objective of acquiring the highest quality programs affordable regardless of source from the objective of building the stations' ability to produce programs. This policy eventually produced a wide rift between the stations and the NETRC.

The Fourth Network Concept

Practically all of the center's activities from April 1959 until July 1963 were designed to make itself the "fourth network." One dramatic change was the introduction of "prime time" scheduling in September 1961. Moreover, the prime time plan permitted national promotion and publicity. However, not all of the affiliated station managers accepted White's concept of modeling a national ETV service after a commercial network.

In 1959-1960, Westinghouse gave the center the means to produce the series *Reading Out Loud*; the Humble Refining Company underwrote the distribution of the BBC Shakespeare cycle, *An Age of Kings*, in 1962, and Pyramid Books published study guides to accompany the series. In May 1960, White announced that the center had received from the Ford Foundation a supplemental grant of about $2.7 million for videotape recorders, $350,000 from Ampex Corporation for the same purpose, and $750,000 from the Minnesota Mining Corporation for videotapes. Meanwhile, the Ford Foundation allotted another $500,000 for support of the Broadcasting Foundation of America when it was taken over by the center. Another supporting grant of $350,000 came from the U.S. Office of Education.

An international division was established in the center in 1960 to bring about the exchange of programs with other countries. Production contracts were made with Canada, Great Britain, Australia, Yugoslavia, the USSR, France, Italy, and West Germany.

The suggestion of a "university of air" is embodied in the center's departmental divisions of programming into humanities, fine arts, science, social science, public affairs, and children's programs. This was supplemented by a television academic faculty concept. For example, Mme. Anne Slavk spent three years in Boston preparing and recording *Parlons Francais* for use in elementary schools; Professor Harvey White of the University of California spent a year in Pittsburgh broadcasting and recording a high school physics course and another year in New York City developing a graduate physics television course for teachers; John Dodds of Stanford University took a year off to work on *American Memoirs*; Huston Smith and Ralph Patrick of Washington University spent a semester preparing *Search for America*; and Professor Zechariah Chafee, Jr., of Harvard, spent the last year of his life broadcasting and recording his course on constitutional law.

In the humanities and the arts, aside from the productions of Shakespeare, Tolstoy, Ibsen, and Gorky, programs in the 1960s included a series on photography as a fine art, ballet programs, and symphony concerts. In American public affairs, there were such programs as *History of the Negro People, Metropolis,* and *Capitol Hill*. Also, science programs were enriched through collaboration with the NSF, Westinghouse Laboratories, the American Medical Association, the Public Health Service, and pharmaceutical companies.

Interconnection and Communications Satellites

In 1963, NETRC became NET—National Educational Television. At this juncture, NET was supplying ten hours of programming per week, including reruns. However, NET was a network in name only since there was no direct interconnection between the stations. Program distribution involved circulating programs on films or videotape by mail and it was therefore impossible for stations to show given programs simultaneously. Sometimes films and tapes got lost and showed up days after they were scheduled. A possible solution to this persistent problem came from an unexpected source in 1965 when ABC asked the FCC to construct a communications satellite for use in distributing its own programs and volunteered to provide a free channel to educational broadcasters. The FCC responded by inviting interested parties to comment on the broad question of the domestic use of satellite communications facilities by the broadcasting networks. Among the parties that responded were Comsat, AT&T and other communications common carriers, the commercial television networks, various federal agencies, and the Ford Foundation.

Fred Friendly (who became the Ford Foundation's advisor on educational television after his resignation from CBS) suggested an imaginative proposal that the Ford Foundation placed before the FCC in 1966.[41] The Ford Foundation proposed the creation of a nonprofit corporation that would own and operate satellite relay facilities for domestic use by commercial and noncommercial television broadcasters, with the commercial networks sharing the costs and NET getting the service free. Moreover, this proposal called for a built-in margin above operating costs to be used for programming funds for educational broadcasting. The foundation estimated that $30 million per year could be realized in this way, while commercial networks would be paying less than they had been paying AT&T for the use of land circuits. AT&T and Comsat immediately opposed the proposal, even though the three commercial networks endorsed it.[42] The Johnson administration and the educational broadcasters also supported the idea. It appeared that in a short time the entire television industry would shift to satellites, but this vision of the future came to nothing because of an unfortunate coincidence. President Lyndon Johnson had just arranged for the Carnegie Corporation to conduct a major study of educational television's future and everyone agreed that no decision should be made until the Carnegie study was completed.

As the Carnegie Commission was drafting its historic report, the Ford Foundation was turning its attention to other means of promoting educational television. In anticipation of the Carnegie's report calling for a network interconnection, the Ford Foundation decided to sponsor a demonstration project showing what interconnection could accomplish, announcing in December 1966 a $10 million appropriation to develop a Public Broadcast Laboratory.

A Major Turning Point for NET

The year 1967 brought a major transformation for NET, when it ceased to function as a primary distribution agency for educational television stations and shifted its focus to program production. This was in line with its objective to provide programming that would be suitable quality for a fourth network. As well, other agencies and systems were being formed to assume the responsibility for networking programs. John White decided to retire in 1968 and James Day, general manager of the innovative educational television station KQED, San Francisco, was selected as the new NET president. Under Day, NET continued to play a major role in the production of quality educational programming. Then in 1969, NET merged with WNDT (a New York City educational television station) so that they would have access to their own production studios. The new organization took WNDT's corporate name, the Educational Broadcasting Corporation (EBC), and EBC established two divisions—the national production center, still to be known as NET, and the station, which changed its call letters to WNET.

In 1969, historic changes occurred in the national educational television movement. The evolution of new institutions and new leadership as well as the development of new concepts of educational television produced unprecedented changes and political conflicts. The next section of this chapter is a discussion of these events.

The Public Broadcasting Act of 1967

The Carnegie Corporation established a Carnegie Commission on Educational Television in November 1965. The commission, chaired by MIT president James R. Killian, Jr., issued its report in January 1967. In essence, the Carnegie Commission recommended that educational television be transformed to "public television" and become something more than just educational or instructional. Toward this end, the commission recommended that the federal government establish an independent, nonprofit Corporation for Public Television that would receive money from the government and other sources and distribute these funds to individual stations and independent production centers like NET. The report also recommended approval of the Ford Foundation satellite proposal or one of the other alternative proposals by ABC or Comsat.

The Ford Foundation, the educational broadcasters, and President Johnson enthusiastically supported the Carnegie Commission's recommendations. President Johnson submitted his Public Broadcast Act to Congress in March 1967; the bill was signed into law on November 7, 1967.

The Public Broadcasting Act had three parts. Part one was an extension of the Educational Television Facilities Act of 1962, which authorized expenditures of $38 million for educational television and radio during the next three years. Part two established the Corporation for Public Broadcasting (CPB), which would be charged with assisting new stations in getting on the air, establishing one or more systems of interconnection, obtaining grants from federal or other sources, providing funds for program production, making grants to stations for local programming, and initiating research and training projects.[43] Part three authorized $500,000 for a comprehensive study of instructional television and radio.[44]

The Corporation for Public Broadcasting (CPB)

In his January 1968 budget message, President Johnson's appropriation of only $4 million for CPB was less than half of the $9 million authorized in the original act. Consequently, the creation of CPB was delayed until Congress finally appropriated $5 million for fiscal 1969. Meanwhile, the Carnegie Corporation, Ford Foundation, United Auto Workers, Communications Workers of America, the CBS television network, and others immediately donated several millions to help get CPB started.

Most of 1968 elapsed before a board of directors was complete. As chairman of the board, President Johnson appointed Frank Pace, former secretary of the army. In February 1969, the CPB board selected John W. Macy, former head of the U.S. Civil Service Commission, to serve as its president. Meanwhile, the CPB formed a skeleton staff in its Washington offices and began to plan for program grants and interconnection. During this period, the bulk of the programming and interconnection for the public television system was still being performed by the Ford Foundation through grants to NET. In fact, although the Ford Foundation had yielded leadership to CPB, it made more than $90 million of grants for public television between 1968 and 1972.[45]

In April 1969, CPB announced that it intended to create the Public Broadcasting Service (PBS), which would take responsibility for interconnection from NET; simultaneously, the Ford Foundation announced that it would end support for the Public Broadcast Laboratory.

The Public Broadcasting Service (PBS)

The Public Broadcasting Act of 1967 called for the CPB to arrange for some agency other than itself to perform interconnection. Since the Ford Foundation had ended its support for NET's networking efforts, the CPB established the Public Broadcasting Service in November 1969 to select and distribute programming to public television stations. The primary function of PBS was to help CPB and the Ford Foundation develop suitable programs among the major production centers, which PBS would then distribute by interconnection. PBS was not to produce programs and would be a station-operated interconnection. The station managers elected their own representatives to serve on the PBS board of directors; Hartford Gunn, Jr., general manager of the Boston public television station WGBH was chosen president of PBS in February 1970. PBS immediately took over interconnection responsibilities and began preparing a schedule of evening programming for the fall of 1970. Most of the PBS funds came from CPB, although the Ford Foundation granted $1.2 million in the first year.

The Founding of National Public Radio (NPR)

The scope of the Public Broadcasting Act of 1967 also covered radio, and it was logical that CPB should also establish a comparable public radio network. Just as NET had been passed over in favor of creating a new educational television network, so was the National Educational Radio (NER) division of the NAEB (which ran the bicycle network) passed over in favor of creating a new operation and a new concept for radio.

An interconnected NPR network was begun in May 1971. Unlike PBS, NPR was to produce programs as well as acquire them from other sources, particularly from member stations. NPR was funded by CPB. The NPR board consisted of twenty-five persons, twelve elected by member stations, twelve selected from the general public, and the NPR president. The first president was Donald N. Quayle, former executive director of the Eastern Educational Network.

CPB approached public radio in a different manner than public television. One reason is that the Land report, *The Hidden Medium: Educational Radio* did not propose a plan for developing educational radio by federal funds, whereas the Carnegie Commission report did provide such a plan.[46] CPB adopted the "Policy of Public Radio Assistance," which set the criteria for grants to individual stations and outlined a five-year development plan. In contrast to public television, educational radio stations were much less fearful of being dominated by the White House, Congress, or the CPB.

As the NPR became the dominant force in public radio activities, the NAEB discontinued both its television and radio operations and formed a new organization—the Association of Public Radio Stations (APRS) to handle some of the radio functions previously assumed by the NER.

Less than one-fifth of all noncommercial, nonprofit radio stations became members of NPR. NPR has traditionally programmed news, public affairs, art, music, and drama. The two most distinguished programs became *Morning Edition* and *All Things Considered*. Programs were fed to the stations from NPR headquarters in Washington, D.C., and individual stations sent programs and reports to NPR for national distribution.

In the early 1980s, the Reagan administration produced a financial crisis by proposing that federal funding for NPR be phased out. In response, NPR developed NPR Ventures in 1983, in an attempt to become financially independent. However, this effort, which involved joining with commercial partners in new business activities, proved to be unsuccessful and costly. NPR was saved from bankruptcy by a $9 million loan from CPB. NPR member stations agreed to pay $1.6 million annually for three years (1984-1986) to assist in paying back the loan. CPB forced NPR to assist in paying the loan by getting it to sell its satellite equipment as security in the event of a loan default. Meanwhile NPR's president and several NPR officers were forced to resign as a result of the financial crisis, and more than 140 NPR employees lost their jobs. Most of NPR's cultural and arts programs were lost, with the exception of classical and jazz music and the two programs *Morning Edition* and *All Things Considered*.[47]

By the early 1980s, it became clear that NPR would not continue to be the dominant noncommercial or public radio system. New public networks were beginning to develop an alternate programming that brought about increasing competition for program support.[48] It appeared that the principal threats to NPR in the 1980s would be the continued lack of funding and the incessant obstructionism of government bureaucracies. If NPR can survive these threats and maintain its existing structure, it has a good chance for the future.

Nixon and the Politics of Public Television

Just before President Johnson left office in January 1969, he recommended authorization of $20 million for CPB for fiscal 1970. In February, the new president, Richard Nixon, recommended only $10 million. Not until March 1970 did the White House and the Congress agree upon a compromise appropriation of $15 million. In September 1970, the White House and the Congress agreed upon an authorization of $35 million for the CPB for fiscal years 1971 and 1972. Consequently, in 1970, there was high optimism for the prospects of public television.

However, there were already some signs of conflict and frustration ahead.[49] In September 1970, President Nixon established the Office of Telecommunications Policy (OTP) and appointed Clay T. Whitehead as its director. Almost immediately, President Nixon and his OTP director began to include public broadcasting in their statements criticizing the lack of "fairness" in the news media's reporting concerning Nixon's handling of the Vietnam War and the domestic civil disorders. One of the direct attacks came in October 1970 when Whitehead complained to the NAEB at its convention that CPB and PBS had "over-centralized" public broadcasting, creating a "fourth network" and depriving stations of their autonomy. Moreover, he declared that public broadcasting had become captive of the "liberal Eastern establishment," as reflected in PBS news and public affairs programs. Then Whitehead made the threat that public broadcasting was doomed unless it changed such programming and gave more control to the individual stations.[50]

Meanwhile, the confrontation between the Nixon administration and public broadcasting was exacerbated by the establishment of the National Public Affairs Center for Television (NPACT) and the hiring of Sander Vanocur and Robert MacNeil in August 1971. NPACT was to provide the central control essential for national long-range planning and programming. NPACT's activities would focus on the coverage of important political events, congressional hearings, presidential addresses, and the upcoming 1972 campaign. NPACT's formation represented CPB, PBS, and the Ford Foundation's most decisive step away from the programming dominance of NET.[51]

From the outset, the Nixon administration saw the creation of NPACT as a threat and criticized the staff as "liberals," asserting that Vanocur and MacNeil and several CPB executives were paid excessive salaries.[52] They even complained about the rich interior decor in the CPB offices!

The Nixon administration attacks achieved their goal, making it increasingly difficult to obtain congressional support of public broadcasting, which began to generate internecine quarrels in the public broadcasting community. For example, Whitehead's speech skillfully exploited the television station managers' suspicions of national broadcasting agencies and ignited a debate of local versus national control. Another issue present but not openly discussed with the irritation still felt by NAEB and NET about being overlooked when public television was first organized. In addition, PBS was annoyed at being held responsible for programming when they had no say about what programs would receive federal or foundation dollars. One illustration of the problem of programming occurred when PBS decided on one occasion to refuse to carry "The Politics—and Humor—of Woody Allen," which included a half-hour satire on President Nixon. This assertion of control disturbed CPB because they considered themselves the sole arbiter of what should be distributed over PBS. Meanwhile, even within the CPB there was not complete harmony. Pace and Macy, who had been appointed by President Johnson, were beginning to have trouble working with a board that was increasingly being filled with Nixon appointees.

On June 22, 1972, Congress sent to the White House a bill authorizing an appropriation for the CPB of $155 million for two years ($65 million for 1973, and $90 million for 1974). On June 30, Nixon vetoed the bill on the grounds that "an organization, originally intended to serve the local stations, is becoming instead the center of power and the focal point of control for the entire public broadcasting system." He asked Congress to enact a one-year extension of the corporation's authorization and to provide it with $45 million. Congress did not override the veto.[53]

After the veto, the president and chairman of CPB promptly resigned in protest, as did a number of other public broadcasting officials. President Nixon just as promptly filled the vacancies with his own people. However, he underestimated his appointment of Thomas B. Curtis, a former congressman from St. Louis, as chairman of the CPB board. Curtis selected Henry Loomis, deputy director of the U.S. Information Agency, to succeed Macy as CPB president. Curtis and Loomis immediately began to take over from PBS the program planning and scheduling process of the public television interconnection, relegating PBS to the status of a bookkeeper in charge of interconnection. The first step was for the two agencies to negotiate an agreement. PBS officials angrily charged that CPB was undermining the entire public broadcasting system. On the other hand, some of the station managers were denouncing both CPB and PBS. They criticized CPB for knuckling under to the Nixon administration and forcing the cancellation of the public affairs programs while they took offense at PBS for arbitrarily choosing what programs to send and when to send them. Meanwhile, CPB and PBS were drafting position papers, each side claiming responsibility for national program-making decisions.

When it became obvious that OTP would not be submitting a long-range funding bill to Congress, the chairman of the House Subcommittee on Communications and Power, Torbert Macdonald, introduced a bill providing for five-year funding of public broadcasting at levels approximating the recommendations of the Carnegie Commission. After a series of hearings, in the summer of 1972 both the House and Senate voted for it by overwhelming margins (254 to 69 and 82 to 1). Whitehead assured both broadcasters and congressmen that Nixon would sign the bill, but without warning, Nixon vetoed the bill and repeated his concern that localism was being undermined by both CPB and PBS.

Meanwhile, as the CPB-PBS feud continued, it was clear there was a need for a strategy to restructure these two organizations. With the help of a Ford Foundation grant and through organizational work by the Educational Television Stations division of the NAEB, the National Coordinating Committee of Governing Board Chairmen of public television stations was formed with Ralph B. Rogers (chairman of the board of the Dallas public television station KERA and formerly an executive of Texas Instruments) as its chairman. The object of this committee was to bring together the station managers, representatives of the NAEB, and others who saw a threat to public broadcasting. This ad hoc group developed an entirely new structure for PBS and created a new entity, the Station Program Cooperative (SPC). The basic idea of the SPC was that stations should control the acquisition of programs and decide which programs they are willing and able to buy, using the funds they had received or expected to receive from the CPB, foundations, or local contributors.

President Nixon's veto accelerated two developments within PBS. The first was what PBS president Hartford Gunn, Jr., called a "market plan"—a plan that enabled local stations to select and fund national programs. A second development was a plan that called for long-term federal financing. Unfortunately, contradictory public statements by CPB, PBS, NAEB, and the National Coordinating Committee of Governing Board Chairmen gave the negative impression to Congress and the American people that public broadcasting was in complete disarray.[54] CPB attempted to solve this impasse by making it clear that an accommodation was possible if only the differences could be resolved. Avery and Pepper have described in detail the many careful steps that had to be taken before a resolution could be reached.[55]

In the meantime, on March 30, 1973, PBS was reborn. By a 124 to 1 margin the public television licensees voted to be represented by the new Public Broadcasting Service. The new organization included what had previously been PBS, ETS, and the Governing Board Chairmen's coordinating committee. Two separate boards, a twenty-five member laymen's group of station board members and a twenty-one member professional group of station managers, would work together to govern the new PBS. As a result of this reorganization, the new PBS *was* the stations rather than the *representative* of the stations.

Finally, the feud between CPB and PBS officially ended in May 1973 when a joint resolution, accepted by the CPB and PBS boards, left the decision on CPB-funded programs to the CPB program department but provided a way for PBS to dissent. The significance of the May joint resolution is best summed up by James Killian:

> When the history of the Corporation for Public Broadcasting is written 1973 will be remembered for its new focus and the renewed strength that has emerged.
>
> The new focus of the Corporation comes out of a long dispute that ended in a landmark partnership agreement with the Public Broadcasting Service representing the local noncommercial television stations. Under this agreement ... an increased portion of CPB's funding will flow to the individual stations.[56]

After the CPB-PBS compromise and the rapid descent of President Nixon during the Watergate scandal, there was an end to the organized attack on public broadcasting.[57] Even so, Tom Curtis, chairman of the CPB board of directors, resigned in protest of the Nixon administration's constant interference, and James R. Killian, Jr., who had chaired the Carnegie Commission on Educational Television, succeeded Curtis as chairman. The Senate appropriated funds for public broadcasting for two years and for educational broadcasting facilities for five years. The bill passed the House with minor changes and, this time, it was signed by President Nixon in August 1973. Thus ended the first significant threat to public broadcasting.[58]

The Aftermath of the Nixon Years

In July 1974, the Office of Telecommunications Policy along with CPB, PBS, and NPR prepared a proposal for long-term funding of public broadcasting. President Ford submitted an authorization bill to Congress in mid-1974 that provided for an initial $70 million, increasing to a final $100 million by 1981. After a year and a half of debate, the Public Broadcasting Financing Act of 1975 was signed into law on the last day of 1975. However, the battle for five-year funding was lost and CPB had to continue to go to Congress each year for additional funds. Implicit in the failure to secure automatic appropriations was the lingering threat that the administration or Congress could reduce or withhold funding whenever CPB-PBS programming was seen as too liberal or too controversial.

With Nixon gone, the issue of how to balance local and national priorities still remained. Public broadcasting was still sensitive to the threats of the Nixon years and emphasis was placed on the safe and the noncontroversial in news and public affairs. As a consequence, through the 1970s adventuresomeness and forthright journalism became a rare commodity. In recognition that all was not well with public broadcasting, James R. Killian, Jr., upon resigning from the CPB board in January 1975, suggested the need for another Carnegie-type study of public broadcasting. A second Carnegie Commission was formed in 1977 to examine what had happened in the ten years since the first commission had issued its report and to make recommendations for the future of public broadcasting. "What public broadcasting tried to invent," reported Carnegie II, "was a truly radical idea: an instrument of mass communication that simultaneously respects the artistry of the individuals who create programs, the needs of the public that form the audience, and the forces of political power that supply the resources. Sadly, we conclude that the invention did not work, or at least not very well."[59] The second Carnegie Commission declared that the only way to shield public broadcasting from political pressure was to have a Public Telecommunications trust that would be more independent of government than the CPB. The Carnegie Commission concluded that the events of 1971-1973 "slowed the growth of public broadcasting and left a psychological scar on the stations—an enhanced sensitivity to perceived threats to their independence—which persists today."[60]

On October 6, 1977, President Jimmy Carter submitted to Congress proposals "to strengthen our public broadcasting system and to insulate it from political manipulation."[61] He proposed a renewal of the five-year authorization measure from fiscal 1981 to fiscal 1985, and a five-year authorization for CPB—$180 million in 1981, and $200 million in each of the four succeeding years. He also proposed $30 million annually in fiscal 1979 and 1980 for facilities, and $1 million in fiscal 1979 for telecommunications demonstration projects. The House and Senate Conference Committee modified Carter's proposal so that it authorized appropriations for CPB for only three years—fiscal 1981, 1982, and 1983—and authorized $40 million for the facilities program for each of the fiscal years 1979, 1980, and 1981. The act was passed by Congress and President Carter signed it into law in October 1978. The reduced amounts appropriated by Congress were a direct result of the report and recommendations of the Carnegie Commission and the House and Senate bills to revise the Communications Act of 1934.

One of the features of the Public Telecommunications Financing Act of 1978 that provoked considerable criticism was the restrictions it placed on the freedom of the public broadcasting system to manage its own affairs. These restrictions included a limit on the salaries that CPB, PBS, and NPR could pay its employees; the requirement of open meetings by the governing boards of CPB, PBS, NPR, and the stations; and the requirement that public telecommunications entities other than public broadcasting have access to satellite interconnection. Moreover, certain members of Congress were concerned about the trend toward too much central control in the public television system. These pungent criticisms did not only have implications for PBS, but for NPR, which in 1977 merged with the Association of Public Radio Stations (APRS) and became like PBS, both an agency for interconnection and a trade association. Thus, it was clear that the negative influence of the Nixon years was still being felt in public broadcasting.

The PBS Satellite System

In 1976, PBS announced a new plan to transmit its programs via Westar, a domestic communications satellite that had been launched by Western Union in 1974. Huge loans had been obtained and construction of ground stations in the southeastern United States was completed by February 1978; the use of AT&T lines in that area was discontinued. By 1980, the PBS satellite system was complete and in operation.

In assessing this system, Blakely has noted these sobering facts:

> First, although the system has the capability for multichannel distribution, that expanded capability ends at the station: a broadcasting schedule of sixteen hours a day will not likely be extended because the range of program choice is wider. Second, although the system has the capacity of multiprogram distribution, the cost of producing extra programs will not be provided or reduced by the mere fact of satellite interconnection. Third, by opening up the capability of providing many more public services by and for many more noncommercial and/or nonprofit groups—through various methods of ground distribution from the satellite terminals, including multichannel cable systems—public broadcasting has opened also a Pandora's box of competition. Because the increased capability for more and wider public services are needed and welcome, public broadcasting will inevitably face increased competition for support from both tax-based and private sources at all levels.[62]

Although the immediate future of public broadcasting appears secure since Congress now appropriates funds for CPB and for public broadcasting facilities construction on a three- to five-year basis, the future may threaten public broadcasting again when the whole concept of broadcasting or distributing television signals becomes obsolete in the face of cable.

PBS Programming Philosophy and Practice

There has been a debate concerning programming content since educational television first began. One point of view defines *educational* in terms of instruction while others define *educational* in the broadest possible sense. The Carnegie Commission on Educational Television introduced the term *public television* in 1967 because the commission felt that the word *educational* would be an impediment to the support of television for noncommercial purposes. As a result, a distinction has been erected between instructional television and public television—a distinction that has transformed the original concept of educational television.

Today public television has become more like a commercial fourth network, and has adopted much of the commercial program philosophy. For example, the original philosophy that guided the programming service of educational television was: "Foremost ... an educational television program must in fact be educational ... it must effect changes in the viewer of an educational nature."[63] The goal, as Blakely has pointed out, was "to achieve desired effects from programs rather than to attract large audiences."[64] Clearly, public television has changed this view and PBS programmers have become primarily concerned with maximizing audiences, programming what appears to be most "popular" and attempting to compete with commercial networks. PBS programmers have also resorted to studying national Nielsen data and have tried to avoid placing certain programs against a hit series in the commercial schedules.[65]

The most important source of PBS programs is the Station Program Cooperative (SPC) that went into effect in 1974. Although this approach was a cumbersome and time-consuming procedure when it began, it has proved to be quite successful. PBS funds and manages the SPC, in which most stations participate. Representatives of the stations meet every October at the PBS Program Fair to screen programs submitted by stations and independent producers. Suitable and affordable programs are selected for which the stations pay and which become part of the program schedule for the next season. This system tends to bypass untried programs, programs that may be perceived as too controversial, or those that appear unattractive to general audiences. The predictable choices are the long-running series that continue from year to year.

Most programs that PBS distributes are not bound by any set of programming priorities or policies. Essentially, PBS produces what the various funders are willing to fund. Those programs that are funded and become a part of the PBS national schedule do not reflect any particular philosophy or set of objectives. In other words, there is no guiding philosophy or organized educational plan in public broadcasting.[66]

Developments in Instructional Television

The development of public broadcasting has produced an increasing separation from instructional television as it was originally conceived. For example, Bronson has stated that the CPB approach "indicates a questionable bureaucratic concern with directing social change rather than in promoting the development of educational broadcasting."[67] Meanwhile, instructional television has not been particularly successful. Since instructional television was initially seen as a money saver and a panacea for the teacher shortage and crowded classrooms of the 1950s and 1960s, it was not expected to require radical organizational changes or the extent of financial support needed to sustain its use. Moreover, the utilization of local talent and materials "displayed in public what had heretofore gone on behind too many closed classroom doors as uninspired teaching."[68] Koerner and others have noted that instructional television has been a disappointment and some have even used such terms as "disaster" and "enormous failure."[69]

One of the most detailed of the media use studies in the 1970s was conducted by Dirr and Pedone.[70] They surveyed carefully drawn samples totaling almost 6,500 superintendents, principals, and teachers of elementary and secondary schools. They found that 72 percent had instructional television programming available to them, but only 59 percent used it to some degree and about 46 percent used at least one series regularly. Elementary school teachers used instructional television almost twice as much as secondary school teachers. Interestingly, about one quarter of the teachers mentioned commercial station programming as a source of educational materials; cable television was mentioned by 15 percent; and ITFS was mentioned by only 3 percent. School districts, on the average, reported expenditures of only $3.27 per student per year in support of instructional television. Also, only one-third of the respondents in this study reported seeing at least one instructional television program during a four-week period.

By the 1980s, more than one hundred of the nation's noncommercial television stations were part of state networks operated by broadcasting agencies in some twenty-three states. Most of them were first authorized to provide instructional television for the schoolchildren of each state. State networks such as those in South Carolina, Maryland, Kentucky, Nebraska, and Iowa have been active in the production and distribution of instructional television programs for primary and secondary grades on up to graduate degree courses.[71] Also, some local school systems have utilized noncommercial stations for purposes of instructional broadcasts, but by the 1980s, only fourteen of these school licenses remained.

Educational uses of broadcast television began a new era in reaching mass audiences when *Sesame Street* first went on the air in 1971. Developed by the Children's Television Workshop (CTW) with funding primarily from the U.S. Office of Education and the CPB, its purpose was to teach children of ages three to five years basic skills such as recognition of letters and numbers. The program proved to be an immediate success and has consisted of 130 one-hour shows that have been partially revised each year.

Based on the success of *Sesame Street* CTW introduced *The Electric Company* in 1973 to teach basic concepts and reading skills. In 1980, the *3-2-1 Contact* series was introduced to teach basic skills in science. These programs are reportedly viewed in about half of the nation's homes where there are children under the age of six, and also in at least 30 percent of the elementary schools in the country.

The success of CTW and, more specifically, that of *Sesame Street*, is not recognized in all quarters, not even by those who had a hand in developing it. In his 1974 book *Children and Television*, Lesser, one of the principal creators of the program, expresses doubts and reservations about the value of *Sesame Street* and discusses CTW's "failure to create a movement toward general improvement in the quality of children's programs."[72]

Instructional television in most schools of the United States involves the use of the local PBS station's instructional programs. Typically, classes view *The Electric Company* or even *Sesame Street*. The local PBS station does not schedule a particular program at times when it would be most convenient for the teacher to utilize it for classroom activities and, therefore, the program must be turned on when it is being broadcast.[73] If the school district is financially able to provide an alternative in an ITFS system, two to four channels of instructional programming each day may be possible. However, to date, very few school districts utilized this form of broadcasting.[74] Meanwhile, the rapid growth of cable television has created an alternative to ITFS and may be used extensively in the future.

During the decade of the 1980s, one major application of educational broadcasting was the joint project of the CPB and the Annenberg School of Communications at the University of Pennsylvania. Its stated purpose was to prepare "college credit courses to be offered through radio and television and other telecommunications media." Beginning in 1981, an Annenberg donation of $150 million, at the rate of $10 million a year spread over fifteen years, has the potential of producing an impact similar to that of Britain's Open University.

Another important development was the establishment of the PBS Adult Learning Service in the fall of 1980. This service provides college credit courses via television to adults throughout the United States and was founded on the concept of a partnership among PBS, local television stations, and the local colleges and universities. In 1983/84, over 100,000 students were enrolled.

Experimental Communications Satellites

Several educational uses have been made of experimental communications satellites in recent years. The first of these, the ATS-1, was launched by NASA in December 1966. It had no video capability, but it was utilized for educational purposes by the University of Hawaii in 1971 in what was called PEACESAT (Pan Pacific Educational and Communication Experiments by Satellite). A more powerful version of the ATS-1, the ATS-6, was launched (also by NASA) in May 1974. The ATS-6 had video capability and was used for a series of six health and education experiments in rural areas of the United States (the Rocky Mountain region and Appalachia and Alaska). ATS-6 was not originally designed for educational purposes, but it did provide a model for designers and engineers for future instructional use of communications satellites.

Instructional Cable Television

Although educational programming is part of a number of cable services, the Appalachian Community Service Network, now called The Learning Channel, is the only network to date that has concentrated on instructional cable television. It offers sixty-four hours per week of college credit courses, adult education programs, seminars, and community-interest programming to over 4.5 million homes on about 500 cable systems, largely in the Appalachian mountain regions of Ohio, Kentucky, and Pennsylvania.

The Enigma of Instructional Television

Friedlander has stated, "whether or not instructional television in American schools and colleges is in trouble depends a great deal on how one is inclined to see things."[75] One view is that expressed by Gordon:

> Ever since Comenius and probably before, there has been no shortage of clowns, mountebanks, jugglers and recreation directors who have thoroughly convinced themselves that, given the opportunity, they would turn out to be entirely competent to teach anything to anybody better than professional teachers. After all, they know how to sell snake oil on the midway, don't they? Well, kid, why not sell education in the same way....

> It was inevitable that instructional video could not survive the success of Sesame Street. For far more complex reasons ... neither could it survive the media hype that attended Sir Kenneth Clark's "Civilization" and Jacob Bronowski's "The Ascent of Man."

... Clark and Bronowski were responsible for two series of really fine television programs. But they were—and are—in the end, television programs, not ITV. I know a clutch of cultural illiterates who enjoyed them both, but I doubt that any fundamental educational change resulted in them from the experiences.

Ill-conceived as educational communications (but superbly conceived as serious, inspirational home entertainments), they seem to have left our educational landscape pretty much the same as it was before they came. Ditto Sesame Street. All have probably given dreary lives a bit more color than they had. But asks the professional teacher, have they dispelled the educational miasma that foredooms formal basic education in the ghettos? Have they helped lead older minds to directed, disciplined inquiry into the past, present or future? Have they even exerted cultural forces comparable to yesterday's Chautauqua lecturers, or Sunday sermons? Once the testimonials quieted down, what have they, what could they accomplish?[76]

Berkman contends that instructional television is a medium whose future has passed. He says:

If ITV ever did have a chance to take off, it was in the late 1950's through the mid 1960's. This was the era of the teacher and physical plant shortages, and of the mythic Crisis in Education.

... it was also the era of when the Ford Foundation put some $25 million into proving the worth of instructional television through the National Program for the Use of Television in the Public Schools.... I defy anybody to show me where this multi-megabuck-backed experiment—by far the largest ever in American education—rates even a footnote in the education texts. If, given these conditions ... ITV couldn't make it back then, why do we think that the time when ITV will play even a minor role in formal learning is only a short time away?[77]

Rockman, on the other hand, considers instructional television to be alive and well. He says:

Quality programs are increasingly available, although merely broadcasting them is not going to stimulate the acquisition of television sets or their use. If enough quality instructional television series are available and, more important, are desired by the schools for use in the schools, then instructional television will become another major instructional resource, like textbooks, and will be solidly incorporated into the educational system.[78]

Finally, a more recent analysis by Tucker pinpoints the major problems of instructional television. He observes:

notwithstanding the efforts of many able and dedicated people and the many creative projects of significant value, the application of telecommunications technology to education since World War II has warranted at best a footnote to the history of education in that period.

... Telecommunications has tended to be used only when someone else (usually the federal government) has been willing to foot all or most of the bill and only for so long as that external support has been provided. And, as a funding priority, telecommunications has not been high on educators' lists.[79]

When the final chapter of the history of instructional television is written, it may be that, like the slide, film, radio, and teaching machine, television as an instructional medium will fall into general disuse.

Notes

[1]Carnegie Commission, *Television: A Program for Action*. New York: Bantam, 1967, 1.

[2]David Hawkridge and John Robinson, *Organizing Educational Broadcasting*. London: UNESCO Press, 1982, 25.

[3]Frieda Barkin Hennock was the first woman member of the FCC. Brought to the 1948 Institute of Education by Radio by Clifford Durr (whom she succeeded as commissioner), she knew little about broadcasting at first but learned rapidly. She saw the issue of reserved television channels for education as a means of increasing competition and public responsibility in broadcasting. She had a vision of a national educational television system and played a significant role in the movement toward educational television.

[4]Testimony of U.S. Commissioner of Education Earl J. McGrath before the FCC on November 27, 1950. Docket nos. 8736, 8975, and 8976.

[5]Dallas W. Smythe and Donald Horton, *New York Television*, January 4-19, 1951. Monitoring Study 1, NAEB, 1951.

[6]The Rockefeller Foundation has had a beneficial role in the early history of educational broadcasting. For example, the General Education Board of the foundation made grants for research to the Office of Radio Research at Columbia University and the Bureau of Educational Research at Ohio State University. Robert B. Hudson was trained under a Rockefeller grant before becoming director of the Rocky Mountain Radio Council. Carl Menzer, WSUI, University of Iowa, received a Rockefeller grant. Ralph Steetle became involved in educational broadcasting as a result of a Rockefeller fellowship. Harold McCarty studied broadcasting in Great Britain in the fall of 1935 under a Rockefeller grant. Charles Siepmann, director of talks and latest director of regional planning for BBC came to the United States on a Rockefeller grant and later emigrated to this country.

[7]Robert B. Hudson, "Allerton House 1949, 1950," *Hollywood Quarterly* 5 (1950-1951), 238-39.

[8]KTHE experienced the problems that many early educational television stations faced. With the pressure of commercial broadcasters for VHF channels, a number of valuable VHF channels were lost to commercial interests. The sole support of KTHE was a grant from the Hancock Foundation, and funds were cut off when Hancock resigned as head of the foundation. However, KCET Channel 28, Los Angeles, reinstated educational television in Los Angeles on September 28, 1964. The station was licensed to Community Television of Southern California.

[9]For a detailed history of some of the pioneering educational television stations, see John Walker, *Channels of Learning*. Washington, D.C.: Public Affairs Press, 1962.

[10]Philip Lewis, *Educational Television Guidebook*. New York: McGraw-Hill, 1961, 28-29.

[11]Sydney W. Head, "A Friendly Critic on ETV Programs," in *Educational Television the Next Ten Years*. Stanford, Calif.: Institute for Communication Research, Stanford University, 1962, 126.

[12]Ibid., 129.

[13]Irving Gitlin, "A Commercial Broadcaster on ETV Programs," in ibid., 138.

[14]Robert B. Hudson, "How the National Program Center Sees the Outlook," in ibid., 153.

[15]Stations also have periodic "pledge nights" when volunteers man telephones on camera to receive membership pledges. Another device is to cancel pledge nights if sufficient money is received to make subscription goals.

[16]The Television Programs Institute at Pennsylvania State College, April 21-24, 1952, was called by the ACE at the inducement of the Fund for Adult Education. The institute was attended by 116 leaders in education. Significant developments were made in proposals and plans for a national citizens committee to supplement the JCET, for a scheme of financial aid for bringing stations into being, and for a national center for the exchange and distribution of programs. One of the immediate effects of the Pennsylvania State Institute was the stimulation of other regional conferences in states across the country.

[17]The first regional network (established in 1960), the Eastern Educational Network (EEN) served as the prototype for the regional networks which were developed later. EEN included more than forty stations in ten states, from Maine to Virginia and inland to Pennsylvania. The second regional network, Midwestern Educational Television (MET) was established in 1961 with ten affiliates in the Minnesota-North Dakota—South Dakota area. The Southern Communications Association (SECA) was formed in 1967 and includes more than fifty stations in more than a dozen states, from Maryland and West Virginia and west to Texas and Arkansas. The Central Educational Network (CEN) was also founded in 1967 as a counterpart to EEN. More than thirty stations in a dozen states were included in the Chicago-based network. The Western Educational Network (WEN) has existed since 1968 and involved more than twenty stations, from Alaska and Hawaii inland to New Mexico, Utah, and Idaho. Finally, the Rocky Mountain Public Broadcasting Network (RMPBN) was established in 1969 and consisted of ten stations in five states: Colorado, New Mexico, Arizona, Utah, and Idaho.

[18]A similar early college credit series has been *Sunrise Semester*, presented by New York University and produced and distributed by CBS.

[19]See Early G. Herringhaus, *An Investigation of Television Teaching.* St. Louis, Mo.: St. Louis Public Schools, 1957.

[20]EBF filmed White's entire physics course of 162 half-hour lessons in both color and black-and-white. This series was offered to any school or school system for use as a film or television presentation. It had an important influence on the initiation of the *Continental Classroom* national television series.

[21]*Teaching by Television*, a report from the Ford Foundation and the Fund for the Advancement of Education. New York: Ford Foundation, 1959, 37-39.

[22]Clifford G. Erickson and Hyman M. Chausow, *Chicago's TV College.* Chicago: Chicago Junior College, August 1960.

[23]During the 1956-1961 period, a study known as the Washington County Closed-Circuit Educational Television Project was conducted. Details of this study are discussed in chapter 15.

[24]See Washington County Board of Education, *Washington County Closed-Circuit Television Report.* Hagerstown, Md.: Ford Foundation, 1963.

[25]The technique of rebroadcasting television signals from aircraft was first developed by Charles E. Nobles, an engineer in the Westinghouse Baltimore laboratory, in 1944.

[26]Wilbur Schramm et al., *Bold Experiment.* Stanford, Calif.: Stanford University Press, 1981.

[27]Ibid., 184-85.

[28]Ibid., 187.

[29]Ibid., 188.

[30]Ibid., 189.

[31]Ibid., 193-97.

[32]Jack McBride and W. C. Meierhenry, *Final Report of the Study of the Use of In-School Telecast Materials Leading to Recommendations as to Their Distribution and Exchange.* Lincoln, Nebr.: U.S. Office of Education, 1961.

[33]Renata von Stoephasius and Judith Murphy, *Decade of Experiment.* New York: FAE, 1961.

[34]To distinguish the Fund for the Advancement of Education from the Fund of Adult Education, TFAE was used for the Fund for the Advancement of Education and FAE for the Fund of Adult Education.

[35]The "Continental Classroom," a nation-wide college course by television, began in 1958, with most of the costs being underwritten by TFAE, over more than 150 NBC outlets. The original purpose was to bring high school teachers up to date in their subjects by exposing them to current developments and to distinguished scientists and scholars. The program was designed so that any college or university in the United States could utilize the program for credit purposes. The program was discontinued in 1961 after it achieved an impressive record of participating colleges and active viewers.

[36]Judith Murphy and Ronald Gross, *Learning by Television.* New York: TFAE, 1966, 9.

[37]See Paul Woodring, *Investment in Innovation: An Historical Appraisal of the Fund for the Advancement of Education.* Boston: Little, Brown, 1970.

[38]John Walker Powell, *Channels of Learning: The Story of Educational Television.* Washington, D.C.: Public Affairs Press, 1962, 89.

[39]An NAEB advisory committee to the center (Burton Paulu, Graydon Ausmus, Harold McCarty, George Probst, and Richard Hull), along with Harry Skornia, Robert Hudson, Ralph Steetle, James Miles, and Frank Schooley met at the second Gunflint Lodge Conference in August 1953 and expressed their concern that stations were getting on the air faster than the center was ready to supply them with programs. They also recommended that the center establish network charters for programs provided to affiliated stations and that it should make grants or pay commissions to stations that produced programs for the center.

[40]During the Newburn administration, Robert Hudson was the only professional broadcaster on the NETRC staff. More than any other person, he was the guiding leader of ETV from the time the FCC proposed making no reservations for educational television in 1949 until the Corporation for Public Broadcasting began operating in 1969.

[41]See Fred W. Friendly, *Due to Circumstances beyond Our Control.* New York: Random House, 1967, 302-22.

[42]For an account of the hearings, see U.S. Congress, Senate Subcommittee on Communications, Committee on Commerce, *Hearings, Progress Report on Space Communications*, 89th Congress, 2nd Session, 1966, 230.

[43]See Allen E. Koenig and Ruane B. Hills, eds., *The Farther Vision: Educational Television Today.* Madison: University of Wisconsin Press, 1967, 380.

[44]The commission's report was submitted to Congress in March 1970. See *To Improve Learning: A Report to the President and Congress of the United States, Commission on Instructional Technology.* Washington, D.C.: U.S. Government Printing Office, March 1970.

[45]The Ford Foundation, along with the Carnegie Corporation, the Markle Foundation, and the U.S. Office of Education, formed the Children's Television Workshop in 1968. The Carnegie Corporation took the lead in developing "Sesame Street" with the Ford Foundation, making grants totaling $5 million in 1970, 1971, and 1972, to continue production of "Sesame Street" and to develop and produce "The Electric Company," an advanced series to teach reading skills. These two successful programs that

have captured a large portion of the public television audience were originally produced as instructional programs, as an effort to aid learning in children' they did not evolve from public television. For a complete account of this development, see Richard M. Polsky, *Getting to Sesame Street: Origins of the Children's Television Workshop.* New York: Praeger Publishers, 1974.

[46]NAEB, *The Hidden Medium: A Status Report on Educational Radio in the United States.* New York: Herman W. Land Associates, 1967.

[47]Susan Tyler Eastman et al., *Broadcast/Cable Programming*, 2d ed. Belmont, Calif.: Wadsworth Publishing, 1985, 437-56.

[48]The Pacifica Stations, founded in 1949, was one of the first listener-supported, noncommercial stations in the United States. The Pacifica Stations consist of KPFA-FM, Berkeley, California; KPFK-FM, Los Angeles, California; WBAI-FM, New York City; WEFM-FM, Washington, D.C.; and KPFT-FM, Houston, Texas. The Pacifica Foundation, licensee of the stations, has a specific social and political purpose and they dramatically demonstrate the important role of broadcasting that is free from commercial restraints in their reporting of the news and public affairs. Other competitive noncommercial networks include the American Public Radio Network, composed of Minnesota Public Radio; KUSC-FM, Los Angeles; KQED, San Francisco; WNYC AM/FM, New York City; and WGUC, Cincinnati. American Public Radio differs from NPR in two ways. First, it is not a membership organization but a network of affiliated stations paying fees to be the primary or secondary outlet for APR programs. Also, unlike NPR, APR offers its programs to only one station in each market. Moreover, APR's charter does not permit it to become a national production center. Another national distributing organization, U.S. Audio, was formed by Eastern Public Radio, Audio Independents, and the Longhorn Network.

[49]One of the best sources of the history of the struggles of public television during the Nixon years is: David M. Stone, *Nixon and the Politics of Public Television.* New York: Garland Publishing, 1985.

[50]Fred C. Esplin, "Looking Back: Clay Whitehead's OTP," *Public Telecommunications Review* 3 (March/April 1975), 17-22.

[51]Jim Karayn, firm chief of NET's Washington bureau, was selected to manage NPACT. NET's James Day, predictably, opposed the creation of NPACT. The Ford Foundation, he claimed, had told him that NET's major responsibility was public affairs. Meanwhile, NPACT took over production responsibilities for two current political programs, Elizabeth Drew's highly acclaimed weekly interview program, *Thirty Minutes with ...* and the popular *Washington Week in Review*, a round-table discussion with four of the capitol's leading reporters on major news stories of the week.

[52]Both Vanocur and MacNeil took one-third salary cuts to come to NPACT. Originally, Karayn wanted NBC's Edwin Newman and offered him $150,000 a year to leave NBC for NPACT. Newman decided not to accept the offer and Vanocur was offered $85,000 a year and MacNeil $65,000 a year. Although this was not much money by industry standards, it immediately created problems because this was considerably higher than the salaries of congressmen and most civil servants at this time.

[53]Nixon's veto of a bill designed to bring CPB funding to a level approaching that recommended by the Carnegie Commission created a chaotic situation for public broadcasting. All planning had been based on the assumption that public broadcasting would be funded for two years. The system had to scramble desperately to receive supplementary funds during fiscal 1973 at the $35 million level it had received in fiscal 1972. In addition, President Nixon nominated even more of the CPB board. By the summer of 1972, Nixon had named eleven of the fifteen directors.

[54]Most of the viewing audience of public television had very little knowledge of what was going on during this period. However, in March 1973, Patrick Buchanan, an assistant and advisor to President Nixon, appeared on Dick Cavett's late-night talk program on ABC and gleefully admitted that the administration had throttled public broadcasting. According to Buchanan, Nixon had orchestrated a campaign of harassment and intimidation in retaliation for the failure of public broadcasting to give complete loyalty to him by airing critical public affairs programs. By that time PBS had cancelled practically all of its news and public affairs programs.

[55]See Robert K. Avery and Robert Pepper, *The Politics of Interconnection: A History of Public Television at the National Level*, Washington, D.C.: NAEB, 1979; and Robert Pepper, *The Formation of the Public Broadcasting Service*, New York: Arno Press, 1979.

[56]James R. Killian, Jr., "The New Focus," *Corporation for Public Broadcasting Annual Report*, 1973, 1.

[57]A historic series of broadcasts for public television occurred when NPACT correspondents Robert MacNeil and Jim Lehrer covered the Senate Watergate Committee hearings. Ironically, one station that did not agree until the very last minute to carry the event in prime time was Washington's WETA Channel 26. The hearings were a watershed for public television and a turning point for its future. In May and June and throughout the entire summer of 1973 the public response to the hearings was sensational. Evening audience ratings were five or six times normal and on some evenings, New York's Channel 13 exceeded two of the three commercial networks with their videotaped coverage. Viewer support through membership contributions increased tremendously. WNET Channel 13 in New York City averaged about 1,200 new subscribers a week during the Watergate hearings.

[58]A documentary history of the Office of Telecommunications Policy regarding their handling of public broadcasting during the Nixon administration can be found in *The Nixon Administration Public Broadcasting Papers: A Summary 1969-1974*. Washington, D.C.: NAEB, 1979.

[59]The Carnegie Commission on the Future of Public Broadcasting, *A Public Trust*. New York: Bantam, 1979, 11.

[60]Ibid., 49.

[61]See *Public Telecommunications Review* 5 (September/October 1977), 58-62.

[62]Robert J. Blakely, *To Serve the Public Interest*. Syracuse, N.Y.: Syracuse University Press, 1979, 215.

[63]This quoted statement was not published until 1955, but these principles guided the Educational Television Radio Center from its inception. See Educational Television and Radio Center, *Presenting National Educational Television*. Ann Arbor: ETRC, 1955.

[64]Ibid., Blakely, "To Serve," 104.

[65]Another competitive PBS strategy was bridging. Since most viewers stay with a program from start to finish, lengthy programs were scheduled by PBS to prevent an audience from switching to the competition's programs at the time where one network's programs end and others begin.

[66]British programs such as *Masterpiece Theater* and *The Shakespeare Plays* appear on American public television because they are high-quality programs at one-tenth the cost of producing comparable programs in the United States. Unfortunately, PBS lacks a unified national authority necessary for coordinated planning.

[67]Vernon Bronson, "When Educational Television Goes Public," *Educational Broadcasting Review* 3 (December 1969), 13.

[68]Ibid., Murphy and Gross, "Learning by Television," 10.

[69]J. D. Koerner, *The Present and the Future in Educational Technology*. New York: Alfred P. Sloan Foundation, 1977.

[70]P. J. Dirr and R. J. Pedone, *Uses of Television for Instruction: 1976-77*. Washington, D.C.: Corporation for Public Broadcasting, 1979.

[71]South Carolina has developed an extensive ITFS system to provide instructional programming. The system replaces the state-wide closed-circuit system, relying on microwave and cable networks.

[72]G. S. Lesser, *Children and Television.* New York: Random House, 1974, 241.

[73]The 1960s and 1970s brought an increase in the use of videotape recorders, which gave teachers more control over classroom television.

[74]Some notable uses of ITFS systems have been demonstrated by Stanford University, the University of Southern California, and the State University of California at Chico.

[75]Bernard Z. Friedlander, "Instructional Television: An Agenda for Self-Analysis," in Douglass Cater and Michael J. Nyhan, eds., *The Future of Public Broadcasting.* New York: Praeger Publishers, 1976, 95.

[76]George N. Gordon, "Instructional Television: Yesterday's Magic," in Jerold Ackerman and Lawrence Lipsitz, eds., *Instructional Television.* Englewood Cliffs, N.J.: Educational Technology Publications, 1977, 149-51.

[77]David Berkman, "Instructional Television: The Medium Whose Future has Passed," in ibid., 95-108.

[78]Saul Rockman, "Instructional Television Is Alive and Well," in Cater and Nyhan, 71-93.

[79]Marc S. Tucker, "The Turning Point: Telecommunications and Higher Education," *Journal of Communication* 33 (Winter 1983), 119.

Select Bibliography

Avery, Robert K., and Robert Pepper. *The Politics of Interconnection: A History of Public Television at the National Level.* Washington, D.C.: NAEB, 1979.

Blakely, Robert J. *To Serve the Public Interest.* Syracuse, N.Y.: Syracuse University Press, 1979.

Cater, Douglass, and Michael J. Nyhan, eds. *The Future of Public Broadcasting.* New York: Praeger, 1976.

Dirr, P. J., and R. J. Pedone. *Uses of Television for Instruction: 1976-77.* Washington, D.C.: Corporation for Public Broadcasting, 1979.

Gibson, George H. *Public Broadcasting: The Role of the Federal Government, 1912-76.* New York: Praeger, 1977.

Gordon, George. *Educational Television.* New York: Center for Applied Research in Education, 1965.

Head, Sydney W. *Broadcasting in America: A Survey of Electronic Media,* 5th ed. New York: Houghton Mifflin, 1987.

Horwitz, Robert B. *The Irony of Regulatory Reform.* New York: Oxford University Press, 1989.

Lesser, G. S. *Children and Television.* New York: Random House, 1974.

NAEB. *The Hidden Medium: A Status Report on Educational Radio in the United States.* New York: Herman W. Land Associates, 1967.

Schramm, Wilbur, et al. *The People Look at Educational Television: A Report on Nine Representative ETV Stations.* Stanford, Calif.: Stanford University Press, 1963.

Stone, David M. *Nixon and the Politics of Public Television.* New York: Garland Publishing, 1985.

Tyler, Susan E., et al. *Broadcast/Cable Programming.* Belmont, Calif.: Wadsworth Publishing, 1985.

Wood, Donald N., and Donald G. Wylie. *Educational Telecommunications.* Belmont, Calif.: Wadsworth Publishing, 1977.

14

Educational Technology and the Emergence of the Information Society: 1950–1980

The primary objective of this chapter is to show the relationship of educational technology to the rapidly developing information society. This historic societal transformation has produced dramatic and sweeping changes by making information processing, communication, and control the central aspects of human society and social behavior. Although the impact of the information society on education has been relatively minor thus far, when compared to other institutional sectors of our society, its potential for the future promises epoch-making innovations in educational technology. For example, it is likely that the nature of our present formal school systems will be radically altered by the creation of computerized knowledge networks and long-distance systems. The traditional uniform method of collective education promises to be replaced by individualized approaches geared to individual ability and choice and by systems of self-learning that will change the traditional role of the teacher as a transmitter of information. Moreover, it is probable that greater emphasis will be placed on the education of adults and elderly people so that they may be able to adapt to the changes of the information society and develop their abilities for the society as a whole.

It is the purpose of this chapter to look broadly at the relationship between educational technology and the emergence of the information society by (1) providing a brief historical background of the rise of the information society and a description of its characteristics; (2) exploring the prevailing visions of the information society; and (3) assessing the impact of the information society on educational technology during the period covered by this chapter.

Historical Background of the Information Society

According to Beniger, the information society emerged from what he calls the control revolution in the 1950s. Beniger describes the control revolution, beginning in the late nineteenth century, as representing the beginning of a restoration—although with increasing centralization—of the economic and political control that was lost at more local levels of society during the Industrial Revolution. Before this time, control of government and markets had depended on personal relationships and face-to-face interactions; now control came to be reestablished by means of bureaucratic organization, the new infrastructures of transportation and telecommunications, and system-wide communication via the new mass media.[1]

The concept of the information society dates from the late 1950s and the pioneering work of an economist, Fritz Machlup, who in 1962 first measured that sector of the U.S. economy associated with what he called "the production and distribution of knowledge."[2] Under this classification Machlup grouped thirty industries into five major categories: education, research and development, communications media, information machines such as computers, and information services such as finance, insurance, and real estate. He estimated from 1958 data that the information sector accounted for 29 percent of gross national product (GNP) and 31 percent of the labor force. He also estimated that between 1947 and 1958, the growth rate had doubled and that the United States was rapidly becoming an information society.

Over the past decades several other analyses have updated the original Machlup estimates of the extent of the information society. For example, Burch[3] calculated the information sector had reached 33 percent of GNP by 1963 and Marshak[4] predicted that the sector would approach 40 percent of GNP in the 1970s. One of the most innovative efforts to date has been the work of Marc Uri Porat of the Office of Telecommunications in the U.S. Department of Commerce. In 1967, according to Porat, information activities (defined differently than those of Machlup) accounted for 46.2 percent of GNP—25.1 percent in a "primary information" sector and 21.1 percent in a "secondary information" sector.[5]

An entirely new stage in the development of the information society arose in the early 1970s through the proliferation of microprocessing technology and the convergence of telecommunications and computing into a single infrastructure of control. The name given to this synthesis is information technology. The French call it *la telematique*, a neologism coined by Nora and Minc in their famous 1978 report to the president of France, in which they viewed the growing interconnection of information processing, communication, and control technologies as analogous to "the entire nervous system of social organization."[6] Instead of *telematics*, Oettinger and his colleagues at Harvard's Program on Information Resources Policy have suggested compunications (for "computing + communications").[7]

The critical aspect of the information society is increasing digitalization of mass media and telecommunications content. Digitalization makes communication possible from humans to machines, between machines, and from machines to humans as easy as personal conversation. In the process,

> digitalization promises to transform currently diverse forms of information into a generalized medium for processing and exchange by the social system, much as, centuries ago, the institution of common currencies and exchange rates began to transform local markets into a single world economy.[8]

Ruben points out that the information society involves a number of issues. For example, he observed that the information age has brought about such an increase in the volume of data that many personal and social problems relate to the impossibility of absorbing more than a small percentage of the information available. Ruben raises such complex issues as the following:

> What is the relationship between varying levels of information availability and various individual and social outcomes: Is it possible to develop methods to

determine what is the "right" amount of information for the purposes and decision at hand, on an a priori basis? How can we apply knowledge relative to human information processing, attention, information reception, information selectivity, source selection, and use? Can methods be developed that will assist with the personal and social management of information?[9]

Ruben also noted issues in the information society relating to:

the shift from linear to interactive media; a broadening concept of literacy; a merging of information-processing and transportation technology; regulation of new technologies; freedom and privacy; the relationship between available information and use; and variety and constraint in media and society.[10]

With reference to literacy, Ruben suggests that the formerly distinct operational competencies of the journalist, the librarian, the communications specialist, and the lawyer may now overlap as a result of common information-handling technologies and processes. Reading and writing may well come to be seen as examples of information-processing competencies and today's concepts of computer literacy might be viewed "as tapping only the most superficial and transitory of the necessary skills and competencies."[11]

It must be emphasized that the information society has not evolved from recent changes, but rather with increases in the speed of material processing more than a century ago. Likewise, microprocessing and computing technology does not represent a new force, as some seem to think, but is, in effect, the continuation of the control revolution. The information society that has emerged is the result of a number of factors or societal changes that have been noted by a number of contemporary observers. These include the rise of a new information class;[12] meritocracy of information workers;[13] a global village based on new mass media and telecommunications;[14] a technetronic era;[15] and the micro millennium.[16]

Visions of the Information Society

A number of philosophers and social scientists have concerned themselves with the important issues about how computerization works and whether or not it is likely to affect society negatively or positively.[17] Most of the writing on the information society has reflected a fantastic futurism. For example, Feigenbaum and McCorduck exclaim:

The world is entering a new period. The wealth of nations, which depended on land, labor, and capital during its agricultural and industrial phases—depended upon natural resources, the accumulation of money, and even upon weaponry—will come in the future to depend upon information, knowledge, and intelligence.[18]

Martin forecasts that:

The electronic revolution will not do away with work, but it does hold out some promises: Most boring jobs can be done by machines; lengthy commuting can be avoided; we can have enough leisure to follow interesting pursuits outside our work; environmental destruction can be avoided; the opportunities for personal creativity will be unlimited.[19]

Hiltz and Turoff see "no limits in telecommunications and electronic technology. There are no limits in the consumption of information, the growth of culture, or the development of the human mind."[20]

Writing of the "fifth generation" supercomputers, Masuda predicts:

> freedom for each of us to set individual goals of self-realization and then perhaps a worldwide religious renaissance, characterized not by a belief in a supernatural god, but rather by awe and humility in the presence of the collective human spirit and its wisdom, humanity living in a symbolic tranquility with the planet we have found ourselves upon, regulated by a new set of global ethics.[21]

Anthony Oettinger, chairman of the Program on Information Resources Policy at Harvard, maintains that information is a basic resource like materials and energy—in the future, those who have more of it will tend to be materially better off, and those with less may be worse off:

> By widening the range of possible social "nervous systems" the continuing growth of information resources is upsetting the world order just as the Industrial Revolution upset it by widening the range of physical modes of production. Where this will lead is as hard to foretell as predicting today's world when the steam engine was invented. However, the timeless truth that knowledge is power once again needs reinterpretation because of newly abundant, varied, and versatile modes of gathering, storing, processing, transmitting, and exploiting information that contrast with even scarcer and costlier materials and energy.[22]

Toffler writes of the "great, growing engine of change—technology" and sees a "dramatically new techno-structure for a Third Wave civilization."[23] Williams proclaims that "our lives will never be the same again" because of the "miracles of electronic communications."[24] These speculations and many others in a similar vein tend to "dominate discussion in a straightforwardly quantitative manner which makes it difficult for alternative perspectives to be heard" and "to create a general sense of acquiescence to innovation."[25]

But these visions of the information society as accurate predictions of social and economic futures are not accepted by everyone. Winner, for example, has characterized such rhapsodic statements and beliefs as "mythinformation." He says they carry with them "the almost religious conviction that a widespread adoption of computers and communications systems along with easy access to electronic information will automatically produce a better world for human living."[26] Winner points out that the political arguments of "computer romantics" draw upon the assumptions that: people are bereft of information; information is knowledge; knowledge is power; and increasing access to information enhances democracy and equalized social power.[27] Winner views these assertions as providing a distorted picture of the role of electronic systems in social life and asserts that "the formula information-knowledge-power-democracy lacks any real substance."[28]

Winston, in his book *Misunderstanding Media*, views the so-called information revolution as an illusion and "a rhetorical gambit, an expression of profound ignorance, a movement dedicated to purveying misunderstanding and disseminating disinformation."[29] He states there are three central assertions made about the nature of innovation in telecommunications that he finds faulty. They are:

(a) that there is an exponential increase in the amount of information in the world;

(b) that the pace of change is faster now than it was in the past and is looking to get faster yet;

(c) that the nature and locus of innovation is now very different from what it was even in the immediate past of the last century.[30]

Taking these points in order, Winston asserts that "there is not one scrap of evidence that our capacity to absorb information has markedly changed because of this monstrous regiment of data, print, and images, nor that the regular provision of 'facts' beyond our limited capacity to absorb them materially alters our ability to run our lives and societies."[31]

Winston refutes the second assertion by saying that the pace of change is deceptive. In the case of telecommunications, he states "there is no evidence of speed-up at all." For example,

> electronic television was described in 1908, partially demonstrated in 1911, patented in 1923, perfected (or invented) a decade later and it took a quarter of a century for it to be diffused. Video recording was proposed in 1927 and demonstrated in 1953. The first cassette appeared in 1969. Diffusion was to take a further decade and a half.[32]

The concept of a computer

> as a stored program device was first made in 1944, although glimmers of it as a possibility can be traced back to the previous century. Five years later the first giant machines worked: 10 years later there were a couple of hundred computers in the world; 20 years later, some 30,000. In 1976 the first microcomputer appears, although throughout the 40 year period of the giants, various "baby" machines had been stillborn.[33]

Thus, Winston says that this history refutes the idea, for telecommunications at least, that there has been a general technological speed-up.

Winston also challenges the third assertion, that the nature and locale of innovation and the type of inventor has significantly changed. He says "the men who made the telegraph and the telephone were every bit aware that solutions existed to the problems they had determined to solve as their descendants who grappled with television, microelectronics, laser, and the rest."[34]

According to some critics, the visions of the information society do not explain what policies are necessary to assure a highly productive, democratic, and socially stable society rather than an oppressive one. For example, Marien writes:

> unemployment caused by the automation of office work and other informational services may be extensive and, if not compensated by an equal number of new jobs in the information sector, could result in a labor force no longer dominated by information-related occupations. The major activity of society would then be some other occupation, or even involuntary idleness—the lack of any occupation—a condition that already characterizes some Third World nations.[35]

For Roszak, the visions confuse information with knowledge and tend to make the two synonymous. This leads inexorably and incorrectly, according to Roszak, to the identification of computer-related skills with overall creativity, learning, and understanding when, in fact, there is no evidence that this is the case.[36]

Siegel and Markoff make the point that much of the most advanced new microelectronic technology has been developed and continues to be developed for military uses and is not particularly oriented toward or designed for the solution of basic human problems, such as eliminating pollution or developing more effective teaching and learning.[37]

Despite these negative overtones, none of these criticisms negates the fact that our industrial society will tend to become increasingly information-oriented in the future.

The Impact of the Information Society
on Educational Technology

Beginning in the 1950s the Ford Foundation supported a variety of projects to utilize the new technology that was destined to begin "a new era in American education."[38] Other foundations, particularly Carnegie and Kettering, also supported and promoted new information technology in education. Through the National Defense Education Act of 1958 and the Elementary and Secondary Education Act of 1965, the federal government became the primary source of funds for the promised technological revolution in education. However, by the 1970s, the impact of the information society had yet to be fully felt. Much of the reason for this minor impact was that technology was still too complicated for use with relatively simple tasks but beyond the expertise of most educators to apply to more complex tasks. The large expense involved as well as rigid resistance to innovations constituted other formidable barriers.

It must be mentioned that a hidden agenda was involved in advocating the incorporation of the new technology into education. Technological innovations were seen essentially as the improvement of managerial efficiency in the educational process, whereby more students would be taught in less time with fewer teachers and with more efficient utilization of space at lower cost. Consequently, the major innovations promoted during this period were (1) televised instruction, (2) programmed instruction, (3) team teaching, (4) modular-flexible scheduling, (5) differentiated staffing, (6) learning resource centers, (7) individualized instruction, (8) independent study, (9) language laboratories, (10) nongraded schools, (11) open-plan schools, (12) behavioral objectives, (13) performance contracting, and (14) computer-assisted instruction.

The early impact of the information society on educational technology was primarily focused on educational television, programmed instruction, and computer-assisted instruction. Unfortunately, the early glowing promises that these technological innovations would revolutionize education failed to materialize for a variety of reasons. These early failures have been well documented by Smith and Smith,[39] by Tyack and Hansot,[40] and Levin et al.,[41] as well as by a number of other researchers. In each case, evaluations of these and other technological approaches were shown to be designed primarily to prove their success rather than to find solutions to perennial educational problems. The prevailing impulse of these innovations and reforms were characterized solely by a desire for improvisation and typically they lacked any sound theoretical or experimental foundation. The result was that these innovations and reforms were often of short duration and quickly faded away as each societal crisis called for a return to traditional educational practice or for implementation of another technological innovation.

This section is a review of the technological impact areas during the 1950-1980 period. An extended review of the period after 1980 will follow in chapter 17.

A Historical Evaluation of
Instructional Technology

Perhaps, the best historical benchmark of the impact of the information society on educational technology in the 1970s was the report *To Improve Learning*.[42] The report by the Commission on Instructional Technology, which grew out of Title III of the Public Broadcasting Act, reviewed the use in the educational process not only of television, but of all methods of communication. Within two volumes containing the recommendations of the commission, together with 113 papers prepared by a prominent array of education scholars, the report contains the most comprehensive discussion of educational technology made to date. Volume 1 (1970) is divided into two parts, one a report of the commission, the other containing the first 22 of the 113 papers, and focused on The State of the Art. Volume 2 (1971), containing papers 23 through 113, deals with the following topics: Theories and General Applications; Practical Considerations; Implications for Business and Industry; and Economic Evaluations.[43]

The commission's study revealed that the most basic problems are not peculiar to technology per se, but pervade all of American education. These are: (1) the lack of practical understanding about the processes of human learning; (2) insufficient money for systematic R&D; and (3) the rigidity of the educational structure with its patterns of grades, courses, credits, departmentalization, and prescribed years of attendance at each level. With reference to the low use and quality of instructional technology, the commission cited: (1) indifference or antipathy toward using technology in education; (2) poor programs available via television, programmed instruction, and through other media; (3) inadequate and inappropriate equipment; (4) inaccessibility to instructional materials; (5) teachers not trained in instructional terminology; and (6) media specialists excluded from central planning.[44]

The report summary stated that:

> today technology touches only a fraction of instruction. Colleges, universities, and schools have been using television, films, computers, or programmed texts in instruction, but to a limited extent. The results are mixed, with some institutions making a creative and sustained use of the new media while others, after an initial burst of enthusiasm, quickly lose interest.[45]

In order to bring about an improvement in the low impact of educational technology in the schools, the commission made six recommendations, as follows:

1. to establish the National Institutes of Education within the Department of Health, Education, and Welfare "with broad authorization to support and fund greatly strengthened programs in educational research, development, and application."

2. to establish a National Institute of Instructional Technology "to work closely with existing agencies concerned with instructional technology and to establish such other regional centers and programs as it deems necessary." (It would concentrate on research, development, and application of technology.)

3. to establish "a center or 'library' of educational resources."

4. to establish "projects to demonstrate the value of technology for instruction." (These would be initiated by the National Institute of Instructional Technology.)

5. to develop programs (proposed by the National Institute of Instructional Technology), "based on stepped-up research and development, to train and retrain teachers, administrators, and a variety of specialists."

6. to develop "a mechanism whereby the National Institute of Instructional Technology could bring education and industry together in a close working relationship to advance the effectiveness of instruction through technology."[46]

Curiously, the definition of instructional technology used in this report emphasized hardware or media rather than process. The rationale for this emphasis on an obsolete concept of instructional technology undoubtedly rested on the fact that this was the conception that many people held at the time and, as a matter of fact, still hold today. Simultaneously, a second definition, or a process definition was offered, but the commission decided that it "belongs to the future."[47]

There were mixed reactions to the report. Ely, for example, observed that:

> there is an honest balance between reporting actual performance and citing potential contributions, between the myths and the realities of instructional technology. The deterrents to progress are documented and diagnosed. The relative insignificance of current technological applications to education is painfully displayed. The failure of the educational community to respond to new demands in a new day is the context for the critique of instructional technology. These realistic perceptions save the report from being a "whitewash" for instructional technology.[48]

Briggs commented that:

> by defining technology as media, the report repeats the historical error of putting the cart of the machine before the horse of purpose. The use of television for instruction over the past ten or fifteen years provides us with an excellent example of this problem. The fact that television is a powerful communications medium has in no appreciable way led to an increase in the application of what we know about learning to the process of instruction, particularly in regard to the range of individual differences among students. In fact, television has not demonstrated any capacity to provide instruction that is truly tailored to each individual student. Nor have motion pictures and overhead projectors. Indeed, all of these media in their present formats, because they are instruments of mass or group communications, work against tailoring instruction to the needs of individual students. Moreover, neither television nor motion pictures can be compared to textbooks, which have a relatively high degree of flexibility, and to teachers, whose inherent capability for flexibility approaches the infinite.[49]

Torkelson noted that the commission report contained "numerous specifications and plans for improving learning through the applications of instructional technology" and concluded that "educators must open their doors to collaborative efforts with interested parties outside the educational establishment" and that "national programs of research, development, and demonstration must be launched to derive defensible expenditures related to the applications of instructional technology and to provide exemplars of effectiveness and efficiency."[50]

Unfortunately, the major recommendation of the commission, to establish a National Institute of Instructional Technology, was never implemented. Instead a National Center for Educational Technology (NCET) was established by the U.S. Office of Education early in 1972 and Robert T. Filep became the first associate commissioner for educational technology in October 1972. However, in the following year, federal funds were withdrawn for administrative and research and development support, and the new director was forced to resign when NCET was reorganized within the National Institute of Education.

Impact of Educational Television

During the early 1950s, the most vocal advocates of educational television proclaimed that television would provide a solution to such problems as teacher shortages (particularly in the sciences, mathematics, and specialized subjects), overcrowded classrooms, and poorly prepared teachers. Educators were told that television could solve all these problems and that expert, skilled science teachers, for example, could provide effective lessons to wide audiences at low cost. Thus, it was not surprising that many educational administrators, inspired by educational television's potential and spurred by the availability of federal NDEA and Title I funds, purchased closed-circuit television systems and videotape recording equipment, and employed the necessary personnel to make instructional television possible.

In the process of developing programs for instructional television, a number of unexpected technical problems arose. For example, aggressive television equipment salesmen from competing manufacturers pressed naive educators to sign on the dotted line as quickly as possible. Only later did educators come to the realization that components from different manufacturers were incompatible or that the equipment was not always adequate to perform the service they had envisioned. Another complication was that states could not recommend what kinds of equipment were best suited for school use and some states even passed legislation requiring that contracts go to the lowest bidder regardless of the quality of the equipment. Another problem was created when many schools purchased a large number of 17-inch rather than 21-inch monitors. Educators soon realized that 17-inch monitors were inadequate for classroom viewing. When portable videotape recording equipment became available, salesmen claimed that schools could now record off the air, stockpile tapes, and ultimately dispense with the use of local instructional broadcast television service. History repeated itself again when educators found that tape recorders proved to be incompatible and, as a result, greatly increased the cost of making instructional television programming available. Meanwhile, when it came to programming and production, educators experienced more disappointment. Because of inadequate equipment and lack of production expertise, low quality productions were the usual result. By the beginning of the 1970s, the schools had a hodgepodge of television equipment, much of which had been relegated to storage. At the same time, their instructional budgets were insufficient to replace obsolete black-and-white sets (many of which had been stolen or damaged) with color sets as well as to purchase needed compatible videotape recorders and other new equipment.

The development of delivery systems to the schools proved to be almost as chaotic as that within the schools. Most schools received an open broadcast signal from the local public television station. However, this delivery for the most part limited reception to one program choice at any particular time over the broadcast channel. This problem was further complicated by the fact that many public television stations were licensed to operate on ultra high frequency (UHF) channels that required good master antennas for satisfactory reception and that were unavailable in many schools. Because of this limitation, many schools had to rely on media centers to deliver tapes or films, either by truck or over their own closed-circuit or Instructional Television Fixed Service (ITFS) 2500 megahertz systems.

In order to solve the delivery problem, some states established Educational Television Commissions or gave mandates to state boards of education to develop delivery networks that would make educational television available to all citizens. Some of the more notable of these state-wide systems that best utilized television services to the schools were established in Wisconsin and South Carolina. In 1973, the Agency for Instructional Television was created in response to a need for a permanent American-Canadian organization to work closely with the states and the provinces to expand and improve cooperative production activities originated earlier by the National Instructional Television Center (NIT).

In 1971, an American version of the Open University of Great Britain, the University of Mid-America (UMA), began as a consortium of four universities (Nebraska, Iowa, Missouri, Kansas) that was intended to bring the opportunity of a complete college degree directly into the homes of residents. By the late 1970s, the alliance had spread to eleven institutions, offering a dozen or more courses taught mostly through broadcast television. However, by 1982 UMA had closed down, its demise brought on by insecure federal funding, poor coordination among technical teams, over-concentration on teaching via television while neglecting other media, lack of clarity about who held decision-making authority, and lack of expertise in marketing the courses.

Cable television was also seen in the 1970s as a means of providing flexibility of choice for teachers, but several different companies with different channel capacities in the same educational community made coordination of scheduling difficult. Also, after the experiences of the past, many educators moved cautiously into this new field of technology.

Another formidable barrier to the utilization of television for instructional purposes was found in the persistent resistance of teachers to altering their traditional methods of instruction. Such resistance constituted a number of factors. It involved teachers' inertia, dislike of outside interference in planning instruction, an unwillingness to yield instructional control to audio or video technologies, or an outright fear of using an unfamiliar instructional technique. In Evans's study of college professors' resistance to instructional television, he concluded that:

> the degree of acceptance of an innovation by professors may partly depend on whether they viewed the innovation as being instituted or imposed by the university administration or whether they felt that it originated within their own academic departments as a result of their own planning.[51]

It became clear in the late 1970s that instructional television would not be able to reach its full potential until it became fully integrated into the curriculum and into teaching. As the 1983 Corporation for Public Broadcasting (CPB) study of educational television concludes,

> until educators allow instructional television programming to be developed as an integral part of the core curriculum, it will continue to be peripheral to teacher, textbook, and blackboard. Substantive change does not occur with one fifteen-minute exposure per school week.[52]

Educational television was at its height in the 1960s and declined through the 1970s so that it served only occasionally to supplement classroom instruction.

According to studies based on self-reports between 1970 and 1981, teachers in three states who said they used television reported that they viewed programs between 2 and 4 percent of the instructional time available to them each week. Some teachers never turned to television for lessons. For example, in Maryland, 13 percent of the elementary, 43 percent of the junior high, and 60 percent of the high school teachers reported no use whatever in 1981.[53] The pattern of greatest use, in the elementary grades, was found in a national study completed by Dirr and Pedrone in the year 1976/77.[54] Their study, the first indepth study of the public school use of television since the early 1950s, reported that teachers averaged between thirty to sixty minutes of television per week in 1977. The highest use was by elementary teachers (66 minutes a week), and the lowest by junior-high school teachers (45 minutes per week).

There has been some recent evidence which indicates that instructional television had begun to be used more frequently in the 1980s, but it appears that little has changed in the classroom use of television since it first became available. Since the problem of technological innovation has persisted in the history of educational technology, it will be discussed in some detail in chapter 16.

The Impact of Programmed Instruction and Computer-Assisted Instruction

A number of independent historical threads have run through the development of computer-assisted instruction since its inception. The first computer-assisted instruction grew out of the early work on self-scoring tests and mechanical teaching machines by Pressey in the early 1920s. Further development by Pressey and others was supported by the U.S. military. Major theoretical foundations were supplied by B. F. Skinner's techniques of operant conditioning in the development of programmed instruction. However, studies of programmed instruction materials made during the 1960s showed that between 50 and 90 percent of the text material could have been deleted without diminishing the student's ability to answer questions for any particular block of text. In effect, programmed instruction failed in the classroom because of inferior and superfluous material that did not contribute to an understanding of the text.

Computer-assisted instruction (CAI) and the use of courseware has a long history of optimism associated with it even though much of what was first put into computers as CAI was just programmed instruction material that had been repackaged. In 1966, a fully developed CAI was seen as only being a few years away. Charles E. Silverman, a senior editor of *Fortune* magazine, viewed the computer as offering "a technology by which, for the first time, instruction really can be geared to the specific abilities, needs, and progress of each individual," and went on to say, "this quest for ways to individualize instruction is emerging as the most important single force for innovation and reform."[55] Patrick Suppes of Stanford University stated at the same time, "One can predict that in a few more years millions of school children will have access to what Philip of Macedon's son Alexander enjoyed as a royal prerogative: the personal services of a tutor as well-informed and responsive as Aristotle."[56]

However, by the 1970s, both Silverman and Suppes had a different assessment of the impact of the computer in the classroom. Silverman in his 1970 report for the Carnegie Corporation criticized the "advocates and prophets" of computer-assisted instruction for having made "extravagant predictions of wonder to come."[57] In 1974, in reviewing the research on the effectiveness of computer learning, Suppes and his associates acknowledged that "findings of 'no significant differences' dominate the research literature in this area," but that "it may be useful in small doses as a supplement to regular instruction with regard to elementary skill-drill practices."[58]

Because the development of CAI was already lagging some twenty years or more after the early glowing predictions of the 1950s, a certain amount of skepticism had arisen by the middle 1970s. For example, Control Data was reported to have invested more than $900 million in its PLATO CAI systems without making a profit, although their hopes were for billions in return. When the prospect for CAI appeared most bleak, the development of the microcomputer in the late 1970s injected a new enthusiasm in the CAI movement. However, in a pessimistic vein, Seymour Papert, author of *Mindstorms* and a major influence in the development of LOGO—a programming language designed to allow children to program computers—noted that:

> Computers are not having any effect now. There's been a lot of ballyhoo about computers revolutionizing the schools, but in fact the relative number of computers in schools is so small that it's negligible. They aren't having any effect. They can't have any effect.[59]

Perhaps, Papert's 1984 opinion is now unduly negative but may have been close to summarizing the conditions that prevailed at that time. It is still not clear what the future history of the use of microcomputers in schools will be, but it appears likely that still another technology may eventually displace even the microcomputer.

A Lesson from History

Past history has clearly shown that before one technology can be developed in an orderly process for maximum efficiency, a new one appears on the horizon. Beginning with the instructional slide, a kind of media bandwagon syndrome has influenced educators' decisions about new media superimposed on the educational system implying that existing educational ills or problems could be cured by the use of this new medium or mode of technology. The result has been that these technological innovations have achieved marginal instructional benefits and have often ended in disillusionment. The euphoric atmosphere that prevailed with regard to the use of classroom television and programmed instruction in the 1950s may be repeated with other technological innovations if the broad problems of education continue to be ignored.

Although educators have been optimistic about the use of computers in education for more than thirty years, the current advocates of computer-assisted instruction are voicing the same arguments about its educational potential as was given by many enthusiastic proponents of educational television over thirty years ago. As educators consider the role that computers will assume in educational programs, it is easy to detect similarities between what the schools are doing and thinking about microcomputers today and what they did and thought about television three decades ago. Wagschal, for example, argues that the typical day in American schools proceeds as if television did not exist. He says:

> There are at least three explanations for the failure of television to capture the interest and imagination of public school educators, and these explanations will prove instructive for educators who are now coming to grips with the computer revolution. First, the schools that purchased television sets rarely had the foresight to set aside money for equipment repairs and maintenance. Second, these schools never found an effective way to train teachers to integrate television into their ongoing instructional programs. Third, and perhaps most important, a majority of teachers had (and still have) an extremely snobbish attitude regarding the quality of commercial television and its consequent usefulness in the classroom.[60]

Wagschal then compares the educational television experience to what he perceived to be occurring with the use of computers in the school. He observes:

> As the case with television, most schools have stretched their budgets to the limit to purchase computer hardware and software. Therefore, they have little money set aside to repair and maintain the machines they have purchased. Moreover, as was true in the case of television, few schools have been able to afford the large-scale teacher retraining efforts that will enable teachers to make computers an integral part of classroom instruction. Most discouraging, however, is the fact that teachers' attitudes toward computers in the schools have some striking parallels with their previous and present attitude toward television.[61]

Thus, history appears to be repeating itself and bringing with it an even more complex set of problems involving adequate funding, programmatic utilization, and cost-effectiveness as well as a host of technical problems. As historians Tyack and Hansot have noted, "in successive waves of four to eight years, the number of articles on radio, film, television, and programmed instruction tended to peak and then fall off as a new cure-all appeared."[62] Even though some may protest that the computer is different and that it will not repeat this pattern, history teaches us that it is still too early to reach a definitive conclusion. The verdict is not yet in.

Notes

[1]James R. Beniger, *The Control Revolution.* Cambridge, Mass.: Harvard University Press, 1986, 7.

[2]See Fritz Machlup, *The Production and Distribution of Knowledge in the United States.* Princeton, N.J.: Princeton University Press, 1962. For an updated version, see Fritz Machlup, *Knowledge: Its Creation, Distribution, and Economic Significance,* Vol. 1. Princeton, N.J.: Princeton University Press, 1980.

[3]Gilbert Burch, "Knowledge: The Biggest Growth Industry of Them All," *Fortune* 7 (November 1964), 128-31.

[4]Jacob Marschak, "Economics of Inquiring, Communicating, and Deciding," *American Economic Review* 58 (March-May 1968), 1-8.

[5]Marc Uri Porat, *The Information Economy: Definition and Measurement.* Washington, D.C.: Office of Telecommunications, U.S. Department of Commerce, 1977.

[6]Simon Nora and Alain Minc, *The Computerization of Society: A Report to the President of France.* Cambridge, Mass.: MIT Press, 1980, 3.

[7]See Anthony G. Oettinger et al., *High and Low Politics: Information Resources for the 80s.* Cambridge, Mass.: Ballinger, 1977.

[8]Beniger, *Control Revolution,* 25-26.

[9]Brent D. Ruben, ed., *Information and Behavior,* Vol. 1. New Brunswick, N.J.: Transaction Books, 1985, 8.

[10]Ibid., 7.

[11]Ibid., 10.

[12]See Milovan Djilas, *The New Class: An Analysis of the Communist System.* New York: Praeger Publishers, 1957.

[13]See Alvin W. Gouldner, *The Future of Intellectuals and the Rise of the New Class.* New York: Seabury Press, Continuum, 1979.

[14]See Marshall McLuhan, *Understanding Media: The Extensions of Man.* New York: McGraw-Hill, 1964.

[15]See Zbigniew Brzezinski, *Between Two Ages: America's Role in the Technetronic Era.* New York: Viking Press, 1970.

[16]See Christopher Evans, *The Micro Millennium.* New York: Washington Square/Pocket Books, 1979.

[17]Daniel Bell, *The Coming of Post-Industrial Society.* London: Penguin Books, 1976. Among the important writings in this vein are David Burnham, *The Rise of the Computer State,* New York: Random House, 1983; Abbe Moshowitz, *The Conquest of Will: Information Processing Human Affairs,* Reading, Mass.: Addison-Wesley, 1976; Joseph Weizenbaum, *Computer Power and Human Reason: From Judgment to Calculation,* San Francisco: W. H. Freeman, 1976; and William J. Donnelly, *The Confetti Generation,* New York: Henry Holt, 1986.

[18]Edward A. Feigenbaum and Pamela McCorduck, *The Fifth Generation: Artificial Intelligence and Japan's Computer Challenge to the World.* Reading, Mass.: Addison-Wesley, 1983, 14.

[19]James Martin, *Telematic Society: A Challenge for Tomorrow.* Englewood Cliffs, N.J.: Prentice-Hall, 1981, 172.

[20]Ibid., 4.

[21]Feigenbaum and McCorduck, *Fifth Generation*, 240.

[22]Anthony B. Oettinger, "Information Resources: Knowledge and Power in the 21st Century," *Science* 209 (July 1980), 191-98.

[23]Alvin Toffler, *The Third Wave*. New York: Bantam Books, 1980, 164.

[24]Frederick Williams, *The Communications Revolution*. Beverly Hills, Calif.: Sage Publishers, 1982, 9.

[25]Frank Webster and Kevin Robins, *Information Technology: A Luddite Analysis*. Norwood, N.J.: Ablex, 1986, 29.

[26]Langdon Winner, *The Whale and the Reactor*. Chicago: University of Chicago Press, 1986, 105.

[27]Ibid., 108.

[28]Ibid., 113.

[29]Brian Winston, *Misunderstanding Media*. Cambridge, Mass.: Harvard University Press, 1986, 363.

[30]Ibid., 372.

[31]Ibid., 367.

[32]Ibid., 372.

[33]Ibid., 372.

[34]Ibid., 374.

[35]Michael Marien, "Some Questions for the Information Society," in Tom Forester, ed., *The Information Technology Revolution*. Cambridge, Mass.: MIT Press, 1985.

[36]Theodore Roszak, *The Cult of Information*. New York: Pantheon, 1986.

[37]See Leonard Siegel and John Markoff, *The High Cost of High Tech*. New York: Harper & Row, 1985.

[38]The Ford Foundation, *Teaching by Television*. New York: The Ford Foundation, 1961, Preface, n.p.

[39]See Karl U. Smith and Margaret Foltz Smith, *Cybernetic Principles of Learning and Educational Design*. New York: Holt, Rinehart, & Winston, 1966.

[40]See David Tyack and Elizabeth Hansot, "Futures That Never Happened: Technology and the Classroom," *Education Week* 5 (September 4, 1985), 40.

[41]See H. M. Levin et al., "Cost-Effectiveness of Four Educational Interventions," Institute for Research on Educational Finance and Governance, Stanford University, Report No. 84-A11, 1984.

[42]Sidney G. Tickton, ed., *To Improve Learning: An Evaluation of Instructional Technology*, 2 vols. New York: R. R. Bowker, 1970, 1971.

[43]The Commission on Instructional Technology was commissioned by the Democratic administration in April 1968. The commission was chaired by Sterling M. McMurrin, dean of the Graduate School, University of Utah. Other members of the commission were: David E. Bell, Ford Foundation; Roald Campbell, University of Chicago; C. Ray Carpenter, Pennsylvania State University; Neil P. Eurich, Vassar College; Harold B. Gores, Educational Facilities Laboratories; A. Leon Higginbotham, judge, U.S. District Court, Eastern District of Pennsylvania; Kermit C. Morrissey, Community College of Allegheny County, Pennsylvania; and Kenneth E. Oberholtzer, former superintendent of schools, Denver, Colorado. The report was submitted fifteen months later, to a Republican administration,

which kept it under wraps for six months before sending it to a Congress controlled by Democrats. The commission's half-million dollar study was supplemented by over 130 original papers, which were published in Volume 2 in 1971.

[44]Sidney G. Tickton, ed., *To Improve Learning: An Evaluation of Instructional Technology*, Vol. 1. New York: R. R. Bowker, 1970, 77-81.

[45]Ibid., 9.

[46]Ibid., 41-62.

[47]Ibid., 27.

[48]Donald P. Ely, "Comment on the Report of the Commission on Instructional Technology," *A V Communication Review* 18 (Fall 1970), 310.

[49]Leslie J. Briggs, ibid., 316.

[50]Gerald M. Torkelson, "Review of *To Improve Learning*," *A V Communication Review* 20 (Spring 1972), 91-92.

[51]Richard I. Evans, *Resistance to Innovation in Higher Education*. San Francisco: Jossey-Bass, 1968, 153.

[52]*Telecommunications and the Schools*, a report to the Corporation for Public Broadcasting. Concord, Mass.: Designs for Education, 1983, 25.

[53]R. W. Faunce, *Use of and Reaction to Educational Television Lessons (KTCA Channel 2) by Minneapolis Elementary School Teachers, 1970-71*, Minneapolis: Minneapolis Special School District, June 1, 1971, ERIC No. ED 069 142; John Willis, *The Use of Instructional Television in West Virginia Elementary Schools, 1977-1978*, Charleston, West Virginia State Department of Education, Bureau of Planning, Research and Evaluation, October 1978, ERIC No. ED 168 554; Kerry Johnson and Paul Keller, *Television in the Public Schools: Final Report of the Maryland ITV Utilization Study*, College Park, Md.: Maryland University, School of Library and Information Services, December 1981, ERIC No. ED 213 394.

[54]Peter Dirr and Ronald Pedrone, "A National Report on the Use of Instructional Television," *A V Instruction* 23 (January 1978), 11-13.

[55]Charles E. Silverman, "Technology Is Knocking at the Schoolhouse Door," *Fortune* 74 (August 1966), 207.

[56]Patrick Suppes, "The Uses of Computers in Education," *Scientific American* 215 (September 1966), 207.

[57]Charles E. Silverman, *Crisis in the Classroom*. New York: Random House, 1970, 186.

[58]Dean Jamison et al., "The Effectiveness of Alternative Instruction Media: A Survey," *Review of Educational Research* 44 (Winter 1974), 56.

[59]Seymour Papert, "Computer Criticism vs. Technocentric Thinking," *Educational Researcher* 16 (January-February 1987), 22-30.

[60]P. H. Wagschal, "A Last Chance for Computers in the Schools?" *Phi Delta Kappan* 66 (December 1984), 252.

[61]Ibid.

[62]Tyack and Hansot, "Futures That Never Happened," 40.

Select Bibliography

Beniger, James R. *The Control Revolution*. Cambridge, Mass.: Harvard University Press, 1986.

Dewey, John. *Philosophy and Civilization*. New York: Milton Balch, 1931.

Ellul, Jacques. *The Technological Society*, tr. John Wilkinson. New York: Knopf, 1964.

Feigenbaum, Edward A., and Pamela McCorduck. *The Fifth Generation: Artificial Intelligence and Japan's Computer Challenge to the World*. Reading, Mass.: Addison-Wesley, 1983.

Machlup, Fritz. *The Production and Distribution of Knowledge in the United States*. Princeton, N.J.: Princeton University Press, 1962.

_____. *Knowledge: Its Creation, Distribution, and Economic Significance*, vol. 1. Princeton, N.J.: Princeton University Press, 1980.

Martin, James. *Telematic Society: A Challenge for Tomorrow*. Englewood Cliffs, N.J.: Prentice-Hall, 1981.

Nora, Simon, and Alain Minc. *The Computerization of Society: A Report to the President of France*. Cambridge, Mass.: MIT Press, 1980.

Oettinger, Anthony G. *Run, Computer, Run*. Cambridge, Mass.: Harvard University Press, 1969.

Porat, Marc Uri. *The Information Economy: Definition and Measurement*. Washington, D.C.: Office of Telecommunications, U.S. Department of Commerce, 1977.

Roszak, Theodore. *The Cult of Information*. New York: Pantheon, 1986.

Ruben, Brent D., ed. *Information and Behavior*, vol. 1. New Brunswick, N.J.: Transaction Books, 1985.

Siegel, Leonard, and John Markoff. *The High Cost of High Tech*. New York: Harper & Row, 1985.

Toffler, Alvin. *Future Shock*. New York: Bantam Books, 1971.

_____. *The Third Wave*. New York: William Morrow, 1980.

15

Educational Technology and Related Research; Bureaucracy and Politics in Educational R&D: 1950–1980

The intention of this chapter is threefold: (1) to provide a brief historical perspective of educational technology and research; (2) to review the bureaucratic and political aspects of research and development in education as it emerged under the sponsorship of the federal government; and (3) to summarize selective research related to educational technology.

Since research studies concerning various aspects of educational technology have been cited throughout Part III of this book, the attempt in this chapter is not intended to be comprehensive or exhaustive, but focuses on exemplary reviews of relevant research. Chapter 17 in Part IV of this book completes the summarization of exemplary research studies of the 1980s related to educational technology.

Historical Perspective

At the beginning of this century, many educators and scientists were energized by the belief that research could bring about a new era in educational practice. Edward Thorndike, for example, was intensely involved in laboratory work on the psychology of learning and systematically applied the theory of S-R bonds to the technology of instruction in various subject matters. John Dewey envisioned a linking science or a connection between scientific theory and practical application. For a short period after the strong influence of Thorndike and Dewey and others like Maria Montessori and Sidney L. Pressey, there was a strong linkage between educational technology and psychology. However, by the early 1930s, these two fields became separated from each other and this, in turn, transformed the nature of the research undertaken. Psychology adopted the natural sciences as its model and proceeded to develop experimental techniques that were more appropriate for theoretical purposes rather than being concerned with the problems of learning in various educational contexts. Koch concluded after years of scholarly research that the entire "100-year course of scientific psychology can now be seen to be a succession of changing doctrines about what to emulate in the natural sciences," and that "each such strategic doctrine was entertained not as conditional upon its cognitive fruits but functioned rather as a security fetish bringing assurance to the psychologist, and hopefully to the world, that he was a scientist."[1]

Educational technology, during this period of separation, focused on the practical problems of teaching, but, in particular, conducted research on the materials, devices, and/or media of instruction. This type of research, based on the comparative media paradigm, began during World War I and grew with the development of films and radio. As each new medium was introduced into the classroom, the prevailing research assumed that learning would be enhanced by the proper combination of medium, learner, subject-matter content, and learning task. However, as we have seen, consistent "no-significant difference" findings confirmed the fact that this kind of media research was inadequate. Gradually, it became apparent that learning as measured is largely independent of the means of delivery and that the issues of learning method and content must be resolved on other research grounds.

Following World War II and during the 1950s, two major developments began to bring psychology and educational technology together again. The first was associated with a large research effort sponsored by the military in which psychologists and communication engineers worked together to solve training problems. For example, in solving training problems associated with developing guidance systems for missiles and for aircraft, psychologists developed new ways for studying psychological problems and constructing theories while engineers taught psychologists how to analyze a working system and explore methods by which such a system might be more effective in meeting its objectives. Such analysis involved the experimental testing of various methods, techniques, and materials in military training. The second development was the emergence of Skinner's operant conditioning and its application to education in the form of teaching machines and programmed instruction.

The curriculum reforms of the 1950s and 1960s brought about another important linkage between psychology and educational technology and established a new integration of psychological theory and educational practice. Modern cognitive psychology began to replace behavioristic theories of learning in the 1970s in educational technology and, as a result, a new era in research began. Thus, research in such areas as problem solving, thinking, memory, imagery, and understanding is creating new approaches toward the application of an educational technology based on "a prescriptive theory of instructional design" and "a descriptive science of human learning and performance."[2]

Impact of Federal Aid on Educational Technology Research

Educational research since mid-century changed largely because of the intervention of the federal government in terms of increased funding and a change in the locus of control. Simultaneously, the bureaucratic and political nature of the federal government expanded and became increasingly specialized and groups of specialists made up the so-called "professional-bureaucratic complex." These developments led to what Samuel H. Beer calls "technocratic politics" whereby every educational research program launched in the federal government was initiated by a small handful of persons, or those composing the professional-bureaucratic complex.[3]

Federal support of science R&D grew rapidly after World War II and became the model for educational research. This model is based on the belief that knowledge is in itself good and that more knowledge is better. The scientific model assumes that it is possible to isolate phenomena, subject them to examination under specified conditions, and to predict their behavior. When this model is applied to education, complications arise because of the weak knowledge base of the social sciences, adverse political constraints, and inadequate communication both within and between the researcher and the practitioner.[4]

The launching of *Sputnik I* in 1957 provided the major impetus for science R&D in the 1960s. Meanwhile, in education four agencies of the federal government were supporting R&D activities: the U.S. Office of Education (USOE); the National Science Foundation (NSF); the National Institutes of Mental Health (NIMH); and the Office of Economic Opportunity (OEO). In 1972, most of the R&D programs in USOE were shifted to the newly created National Institute of Education (NIE), and some of the projects of the OEO were moved to the newly created Office of Child Development (OCD). Also, other government agencies sponsored R&D related to educational technology, such as computer-aided instruction by the Office of Naval Research (ONR) and programmed instruction by the Department of Defense (DOD). However, the focus in this chapter will be on USOE and NSF since this is where the bulk of R&D funds on education were spent during this period.

The Cooperative Research Act

During the first half of the twentieth century, most educational research was undertaken by outstanding figures in education or psychology and was pursued on an unsystematic, individual, or part-time basis. The first improvement in the support of education R&D within the Office of Education came in 1954 with the establishment of the Cooperative Research Program (CRP). Proposed by President Eisenhower in 1953, the CRP funded a modest amount of university and college research, but the products were of considerable significance. The CRP did much to encourage research in classrooms and resulted in the development of many instruments for evaluating aspects of teaching. The primary impact of the CRP was that it provided a stimulus for development of research within schools and colleges of education.

Enactment of National Defense Education Act

The Cooperative Research Program was in its second operating year when the USSR launched *Sputnik I* and Congress, perceiving the weakness of the educational system, drafted the National Defense Education Act (NDEA) of 1958 and gave authority to CRP for two more research support programs. The NDEA consisted of ten titles, two of which authorized funds for studies and research.

Title VI empowered the U.S. commissioner of education

> directly or by contract, to make studies and surveys to determine the need for increased or improved instruction in modern foreign languages and other fields needed to provide a full understanding of the areas, regions, or countries in which such languages are commonly used, to conduct research for more effective methods of teaching such languages and in such other fields, and to develop specialized materials or use in such training, or in training teachers of such languages or in such fields.[5]

Title VII consisted of two parts: Part A authorized the commissioner through grants and contracts to conduct, assist, and foster research and experimentation (1) on a variety of audiovisual aids, (2) for training teachers to use these aids, and (3) for presenting academic subject matter through such media; Part B authorized the commissioner to disseminate information about new technologies and the research about them by (1) studies and surveys to determine need, (2) catalogs, reviews, bibliographies, abstracts, analyses of research, and experimentation to encourage more effective use, and (3) advising, counseling, and demonstrating to state and local educational agencies and institutions of higher education.[6]

It is interesting to note that Title VII, which promoted "research and experimentation in more effective utilization of television, radio, motion pictures, and related media for educational purposes," did not appear in the original draft of this hastily drawn bill, but was written at the last minute by the congressional staff from materials prepared by Henry Ruark and Donald White, then officers of the National Audiovisual Association, lobbyists for the audiovisual industry. Dershimer notes that "not a single researcher or scholar from the educational research community testified in its behalf; neither Secretary Folsom nor Commissioner Derthick mentioned research in their testimony."[7] This pattern of participation reflected a trend that continued to shape the policies related to the initiation of national research policies in education. Thus, research programs in education were typically launched by a small group of persons without any particular or widespread support either in or outside the Office of Education.

Shortly after the enactment of NDEA, the U.S. Office of Education established an Educational Media Branch to administer the research and development program included under Title VII.[8] The three original staff members consisted of Kenneth Norberg, coordinator of the media center at California State University, Sacramento; Clarence W. Stone, a professor of library sciences from the University of Illinois at Urbana; and Calvin Stordahl, an educational psychologist and formerly research administrator with the Department of Defense. During the first year, the Title VII program spent or committed almost $1.6 million and the staff processed approximately 250 proposals of which 45 were approved. In 1965, Francis Keppel, commissioner of education, reorganized the U.S. Office of Education and in the process eliminated the Educational Media Branch, separating its functions under Title VII, Parts A and B, within a larger administrative unit known as the Bureau of Research.

Impact of Title VII Program

There appears to be a general consensus of opinion, with the exception of some, that the Title VII influence was a positive force for educational technology. Some reviewers have been critical of the design and methodology of some projects. MacLean, for example, was not only critical of statistics and design, but was concerned with other aspects. He states that

> the problems are really much broader, and are all mixed up with scientific and human values. They are summed up in a question which I hate to hear asked of my own research findings, but which I think needs to be asked of all studies of problems in education and communication: So what?[9]

MacLean says further that

> I have yet to see a Title VII project which makes good use of the methods developed by social anthropologists and sociologists for studying large social systems. Nor have I seen any which takes advantage of the richly fruitful and rigorous methods for exploring self-orientations and defining belief-hierarchies or patterns.[10]

A study of the impact of Title VII in achieving its stated goals of encouraging "research and experimentation in the more effective utilization of television, radio, motion pictures, and related media" was commissioned by the Office of Education in early 1969. The principal investigator for the project was Sidney P. Marland, Jr., at the time president of the Institute for Educational Development and later the U.S. commissioner of education. Assisting Robert Filep as director of the project were several individuals who had been involved with the Title VII program over the years. These included among others, C. Ray Carpenter, Thomas Clemens, Robert M. Gagnè, Wilbur Schramm, and William Allen. A final complete report was made by Robert Filep (ERIC No. ED 042 064) and an overview report by Filep and Schramm.[11] The overview concerns itself with such questions as the impact of Title VII in terms of bringing researchers into the field of instructional media, the quality of the research, its role in educational television and information system development, and concludes with a series of thirty-four recommendations with regard to the nature of future legislation and the type of administration required for programs of this kind.

As to the overall impact of Title VII, the final report provides this summation:

> It is shown that Title VII had a substantial impact on educational scholarship and brought numerous new researchers into the field of educational media and technology. It also helped upgrade the quality of the research effort and contributed to the growth of many departments of instructional technology and related institutions. It was instrumental in several developments toward quality educational television and helped in the establishment of educational information dissemination institutions such as the ERIC Clearinghouses. In general, funding from Title VII did contribute to the application of the systems approach to education, to providing more individualized instruction, and to securing greater teacher acceptance of the new media.[12]

Torkelson has noted that "it would be interesting to compare differences in educational practice of today with those of the era of Title VII, particularly to identify, if possible, the threads of Title VII influence on current practices."[13] He felt that probably the Part B influences would be more obvious than those of Part A because of the developmental aspect of Part B. McKeegan, after analyzing Title VII, stated:

> Until both teachers and school administrators are prepared in programs which emphasize the critical role of theory development and research in effective instruction, there can be little hope for widespread use of research findings in education. To expect administrators and teachers trained in a theoretical or antitheoretical methodologically oriented programs to become highly flexible evaluators and adopters of research is to expect what cannot be. Perhaps it is time we faced up to the questions of how we go about developing experimentalism as an outlook in professional preparation programs if we are ever to secure much real gain from our investment in educational research.[14]

Title VII contained the provision that a committee composed of representatives from the lay and educational communities would evaluate proposals for research grants and contracts. Although the committee was considered "advisory," it had preemptive authority over Part A (research) and the commissioner could fund only those projects approved by the committee. The committee's role in Part B (dissemination) projects was advisory only and Title VII staff had more leeway in authorizing these projects. The advisory committee was generally poorly equipped to evaluate the quality of research proposals and spent a considerable amount of time on technical matters rather than on long-range policy planning.

The Filep and Schramm final report indicated that "the reorganization of 1965 diffused the Title VII projects throughout the Office of Education and left the advisory committee with less than a clear mandate." Despite this problem, it was during the period 1965-1968 that "members were able to realize the committee's most useful function—policy advice." The report also suggests that "when the research results began to be reported in 1963, the weight of spending shifted to Part B since there was now more knowledge, techniques, etc., to disseminate."[15] For example, Part B addressed such questions as innovation and change and the systems approach to instruction as well as providing an impetus for television libraries and ERIC projects. Unfortunately, however, at this time, there were no vehicles whereby research results could be effectively disseminated and the model proposed for research and dissemination in Title VII, according to Hugh F. McKeegan, former administrator of Title VII projects, "was fragmentary, incomplete, and based on an oversimplified view of how change can be brought about in our schools."[16] In retrospect, Gerald M. Torkelson, another former administrator of Title VII projects observed "that goals and language of Title VII ... represented a form of naivete about the processes of dissemination."[17]

Education R & D Centers

By the beginning of the 1960s, it was apparent to federal policy makers that the research programs of the Cooperative Research Act were fragmented and inconclusive and failed to lead to notable improvements in educational practice. Sterling McMurrin was commissioner of education in the early 1960s and he had the concept of reviving the old idea of a half century earlier of the development of Research and Development Centers. Despite opposition within the staff of the Office of Education, McMurrin appointed committees to consider the possibility of developing Research and Development Centers related to education.[18] In 1963, an advisory panel was appointed with Ralph Tyler as its chairman.[19] The panel produced the first set of guidelines, solicited proposals, and set up the first site visits.

The R & D Centers were seen as analogous to federally sponsored scientific laboratories. The Office of Education held the view that university-based R & D Centers could overcome the shortcomings of the previous CRP effort because it was believed that any practical problem in education could be solved by assembling a group of scientists and providing them with the necessary resources to solve the problem. Moreover, the prevailing concept of educational technology was that it was the result of scientific development and that it could not develop until the necessary underlying sciences had made sufficient progress. As Travers observes, "this is a modern, and parochial view of technology, for the fact is that technology has had a history of development at least back to the time of the cave men" and that "much of modern technology, if not most technology, is based on inventions made prior to the scientific era."[20]

The First R & D Centers

The Learning Research and Development Center (LRDC) at the University of Pittsburgh, one of the first two centers funded in 1964, focused on research and product evaluation. In 1964, three more centers were created: the Center for Advanced Study of Educational Administration at the University of Oregon at Eugene; the Center for Research and Development for Learning and Reeducation at the University of Wisconsin at Madison; and the Center for Research and Development on Educational Differences at Harvard University. A sum of $500,000 each was committed to these institutions annually through a five-year cost reimbursement contract. Eventually, a total of ten R & D Centers were established.

The Emerging Government-Sponsored Educational Technology

The development of federally sponsored education R & D Centers reflected a new federal emphasis on cost-benefit analysis and a behavioristic bias. The emphasis was on achieving the traditional goals of education more efficiently at less cost and to develop cultural conformity of ghetto children and minority groups. These R & D Centers were seen as sources of a packaged technology of instruction and were based on the assumption that the behavioral sciences had produced a reliable body of knowledge that could be systematically applied to the problems of education.

The Learning Research and Development Center at the University of Pittsburgh was primarily influenced by the concepts of operant psychology. For example, programs such as the Individually Prescribed Instruction, developed in the Oakleaf School by the LRDC, represents an extreme form of the use of the principles of operant conditioning in designing individualized programs of instruction in the elementary schools. As Travers states, "this kind of training, for one can hardly call it education, is surely designed to fit individuals into an industrial system in which they will show the same passive acceptance of control as they did in their days in the classroom."[21]

The real supporters of the new education R & D Centers were those few universities where these R & D Centers had been established. Others saw the new centers as draining away the funds that might enable them to develop viable research centers for graduate training. Meanwhile, as the new education R & D Centers were organized as independent enterprises outside of the schools and departments of education, the staff of these R & D Centers viewed educationists as their chief adversary. For example, Robert Glaser, director of the LRDC of the University of Pittsburgh, purposely structured the center so that it would be outside of the School of Education.

Problems of Education R & D Centers

Each of the R & D Centers had a different focus and this contributed to an incomplete and unsystematic approach.[22] Also, uncertainties about Office of Education budgets and institutional constraints were other difficulties encountered. The most profound problems, however, were those connected with the research process itself. Even after some of the centers had created reasonably complex research programs, they found that they were ill-equipped to carry development beyond the prototype stage.

The critical problems revolved about the naive view that the behavioral sciences could provide the intellectual foundation for education R & D Centers of the kind that physics provided for the Manhattan project. This was a faulty concept because the Manhattan project was based upon an advanced state of nuclear physics knowledge and only technical problems remained to be solved. In contrast, the behavioral sciences were still in a very primitive state of development and could hardly be expected to provide the knowledge base for R & D Centers to the extent that physics provided for the Manhattan project. Obviously, the lessons of past history had not been learned since the Office of Education had previously attempted the development of educational research centers in the 1920s and those had not survived. At that time, the design of the proposed centers was based on an analogy between educational and agricultural research and focused on the belief that there was a body of scientific knowledge available that could be passed on to practitioners. Thus, again in the 1960s, the same false analogy prevailed when the R & D Centers were formed for the same purposes.

Regional Educational Laboratories

The failure of the Education R & D Centers to achieve their stated objectives of transmitting relevant knowledge to practitioners in the field produced a new initiative by the Office of Education.[23] This was the idea of developing a national chain of regional educational laboratories that would generate new curricula, instructional methods, and materials based on the latest research findings. Governing boards of the laboratories were to be composed of representatives of state departments of education, colleges and universities, private and public schools, and industrial and cultural organizations.

In the early planning stages of the educational laboratories, there were frequent discussions between the Gardner Task Force and the Office of Education staff.[24] Two issues emerged early; whether the laboratories should be nationally or regionally oriented and how many laboratories should be created. The original intent was that the laboratories would be fashioned after the great national laboratories of the Atomic Energy Commission and test the feasibility of new methods. However, the Office of Education felt that they could not get the support of Congress until they replaced the "national" label with "regional" so that every congressman could get one in his own region. Ralph Tyler of the Gardner Task Force originally wanted five or seven laboratories, but others wanted more. At one time, Francis Keppel, commissioner of education, called for ten to fifteen, and later increased the number to fifteen to twenty. There was even talk of forming a laboratory in each state.[25]

President Johnson signed the Elementary and Secondary Education Act into law on April 11, 1965. Authorization for the laboratories was in Title IV of the Act. Over a year elapsed between the passage of the enabling act and the negotiation of the preliminary contracts for laboratories. By September 1966 twenty Regional Education Laboratories had been authorized. Although twenty personnel positions had been allocated for Office of Education administration, only eight positions had been filled. Two years passed before a division chief for the laboratories had been appointed. Meanwhile, staff turnover was high because the laboratories personnel were unhappy with the erratic management of the program. Moreover, hostility developed between the R & D Centers and laboratories personnel because of their competition for funds.[26]

Problems of the Regional Education Laboratories

Soon after their formation, the Regional Education Laboratories were becoming increasingly controversial in terms of how fast they ought to develop, how many there should be, and whether they could truly meet the needs of education. As a consequence, John Gardner, the secretary of HEW, commissioned Francis S. Chase, dean of the School of Education at the University of Chicago, to provide him with "trustworthy information to determine action with respect to the new laboratories."[27] On November 15, 1966, Secretary Gardner placed a thirty-day freeze on the renegotiations of the twenty laboratory contracts scheduled to take effect on December 1.

Chase made a nation-wide survey and interviewed former Gardner Task Force members, former advisors, and those who were planning laboratories. Chase wrote a report in the latter part of 1968 in which he stated that the laboratories must focus on the processes that have been lacking in education and that have prevented the

> systematic adaption of knowledge and technology to educational use through a set of closely related processes ranging from the design of models and prototypes through the successive modification of materials, technologies, strategies, and systems for achievement of specified effects.[28]

They must view research and development as "a closely integrated system for producing specified changes in educational institutions and processes."[29] The resulting products of laboratories must be the "development of tested products, operable systems, or other demonstrably useful combinations to the improvement of educational institutions and processes."[30]

Chase's influence was considerable at this time and contributed to the survival of the laboratories. In March 1967, contracts were renegotiated with twenty laboratories to continue their funding through a nine-month period. By November 1967, full-year contracts had been negotiated with all twenty laboratories. By the end of summer of 1967, Chase had helped to locate Norman Boyan, a professor of education at Stanford, who agreed to direct the Laboratories Division of the Bureau of Research.

The demise of the Regional Education Laboratories began in 1969 when five laboratories were eliminated. Within four years the number of laboratories had been reduced to ten. Several factors produced a diminished enthusiasm for the laboratory program. First of all, there was a growing congressional disenchantment with basic research and the way it was applied to practical educational problems. Perhaps, the major factor was the prevalence of simplistic thinking concerning the nature of educational research. As Travers has aptly stated,

> personnel in the Office of Education had little understanding of the nature of knowledge in the behavioral sciences and even less knowledge of the problems of applying that knowledge. Associate Commissioners for Research had typically no qualifications in the field though they may have had experience in administration.[31]

Moreover, associate commissioners for research in the Office of Education remained isolated from the research community and, simultaneously, "came to assume ever increasing power in the establishment of research policies and decisions related to whether particular projects should or should not, receive support."[32]

Assessment of Regional Education Laboratories

The primary purpose for the founding of Regional Education Laboratories was that of bridging the gap between educational research and educational practice. Further, the regional laboratories were supposed to be unique associations of colleges and universities, state departments of education, schools and other educational enterprises in a given region to accelerate educational innovations and progress. Unfortunately, much of the work of the regional laboratories proved to be disappointing. They generally failed to view educational problems broadly and chose to focus their efforts largely on reform within the existing sacrosanct educational establishment. The relationship of the regional laboratories with schools, colleges and universities, and other educational organizations have tended, on the whole, to be rather peripheral and meaningless. Some notable programs, however, have been developed by some of these laboratories. For example, the Far West Laboratory for Educational Research and Development achieved national prominence with its Beginning Teacher Evaluation Study. The Northwest Laboratory for Educational Research and Development established the Clearinghouse for Applied Performance Testing, which emphasized a broader view of traditional methods of assessment. Finally, Research for Better Schools developed a multimedia package focusing on improving the effectiveness of classroom teachers and based on research on classroom teaching.

Travers has noted that many of the products developed by the laboratories were based on the assumption that educational reform could be achieved by "packaged education backed up by some kind of guarantee concerning utility."[33] He gives as an example *The Alaskan Readers*, developed by the Northwest Regional Educational Laboratory. *The Alaskan Readers* outlines some of the problems of teaching academic skills to minority groups and criticizes the usual Dick-and-Jane approach to the teaching of reading. However,

> the goals of the Dick-and-Jane type readers and *The Alaskan Readers* are essentially the same, but the cultural bias has been altered and vastly greater care has been exercised in the details of design. The materials are not designed to achieve anything radically new but have been prepared to increase the efficiency of conservative and traditional education.[34]

Travers goes on to describe the political character of laboratory products and notes that:

> the materials are developed upon the assumption that if the minority groups can be trained to fit into the system, all will be well. The emerging educational technology is intensely conservative in that it is designed to preserve the world of the establishment, just as all government-sponsored technologies have done in the past.[35]

The Educational Resources Information Center (ERIC)

This section summarizes some of the highlights of ERIC's history and shows its particular relationship to educational technology.[36]

ERIC was the third major initiative launched by the Office of Education in the 1960s. It began in 1964 and was modeled after the Clearinghouse for Federal Scientific and Technical Information to acquire, abstract, index, store, retrieve, and disseminate "exemplary information and research."

Background

ERIC's heritage can be traced to the late 1950s when the Office of Education became concerned with the dissemination of research on the uses of "new" media in education. Maurice F. Tauber and Oliver Lilley of Columbia University were asked to make a feasibility study in 1959 to solve this problem. This report called for the establishment of a Media Research Information Service within the Office of Education, with an initial staff of five.

Thomas Clemens, who had become project officer for the Columbia University study shortly after joining the Office of Education's Media Program in early 1960, disagreed with the recommendation of the Columbia University study that the disseminated information should be limited to media research. He argued that any information service should include the entire field of education. His supervisor agreed and appointed Clemens to head an internal committee to study how a comprehensive information service could be developed. In September 1960, the Clemens Committee submitted its recommendations, but action was deferred. The committee felt that they should not proceed too rapidly and recommended that the information service should first proceed with the abstracting, indexing, and dissemination of current research related only to the subjects of media, cooperative research projects, and library services. When these areas had been substantially tested, then information center activities could be extended to other relevant educational research.

Shortly after the Clemens Committee report, a contract was given to Allen Kent of the Center for Documentation and Communication at Western Reserve University to develop a design for an information service system. Following fourteen months of work, the Western Reserve study appeared in June 1962 under the title *The Library of Tomorrow — Today.* Kent's design called for the organization of a pilot information center that would provide for detailed analysis and selective dissemination of research documents based on individual request. This report provided the first specific description of what was later to become known as ERIC. These services included:

1. Development of a database;

2. Creation of abstract bulletins;

3. Reproduction of source documents;

4. Use of these information tools by ERIC in direct service to educators;

5. Decentralization of the files for local exploitation by other agencies; and

6. Distribution of copies of bulletins and source documents to stock special libraries that could then service their clientele.[37]

By the time the Western Reserve report was received, the term *ERIC*, as the acronym for some type of information service, was already in common use among the members of the Clemens Committee. Also, there was "no dispute with the basic philosophy, the operational characteristics, or the time schedule" for ERIC. It was agreed that ERIC operations should begin in 1964, but some in the Office of Education were anxious to get it started sooner. For example, Harold A. Haswell, director of the Higher Education Programs Branch, read the Western Reserve study and became so enthusiastic about ERIC that he volunteered to head it. His opportunity came in April 1964 when Commissioner Francis Keppel announced a reorganization of the Bureau of Educational Research and Development and made ERIC a branch of the Division of Educational Research, the head of which was Francis A. J. Ianni.[38]

ERIC Begins Operations

On May 15, 1964, ERIC, under the direction of Haswell, began as an office without funds and without a program! Nevertheless, there was considerable demand from within the Office of Education for consultation and technical assistance by the ERIC staff. In July 1964, Ianni asked Haswell to work on projects concerned with cooperative research and educational media. Meanwhile, Fred Goodman, a consultant from the University of Michigan, began to conceptualize the future operations of ERIC, "including indexing, equipment, retrieval, educational literature, and other subjects." During October and November 1964, Goodman and Haswell discussed the options of centralization and decentralization of so-called "acquisition centers."

In 1965, two important events eventually produced the ERIC system we know today: increased funding brought about by the Elementary and Secondary Education Act (ESEA) and the arrival of Lee G. Burchinal as deputy director of the Division of Educational Research. Following the passage of ESEA, Commissioner Francis Keppel directed ERIC to present a plan for quickly disseminating information for use by state and local educational agencies in developing programs for teaching children from disadvantaged backgrounds. This plan, known as Project Fingertip, was developed over a weekend, approved immediately, and implemented about one month later. ERIC managed the acquisition effort; Jonker Business Machine Corporation did most of the abstracting and indexing; the Microcard Corporation produced microfiche; educators were secured to prepare descriptions of programs cited; and ERIC managed the distribution of the data collected. By the time the material was mailed in March 1966, 1,746 documents in microfiche with printed guides were sent to 650 selected locations.[39]

As a result of this successful effort, planning began that would transform ERIC from a national information center to a national system. As a consequence, ERIC became the lead program in a newly created Division of Research Training and Dissemination, headed by Burchinal. Burchinal has been described as a person who "charted a course of action that was direct, relatively noncontroversial, and low profile."[40] He took as his right-hand man Thomas Clemens, who had been on the staff of the NDEA research program since 1959. Together they established clearinghouses at universities and professional organizations so that "leading experts in various fields of knowledge can remain active in their various professional roles and yet contribute to the development of information services for their respective professional fields."[41]

Establishment of ERIC as a National System

ERIC's managers began a development of a decentralized national system during the last half of 1965. The ERIC Document Reproduction Service (EDRS) was established and in November 1965, the Micro-Photo Division of the Bell and Howell Company was awarded the first EDRS contract.

In December 1965, ERIC sought clearinghouse proposals. Two bidders' conferences were held in February 1966 and ERIC received forty-five proposals in sixteen of the nineteen areas of education that had been offered as possible subject areas by the March 15, 1966 deadline. Two proposals arrived early and ERIC selected these two as "prototype clearinghouse." One was a contract with Ohio State University to create a Clearinghouse on Vocational and Technical Education; the other was with the City University of New York for a Clearinghouse on Urban School Personnel. Both contracts became effective on March 1, 1966.

After considerable evaluation, discussion, and negotiation, ten other clearinghouses were selected to begin operation on June 1, 1966. The next component of the system was installed in November 1966 when the first issue of *Research in Education* (later renamed *Resources in Education*) was printed. Since the establishment of a national system in 1965, ERIC has been substantially unchanged except for changed sponsors and locations of clearinghouses as a result of requiring recompetition on three-year cycles, and the consolidation of some clearinghouses for greater effectiveness and continual budget constraints.[42]

Clearinghouse for Educational Media and Technology

The primary reason why only twelve clearinghouses were established during the spring of 1966 was a budgetary limitation. However, at the beginning of 1967 a bidders' conference was held covering six areas, one of which was educational media and technology. As a consequence, Stanford University, with Wilbur Schramm as director, was awarded the contract for the first Clearinghouse on Educational Media and Technology. This contract was later renewed, with reduced funding, in 1971.

The continual erosion of the budget brought another change in 1973 when proposals were solicited for a contractor to operate a combined clearinghouse on educational media and technology and library and information science, to be renamed information resources. The new contract became effective on January 1, 1974, and was awarded to Stanford University with Lewis Mayhew as director. Another competition during 1976 resulted in a shift of locale for the Clearinghouse on Information Resources from Stanford University to Syracuse University with Donald P. Ely as director. The starting date was January 1, 1977.[43]

Assessment of ERIC

ERIC has been praised highly by many, but it has also been widely criticized. Certainly, it made many of the studies conducted with Cooperative Research Program (CRP) funds in the 1960s more easily accessible to teachers and school administrators. However,

> like the laboratories and centers, ERIC and its adjunct were judged by some to be a disappointment. School professionals, by and large, did not know what was in the ERIC system, did not know how to gain access to it because most ERIC facilities were on university campuses rather than on school sites.[44]

Moreover, "when teachers and administrators did find a reference in ERIC to a report or document that appeared to meet their needs, their written request for copies often met with delays. When the material did arrive, it was often of doubtful relevance or quality."[45]

The Fry study conducted in 1970/71 provided the first nation-wide data on uses of ERIC.[46] Over 190,000 people per week, close to one million people per year, were reported to have used various ERIC products or services. In 1980, another study was launched with King Associates to update the earlier results. The King study showed increased and broader use of ERIC resources.[47] At this time, ERIC resources were used more than 2.7 million times annually. Moreover, ERIC resources were available at an estimated 3,269 locations throughout the United States; about 53 percent of these were located at institutions of higher learning; 25 percent were managed by elementary or secondary education organizations; and the remainder were located within public, state, or federal libraries, professional societies, research centers, business organizations, and federally supported centers. The majority of the users (63 percent) were students or persons providing educational services (teachers, counselors, administrators); researchers and others accounted for 37 percent of the usage. In addition, Central ERIC collects data on the searches of ERIC tapes. In 1980, about 340,000 computer searches, or over 1,500 per day, were conducted. Despite this impressive data, the paucity of funds has been a persistent problem for ERIC. Even though the ERIC budget began increasing in 1975, the purchasing power of funds available for the system has steadily declined.

The National Institute of Education

In the latter years of the 1960s, the Office of Education Bureau of Research was reorganized by the commissioner of education and found itself in fierce competition with other Office of Education bureaus for reduced budgets, external reviews, and congressional pressure to show quick, tangible results. Once the enthusiasm and support for R & D Centers and Regional Laboratories had faded, there was increasing difficulty to continue programs or to maintain them at former levels of activity.

In part the reorganization was designed to meet past criticisms concerning the impact of research and development. It brought all research programs into the Bureau of Research while the bureau was subject to policy review by the assistant secretary of planning and evaluation (ASPE), by the HEW budget analysts, and by staff assistants to the HEW secretary. In the Executive Office of the President, the research budget had to gain approval from the Bureau of the Budget (renamed the Office of Management and Budget in 1970). In addition, all education research activities were monitored by the Office of Science and Technology and its President's Science Advisory Committee. In the early days of the Nixon administration, the degree of staff monitoring of the Office of Education research was so excessive that representatives of the OMB, OST, and ASPE became known as the "unholy trinity."

The unholy trinity, consisting of three men who would later occupy top posts in the NIE, provided continuous harassment for the Bureau of Research. This conflict between the Bureau of Research and its antagonists arose for several reasons. Probably the dominant factor was that most of the staff review roles were filled by men with backgrounds in the natural sciences who were convinced that the natural science model was the appropriate one for "scientific" R&D in education. They were unanimous in their "disdain for 'educationists' in the Bureau of Research and in schools of education."[48] They also were convinced that the Bureau of Research was administered incompetently and reflected the biases of traditional education researchers. These attitudes were reinforced further with the publication of the Coleman survey on equality of educational opportunity, which cast doubts concerning the effectiveness of schools in reducing social and economic inequality. Finally, there came to be a growing disillusionment with the Great Society programs. Congress had become impatient with education research and development by the end of the 1960s. This was evident in that the staff of the Bureau of Research was cut in half from 1967 to 1971.

Nixon had proposed in his campaign that, if elected, he would create a "National Institute for the Educational Future," and that all programs would be cut that could not be justified in terms of results. After Nixon was elected, there began a lengthy planning period, from April 1970 to June 1972, for a National Institute of Education (NIE). Because there were few planning models to imitate and because NIE planners wanted to create a unique agency, different from all that had gone before, the planning period was characterized by uncertainty as well as optimism. When James Allen, the commissioner of education, asked the White House group if they could recommend someone to direct the planning effort, they suggested Roger Levien of the Rand Corporation.

Levien, with his one-man staff and two consultants, interviewed many people in education and research, and after six months, presented a preliminary draft of his report to HEW. His report identified five deficiencies in USOE's R&D activities: "lack of funds; lack of bureaucratic status and power; lack of program continuity and focus; lack of high-quality personnel; and lack of linkages among research, development, and practice."[49]

With the appointment of Sidney P. Marland as commissioner of education in December 1970, Levien was not asked to continue his planning efforts. Marland then hired Harry Silberman (formerly of the System Development Corporation) from the National Center for Educational Research and Development as associate commissioner and asked him to establish an NIE Planning Unit task force. By September 1971, Marland was receiving considerable criticism from the unholy trinity and others because they felt that the Planning Unit was being dominated by USOE and the educationists. He responded to these criticisms by moving the Planning Unit out of the USOE building and established Silberman in his own quarters. During the next months, much effort was focused on developing an interim report, but after approximately nine months of work, the Planning Unit "found itself buffeted by external criticism, bedeviled by advice-givers, somewhat estranged from Marland, and unsure of what to do next."[50]

Silberman was urged to involve planners from policy research groups. As a result, he organized four teams of planners. One was directed by Amitai Etzioni of the Columbia University Center for Policy Analysis; another was directed by O. W. Markley of the Stanford Research Institute Educational Policy Research Center; Beverly Kooi directed the third team, composed of Planning Unit and USOE staff and consultants to USOE-supported R&D centers and laboratories; and Senta Raizen from the NSF, where she was special assistant to associate director for education, chaired the fourth team. The four planning analyses were completed and distributed April 20, 1972, and this, in effect, marked the end of the Planning Unit program planning for the NIE. Finally, in June 1972, twenty-six months after Levien had begun work on a preliminary plan, President Nixon signed the legislation that created the National Institute of Education. On August 1, 1972, NIE began its operational life. On that date Emerson Elliott became acting director; he was soon succeeded by Thomas K. Glennan, formerly assistant director for planning, research, and evaluation of the Office of Economic Opportunity.

The NIE inherited $144 million worth of programs from the Office of Education. The R & D Centers and the Regional Laboratories constituted the largest inherited programs. Also transferred was the $15 million dissemination program that included as its largest component ERIC, the network of eighteen clearinghouses for computerized storage and retrieval of education documents. In addition, the Career Education and Experimental Schools program as well as a number of smaller miscellaneous programs were transferred. At the beginning of its second year in July 1973, NIE inherited three more programs: the OEO Education Voucher Experiment, the OEO Teacher Competence Study; and the USOE Education Technology Program. One major component of the technology program was a regional educational television-based open university conducted by the State University of Nebraska, offering courses for college credit to students unable to attend the university; and an education satellite project for the development of curriculum materials and the use of a NASA communications satellite to beam educational programs to remote portions of the Rocky Mountain states and Alaska. During its first year of operation, NIE began only one program of its own, Field Initiated Studies, a $10 million basic research support program. It funded research proposals from established research investigators in the areas of learning and instruction; human development; objectives; measurement and evaluation; social thought and processes; and organization and administration. Meanwhile, "the fate of these programs within NIE was shaped by a complicated interaction among personalities, bureaucratic momentum, politics, and the initial expectations for rationality and comprehensiveness."[51]

In their excellent, well-documented history of the NIE, Sproull et al. explore the underlying concepts, actions, external events, and beliefs associated with the creation of the NIE in great detail. This document constitutes the most important source of material for this section. Their history is in large part the story of how able people failed to lead an organization in the direction they sought. Unfortunately, the NIE, almost immediately after it was founded, proceeded on an entirely different course from that which research workers had hoped. It was taken over almost completely by the same bureaucracy that had failed to develop a useful research program in the R & D Centers and the Regional Education Laboratories.[52] Policies were set by federal officials rather than by research workers and scholars. As a consequence, the NIE failed to develop a viable program of educational research.

Research on the Impact of Television on Learning and Behavior

The armed forces were the first to experiment with television as an instructional medium because of its promise in meeting the mass instruction requirements demanded by military training. As early as 1950, the navy began some of the first studies of the instructional effectiveness of television. Shortly afterward, the Human Resources Research Office at George Washington University conducted for the army a study comparing television with conventional instruction in teaching effectiveness. It was not until 1955 that full-scale instructional television began in schools and colleges with financial support from the Ford Foundation. The National Defense Education Act of 1958 provided financial grants through Title VII that spurred the development of instructional television research in the late 1950s and the early 1960s.

Another early area of investigation concerned studies of the effects of television on children. No one knew, for example, whether television could change attitudes or values or whether television could create passivity or aggression. It was also unknown to what extent television could enlarge or limit children's intellectual boundaries. In the late 1960s and early 1970s, there came to be increasing concern with regard to the effect of television on social behavior. As a consequence, the U.S. Congress was prompted to appropriate $1 million to fund research studies on violence portrayed on television and the behavior of children and adolescents.[53]

Pennsylvania State University

The Fund for the Advancement of Education began its support for a closed-circuit instructional television project at Pennsylvania State University in 1954. Subsequently, the fund agreed to finance the project until 1959, with the university increasing its contribution each year and eventually assuming the entire expense of regular operation of the instructional television system.

The experimental phase of this project was carried out during the spring semester of 1955 and the fall semester of 1956/57. By 1958, 3,700 (out of a total of 14,000) students were taking one or more of 13 television courses offered. The initial experiments of this closed-circuit television project, under the direction of C. R. Carpenter and L. P. Greenhill, were designed to determine whether television could be used effectively in regular undergraduate courses and what its effects would be on instructors, students, and on the institution itself. In one phase of experimentation, a course taught in the traditional manner was compared with the same course taught by an instructor over television. New courses and materials were prepared for further comparisons. The primary focus was on extending the influence of superior teachers in those introductory courses attended by large numbers of students, which were usually taught by the lecture or lecture-demonstration method. When the students were tested at the end of the courses, it was found that there were no significant differences in achievement. It also appeared that teachers and students did not like television very much, although most instructors were willing to experiment with it and most students preferred it to live presentations in very large classes. These studies did demonstrate, however, that the influence of outstanding teachers could be extended to large groups of students without measurable loss of learning and that television could be economically feasible if the type of equipment chosen is appropriate to the task and if the system is used for a sufficiently large group (several courses involving 300 to 400 students).

The results of the Pennsylvania State University closed-circuit television project proved a great disappointment to those who thought that television instruction would revolutionize education. In addition, accumulating evidence from the majority of similar studies also revealed "no significant differences" between televised instruction and direct instruction. Thus it became apparent to some researchers that new experimental approaches were needed to replace the stereotyped instructional media comparisons design in order to understand and develop the potential of instructional television.[54]

Washington County Closed-circuit Educational Television Project

One of the largest single experiments in the use of closed-circuit television for instruction started in 1956 in Hagerstown, Washington County, Maryland. The Washington County Board of Education had first considered using television in the schools in 1954. Although the board was unaware of it then, the Ford Foundation's Fund for the Advancement of Education and the Electronic Industries Association had formed a joint committee for the purpose of starting a large-scale project in instructional television—a model program that would provide for regular, direct instruction by television rather than for a supplemental use of it. On the basis of the Washington County Board of Education's proposal to use television for instruction at all grade levels and in basic subject areas, as well as for teacher education, the fund chose Washington County as the site for its first comprehensive test of instructional television in the public schools.

The project extended over a period of five years (1956-1961), starting in the summer of 1956 when approximately one hundred teachers and administrators gathered at a workshop for the purpose of planning the new instructional television program. Simultaneously, engineers began stringing cable for the television network. The first instructional telecasts were beamed to eight schools in the fall of 1956, and by the end of the project in 1961, every public school in Washington County was linked to the television circuit.[55]

This project cannot be considered a formal experiment, for it was largely exploratory. As it developed, television came into use at all grade levels and in most subject areas. One of the most interesting aspects of this project was the successful application of television within a district-wide guidance program. In brief, the results of this study showed that television produced substantial increases in achievement and indicated that this gain was statistically significant in some course areas. For example, in fifth-grade arithmetic, pupils made almost two years' growth in arithmetic—from five months below grade level to four months above it.[56] Although the project staff did not claim that television per se was totally responsible for learner achievement, they saw educational value in television because:

1. It focused attention on problems in a way never before possible.

2. It stimulated teamwork and planning.

3. It created interest in curriculum development and teaching procedures.

4. It required pupils to assume more responsibility.

5. Parents took a greater interest than formerly in the school program and in the progress of their children.[57]

Much of the success of the Washington County project was a direct result of the way television was introduced into the system. During the five-year experiment, summer workshops were continued, frequently supplemented during the regular school terms with consultant service, as well as field trips. Also, there was no lack of emphasis on the fact that the teacher in the classroom, who followed the instructional telecasts, was the key person in the teaching team.[58]

Instructional Television Research in the 1960s

By the 1960s there was no longer any doubt that students could learn effectively from instructional television. It had been demonstrated—in approximately four hundred quantitative studies in which television instruction was compared to conventional instruction—that students in some cases will learn more, and in some, less. However, the overall conclusion was that there was "no significant difference." Relative to this conclusion is the evidence presented by Kumata as follows:

> In the United States, we have put most of our bets on the discovery of some effect which is directly attributable to the means of message transmission and hundreds of similar studies have been conducted. Almost all of them say that it makes no difference whether television is present or absent. They say that if you ignore audience variables, the nature of the student; if you ignore the nature of the source, those who put on the program; and if you look just at the media of transmission, you will get rather ambiguous results.
>
> We have been insisting that perhaps we should look at television instruction as part of a general communication process and that we may get some valuable hints from other research which has been done in the communications field.
>
> If we were to characterize the research done, I think four points would stand out. First, *no particular theoretical framework has been apparent in most of the studies* [italics mine]. Almost all of the studies have been of an applied nature.... Further there has been very little dependence on prior research. Second, the overwhelming majority of these studies have been what we call "comparability" studies, and almost all of these have been comparisons of television versus face-to-face instruction. Very few studies have been done as comparisons of radio, film, and television. Third, almost all of the main dependent variables in these investigations have been some measure of students' information gain.... Most examinations have been in the nature of requests for students to reproduce

information previously supplied by the instructor. Fourth, most research in instructional television has been done in the classroom situation, with regularly enrolled students. In other words, research has concentrated upon the captive audience aspects of educational television.[59]

The implication for the researcher and the educator is that areas of new research must be conceived and that the emphasis should be shifted to the totality of the teaching-learning process. When Carpenter, for example, talked about instructional television research as systems research, he was, in effect, asking that we determine the place of television within an instructional system or within the context of a technology of instruction.[60]

The Denver-Stanford Project

One of the first extensive research projects that attempted to measure combinations of instructional media, as well as combinations of related activities with television, was conducted jointly over a three-and-one-half year period (1960-1964) by the Denver Public Schools and the Institute for Communication Research at Stanford University. When it became apparent that there was need for an investigation of the context of instructional television, in late 1959, the National Educational Television and Radio Center brought together representatives of the Denver Public Schools and Stanford's Institute for Communication Research. From this meeting emerged a proposal for a joint project financed under Title VII (NDEA), and funds were granted. The project was officially titled "Four Years of Research on the Context of Instructional Television," but it has come to be known as the Denver-Stanford project.

Beginning with the 1960/61 school year, the Denver Public Schools made foreign language mandatory for all fifth- and sixth-graders, and pupils were permitted to choose between Spanish and French. Since some 80 percent chose Spanish and since there was a shortage of elementary teachers qualified to teach Spanish, the problem of the study was how to introduce and teach Spanish most effectively in elementary school under the conditions pertaining in Denver. In more general terms, the problem was to determine the kind of teaching and learning context that would make for maximum learning from instructional television. This is what Denver and Stanford were working on from 1960 to the beginning of 1964.

The findings of the Denver-Stanford project showed that the most effective context for instructional television in the audio-lingual year was provided by classroom teacher-conducted practice plus practice with an electronic aid, such as a dual-channel tape recorder. In general, an eclectic method including structure drill, dialogue drill, and narrative drill proved effective. The most effective classroom combination for the second year of the language—the sixth-grade audio-lingual-reading-writing year—proved to be teacher-directed practice, programmed instruction in school, and a Spanish corner for individual use in the classroom. A striking relationship was noted between pupil performance and the preparation of the teacher. It was found, for example, that a pupil could work independently with programmed instruction, extending reading, etc., to the extent that the teacher was prepared and experienced. Another finding was that for teacher-directed activities, small classes tended to perform better, but for individual activities like programmed instruction, large classes tended to perform better.

The aspect of the Denver-Stanford project that attracted the most interest was the direct involvement of parents in the instructional process. In all three years of the project, parents were invited to help their children learn Spanish, a practice that ran contrary to the trend of public school methods over the last fifty years. This part of the project was administered through the local PTA. The PTA secured the volunteers, instructed them in the procedures they were to follow, supplied them with special materials, and provided them with the information needed to evaluate their procedures. The best school performance in Spanish was associated with high amounts of practice and viewing by parents and children. Attitudes were associated with participation. When family participation was high, favorable parental attitudes made relatively little difference in the learner's school performance; but when family participation was low, favorable parental attitudes made a significant difference in how well the child did in school. Thus, these results constituted an important instructional resource that had been largely overlooked.[61]

Television in the Lives of Our Children:
The Early Years

Television in the Lives of Our Children was the first major North American study investigating the effects of television on children and the only large-scale investigation conducted until the Surgeon General's Report on Television and Social Behavior in 1972.[62] In many ways, this study resembled the milestone Payne Fund studies on the effects of films. (See chapter 8 of this book.)

This study involved eleven investigations between 1958 and 1960 in ten communities of the United States and Canada. The focus of these studies, conducted by Wilbur Schramm, Jack Lyle, and Edwin Parker, was on the uses and functions of television by children and was based on the view that children were not passive receivers, but were active agents who selected material from television that best met their needs and interests. The research design provided for a comparison of children in communities with television and without it, an analysis of the influence of fantasy and reality in the content of programs, and an exploration of the potential physical, emotional, cognitive, and behavioral problems of children that might be due to viewing television. The study also focused on children's learning from television and on the conditions of learning, including homework habits, bedtime hours, and program choices.

The findings are rather complicated to be discussed in detail. In summary, it was found that there were considerable differences among the children in their use of television and that these differences were not only age differences, but such factors as the child's IQ, social class background, and the quality of each child's social relations with both parents and peer groups were influential. Although these investigators placed great importance on the role of television in the lives of children, they concluded that:

> For some children, under some conditions, some television is harmful. For other children under the same conditions, or for the same children under other conditions, it may be beneficial. For most children, under most conditions, most television is probably neither harmful nor particularly beneficial.[63]

Lowery and DeFleur point out that this study's conclusions are self-contradictory. They pointed out that:

> it was not surprising that many researchers interpreted this work as supporting the minimal-effects hypothesis. Yet public opinion was not satisfied. Perhaps it was the conflicting conclusions that bothered many people. How could something that occupied so much of children's time and was so important in their socialization be so innocuous?[64]

Although Schramm et al. stated that television was fulfilling the fantasy needs of children, the lingering fear remained alive concerning the negative effects of television on children.

Learning from Television

In their classic work, *Learning from Television: What the Research Says,* Godwin Chu and Wilbur Schramm summarized hundreds of research studies by attempting to take a "wide-angle view of the field with low definition."[65] Although their first report was released in 1968 and subsequent reports were reprinted in 1974 and 1979, Chu and Schramm's conclusions are essentially based on television research available in 1967.[66]

Chu and Schramm concluded that:

> it has become clear that there is no longer any reason to raise the question whether instructional television can serve as an efficient tool of learning. This is not to say that it always *does*. But the evidence is now overwhelming that it can, and, under favorable circumstances, does. This evidence comes from many countries, from studies of all age levels from preschool to adults, and from a great variety of subject matter and learning objectives. The questions worth asking are no longer whether students learn from it, but rather, (1) does the situation call for it? and (2) how, in the given situation, can it be used effectively?[67]

Schramm summed up 393 experimental comparisons of television and classroom teaching. "He reported that 255 of these comparisons showed no significant differences, 83 were significantly in favor of televised teaching, and 55 significantly in favor of conventional teaching."[68] As Chu and Schramm state,

> this is an unreal comparison, because almost nowhere in the world is television being used in the classrooms without being built into a learning context managed by the classroom teacher. Indeed, some of the most successful uses seem to depend on the studio teacher and the classroom teacher working as a team, toward the same learning goals. Therefore, the finding of "no significant differences" seems to mean that television can do its part in this combination, and one goal of future research and practice is to find what combinations will be more efficient than either classroom teaching or television teaching alone.[69]

This only summarizes some of the more important Chu and Schramm conclusions. In all, they state sixty conclusions under six broad headings:

1. Do pupils learn from instructional television?

2. What have we learned about the efficient use of instructional television in a school system?

3. What have we learned about the treatment, situation, and pupil variables?

4. Attitudes toward instructional television.

5. Learning from television in developing regions.

6. Learning from television: Learning from other media.

Since Chu and Schramm completed their work, major paradigm shifts have occurred in media research as the result of a number of new insights concerning the function of media in the teaching-learning situation. Some of these concepts will be discussed in the last section of this chapter.

Children's Television Workshop (CTW)

The Children's Television Workshop became the dominant model of educational television programming for children in the 1970s. Much of the success of two of its programs, *Sesame Street* and *The Electric Company*, evolves from its conceptual and operational model, which has been described as a "forced marriage of educational advisors and professional researchers with experienced television producers."[70] For each CTW series, there have been extensive initial planning sessions by producers, researchers, content experts, and advisors.

The development of the CTW demonstrated that the most innovative projects in the use of television for learning have come from outside the traditional educational institutions. Prior to *Sesame Street*, televised instruction was very much of the "talking head" variety. *Sesame Street* differed dramatically from its predecessors in educational television by bringing together entertainment and instruction and by exploiting the medium in a new way.

The Use of Formative Research

Formative research played a vital role in the CTW production of *Sesame Street, The Electric Company,* and *3-2-1 Contact.* The formative research model developed by CTW in the late 1960s provides an excellent example for building a stronger connection between the science and technology of learning. In the case of *Sesame Street* and *The Electric Company*, formative research developed principles of presentation design appropriate to the educational goals, the viewers, and production techniques. One important aspect of the formative model was the identification of and definition of program designs that could provide reliable predictors of learning for particular learners. Although the formative model developed by CTW was a significant landmark in the technology of instructional design, it is still tentative and should be seen more as a point of departure rather than a fixed formula.[71]

Summative Evaluations

Summative research should be clearly distinguished from formative research. While formative research is used to refine goals and evolve strategies for achieving goals, summative research is undertaken to test the validity of a theory or determine the impact of an educational practice so that future efforts may be improved or may be modified.

The rationale for *Sesame Street* was based on helping prepare disadvantaged children for school and teaching young children how to think as well as master normative factual content. Ball and Bogatz made a study of the first year of *Sesame Street* on 943 children, 731 of whom were "disadvantaged."[72] They found gains in achievement in direct proportion to the amount of viewing for all groups. For similar viewing amounts, younger children achieved larger gains. It was found that advantaged children watched more of *Sesame Street* than did any group of disadvantaged children and achieved the highest pretest and posttest scores of all groups. Spanish-speaking children achieved notable gains.

Bogatz and Ball analyzed the second year to replicate the first year study and examined the impact of new goals added to the program.[73] Test sites were used where *Sesame Street* was becoming available for the first time via cable. The second-year sample showed an increase in disadvantaged children in a number of areas.

There is no question that *Sesame Street* has been the most widely viewed and researched educational television program in history. Even today it still maintains the largest number of young viewers.

The Electric Company was designed by CTW to increase reading skills among primary school children grades one through four. The reading skills emphasized were symbol and sound analysis and meaning. Like *Sesame Street, The Electric Company* utilized a number of attention-getting production techniques.

Ball and Bogatz reported findings of summative research indicated that the program generated significant positive effects on reading among children in grades 1-4, with the largest improvement among first-graders. No differences in effects were found for viewing in black-and-white versus color.[74]

The research on *Sesame Street* and *The Electric Company* indicated both the strengths and limitations of television. Although the data show that television can teach certain academic skills to children ranging in age from three to ten, its effectiveness is limited in the absence of support materials and an interested adult who can encourage viewing and enrich the lesson.

Programmed Instruction Research

Programmed instruction research, in contrast to instructional media research, has been linked to a greater extent with basic and applied research. Such research can be classified into two broad categories: (1) field-study experiments involving the use of programmed materials in actual classroom situations or (2) laboratory studies in which relatively small groups of experimental subjects have been given programmed materials outside of classroom situations. In the laboratory experiments, two different versions of a program might be written and each version given to a different group of subjects. Their relative achievement scores would then be compared. Or these studies might involve such theoretical problems as the comparison of different response modes and of different prompting and confirmation methods, ways of eliciting desired responses, or adapting programs to individual differences.

This section focuses on a very few studies selected as representative of the types of problems that were investigated most frequently when the programmed instruction movement was at its apex.

Effectiveness of Programmed Instruction

More than three-fourths of all the research on programmed instruction was conducted during the 1960-1970 period. The general conclusion from this research was that no significant difference was found among treatment comparisons, and when significant differences were obtained, they seldom agreed with other findings on the same problem.

Research has disclosed that self-instructional approaches in the form of linear and branching programs promote learning. Numerous other studies comparing programmed instruction with so-called conventional teaching procedures have demonstrated that students learn from programmed instruction. But the basic question—how well do they learn from programs, as compared to how well they learn from other methods of instruction—has produced no definitive answers. Silberman has reported, for example, that in fifteen field-study comparisons of programmed and conventional instruction, nine favored the programs with respect to criterion scores and six showed no significant differences.[75] All fifteen comparisons showed that programmed instruction took less time. This general pattern of results has been reflected in most research, although the results of some studies have actually favored conventional instruction.

Concern with evaluative criteria for assessing the quality of programmed materials was primarily responsible for the formation in 1961 of the Joint Committee on Programmed Instruction (JCPI), representing the American Educational Research Association (AERA), the American Psychological Association (APA), and the Department of Audiovisual Instruction (DAVI) of the National Education Association (NEA). In 1964, the JCPI made the following three general recommendations about the reporting of evidence on a program's effectiveness:

> First: Evidence for the effectiveness of a program should be based on a carefully conducted study which shows what the program's use accomplished under specified conditions.
>
> Second: The results of the evaluation study should be carefully documented in a technical report prepared in keeping with accepted standards of scientific reporting.
>
> Third: All claims of statements about the effectiveness of a program should be supported by specific reference to the evidence contained in the technical report.[76]

The substance of the committee's further recommendations, made in 1965, indicates that prospective purchasers or users should evaluate each program on its own merits and determine the suitability of the program for their own purposes. Moreover, the prospective user was advised to ignore all claims for the effectiveness of a program that were not supported by appropriate data that had been subjected to competent evaluation. Other comprehensive recommendations were offered by the JCPI to program publishers, reviewers, producers, and technical advisers.[77]

Pressey Studies

Some of the earliest investigations of programmed instruction were made in the 1920s by Sidney L. Pressey at Ohio State University as part of a course in educational psychology. These studies were designed to show that automated instruction facilitated learning by providing for immediate reinforcement, individual pace setting, and active responding.

The technique Pressey developed was to expose a question to a student and permit him to answer by pressing a key, by inserting his pencil tip in a punchboard, or by means of chemically treated paper. In addition, the student was referred to a specific textbook for supplementary information or his error was discussed with the instructor.

Pressey reported that his experimental students learned new material successfully from these automated programs and demonstrated significant reductions in errors when the same programs were taken a second time. He also found that the subject matter was learned faster and retained longer from his multiple-choice programs than from textbook reading.[78]

The Roanoke Experiment

One of the first extensive field tests of programmed instruction was conducted in the Roanoke (Virginia) city schools in 1960.[79] The Roanoke experiment began as a result of an invitation by Allen Calvin, a psychologist at Hollins College, to Edward Rushton, Roanoke's superintendent. Calvin, who had earlier become interested in programmed instruction, had applied for and received a grant from the Carnegie Foundation to develop an experiment utilizing an automatic teaching device to assess the possibilities of programmed instruction. Soon after, Encyclopaedia Britannica Films (EBF) became interested in his work and established, first at Hollins College and later in Palo Alto, California, its Center for Studies in Learning and Motivation.

EBF also worked with the Roanoke schools in the Roanoke experiment. The arrangement was that Roanoke would set up the demonstration class and that EBF and Hollins College would provide Roanoke with teaching machines, the programmed course, and consultation services. In February 1960, eighth-grade students, working at their own speed and receiving no help from the teacher, worked directly with ninth-grade algebra programmed materials, using lightweight Foringer teaching machines. The results of this pilot study were favorable, and in the fall of 1960 some nine hundred ninth-graders in all of the Roanoke secondary schools participated in a field test of three mathematics programs, Algebra I and II and Plane Geometry. Classes were conducted in three ways. The so-called conventional class was taught as usual except that the students were told they would be part of an experiment. In the second, the programmed material was used with no help from the teacher except to discuss examination results. In the third, the programmed material was used with help from the teacher. The experimental classes had no homework but the conventional classes had homework as usual.

No definite conclusions were drawn from this study inasmuch as the study had a number of uncontrolled variables (for example, one teacher who failed 30 percent of the program group was described as hostile), and the data are not entirely consistent. Nevertheless, Roanoke decided that student and teacher attitudes warranted the continued use of programmed instruction.

Klaus and Lumsdaine Study

Another early large-scale field study designed to test the effectiveness of programmed instruction was conducted by Klaus and Lumsdaine in the Pittsburgh (Pennsylvania) secondary schools, with 450 students.[80] This study, however, compared programmed instruction and conventional instruction in a somewhat different way. Of fifteen physics classes that were receiving regular instruction by lectures, viewing televised Harvey E. White physics films, using a textbook, and carrying out laboratory exercises, some were given, in addition, self-instructional programs in physics for six weeks. Although the use of these programmed materials was not required, the classes in which they were used showed a substantial increase in test scores when compared with those classes without programs. There was no significant difference in achievement between students who received programmed instruction and those who had lectures by their regular teachers. This suggests the possibility of substituting programmed instruction for the lecture aspects of instruction and releasing teachers for more creative instructional tasks.

Teaching Machines versus Programmed Texts

In the early years of the programmed instruction movement, many assumptions were made about how best to present material in a self-instructional program, but experimental studies have given little support to these judgments, demonstrating that programming is still more an art than a science.

One common early assumption was that the machine was the superior learning mode. However, the dominant conception, supported by research, was that the teaching machine was less important than the program.[81] Moreover, studies involving linear programs indicated that there were no significant differences between the two presentation modes of devices and texts.[82]

Small Step versus Large Step

One programming variable that has been frequently investigated is size of step. An early study by Evans et al. using four alternate versions of a program, found that graduate students with 51 and 68 steps did significantly better than other students using programs containing 30 or 40 steps, on the basis of posttest criteria.[83] However, Smith and Moore found no significant differences in the rates of learning to spell when pupils were taught 166 words by means of programs of 1,128 and 546 steps, respectively.[84] Weiss et al. found that more learning came from gradually increasing the step size than from maintaining either very short or very long steps. They also discovered that when the learner was permitted to select his own size of step before practice, he chose a gradually increasing length. Those who were permitted to practice only short steps were negatively affected in their level of performance.[85]

Overt versus Covert Responses

The experimental comparison of overt and covert responses in programmed instruction has been investigated in a number of studies, but the basic difficulty, as with so many other programming variables, has been a lack of precise, careful definition. For example, the overt-covert response mode issue is further confused because of the inadequate definition of what constitutes an overt or covert response. Although the great majority of the studies find no significant differences between the amount of learning from overt or covert responses, results from studies by Gropper and Lumsdaine indicate overt responding may not be necessary in some situations or it may be very helpful in certain programmed situations.[86]

Immediate Knowledge of Results

The majority of the studies in programmed instruction support the general assumption that immediate knowledge of results contributes to learning. On the other hand, a few studies found no significant differences attributable to knowledge of results.[87]

Learner Pacing

Somewhat surprisingly, studies have not demonstrated any significant advantage for individual learner pacing. For example, Carpenter and Greenhill compared an externally paced television program with self-paced teaching-machine programs in three experiments, and externally paced films with a self-paced programmed text in another. In each instance they found no significant difference related to pacing.[88]

The Problem of Reinforcement

The attempt to reduce all learning to the reinforcement (or operant conditioning) model of Skinner has found many in disagreement and considerable contradictory experimental evidence. One study by Rigney and Fry, for example, casts doubt on the reinforcement interpretation and indicates that linear programs, if prolonged, induce boredom.[89] Snygg's analysis of reinforcement theory showed it to be relatively useless for two reasons: First, the basic problem of how to get the learner to elicit the desired response for the first time is neither posed nor answered; and second, the reinforcement theory offers no guide for predicting what will be reinforcing to learners.[90] Clearly, Skinner was prematurely optimistic when he claimed that "the basic process and relations which give verbal behavior its special characteristics are now fairly well understood."[91]

Long-Term Effects of Programmed Instruction

During the early 1960s, programmed instruction, after a short period of enthusiasm, had already begun to wane. Unfortunately, as Lange observed, the early proponents of teaching machines and programs often permitted their claims to outdistance reality with the inevitable consequence of mounting criticism that was often quite severe.[92] Much of the reason for the rapid decline of programmed instruction was that the teaching machine came on the market long in advance of the appropriate software. Moreover, there was no evidence of pretesting despite the fact that programmed instruction was touted as the first real application of scientific principles of learning. Many educators never understood the full implication of programmed instruction and perceived it as another "medium" of instruction rather than a process for specification, design, and validation of instruction.[93]

Despite its failure as a movement in education, the programmed instruction movement has produced some important long-term effects on the history of educational technology. First of all, programmed instruction strongly influenced the development of the "systems approach" whereby emphasis is placed on the process of instruction rather than on media. Second, programmed instruction opened up new possibilities for individualizing instruction, for teaching diagnostically, and for providing a real school situation for the scientific study of learning.

Research on Computer-Assisted Instruction (CAI)

Since the 1960s, considerable research has been conducted on computer-assisted instruction. The studies that have evaluated CAI as a replacement for conventional classroom instruction found little or no significant difference in student achievement between CAI lessons and classroom learning, although there was some reduction in the amount of time needed for instruction.[94] In some of the studies, children who learned from CAI retained less of the material over a period of time than those children who were taught in the traditional manner.[95] A review of twenty studies comparing CAI with classroom instruction found nine studies showing CAI to be more effective, eight that showed no significant difference, and three that showed mixed results.[96]

Most studies focused on CAI as a supplement rather than a replacement for conventional instruction, and, in general, found positive results on learning for low-achieving or slower children as measured by standardized achievement test scores.[97] Other reviews of research showed a predominance of positive effects of CAI as a supplement to classwork, along with an increase in positive attitudes toward CAI after use.[98]

By the end of the 1960s, most of the computer-assisted learning projects were beginning to fade. Despite this negative climate, the National Science Foundation of America (NSF) decided to launch a $10 million project over five years in two demonstrations of computer-assisted learning: the TICCIT and the PLATO projects. At the conclusion of these projects, the PLATO evaluation found no significant impact on student achievement and TICCIT's positive result was complicated by high drop-out rates.[99] Jamison et al. concluded that computer-assisted instruction was effective at the elementary school level, but was about as effective as conventional instruction at the secondary school and college levels.[100]

In a review of fifty-nine independent studies of computer-assisted college teaching by Kulik, Kulik, and Cohen, they concluded that in comparison with conventional instruction CAI made small but significant contributions to course achievement, produced slightly more favorable attitudes toward instruction, and substantially reduced the amount of time needed for instruction.[101]

Kulik, Bangert, and Williams used results from fifty-one independent evaluations of CAI in grades 6-12. Their findings indicated: (1) higher performances on final examinations, (2) smaller positive effects on follow-up examinations, (3) substantial savings in learning time, and (4) very positive attitudes by students toward both the computer and their courses.[102]

The most rigorous studies of CAI effectiveness have been conducted by James Kulik and his colleagues at the University of Michigan (Kulik, Kulik, and Bangert-Drowns, 1985;[103] and Bangert-Drowns, Kulik, and Kulik, 1985).[104] These reviews all report reliable modest positive effects of CAI at all levels of formal education. These researchers used a statistical approach called meta-analysis, which in recent years has become increasingly popular to integrate findings from a large number of studies. Ironically, the meta-analysis approach itself has been a subject for debate and has become the basis for the most persistent assault on past CAI research.[105]

It must be pointed out at this juncture that most CAI studies made thus far were completed in the 1960s and 1970s on mainframe computers. In fact, the most comprehensive study of the effectiveness of CAI in the elementary school, for example, included thirty-two studies of which only five were made in the 1980s. While some contend that microcomputers are automatically superior to mainframe computers in terms of instructional effectiveness, the evidence to date is limited and inconclusive. While studies of microcomputer CAI applications have yielded effectiveness results stronger than those discovered in studies of CAI on terminal-to-mainframe configurations, studies made to date have been too few in number and too varied in design to allow us to draw any definitive conclusions regarding the differences in instructional effectiveness between mainframe and microcomputers. (See, for example, Carnoy et al.)[106] Since most of the history of microcomputer research has occurred in the 1980s, a complete discussion of microcomputer research will follow in chapter 16.

Finally, it is important to note that in many cases, CAI has been only a part of a larger intervention that has included other components. Thus, it has been argued persuasively by Salomon and Gardner that evaluations of CAI have often overlooked the unique effects of CAI by attributing both CAI and non-CAI impacts in such studies to CAI.[107] For example, many of the studies were not designed to separate the unique effects of CAI from those associated with other aspects of the instructional situation. A good example of such a situation is the nationally-known Writing to Read program associated with IBM whereby computers are used by young children to write words from which they learn to read. (See Murphy and Appel, 1984.)[108]

Research on Instructional Design and Media Selection

It seems clear on the basis of research that no single medium is superior in all respects in any instructional situation, but it is also apparent that any medium can make a viable contribution to almost any learning task.[109] Nevertheless, research in the 1950-1980 period offered only limited or incomplete guidance to the instructional designer in the selection and use of media for instruction. This need had been evident for a long time, but an adequate solution was not forthcoming. At a more theoretical level, both educational and psychological research has been seriously hampered by the absence of a theory of the structure of the symbol systems that constitute such an important part of our environment, the media that transmit these symbols, and the cognitive transformations that take place in those exposed to them. Research on media, without this framework, reflected this limitation.[110]

Some time ago, this author stated that "an urgent need exists for a taxonomy of instructional media which can provide a systematic approach to the selection and uses of media for educational purposes."[111] Since that time, important work has been done, but the need still existed in the 1970s. After reviewing the research in the hope of finding some source of help on this matter, Campeau summed up her conclusions as follows:

> In brief, an extensive literature search was for research evidence relevant to selecting appropriate media for specified learning tasks. In particular, it was hoped that results of studies on the instructional effectiveness of media under a variety of learner and treatment conditions could be applied to the task of attempting to construct a media taxonomy. The disappointing result of the literature search was that little more than a dozen experimental studies were found to meet criteria that gave them some assurance that findings were interpretable.
>
> What is most impressive about this formidable body of literature surveyed for this review is that it shows that instructional media are being used extensively, under many diverse conditions, and that enormous amounts of money are being spent for the installation of very expensive equipment. All indications are that decisions as to which audiovisual devices to purchase, install, and use have been based on administrative and organizational requirements, and on evidence of instructional effectiveness — and no wonder. To date, media research in post-school education has not provided decision makers with practical, valid, dependable guidelines for making these choices on the basis of instructional effectiveness.[112]

Commenting further in this same report, Campeau writes:

> The question of which media to compare, or which learner and media characteristics to examine should be determined in the light of subject matter and task characteristics. At present, an entire unit or course is programmed, or produced as a series of televised lessons, or filmed, or tape recorded, or produced in multimedia format, without identifying specific instructional objectives to be met and without analyzing the types and conditions of learning required. Learners are assigned to these experimental treatments without regard for traits that might interact with media and task characteristics.[113]

It is clear from the Campeau study that a comprehensive analysis is required of the types of learning tasks and instructional events that make up teaching as well as an analysis of the media of instruction so that their characteristics and the ways of using them can be incorporated into a design that includes the total learning situation. Moreover, such an analysis must include data concerning individual differences and the classification of different learning conditions.

In the 1970s, the state of the art was unable to solve the persistent problem of instructional design and media selection. As Heidt said, "Most classification systems claim to be applicable to the solution of practical problems of media design and instruction. Such pretensions, however, prove to be illusory as soon as a media designer or teacher attempts to use them for one of his everyday problems."[114] Heidt says further:

> The criterion of categorization is too general or too complex, so that the classification results only in trivial statements, as for example in Gagne's table where all media are said to be suitable for the presentation of the instruction stimulus, either with or without limitations.
>
> It is difficult to realize the instructional relevance of the principle of arrangement chosen. What would be the instructional consequences if we could detect that two media under discussion differ with respect to the quantity of sensory cues they provide?

The concept of medium is too complex and too wide. What, for example, does Gagnè mean by "teaching machine"? The differences between the devices covered by that term are immense. Or what does Briggs mean by "TV"? To what form of organization (public broadcast, CCTV, etc.) and to what aspect (transmission, video-tape production, etc.) do his statements refer?

The matching of media with the respective categories by means of ratings like "yes-limited-no" is too comprehensive and too general, and often incomprehensible without further information. What help is it for a teacher to learn that he may use sound movies in nearly all instructional situations as Briggs suggests? Why are printed media supposed to be suitable for directing attention while moving pictures are said to be unsuitable? On such a general level it is possible to give quite a number of good reasons for a reverse rating.[115]

The development of differential learning psychology in the 1970s resulted in a particular learning research known as *aptitude-treatment interaction* (ATI) or *trait-treatment interaction* (TTI) research, which considers the connections between personality traits of the learner and variables of the instructional situation. Consequently, the introduction of modern media into instruction and learning offered an opportunity to take into account the treatment of instructional design and media as part of the learning environment. Allen reviewed research concerning aptitude-treatment interaction and, simultaneously, developed an extensive list of generalizations for instructional designers. When Allen looked at the research evidence itself, he said:

There is little definitive evidence from the aptitude treatment interaction research that points conclusively to the employment of practices that might guide the selection of the more general instructional strategies, much less lead to the design of specific instructional media. The research results are so fragmentary and diverse that generalizations from these alone are virtually impossible....

We must look beyond the experimental data and base our decisions also on theories about how individuals learn and process information and upon the apparent directions suggested by the findings.

The translation of research and theory into real-life applications is desperately needed.[116]

A provocative approach to instructional design and media use was offered by Salomon. According to Salomon, "The better a symbol system conveys the critical features of an idea or event, the more appropriate it is."[117] Therefore, in choosing a medium of instruction, one analyzes what is to be taught, then searches for the symbolic coding system and the method of presentation that best fits the key elements of the information to be transmitted. Thus, "if the simultaneous operation of valves in an engine is taken as the critical feature, language would not be the appropriate medium to convey that sort of information."[118] Salomon makes the point that "since the requirements of task and the effects of media differ, there can be no best technique, method, or medium for the attainment of a general educational objective."[119] Thus, "the search for the 'best' mode of presentation for such general goals is therefore bound to fail, as indeed it has failed in the past."[120]

By the 1970s, researchers had not characterized instructional tasks and medium potentials precisely enough to reach any definitive conclusions about which medium was better suited to which educational objective. As Schramm concluded after a comprehensive review of the research, instructional media may be equally useful for most educational tasks.[121] However, the quality of media research is probably the real issue. It appears likely that more quality research will be conducted in the next decades for the purpose of determining the total effects of a given medium or combination of media in particular learning situations. Probably the crucial question will focus on the question of whether or not individual learners process information more effectively via print, visual, or audio media. Moreover, it became clear that educational technology could no longer afford to remain isolated from the fields of development psychology, differential psychology, and neuropsychology.[122]

Instructional Research in Transition

By the late 1970s, educational technology was beginning to replace the dominant behaviorist views with more cognitively oriented views. As cognitive science strived for theoretical organization, research began to be focused on new ways of learning and a deeper understanding began to develop concerning human cognition and knowledge. For example, research in educational technology has reflected a tendency to study learning as a result of the mental activities of learners, including images, motives, feelings, thoughts, attention, and memory, rather than as the direct consequence of environmental stimuli. Thus, the central focus of research in educational technology began to shift to the study of learners' cognitive processes in learning and memory.

Research on the psychology of perception since mid-century began to introduce dramatic changes in traditional concepts of learning. For example, most psychologists had held that learning could only take place through reinforcement. However, more recent research indicated that learning can take place without external feedback or reinforcement and opened the way to a new understanding of perceptual learning. Moreover, research produced models of the brain that brought about the recognition that the brain can simulate external conditions and imagine events that have not yet occurred. Much has been discussed about the right-versus-left side brain functions, but the precise application to educational technology still remains to be applied.

Another important area of research came out of the revolutionary ideas flowing from the work of Noam Chomsky. Aside from Chomsky's far-reaching impact on linguistic research, his work has influenced anthropology and philosophy as well as holding important implications for learning and instruction. This new research has illustrated the creative aspect of language reflected in the ability of the infant to produce novel sentences and demonstrate native competence in the rules of language, even in the second year of life.

In more recent times, the work of Piaget has developed the foundation for developing the psychology of acquiring scientific knowledge. More significantly, in terms of educational technology, the concepts of Piaget promise to transform the nature of educational technology from a mechanistic, impersonal approach to learning to a more humanistic approach in which children interact with the real world. Also, in the Piagetian approach, curriculum content becomes of prime importance because of its relationship to the conditions of effective learning.

Paradigm Shift

By the late 1970s, it was evident that a paradigm shift from behaviorist to cognitive theories was beginning to take place in instructional media research (see Clark and Salomon, 1986).[123] Although most early researchers on the use of media in teaching were convinced that specific media were superior to others in influencing learning, the empirical findings of over half a century of research on media in teaching have consistently shown "no significant differences" in improved learning when experimental comparisons of different treatments, such as film versus print versus live teachers, were made. Despite these results, there continued to be widespread sentiment that media could make education more productive and produce effective learning. Part of the reason that researchers have been reluctant to discontinue media comparison studies was their perception that earlier studies were based on a lack of adequate theory and poor research design. In any event, it is clear that, to date, we know neither how to measure the psychological effects of media nor how to adapt them to the goals and functions of education, but new guidelines are beginning to be formulated.

It is also important to note that the behaviorist influence on educational technology during the 1950s and 1960s provided an additional stimulus to the media comparison syndrome. Since behaviorist perceptions of learners was seen as reactive and under stimulus control, this led to an intensive search for the most effective medium. Thus the appearance of each new medium brought with it the hope that it would transform education.

As Clark says, "even in the few cases where dramatic changes in the achievement or ability have followed the introduction of a medium, as was the case in El Salvador, it was not the medium that caused the change, but rather a curricular reform that accompanied the change." He says that "the best current evidence is that media are mere vehicles that deliver instruction but do not influence student achievement any more than the truck that delivers our groceries causes changes in our nutrition."[124]

During the 1970s, due to the influence of the cognitive impact on educational technology, media comparison studies were generally discarded and an emphasis began to be placed on the attributes of media rather than on media per se. This particular focus was on the way that information is processed in learning. Thus specific elements of an instructional message came to be analyzed in terms of how it might affect particular learners under specific task conditions. For example, such media attributes as animated motion or zooming were studied to determine what systems of symbols could produce the required learning. Obviously, this research approach is far removed from the traditional conceptions of the role of media in instruction and learning. This orientation reflects the idea that learning will take place when the medium transmits a symbol system that is isomorphic with the critical aspects of the task to be undertaken.

The shift in media research created a need to identify certain media attributes that have a significant relationship to learning. Also, this new research view brought about the generation of a number of symbol system theories that had the potential of providing a bridge between research on media in teaching and research on cognition and symbolic behavior.

Although the concept that media attributes or modes of information played crucial roles in learning was not new, the development of symbol system theories did not appear until the 1970s. Gardner et al. introduced Goodman's theory of symbol systems in 1974 stating that "an analysis in terms of symbol system is required for an understanding of media."[125] Goodman's classification of symbol systems, and particularly his notion of notationality, has provided a basis for the comparison of diverse symbols, a challenge to traditional classifications of media, and the generation of a number of hypotheses concerning the processing of different kinds of symbols.

Olson and Bruner proposed that the content or the knowledge that is coded and communicated by different symbol systems through diverse media is widely generalizable, but skills or activities that are utilized in extracting any particular knowledge is unique to each medium experience. In Olson and Bruner's words, "media converge as to knowledge conveyed, but they diverge as to the skills they assume and develop."[126] Consequently, Olson and Bruner conclude that "instructional media, therefore, cannot be chosen simply in terms of their ability to convey certain kinds of content, but must also be chosen in terms of their ability to develop the processing skills that make up such an important part of human intelligence."[127]

Clark and Salomon developed a media attributes theory based on the assumption that (a) both the media and the human mind employ symbols to represent, store, and manipulate information; and (b) some of the symbol systems employed in cognition are acquired from the symbol systems employed by media. They hypothesized that:

> instruction presentation can be "closer to" or "more distant from" the way a learner tends mentally to represent the information presented under given task requirements. The closer the match between the communicational symbol system

and the content and task-specific mental representations, the easier the instructional message is to recode and comprehend.[128]

A second feature of the Clark and Salomon theory is their view that some of the symbolic features of instruction, under some conditions, can be internalized by learners and thus serve as tools of mental representation.[129]

Clark and Salomon have listed some lessons for future research in new media. Their summary of some of the most important lessons follows:

1. Past research on media has shown quite clearly that no medium enhances learning more than any other medium regardless of learning task, learner traits, symbolic elements, curriculum content or setting.

2. Any new technology is likely to teach better than its predecessor because it generally provides better prepared instructional materials and its novelty engages learners.

3. Future research on media should be conducted in the context of and with reference to similar questions in the general cognitive sciences.

4. In the future, researchers might ask not only how and why a medium operates in instruction and learning, but also why it should be used at all.[130]

Clark and Salomon also make the important point that:

most new media are not developed with educational applications as their foremost goal. Consequently, decisions to adopt them occur before there is a clear evidence about their efficacy or the availability of superior materials. This was certainly the case with television and is clearly the case with microcomputers. While the enthusiasms that surround the introduction of a new medium lend a certain currency and legitimacy to schools, they also take scarce resources away from already identified priorities.[131]

A further review of the history of research in educational technology during the 1980s is contained in chapter 17.

Notes

[1]Sigmund Koch, "Psychology Cannot Be a Coherent Science," *Psychology Today* 3 (September 1969), 64.

[2]Robert Glaser, "The Contributions of B. F. Skinner to Education and Some Counter Influences," in Patrick Suppes, ed., *Impact of Research on Education: Some Case Studies.* Washington, D.C.: National Academy of Education, 1978, 260.

[3]Samuel H. Beer, "The Modernization of American Federalism," *Publius* 3 (Fall 1973), 75.

[4]Historically, the federal government has usually supported those research and development activities that appeared to have the potential for solving current problems immediately. In education, for example, the concern for the development of trained manpower for the national defense was manifested in increased funding for science curriculum development in the late 1950s and early 1960s. Improving education as a process of educational technology has never been seen as a need or a pressing concern for the federal government. By the end of the 1960s, it was clear that the abundance of pressing social problems could not be cured by education or that more money for education R&D would assure

success. Moreover, it was becoming more apparent that the scientific natural science model was not appropriate for educational research.

[5]Public Law 85-864, September 2, 1958, 72 Statutes, 1959.

[6]Ibid.

[7]Richard A. Dershimer, *The Federal Government and Educational R & D*. Lexington, Mass.: D. C. Heath, 1976, 44.

[8]The NDEA encountered considerable opposition in Congress, but was finally passed and signed into law on September 2, 1958. It authorized $3 million in fiscal year 1959 for Title VII, but increased this to $5 million for each of the next three fiscal years. Studies under Title VI received an authorization of $1 million each year.

[9]Malcolm S. MacLean, Jr., "Critical Analysis of 12 Recent Title VII Research Reports," *AV Communication Review* 10 (Summer 1962), A103.

[10]Ibid., A105.

[11]Robert Filep and Wilbur Schramm, *A Study of the Impact of Research on Utilization of Media for Educational Purposes Sponsored by NDEA Title VII 1958-1968. Final Report: Overview*. El Segundo, Calif.: Institute for Educational Development, 1970, i. (ERIC No. ED 042 064.)

[12]Ibid., 1.

[13]Gerald M. Torkelson, "AVCR — One Quarter Century: Evolution of Theory and Research," *AV Communications Review* 25 (Winter 1977), 350-51.

[14]Hugh F. McKeegan, "Title VII in the Rearview Mirror," *AV Communication Review* 19 (Fall 1971), 329.

[15]Filep and Schramm, *Final Report: Overview*, 17.

[16]McKeegan, "Title VII," 329.

[17]Torkelson, "AVCR — One Quarter Century," 350.

[18]In 1962, Commissioner McMurrin appointed an ad hoc advisory committee of twenty-seven scholars who made a series of recommendations for ways the Office of Education might proceed.

[19]Ralph Tyler was assisted by Alan Pifer, vice president of Carnegie Corporation; Thomas Eliot, chancellor, Washington University at St. Louis; William Robinson, commissioner of education, Rhode Island; and Benjamin Bloom, professor of educational psychology, University of Chicago.

[20]Robert M. W. Travers, "Educational Technology and Related Research Viewed as a Political Force," in Robert M. W. Travers, ed., *Second Handbook of Research on Teaching*. Chicago: Rand McNally, 1973, 980.

[21]Ibid., 989.

[22]Sproull et al.'s study of the R & D Centers has indicated that "no federal master plan of identified priorities existed at the time of their creation" and that each of the centers had a different focus. They concluded that "the system of centers seemed incomplete and unsystematic." See Lee Sproull et al., *Organizing an Anarchy*. Chicago: University of Chicago Press, 1978, 18.

[23]Federal educational research laboratories had the responsibility to disseminate research findings. However, Marilyn Rauth in her study has indicated that "front-line educators claimed they never saw the fruits of this labor." She said "the labs claimed research was being disseminated, but lab visibility was lost because labs worked through school administrators, who acted as knowledge brokers." She

found that "significant educational research findings ... sat on the shelves of research institutions and libraries." See Marilyn Rauth, "The Federal Research Agenda and Professional Organizations," in Manual J. Justiz and Lars G. Bjork, eds., *Higher Education Research and Public Policy*. New York: ACE and Macmillan, 1988, 189.

[24]On May 22, 1964, at the University of Michigan, President Johnson announced that he was assembling a series of working groups to help him design the Great Society. One of these was the Task Force on Education, chaired by John Gardner, then president of the Carnegie Corporation. Gardner, a psychologist, had shown an interest in education for years. Joining Gardner's task force were the following twelve members: James E. Allen, Jr., commissioner of education, New York State Department of Education; Hedley W. Donovan, editor in chief, *Time*; Harold B. Gores, president, Educational Facilities Laboratories; Clark Kerr, president, University of California; Edwin H. Land, president, Polaroid Corporation; Sidney P. Marland, superintendent of schools, Pittsburgh; David Reisman, professor of the social sciences, Harvard; The Reverend Paul C. Reinet, president, St. Louis University; Mayor Raymond R. Tucker, St. Louis, Missouri; Ralph W. Tyler, director, Center for Advanced Study in the Behavioral Sciences; Stephen J. Wright, president, Fisk University; and Jerrold R. Zacharias, professor of physics, MIT. This task force recommended the creation of the Regional Education Laboratories. The Gardner Task Force had visualized the laboratories as few in number but high in excellence.

[25]Dershimer, *Educational R & D*, 87.

[26]See Sproull et al., *Organizing an Anarchy*, 19.

[27]Francis Chase, "Educational Research and Development in the Sixties: The Mixed Report Card," in *Educational Research: Prospects and Priorities*, Appendix 1 to hearings on the National Institute of Education. House Select Subcommittee on Education, 92d Congress, 1st sess., 2.

[28]Francis Chase, "The National Program of Educational Laboratories." Bureau of Research, Office of Education, Department of Health, Education and Welfare, Washington, D.C., December 17, 1968, 8.

[29]Ibid., 22.

[30]Ibid., 37.

[31]Robert M. W. Travers, *How Research Has Changed American Schools*. Kalamazoo, Mich.: Mythos Press, 1983, 538.

[32]Ibid., Travers, *Second Handbook of Research on Teaching*, 985.

[33]Ibid.

[34]Ibid.

[35]Ibid.

[36]For a complete, well documented history of ERIC, see Delmer J. Trester, *ERIC—The First Fifteen Years*. Columbus, Ohio: Ohio State University, 1981.

[37]Lee G. Burchinal, "ERIC: The International Education Information System," in William J. Paisley and Matilda Butler, eds., *Knowledge Utilization Systems in Education*. Beverly Hills, Calif.: Sage Publications, 1983, 45.

[38]Trester, *First Fifteen Years*, 1-12.

[39]Ibid., 13-34.

[40]Dershimer, *Educational R & D*, 109.

[41]Ibid.

[42]Burchinal, "ERIC," 51.

[43]Trester, *First Fifteen Years*, 15.

[44]Lee Sproull et al., *Organizing an Anarchy: Belief, Bureaucracy, and Politics in the National Institute of Education*. Chicago: University of Chicago Press, 1978, 19.

[45]Ibid.

[46]See B. M. Fry, *Evaluation Study of ERIC Products and Services: Summary and Volumes 1-4*, March 1972 (ERIC No. ED 060 922-ED 060 926).

[47]See D. McDonald et al., *Cost and Usage of the Educational Resources Information Center (ERIC) System, Final Report*, Rockville, Md.: King Research, 1981 (ERIC No. ED 208 902); J. L. Heinmiller, *Cost and Usage Study of the Educational Resources Information Center (ERIC) System: A Descriptive Summary*, Washington, D.C.: National Institute of Education, December 1981 (ERIC No. ED 208 903).

[48]Ibid., *Organizing an Anarchy*, 28.

[49]Ibid., 40.

[50]Ibid., 52-53.

[51]Ibid., 130.

[52]The surviving R & D Centers and Regional Education Laboratories and other miscellaneous organizations formed a coordinating organization called the Council for Educational Development and Research, referred to as CEDAR. The council published summaries of the accomplishments of the organizations listed in terms of products that were available. This compilation was called the *Cedar Catalog*. The *Cedar Catalog* appeared annually through 1974, but when the National Institute of Education took over this program, a complete catalog was never published. The *Cedar Catalog* included a section of summaries of what was called "Basic Research." However, the products in this section were mainly annotated bibliographies and summaries. Another section called "Product Evaluation" was mostly blank. Some entries stated that the product was tried out on children and the children seemed to enjoy the materials, but it was not clear how they determined whether the children did or did not enjoy the materials. Orlick has observed that "there is a tendency to fund poorly conceptualized and politically motivated R & D projects, rather than to fund well-planned research proposals. The USOE is looking for quick payoffs which never tend to materialize," (see Orlick, "Federal Educational Policy: The Paradox of Innovation and Centralization," *Educational Research* 8 (1979), 4-9).

[53]See Surgeon General's Scientific Advisory Committee on Television and Social Behavior, *Television and Growing Up: The Impact of Televised Violence*. Report to the Surgeon General, United States Public Health Service, Washington, D.C.: GPO, 1971.

[54]See, for example, L. Siegel and L. C. Siegel, "The Instructional Gestalt: A Conceptual Framework and Design for Educational Research," *A V Communication Review* 12 (Spring 1964), 16-45.

[55]Throughout the five years of the project, the Washington County school system received support from two major sources—the Electronic Industries Association and the Fund for the Advancement of Education. Seventy-five manufacturers donated the equipment valued at $300,000, and the fund contributed about $200,000 each year.

[56]Washington County Board of Education, *Washington County Closed-Circuit Report*. Hagerstown, Md., 1963, 47-53.

[57]Ibid., 73.

[58]Since the Fund for the Advancement of Education considered the Washington County closed-circuit educational television project a success, funds were provided in 1957 to launch a nation-wide

experiment in instructional television known as the National Program in the Use of Television in the Public Schools. The main thesis of *Schools for Tomorrow*, a report by Alexander J. Stoddard of the fund, was that television is an effective medium of instruction for the teaching of large groups. In an effort to test this hypothesis, the fund involved over two hundred thousand students in more than eight hundred elementary and secondary schools throughout the country. Public school systems participating in this program were the following: Anaheim, California; Atlanta, Georgia; Buena Vista No. 9 School District, Saginaw, Michigan; Cincinnati, Ohio; Dade County (Miami), Florida; Detroit, Michigan; Jefferson County, Kentucky; Milwaukee, Wisconsin; Norfolk, Virginia; Oklahoma City, Oklahoma; Philadelphia, Pennsylvania; and Wichita, Kansas, as well as schools in central Michigan; the Columbus, Ohio, area; Evansville and vicinity; western Florida; Des Moines, Iowa; and Kansas City, Missouri. During the first two years of the national program, the participating schools made many comparisons between achievement of television students and conventionally taught students. In the second year of the experiment, the number of comparisons favoring television students was more than twice the number of comparisons favoring control groups, while the number of significant differences favoring television was more than three times the number favoring conventional teaching. The most obvious thing was the large number of *no significant difference* results. However, the difference between the results for the younger and older students was highly significant, showing that television has been a more effective medium for younger students than for older. See *Teaching by Television*. New York: Ford Foundation and Fund for the Advancement of Education, 1961.

[59]Report presented by Hideya Kumata at the International Seminar on Instructional Television, Purdue University, Lafayette, Ind., October 8-18, 1961. From *History and Progress of Instructional Television Research in the United States*, Hideya Kumata, ed.

[60]C. R. Carpenter, "Approaches to Promising Areas of Research in the Field of Instructional Television," in *New Teaching Aids for the American Classroom*. Stanford, Calif.: Institute for Communications Research, 1960, 73-94.

[61]See Denver Public Schools-Stanford University, *The Context of Instructional Television — Summary Report of Research Findings 1960-1964*. NDEA Title VII Project 354, U.S. Office of Education, June 1964.

[62]Wilbur Schramm et al., *Television in the Lives of Our Children*. Palo Alto, Calif.: Stanford University Press, 1961.

[63]Schramm et al., *Lives of Our Children*, 13.

[64]Shearon Lowery and Melvin L. DeFleur, *Milestones in Mass Communications Research: Media Effects*. New York: Longman, 1983, 294.

[65]Godwin Chu and Wilbur Schramm, *Learning from Television: What the Research Says*, 4th ed. Washington, D.C.: National Association of Educational Broadcasters, 1979, i.

[66]The 1974 version of the Chu and Schramm report did not contain any new reviews, but Monty Stanford added a chapter on instructional radio research and provided three generalizations based on a review of instructional television research completed between 1967 and 1972.

[67]Ibid., *Learning from Television*, 98.

[68]Ibid., 5.

[69]Ibid., 6.

[70]G. S. Lesser, *Children and Television: Lessons from* Sesame Street. New York: Random House, 1974, xv-xvi.

[71]For a detailed account of the use of formative research in CTW, see E. L. Palmer, "Formative Research in Educational Television Production: The Experience of the Children's Television Workshop," in Wilbur Schramm, ed., *Quality in Instructional Television*. Honolulu, Hawaii: University Press of Hawaii, 1972.

[72]See S. Ball and G. A. Bogatz, *The First Year of* Sesame Street: *An Evaluation*. Princeton, N.J.: Educational Testing Service, 1970.

[73]See G. A. Bogatz and S. Ball, *The Second Year of Sesame Street: A Continuing Evaluation*, 2 vols. Princeton, N.J.: Educational Testing Service, 1972.

[74]See S. Ball and G. A. Bogatz, *Reading with Television: An Evaluation of* The Electric Company, a report to the Children's Television Workshop. Princeton, N.J.: Educational Testing Service, 1973.

[75]H. F. Silberman, "Characteristics of Some Recent Studies of Instructional Methods," in J. E. Coulson, ed., *Programmed Learning and Computer-Based Instruction*. New York: John Wiley & Sons, 1962, 13-24.

[76]American Educational Research Association, American Psychological Association, Department of Audiovisual Instruction, National Education Association: Joint Committee on Programmed Instruction and Teaching Machines, *Recommendations for Reporting of Information on the Performance Characteristics of Programmed Learning Materials: Third Interim Report*. (Preliminary edition.) Berkeley: University of California Press, 1964.

[77]For further details on the effectiveness of programs, the reader may wish to consult Arthur A. Lumsdaine, "Assessing the Effectiveness of Instructional Programs," in Robert Glaser, ed., *Teaching Machines and Programmed Learning, II: Data and Directions*. Washington, D.C.: DAVI, 1965, 267-320.

[78]S. L. Pressey, "Development and Appraisal of Devices Providing Immediate Automatic Scoring of Objective Tests and Concomitant Self-Instruction," *Journal of Psychology* 29 (1950), 417-47.

[79]E. W. Rushton, *Programmed Learning: The Roanoke Experiment*. Chicago: Encyclopaedia Britannica, 1965.

[80]David J. Klaus and A. A. Lumsdaine, *An Experimental Field Test of the Value of Self-Tutoring Materials in High School Physics*, an interim report of progress and findings. Pittsburgh, Pa.: American Institute for Research, 1960.

[81]L. S. Goldstein and L. G. Gotkin, "A Review of Research: Teaching Machines vs. Programmed Textbooks as Presentation Modes," *Journal of Programmed Instruction* 1 (1962), 29-36.

[82]Research on the techniques of programming has been largely concentrated on linear Skinnerian programs. It is interesting to find that only a few experiments have made use of other kinds of programming, such as the "intrinsic" kind of Norman Crowder, the "adjunct" type of Sidney L. Pressey, or the adaptive programming of Pask and others.

[83]J. L. Evans et al., "A Preliminary Investigation of Variations in the Properties of Verbal Learning Sequences of the 'Teaching Machine' Type," in Arthur A. Lumsdaine and Robert Glaser, eds., *Teaching Machines and Programmed Learning: A Source Book*. Washington, D.C.: DAVI, 1960, 446-51.

[84]Wendell Smith and J. William Moore, *Size-of-Step and Achievement in Programmed Spelling*. Lewisburg, Pa.: Bucknell University Press, 1961.

[85]Walther Weiss et al., "Combining Practice with Demonstration in Teaching Complex Sentences: Serial Learning of a Geometric-Construction Task," in A. A. Lumsdaine, ed., *Student Response in Programmed Instruction*. Washington, D.C.: National Academy of Sciences, National Research Council, 1961, 55-76.

[86]George L. Gropper and A. A. Lumsdaine, *An Investigation of the Role of Selected Variables in Programmed TV Instruction. Studies in Televised Instruction, Report No. 4*. Pittsburgh, Pa.: Metropolitan Pittsburgh Educational Television Stations WQED-WQEX and American Institute for Research, 1961.

[87]See, for example, J. William Moore and Wendell I. Smith, "Knowledge of Results in Self-Teaching Spelling," *Psychological Reports* 9 (1961), 717-26.

[88]Carpenter and Greenhill, *Comparative Research on Methods and Media for Presenting Programmed Courses in Mathematics and English*. University Park, Pa.: Pennsylvania State University, 1963.

[89]See, for example, J. W. Rigney and E. B. Fry, "Current Teaching-Machine Programs and Programming Techniques," *A V Communication Review* 9, supplement 3 (May-June 1961).

[90]D. Snygg, "The Tortuous Path of Learning Theory," *Audiovisual Instruction* 7 (1962), 8-12.

[91]B. F. Skinner, *Verbal Behavior*. New York: Appleton-Century-Crofts, 1957, 3.

[92]See P. C. Lange, "Future Developments," in P. C. Lange, ed., *Programmed Instruction*. Chicago: National Society for the Study of Education, 1967, 319.

[93]Susan Markle made an early contribution to the understanding of programmed instruction by defining it as a "reproducible sequence of instructional events designed to produce a measurable and consistent effect on the behavior of each and every acceptable student." In this sense, programmed instruction became synonymous with the term "validated instruction." See Susan Markle, "Empirical Testing of Programs," in Phil C. Lange, ed., *Programmed Instruction*, Part II, yearbook of the National Society for the Study of Education. Chicago: University of Chicago Press, 1967, 104. Susan Markle also made an important contribution to programming. Since guidance for the beginning programmer was seriously limited in the 1960s, she provided a useful text, *Good Frames and Bad*. New York: John Wiley & Sons, 1969.

[94]D. Jamison et al., "The Effectiveness of Alternative Instructional Media: A Survey," *Review of Educational Research* 44 (Winter 1974), 1-61.

[95]P. Suppes and M. Morningstar, *Computer-Assisted Instruction at Stanford, 1966-1968: Data, Models, and Evaluations of the Arithmetic Programs*. New York: Academic Press, 1972.

[96]J. Edwards et al., "How Effective Is CAI? A Review of the Research," *Educational Leadership* 33 (November 1975), 147-53.

[97]L. N. Simmons, *Effects of Educational Technology: A Review of the Literature*, research report no. IR76-800-71-14. Dallas: Dallas Independent School District, Department of Research, Evaluation and Information System, 1975.

[98]J. Feldhusen and M. Szabo, "The Advent of the Educational Heart Transplant, Computer-Assisted Instruction: A Brief Review of Research," *Contemporary Education* 40 (February 1969), 265-74.

[99]Jamison et al., "Alternative Instructional Media," 1-61.

[100]Ibid.

[101]J. Kulik, C. Kulik, and P. Cohen, "Instructional Technology and College Teaching," *Teaching of Psychology* 7 (December 1980), 199-205.

[102]J. A. Kulik, R. L. Bangert, and G. W. Williams, "Effects of Computer-Based Teaching on Secondary School Students," *Journal of Educational Psychology* 75 (February 1983), 19-26.

[103]James A. Kulik, Chen-Lin C. Kulik, and Robert L. Bangert-Drowns, "Effectiveness of Computer-Based Education in Elementary Schools," *Computers in Human Behavior* 1 (1985), 59-74.

[104]Robert L. Bangert-Drowns, James A. Kulik, and Chen-Lin C. Kulik, "Effectiveness of Computer-Based Education in Secondary Schools," *Journal of Computer-Based Education* 12 (January 1985), 59-68.

[105]Richard E. Clark, "Evidence for Confounding in Computer-Based Instruction Studies: Analyzing the Meta-Analyses," *Educational Technology and Communication Journal* 33 (Winter 1985), 249-62.

[106]Martin Carnoy et al., *Education and Computers: Vision and Reality.* Stanford, Calif.: CERAS, School of Education, 1986, 53.

[107]Gavriel Salomon and Howard Gardner, "The Computer as Education: Lessons from Television Research," *Educational Researcher* 15 (January 1986), 13-19.

[108]Richard T. Murphy and Lola Rhea Appel, *Evaluation of the Writing to Read Instructional System*, second-year report. Princeton, N.J.: Educational Testing Service, 1984.

[109]See Wilbur Schramm, *Big Media Little Media.* Beverly Hills, Calif.: Sage Publications, 1977.

[110]See W. H. Allen, "Instructional Media Research: Past, Present, and Future," *AV Communication Review* 1 (Spring 1971), 5-18.

[111]Paul Saettler, "Design and Selection Factors," *Review of Educational Research* 38 (April 1968), 115-28.

[112]P. L. Campeau, "Selective Review of the Results of Research on the Use of Audio-Visual Media to Teach Adults," *AV Communication Review* 22 (Spring 1974), 31.

[113]Ibid.

[114]Erhard U. Heidt, *Instructional Media and the Individual Learner.* New York: Nicholas Publisher, 1976, 37-38.

[115]Ibid., 38.

[116]Allen, "Instructional Media Research," 139.

[117]G. Salomon, "What Is Learned and How Is It Taught: The Interaction between Media, Message, Task, and Learner," in D. Olson, ed., *Media and Symbols: The Forms of Expression, Communication, and Education*, Part I, 73rd yearbook of the National Society for the Study of Education. Chicago: University of Chicago Press, 1974, 392.

[118]Ibid., 392.

[119]Ibid., 395.

[120]Ibid., 395.

[121]Ibid., Schramm, *Big Media.*

[122]See M. C. Wittrock, "Education and the Cognitive Processes of the Brain," in Jeanne S. Chall and Allen F. Mirsky, eds., *Education and the Brain*, Part II, 77th yearbook of the National Society for the Study of Education. Chicago: University of Chicago Press, 1978, 61-102.

[123]R. E. Clark and Gavriel Salomon, "Media in Teaching," in Merlin C. Wittrock, ed., *The Third Handbook of Research on Teaching.* Chicago: Macmillan, 1986, 468.

[124]R. E. Clark, "Reconsidering Research on Learning from Media," *Review of Educational Research* 53 (Winter 1983), 445.

[125]Howard Gardner et al., "Symbol Systems: A Philosophical, Psychological, and Educational Investigation," in *Media and Symbols: The Forms of Expression, Communication, and Education* 31.

[126]Ibid., David R. Olson and Jerome S. Bruner, "Learning through Experience and Experience through Media," 149.

[127]Ibid.

[128]Ibid., Clark and Salomon, "Media in Teaching," 468.

[129]Ibid., 474.

[130]Ibid., 475.

[131]Ibid.

Select Bibliography

Allen, William H. "Instructional Media Research: Past, Present, and Future." *AV Communication Review* 1 (1971): 5-18.

Chu, Godwin, and Wilbur Schramm. *Learning from Television: What the Research Says*, 4th ed. Washington, D.C.: NAEB, 1979.

Clark, Richard E., and Gavriel Salomon. "Media in Teaching," in Merlin C. Wittrock, ed., *The Third Handbook of Research on Teaching*. Chicago: University of Chicago Press, 1986.

Dershimer, Richard A. *The Federal Government and Educational R & D*. Lexington, Mass.: D. C. Heath, 1976.

Filep, Robert, and Wilbur Schramm. *A Study of the Impact of Research on Utilization of Media for Educational Purposes Sponsored by NDEA Title VII 1958-1968. Final Report: Overview*. El Segundo, Calif.: Institute for Educational Development, 1970. ERIC No. ED 042 064.

Glaser, Robert, ed. *Teaching Machines and Programed Learning, II: Data and Directions*. Washington, D.C.: DAVI, 1965.

Heidt, Erhard U. *Instructional Media and the Individual Learner*. New York: Nicholas Publishing, 1976.

Lowery, Shearon, and Melvin L. DeFleur. *Milestones in Mass Communications Research*. New York: Longman, 1983.

Paisley, William J., and Matilda Butler, eds. *Knowledge Utilization Systems in Education*. Beverly Hills, Calif.: Sage Publications, 1983.

Schramm, Wilbur et al. *Big Media, Little Media*. Beverly Hills, Calif.: Sage Publications, 1977.

_____. *Television in the Lives of Our Children*. Palo Alto, Calif.: Stanford University Press, 1961.

Sproull, Lee, et al. *Organizing an Anarchy: Belief, Bureaucracy, and Politics in the National Institute of Education*. Chicago: University of Chicago Press, 1978.

Suppes, Patrick, ed. *Impact of Research on Education: Some Case Studies*. Washington, D.C.: National Academy of Education, 1978.

Torkelson, Gerald M. "AVCR—One Quarter Century: Evolution of Theory and Research." *AV Communications Review* 25, 4 (Winter 1977): 317-58.

Travers, Robert M. W. "Educational Technology and Related Research Viewed as a Political Force," in Robert M. W. Travers, ed., *Second Handbook of Research on Teaching*. Chicago: Rand McNally, 1973.

_____. *How Research Has Changed American Schools*. Kalamazoo, Mich.: Mythos Press, 1983.

Trester, Delmer J. *ERIC—The First Fifteen Years*. Columbus, Ohio: Ohio State University Press, 1981.

Part IV

Educational Technology in the 1980s and Beyond

The final part of this book is composed of four chapters. Chapter 16 reviews the evolution of new information technologies and their present and potential implementation in educational technology, and provides a historical analysis of the adoption and use of information technologies. Chapter 17 explores the new theoretical and research horizons in educational technology and reviews exemplary related research. Chapter 18 focuses on the professional organization of educational technology, including professional education programs and certification. Chapter 19 reviews the state-of-the-art of educational technology and explores its future prospects.

16

Educational Technology and New Information Technologies

It is the purpose of this chapter: (1) to draw a conceptual distinction between educational technology and new information technologies; (2) to describe the historical background, meaning, and characteristics of the new information technology; (3) to provide an overview of new information technologies and their relationship to educational technology; and (4) to offer a historical analysis of the problems of adoption and use of new information technologies within the traditional school organization.

A Conceptual Distinction

With the rise of new information technologies, there has been widespread confusion concerning their meaning and function within the instructional process. Many people, including some educators, have equated new information technologies with educational technology and have used the terms interchangeably. New information technologies refers to electronic media that may or may not be used for instructional purposes, while educational technology is concerned with the total process of instructional design and learning. Moreover, what is more important, it is now known that technologies do not mediate learning, but that knowledge is mediated by the cognitive processes produced by technologies. According to Clark and Sugrue, "media attributes studies indicate that media are best conceptualized as delivery vehicles for instruction and not as variables that directly influence learning."[1] Consequently, the function of educational technology involves the development of powerful instructional designs that generate the most productive cognitive processes required for particular learning tasks. The conception of educational technology as consisting primarily of hardware or machines reflects the earlier media concept that equated a technology of learning with information technologies.

Background and Meaning of New Information Technologies

The term *information technology* is of relatively recent origin and did not evolve until the 1970s. However, its basic concepts can be traced to the World War II alliance of the military and industry in the development of electronics, computers, and information theory.[2] Following the war, the military remained the major source of research and development funding for the expansion of automation to replace manpower with machine power, and thus enable industry to strengthen the control of management.

Although earlier stored-program computers, such as EDVAC and EDSAC, were developed, the computer first entered public consciousness when Eckert and Mauchly completed UNIVAC I, the first commercial computer, in 1951. Shortly thereafter, UNIVAC was delivered to the Census Bureau and was used by CBS to predict the 1952 presidential election. A new phase in the history of computers began in 1975 with the development of microcomputers by MITS. This was quickly followed by Tandy Corporation's first Radio Shack computer in 1976, and by the Apple microcomputer in 1977. During the next years, thousands of companies went into the microcomputer business, selling both hardware and software. The market then increased dramatically when IBM introduced the first personal computer in the fall of 1981.

Since the 1950s, four generations of computers have evolved. From the first generation to the fourth, the trend has been to produce smaller, more powerful, more reliable, and less expensive computers. The first generation of computers (1951-1958) began with the introduction of UNIVAC in 1951. This computer, as well as others of this generation, used vacuum tubes to control operations. The second generation of computers (1958-1964) was a direct result of the invention of the transistor by Bell Labs in 1947. Transistors were faster, more reliable, and much smaller than vacuum tubes. The third generation of computers (1964-1974) was also characterized by a continuing trend in the diminishing size of components. The integrated circuit containing numerous components fused on a single silicon chip was the major technological achievement of this era. The fourth generation of computers (1974-) was a direct result of the microprocessor, or computer on a chip. Microcomputers have brought about further miniaturization of components, increased speed, greater reliability, and have vastly increased storage capacities. The fifth generation of computers, which are still in the experimental stage, will be characterized by advances in artificial intelligence that will minimize the need for complex programming.[3] Despite all the advances that have been made in the technology (the hardware) and the programs (the software), computers today still belong to the fourth generation because they still follow what is known as the von Neumann architecture—the logic of computer theory and design proposed by John von Neumann. Many are working toward a fifth-generation of computer, but before this can be accomplished, a new level of theory for *knowledge information processing* beyond knowledge engineering needs to be achieved. It is to be demonstrated in the years ahead what extent computers can think or learn. Some believe that advances in neural science may eventually provide the significant breakthrough.

Gerstein defines information technology by stating that it "refers to the collective means to assemble and electronically store, transmit, process, and retrieve words, numbers, images, and sounds, as well as the electronic means to control machines of all kinds."[4] Webster and Robins define information technology as that "which encompasses word processors, office equipment, electronic mail, cable television, videotext, robotics, television games, computer networks, and satellite communications."[5]

In a 1983 report issued by the Office of Technology Assessment of the United States Congress—*Information Technology and Its Impact on American Education*—information technology is defined as including communications systems such as direct broadcast satellite, two-way interactive cable, low-power broadcasting, computers, and video technology. This report also stated that

> the full range and form of the technologies are yet to be determined, but it is most likely that hardware and software developments will be integrated to form new, yet to be specified types of information products and services that will blur the traditional distinctive characteristics between and among media.[6]

Convergence of Computing and Telecommunications

New information technologies, such as computers, cable television, videocassettes, satellites, and lasers, are blending into new media configurations. Technological convergence, due largely to the computer's manipulation of images, sounds, and text, is occurring with increasing speed with each new technological advance. These information technologies provide new alternatives to existing communications systems. For example, videocassettes or videodiscs "store" forms of television that can be transported and played at more convenient times. Communication satellites constitute another form of broadcasting whereby digital radio or television signals are received and transmitted in the electro-magnetic spectrum. Likewise, videotext or teletext are alternative coding systems that provide means of delivering print and graphic materials by broadcast or wire transmission. Cable television is simply a form of traditional broadcasting that provides for the simultaneous transmission of many radio and television signals or textual information by means of either one-way or two-way interactive wired systems.

The explanation of the convergence between historically separated communications media lies in digital electronics. Therefore,

> communications of all kinds, when transformed into digitized form, cannot only be transmitted but also stored and modified as desired. Computers can manipulate communications in all media so as to synthesize graphic patterns or voice, to edit text or video tapes, to write abstracts without a human author, to draw inferences, or to find proofs. Thus a broadband digital communication system is likely in the end to become a vehicle not only for data communication but also for other kinds of communication, including voice and pictures, publishing, broadcasting, and mail.[7]

One generalization about information technology is that the new media forms have rarely replaced the old media, but simply utilized the newer forms for more specialized purposes and combined particular media capabilities with the use of computers and digital encoding. For example, the convergence of print and electronics illustrates how the historically wide separation of print media from the electrical ones were brought together with data or computer networks. It now appears likely that digital electronic networks may, in the twenty-first century, carry much of what today is delivered as a printed paper. Moreover, electronic technologies are challenging the old process of print publishing and the means by which copy is delivered to the reader. In the not too distant future, anything that is published in print will be typed on a word processor or typeset by use of a computer. Simultaneously, the issues of telecommunications will soon become issues for all communications as they all become forms of electronic processing and transmission.

Information Technology as Extensions of Media

Before the development of the term *information technology*, the prevailing term that referred to the use of devices or instruments in education was *instructional media*. Since new information technology is extending and bringing about a convergence of traditional media, it is important to examine the historical conceptions of media.

Although the term media was widely used in education, beginning in the period after World War II, very few definitions were proposed nor was there a general agreement on the meaning or function of media in the educative process. Usually, definitions of instructional media have merely enumerated lists of devices or aids such as projected media and audio or visual media. Frequently, the word *means* has been used to express the concept that the medium is differentiated from the content or message of a communication. Reiser and Gagnè, for example, define "instructional media as the physical means by which an instructional message is communicated."[8] Romiszowski defines media "as the carriers of messages, from some transmitting source to the receiver of the message."[9] Moeller views the medium as "a mechanical device which 'mediates' between the source or communicator and audience, whether the medium be a printing press or a transmitter or a projector."[10] Thayer expresses a broad definition of media when he states that "by the term media, we should be referring to all of the means—all of the devices, technologies, etc.—utilized for acquiring, storing, transporting or displaying messages." Thus, he says, "the human ear is a medium, as are human languages. The microscope and the telescope are media. A piece of parchment, like the wall of an inhabited cave, when used to inscribe messages, is also a medium."[11]

Salomon proposed that media be defined in terms of unique presentation modes that fulfill unique psychological functions. According to Salomon, the factors that underlie the use of media are the symbol system, the message, the learner, and the educational task. He says that "it is the symbol system rather than the technology of transmission that is crucial for instruction."[12] Gross echoes a similar concept when he says that "the central goal of education must be the acquisition of competence in the modes of symbolic behavior."[13] And further, he says "the modes of symbolic communication must precede the development of whatever technological media may be used to store and transmit their coded products."[14]

Still another entirely different concept of media has been offered by Gordon when he says we have "fallen into the habit of regarding our attractive technology—movie projectors, television receivers, etc.—not only as mediums but as messages." In the first place, he says, "they are not mediums, and, in the second place, they are not messages. They are, of course, extremely effective devices which serve as instruments by which mediums of communication of three sorts (narrative, picture, and impersonation) may be distributed."[15] Gordon says further that "we concentrate on techniques or instruments for spreading pictures abroad to the public, like museums, magazines, newspapers, movies, television, etc., and call these instruments 'media' when in fact they mediate little or nothing."[16]

Microcomputers and Education

The use of computers in education began in the 1960s with the introduction of computer-assisted instruction (CAI). Prominent examples of this era were the Stanford CAI project and the IBM 1500 CAI system (with author language "Coursewriter") that became a model for most of the author languages provided by computer manufacturers. It also became apparent in the early 1970s that CAI had not realized its early expectations for a number of reasons.[17] Nevertheless, a wave of new systems came into existence, led by the PLATO (Programmed Logic for Automated Teaching Operations) project at the University of Illinois, and followed by the TICCIT (Time-Shared Interactive Computer-Controlled Information Television) project at Brigham Young University. But these projects affected student achievement less than first hoped. By the middle 1970s, it became clear that CAI in the form of mainframe computers had achieved only modest success and, in addition, its cost was significantly more expensive than conventional instruction.

A new hope for the use of the computer in education arose in the late 1970s when the first microcomputer became available to a growing market. By the early 1980s, school systems began to invest heavily in microcomputers for classroom use, and, by 1985, it was reported that there were at least one million microcomputers in American elementary and secondary schools (see Becker, 1986).[18] By 1988, the estimate was as high as three million! Despite this amazing growth, the average user got to use the computer less than thirty minutes a week, while one-third got it for less than fifteen minutes or less. The drill-and-practice format was the usual activity in the elementary school and programming, along with computer literacy, was the predominant activity in the secondary schools.

It was clear from most of the computer literature that the computer was viewed as the further extension and embodiment of the traditional goals of education. The primary forces that pushed computers on the schools—the computer industry, the parents, and the educators themselves—all called for a return to basics. As a result, an increasingly conservative form of educational software began to be produced by publishers because they knew compliance with the demands of school boards and state-level adoption agencies would make it more likely that their products would be sold to the school system. Thus, so-called wrap-around packages consisting of drill-and-practice type diskettes and correlated textbooks were produced and promoted.

By the late 1980s, the first wave of heavy microcomputer usage in education had reached its peak: an era from 1977 to 1983 when many anticipated unique benefits from computers in education. Although school microcomputer purchases have continued, there were clear indications that educators were beginning to engage in a critical examination of earlier prophesies. A survey by Becker, for example, indicated that there had been a substantial decrease in the number of teachers who viewed computer-assisted instruction as the primary role of computers in education.[19] Brohy and Hannon claimed that

> once the novelty wears off, learning by computer becomes just another method akin to learning with the aid of television, filmstrips, listening centers with headsets, etc. A few students can be expected to retain high enthusiasm indefinitely, but most will not.[20]

Futrell and Geisert have pointed out that "the most basic concepts of curriculum design are not being employed" and that "the situation is counterproductive in the maintenance of a healthy growth of microcomputer use in schools."[21] Early enthusiastic advocates of microcomputers in education assumed that training teachers to produce their own software could be expected, but most teachers lack the time, the energy, or the expertise to engage in such a task. What is more, most teachers did not know how to use computers to promote educational effectiveness nor were they adequately trained. Another reason why computers did not meet their expected potential was that many teachers "became disenchanted with the drill-and-practice software available at the time and have not ventured back to examine more recent software products which schools who more recently became microcomputer owners have been able to use at least somewhat successfully" (Bonner, 1984).[22] Even today, commercially available software tends to be less than adequate because few agreed-upon standards exist for computer courseware (see Cohen, 1983).[23] According to the U.S. Office of Technology Assessment report, *Power On! New Tools for Teaching and Learning*, "there is a general consensus that most software does not yet sufficiently exploit the capacity of the computer to enhance teaching and learning."[24] Roblyer has cautioned that "better design and development methods are an essential component in improving the impact of CAI on education. Without this emphasis, the microcomputer is destined to end up primarily a tool for computer literacy, word processing, and administrative support."[25]

Another early prophesy was that the costs of computers would decrease dramatically because of mass production and competition among the manufacturers. However, even though prices have dropped substantially, books and other media are comparatively much less expensive. Levin's analysis of the cost-benefit and cost effectiveness of CAI concluded "that popular assumptions about costs and cost-effectiveness of CAI are often not supported by evidence. To the degree that decisions to adopt CAI are made on the basis of such assumptions, they may be costly and inefficient."[26]

Despite these waves of criticism of computers in education in the late 1980s, most educators remained largely uncritical and continued to promote computer usage in the schools. Sloan has observed:

> that American educators have made no concerted effort to ask at what level, for what purposes, and in what ways the computer is educationally appropriate and inappropriate, in what ways and to whom we can count on its being beneficial or harmful. The overall picture has been one, instead of educators vying to outdo one another in thinking of new ways to use the computer in all manners and at every level of education possible. Professional responsibility demands more.[27]

Computer Instructional Applications

By the mid-1980s, a national pattern of computer use in the schools could be clearly discerned. The drill-and-practice mode had become dominant as well as teaching about computers (see Walker, 1986).[28] Unfortunately, most of the drill-and-practice programs available were "poorly conceived, limited in their effectiveness, and uninteresting to students" (see Hannafin and Peck, 1988).[29] However, drill-and-practice modes do possess high educational potential if effective design strategies and improved methods can be developed.

Tutorial CAI is sometimes offered as a substitute for tutors and resembles a dialogue between a teacher and a student. Effective tutorials provide appropriate feedback and remediation, and strategies for making instruction more meaningful to the learner. Another aspect of tutorial applications is computer-managed instruction (CMI) in which the computer assesses student mastery by directing the learner to appropriate materials in other media such as print, audio, or video. Some of the major problems with tutorial CAI is that it is difficult to develop, there are few good tutorial programs available, and it is very costly.

Simulations represent another computer approach to instruction. These electronic environments have their own set of rules, and the way a learner plays his or her role determines the outcome of the simulation.[30] A program called *Sell Bicycles* produced for the intermediate grades, for example, involves a sophisticated simulation of running a store. Another example of an excellent simulation is *The Factory*. Produced by Sunburst Communications, it won a best software award in 1983. As the name indicates, the setting for this simulation is a factory. One player selects up to three different types of machines to produce a product. Additional players can be challenged to recreate the product produced by the first player. This is a good example of a simulation designed to develop problem-solving skills—particularly with nine- to fifteen-year-olds.

There is no question that simulations offer a unique application of the computer for instructional purposes. Several studies have focused, for example, on the relationship between effective learning and simulations, but these studies were concerned with non-computer simulations. After critically evaluating the available research, Dekkers and Donatti concluded, "The evidence from these analyses does not support the contention that simulation activities in the classroom result in increased cognitive development or retention when they are compared with other teaching strategies."[31] A later review of the literature on computer based instructional simulations came to the same conclusion. Obviously, a major program of research in this area is still needed.

Instructional CAI games is still another mode. The common characteristic for CAI games is their capacity to provide practice in the applications of information, skills, and concepts, using a motivating, competitive format.[32] One of the first computerized games was developed by Will Crowther and Don Woods at Stanford University. Their game, *Adventure*, provided a fantasy, or simulated environment, that gave the learner imaginary powers for dealing with powerful, magical beings who populated an imaginary world.[33] Games have been criticized for providing only incidental or trivial skill development and for excessive use of computer capabilities.

Hybrid designs have been developed to utilize the advantages or to lessen the disadvantages of the various design options. Many consider problem-solving and inquiry designs as hybrid designs because they incorporate the functions of two or more basic designs rather than developing a separate CAI design. Problem-solving CAI is usually designed to resolve a problem through the application of lesson knowledge while inquiry designs stimulate learning by enabling the learner to solicit information or explanations related to unique needs. These approaches often combine tutorial and simulation designs or may be combined with drills. Hybrid CAI application possibilities are only limited by the designer's creativity.

A major class of computer tools for learning and problem solving has evolved in recent years. These tools, sometimes referred to as "intelligence extenders," make it possible to quickly access or manipulate text and graphics (even sound) to use in various combinations as needed. One of these promising new tools, known as *hypertext* or *hypermedia*, enables the user to access text and graphics in a fashion permitting exploration in a sequence which makes the most sense in terms of the user's knowledge base. A current application at Brown University illustrates the use of hypermedia applied to education.[34] HyperCard, the latest associative tool, enables the user to create and link together intermixed text, graphics, videodisc images, and sound. For example, a laserdisc player, a CD-ROM reader, a modem, a printer, and an external storage and retrieval device can all be connected to a Macintosh computer and accessed through HyperCard.[35]

Still another computer application in education involves programming languages such as BASIC, FORTRAN, COBOL, PASCAL, ADA, or LOGO. In this approach, the purpose is to provide an opportunity for the learner to program the computer rather than programming the learner by the computer. The most famous example of this approach has been Papert's programming language called LOGO, which was designed especially for children. But LOGO is more than just a programming language; it is also a theory about thinking and programming. Papert has demonstrated that it is possible to design computers to enable children to easily program the computer to meet their changing needs in the learning process. He says:

> We are at a point in the history of education when radical change is possible, and the possibility for that change is directly tied to the impact of the computer. Today what is offered in the education "market" is largely determined by what is acceptable to a sluggish and conservative system. But this is where the computer presence is in the process of creating an environment for change.[36]

The introduction of the microcomputer in the classroom has produced a shift of focus in conventional instruction from the products of learning to the cognitive processes of learning, or more specifically, to problem solving. For example, in the area of mathematics, new programs will do most of the mathematical manipulation so that teachers can dispense with these manipulations and focus instead on teaching understanding or problem solving. Likewise, traditional instruction in language arts, which has placed emphasis on such skills as grammar and spelling, can now focus on composition and editing on the monitor screen.

In other subject areas, such as science and social studies, microcomputer simulations can provide insights concerning the consequences of decisions or the ways to search and evaluate information to solve a particular problem.

Microcomputers can also play many supporting roles in what is known as computer-managed instruction (CMI). This might include managing students in individualized programs, maintaining grades, generating tests or worksheets, and performing administrative functions. Electronic spreadsheets may serve as a tool for students, teachers, and administrators. For example, students can use them to manipulate accounting ledgers in business education courses or do economic forecasting in social studies. They can also be applied to problem solving in science and mathematics. The essential feature of the electronic spreadsheet is that the student can change any one of the entries on the sheet, and the computer automatically calculates and changes all the other entries that may be affected by that single change.[37]

Another obvious use of microcomputers as tools is as super calculators. The capacity to carry out fundamental mathematical and logical operations is built into many computers' on-board memory and is available to all computer users through the BASIC language. Moreover, most computers can be programmed to do trigonometric, logarithmic, and other specialized mathematical calculations.

Along with word processing and numerical analysis, information processing is proving to be extremely useful in processing or accessing vast quantities of stored data in computers. These so-called databases may be activated to provide selected information for a wide variety of research or instructional purposes. A number of new technologies have emerged in the 1980s that promise improved access to information. All of them claim greater storage capacity, faster information retrieval, support of multiple concurrent users, and lower costs than existing media such as magnetic storage and microform. The most publicized of these new technologies are the optical media: videodisc, compact disc, CD-ROM, and optical digital storage (on disk, tape, and cards). Videodisc will probably remain the most desirable medium for still and motion video in the early 1990s. Compact discs will likely dominate the audio market through the 1990s. Videodisc currently offers a greater storage capacity than CD-ROM, but CD-ROM offers simpler production techniques, and the promise of more widely available and less costly retrieval equipment. The major appeal of CD-ROM, particularly for educators, is that the small size of the medium and the disk player makes it particularly well-suited to personal and desktop computers. It appears likely that CD-ROM devices will be attached to microcomputers rather than larger computers at libraries or information centers.

Another long-range possibility is networking of instructional information systems in which computers are connected to one another. Thus, the ideal situation is to have a large database tied into offices and schools via terminals, modems on microcomputers, or a computer network. This arrangement makes information easily accessible to those who need it.

Bank and Williams describe such a network or information system. In their words, an Instructional Information System (IIS):

> can link data on pupil characteristics (for example, ethnicity, primary language, and socioeconomic status) with pupil performance on tests; with their instructional history; and with student, parent, and teacher attitudes and opinions. This data may then be combined in any number of ways to provide information to decision makers about how to better manage instruction.[38]

A step in this direction was taken during the 1984-1985 school year when staff members from the Learning Research and Development Center (LRDC) worked with the Pittsburgh Public Schools in the development of a prototype microcomputer information system.

Changing Concepts of Computer Literacy

Discussions about computer literacy began appearing in the literature in the mid-1970s. Early concepts centered on the understanding of computer capabilities, applications, and algorithms. But other writers assumed that computer literacy should also include emphasis on the social issues. For example, Moursund conceptualized computer literacy as "a knowledge of the non-technical and low-technical aspects of the capabilities and limitations of computers, and of the social, vocational and educational implications of computers."[39] Another concept by Bright is that "a fully educated, computer-literate person might be expected to know how to program in one of the standard computer languages and to be able to use the computer to solve simple problems."[40] Bright says further that computer literacy "will become increasingly important in the 1990s and beyond."[41]

Not everyone concurs with these views. In fact, Sloan finds it difficult to understand the prevailing assumption that computer literacy is essential despite the absence of evidence to the contrary. He says that "while most people have not stopped to examine the evidence, it is nevertheless unclear how they arrived at such an assumption in the first place" and "what has apparently convinced an entire population that something as vague and worthless as computer literacy is essential to their lives."[42] Sardello writes that:

> the very term *computer literacy* establishes the computer as far more than a machine; such a term is an assault on the basis of culture itself by assuming that computer programming is truly a language—not a constructed, artificial language, but a language fully capable of expressing the full and complete life of a people.[43]

Broughton sees computer literacy as the political socialization of the child. He says that "the elevation of 'computer literacy' to prominence as a high priority educational objective hides the latent neopositivist curriculum of scientism" and aims to return:

> back to the old basic skills—plus one metaskill. The hard areas are epitomized by those very same domains taken to have pioneered the invention of the micro-computer itself: natural science and mathematics. These are the realms where organized logical, rule governed, algorithmic thinking are at a premium. Here, Piaget's theory is often invoked because of its claim that development moves naturally and inexorably toward the ultimate end point of systemic, logico-mathematical cognition. The supposition (unsupported) that the discovery and perfection of the microcomputer was itself achieved by means of this kind of thinking serves only to confirm its preeminence. To borrow Papert's favorite term, it is "space-age" thinking.[44]

Artificial Intelligence and Computer-Assisted Instruction

Artificial intelligence (AI), like cognitive science, had its origins in the mid-1950s in the work on the Logic Theorists by Newell and Simon at Carnegie-Mellon University and the work of Marvin Minsky, John McCarthy, and others at MIT in the 1960s. McCarthy originated the computer language called LISP for computing with symbolic expressions. Such projects as ELIZA and Papert's work on using the LOGO language and turtle graphics as a powerful teaching tool for young children were begun at this time. Also, Ed Feigenbaum began his work on artificial intelligence at Stanford. In the 1970s, the phenomenal SHRDLU, developed by Terry Winograd at MIT, was a major breakthrough in artificial intelligence because it could respond to questions about its simulated world, execute demands, and report the results. Another flurry of excitement was generated with the development of PERCEPTRON in 1960, a mechanism designed by Cornell's Frank Rosenblatt to recognize letters and other patterns placed in front of its "eyes." Even more impressive accomplishments in the area of visual perception came from another MIT researcher, David Marr, who modeled the early phases of the perception of objects and scenes. This approach has come to be known as intelligent CAI (ICAI). The work that has gone on in the development of instruction strategies in ICAI programs has been extensive in recent years. Artificial intelligence has been applied to computer-assisted instruction primarily in the area of teaching procedural knowledge and reasoning strategies for use in problem solving. So-called generative programs were the earliest application of AI techniques in education. This approach was used primarily in drill-and-practice programs in arithmetic and vocabulary recall. Although generative CAI was an advance over branching programs, it was limited to very simple knowledge domains and few subjects were sufficiently structured to fit into a generative model which required a way of determining the relative difficulty of the material being taught.[45]

Beginning in the 1970s, two different approaches developed with reference to the use of computers in education from the artificial intelligence perspective: intelligence tutoring systems and computer-based learning environments. ICAI has provided for dialogue-based tutorial systems designed to give the student increased control over the machine. Meanwhile, learning environments have been designed to create simulated miniworlds which combine games, simulations, or programming with machine-based tutors capable of engaging the learner in a dialogue.

Intelligence tutoring systems are essentially passive machine-based teachers that answer students' questions, evaluate their responses, and give critiques on their proposed solutions. Moreover, they identify student errors or misunderstandings and provide suggested alternatives. The best known intelligence tutoring systems include SOPHIE, an electronic troubleshooting system; BUGGY, a system relating to elementary algebra and procedural skills in arithmetic; WEST, MYCIN, and GUIDON, devised for medical diagnosis of infectious blood diseases; LMS for simple algebraic equations; and WUMPUS for logic and problem solving.

The Geometry Tutor is one of two ICAI systems being developed by John R. Anderson and his colleagues at Carnegie-Mellon University (the other is the LISP Tutor). The purpose of the Geometry and LISP Tutor research is to understand how learners reach solutions to problems and to determine the major difficulties in developing problem-solving skills. Meanwhile, work is progressing on programs in other centers, including tutors in fractions at the Learning Research and Development Center at the University of Pittsburgh, in physics at the University of California at Berkeley, and in organic chemistry at Carnegie-Mellon University.

Current ICAI research is focused on three areas of most concern. These are the nature of the expertise module, the transfer of meaning, and the sequencing of knowledge. The issue of the expertise module is important because ICAI applications require a type of knowledge representation that can facilitate such capabilities as access, planning, problem solving, reasoning, pattern recognition, question answering, and hypothesis generation/evaluation. Transfer of meaning is also crucial because learning, recall, execution, and adaptation of complex processes are necessarily promoted by provided multiple levels of meaning. Sequencing of knowledge, or the "syllabus" or "scripts" that link knowledge into functional structures or learning strategies, constitutes a vital part of ICAI design. In all these studies, the basic issue is how different learners learn and what approaches or designs are most appropriate or effective for different learners. It is obvious that considerably more research in cognitive science is required in order to resolve these problems.[46]

Early researchers in ICAI were very optimistic about the future possibilities of artificial intelligence, but over the past decades, some degree of skepticism has arisen about claims of

AI revolutionizing the schools in the near future.[47] Aside from the restraints of our current understanding of human learning and the difficulties of designing appropriate intelligent ICAI systems, economic restraints are also hampering the quality and number of these systems. In the light of these factors, it is uncertain what the status of ICAI will be by the year 2000. There is no question that societal pressures will also be influential in determining the future role of ICAI systems in education.

New Information Technologies: Implications for Educational Technology

A whole range of new information technologies became available in the 1980s that had the potential of being utilized in some instructional situation by educational technology. Since this book is not about hardware or media per se, it is not intended to discuss all the technical ramifications of these developments, but merely to point out some of the technological innovations that have implications for teaching, both within the schools as well as outside the schools. Some of these developments are not well known because they originally took place in other countries or because schools have not used them to any degree.

The development of media technologies for instruction has exerted an immense impact on educational technology during the latter years of this century. One important developmental process is reflected in the emergence of simpler, more practical video recorders, cassettes, and discs, and low-cost television equipment. And more recent developments, sometimes called cellular communications, may even render obsolete many present radio, telephone, television, and navigation systems.

New media technologies for the future went in the direction of both macro and micro technologies. At the macro level, where broadcasting was once confined to terrestrial transmission, the development of communications satellite technology has made the idea of a global village a reality. Also, as an alternative to open broadcasting, broadband communications or cable systems involving direct video and audio signals have important implications for educational broadcasting. At the micro level, an increasing miniaturization of equipment, or what has been called "microelectronics," has meant that media can be used more extensively. Micro technologies include such developments as the portapak video camera, the videocassette, and electronic films. As distinguished from photographic film, electronic films are delicate masses of electronically active material condensed, for the most part, from hot vapors onto cold, hard insulating surfaces such as glass. Depending on the materials used, such films, called either thin or thick, are often ten times thinner than an ordinary soap bubble. These films may eventually lead to a television camera only half-an-inch square, a hand-held battery-operated computer, a form of computer that could store a quarter million bits of information on a glass slide half-a-foot square, a new type of videotape that could store pictures optically for later readout by an electron beam, and a revolutionary type of integrated circuitry for application in all forms of electronic equipment.

The application of new media technologies for instruction has occurred in a number of ways in recent decades. One of the more notable applications in the industrialized world was that of the Open University in Great Britain. This system involved multimedia combinations of radio, television, films, and programmed materials. Similar systems have been developed in other regions of the world, notably, the Long Distance Studies Institute in West Germany, Portugal's Telescola, and the Western Australian Correspondence School. Moreover, experimental telecommunications satellite systems have been developed in various parts of the world for educational purposes. In terms of the future applications of satellites for instruction and information, it can be stated with assurance that developments will intensify and expand. Additional experimental communications satellites are in the planning stage.

Communications satellites used for broadcasting as well as telephony unquestionably present opportunities unparalleled by the traditional media technologies, but they lack the kind of interactive communication that the traditional media do provide. For example, posters, filmstrips, films, maps, charts, etc., may more effectively meet such needs as mobility and low cost. The potential of radio, with its easy accessibility, relatively low cost, and its possibilities for two-way interactive communications, have not been fully realized in the industrialized nations. In contrast, too much attention tends to focus on such big, prestigious media as television, computers, and communications satellites. Neither so-called big media nor little media are necessarily better or more effective in instructional situations. It is clear, however, that the increasing diversity and development of media technologies will require serious decisions about a rapidly expanding range of strategic alternatives that will be appropriate for specific educational objectives.

Interactive Video

Probably one of the more interesting technological innovations of recent years has been the use of the videodisc. What has become known as *interactive video* involves the interfacing of small gauge video and microcomputers. One side of a disc can hold 54,000 frames, either pictures or pages of text, along with an accompanying audio track. Thus, the term *videodisc* is misleading insofar as it suggests that the disc is strictly a video medium. The computer can produce text, graphics, and sound, while the video player can produce video and audio output. In addition, an interactive video system may present video with or without audio, video frames with or without computer-generated text or graphics, or computer-generated text or graphics with audio from the video player.

One of the primary applications of interactive video involves an instructional situation whereby a learner is given control so that he may review the material or gain access to remedial instruction. Grabowski and Aggen have noted that interactive video may provide the designer with alternatives such as using cognitive strategies as rehearsal, mnemonics, and imaging to promote the encoding of information.[48] However, interactive video has its limitations. As Schaffer and Hannafin point out, interactive video may require considerable skill in designing and developing instruction and may require additional time and manpower if it is to be properly implemented.[49] Finally, interactive video is very expensive. The cost of videodisc courseware ranges from $35,000 to $100,000 *per hour*. Moreover, the cost of the associated computer courseware that drives the videodisc ranges from $2,000 to $20,000 per hour of instructional video material.

The basic objective of interactive video instruction is to replace the teacher completely. As a result, it must be extremely sophisticated so that it can mimic the best teachers. After the appropriate program and responses are built into the courseware, the videodisc becomes unchangeable once the master is made. Of course, the computer courseware can be altered, but this would be prohibitive since the cost of disc mastering alone is approximately $10,000.

To date, the education community has not seen a great need for videodisc instructional systems. With funding from the Annenberg (CPB) Project the University of Nebraska produced six experimental videodiscs to simulate several science laboratory experiments.[50] At WICAT in Orem, Utah, several discs have been developed to teach Spanish as a second language.[51] Other applications have been described by DeBloois et al.[52]

Teleconferencing

Interest in teleconferencing has increased considerably in recent years because it permits groups separated by long distances to exchange two-way video and audio information as well as engage in interactive question and answer sessions. In order to accomplish teleconferencing, a variety of technologies are used, such as telephones, microwave relays to satellites, computers, and printed materials.

Electronic Blackboard

The electronic blackboard is a device for transmitting visual information to learners at a great distance. As the instructor draws a diagram on the board, it is transmitted, usually over telephone lines, to television sets that have been equipped with special converters, by means of a narrow-band signal. Such signals may also be transmitted by audiocassette.

Slow-Scan Television

This development makes it possible to transmit a moving television picture or a still picture. One possible use of slow-scan television is to supplement a lecture with additional visual information.

Integration of Technology

It is likely that many benefits will come from the implementation of digital integrated networks. These systems, such as the Systems Digital Network (ISDN) will be able to provide digital communications for voice, data, and video signals and will make it possible for any school or home to access any combination of computer programs and video, data, or audio information sources from anywhere in the world.[53]

Rapid Obsolescence of Information Technologies

If there is one lesson to be learned from the past history of educational technology, it is that one can expect the rapid obsolescence of information hardware or media. It is easy to be caught in each media bandwagon as it passes by. It is most important to maintain the focus on the process of educational technology rather than be swept into a kind of media hypnosis.

Task Force Report: *Transforming American Education: Reducing the Risk to the Nation*

In April 1986, *Transforming American Education: Reducing the Risk to the Nation*, the report of the National Task Force on Educational Technology appointed by Terril Bell, then secretary of education, was issued three years to the month after the *A Nation at Risk* report. Finding the United States to be "at risk," the earlier report had stated:

> the educational foundations of our society are presently being eroded by a rising tide of mediocrity that threatens our very future as a nation and a people.
> If an unfriendly foreign power had attempted to impose on America the mediocre educational performance that exists today, we might well have viewed it as an act of war. As it stands, we have allowed this to happen to ourselves. We have even squandered the gains in student achievement made in the wake of the Sputnik challenge. Moreover, we have dismantled essential support systems which helped make those gains possible. We have, in effect, been committing an act of unthinkable, unilateral disarmament.[54]

The Task Force on Educational Technology generally agreed with the recommendations for reform stated in *A Nation at Risk*.[55] One specific recommendation referred to the promise of information technology to improve education. However, the task force believed that the principal obstacles to transforming education into the system it needs to become lie in the lack of all the requisite tools to carry out that transformation effectively. The report stated that "what is new, then, is not the idea of learning for subject matter mastery in individualized programs but the availability of the tools offered by educational technology to implement that idea."[56] Furthermore, "teachers must learn to become managers of a complex educational environment, designers of individualized learning programs for each student, evaluators (and perhaps constructors) of some of the sophisticated tools offered."[57]

The task force report reflected its members' belief in the educational potential of the computer with statements like the following:

> To transform education, we must create a system in which an individual learning plan permits each learner to proceed at a rate and pace that is challenging but achievable, makes no unjust comparisons with the progress of others, prevent students from becoming passive, and assures positive reinforcement and steady progress. Such a plan will allow the most able to move to new realms without restriction and the least able to find their own unique achievement levels.[58]

> The computer is a device uniquely suited for education. With related technology, it enables people to deal with vast amounts of information. It can be programmed to adapt learning to the needs of each student, providing corrective advice and allowing the student to proceed as rapidly or as slowly as he or she is able.[59]

It was clear from this report that the task force believed the computer was capable of revolutionizing education. Although there is no question that the computer can contribute to the educational process in many ways, it is only a tool. Its ultimate educational potential depends on how it is used and how effectively it can be integrated into the total instructional process. By 1990, the federal government had not acted upon its own recommendations. In fact, it had not even made the report public through the usual governmental channels.

Critique of Task Force Report

The direction and context of the reform efforts of the Educational Technology Task Force have drawn criticism from some who believed educators were being made scapegoats for national problems, the solutions of which were beyond the capability of the schools to effectuate. Moreover, many felt that the severe reductions and eliminations of programs by the Reagan administration had seriously threatened American education.

Goldberg, for example, observed that the 1986 report is essentially an echo of the 1970 presidential report, *To Improve Learning*.[60] He says that the 1970 report with a few word changes could easily be invoked today. Also, Goldberg points out that we should note "the use of 'high' in front of technology and try to determine what is high, medium, and low and what the various perceptions mean."[61] Having done that, there is a need "to explore how perceptions and definitions are translated in the various settings, how decisions about technology are made, once the rhetoric and the hype are stripped away."[62]

This author views the 1986 report as essentially a reflection of the hardware or media concept of educational technology discussed in the first chapter of this book. This is the same view that dominated the audiovisual instruction movement during the first half of this century. In this report, educational technology is consistently equated with media or, more specifically, with computers. Since this task force was composed almost entirely of representatives of the computer manufacturers, it is not surprising that the focus is on the educational use of computers rather than films or television and that the report expresses a computer bias. Moreover, it is clear from this report that the computer industry is pursuing educators with one of the most intense mass marketing efforts in business history. As Roszak has cogently observed,

> the goal has been nothing less than to place computers in the hands of every teacher and student. With the help of grants, donations, and stupendous discounts ranging up to 80 percent, the companies have succeeded in striking a number of what many hope will be bellwether deals with schools large and small. The campuses have not displayed much sales resistance to these blandishments.[63]

One of the recommendations of the task force is that "the information technology industry cooperate to perform research and development to transform education through applications of technology, to evaluate the effectiveness of the new methods and materials, and to disseminate successful practices to the field."[64] This is another example of not learning from history. In the mid-1960s, when several electronics companies and publishing houses merged to design complete instructional systems that would train teachers to use them and would also test learners, the systems proved to be faulty and unreliable. School districts that purchased these systems or materials literally "bought" the educational objectives and instructional techniques built into them. Today, just as then, the developers of systems or computer software can hardly be expected to produce empirically tested products when most educational practitioners and academic specialists have failed to do so.

A Historical Analysis of Technological Innovations in Education

Since the study of American educational history clearly documents how difficult it is to effect the adoption and use of new technologies and instructional methods in the classroom, it is appropriate to analyze the historical experience to establish a sound and realistic basis for judging present and future technological developments in education. The historical work of Cuban, for example, demonstrates how little instructional techniques in secondary classrooms have changed from 1900 to 1980.[65] Goodlad and associates found this same occurrence at the elementary level with the exception of instructional methodology from the Progressive movement.[66] In a historical study of the classroom use of technology, Cuban says that one can hardly ignore:

> the persistent core of practices that teachers have found to be efficient and resilient, engineered to fit the physics of the classroom. Thus, while governance, curricula, and organization have altered the district and school terrain sufficiently to be readily observed, shifts over the last century in classroom topography barely can be detected.[67]

Past Uses of Technology

It is appropriate to begin by looking back to the early nineteenth century to see how the use of new technologies was hailed as the way to make schools more efficient, effective, and less expensive. The Lancasterian monitorial schools during the 1806-1853 period used slates, sand tables, wall charts, and chalkboards to achieve mass education at low cost, but the rigid, mechanical recitation method lost favor because little attention was given to individual students. A new instructional reform in the mid-nineteenth century was the use of printed texts whereby students could read at their own pace and less reliance could be placed upon lecture and recitation. However, teacher talk still predominated and classes became rigidly organized around texts, lectures, and recitations. When publishing became more sophisticated in the late nineteenth century, reformers saw a solution to the prevailing instructional problems through the new abundance of books. A number of individualized plans were developed to permit students to work at their own pace and to provide for flexible grouping and grading. Some of these plans were the Dalton plan, the Winnetka plan, and Burk's System of Individualized Instruction, but when educational historians began investigating these plans early in this century, there was little evidence of their existence. Classrooms were still rigidly structured for lecture and recitation, the text was dominant, and the heralded new plans for organizing instruction were nonexistent with hardly any flexible use made of printed materials.

With the rise of industrial technology in the late nineteenth century, educators began to envision the use of such new technologies as photography, the instructional slide, and maps and globes. In the early twentieth century, education reformers argued that the use of motion pictures, filmstrips, and radio could make education more effective, and that even the teacher could eventually be replaced. Despite research that demonstrated the effectiveness of films in the 1920s and 1930s, few teachers used films in their classrooms, largely because of technical obstacles. Since the end of World War II, educational reformers and school critics have pushed for one technological innovation after another, claiming that new technologies would make the classroom more effective and efficient by requiring fewer teachers, providing for individualized instruction, and creating the conditions for making the student less dependent on the teacher.

In the 1950s and 1960s, the advent of educational television led some to suggest that the role of teachers could be radically altered (see Asheim, 1962).[68] Television, it was thought, would provide superior instruction by a few master teachers and relieve overcrowded classrooms. Today, television programs play a small role in many classrooms and they have certainly not altered classroom practices to the extent promised by their most vocal advocates. If the early prophesies can be used as a criterion of success, then television must be considered a failure. If on the other hand, one looks at recent use studies, it may be perceived as a success, depending upon how one evaluates the data (see Riccobono, 1985).[69] However, Cuban has shown that despite extravagant claims for the revolutionary effects of educational programming in instructional television, it has been used very little in the schools.[70] He explains this is partly due to a poor fit between the kinds of materials that are available for viewing and the demands of regular classroom instruction.

Another example of the difficulty of technological innovation is offered by the curriculum reform efforts of the early 1960s, involving new curricula and texts in the sciences and mathematics (for example, BSCS—Biological Sciences Curriculum Study; SAPA—Science, A Process Approach; and MACOS—Man, A Course of Study). Despite the development of so-called "teacher-proof" curricula and a whole variety of instructional media to accompany these efforts, they were hardly used, and when they were, they were usually adapted to fit existing practice (see Atkin and House, 1981).[71]

Of course, the newest technological innovation is computer-assisted instruction. Despite some evidence that teachers hold positive attitudes toward microcomputers in the classroom (see Ingersoll et al., 1983/84),[72] Norris and Lumsden found that teachers were "positive toward computers as long as the function of the computers is removed from their experimental world of practice."[73] They also found that teachers and principals range "somewhere between apathetic and hostile in their attitudes toward computers."[74] It remains to be seen whether computers will follow the path of past technological innovations. Cohen suggests that the great flexibility of the computer "may make it easy for schools to adapt this technology to the inherited organization of instruction," but he cautions that "they may well be disappointed."[75] Cuban makes the prediction that he does not "expect general student use of computers in secondary schools to exceed five percent of the weekly time set aside for instruction."[76] He says further that "I predict no great breakthrough in teacher use patterns at either level of schooling. The new technology, like its predecessors, will be tailored to fit the teacher's perspective and the tight contours of school and classroom settings."[77]

Analysis of the Failure of Technological Innovations in Education

Over the years, many attempts have been made to explain the failure of technological innovations and educational reform. Some of the prevailing explanations refer to insufficient funds, lack of adequate time, poor teacher preparation, or the persistent resistance of teachers to change. Some of these factors may be relevant, but they appear to overlook more basic behavior patterns of individual teachers operating within the school organization.

This historical analysis relies heavily on the work of Cuban[78] and Cohen[79] for explanations for the consistent failure of technological innovations through the years. Their analyses provide the most realistic explanations to date of why it is difficult to expect technological innovations in the typical school organizational setting. Cuban states, for example, that:

> for a teacher, the question of whether she can keep the entire class interested for fifteen minutes in the topic of federal policy toward railroads in the twentieth century is a far more pressing issue to resolve than the problem identified by reformers of whether instructional television will reduce the shortage in qualified teachers. Moreover, teachers will use new instructional tools to the degree that the classroom and the occupational culture finds acceptable. Thus, watching an occasional film or televised lessons is within the norm, but two to three movies a day or television three hours daily would seldom be sanctioned by either administrators or colleagues.[80]

He says further that "radio, film, and instructional television met only marginally most problems that teachers defined as important."[81] With reference to computers, Cuban observes that school administrators:

> faced with uncertainty about computer use and the swift changes in the technology but still hearing a strong signal from parents and school boards to do something with computers, careful superintendents and principals, acting as gate-keepers for innovations entering their schools, have purchased some machines.[82]

He says:

> such token adoption of an innovation, echoing earlier school responses to machines, not only insulates a principal (or superintendent) from static over the presence of modern technology in schools but also buffers unwilling or unconvinced teachers from the intrusive enthusiasm of boosters. Hence the number of machines in schools grows, feeding researchers' appetites for statistics on number of machines per building. As with other innovations, however, such figures seldom bear a strong relationship to the frequency of teacher or student use.[83]

Cohen's analysis of explanations for the failure of technological innovations says "one explanation for the persistence of traditional instruction is that societies get the schools they deserve or want."[84] Furthermore, teachers work under many constraints and "must often trade off academic demands for classroom peace, and protection from complaining parents and principals."[85] Thus, he says, under these circumstances, "one would expect that demanding reforms of instruction would take hold only under special conditions and that inherited instructional forms would persist."[86] Cohen says that if one can expect to find widespread adoption and use, innovations would have to make only modest change in inherited/traditional approaches to teaching and learning.

> The implications for the new technology seem straightforward: cost and promotion aside, if widely used in ordinary school settings it seems likely to be used for standard and relatively underdemanding activities, usually lumped together under the rubric of drill and practice, if used in the service of academically demanding instruction.[87]

Cohen observes that one of the most powerful and appealing features of the new computer technology is that it opens up new approaches to inquiry-oriented instruction. However, he sees important barriers to the success of such instruction. For example, he says there is evidence that students in school and university classrooms find inquiry approaches problematic and that "they prefer rote learning, in part because it is simpler, easier, and less uncertain."[88] Cohen notes that "mass education institutions are likely to select those technology applications that fit established practices of teaching and learning." He observes that technology does not cause educational change, but only enables it. The mere existence of tools, he says, is not sufficient to assure their adoption and use. Cohen concludes his analysis with these words:

> Instructional practice in American education is therefore removed from major influence by the leaders of revisionist thought about learning and instruction. It also swims in a sea of popular traditional practices of teaching and learning. This has meant that teachers who tried to implement inquiry-oriented reforms typically did so without much helpful leadership, and frequently with much unhelpful resistance inside and outside the school. Considered from the perspective of the latest technology, my analysis suggests a paradoxical conclusion: The features that promise the greatest intellectual gains may make the smallest instructional headway.[89]

The Cuban and Cohen analyses indicate that we cannot expect technological change until there are some radical changes within the school organization and structure. Some years ago, this author described the need for truly experimental laboratory schools to be established outside of the traditional school organization.[90] Here, atypical instructional procedures would be the rule, with the support of those cooperating rather than with the threat of interference. It would also be a place for extended observation and testing, where creative experimental treatments could be employed over a relatively long period of time. Also, it seems imperative that drastic changes be made in educational staffing. For example, it is important to realize that the *majority* of the instructional system staff should be *nonteaching* members. The nonteaching staff would assist the teaching members in specialized functions: graphic art, film and television production, photography, secretarial, engineering, computer programming, etc. Other personnel who may or may not be directly attached to the instructional system but who may render a number of valuable services might include counselors, psychologists, curriculum consultants, research workers, librarians, media specialists, and others. Overall, the qualified educational technologist would provide leadership and direction for the entire instructional system. Such a change would require considerable federal and state financial support, but if the lessons of history continue to be ignored, the educational system is destined to follow the same implementation paths of past technological innovations.

Notes

[1]Richard E. Clark and Brenda M. Sugrue, "Research on Instructional Media," in Donald P. Ely et al., eds., *Educational Media and Technology Yearbook*, vol. 14. Englewood, Colo.: Libraries Unlimited, 1988, 34.

[2]Claude Shannon is generally acknowledged as the father of information theory. Information theory was developed in a practical manner during World War II in the process of improving the accuracy of anti-aircraft control systems, developing guidance systems for missiles and anti-aircraft, and experimenting with ways of sending messages without distortion or ways of coding messages that would improve the quality of information transmission. See C. E. Shannon and Warren Weaver, *The Mathematical Theory of Communication*. Urbana: University of Illinois, 1949.

[3]See T. Moko-oka, ed., *Fifth Generation Computer Systems*. Amsterdam: North Holland, 1982.

[4]Marc S. Gerstein, *The Technology of Connection*. Reading, Mass.: Addison-Wesley, 1987, 5.

[5]Frank Webster and Kevin Robins, *Information Technology: A Luddite Analysis*. Norwood, N.J.: Ablex, 1986, 29.

[6]*Information Technology and Its Impact on American Education*, Office of Technology Assessment, U.S. Congress. Washington, D.C.: GPO, 1983, 5.

[7]Ithiel de Sola Pool, *Technologies of Freedom*. Cambridge, Mass.: Harvard University Press, 1983, 53.

[8]Robert A. Reiser and Robert M. Gagnè, *Selecting Media for Instruction*. Englewood Cliffs, N.J.: Educational Technology Publications, 1983, 5.

[9]A. J. Romiszowski, *Designing Instructional Systems*. London: Kogan Page, 1981, 339.

[10]Leslie G. Moeller, "The Big Four Mass Media: Actualities and Expectations," in Richard W. Budd and Brent D. Ruben, eds., *Beyond Media: New Approaches to Mass Communications*. Rochelle Park, N.J.: Hayden Book Co., 1979, 14.

[11]Lee Thayer, "On the Mass Media and Mass Communications: Notes toward a Theory," in Richard W. Bud and Brent D. Ruben, eds., *Beyond Media: New Approaches to Mass Communications*. Rochelle Park, N.J.: Hayden Book Co., 1979, 58-59.

[12]Gavriel Salomon, "What Is Learned and How It Is Taught: The Interaction between Media, Message, Task, and Learner," in David R. Olson, ed., *Media and Symbols: The Forms of Expression, Communication, and Education*, Part I, 73rd yearbook of the National Society for the Study of Education. Chicago: University of Chicago Press, 1974, 384.

[13]Larry Gross, "Mode of Communication and the Acquisition of Symbolic Competence," in David R. Olson, ed., *Media and Symbols: The Forms of Expression, Communication, and Education*, Part I, 73rd yearbook of the National Society for the Study of Education. Chicago: University of Chicago Press, 1974, 57.

[14]Ibid., 60.

[15]George N. Gordon, *The Languages of Communication*. New York: Hastings House, 1969, 158.

[16]Ibid., 142.

[17]Among the many reasons why CAI did not succeed in the 1970s were the engineering problems associated with its development. Frequently, computer companies withdrew from the educational market at a critical time either because the market was not considered profitable or because they were beset with problems of quality control. For example, after Texas Instruments had supported the development of the LOGO project at MIT and the development of TI-99, and after it had captured a significant portion of the market, it withdrew its product and subsequently produced a negative impact

on the production of educational software. Another example is Apple II. Apple II was one of the best available systems for use with small children with its plug-in, sprite board, containing the TI-99 graphics processor as well as providing an increase in memory size and the addition of a drawing capability for the sprites. Nevertheless, the company abruptly decided to discontinue the board and software for both technical and marketing reasons. Meanwhile, the European producer Phillips developed the MSX microcomputers, some of which are the best LOGO-capable systems currently available, but they were not interested in capturing the American education market because they saw it as being saturated with Apple IIs and IBM PCs.

[18]H. J. Becker, *Instructional Uses of School Computers*, Reports from the 1985 National Survey, nos. 1-3. Baltimore, Md.: Johns Hopkins University Center for the Social Organization of Schools, 1986.

[19]Ibid.

[20]J. Brophy and P. Hannon, "On the Future of Microcomputers in the Classroom," *The Journal of Mathematical Behavior* 4 (1985), 52.

[21]M. Futrell and P. Geisert, "A Call for Action to Improve the Design of Microcomputer Instructional Courseware," *Educational Technology* 25 (May 1985), 13-15.

[22]P. Bonner, "Computers in Education: Promise and Reality," *Personal Computing* 8-9 (September 1984), 71.

[23]V. B. Cohen, "Criteria for the Evaluation of Microcomputer Courseware," *Educational Technology* 23 (January 1983), 9-14.

[24]U.S. Congress, Office of Technology Assessment, *Power On! New Tools for Teaching and Learning.* OTA-SET-379. Washington, D.C.: GPO, 1988, 122.

[25]M. D. Roblyer, "Fundamental Problems and Principles of Designing Effective Courseware," in David H. Jonassen, ed., *Instructional Designs for Microcomputer Courseware*. Hillsdale, N.J.: Lawrence Erlbaum, 1988, 8.

[26]Henry M. Levin, "Costs and Cost-Effectiveness of Computer-Assisted Instruction," in Jack A. Culbertson and Luvern L. Cunningham, eds., *Microcomputers and Education*, Part I, 85th yearbook of the National Society for the Study of Education. Chicago: University of Chicago Press, 1986, 173.

[27]Douglas Sloan, ed., *The Computer in Education*. New York: Teachers College, Columbia University, 1985, 1.

[28]Decker F. Walker, "Computers and the Curriculum," in Jack A. Culbertson and Luvern L. Cunningham, eds., *Microcomputers and Education*, Part I, 85th yearbook of the National Society for the Study of Education. Chicago: University of Chicago Press, 1986, 35.

[29]Michael J. Hannafin and Kyle L. Peck, *The Design, Development, and Evaluation of Instructional Software*. New York: Macmillan, 1988, 149.

[30]For an excellent review of educational computing simulations, see Jerry Willis et al., *Computer Simulations*. New York: Garland Publishing, 1987.

[31]John Dekkers and Stephen Donatti, "The Integration of Research Studies on the Use of Simulation as an Instructional Strategy," *Journal of Educational Research* 74 (July/August 1981), 424-27.

[32]C. Crawford, *The Art of Computer Game Design*. New York: McGraw-Hill, 1984.

[33]Willis et al., *Computer Simulations.*

[34]See Nicole Yankelovich et al., "Issues in Designing a Hypermedia Document System: The INTERMEDIA Case Study," in *Multimedia in Education: Learning Tomorrow*. Cupertino, Calif.: Apple Computer, 1987.

[35]HyperCard's lineage can be traced back to Memex, the forerunner of today's "hypertext." For an excellent guide to the current use of HyperCard, see Dennis Myers and Annette C. Lamb, *Developing Desktop Instruction: Macintosh HyperCard for Presentations, Tutorials and Information Exploration.* Orange, Calif.: Career Publishing, 1989.

[36]Seymour Papert, *Mindstorms: Children, Computers, and Powerful Ideas.* New York: Harper & Row, 1980, 36-37.

[37]See Daniel S. Cheever, Jr., et al., *School Administrator's Guide to Computers in Education.* Reading, Mass.: Addison-Wesley, 1986.

[38]Adrianne Bank and Richard C. Williams, eds., *Information Systems and School Improvement.* New York: Teachers College, Columbia University, 1987, 5.

[39]D. Moursund, "What Is Computer Literacy?" *Creative Computing* 2 (November/December 1976), 61.

[40]George W. Bright, "What Is Computer Literacy?" *Creative Computing* 2 (November/December 1976), 55.

[41]Ibid., 157-64.

[42]Sloan, *Computer in Education*, 69.

[43]Ibid., 95.

[44]Ibid., 104.

[45]An excellent account of the first ten years (1957-1967) of ICAI developments and research can be found in Hubert L. Dreyfus, *What Computers Can't Do: The Limits of Artificial Intelligence*, rev. ed. New York: Harper & Row, 1979.

[46]For a collection of papers that virtually defines the field of ICAI, see D. Sleeman and J. S. Brown, eds., *Intelligent Tutoring Systems.* New York: Academic Press, 1982. Other helpful sources include the following: Martha C. Polson and J. Jeffrey Richardson, eds., *Foundations of Intelligent Tutoring Systems*, Hillsdale, N.J.: Lawrence Erlbaum, 1988; and Heinz Mandl and Alan Lesgold, eds., *Learning Issues for Intelligent Tutoring Systems*, New York: Springer-Verlag, 1988.

[47]Some have raised the question of whether an artificial intelligence system can really "know" anything about the world external to the symbols it manipulates. See, for example, J. Searle, *Minds, Brains and Science*, Cambridge, Mass.: Harvard University Press, 1984; and T. Winograd and F. Flores, *Understanding Computers and Cognition: A New Foundation for Design*, Norwood, N.J.: Ablex, 1986.

[48]B. Grabowski and W. Aggen, "Computers for Interactive Learning," *Instructional Innovator* 29 (February 1984), 27-30.

[49]L. C. Schaffer and M. J. Hannafin, "The Effects of Progressive Interactivity on Learning from Interactive Video," *Educational Communications and Technology Journal* 34 (Summer 1986), 89-96.

[50]B. G. Davis, "The Evaluation of Science Lab Videodiscs." Paper presented at the Fifth Annual Nebraska Videodisc Symposium, August 1984.

[51]D. D. Williams et al., "Evaluating the Use and Effect of Student-Controlled Interactive Videodiscs." Paper presented at the annual meeting of the Evaluation Research Society, Chicago, Ill., October 1983.

[52]M. DeBloois et al., *Effectiveness of Interactive Videodisc Training: A Comprehensive Review.* Falls Church, Va.: Future Systems, 1984.

[53]For a discussion of Integrated Systems Digital Network see U.S. Congress, Office of Technology Assessment, *International Competition in Services.* Washington, D.C.: GPO, 1987.

[54]National Commission on Excellence in Education, *A Nation at Risk: The Imperative for Educational Reform*. Report to Secretary Bell of the OSOE. Washington, D.C.: GPO, 1983, 5.

[55]The members of the National Task Force on Educational Technology consisted of the following: William J. Ridley (co-chairman), vice president for academic strategies, Control Data Corporation, Minneapolis, Minnesota; Dr. McAllister Hull (co-chairman), counselor to the president, University of New Mexico, Albuquerque, New Mexico; George J. Adams, president, Mobility Systems and Equipment Company, Los Angeles, California; Dr. Roberta Anderson, academic vice president, Morehead State University, Morehead, Kentucky; Dr. Robert Benton, superintendent, state department of instruction, Des Moines, Iowa; William H. Booz, teacher, Fairfax County Public Schools, Annandale, Virginia; Dr. Barbara Bowen, director, Apple Education Foundation, Cupertino, California; Robert C. Brown, executive vice president of education, publishing, and training, McGraw-Hill Book Co., New York, New York; William H. Bowman, chairman of the board, Spinnaker Software, Cambridge, Massachusetts; Bruce Brombacher, teacher, Joines Middle School, Upper Arlington, Ohio; Richard T. Bueschel, senior vice president of technology, Houghton Mifflin Co., Boston, Massachusetts; Barry J. Carroll, vice president, Katy Industries, Des Plaines, Illinois; Dr. Sylvia Charp, editor-in-chief, T. H. E. Journal, Upper Darby, Pennsylvania; Bobby Goodson, education consultant, Sunnyvale, California; Dr. Gregory Jackson, Graduate School of Education, Harvard University, Cambridge, Massachusetts; Dr. Lorrin Kennamer, dean, College of Education, University of Texas at Austin, Austin, Texas; Dr. Daniel Kunz, executive director, government relations, Commodore Computer, Washington, D.C.; Bernard Oliver, technical advisor to the president, Hewlett-Packard Corp., Palo Alto, California; Joseph F. Potts, product manager, personal and educational software, IBM Corporation, Boca Raton, Florida; Dr. Billy R. Reagan, general superintendent, Houston Independent School District, Houston, Texas; Dr. Judith Schwartz, co-director, Educational Technology Center, Harvard University, Cambridge, Massachusetts; Gordon Stulberg, PolyGram Pictures/PolyGram Corporation, Culver City, California; Dr. William Turnbull, distinguished scholar in residence, Educational Testing Service, Princeton, New Jersey; Richard L. Warner, president, R. L. Warner Enterprises, Salt Lake City, Utah; and Dr. Paul Resta (ex officio member), director, Center for Technology and Education, University of New Mexico, Albuquerque, New Mexico.

[56]"Transforming American Education: Reducing the Risk to the Nation," *Tech Trends* 31 (May/June 1986), 12.

[57]Ibid., 13.

[58]Ibid., 23.

[59]Ibid., 15.

[60]See Sidney G. Tickton, ed., *To Improve Learning*, Parts I and II. New York: R. R. Bowker, 1970. In the opening statement of this report, it was stated that "the Commission on Instructional Technology was established in the belief that technology, properly supported and wisely employed, could help meet some of the nation's most pressing educational needs. The Commission's task was to determine, in a study lasting more than a year, whether this belief in technology's value for education was justified; and if it is justified, to recommend to the President and the Congress specific actions to provide for the most effective possible application of technology to American education" (9).

[61]Albert L. Goldberg, "Another National Report: Some Reflections," *Educational Technology* 26 (September 1986), 32.

[62]Ibid.

[63]Theodore Roszak, *The Cult of Information*. New York: Pantheon, 1986, 57.

[64]"Transforming American Education," 13.

[65]Larry Cuban, "Persistent Instruction: The High School Classroom, 1900-1980," *Phi Delta Kappan* 64 (October 1982), 113.

[66]See John I. Goodlad, *A Place Called School*. New York: McGraw-Hill, 1984.

[67]Larry Cuban, *Teachers and Machines: The Classroom Use of Technology since 1920*. New York: Teachers College, Columbia University, 1986, 104.

[68]L. Asheim, "A Survey of Informed Opinion on Television's Future Place in Education," in *Educational Television: The Next Ten Years*. Stanford, Calif.: Institute for Communication Research, 1962.

[69]J. A. Riccobono, *School Utilization Study: Availability, Use, and Support of Instructional Media (1982-83)*, final report. Washington, D.C.: CPB, 1985.

[70]Cuban, *Teachers and Machines*.

[71]M. J. Atkin and E. R. House, "The Federal Role in Curriculum Development 1950-1980," *Educational Evaluation and Policy Analysis* 3 (1981), 5-36.

[72]G. M. Ingersoll et al., "Attitudes of Teachers and Reported Availability of Microcomputers in American Schools," *International Journal of Instructional Media* 11 (1983/84), 27-37.

[73]C. M. Norris and B. Lumsden, "Functional Distance and Attitudes of Educators toward Computers," *T. H. E. Journal* 11 (November 1984), 129.

[74]Ibid., 132.

[75]David K. Cohen, "Educational Technology and School Organization," in *Technology in Education: Looking toward 2020*. Hillsdale, N.J.: Lawrence Erlbaum, 1988, 246.

[76]Cuban, *Teachers and Machines*, 99.

[77]Ibid.

[78]Ibid.

[79]Cohen, "Educational Technology," 246.

[80]Cuban, *Teachers and Machines*, 66.

[81]Ibid., 67.

[82]Ibid., 77.

[83]Ibid., 77.

[84]Cohen, "Educational Technology," 248.

[85]Ibid., 252.

[86]Ibid., 252.

[87]Ibid., 252.

[88]Ibid., 254.

[89]Ibid., 264.

[90]Paul Saettler, *A History of Instructional Technology*. New York: McGraw-Hill, 1968.

Select Bibliography

Becker, H. J. *Instructional Uses of School Computers:* Reports from the 1985 National Survey, nos. 1-3. Baltimore, Md.: Johns Hopkins University Center for the Social Organization of Schools, 1986.

Cohen, David K. "Education Technology and School Organization," in Raymond S. Nickerson and Philip P. Zohhiates, eds., *Technology in Education: Looking toward 2020*. Hillsdale, N.J.: Lawrence Erlbaum, 1988.

Cuban, Larry. *Teachers and Machines: The Classroom Use of Technology since 1920*. New York: Teachers College Press, Columbia University, 1986.

Culbertson, Jack A., and Luvern L. Cunningham, eds. *Microcomputers and Education*, Part I. 85th yearbook of the National Society for the Study of Education. Chicago: University of Chicago Press, 1986.

Dreyfus, Hubert L. *What Computers Can't Do: The Limits of Artificial Intelligence*, rev. ed. New York: Harper & Row, 1979.

Gerstein, Marc S. *The Technology of Connection*. Reading, Mass.: Addison-Wesley, 1987.

Gordon, George N. *The Languages of Communication*. New York: Hastings House, 1969.

Hannafin, Michael J., and Kyle L. Peck. *The Design, Development, and Evaluation of Instructional Software*. New York: Macmillan, 1988.

Mandl, Heinz, and Alan Lesgold, eds. *Learning Issues for Intelligent Tutoring Systems*. New York: Springer-Verlag, 1988.

Moto-Oka, T., ed. *Fifth Generation Computer Systems*. Amsterdam: North Holland, 1982.

Nickerson, Raymond S., and Philip P. Zohhiates, eds. *Technology in Education: Looking toward 2020*. Hillsdale, N.J.: Lawrence Erlbaum, 1988.

Papert, Seymour. *Mindstorms: Children, Computers, and Powerful Ideas*. New York: Harper & Row, 1980.

Polson, Martha C., and J. Jeffrey Richardson, eds. *Foundations of Intelligent Tutoring Systems*. Hillsdale, N.J.: Lawrence Erlbaum, 1988.

Ragsdale, Ronald G. *Permissible Computing in Education*. New York: Praeger, 1988.

Searle, J. *Minds, Brains, and Science*. Cambridge, Mass.: Harvard University Press, 1984.

Sloan, Douglas, ed. *The Computer in Education: A Critical Perspective*. New York: Teachers College Press, Columbia University, 1984.

Thayer, Lee. "On the Mass Media and Mass Communication: Notes toward a Theory," in Richard W. Budd and Brent D. Ruben, eds., *Beyond Media: New Approaches to Mass Communications*. Rochelle Park, N.J.: Hayden Book Co., 1979.

U.S. Congress, Office of Technology Assessment. *Power On! New Tools for Teaching and Learning*. OTA-SET-379. Washington, D.C.: GPO, September 1988.

Webster, Frank, and Kevin Robins. *Information Technology: A Luddite Analysis*. Norwood, N.J.: Ablex, 1986.

White, Charles S., and Guy Hubbard. *Computers and Education*. New York: Macmillan, 1988.

Williams, Frederick. *The Communications Revolution*. Beverly Hills, Calif.: Sage Publications, 1982.

Willis, Jerry, et al. *Computer Simulations*. New York: Garland Publishing, 1987.

Winner, Langdon. *The Whale and the Reactor*. Chicago: University of Chicago Press, 1986.

Winograd, T., and F. Flores. *Understanding Computers and Cognition: A New Foundation for Design*. Norwood, N.J.: Ablex, 1986.

Winston, Brian. *Misunderstanding Media*. Cambridge, Mass.: Harvard University Press, 1986.

Young, John Z. *A Model of the Brain*. Oxford: Oxford University Press, 1964.

Young, Michael. *The Rise of the Meritocracy 1870-2033: An Essay on Education and Equality*. Harmondsworth, England: Penguin, 1961.

17

Educational Technology in the 1980s: New Theoretical and Research Vistas

The aim of this chapter is threefold: (1) to examine the new theoretical and research horizons of educational technology; (2) to review related exemplary research on media, including instructional television, computer-based-instruction and intelligent tutoring systems; and (3) to trace the federal support for educational technology research and development.

This review of research related to educational technology is not intended to be exhaustive or comprehensive. The primary purpose is to highlight historical directions or trends in theory and research that hold important implications for the future development of educational technology. For example, there is now a substantial body of research on the learning and instruction of school subjects, particularly reading and mathematics, that have the potential of generating new theories and providing the basis of testing the validity of new concepts in the instructional process and, simultaneously, offering provocative guidelines for instructional design.

The Role of Cognitive Processes in Learning and Instruction

Beginning in the 1980s, it had become clear that the information-processing model of cognitive psychology was beginning to replace the behaviorist model with more cognitively oriented theoretical views in educational technology. This new model, according to Hilgard, has "replaced the stimulus-response psychology with an input-output psychology with due attention to transformations taking place between input and output."[1] Thus, the information processing model is based on the idea that learners are processors of information and concerns a series of cognitive operations (or processes) that a learner uses in a given situation. Rather than passively responding to instructional stimuli imposed by a teacher, the learner generates his own meaning of what is experienced. Learning in this view is an active, constructive process which is based on existing knowledge and past experience.

Within the last several years, cognitive processes have acquired increased importance and more research emphasis began to be placed on problems of instruction associated with intelligence and aptitude, motivation, the skills and strategies needed for problem solving, and on the individualistic ways that learners perceive, learn, and remember. Recent research in cognition implies that teaching involves the active design of instructional activities that facilitates the learner's active construction of verbal and mental processes that relates or integrates memories and knowledge with new information and generates a process we call learning.

Pintrich et al. have noted that

> perhaps the most significant contribution made by cognitive theory is the common language it provides for a wide range of educational phenomena. Not only are the most experimental, motivational, and differential psychologists now using the same paradigm, but so are researchers on educational media, instructional design, and classroom teaching. For researchers on classroom teaching and tasks, cognitive science has introduced theory to an area that has been largely atheoretical; for instructional designers, it has provided a shift from examination of instructional stimuli, learners' overt responses, and reinforcement to concerns about the instructional effects on cognitive structures and strategies; for the media researchers, it has resulted in redefinition of media as activities that correspond to required mental operations and as attributed that support these activities. Conceptions of the learner, the task, the medium, and instruction are being reformulated as parallel interacting processes grounded in cognition.[2] (Reproduced, with permission, from the *Annual Review of Psychology*.)

The impact of cognitive science on educational technology in the 1980s opened new vistas and produced a significant retreat from mechanistic, stimulus-response, reductionist theories. An early review of the theoretical developments in cognitive psychology and their relevance to education was published by Calfee.[3] Under the impetus of cognitive psychology, there was an appearance of a new journal, *Cognition and Instruction*, in 1984. Meanwhile, significant research studies in reading, writing, mathematics, science, and problem solving yielded new knowledge concerning the intellectual components involved in the teaching-learning process. The new instructional methods which were implied in these studies gave educational technology a new rebirth and moved it from a hardware or media-oriented approach that had been dominant in earlier years to one increasingly focused on issues related to instructional theory.

Intelligence and Aptitude

Although the concepts of intelligence and aptitude have received considerable research attention in earlier years, interest in intelligence waned preceding the new cognitive perspective of the 1970s. The capabilities of the computer in symbol manipulation, transformation and storage of information, and problem solving has provided an analogy for the operations involved in human intelligence and has stimulated an intense revival of research focused on defining intelligence in terms of the cognitive processes of learning. Much of the focus has been on the processing abilities of individual learners and how they might become the basis for adapting teaching to individual differences among learners. As a consequence, much of the research has been concerned with either aptitude-treatment interactions (ATI) or with exploring the possibilities of teaching general learning strategies.[4]

Corno and Snow have reviewed some of the research literature relating to aptitude development.[5] The research has shown that training in particular cognitive strategies is likely to interact with aptitudes in complicated ways just as instruction has been shown to interact with aptitudes in broader educational contexts. In fact, Koyllonen et al. have shown that aptitudes and strategies not only interact, but that learners of different aptitudes may even change strategies as tasks vary in difficulty or as new experience is gained in completing tasks.[6] Considerable research has also been conducted in recent years studying the development of strategic cognitive and metacognitive activities of learners. This research generally supports the position "that learning and memory skills can be trained, that metacognitive awareness about learning from instruction can be developed, and that transfer to related strategic situations is possible if attention is paid to training the generalization-transfer process."[7]

Corno and Snow point out that available theory of aptitude for learning from teaching indicates that such learning involves accessing, adapting, and applying whatever cognitive systems and structures a learner already has, and inventing new systems and structures as necessary, to overcome whatever instructional barriers each learner may encounter.[8] The use of computerized instruction may be an important instructional approach for the effective application of adaptive teaching because computer programs can be made response sensitive and thus adapted to the individual learner.

Motivation

The shift from a stimulus-response perspective to a cognitive perspective has brought about different research approaches to motivation. Aside from the disequilibrium motivation theory of Piaget, the attribution theory of Weiner has strongly influenced the development of attribution models. The theory developed by Bernard Weiner began with the variables identified in John W. Atkinson's theory of achievement motivation and refers to an individual's perceived causes of an event or an outcome. Weiner has identified four major causes that individuals typically select for success or failure outcomes, namely, ability, effort, task difficulty, and luck. To date, the bulk of the research has been focused on these four attributions described by Weiner.[9]

Consistent findings confirm that mildly handicapped children tend to be self-blaming for failure and studies by MacMillan et al. have shown that individuals who attribute failure to stable internal causes show passivity in learning, anxiety, and lowered self-esteem.[10] Children's concepts of the causes of their successes and failures develop from a relatively undifferentiated state to a more analytic conception in which they believe that the events they experience are under their own control rather than under the control of other people. Research in educational settings has also demonstrated that there are links between expectations, attributions, and teachers' behaviors. Wittrock has proposed that research in motivation should study how attribution to cognitive strategies, rather than ability and effort, might influence learning and achievement.[11]

Metacognition

"Metacognition refers to one's knowledge concerning one's own cognitive processes and products or anything related to them."[12] Although the use of the term is relatively recent, the view of the learner as one who reflects upon or is able to monitor and influence his own learning has a long history. The research appears to indicate that the concept of metacognition can be useful in educational technology not because of what learners know about their own cognition out of context, but rather that such knowledge is manifest in their performance on instructional tasks. It is as Shank succinctly put it: "A child need not know that in order to know how."[13] Miller has suggested a focus for future research in all areas of metacognition, including the social, motivational, and personality context of metacognition.[14]

Reading

Reading has been a focus of instructional research since the earliest research endeavors. However, cognitive psychology has generated new approaches and explored new areas of reading research. For example, one of the recent findings in the area of text comprehension concludes that reading comprehension depends not only on the local properties of the text and the reader's decoding activities at the sentence and paragraph level, but also on the overall, between-paragraph organization of the text. The implication is that learners need to be given the opportunity to work with longer texts rather than with short sentences or paragraphs so that they might develop more effective comprehension of the text.[15]

Before the 1970s, little systematic research was undertaken on the processes of reading comprehension. Much of the earlier research was focused on problems related to processes of word recognition and the early stages of reading development. The influence of cognitive psychology stimulated research about the role of prior knowledge in comprehension and laid the basis for an educational technology of reading instruction. In particular, several theories of comprehension and memory were proposed, and a number of experiments were conducted in the 1970s which clearly demonstrated that prior knowledge played an integral role in the process of comprehending and remembering.[16] Rumelhart's[17] model and the schema-theoretic model of Adams and Collins[18] stressed both bottom-up (from the text) and top-down (from the reader) text processing and hypothesized that skilled readers had a finite number of abstract superordinate schemata that were used in text comprehension. In addition, a large body of research and theory in reading comprehension suggested that reading is an active, constructive, and inferential process.

Instructional research has provided sufficient evidence that learners can learn and apply strategies for comprehension, but there is still a need to know whether these strategies can be developed in typical classroom situations. Palincsar and Brown[19] designed an experimental instructional model, based on Vygotsky's zone of proximal development,[20] which was used to explore strategies for general comprehension skills in remedial seventh graders. For purposes of instruction, they selected the strategies of summarizing, questioning, clarifying, and predicting. On the whole, these children did learn how to ask questions and to express major ideas in brief excerpts, but the small class size, from two to seven students, limits the generalizability of the Palincsar and Brown study to typical classrooms.

Faw and Waller made a comprehensive review of the literature on questioning and found that both factual prequestions and postquestions tend to increase students' abilities to answer these same questions after reading; however, only postquestions facilitate overall comprehension.[21] Singer recommends teaching active comprehension by helping students learn to ask their own questions to guide their processing of a selection.[22] In a search for other methods for improving young children's recall of narrative passages, Levin and Pressley have summarized studies which have utilized pictures and concluded that children who heard the stories accompanied by pictures recalled more information than students who hear stories without pictures.[23]

Research in the 1980s has also focused on varied instructional contexts. For example, Harste et al. found that teacher beliefs about language and literacy influence the decisions they make about what to teach to students.[24] A number of researchers have examined within-school and within-classroom contextual effects, using a variety of methods of investigation and analysis. Despite their differences in methodology, all these studies indicate that practically all aspects of the context in which literacy is acquired affect both attitude toward and performance on literacy tasks. For example, teacher beliefs about language and literacy influence the decisions they make about what to teach students;[25] teachers' expectations about student performance influence the kind of feedback they offer students when they make oral reading errors;[26] teachers' knowledge about student-at-home language traditions influences the kinds of interaction patterns they use when teaching minority children;[27] and task ambiguity and perceived personal risk influence students' recall performance.[28]

Writing

Research on writing has been relatively neglected in the past, but the cognitive movement has brought about new research focuses. Scardamalia and Bereiter have summarized much of this research which has included studies on the "new" rhetoric oriented toward instruction, the composing process, discourse analysis, story grammar, classroom practices, basic writers, early development of written symbolism, interactive kinds of response to student writing, and anxiety toward writing.[29] To date, there is no immediate prospect of a cognitive synthesis of this research even though some cognitive research is being done in all these areas. Beaugrande has made a major contribution to a synthesis of these studies within a cognitive framework.[30]

Innovative work on the application of computers to writing is reflected in the use of word processors, automated editors, dictionaries, encyclopedias, and as components in communication networks. Frase[31] has described an advisory system, *Writer's Workbench*, that was developed to assist students in their composing processes. An evaluative study by Kiefer and Smith[32] of this system found that students improved their editing skills after using *Writer's Workbench* for a semester. Moreover, they found that university students who used these tools showed transfer to stylistic revision without direct instruction.

Mathematics

In earlier years, Piaget proposed a theory of development of the foundations of basic number, measurement, and geometry concepts.[33] In the 1960s the application of cognitive learning theory to the process of mathematics was reflected in a number of theories.[34] Current cognitive research in mathematics has provided us much knowledge about how children learn mathematics. For example, this research on the teaching of mathematics has developed the perspective that learners construct knowledge and do not simply absorb what they are told. In line with this research, Resnick and Omanson have explored instructional procedures that specifically utilize the knowledge of children's constructive processes.[35] Despite these insights, more research is needed to determine how knowledge of children's learning of mathematics can be applied to the design of instruction.

The picture of mathematics instruction drawn from a number of "scientific" and "field-base" studies reviewed by Romberg and Carpenter both supports and contradicts the stereotyped view of traditional mathematics teaching.[36] "Teachers are more concerned with management and control than they are with learning; their 'group' is important, not individuals within the group if mathematics is to be covered in an efficient manner."[37]

It appears clear that a variety of constructs from cognitive research need to be applied to the teaching of mathematics in the years ahead. According to Romberg and Carpenter, instructional research should consider how learning proceeds and examine the processes that learners use to solve mathematical problems. Also, dynamic models are needed "that capture the way meaning is constructed in classroom settings on specific mathematical tasks."[38] In addition, the role of computers must be considered because it may make such traditional mathematics procedures as the text, lecture, blackboard, and worksheet procedures extinct. Since new information about learning and teaching mathematics is emerging, new assessment tools must also be developed. For example, the outdated notion that one can assess the learning of mathematics solely in terms of the ability to produce correct answers must be supplemented by an understanding of how information is organized and how it is connected to past experience.

Science and Problem Solving

Recent research on science learning and problem solving has focused on the ways in which knowledge is organized and assessed and the ways in which specific knowledge and problem solving strategies interact. Piaget's theory of human development has become dominant in science education because it is constructivist and deals with the manner in which the learner builds up his own beliefs and pictures of the world. Other theories brought many new concepts to science instruction such as stages of development, levels of processing, semantic and episodic memory and cognitive style into research.

White and Tisher have summarized a number of important studies related to science instruction.[39] They found that certain classroom strategies have become prominent in science teaching. These include wait-time, questioning skills, questions in text, and teaching styles. For example, Redfield and Rousseau's study concludes that higher cognitive questions have a greater impact on pupils' achievement than lower cognitive ones.[40] Brown, Campione and Day point out that attention should be paid to the role of pupil's questions and to improving their skills in framing them.[41] Holiday found a partial set of study questions motivated pupils to concentrate on selected portions of critical information and resulted in inadequate processing of specialized material.[42] Although there have been a number of studies on wait-time, or the length of pauses between a teacher's question and a pupil's response or between that response and the teacher's subsequent reaction, the research indicates that little is known about what pupils are thinking during science instruction.

Larkin et al. have investigated differences in scientific problem solving between expert and novice students in an introductory physics course.[43] Experts and novices were asked to solve specific physics problems by thinking aloud or describing what they were thinking as they solved the problem. The results indicated that the experts solved the problems in about one-fourth of the time required by novices. Other major differences involved the way knowledge was organized and the procedures employed. For example, experts organized physics formulas into large units while the novices organized formulas in small fragments. Also, novices tended to work backwards from the unknown to the givens; in contrast, the experts tended to work forwards, inserting the givens into a large formula and finding the value for the unknown. Moreover, experts had so much experience with problems that they could rapidly recognize what kind of problem it was and then select a solution equation to solve it. As a way of validating these observations, Larkin et al. produced computer programs to simulate the performance of the novice and expert physics problem solvers.

Research on humans and computers seems to indicate that problem solving and thinking skills are learned within a particular science context, and that becoming an expert problem solver involves a considerable amount of learning. In fact, Simon and Hayes have estimated that the development of an expert problem solver may require at least ten years.[44] Greeno summarizes the research on problem solving by stating "there is no basis in current scientific knowledge for changing our present policy of intensive disciplined training for individuals who aspire to making creative changes in the domains in which they choose to work."[45]

Social Studies

Armento conducted a 1986 review of social studies research of the preceding ten years and found that an empirical-analytic orientation still dominated the field.[46] However, she also noted a shift from a behavioristic to a cognitive orientation that was beginning to take place in the early 1980s. Thus, research on teaching social studies began to focus on such questions as "how can teachers influence students to construct images and meanings of the social world or how to relate prior knowledge to new data rather than the behavioral question of how do teachers and instruction directly influence learning."[47]

Based on research conducted on the brain, on human learning, and memory, Wittrock developed a generative model of teaching.[48] A test of the generative hypothesis was made by MacKenzie and White as they observed the effects of three instructional methods on eighth- and ninth-graders learning geographic principles and skills.[49] One group of students studied the social studies content in a classroom setting using a textbook-discussion approach. A second group studied the same content, but also took a traditional field trip to the site of a neutral setting. The third instructional strategy was based on the generative model whereby the group studied the same content as the other groups, but, on the field trip, were given opportunities to generate data, construct records, and develop some connections between the principles learned on the field trip and the other concepts acquired in the classroom and from the text. The traditional classroom group demonstrated 51 percent retention; the traditional field trip group, 58 percent; and the generative field group 90 percent retention.

Little has been known about the psychological processes involved in social cognition and social inquiry. In order to investigate the processes used in social science problem-solving, Voss et al. used a protocol analysis (or think-out-aloud procedure) with persons with different backgrounds in training and experience.[50] The results of their work show that (1) there appear to be domain-specific skills that are used within specific problem-solving situations; (2) more sophisticated problem solvers spend considerably more time using problem solving strategies; and (3) more sophisticated problem solvers use more social studies-specific knowledge.

Unfortunately, limited information exists concerning the constructivist approach in social studies teaching. It is clear that social studies research cannot significantly progress unless more research is focused on the affective and cognitive processes related to social studies learning.

Instructional Theory and Design

According to Shuell, a theory of instruction

> refers to the specification of the relationship among (1) various instructional variables (as distinguished from learning variables and cognitive variables); (2) learning/cognitive process variables; and (3) the nature of the material or outcome that the student is going to acquire.

He says further that "a theory or science of design would be concerned with the mechanics of developing an instructional program or unit."[51]

The information processing theory, with such constructs as short-term and long-term memory, cognitive strategies, schemata, automaticity of cognitive processes, and metacognition, began to emerge in educational technology in the early 1980s and promises to become the dominant model of instructional design. In a 1983 review of instructional design models, seven of the models described reflected a cognitive orientation.[52] Also, the increasing impact of microcomputers in instruction may generate the development and use of new instructional theories and design models during the remainder of this century. Meanwhile, Mitchell has observed that "the received wisdom in the instructional design movement is, if not wrong, incomplete." He asserts that we need a "feedback-controlled selection of instructional materials (e.g., using computer-aided learning or a human controlled), not a rigid design."[53]

Dynamic Assessment

Cognitive psychology has been an important influence on methods of assessing the processes of thinking and learning. Since traditional psychometric procedures have not addressed the dynamic nature of the teaching, learning, and testing process, dynamic assessment approaches, based largely on the work of Vygotsky, have evolved in recent years.[54] It was during the 1970s that there was great dissatisfaction with assessment practices with suggestions for modifications in the direction of dynamic assessment.[55] Glaser has described the Zeitgeist of the 1980s in terms of

> a shift from the selective system to a system that can be helping, adaptive, and instructionally oriented; the necessity of attaining and assessing high levels of competence; and the presence of a social attitude more willing and scientifically able to unpack the factors of mental abilities and to test the limits of their instructability.[56]

A significant work of the 1980s has been that of Feuerstein[57] and of Brown, Campione, and their associates[58] as well as the research of a number of other investigators. Moreover, the 1980s have seen the applications of dynamic assessment to disadvantaged and educable mentally retarded as well as deaf and reading disabled students. Meanwhile, Ionescu and Jourdan-Ionescu have criticized traditional measures of intelligence for being static and for neglecting the mechanisms of cognitive functioning, for providing insufficient information relating to educational programming, and for cultural bias.[59]

Research on Media

Much of the earlier history of instructional media research tended to be dominated by the use of whatever medium was currently in style. Thus, each new medium took center stage for a time and was typically compared with older media. We have shown that the overall results of these comparisons over a period of more than half a century indicated that there were "no significant differences" between the use of various media and traditional instruction. During the behaviorist era in educational technology, media researchers assumed that learners were reactive and responded to external stimuli which were designed to reinforce and control their behavior. With the growing influence of the cognitive orientation in educational technology in the 1980s, media comparison studies began to be replaced with an increasing body of research concerned with developmental cognitive processes and their relationship to specific media attributes. Thus, aptitude-treatment (ATI) research was undertaken to determine which specific media attributes were most effective.[60] This approach led to clearer distinctions between the means of message transmission and the kinds of mental operations involved. Also, such a media reorientation began to generate the development of symbol systems theories pertaining to the processing of words and pictures.[61]

Instructional media research using the cognitive paradigm is based on the assumption that learners usually affect the manner in which they process the instructional stimulus. The term *mindware* has been coined by Salomon to describe a learner's mental set during an instructional experience.[62] In contrast to the older models which viewed the learner as a passive recipient of instruction, the new cognitive model views the learner as an active participant in the teaching-learning process. According to Clark, "some particular qualities of media may affect particular cognitive processes that are relevant for students with specific aptitude levels to learn particular knowledge or skills."[63]

The new cognitive research approach focused on determining which attributes of media might interact with learner aptitudes or distinctive learner characteristics under different learning environments in terms of learning objectives. Thus, such questions as "the possible cognitive effects of explicit filmic supplantation of cognitive operations on students' mastery of related skills or whether the attributes of a medium may evoke mental operations required for a particular task" may be posed (see Clark and Salomon, 1986).[64]

After an extensive review of instructional media research, Clark asserted that "media are delivery vehicles for instruction and do not directly influence learning" and certain elements of different media, such as animated motion or zooming might serve as sufficient conditions to facilitate the learning of students who lack the skill being modeled. Symbolic elements such as zooming are not media (we can have a film or television show which does not contain zooming) but allow us to create sufficient conditions to teach required cognitive skills.[65]

An illustration of this new research paradigm which focuses on cognitive differences rather than comparing the effectiveness if two or more media can be seen in the study of Beagles-Roos and Gat.[66] When they examined the cognitive differences of children exposed to a television and radio story with the soundtrack in common, they found that those in the television group were better at picture sequencing, recall of details from the story, and making inferences based on actions. Those in the radio group were better at making inferences based on verbal sources, at recognizing expressive language, and on knowledge unrelated to the story.

When a study is made of the instructional media research in the 1980s, it appears to suggest, according to Clark

> that the learning that occurs from well-prepared media presentations is actually due to three factors or types of variables: (1) learning task type (e.g., more procedural or more declarative tasks); (2) individual learner traits (e.g., motivation, general ability, and prior knowledge); (3) instructional methods (e.g., the way that the instructional presentation compensates for deficits in learner traits that are required for learning.[67]

He says further that

> instructional technology research in the next decade might profitably focus on interactions between these variables. In these studies, media should be employed as delivery devices that will aid the researcher's control of treatment duration, reliability, and quality.[68]

New Research Approaches in Instructional Television

Although there has been considerable television research since 1975, a relatively small portion of it has been devoted specifically to instructional television.[69] The two most active areas of television research to date have been the effects of television violence on children's aggressive behavior and studies of the relationship of the social world portrayed on television and the child's conceptions of social reality. Instructional television research, on the other hand, has focused on availability and use studies, the teaching of cognitive skills, exposure effects on affect, moods, and emotions, and on educational television for adults.

The new cognitive research approach was also manifested in the early 1980s when television researchers began to investigate the cognitive processes of a child as an active information processor. As a consequence, new active theories of television viewing were in marked contrast to the older view of the passive television viewer presented in earlier research. Different perspectives could also be seen in the increased attention to the child's background and experiences in the analysis of the cognitive tasks involved in viewing particular television programs.

Instead of past models of learning built upon one-way influence in which the learner is a passive recipient, an interactive reciprocal model became more appropriate when cognitive research was employed. Thus, a learner's perception of the instructional purpose of a television lesson directly and substantially affects what he or she can learn from viewing it. Salomon hypothesized that the Amount of Invested Mental Effort (AIME) in a learning task depends primarily on the learner's perception of the relevant characteristics of the medium and the task, and the perception of his ability to make something meaningful out of the material presented.[70] Interestingly enough, Salomon, in a series of studies, found that television proved to be mentally less demanding than printed text when comparable content was employed. He was also able to influence the amount of effort the learner invested in processing television content by giving them some expectations about the purpose of their viewing.

Availability, Use, and Support of Instructional Television

Although there have been a number of utilization surveys, the most comprehensive one to date has been the Corporation for Public Broadcasting's *School Utilization Study*.[71] Riccobono reported that "the percentage of school districts reporting availability of ITV programming increased sharply from 73 percent in 1976-77 to 91 percent in 1982-83."[72] Riccobono noted that "the percentage change is greatest among the smallest and least wealthy districts, for which the potential for increase typically was greatest."[73] However, he found that the findings were quite different at the classroom level of analysis and observed that "even in the presence of clearly increased availability of television as an instructional medium in the nation's school districts and schools, availability of ITV to individual teachers showed no significant change from 1977 to 1983."[74] In fact, Riccobono states that "taken at face value, the results suggest that relative availability to teachers has declined over the past six years."[75] Moreover, the Riccobono data indicates that approximately 54 percent of teachers with ITV actually used it during the 1982/83 school year. Of these, only 9 percent used an entire series, 33 percent used two or more series, and 58 percent did not use a complete series. Riccobono's data concerning the support for instructional television showed that only 60 percent of the school superintendents provided this information while 40 percent of those indicated a total ITV budget of zero. The budgets ranged widely from a very few dollars to about $1 million with a median total budget of all reporting districts of about $58,000 and $50,000.[76]

Carlisle made an extensive survey of the use of instructional television in the United States.[77] His study commissioned by the Agency for Instructional Technology, included interviews with 158 teachers and administrators in twelve states and seventy communities. While this survey, in Carlisle's own words, was "in no way a clinically pure, national survey," he gathered an impressive number of case histories that illustrated the exemplary use of instructional television. A notable study of the use of instructional television was made in 1982. Created by the Agency for Instructional Television (AIT), the "ThinkAbout" television series was billed as "the most ambitious use of instructional television ever made." The sixty 15-minute programs were designed to help fifth- and sixth-graders "effectively express themselves, manage their own learning, reason systematically, and think flexibly."[78] Thirteen program clusters were developed on topics such as finding alternatives, estimating and approximating, giving and getting meaning, collecting information, etc. Planning began in 1973 and the program was introduced in 1979 to the thirty-eight consortia of state and provincial agencies in the United States and Canada. The program involved hundreds of educators and cost about $5 million in public and private funds.

Three researchers spent up to an entire school year in six suburban elementary classrooms in the Midwest and the West in the early 1980s to evaluate the impact of the "ThinkAbout" program series. With only six teachers, classroom use varied widely in (1) the number of programs used (e.g., one teacher used all sixty, another only twelve), (2) the amount of preparation before each program (e.g., two teachers had preparation discussions based on the teachers' guide; two teachers just turned on the set at the scheduled time), (3) the time and quality of discussions, (4) the level of integration with the school curriculum. In all classes, except one, "ThinkAbout" usually competed with a number of other assigned activities, and in all but one case, "ThinkAbout" was shown in the afternoon when teachers often looked for filler activities after the heavy concentration of basic subjects in the mornings.[79]

Johnston maintains that the research on "ThinkAbout" is limited because the criterion of its effectiveness was unrealistic and because sufficient time had not elapsed to enable teachers to adapt their teaching to the new curriculum.[80]

Basic Research in Educational Television

Basic research has been exemplified by studies of the effects of television in terms of knowledge, attitudes, and behavior. Dorr, Howe, Meyer, and Bryant and Anderson provide excellent overviews of this type of research.[81] In more recent years, a so-called selective-exposure approach has tended to modify and complement much of the impact research. According to Zillmann and Bryant, selective exposure "designates behavior that is deliberately performed to attain and sustain perceptual control of particular stimulus events." Thus, in this definition, selective exposure involves almost every aspect of human behavior and

> subsumes anything from closely watching a poisonous snake in the grass, following the flight of a bumblebee, listening to a birdcall, watching the road and other cars as we travel down the highway, reading the newspaper, listening to records in solitude or while keeping an eye on the children, and watching television intently.[82]

Educational television when used outside of the classroom must maximize gratifications from exposure. Research evidence, for example, has suggested that the use of such clues as puppets or clowns may not be sufficient to hold the attention of young viewers if other gratifications are not forthcoming.[83]

Although the theory of gratifiers and the law of effect are clearly understood, little is known about what televised cues are sufficiently gratifying to produce desired effects on exposure. However, some recent research has been highly suggestive (e.g., Anderson and Lorch, 1983;[84] Rice et al., 1982).[85] Such attributes, for example, as humor, sound effects, long zooms, background music, etc., require further experimentation to determine how they may be used to facilitate exposure to educational television.

The Cognitive Impact of Microcomputers

Early microcomputer research studies were in some respects, similar to audience surveys in the early days of radio education and instructional television. There were at first studies of utilization that investigated the extent of school computer use. Some studies of microcomputer utilization emphasized that research must investigate software applications as well as hardware acquisition. Later microcomputer research shifted its emphasis from diffusion and organization processes to studies of the cognitive, attitudinal, and behavioral effects. There have also been a number of cost-effectiveness studies of the microcomputer. However, this section focuses on a review of some of the significant studies relating to the instructional effectiveness of the microcomputer.

There is still insufficient evidence to reach any firm conclusions regarding the importance of the difference in technology between the mainframe computer and the microcomputer with reference to instructional achievement. Preliminary indications are that computer-assisted interventions using microcomputers are at least as effective as applications on mainframe computers.

Considerable research on the microcomputer has concerned itself with drill and practice programs. Typically the results have shown that students learn about the same amount of material through the computer as through conventional instruction, but that this learning takes place in less time or at a faster rate. These results have been consistently obtained with elementary through college students and has included content as diverse as mathematics, science, and typewriting.

Kearsley et al. reviewed fifty major computer projects and reached a number of conclusions. Their first conclusion: "While technology can be a tremendous multiplier of good ideas, it does not, in itself, produce them."[86] Other conclusions of these reviewers: (1) We know very little about individualized instruction; (2) We do not know very much about the effects of instructional variables; (3) There is a need for new software tools and techniques; (4) We have just scratched the surface of the computer's potential; (5) Twenty years ago the same issues were being discussed that are being discussed today.

One perspective flowing out of microcomputer research is that mastery of a programming language is the most effective and direct way to attain the cognitive benefits of computer use. Another competing perspective maintains that learning to program will not serve the needs of most students and that future computer software promises to provide more powerful "tool software" which can facilitate an easier user interface.

The Motivational Impact of Computers

Most of the major studies of the effects of computers in education have been concerned with the motivational impacts. However, in recent years, increasing attention has been focused on the possible effects on attitudes toward learning as well as the broad implications of exposure to computers. A two-year case study of a high school in California's Silicon Valley illustrates the way in which computers are being experienced by students and the potential impact of computers on student attitudes.[87] The principal point of agreement among almost all of the students was the necessity of learning about computers so that they may be able to cope with the future. There were students who were intensely enthusiastic about computers and who spent many hours writing or copying computer programs while there were others who were literally struggling to use the computer or those who dropped out in frustration. There were students who saw a distinct benefit in taking a computer course while others were less enthusiastic and were even cynical of the value of computer classes from an academic point of view.

Kulik et al. used results from fifty-one independent evaluations of CAI in grades 6-12. Their findings showed: (1) higher performances (a gain of 0.32 standard deviations) on final examinations, (2) smaller positive effects on follow-up examinations, (3) substantial savings in learning time, and (4) very positive attitudes by students toward both the computer and their courses.[88] Another study showed that student encounters with computers will not necessarily be positive. Carnegie-Mellon University in Pittsburgh adopted a requirement that all students learn to program a computer, but a study of the student attitudes of those involved in this program found that students were often confused, angry, and discouraged by trying to master computer programming.[89] In still another interesting study, it was found that students blame themselves for computer problems or breakdowns. When computer breakdown was deliberately caused by the researchers, 42 percent of the students blamed themselves, 26 percent blamed the computer, and 32 percent blamed both the computer and themselves.[90]

The Roblyer, Castine, King Research Review: Assessing the Impact of Computer-Based Instruction

One of the most comprehensive reviews of research on the impact of computer-based instruction during the 1980s was the Roblyer, Castine, King review.[91] This research review, as Cleborne D. Maddux wrote in the preface, "focuses attention on our problems and our shortcomings" and "draws attention to what we know, and it makes devastatingly clear how much we do not know."[92] Maddux says further that there is an Everest Syndrome in educational computing and that there are those who "believe that computers should be brought into educational settings simply *because they are there.*"[93] The result of the Everest Syndrome, according to Maddux "is an improper emphasis on computer hardware, and a consequent underemphasis on other, frequently more powerful variables affecting the computer user."[94] Thus, he says, "this may result in computer implementations that over-emphasize what hardware can be made to do, rather than what children using computers can be empowered to do."[95] Maddux says "another manifestation of the Everest Syndrome may be the most serious of all."[96] It is, he says, "the neglect of philosophy and theory as it applies to educational computing."[97] For example, Maddux says that the host of textbooks now available for introductory courses in educational computing "are not really books about educational computing at all," but are rather books "about how to operate computers using specific software."[98] He says, "they teach teachers-in-training how to use word processing, data base management, and spreadsheets, for example, but they devote little, if any space to why and how such applications should be taught to children."[99] Finally, Maddux says the common myth about computers is "that all we need to do is place a computer and a child in the same room and wonderful things will happen."[100]

The Roblyer, Castine, King research review provides a summary of literature reviews and findings from 1975 to 1987, meta-analyses of studies from 1980 to 1987, reviews of findings from areas of interest, and ends with a discussion of findings and implications for computer use and research. As in past reviews, the Roblyer, Castine, King review found that most of the studies were in mathematics and reading, most of these in basic skills, and about half of the total from elementary grades. They found that due to study flaws and lack of data, only a fraction of the total number of research reports available could be used. While studies in the past frequently measured learning retention and learning time, Roblyer, Castine, and King found little emphasis on these variables. They also found almost no studies on computer applications as a total replacement for traditional methods.

In terms of research characteristics, Roblyer, Castine, and King found that only about 40 percent of the achievement studies were able to accomplish random assignment controls. Also, most studies that used random assignment also used pretest-posttest control group designs. Fewer than 30 percent of the studies had the control group use some form of computer application. Moreover, researchers used a variety of tests, about 30 percent were locally-developed, usually by the experimenter. Word processing studies most often used a wholistic scoring method designed by the experimenter. When student attitudes or cognitive skills were being studied, "no two experimenters seemed to use the same instruments."[101] The sample size varied from a low of 16 to a high of about 4,000. Most studies had a total N of around 100 students.

The Roblyer, Castine, King review revealed that "attitudes toward school and subject matter seemed most affected by computer use, and was the most studied."[102] Although only three studies with data were located which measured this variable, the results were consistently positive. Little data was available on attitudes toward computers as instructional media.

In the content area, this review confirmed the trend identified by past studies that computer applications are more effective in teaching mathematics than reading/language skills.

However, unlike past reviews, no significant differences were found between effects for reading and mathematics. There also was great variability between effects for reading. Science achieved the highest overall effect size, but the small number of studies from this area limits the conclusions one can draw. Roblyer, Castine, and King found it to be most surprising to find "that using computer applications to teach cognitive skills (problem-solving, critical thinking) yielded about the same effects as for reading and mathematics."[103]

With regard to specific applications of the computer in instruction, the only areas with sufficient numbers of studies to analyze were reading and mathematics. Various applications for mathematics were about equally effective. In reading, tutorial applications achieved higher effects than other types. However, effects among applications types were not found to be significantly different ($p < .05$). High positive effects were achieved in social studies when simulations were used for unstructured work. When drill software was used in science or when simulations were used for drill, much lower effects resulted.

The only significant differences among groups included in any metanalysis occurred in comparisons of elementary, secondary, and college levels. In contrast to past studies, the Roblyer, Castine, King review found significantly higher results at college/adult levels. Effects from elementary levels were higher than those at secondary levels, but the differences were not very great. The general results indicated that computer applications can be as successful at higher levels and may be even more effective than at lower levels. No significant differences were found with the effectiveness of computer applications among lower-achieving students compared to regular students. There were also no significant differences between males and females in achievement using computer-based methods. However, the results clearly showed that computer-based instruction with Spanish-speaking populations was not as effective as other methods.

Roblyer, Castine, and King also point out the need for more substantial research in such areas as computer applications in various skills and content areas, word processing use, creativity and problem solving with LOGO and CAI, computer applications for ESL students, studying the effects of computer use on attitudes and dropout rate, and the effects of computer use on achievement of males and females. They also see the need for more cost-effectiveness studies and a higher standard for research reports.

Roblyer, Castine, and King conclude their review with a cautionary word for the future. They say, "there is, of course, never a final word on the future: it is always before us. But the opportunity now before us will not always be there. Educators are currently enthusiastic and supportive of computer-assisted instruction, computer-based discovery-learning materials, and computer productivity tools. But the enthusiasm will wane, as it does with all new things. Unless a clear case can be made soon with research and evaluation results for keeping a computer application in use, it may be one of the methods in danger of faddish discard."[104]

Intelligent Tutoring Systems

The most notable contribution of cognitive science to educational technology is what has come to be known as intelligent computer-assisted instruction (ICAI) or intelligent tutoring systems (ITS). Although computers have been used in education for over thirty years, there is still no fully functioning intelligent tutoring system. However, in recent years, a number of ITS systems have been developed as research prototypes (e.g., GUIDON by Clancey, 1983;[105] SOPHIE by Brown et al., 1982;[106] WEST, by Burton and Brown, 1979;[107] the BUGGY/DEBUGGY series by Burton, 1981;[108] and Anderson's LISP Tutor (Anderson et al., 1985).[109] Most ITS systems are either problem-solving tutors or simulations. A recent prototype, SMITHTOWN places special emphasis on discovery learning and on the coaching of metacognitive process of learning.[110]

ITS constitutes a highly sophisticated form of CAI which usually consists of four major components: the expert knowledge component, the learner modeling component, the tutorial planning component, and the communication component. The expert knowledge component comprises the knowledge of experts: the facts and rules of a particular domain. The learner modeling component involves the dynamic representation of the emerging knowledge and skill of the learner. The tutorial planning component is the part of the ITS that designs and regulates the instructional or "intelligent" dialogue with the learner. The fourth or communication component controls interactions between the system and the learner.[111]

There are many issues and problems that will have to be resolved before there is much future progress in the development of ITS. It is still not clear whether the current limits of intelligent tutoring reflects an early stage of development or whether there are fundamental limits. Much additional basic research is required in building a metatheory of expert knowledge that shows how declarative, procedural, and causal knowledge relate and "a theoretical approach needs to be developed for investigating the linguistic character of tutorial discourse."[112] Moreover, as Littman and Soloway point out, "because evaluation of ITSs is an issue for both the present and the future, it is appropriate to identify some problems that could lead to progress for the field."[113] In the meantime, Burton sees an enrichment of traditional instruction as a result of new technology and the cognitive perspective that ITS research brings to defining the content of instruction. For example, research on the machine learning of semantic networks, rule systems, and mental models has provided a basis for a new generation of ITS.[114]

Federal Support for Educational Technology R&D

This section draws heavily on the 1988 Office of Technology Assessment report, *Power On! New Tools for Teaching and Learning*.[115] According to this report, three federal agencies have been the major funders of research and development in educational technology during the 1980s: the Department of Defense (DoD), the National Science Foundation (NSF), and the Office of Education/Department of Education. Direct federal funding for educational technology R&D accounted for a total spending of approximately $240 million per year.

DoD's R&D effort has focused essentially on computer technology and its applications to education. Their research has ranged from basic cognitive science investigations to applied development of course materials and electronic teaching machines.

The NSF took the lead in educational technology research in the 1960s and 1970s in supporting computer use in schools, but when schools were beginning to acquire microcomputers in large numbers, NSF had no program focused on educational technology. However, beginning in 1984, R&D activity in educational technology expanded with emphasis on science and engineering education. The Informal Science Education Program supports several media projects and the Research in Learning and Teaching Program funds several projects in cognition and studies of student problems in understanding scientific and mathematical concepts. Computer-based projects include a study of the effects of computer-based curricula in school algebra, a project concerned with how high school students and teachers solve problems in genetics using computer simulations, and an assessment of elementary and middle school children's LOGO debugging skills.

The Office of Education/Department of Education's support for educational technology spans three decades. In the 1980s, much of the department's funding for educational technology was in the form of grants to school districts to purchase computers, videocassette recorders, and software. However, the department has spent a limited amount of money on research. Not even half of one percent of the Department of Education budget has gone to research in the 1980s. From 1981 to 1987, an estimated $129 million was spent on educational technology R&D and demonstration projects with computers. Several computer projects were supported in the early 1980s under Secretary Bell's Technology Initiative. Twelve technology demonstration projects involved the study and demonstration of computer applications. Moreover, the department sponsored a research conference in November 1982 on the potential of computers for education and supported the establishment of the Educational Technology Center at the Harvard Graduate School of Education.[116] The center, funded at $7.7 million over five years, conducted R&D on the role of educational technology in the teaching of mathematics, science, and computing. The center focused on the nature of learner difficulty in understanding and exploiting the educational capabilities of computer-based learning and designed experimental lessons using computers.

Further department involvement in educational technology during the 1980s occurred when Secretary Bell created a National Task Force on Educational Technology in 1983 "to investigate the potential of appropriately integrated technology to improve learning in our nation's schools."[117] It was Bell's hope that this Task Force would set a national agenda for educational technology. However, when Bell left the Department of Education in 1984, the computer initiative came to a virtual halt. The new secretary, William Bennett, did not share Bell's vision of using computers to improve education, and, as a result, educational technology was given a low priority. As a matter of fact, the task force report was held up several months and was never printed or made available to the public through the usual Government Printing Office channels. Meanwhile, there were severe reductions in computer-related R&D. During most of the 1980s, educational technology R&D projects have received only short-term support and did not have the opportunity to progress from laboratory research to the development of products and testing.

In late 1989, the Educational Technology Center at Harvard was funded for another five years, but at a reduced level of $1 million rather than $7.7 million. The new center will be responsible for all curriculum areas, not just mathematics and science and will be concerned with the areas of teaching, learning, assessment, and school leadership. The department's 1989 budget did not provide for any new instructional television initiatives, and no new funds were authorized for the continuance of the Star Schools Program for distance learning.

Other agencies have supported educational technology R&D. For example, the National Institutes of Health, the Department of Labor, and the State Department have instituted various training programs that use computers. However, it is difficult to identify many of the more promising projects because there is a reluctance to share programs or approaches which may have potential application in the schools.

Notes

[1]E. R. Hilgard, "The Trilogy of Mind: Cognition, Affection, and Conation," *Journal of the History of the Behavioral Sciences* 16 (April 1980), 115.

[2]Paul R. Pintrich et al., "Instructional Psychology" in Mark R. Rosenzweig and Lyman W. Porter, eds., *Annual Review of Psychology*, vol. 37. Palo Alto, Calif.: Annual Review, 1986, 617.

[3]B. C. Calfee, "Cognitive Psychology and Educational Practice," in David C. Berlinet, ed., *Review of Research in Education* 9. Washington, D.C.: American Educational Research Association, 1981, 3-72.

[4]See Richard E. Snow and M. J. Farr, eds., *Aptitude, Learning, and Instruction: Vol. 3: Cognitive and Affective Process Analysis.* Hillsdale, N.J.: Lawrence Erlbaum, 1987.

[5]Lyn Corno and Richard E. Snow, "Adaptive Teaching to Individual Differences among Learners," in Merlin C. Wittrock, ed., *Handbook of Research on Teaching*, 3d ed. New York: Macmillan, 1986, 605-29.

[6]P. C. Koyllonen et al., *Models of Strategy and Strategy-Shifting in Spatial Visualization Performance,* tech. report 17. Stanford, Calif.: Stanford University, Aptitude Research Project, School of Education, NTIS No. AD-A108 003, 1981.

[7]Corno and Snow, "Adaptive Teaching," 623.

[8]Ibid., 625.

[9]The acknowledged founder of the attribution concept is Fritz Heider who identified the basic framework in his 1958 text *The Psychology of Interpersonal Relations.* The attribution theory was first developed by Bernard Weiner in 1972. The early development of Weiner's attribution theory began with the identification of the four major causes of motivation. More recent work describes the role of the affective reactions of others on an individual's attributions for success or failure. See Bernard Weiner, *An Attributional Theory of Motivation and Emotion.* London: Springer-Verlag, 1986.

[10]Donald L. MacMillan et al., "Special Educational Research on Mildly Handicapped Learners," in Merlin Wittrock, ed., *Handbook of Research on Teaching,* 3d ed. New York: Macmillan, 1986, 703-5.

[11]Merlin C. Wittrock, "Students' Thought Processes," in Merlin C. Wittrock, ed., *Handbook of Research in Teaching,* 3d ed. New York: Macmillan, 1986, 304-6.

[12]J. H. Flavell, "Metacognitive Aspects of Problem Solving," in L. B. Resnick, ed., *The Nature of Intelligence.* Hillsdale, N.J.: Lawrence Erlbaum, 1976, 232.

[13]R. C. Shank, *Reading and Understanding: Teaching from the Perspective of Artificial Intelligence.* Hillsdale, N.J.: Lawrence Erlbaum, 1982, 56.

[14]Patricia H. Miller, "Metacognition and Attention," in D. L. Forrest-Pressley et al., eds., *Metacognition, Cognition, and Human Performance.* New York: Academic Press, 1985, 218.

[15]See Bonnie J. F. Meyer, "Following the Author's Top-Level Organization: An Important Skill for Reading Comprehension," in Robert J. Tierney et al., eds., *Understanding Readers' Understanding.* Hillsdale, N.J.: Lawrence Erlbaum, 1987, 59-76.

[16]See, for example, W. Kintsch and T. A. van Dijk, "Toward a Model of Text Comprehension and Production," *Psychological Review* 85 (September 1978), 363-94; R. Shank and R. Abelson, *Scripts, Plans, Goals, and Understanding,* Hillsdale, N.J.: Lawrence Erlbaum, 1977; and D. E. Rumelhart and A. Ortony, "The Representation of Knowledge in Memory," in R. C. Anderson et al., eds., *Schooling and the Acquisition of Knowledge,* Hillsdale, N.J.: Lawrence Erlbaum, 1977. For examples of landmark experiments, see R. C. Anderson et al., "Frameworks for Comprehending Discourse," *American Educational Research Journal* 14 (Fall 1977), 367-81; and M. S. Steffensen et al., *A Cross-Cultural Perspective on Reading Comprehension,* tech. report no. 97, ERIC No. ED 159 660, Urbana: University of Illinois, Center for the Study of Reading, 1978.

[17]D. E. Rumelhart, "Understanding and Summarizing Brief Stories," in D. LaBerge and J. Samuels, eds., *Basic Processes in Reading: Perception and Comprehension.* Hillsdale, N.J.: Lawrence Erlbaum, 1977.

[18]M. J. Adams and A. Collins, "A Schema-Theoretic View of Reading," in R. O. Freedle, ed., *Discourse Processing: Multidisciplinary Perspectives.* Norwood, N.J.: Ablex, 1979.

[19]A. S. Palincsar and A. L. Brown, "Reciprocal Teaching of Comprehension-Fostering and Monitoring Activities," *Cognition and Instruction* 1 (1984), 117-75.

[20]See James V. Wertsch, ed., *Culture, Communication, and Cognition: Vygotskian Perspectives.* Cambridge: Cambridge University Press, 1985.

[21]H. W. Faw and T. G. Waller, "Mathemagenic Behaviors and Efficiency in Learning from Prose Materials: Review, Critique, and Recommendations," *Review of Educational Research* 46 (Fall 1976), 691-720.

[22]H. Singer, "Active Comprehension: From Answering to Asking Questions," *The Reading Teacher* 31 (May 1978), 901-8.

[23]J. R. Levin and M. Pressley, "Improving Children's Prose Comprehension: Selected Strategies That Seem to Succeed," *Comprehension: Research and Practice*. Newark, Del.: International Reading Association, 1981, 44-71.

[24]J. C. Harste et al., *Language, Stories, and Literary Lessons*. Portsmouth, N.H.: Heinemann, 1984.

[25]D. DeFord, "Validating the Construct of Theoretical Orientation in Reading Instruction," *Reading Research Quarterly* 20 (1985), 351-67.

[26]J. V. Hoffman et al., "Guided Oral Reading and Miscue Focused Verbal Feedback in Second-Grade Classrooms," *Reading Research Quarterly* 19 (1984), 367-84.

[27]K. H. Au and J. M. Mason, "Social Organizational Factors in Learning to Read: The Balance of Rights Hypothesis," *Reading Research Quarterly* 17 (1981), 115-52.

[28]P. Mosenthal and T. Na, "Quality of Children's Recall under Two Classroom Testing Conditions: Toward a Socio-Psycholinguistic Model of Reading Comprehension," *Reading Research Quarterly* 15 (1980), 504-28.

[29]Marlene Scardamalia and Carl Bereiter, "Research on Written Composition," in Merlin C. Wittrock, ed., *Handbook of Research on Teaching*, 3d ed. New York: Macmillan, 1986, 788-803.

[30]See R. de Beaugrande, "Psychology and Composition: Past, Present, and Future," in M. Nyustrand, ed., *What Writers Know: The Language, Process, and Structure of Written Discourse*. New York: Academic Press, 1982, 211-67.

[31]L. T. Frase, "Knowledge, Information and Action: Requirements for Automated Writing Instruction," *Journal of Computer-Based Instruction* 11 (January 1984), 55-59.

[32]K. E. Kiefer and C. R. Smith, "Textual Analysis with Computers: Tests of Bell Laboratories' Computer Software," *Research Teaching English* 17 (1983), 201-14.

[33]See, for example, J. Piaget, *The Child's Conception of Number*, New York: Humanities Press, 1952; and J. Piaget et al., *The Child's Conception of Geometry*, New York: Basic Books, 1960.

[34]The theories of Ausubel, Bruner, and Gagnè focused explicitly on the structure of content to be learned. Gagnè probably provided one of the clearest specifications of how the mathematics curriculum could be analyzed and researched. See D. P. Ausubel, *Educational Psychology: A Cognitive View*, New York: Holt, Rinehart and Winston, 1968; J. S. Bruner, *Toward a Theory of Instruction*, Cambridge, Mass.: Harvard University Press, 1966; and R. M. Gagnè, *The Conditions of Learning*, New York: Holt, Rinehart and Winston, 1965.

[35]L. Resnick and S. Omanson, "Learning to Understand Arithmetic," in Robert Glaser, ed., *Advances in Instructional Psychology*, vol. 3. Hillsdale, N.J.: Lawrence Erlbaum, 1985.

[36]Thomas A. Romberg and Thomas P. Carpenter, "Research on Teaching and Learning Mathematics: Two Disciplines of Scientific Inquiry," in Merlin C. Wittrock, ed., *Handbook of Research in Teaching*, 3d ed. New York: Macmillan, 1986, 850-73.

[37]Ibid., 868.

[38]Ibid., 868.

[39]Richard T. White and Richard P. Tisher, "Research on Natural Sciences," in Merlin C. Wittrock, ed., *Handbook of Research on Teaching*, 3d ed. New York: Macmillan, 1986, 874-905.

[40]D. L. Redfield and E. W. Rousseau, "A Meta-Analysis of Experimental Research on Teacher Questioning Behavior," *Review of Educational Research* 51 (Summer 1981), 237-45.

[41]A. L. Brown et al., "Learning to Learn: On Training Students to Learn from Texts," *Educational Researcher* 10 (February 1981), 14-21.

[42]W. G. Holiday, "Selective Attentional Effects of Textbook Study Questions on Student Learning in Science," *Journal of Research in Science Teaching* 18 (July 1981), 283-89.

[43]J. Larkin et al., "Expert and Novice Performance in Solving Physics Problems," *Science* 208 (June 1980), 1335-42.

[44]J. R. Hayes, "Three Problems in Teaching General Skills," in S. F. Chipman et al., eds., *Thinking and Learning Skills: Volume 2, Research and Open Questions.* Hillsdale, N.J.: Lawrence Erlbaum, 1985.

[45]J. C. Greeno, "Some Examples of Cognitive Task Analysis with Instructional Implications," in R. E. Snow et al., eds., *Aptitude, Learning, and Instruction*, vol. 2. Hillsdale, N.J.: Lawrence Erlbaum, 1980, 21.

[46]Beverly J. Armento, "Research on Teaching Social Studies," in Merlin Wittrock, ed., *Handbook of Research on Teaching*, 3d ed. New York: Macmillan, 1986, 942-51.

[47]Ibid., 946.

[48]M. C. Wittrock, *The Human Brain.* Englewood Cliffs, N.J.: Prentice-Hall, 1977.

[49]A. A. MacKenzie and R. T. White, "Fieldwork in Geography and Long-Term Memory Structures," *American Education Research Journal* 19 (Winter 1982), 623-32.

[50]J. F. Voss et al., "Problem Solving Skill in Social Sciences," in G. Bower, ed., *The Psychology of Learning and Motivation: Advances in Research Theory.* New York: Academic Press, 1984.

[51]Thomas J. Shuell, "Learning Theory, Instructional Theory, and Adaptation," in Richard E. Snow et al., eds., *Aptitude, Learning, and Instruction*, vol. 2. Hillsdale, N.J.: Lawrence Erlbaum, 1980, 284-86.

[52]See Charles M. Reigeluth, ed., *Instructional-Design Theories and Models.* Hillsdale, N.J.: Lawrence Erlbaum, 1983. Many of the instructional design models discussed in this book have been described in chapter 12 of this book.

[53]David Mitchell, "The Concept of Individualized Instruction in the Microelectronics Era," in Nick Rushby, ed., *Technology Based Learning.* New York: Nicholas Publishing, 1987, p. 97.

[54]In outlining the concept of the *zone of proximal development*, Vygotsky proposed a new theoretical framework for analyzing the child's current state of development and for predicting the next or proximal level of development that the child might be expected to attain. That is, Vygotsky was concerned not with the quantitative assessment of learning ability or intelligence, but with the qualitative assessment of psychological processes and the dynamics of their development. The term *proximal* has traditionally been used in translating the Russian term *blizhaishei* in this context, although the term *nearest* would represent a more literal translation. For a fuller discussion of Vygotskian perspectives, see James V. Wertsch, ed., *Culture, Communication and Cognition.* Cambridge: Cambridge University Press, 1985.

[55]For a historical perspective of dynamic assessment, see Carol Schneider Lidz, "Historical Perspectives," in Carol Schneider Lidz, ed., *Dynamic Assessment.* New York: Guilford Press, 1987, 3-32.

[56]R. Glaser, "The Future of Testing: A Research Agenda for Cognitive Psychology and Psychometrics," *American Psychologist* 36 (September 1981), 925.

[57]See R. Feuerstein, *Instrumental Enrichment: An Intervention Program for Cognitive Modifiability*. Baltimore, Md.: University Park Press, 1980.

[58]See A. L. Brown and J. C. Campione, "Cognitive Science and Learning Disabilities," *American Psychologist* 41 (October 1986), 1059-68.

[59]See S. Ionescu and Jourdan-Ionescu, "La Mesure du potential d'apprentissage: Nouvelle approche dans l'evaluation des deficients mentaux," *Apprentissage et Socialisation* 6 (1983), 117-24.

[60]Cronback and Snow provided the procedures for ATI analysis. See L. J. Cronback and R. E. Snow, eds., *A Handbook for Research on Interactions*. New York: Irvington, 1977.

[61]Some of the symbol system theories are discussed in chapter 14 of this book.

[62]Gavriel Salomon, "Information Technologies: What You See Is Not (Always) What You Get," *Educational Psychologist* 20 (Fall 1985), 207-16.

[63]Richard E. Clark and Brenda M. Surgru, "Research on Instructional Media," in Donald P. Ely et al., eds., *Educational Media and Technology Yearbook*, vol. 14. Englewood, Colo.: Libraries Unlimited, 1988, 21.

[64]Richard E. Clark and Gavriel Salomon, "Media in Teaching," in Merlin Wittrock, ed., *Handbook of Research on Teaching*, 3d ed. New York: Macmillan, 1986, 473.

[65]Richard E. Clark, "Reconsidering Research on Learning from Media," *Review of Educational Research* 53 (Winter 1983), 453.

[66]J. Beagles-Roos and I. Gat, "Specific Impact of Radio and Television on Children's Story Comprehension," *Journal of Educational Psychology* 75 (February 1983), 128-37.

[67]Clark, "Research on Instructional Media," 34.

[68]Ibid.

[69]A summary of television research by the National Institute of Mental Health cites a 1980 bibliography of 2,800 research articles, books, and other materials published in English between 1946 and 1980. Before 1970, 300 titles were published; between 1970 and 1980, 2,500 were published, with more than two-thirds published since 1975. See National Institute of Mental Health, *Television and Behavior: Ten Years of Scientific Progress and Implications for the 80s*. Vol. 10, Summary Report. Washington, D.C.: U.S. Department of Health and Human Services, 1983.

[70]Gavriel Salomon, "Television Watching and Mental Effort: A Social Psychological View," in J. Bryant and D. R. Anderson, eds., *Children's Understanding of Television: Research on Attention and Comprehension*. New York: Academic Press, 1983.

[71]J. A. Riccobono, *School Utilization Study: Availability, Use and Support of Instructional Media*. Washington, D.C.: CPB, 1985.

[72]Ibid., 45.

[73]Ibid., 46.

[74]Ibid., 46.

[75]Ibid., 46.

[76]Ibid., 52.

[77]Robert D. Carlisle, *Video at Work in American Schools*. Bloomington, Ind.: Agency for Instructional Technology, 1987.

[78]James Sanders and Subhash Sinnad, *Research in the Introduction, Use, and Impact of the "Think-About" Instructional Television Series.* Technical Report, vol. 1. Bloomington, Ind.: Agency for Instructional Television, 1982, 114.

[79]See the following: Harry Wolcott, *A View of Viewers: Observations on the Response to and Classroom Use of "ThinkAbout,"* Technical Report, vol. 4, Bloomington, Ind.: Agency for Instructional Television, 1982; Marilyn Cohn, *Teacher Use and Student Response in Three Classrooms,* Technical Report, vol. 2, Bloomington, Ind.: Agency for Instructional Television, 1982; Sylvia Hart-Landsberg, *Toward a Clear Picture of "ThinkAbout": An Account of Classroom Use,* Technical Report, vol. 3, Bloomington, Ind.: Agency for Instructional Television, 1982.

[80]Jerome Johnston, *Electronic Learning.* Hillsdale, N.J.: Lawrence Erlbaum, 1987, 46.

[81]See Aimee Dorr, *Television and Children: A Special Medium for a Special Audience*, Beverly Hills, Calif.: Sage Publications, 1986; M. J. A. Howe, *Learning from Television: Psychological and Educational Research*, New York: Academic Press, 1983; M. Meyer, ed., *Children and the Formal Features of Television*, New York: K. G. Saur, 1983; J. Bryant and D. R. Anderson, eds., *Children's Understanding of Television: Research on Attention and Comprehension*, Hillsdale, N.J.: Lawrence Erlbaum, 1985.

[82]D. Zillman and J. Bryant, eds., *Selective Exposure to Communication.* Hillsdale, N.J.: Lawrence Erlbaum, 1985, 2.

[83]J. J. Wasshag et al., "Selective Exposure to Educational Television Programs as Function of Differently Paced Humorous Inserts," *Journal of Educational Psychology* 73 (February 1981), 27-32.

[84]D. R. Anderson and E. P. Lorch, "Looking at Television: Action or Reaction?" in J. Bryant and D. R. Anderson, eds., *Children's Understanding of Television: Research on Comprehension.* New York: Academic Press, 1983, 1-33.

[85]M. L. Rice et al., "The Forms of Television: Effects on Children's Attention, Comprehension, and Social Behavior," in D. Pearl et al., eds., *Television and Behavior: Ten Years of Scientific Progress and Implications for the Eighties: Vol. 2, Technical Reviews.* Washington, D.C.: U.S. Department of Health and Human Services, Publication No. ADM 82-1196, GPO, 1982, 24-38.

[86]G. Kearsley et al., "Two Decades of Computer-Based Instruction Projects: What We Have Learned," *Technological Horizons in Education Journal* 10 (1983), 90-94; 10 (1983), 88-96.

[87]Robert B. Textor et al., "Anticipatory Anthropology and the Telemicroelectronic Revolution: A Preliminary Report from Silicon Valley," *Anthropology and Education Quarterly* 16 (1985), 3-30.

[88]J. A. Kulik et al., "Effects of Computer-Based Teaching on Secondary School Students," *Journal of Educational Psychology* 75 (February 1983), 19-26.

[89]See Lee Sproull et al., *Encountering an Alien Culture.* Pittsburgh, Pa.: Carnegie-Mellon University, 1984. (Mimeographed.)

[90]Minnesota Educational Computing Corporation, *Highlight Report: A Story of Computer Use and Literacy in Science Education.* Minneapolis, Minn.: MECC, 1980.

[91]M. D. Roblyer et al., "Assessing the Impact of Computer-Based Instruction," *Computers in the Schools* 5. New York: The Haworth Press, 1988.

[92]Cleborne D. Maddux, "Preface," 1.

[93]Ibid., 5.

[94]Ibid.

[95]Ibid.

[96]Ibid., 6.

[97]Ibid., 7.

[98]Ibid.

[99]Ibid.

[100]Ibid., 8.

[101]Ibid., 120.

[102]Ibid.

[103]Ibid., 122.

[104]Ibid., 131.

[105]W. J. Clancey, "GUIDON," *Journal of Computer-Based Instruction* 10 (1983), 8-15.

[106]J. S. Brown et al., "Pedagogical Natural Language and Knowledge Engineering Techniques in SOPHIE I, II, and III," in D. Sleeman and J. S. Brown, eds., *Intelligent Tutoring Systems.* New York: Academic Press, 1982.

[107]R. R. Burton and J. S. Brown, "An Investigation of Computer Coaching for Informal Learning Activities," *International Journal of Man-Machine Studies* 2 (1979), 5-24.

[108]R. R. Burton, "Diagnosing Bugs in a Simple Procedural Skill," in D. Sleeman and J. S. Brown, eds., *Intelligent Tutoring Systems.* New York: Academic Press, 1982.

[109]J. R. Anderson et al., *Intelligent Tutoring Systems.* Pittsburgh, Pa.: Carnegie-Mellon University Advanced Computer Tutoring Project, 1985.

[110]V. Shute and R. Glaser, "An Intelligent Tutoring System for Exploring Principles of Economics," in R. Snow and D. Wiley, eds., *Straight Thinking.* San Francisco, Calif.: Jossey-Bass, in press.

[111]Martha C. Polson and J. Jeffry Richardson, eds., *Foundations of Intelligent Tutoring Systems.* Hillsdale, N.J.: Lawrence Erlbaum, 1988.

[112]Ibid., 246.

[113]Ibid., 234-35.

[114]R. S. Michalski et al., eds., *Machine Learning*, vol. 2. Los Altos, Calif.: Morgan Kaufmann, 1986.

[115]U.S. Congress, Office of Technology Assessment, *Power On! New Tools for Teaching and Learning*, OTA-SET-379. Washington, D.C.: GPO, September 1988, 151-71.

[116]See Alan Lesgold and Frederick Reif, *Computers in Education: Realizing the Potential*, Report of a Research Conference. Washington, D.C.: U.S. Department of Education, August 1983; Educational Technology Center, Harvard Graduate School of Education, "Making Sense of the Future." Position paper on the role of technology in science, mathematics, and computing education, January 1988, 1.

[117]National Task Force on Educational Technology, "Transforming American Education: Reducing the Risk to the Nation." Report to the Secretary of Education, unpublished manuscript, April 1986, 1.

Select Bibliography

Anderson, J. R., et al. *Intelligent Tutoring Systems*. Pittsburgh: Carnegie-Mellon University Advanced Computer Tutoring Project, 1985.

Bryant, J., and D. R. Anderson, eds. *Children's Understanding of Television: Research on Attention and Comprehension*. New York: Academic Press, 1983.

Dorr, Aimee. *Television and Children: A Special Medium for a Special Audience*. Beverly Hills, Calif.: Sage Publications, 1986.

Michalski, R. S., et al., eds. *Machine Learning*, vol. 2. Los Altos, Calif.: Morgan Kaufmann, 1986.

Riccobono, J. A. *School Utilization Study: Availability, Use and Support of Instructional Media*. Washington, D.C.: CPB, 1985.

Roblyer, M. D., et al. "Accessing the Impact of Computer-Based Instruction: A Review of Recent Research." *Computers in the Schools*, vol. 5, nos. 3/4. New York: Haworth Press, 1988.

Rushby, Nick, ed. *Technology Based Learning*. New York: Nicholas Publishing, 1987.

Shank, R. C. *Reading and Understanding: Teaching from the Perspective of Artificial Intelligence*. Hillsdale, N.J.: Lawrence Erlbaum, 1982.

Sleeman, D., and J. S. Brown, eds. *Intelligent Tutoring Systems*. New York: Academic Press, 1982.

Snow, Richard E., and M. J. Farr, eds. *Aptitude, Learning, and Instruction: Vol. 3. Cognitive and Affective Process Analyses*. Hillsdale, N.J.: Lawrence Erlbaum, 1987.

Snow, Richard E., and David E. Lohman. *Implications of Cognitive Psychology for Educational Measurement*. Stanford, Calif.: CERAS, School of Education, Stanford University, March 1988.

Wertsch, James V., ed. *Culture, Communication, and Cognition: Vygotskian Perspectives*. Cambridge: Cambridge University Press, 1985.

Wittrock, Merlin C., ed. *Handbook of Research on Teaching*, 3d ed. New York: Macmillan, 1986.

18

The Professional Organization of Educational Technology: Scholars and Practitioners

Although the process of educational technology can be traced back to ancient Greece, the term *educational technology* was almost unknown until the middle of this century. Moreover, even though the concepts of educational technology have permeated instructional method throughout the centuries, educational technology has not been identified as a unique and distinctive field or profession until recently. It has been frequently and incorrectly stated that educational technology evolved out of the visual education movement of the 1920s, but, as we have seen, the visual education (later audiovisual education) movement was a development of this century and has been almost completely separated from mainstream educational technology going back to the era of the Elder Sophists. In fact, it was in the early marriage of educational technology and psychology just at the turn of the century that educational technology first came into its modern heritage. It was at this time when empirical research, primarily psychological, appeared to be developing the first scientific underpinnings of instructional practice. This is when educational technology and psychology first merged to begin the scientific study of the methods of teaching and learning, the organization of instructional groups, and the particular problems associated with such subject areas as reading, writing, language learning, and arithmetic. The early yearbooks of the National Society for the Study of Education provide ample testimony to these early developments.

The work of Maria Montessori in the first decade of this century anticipated the programmed instruction approaches of Pressey in the 1920s while the young science of psychology was making an impact on educational technology with reference to the sequencing of instruction, the organization of practice, transfer of learning, and testing of comprehension. Unfortunately, the application of psychology to the process of educational technology declined after the 1930s when they moved apart. Thus, it was not until World War II that the two began to come together again when the military experience generated the application of psychological concepts and principles to the problems of instruction and learning. With the rise of Skinner's behaviorism in the 1960s and the emergence of cognitive psychology in the 1970s, educational technology began to be recognized for the first time as a distinct field and profession in its own right.

Even today, there is very little cooperation or coordination among the various groups that identify themselves as being scholars or practitioners in educational technology. Also, there is a wide disparity concerning the definition, theory, intellectual technique, training, and relationship to other professions. It still remains to be seen whether the various fields and disciplines can be synthesized into a unified field and profession known as educational technology.

The purpose of this chapter is (1) to describe the professional organizations associated with educational technology; (2) to review the professional preparation and certification of educational technology practitioners; (3) to look at the state of the art of instructional development; and (4) to analyze the professional changes in educational technology.

The Association for Educational Communications and Technology (AECT)

The Association for Educational Communications and Technology (AECT) began in 1923 as the Department of Visual Instruction of the NEA. In 1947, it changed its name to the Department of Audiovisual Instruction (DAVI) and in 1971, DAVI changed its name to AECT. Part of the reason for this last change was that DAVI was no longer an official department of the NEA and that the label "audiovisual instruction" had become outmoded in theory and practice.

The AECT claims that it serves as an umbrella organization for all persons interested in educational technology, but, in actuality, the majority of its programs are directed toward a minority of its profession and membership. For example, a survey by Molenda and Cambre indicated that only 39 percent of AECT members come from the elementary/secondary level, and business/industry.[1] A 1986 survey for Hutchinson and Rankin revealed that only 16.63 percent of AECT members came from the elementary/secondary level.[2] Nevertheless, much of the AECT program, including its publications, leadership development activities, organizational structure, and other organizations to which it chose to relate continued to be directed toward its elementary/secondary members. There has been ample evidence of this orientation, particularly in the close relationship AECT has had with AASL (American Association of School Librarians) rather than with close relationships with such organizations as AERA (American Educational Research Association), APA (American Psychological Association), NSPI (National Society for Performance and Instruction), or the ASTD (American Society for Training and Development). According to Silber, this limited the orientation of AECT, "rather than fostering the development of the conceptual and practical configuration needed for the subprofessions of educational technology to work together, this one-sided orientation promotes professional jealousy among the different subprofessions and infighting among the various interest groups for power, resources and programs." Silber says that these problems are only symptomatic of a more basic problem and makes the serious indictment that "the Association does not understand or represent the total conceptual framework of the profession of educational technology."[3] Silber notes that the posing of the question, "Should AECT merge with AASL? clearly demonstrates the misunderstanding."[4]

Although Silber launched his criticism of AECT several years ago, the problems he identified still exist. In the meantime, a serious decline in AECT membership occurred in the 1980s because it no longer represented a unified voice for the changing field of educational technology. However, in the late 1980s, AECT began to make an effort to stem this membership and subsequent financial decline by establishing three primary goals as basic to its future success: "(1) to place AECT on firm financial grounds; (2) to recreate a viable organizational structure; and (3) to assert a leadership role in defining the intellectual scope of the field and disseminating the results of research and practice."[5] In the area of finance, AECT was totally out of debt by 1988 because many members contributed to the debt retirement fund and absorbed miscellaneous expenses. Simultaneously, AECT's organizational structure was reviewed and continuous discussion and refinement was undertaken. Considerable efforts were also devoted to AECT's responsibility to define the intellectual scope of the field and disseminate relevant research. In addition to AECT's primary goals, there was considerable improvement in association communications and in the area of leadership development.

Unfortunately, AECT has tended to ignore the whole of educational technology by focusing on particular subfields within educational technology. But in an attempt to overspecialize, "the concept of an 'umbrella professional organization' may no longer be viable either, for there may be too many specialties with the practitioners in too many diverse settings for one organization to provide state-of-the-art services to each of them."[6]

AECT Divisions

To date, nine special interest divisions have been organized that reflect different functions and interests. These include:

1. Division of Educational Media Management for professionals who have major responsibility for planning and administering media programs.

2. Division of Information Systems and Computers for those interested in the development and implementation of processes that will make information, in any form, available to users within an educational environment.

3. Division of Instructional Development for those concerned with the development of instruction and the engineering of solutions to instructional problems.

4. Division of School Media Specialists for those concerned with the development and implementation of sound school media programs, and who want a voice for school media programs within the media professions.

5. Division of Telecommunications for those concerned with educational television, radio, and other electronically mediated instruction with an emphasis on the systematic design and production of content distributed by those media.

6. Industrial Training and Education Division for those interested in and involved with designing, organizing, and managing training programs within the private sector.

7. International Division for those concerned with the worldwide development and application of educational communications and technology.

8. Media Design and Production Division for those concerned with local production skills, and for those interested in promoting and facilitating interaction between commercial and noncommercial media producers and consumers.

9. Research and Theory Division for those interested in and concerned with research in the fields of instructional technology and communications.[7]

In addition, fourteen national associations representing specialized interests within educational technology are affiliated with AECT.[8]

Analysis of AECT Presidents: 1923-1988

Study and analysis of the presidential roster of AECT provides insight into the nature of leadership exerted on the field or profession of educational technology during the major portion of this century. An analysis by McClusky in 1981 showed there had been forty-nine presidents and that forty-seven of the presidents had been employed in positions directly related to audiovisual instruction.[9] The first four presidents represented city school systems, i.e., Berkeley, California, New York City, Pittsburgh, and Detroit. Five state departments of education were represented in the presidency. Three presidents, McClusky, Dale, and Meierhenry, entered the field via research. One early president, Nelson L. Greene (1935-1937), came from the publishing field. Another early president, Grace Fisher Ramsey (1933-1934), was a museum specialist. Greene and Ramsey were the only presidents who did not receive salaries from public education. Beginning with Edgar Dale (1937-1938), most subsequent presidents up to and including 1989, have come from university positions.

Publications

The membership and influence of AECT grew rapidly after World War II. This was particularly reflected in a number of print and nonprint publications. A historical event took place in 1953 with the publication of AECT's first professional journal known as *A V Communication Review*. The title was later changed to *Educational Communication and Technology Journal (ECTJ)* when the label "audiovisual instruction" had become outmoded in theory and practice.[10] To reflect this change, AECT published *Instructional Materials* (Vol. 1, no. 1-4, February-June 1956). However, heated discussions immediately ensued concerning the implications of the title, and within six months, the title was changed to *Audiovisual Instruction*. It had seemed to some that the loss of the term "audiovisual" had indicated a premature redefinition of the field. *Audiovisual Instruction* was later renamed *Instructional Innovator* and subsequently replaced by *TechTrends* in 1985. Still another AECT magazine, the *Journal of Instructional Development* was published in 1977.[11]

Beginning in January 1989, *Educational Communication and Technology Journal* and the *Journal of Instructional Development* were merged under the title *Educational Technology, Research and Development*. Although this merger was prompted to a large extent by financial considerations, it was seen by AECT as an effort to create a unified voice in the field. However, the elimination of "communication" from its title sent a historical signal to the professional community that educational communication was no longer considered to be a generic area of study for the field of educational technology.

Conferences

From the earliest years of its existence, AECT has held national conferences in association with the national NEA conferences. A historical event took place in 1952 when AECT broke with tradition and held its annual convention separate from the NEA in the spring, rather than winter and summer. By 1971, AECT was no longer an official department of the NEA.

In 1980, the AECT board of directors decided to make a major change in the configuration of the national meeting by co-sponsoring, along with the National Audio Visual Association, an international exposition of communication materials and devices. This combination exposition, called COMMTEX International, was designed to attract a larger attendance and to counterbalance a serious decline in AECT membership.[12] In 1989, AECT began the co-sponsorship of this national meeting with the International Communications Industries Association and it became known as INFOCOMM International.

Relationship to Other Professions

Since AECT is the only organized entity of the profession, it has been viewed by both its members and those outside of the organization as representative of the profession of educational technology. But, as we have seen, the philosophical orientation is oriented primarily to its elementary/secondary members, or more specifically, to its membership drawn from state library/media groups. According to Silber, the needed direction of AECT in the area of association and relationship to other professions should be as follows:

(a) AECT must understand and accept the broad concept of the total educational technology profession and recognize that its subprofessions are merely that— subprofessions; (b) AECT must communicate this concept of educational technology to all members of the profession and to all other associations and professions to which it, as the official representative of the profession, relates; (c) AECT must relate equally with all other professions and professions that have some connection with the subprofessions of educational technology; (d) AECT must develop a more balanced program, one designed to serve all subprofessions of educational technology and educational technologists who work in all settings; (e) AECT must take a leadership role in the development of the conceptual and practical configurations needed for the subprofessions of educational technology to work together.[13]

Silber then poses the question of who is to lead the profession to face the problems of the future? He says the past leadership development efforts of AECT have not been adequate to meet leadership needs.[14] Silber sees the immediate years ahead as a time when educational technology "can take either a giant leap forward to a leadership role in the educational community or a giant leap backward to a subservient role."[15]

Contributions to Educational Technology

Despite the current criticisms of AECT, there is no question that the Association has made many significant contributions to the field of educational technology since the earliest days of its founding. Certainly it has remained the oldest and strongest supporter of educational technology through the years and has served a vital function in its development throughout this century. Through its many publications and national conferences, and its efforts in providing a national clearinghouse and a collective voice for educational technology, it has continued to serve as a catalyst for advancing the technology of instruction.

In 1972, AECT made a historical contribution when it published a task force report that named the field "educational technology" and finally solidified the conceptual framework of educational technology with the publication of AECT's official definition statement of the profession, *Educational Technology: Definition and Glossary of Terms*.[16] Moreover, since the early 1970s, AECT has taken an active lead in the accreditation of professional preparation programs in educational technology. In 1976, AECT developed a Code of Ethics that addresses values by its stands for intellectual freedom and affirmative action and against stereotyping in instructional materials.[17]

AECT has sponsored two organizations which are worthy of mention. First, the AECT Archives which is maintained by the University of Iowa in cooperation with AECT, provides the only collection of media, projection and reproduction equipment, photographic devices, manuscripts, and related materials concerned with important historical developments in the field of visual and audiovisual education and/or instructional/educational technology. Secondly, AECT has founded the ECT Foundation, a nonprofit organization whose operation is based on the conviction that the improvement of instruction can be accomplished, in part, by the continued investigation and application of new systems for learning and by the periodic assessment of new technologies of instruction. In addition to awarding scholarships, internships, and fellowships, the foundation develops and conducts leadership training programs for emerging professional leaders.

American Society for Training and Development (ASTD)

ASTD was first established in 1947 for the purpose of providing a forum for professional learning, sharing, and dissemination of information and knowledge regarding media in the training and development process. ASTD is primarily related to the need by business and industry for more well-trained media professionals. This organization has dramatically expanded in recent years because it obviously meets the media professional training objectives of business and industry, health care, the military, software development companies, and private consulting firms. As a consequence, ASTD has become the major U.S. association for training professionals.[18]

Divisions

ASTD divisions consist of the following: Career Development, Organization Development, Technical and Skill Training, Sales Training, International, and Media. The Media Division present their own programs and conduct local workshops in more than 100 chapters throughout the United States. A *Media Resource Directory* contains addresses and names for all Media Division members. Moreover, a Member Information Exchange (MIX) provides an in-house database of members' experience profiles that can be tapped by other members seeking information on specific training topics.

The Media Division has provided many services to the total membership of the society. The dominant services include:

- An annual video tape program containing excerpts from successful training programs

- An ASTD visual resource file (reference slides)

- A media resource bibliography (to be published shortly)

- A media resource directory of membership

- A growing library of resource materials including Ron Anderson's book *Selecting and Developing Media for Instruction*

- A quarterly newsletter, *Media Communicator*

- Participation in the development of a regional and eventually national computer network databank.

Practitioner Publications and Seminars

ASTD publications include the *ASTD Buyer's Guide and Consultant Directory, Info-Line* (a monthly booklet series devoted to a single topic), *ASTD Training Video Directory,* monthly *Training and Development Journal,* and the *Training and Development Handbook.*

A diverse number of seminars are offered each year. TRAINET Seminar Database, a computerized database of 100,000 public seminars are accessible over personal computer or terminal for ASTD members. Audio Cassettes and Videotapes are also available.

Conferences

An ASTD National Conference and Exposition is held annually.

National Society for Performance and Instruction (NSPI)

What was originally called the National Society for Programmed Instruction, was first founded in San Antonio, Texas, in January 1962 by a group of educational researchers working on programmed instruction. The National Office of the Society remained in San Antonio until June 1971, when it was moved to the Catholic University campus in Washington, D.C. Later, under the management of Leanore and Ivan Horabin, it moved to Charles Town in West Virginia. In 1978, it returned to Washington, D.C.

Originally, the National Society for Programmed Instruction was formed to disseminate information on programmed instruction in the *NSPI Journal.*[19] However, over the past years, the Society's goals were expanded to include the instructional field along with most aspects of human performance. Reflecting these broadened concerns, the society changed its name to the National Society for Performance and Instruction in 1974. It has since been committed to a systematic process of analysis, tryout, and data-based revision for identifying, developing, and implementing solutions to human performance problems—and to the continual improvement of all aspects of that basic process. In the 1980s, NSPI enlarged its scope and became an international organization, holding its first international conference in Montreal, Canada, in 1981.

NSPI is composed of 15 geographical chapters throughout the United States and Canada as well as an armed forces chapter. NSPI's annual conference, usually held in the spring, highlights the year's activities. Its membership in recent years has grown from 1,300 to over 2,000 and has included professionals and practitioners from diverse fields.[20]

NSPI's Mission and Goals

The primary mission of NSPI is to enable individuals and organizations to apply systematic approaches to achieve excellence in human performance. Its strategic goals are listed as follows:

1. NSPI will achieve recognition as the leader in the advancement and application of systematic approaches to achieving excellence in human performance.

2. NSPI will expand the application of our systematic approaches by individuals and organizations who affect human performance.

3. NSPI will support its membership in the application of systematic approaches.

4. NSPI will establish collaborative relationships among its members, educational institutions, business, industry, government agencies, medical institutions and other professional societies.

5. NSPI will provide a viable organization to support and accomplish the above goals.[21]

NSPI's Award Program

NSPI's Awards of Excellence Program plays an important part in providing recognition to individuals and to organizations which have excelled at improving human performance. Submissions are solicited in the *Performance and Instruction Journal* and undergo peer evaluation. Those submissions which meet the criteria become finalists and are honored throughout the annual conference and at the Awards Finalists' Reception. Award categories include Outstanding Organization, Instructional Communication, Student Research, Systematic Approach, Non-Instructional Intervention, Instructional Product, *Performance and Instruction* articles, NSPI Member, NSPI Chapter, and Chapter Publication.[22]

Professors of Instructional Design and Technology

On April 20-23, 1985, a historic meeting was held at Indiana University for the purpose of forming an organization known as the Professors of Instructional Design and Technology. The meeting was organized by the University Consortium for Instructional Development and Technology (UCIDT), whose members included Indiana University, Florida State University, Syracuse University, Michigan State University, the University of Southern California, and the University of Georgia.[23] The primary purpose of the first meeting was to explore the current trends and future directions of educational technology as they related to the academic preparation of students. A second purpose was to improve communications among academic programs.

Three leaders in the field made presentations, i.e., Robert Heinich, Robert Gagnè, and Charles Schuller. Following the April 1985 meeting, several working committees were formed. A committee on planning for the future of the society developed two goal statements and identified seven activities in which the society might become involved.[24] The goals were as follows:

1. To encourage and facilitate exchange of information among members of the Instructional Design and Technology community.

2. To promote excellence in the academic programs in Instructional Design and Technology.[25]

The seven activities proposed by the planning committee were as follows:

1. Encourage the use of electronic and other communication networks

2. Collect and disseminate the names and addresses of professors

3. Encourage and sponsor events of conferences

4. Promote sharing of curriculum materials and research

5. Present contemporary issues through publications and forums

6. Encourage inquiry in all forms in the Instructional Design and Technology field

7. Monitor the status of academic programs.[26]

The Public Education Committee suggested the following actions as necessary to the continued involvement of academic institutions with schools:

1. At the national level, professionals should be active on NCATE evaluation teams and ensure its guidelines are being met.

2. Professionals should actively seek opportunities to work with state departments of education on school curriculum development, textbook selection and evaluation.

3. At the regional and state level, academic faculty should be active in the professional organizations since this is where most school people are active.

4. Closer ties should be developed with our colleagues in the colleges of education including joint research, publication and demonstration activities.

5. Greater participation and teacher-in-service activities.[27]

Since its founding in 1985, the Professors of Instructional Design and Technology have met in Shawnee Bluffs, Indiana for their annual conference. Each year, a leader in the field is invited to give a keynote address. At the May 19-21, 1989 conference, for example, this author was invited to give the keynote address in which he called for a revision of the obsolete definition of educational technology and for extended theoretical and research horizons embracing such areas as cognitive science, neuroscience, semiotics, and hermeneutics.

Professional Preparation and Certification of Educational Technology Practitioners

The theoretical and conceptual aspects of educational technology have been an issue for a number of years and this is clearly reflected in the kinds of professional preparation proposed. The basic problem has been to know what the characteristics of a profession are. Finn provided this answer some years ago when he said:

> A profession has, at least, these characteristics: (a) an intellectual technique, (b) an application of that technique to the practical affairs of man, (c) a period of long training necessary before entering into the profession, (d) an association of the members of the profession into a closely knit group with a high quality of communication among members, (e) a series of standards and a statement of ethics which is enforced, and (f) an organized body of intellectual theory constantly expanding by research.[28]

This was later expanded by AECT to include:

1. The ability to exercise its own leadership

2. An association of members of the profession into a closely knit group with a high quality of communication among members

3. Acknowledgement as a profession

4. Professional concern for the responsible use of its work

5. An established relationship with other professions.[29]

Brief Historical Background

Professional preparation and certification in educational technology remained a problematic issue in the 1980s despite its long history as an educational process. The essential problem was that much of contemporary educational technology was viewed from the perspective of the earlier audiovisual instruction movement or from the perspective of a particular media specialty. To complicate this further, some considered the professional preparation in educational technology and the preparation in a library science program as having some of the same competencies.

The earlier impetus for certification came about as a result of a concern with professional certification from audiovisual personnel. The first proposal for certification came at a California audiovisual administration workshop in 1947. This workshop group recommended that an audiovisual director should be required to complete either a supervisory or administrative credential on the elementary or secondary level, plus one course in the administration of audiovisual programs and another in supervision of instruction and curriculum in audiovisual education. Later, in 1951, a more detailed credential program was suggested by the Audio-Visual Instructional Directors of Indiana. The Indiana Teacher Training and Licensing Commission approved these requirements, and in 1952 a special credential was offered by the Indiana State Department of Education. The Indiana credential program was presented to the Committee on Professional Education of the NEA Department of Audiovisual Instruction (DAVI) and was approved at the February 1952 meeting. The following recommendations were made:

1. That DAVI go on record using appropriate state groups to take steps in their individual states to bring about suitable action to establish certification requirements for audiovisual directors.

2. That DAVI assist appropriate state groups by supplying them with a suggested pattern of requirements for certification of audiovisual directors.

3. That DAVI recommend that experience as an audiovisual director prior to the effective date of certification be counted toward professional course requirements in audiovisual education.

4. That DAVI recommend that such state certification requirements become effective within three to five years.[30]

In calling for "a technological leap forward in education," a DAVI task force ten years later realized that:

A new kind of professional will be required to provide leadership in design, implementation, and evaluation of programs in education which make the fullest use of new media. The functions performed by this leader and the resources he brings will be among the essential determinants of success or failure in tomorrow's schools.[31]

Recommendations were made by a number of task forces during the 1960s, but no certification requirements or standards were developed. The 1970s were essentially a recapitulation of the 1960s with respect to certification and accreditation efforts. The Committee on Professional Education of DAVI developed into the Professional Education of Media Specialists (PEMS) Committees of AECT, with subcommittees concerned with such areas as professional programs, media support services, certification, manpower needs, and teacher education. In 1971, the Task Forces on Accreditation and Certification were established. Moreover, the initial document, *Basic Guidelines for Media and Technology in Teacher Education*, was adopted by the AECT in 1971. In 1974, the AECT adopted guidelines for *Advanced Programs in Educational Communications and Technology* which addressed requirements for professional training programs of media and practitioners. These documents were revised in 1977 to conform with the revised standards issued by the National Commission for the Accreditation of Teacher Education (NCATE) in that same year. In recognition of this effort by the AECT, the NCATE granted Associate Membership status to AECT in 1977 and in 1980 admitted AECT to full constituent membership on the Council.

In 1977, AECT created another special task force to study professional certification and develop a set of recommendations. After two years of work, the task force reported in 1979 and recommended (1) that AECT undertake the development of a professional certification program, and (2) that the three largest AECT divisions, Instructional Development, Media Management, and Media Design and Production be responsible for delineating the competencies in each area and specifying the assessment procedures. The task force also called for the creation of a Certification Institute Board to oversee the certification program once it was developed. The board would consist of persons representing practitioners, employers, academic programs, and the three AECT divisions. However, despite the continual interest that had been manifested in the formation of task forces over a period of years, the issuance of many publications, and the frequent discussions of certification at the annual conventions, the 1970s had still not produced a decisive document concerning what competencies should be required or what should constitute the training program for an educational technologist.[32]

Certification and Accreditation: The 1980s

AECT appointed another task force in 1980 to develop a set of core competencies for instructional development professions which could be used as standards for certification of those professions. The task force spent three years revising these sets of competencies. Throughout their years of work, the task force members followed these guidelines:

1. The competencies would reflect the skill of a professional instructional/training designer, regardless of her/his current job, position, academic degree or type of training.

2. The competencies would be performance-oriented rather than academic-oriented.

3. While some employment situations may prevent a designer from exercising every competency, all professionally competent designers should be able to perform most, if not all, of the competencies when given the opportunity to do so.

4. The competencies reflect the skills of experienced, professional designers—as opposed to students, trainers, or entry-level designers.[33]

Figure 18.1 contains the list of AECT instructions-training design competencies.

Fig. 18.1. AECT Instructional/Training Development Competencies.

A competent instructional/training development specialist is able to:

1. Determine Projects Appropriate for Instructional Development

    Analyze information regarding potential projects and decide if instruction development is appropriate.

    Discriminate situations requiring instructional solutions from those requiring other solutions (e.g., job redesign, organizational development, etc.).

    Judge the appropriateness of project selection decisions and provide a rationale for the judgment.

2. Conduct Needs Assessments

    Develop a needs assessment plan including selection of procedures and instruments.

    Conduct a needs assessment and interpret results to suggest appropriate actions.

    Judge the appropriateness, completeness, and accuracy of given needs assessment plans and results.

3. Assess Learner/Trainee Characteristics

    Distinguish among entry skills assessment, prerequisite assessment, and aptitude assessment.

    Identify a range of relevant learner/trainee characteristics and determine methods for assessing them.

    Develop and implement a plan for assessing learner/trainee characteristics.

    Judge the appropriateness, comprehensiveness, and adequacy of a given assessment of learner/trainee characteristics.

4. Analyze the Structural Characteristics of Jobs, Tasks, and Content

    Select and use a procedure for analyzing the structural characteristics of a job, task, or content which is appropriate to that job, task, or content and state a rationale for the selection.

5. Write Statements of Learner Outcomes

    Distinguish objectives stated in performance/behavioral terms from instructional goals, organizational goals, learner activities, teacher activities, and objectives written in other styles.

From *Journal of Instructional Development*, Vol. 5, no. 1, AECT Task Force on ID Certification, pp. 14-15, by permission of the Association for Educational Communications and Technology, 1981.

State an outcome in performance terms which reflects the intent of instruction.

Judge the accuracy, comprehensiveness, and appropriateness of statements of learner outcomes in terms of the job, task, or content analysis, and/or judgment/opinion of the client (e.g., subject matter expert, faculty, etc.).

6. Analyze the Characteristics of a Setting (Learning Environment)

   Analyze setting characteristics and determine relevant resources and constraints.

   Judge the accuracy, comprehensiveness, and appropriateness of a setting analysis.

7. Sequence Learner Outcomes

   Select a procedure for sequencing learning outcomes appropriate to a given situation, sequence the outcomes and state a rationale for the sequence.

   Judge the accuracy, completeness, and appropriateness of a given sequence of learner outcome.

8. Specify Instructional Strategies

   Select a strategy which is appropriate to information about the learner characteristics, resources, and constraints, desired learner outcomes, and other pertinent information and state a rationale for the selection.

   Judge the accuracy, completeness, and appropriateness of a given sequence of learner outcomes.

9. Sequence Learner Activities

   Specify a sequence of learner activities appropriate to the achievement of specified learner outcomes and state a rationale for the sequence.

10. Determine Instructional Resources (Media) Appropriate to Instructional Activities

    Develop specifications for instructional resources required for explicit instructional strategies and learner outcomes.

    Evaluate existing instructional resources to determine appropriateness for specified instructional strategies and learner outcomes.

    Adapt existing instructional resources.

    Prepare specifications for the production of materials where required (e.g., storyboards, lesson plans, script outlines, etc.).

(Fig. 18.1 continues on page 514.)

Fig. 18.1—*Continued*

11.   Evaluate Instruction/Training

Plan and conduct a formative evaluation (e.g., trials with subjects, expert review, analysis of implementation consideration, etc.).

Develop a range of information-gathering techniques (e.g., questionnaires, interviews, tests, simulations, observations, etc.).

Generate specifications for revision based on evaluation feedback.

Judge the appropriateness, comprehensiveness, and adequacy of given formative evaluation plans, information-gathering techniques, and revision specifications.

12.   Create Course, Training Package, and Workshop Management Systems

Determine the components of a course/training package/workshop management system and state a rationale for the selection.

Judge the appropriateness, comprehensiveness, and adequacy of a given management system.

13.   Plan and Monitor Instructional Development Projects

Develop and monitor an instructional development project plan (including timelines, budgets, staffing, etc.) which is appropriate to the nature of the project and the setting.

14.   Communicate Effectively in Visual, Oral, and Written Form

15.   Demonstrate Appropriate Interpersonal, Group Process, and Consulting Behaviors

Demonstrate interpersonal behaviors with individuals and groups and state a rationale for using the behaviors in given situations.

Demonstrate group process behaviors and state a rationale for using the behaviors in given situations.

Demonstrate consulting behaviors with individuals and groups and state a rationale for the behaviors in given situations.

Judge the appropriateness of interpersonal, group process, and consulting behaviors in given situations.

16.   Promote the Diffusion and Adoption of the Instructional Development Process

Select strategies appropriate for promoting the diffusion and adoption of the instructional development process in a given setting and state a rationale for the strategies.[34]

A second study of competencies was conducted in 1983 by the American Society for Training and Development (ASTD) and was titled *Models for Excellence*. ASTD identified thirty-one training and development competencies. For each competency, behavioral examples were shown at three different levels of expertise: basic, intermediate, and advanced. Since it could not be expected that all individuals possessed all of these skills, fifteen key training and development roles were identified. For each role, the report identified the critical competencies as well as the products that represented competence, their relationships to other competencies, and predictions about future needs. Figure 18.2 contains the list of ASTD competencies.

Fig. 18.2. ASTD training and development competencies.

1. Adult Learning Understanding. Knowing how adults acquire and use knowledge, skills, attitudes. Understanding individual differences in learning.

2. A/V Skill. Selecting and using audio/visual hardware and software.

3. Career Development Knowledge. Understanding the personal and organizational issues and practices relevant to individual careers.

4. Competency Identification Skill. Identifying the knowledge and skill requirements of jobs, tasks, roles.

5. Computer Competence. Understanding and being able to use computers.

6. Cost-Benefit Analysis Skill. Assessing alternatives in terms of their financial, psychological, and strategic advantages and disadvantages.

7. Counseling Skill. Helping individuals recognize and understand personal needs, values, problems, alternatives and goals.

8. Data Reduction Skill. Scanning, synthesizing, and drawing conclusions from data.

9. Delegation Skill. Assigning task responsibility and authority to others.

10. Facilities Skill. Planning and coordinating logistics in an efficient and cost-effective manner.

11. Feedback Skill. Communicating opinions, observations and conclusions such that they are understood.

12. Futuring Skill. Projecting trends and visualizing possible and probable futures and their implications.

13. Group Process Skill. Influencing groups to both accomplish tasks and fulfill the needs of their members.

From *Models for Excellence* by permission of the American Society for Training and Development, Washington, D.C., 1983.

(Fig. 18.2 continues on page 516.)

Fig. 18.2—*Continued*

14. Industry Understanding. Knowing the key concepts and variables that define an industry or sector (e.g., critical issues, economic vulnerabilities, measurements, distribution channels, inputs, outputs, information sources).

15. Intellectual Versatility. Recognizing, exploring and using a broad range of ideas and practices. Thinking logically and creatively without undue influence from personal biases.

16. Library Skills. Gathering information from printed and other recorded sources. Identifying and using information specialists and reference services and aids.

17. Model Building Skill. Developing theoretical and practical frameworks which describe complex ideas in understandable, usable ways.

18. Negotiation Skill. Securing win-win agreements while successfully representing a special interest in a decision situation.

19. Objectives Preparation Skill. Preparing clear statements which describe desired outputs.

20. Organization Behavior Understanding. Seeing organizations as dynamic, political, economic, and social systems which have multiple goals; using this larger perspective as a framework for understanding and influencing events and change.

21. Organization Understanding. Knowing the strategy, structure, power networks, financial position, systems of a SPECIFIC organization.

22. Performance Observation Skills. Tracking and describing behaviors and their effects.

23. Personnel/HR Field Understanding. Understanding issues and practices in other HR areas (Organization Development, Organization Job Design, Human Resource Planning, Selection and Staffing, Personnel Research and Information Systems, Compensation and Benefits, Employee Assistance, Union/Labor Relations).

24. Presentation Skills. Verbally presenting information such that the intended purpose is achieved.

25. Questioning Skill. Gathering information from and stimulating insight in individuals and groups through the use of interviews, questionnaires and other probing methods.

26. Records Management Skill. Storing data in easily retrievable form.

27. Relationship Versatility. Adjusting behavior in order to establish relationships across a broad range of people and groups.

28. Research Skills. Selecting, developing and using methodologies, statistical and data collection techniques for a formal inquiry.

29. Training and Development Field Understanding. Knowing the technological, social, economic, professional, and regulatory issues in the field; understanding the role T&D plays in helping individuals learn for current and future jobs.

30. Training and Development Techniques Understanding. Knowing the techniques and methods used in training; understanding their appropriate uses.

31. Writing Skills. Preparing written material which follows generally accepted rules of style and form, is appropriate for the audience, creative, and accomplishes its intended purposes.[35]

On September 1, 1984, the accreditation guidelines for programs in educational technology became effective. With the adoption of AECT guidelines, NCATE adopted a process which was called "Program Folio Review." In preparation for an NCATE review, an institution develops an Institutional Report (IR) based on its self study. This IR folio presents a description or folio of all programs and degrees to be considered and reviewed by the NCATE visitation team. The folios are then sent to AECT for review and evaluation. After AECT reviews the program folio, a summary is sent back to NCATE. NCATE places this report in the hands of the evaluation team before the team visits the campus to conduct its on-site review. In effect, this process provides AECT with folios of all programs in the field and enables it to write a review of each program before returning it to the NCATE. In addition, NCATE added a category entitled "Educational Communications and Information Technologies" to its Annual List. The Annual List, published each year by NCATE, identifies accredited programs in teacher education in American colleges and universities. Also, AECT and NCATE have jointly conducted annual training workshops for individuals interested in serving on NCATE evaluation teams. Silber has criticized the intrusion of NCATE state departments of education or other agencies into the certification process involved in the field of educational technology. He says that "professional educational technologists have little input into the criteria for certification and accreditation used in these agencies" and, "as a result those criteria often have little to do with skills educational technologists actually use."[36] However, the major arguments against the establishment of an AECT accreditation program have been economic and political in nature. The cost alone is considerable and many institutions are not willing to bear the burden of such costs when they are already supporting the expense of a regional, NCATE, and state accreditation for identical programs. Moreover, federal regulations discourage the recognition of more than one accreditation organization within a program specialization unless each of the concerned organizations demonstrates a need for its services.

Training Programs for Instructional Developers

Silber has summarized the state of instructional development training and proposed a direction for the field. He states:

It does not understand the process of training instructional developers like it understands the processes of doing it. More importantly, it does not know that it is not training as well as it should be, and certainly has no idea what is needed to improve itself ... the field of ID must undertake systematic data-based analyses of (a) what makes a "good" instructional developer, (b) what skills and competencies do they need to possess to be "good" and (c) what kind of training/educational program can best help people gain these skills and competencies they need to be good.[37]

In a study by Partridge and Tennyson, faculty members from major institutions that offered both master's and doctoral degree programs in educational technology were asked to rank instructional development and related competencies in terms of emphasis they received at respective institutions.[38] The results from six of these programs are shown in Figure 18.3.

Fig. 18.3. Ranking of student competencies in an ideal program.

Institution	Masters	Doctorate
Brigham Young University	1 — Development of a curriculum.	1 — Development of a unit (course or program of instruction.
	2 — Experimental design.	2 — Development of a curriculum.
	3 — Theories of instruction.	3 — Product evaluation.
	4 — Theories of learning.	4 — Course evaluation.
	5 — The management of programs and personnel.	5 — Evaluation of media materials.
	6 — The administration of programs and personnel.	6 — Program evaluation.
	7 — The use of media equipment: video.	7 — Design of media hardware/facilities.
	8 — The use of media equipment: visual (photographic, graphics).	8 — Data analysis.
	9 — Course evaluation.	9 — Theories of instruction.
	10 — Program evaluation.	10 — Experimental design.
Florida State University	1 — Development of a unit (course or program) of instruction.	1 — (Other) Needs assessment /analysis.
	2 — Development of a curriculum.	2 — (Other) Design of instructional systems.

From M. J. Partridge and R. D. Tennyson, "Graduate Education in Instructional Systems: A Review of Selected Programs," *Journal of Instructional Development*, Winter, 1978-79, Vol. 2, No. 2, pp. 18-25.

Florida State University— *Continued*	3—Test and measurement techniques.	3—Development of a unit (course or program) of instruction.
	4—Theories of learning.	4—Theories of learning.
	5—Theories of instruction.	5—Theories of instruction.
	6—Product evaluation.	6—Development of a curriculum.
	7—Program evaluation.	7—Product evaluation.
	8—Course evaluation.	8—Evaluation of media materials.
	9—Evaluation of media materials.	9—Theories of instruction.
	10—Use of computers.	10—Course evaluation.
Indiana University	1—Development of a curriculum.	1—Development of a curriculum.
	2—Development of a unit (course or program) of instruction.	2—Development of a unit (course or program) of instruction.
	3—The use of media equipment: visual.	3—The use of media equipment: visual.
	4—Evaluation of media materials.	4—Production of media materials: visual.
	5—Production of media materials: visual.	5—Theories of instruction.
	6—The management of media resources.	6—Evaluation of media materials.
	7—The management of programs and personnel.	7—The management of media resources.
	8—The administration of programs and personnel.	8—The management of programs and personnel.
	9—Design of media hardware/facilities.	9—Product evaluation.
	10—Product evaluation.	10—The administration of programs and personnel.

(Fig. 18.3 continues on page 520.)

Fig. 18.3—*Continued*

Institution	Masters	Doctorate
Syracuse University	1—Experimental design.	1—Experimental design.
	2—Theories of learning.	2—Theories of learning.
	3—Test and measurement techniques.	3—Test and measurement techniques.
	4—Data analysis.	4—Data analysis.
	5—Theories of instruction.	5—Theories of instruction.
	6—Program evaluation.	6—Program evaluation.
	7—The management of programs and personnel.	7—Course evaluation.
	8—Development of a curriculum.	8—Product evaluation.
	9—Course evaluation.	9—All others.
	10—Production of media materials.	
University of Iowa	1—Development of a unit (course or program) of instruction.	1—Development of a curriculum.
	2—Evaluation of media materials.	2—Theories of instruction.
	3—Management of media resources.	3—Program evaluation.
	4—Product evaluation.	4—Experimental design.
	5—Production of media materials: visual.	5—Course evaluation.
	6—Production of media materials: video.	6—Administration of programs and personnel.
	7—Production of media materials: audio.	7—Development of a unit (course or program) of instruction.
	8—Theories of instruction.	8—Evaluation of media materials.
	9—Test and measurement techniques.	9—Data analysis.

	10 — The management of programs and personnel.	10 — Theories of learning.
University of Minnesota	1 — Development of a unit (course or program) of instruction.	1 — Theories of instruction.
	2 — Theories of instruction.	2 — Theories of learning.
	3 — Product evaluation.	3 — Data analysis.
	4 — Program evaluation.	4 — Experimental design.
	5 — Development of a curriculum.	5 — Test and measurement techniques.
	6 — Theories of learning.	6 — Product evaluation.
	7 — Course evaluation.	7 — Program evaluation.
	8 — Evaluation of media materials.	8 — Course evaluation.
	9 — Test and measurement techniques.	9 — Development of a unit (course or program) of instruction.
	10 — Management of media resources.	10 — Development of a curriculum.

The best illustration of how specific instructional development and their relative emphases are blended into an ID curriculum is that of Syracuse University. The process developed at Syracuse is particularly unique because it provides practicing instructional developers the opportunity to apply the "ID approach" to the redesign of the training curriculum and course design. The curriculum of the Syracuse IDDE Program is shown in outline form in figure 18.3.

The Media Laboratory: An Innovative Research and Training Program

An innovative doctoral studies program in media technology began at the Massachusetts Institute of Technology (MIT) in September 1986. The program began with three initial areas of concentration: Electronic and Communications Media, Epistemology and Learning, and Music and Music Cognition. Electronic and Communications Media focused on the theory and applications of human and computer interaction and students were expected to have either a strong technical and scientific background or extensive knowledge of the social and human sciences. Epistemology and Learning concentrated on the redefinition of education, work and play and how children learn. Students were required to do field and laboratory work and were expected to become a new kind of educator, with a tradition of computers and electronic communications, and with attitudes primed for innovation. The third area of concentration, Music and Music Cognition, emphasized the connection between art and science or the relationship between structures of music and mathematics. In this program, three kinds of students were encouraged to apply: those wishing to innovate in music and musicology, those wishing to study new musical tools and instruments, and those wishing to use the musical world as the object of their epistemological pursuits.

In order to implement this program, a Media Laboratory was established in September 1985 to provide a research setting for the study of modern communications and the human sciences. Financially supported by more than 100 business and government sponsors, the new $45 million facility with a group of 120 gifted researchers was housed in a new I. M. Pei structure on MIT's East Campus. The faculty included Marvin Minsky, dean of artificial intelligence research; Seymour Papert, the developer of the LOGO system; and Alan Kay, one of the prominent designers of personal computers. As Nicholas Negroponte, the founder and director of the Media Laboratory at MIT states, the Media Lab was set up to collect and process all communications media and technologies that are posed for redefinition and the Media Lab is designed to lead the way to the future.

Many visionary projects are underway, but several have already resulted in working products and prototypes. The laboratory's unique mission is to transform today's passive media, particularly television, into flexible technologies that can respond to individual needs and interests. One of the most ambitious Media Laboratory projects is what is known as Vivarium and designed for grade-school children. The founder of the project, Alan Kay, is attempting to develop an artificial intelligence learning environment which needs new kinds of animation and robotics, new kinds of interface with the user, and an entire new computer architecture. In essence, researchers at the Media Laboratory, like all who are involved in artificial intelligence, are working for parallel processing rather than "serial" in the future (see Stewart Brand, 1987).[39]

The training program associated with the Media Laboratory suggests new training approaches in educational technology. In the process of being involved in real teaching-learning situations in an experimental setting, the potential educational technologists would also be directly involved in the planning of and development of learning environments and teaching materials. A major task would involve the preparation of design specifications for educational products (materials, equipment, learning packages, systems, etc.). But more important, the future educational technologist would be given the opportunity and the learning experience of interacting with the diversity of disciplines found in a college or university community. For example, the biochemist could contribute to the understanding of drugs and brain extract to enhance learning; the neurologist to the functioning of internal neural systems (neural communications); the architectural psychologist to the relationship of space and form to effective learning environments; the human factors engineer to the study of living systems in transactions with their environments; the communications specialist to the use of media and message forms; the social psychologist to the construction of models of small groups and interpersonal behavior; the computer specialist to methods for developing sophisticated interactions-computerized educational approaches; and cognitive psychologists to an understanding of cognition and problem solving. In this sort of learning environment, educational technology students could pursue their interests while becoming involved in ongoing research projects. It appears obvious that if an educational program such as proposed here were developed, there would need to be radical transformation in the kinds of programs which now exist. Perhaps the Media Laboratory of MIT is pointing the way to a beginning in developmental programs for educational technologists.

State of the Art of Instructional Development

Bass and Dills have provided an excellent state of the art summary statement for instructional development for the mid-1980s. They stated that:

We see a field in which practitioners are working very hard to describe themselves and to delineate their activities.

We see a field which has moved from a predominantly higher education orientation to a more universal orientation ... public school.

We see a field which for the most part is taking a careful look at the evaluation of the product/processes it produces in the traditional sense and is even posing other ways of viewing/evaluating its products/processes.

We see a field which is deligently trying to find its place in space and is searching for a delineation of its basic scientific underpinnings as well as for the theories which can form the basis for the design which instructional developers undertake.

We see a field which is interested in interacting with ID clients as effectively as possible, interacting with support personnel as effectively as possible and interacting with understanding subgroups within the field.

We see a field which is interested to some degree in dealing with the cost-effectiveness of ID, but a field which has not devoted as much attention to this concern as would be justified by the austerity of the times or by the accountability demands which are sure to be made of it.

We see a field that lacks a unified underlying literature.

We see a field in which the Division of Instructional Development (DID) of the AECT was once clearly the leading organization but is rapidly losing influence as other organizations turn their attention to ID (i.e., the NSPI and ASTD). We see less emphasis upon the utilization of ideas in higher education in the broad sense while we are seeing more emphasis on the use of ideas in the health sciences areas of higher education and in business and industry.

We see a field which will undoubtedly take a closer look at the individual differences among the trainees for which the instruction is being designed.

We see a field which wishes to become a profession. This means among other things, a field whose practitioners regulate their own behavior according to agreed-upon ethical standards. It also means that those practitioners understand their own professional behavior patterns, since such an understanding must underlie any rational attempt to formulate such an ethical system. We see a field, however, which has devoted little time or thought to the systematic investigation of its own behavior, with the single exception of investigations of consulting behavior.

We see a field which is in need, therefore, of an investigation of many other aspects of its own behavior, and of that of its members.

We see a profession which exists for no other reason than to produce symbol systems and concrete embodiment of these systems, and to distribute them. We see a profession which is in need of an understanding of how its members interact in the production of these symbols and their embodiments. This understanding requires both a sociological analysis of how ideas interact as a culture, and an analysis of our symbol systems in terms of symbology, an aspect both of linguistics and of anthropology.

We see a field which rejects much. Although there are notable exceptions, ideas have mostly rejected, or ignored, techniques derived from behavior modification, the experimental analysis of behavior, and programmed instruction.

We see a field which will become even more sophisticated in knowledge of neurological science and will begin to use in a meaningful way research on the brain. We see a field which will be confronted with new concerns for individuals, which will affect the design of instruction. An example of these concerns would be "stress."

And, at the same time, we see a field which is attempting to better understand the most basic of our tools for distribution of instruction ... the textbook.[40]

Current Status of Curricula in Educational Communications and Technology

A recent international survey of the masters curricula in educational communications and technology provides an excellent picture of its current status.[41] This survey revealed that educational communications and technology is being recognized by higher education as a field within education and the names of degrees in this field are not only in education, but include specific aspects of educational communications and technology such as *computer-based education* or *instructional systems design*. No common core curricula was required. The use of the term *media* occurred only 10 times in this survey while such terms as *educational* or *instructional technology* or *computers in education* were used more often.

Among a total of 170 programs included in this survey, the number of faculty involved represented a mean of 4.0 fulltime and 2.3 parttime positions for each institution. Current research topics covered a wide range of subjects but tended to focus on topics involving computers and/or interactive video. However, it was noted in the survey that these topics decreased by some 6 percent since 1985.

Since 1985, 44 programs had been discontinued, 13 in the states of New York and Illinois. Nevertheless, the total number of masters programs in the United States has steadily grown.

The administrative responsibility has tended to shift with many of the programs, for example, 50 programs have changed their department affiliations since 1985; 21 have changed twice in an eight-year period. A program that was under the Education Department in 1981 was in the Educational Media and Interdisciplinary Studies Department in 1985 and is currently in the Department of Computer Education and Cognitive Systems. Another example is a program that was in the Department of Media Arts in 1981, moved to the Communication Arts Department by 1985, and by 1989 was in the Department of Training and Learning Technology.

The Johnson survey disclosed that more programs are now identified with an instructional (educational) technology department than any other. Other disciplines responsible for educational technology programs include library and information science, journalism and mass media, and biomedical communications.

Trends and Issues in Graduate Program Development in Educational Technology

A recent National Research Council report indicated that there are almost as many doctorates in education as in either biological sciences or engineering. Simultaneously, there has been a substantial decline in the employment of graduates in educational technology in the public schools and an impressive increase in industry and military placements. Moreover, industry is more interested in retraining their employees rather than in hiring new employees.[42]

Knirk pointed out at the 1989 Professors of Instructional Design and Technology conference that there are many important issues facing educational technology today. For example, AECT has substantially decreased in size and influence in the last fifteen years. ASTD, NSPI, and other organizations have increased their meaning to graduate students because instructional development as a process is perceived as having no practical relevance to public teaching and educational practice. In fact, as Knirk observed, "the vast majority of schools do not have enough computers to make them a central element in instruction" and that they "may never find acceptance in the schools any more than instructional television or other media."[43] The content of instructional development courses has given way to computers and instructional systems. However, the software market is fading away rapidly because the enforcement of intellectual property rights is driving publishers and developers away from the school doors. Moreover, only about one-third of all K-12 teachers have had even 10 hours of computer training. Knirk stated that almost two-thirds of the states are financially unable to provide for additional training and support of educational computing.

At this same 1989 conference, Knirk asked these questions:

1. Does the increasing percentage of "limited English" speaking students adversely affect the quality of our graduate instructional development programs?

2. Should we attempt to assist our students in defraying their graduate costs? How?

3. What professional organizations should we support?

4. What should be the content of instructional development courses?

New questions and issues will continue to arise in years to come about graduate program development as the apparatus, philosophy, and direction of educational technology grows and changes.

The deep concern of the professions in the field of educational technology is dramatically reflected in the entire first issue of the new journal, *Educational Technology Research and Development*.[44] Reigeluth, for example, views educational technology as being at the crossroads and believes that some important new directions need to be taken. He would include among these directions the development of the following kinds of strategy prescriptions:

1. prescriptions for types of learning which have been largely ignored by the field, such as understanding and generic skills.

2. prescriptions which take advantage of the unique capabilities of new technologies, such as simulations and intelligent tutors.

3. prescriptions for midlevel strategies.

4. prescriptions for most macro organizational methods, especially structuring and sequencing a course or curriculum and synthesizing ideas.

5. prescriptions for selecting mediational systems.

6. prescriptions for designing instructional-management systems.

7. prescriptions for motivating learners.

8. prescriptions for complete, restructured educational systems.[45]

Clark reiterates Reigeluth's view when he says that researchers in educational technology need to "direct efforts to the achievement of a prescriptive technology" and to "conduct more front-end analysis that produces a distinction between instructional design research and instructional development research."[46]

Heinich has even proposed that educational technology be considered a subset of technology rather than of education. His argument is based on the assumption that education as a professional field will not or cannot produce a viable environment for the development of an educational technology that may provide an effective alternative to the prevailing and failing model of public education.[47] Winn concludes that "we need to upgrade the status of instructional design from a technique to a true profession, maybe even an art." Moreover, Winn agrees with Heinich when he says that "educational technology can only thrive and prosper outside of the traditional institutions of public education."[48]

It was clear by the late 1980s that the AECT Task Force on Definition and Terminology (1977) was no longer viable in the changing currents of professional educational technology. The impact of cognitive science and the emergence of new specialties make the AECT (1977) definition of educational technology obsolete. A new conception of educational technology demands expanded theoretical, research, and development vistas if it is to match the needs of the next century.

New Professional Currents in Educational Technology

There have been dramatic changes within the field of educational technology during the 1980s. Major changes which have affected educational technology have occurred in business and industry. Training has become a primary focus and the concepts of educational technology are becoming more widely used by business, industry, the military, the health professions, and software development companies. Meanwhile, the impact of the computer and other new information technologies is being felt at all levels of education. It is still not clear what the long range effects will be on the traditional roles of library/media specialists or on the future role of the educational technologist. For example, those individuals who work in such traditional educational settings as media specialists who possess only media production or management skills may be at risk. Likewise, those individuals who are in traditional academic roles may find it difficult to cope with the new demands made by new CAI/interactive technologies and the necessity of creating new kinds of instructional software.

AECT has been adversely affected by these developments because it has not changed its focus rapidly enough. For example, in the 1970s, most of the educational technology publications dealt with such subjects as media management/production, instructional development, and performance technology. In contrast, most of the subjects today deal with CAI and interactive video, performance technology, and evaluation.

Notes

[1]Michael Molenda and Marjorie Cambre, "The 1976 Member Opinion Survey: Opinions on Issues Facing AECT," *Audiovisual Instruction* 22 (April 1977), 46-49.

[2]See Joseph A. Hutchinson and Pauline M. Rankin, "Employment Profiles and Compensation for Educational Technologists, 1983-1986," in Elwood E. Miller and Mary Louise Mosley, eds., *Educational Media and Technology Yearbook*, vol. 13. Littleton, Colo.: Libraries Unlimited, 1987, 100-12.

[3]Kenneth H. Silber, "Problems and Needed Directions in the Profession of Educational Technology," *ECTJ* 26 (Summer 1978), 182.

[4]Ibid., 183.

[5]Ibid.

[6]Barry Bratton and Kenneth H. Silber, "Changing Professional Prospects in Educational Technology," in James W. Brown, ed., *Trends in Instructional Technology*. Syracuse, N.Y.: ERIC Clearinghouse on Information Resources, 1984, 44.

[7]Stanley D. Zenor, "AECT, The Association for the Media Profession," in Elwood Miller and Mary Louise Mosley, eds., *Educational Media and Technology Yearbook*, vol. 13. Littleton, Colo.: Libraries Unlimited, 1987, 123-24.

[8]The organizations affiliated with AECT include the Association for Media Educators in Religion; the Association for Multi-Image International; the Association for Special Educations Technology; the Community College Association for Instruction and Technology; the Consortium of University Film Centers; the Federal Educational Technology Association; the Health Educational Media Association; the International Visual Literacy Association; Minorities in Media; the National Association of Regional Media Centers; the New England Educational Media Association; the State University of New York Educational Communications Centers; the Southeastern Regional Media Leadership Council; and Women in Instructional Technology.

[9]F. Dean McClusky, "DVI, DAVI, AECT: A Long View," in James W. Brown and Shirley N. Brown, eds., *Educational Media Yearbook*. Littleton, Colo.: Libraries Unlimited, 1981, 9-17. A complete roster of AECT presidents from 1923 to 1981 can be found in this reference.

[10]To date, the *Educational Communication and Technology* journal has had five editors. William H. Allen was the first editor for seventeen years. Robert Heinich served as the second editor for the next thirteen years. William Winn was the third editor who served from 1983 to the end of 1988. Beginning in 1989, the journal title was changed to *Educational Technology Research and Development* (*ETR&D*), and Howard Sullivan and Norman Higgins were chosen as co-editors. Sullivan became editor of the research section and Higgins edited the development section. A declining trend in circulation in recent years produced some financial restrictions which seriously affected consistent monthly publication. On one occasion, the printer refused to print the journal because previous bills had not been paid. The current financial situation has improved considerably and publication dates are now on schedule. The new journal was created as the result of a merger of *ECTJ* and *JID*, *ETR&D*'s progenitors. There were a number of reasons for this merger. Some were fiscal, others political, and some theoretical. For example, it was realized that it did not make any sense to keep AECT's "theory" and "application" publications separate.

[11]Due to financial hardship, the management and publication of the *Journal of Instructional Development* was assumed by the Learning Systems Institute of Florida State University in 1981. This journal was combined with *ECTJ* in 1989.

[12]In the early days of 1932, the membership of what was then called the Department of Visual Instruction (DVI) was only about 50. Ten years later, it had grown to 500. By 1945, following the establishment of a paid secretarial staff at the NEA headquarters in Washington, D.C., it had reached 3,000. In the middle 1970s, the AECT membership had reached 10,000. However, by the middle 1980s, it had fallen to 6,000. Changes in society and education have produced dramatic changes in membership as the result of job roles and job settings in educational technology.

[13]Silber, "Problems and Needed Directions," 183.

[14]Ibid., 194.

[15]Ibid., 184.

[16]See AECT, *Educational Technology: Definition and Glossary of Terms*, vol. 1. Washington, D.C.: AECT, 1977.

[17]See AECT, *AECT Code of Ethics*. Washington, D.C.: AECT, 1976.

[18]The ASTD has increased from 9,000 to 28,000 in recent years. No other organization in the field has increased to this extent.

[19]The name of the *NSPI Journal* was changed to *Performance and Instruction* in 1981. John Olsen was the first editor. The current editor is Sivasailam Thiagarajan.

[20]The source of much of the material in this section is *Performance and Instruction* 26 (March 1987), 28.

[21]Ibid., 14.

[22]Ibid., 31.

[23]The University Consortium for Instructional Development and Technology began in 1964 when James D. Finn, Donald Ely, and Charles Schuller created a university consortium in conjunction with the Special Media Institutes program that had been established under the old NDEA Title VII(b) to provide special training institutes in media for classroom teachers in various subject areas. The original members of the consortium were Michigan State University, Syracuse University, and the University of Southern California.

[24]The planning committee consisted of the following: John Wedman, University of Missouri-Columbia; Ann Becket, University of Wisconsin; Barbara Seels, University of Pittsburgh; and Barry Bratton, University of Iowa.

[25]Kent L. Gustafson, "Formation of a Society for Professors of Instructional Technology," in Elwood E. Miller and Mary Louise Mosley, eds., *Educational Media and Technology Yearbook*, vol. 12. Littleton, Colo.: Libraries Unlimited, 1986, 64.

[26]Ibid.

[27]Ibid., 65.

[28]James D. Finn, "Professionalizing the Audiovisual Field," *AV Communication Review* 1 (Winter 1955), 6-17.

[29]AECT, *Educational Technology: Definition and Glossary of Terms*, vol. 1. Washington, D.C., 1977, 15-16.

[30]*Boston Conference Proceedings*, NEA, DAVI, Washington, D.C., 1952, 15-16.

[31]Barry Morris, ed., "The Functions of Media in the Public Schools," *Audiovisual Instruction* 8 (January 1963), 11.

[32]The various early attempts to establish training standards are documented in the following sources: *Audiovisual Instruction* (November 1974), entire issue; *Basic Guidelines for Media and Technology in Teacher Education*, Washington, D.C.: AECT, 1971; Minaruth Galey and William F. Grady, *Certification: Guidelines for Certification of Media Specialists*, Washington, D.C.: AECT, 1977.

[33]Barry Bratton, "The Potential for Professional Certification in the Field of Instructional/Training Design," in Ronald K. Bass and Charles R. Dills, eds., *Instructional Development: The State of the Art* 2. Dubuque, Iowa: Kendall/Hunt Publishing, 1984, 566-67.

[34]AECT Task Force on ID Certification, "Competencies for the Instructional/Training Development Professional," *Journal of Professional Development* 5 (1981), 14-15.

[35]American Society for Training and Development, *Models of Excellence.* Washington, D.C.: ASTD, 1983.

[36]Silber, "Problems and Needed Directions," 178.

[37]Kenneth H. Silber, "Training Instructional Developers: A Review of Current Practice and Directors for the Future," in Ronald K. Bass and Charles R. Dills, eds., *Instructional Development: The State of the Art* 2. Dubuque, Iowa: Kendall/Hunt Publishing, 1984, 513.

[38]M. J. Partridge and R. D. Tennyson, "Graduate Education in Instructional Systems: A Review of Selected Programs," *Journal of Instructional Development* 2 (Winter 1978-79), 18-25.

[39]Stewart Brand, *The Media Lab.* New York: Viking, 1987.

[40]Bass and Dills, *Instructional Development,* 594-95.

[41]Johnson, Jenny K., ed., *Masters Curricula in Educational Communications and Technology: A Descriptive Directory.* Washington, D.C.: AECT, 1989.

[42]National Research Council, *Summary Report 1987: Doctorate Recipients from United States Universities.* Washington, D.C.: GPO, 1989.

[43]Fred Knirk, "Reactive or Proactive Graduate Program Development: Trends Affecting Instructional Development Programs in 2001." Address to the annual conference of Professors of Instructional Design and Technology, Shawnee Bluffs, Indiana, May 19-21, 1989.

[44]See *Educational Technology Research and Development (ETR&D)* 37 (1989).

[45]Charles M. Reigeluth, "Educational Technology at the Crossroad: New Mindsets and New Directions," *ETR&D* 37 (1989), 79.

[46]Richard E. Clark, "Current Progress and Future Directions for Research in Instructional Technology," *ETR&D* 37 (1989), 60-61.

[47]Robert Heinich, "The Proper Study of Educational Technology," *Educational Communication and Technology Journal* 32 (1984), 67-87.

[48]William Winn, "Toward a Rationale and Theoretical Basis for Educational Technology," *ETR&D* 37 (1989), 43.

Select Bibliography

American Society for Training and Development. *Models of Excellence.* Washington, D.C.: ASTD, 1983.

Association for Educational Communications and Technology. *The Definition of Educational Technology.* Washington, D.C.: AECT, 1977.

Association for Educational Communications and Technology. *Guidelines for the Accreditation of Programs in Educational Communications and Information Technologies.* Washington, D.C.: AECT, 1983.

Brand, Stewart. *The Media Lab.* New York: Viking, 1987.

Brown, James W., ed. *Trends in Instructional Technology.* Syracuse, N.Y.: Syracuse University, ERIC Clearinghouse on Information Resources, 1984.

Educational Technology Research and Development (ETR&D), vol. 37, no. 1 (1989).

Gustafson, Kent L. "Formation of a Society for Professors of Instructional Technology," in Elwood E. Miller and Mary Louise Mosley, eds., *Educational Media and Technology Yearbook*, vol. 12. Littleton, Colo.: Libraries Unlimited, 1986.

Johnson, Jenny K., ed. *Masters Curricula in Educational Communications and Technology: A Descriptive Directory*, 3d ed. Washington, D.C.: AECT, May 1989.

19

Educational Technology in the 1990s and Beyond: State of the Art and Future Prospects

In this final chapter, an attempt will be made to give this history some sense of conclusion, but just as differing points of view or diverse understanding of what constitutes the nature of educational technology exist, there should be no expectation that some definitive general conclusion will bring this history to a tidy end.

The aim of this chapter is twofold: (1) to briefly assess the state of the art of selected aspects of educational technology in the early 1990s, and (2) to explore the future prospects of educational technology.

State of the Art: Instructional Television

It has been shown that instructional television was faced with a number of serious problems during the 1950s to the late 1970s. For example, the master teacher concept did not necessarily transfer a masterly performance to the classroom by means of television. Also, instructional telecasts were hampered by low-quality productions and by many critical technical problems involving inadequate equipment and lack of compatibility of diverse hardware. Unfortunately, many teachers frequently did not know what instructional television programs existed nor did they know how to use them effectively in the classroom. In any case, instructional television programs were usually considered to be entertainment rather than instruction and were therefore not considered to be a regular part of the curriculum.

There were, however, some positive aspects. Many teachers and schools did make excellent use of instructional television programs, using instructional television programs in a creative and imaginative fashion. In addition, there were schools whose equipment was up-to-date and accessible, whose faculty was sophisticated in the use of television, and whose parents and communities were enthusiastic supporters of instructional television. There were also school systems and regional and state networks that provided excellent technical assistance to schools and who made a systematic effort to integrate instructional television programs with the curriculum as well as assisting schools in integrating new technologies like the computer and cable television into daily instruction. Moreover, after years of ITV research on learning, there was no doubt

> that a well-designed and well produced television program can and does teach. This is especially verifiable when the potentials of the medium are exploited and content visualization is maximized. It is most especially true when the medium is in the hands of a skilled teacher.[1]

National Instruction Television formed nine consortia of state (USA) and provincial (Canada) educational agencies before becoming the Agency for Instructional Television (AIT, now Agency for Instructional Technology). Its mandate was the pooling of resources, leadership, production expertise, and finances to achieve mutually agreed on goals. One of its basic aims was that it would provide sufficient programming for elementary and secondary schools so that the content might effectuate changes in classroom practice. This system was further augmented by the development of the Public Broadcasting Service (PBS).

Another major contribution to educational programming in the 1970s was the Children's Television Workshop's (CTW) innovative development of *Sesame Street* and *The Electric Company* programs and its application of a formative research approach which subsequently became a model for educational television design. CTW also demonstrated what could be accomplished with a unique blend of educational leadership, high purpose, quality research, professional writing and production, and adequate financial support.

Despite positive examples of excellence in the 1970s, the creative use of instructional television in the 1980s was uncommon. There was still an urgent need for information about program availability and a general lack of curriculum integration. A need still existed for more effective and widespread teacher education, both pre-service and in-service, in the effective use of instructional television. Another urgent need was the required leadership in basic and action research. Some excellent overviews of basic research have been made by Dorr,[2] Howe,[3] Meyer,[4] and Zillmann and Bryant,[5] but more intensive and extensive inquiries are needed into the nature of visual and verbal learning and their relationship to television. Equally important is the need for studies of cognition, emotion, motivation, and personality development to determine what elements are necessary in schools to make more effective use of instructional television.

The technical problems which beset the early years of educational television shrank in the 1980s with the development of microwave transmission, satellites and videotape recording systems. However, schools still desperately needed disinterested professional advice about what hardware to buy. Frequently, salesmen convinced educators to buy hardware which became quickly obsolete or which was either not compatible with previous purchases or newer, developing hardware. Another serious factor was the increasingly competitive budgetary considerations with regard to the purchase of television hardware or microcomputers. For example, school administrators openly admitted that money was found for computer purchases when there was no budget item for television sets. The argument was that parents and the public viewed instructional television as "entertainment" and computers as "business." They also asserted that home familiarity forced schools to adopt computers. Of course, the same argument could be made for television, but computer advocates are certain that the new technology will bring cost-effectiveness and reduce the teacher load. Ironically, instructional television advocates originally made the same claim that computer advocates make today.

Instructional television faces a critical era in the 1990s. For example, public television may decrease the amount of satellite transmission time that it now designates for in-school programming and may concentrate more on general programming. Also, as new technologies appear, such as cable television, direct broadcast satellites, VCRs, and microcomputers, they supersede the local public television station. There is also the possibility that teletext, videotext, interactive cable, interactive videodiscs, and microcomputers may be linked with instructional television programming in the future. Meanwhile, instructional television is beginning to be severely affected by the economy. National and regional distribution costs are becoming line items in public television budgets, and instructional television income is expected to assume these costs. Production centers are diminishing in both staff and programming output as costs accelerate. Today, public television stations are cutting back on instructional television service staffs and the amount of time being broadcast for the schools.

Although CTW has had the advantages of over $100 million in funding and an exempt tax status, it now faces economic hardships. Public broadcasting provides only 5 percent of CTW's budget and federal funding has been erratic. CTW's two shows for older children, *The Electric Company* and *3-2-1 Contact*, which relied on government and private underwriting, have now come to an end. New episodes of *Sesame Street* now cost more than $9 million a year. With CTW facing evaporating funds, they are turning toward the creation of commercial programming and commercial exploitation. For example, CTW now licenses more than 1,700 items for children under the *Sesame Street* name which produces revenues of more than $40 million a year.

With the demise of the National Association of Educational Broadcasters and the uncertain future of PBS educational services, instructional television professionals are exploring new organizational configurations. Others feel that after more than a quarter-century of PBS/CPB service to schools, the schools must begin to bear the responsibility of instructional television.

In order to deal with the major issues facing the field, the Office of Policy Development and Planning of the Corporation for Public Broadcasting (COB) circulated in May 1984 a "Research Plan for Evaluating the Educational Uses of Technologies." The purpose of the document was to provide a blueprint for the next five years of research into the educational uses of technology. As a result, the ITV Futures Planning Group was formed in 1985 to provide "a means of staffing the work necessary for systemwide consideration of issues facing learning technologies in the future."[6] This group consisted of administrative officers of the three regional networks, administrations from the Corporation of Public Broadcasting and Public Broadcasting System, and directors of ITV operations at state and local levels. The first significant decision was to exchange the term instructional television for the term *learning technology* because it was seen as a more accurate reflection of the historical development of electronic media for instructional purposes. Secondly, the ITV Futures Planning Group identified twenty-three issues facing the future of learning technologies and established nine working groups, each focusing on different needs which had been identified. The result of this effort was "ITV Futures: The Next Step." Other projects have grown out of these efforts, such as the CPB mandate to the Public Broadcasting Service (PBS) to revitalize public television's role in elementary/secondary education.[7] However, it is still too early to know if this reappraisal of instructional television will lead to a more productive future in view of the increasing economic pressures and the rapidly changing impact of new technologies.

It is clear that PBS needs educational technologists to design and implement instructional programs. Aside from such programs as *Sesame Street*, the new development of narrowcasting has opened an intriguing set of possibilities for instructional programs for a variety of institutions.

A controversial development in commercial television posed a new challenge to instructional television in 1989. Although corporate-underwritten educational films and educational radio have been distributed free to schools since the 1920s, the current development is strikingly different because students are being valued for their potential as consumers rather than as young learners.

Whittle Communications assembled a board of twelve educators and public figures to provide advice and direction for Channel One, a satellite-received news programming venture aimed at elementary schools. The board is headed by Terril H. Bell, former Secretary of

Education under President Ronald Reagan. In the spring of 1989, Whittle Communications began seven weeks of field testing in six elementary schools across the country, providing twelve-minute news programs (Channel One), including compulsory viewing of two minutes of paid commercials in exchange for a gift to the school. Specifically, the schools that agreed to use the news programs were offered the use of the following equipment: a monitor for each classroom in which the program was shown; a fixed satellite-receiving dish wired for Channel One; wiring for a second disk; two VCR systems, one for Channel One, another for customizing; plus a centralized control room and wiring for every classroom. In order to provide additional incentive, Whittle Communications provided 1,000 free hours of educational programming to participating schools. The one condition placed on the use of the equipment was that all students in school be required to watch Channel One (the number of students required was later reduced to about 70 percent). If the school were not to deliver the viewership required, the equipment could be immediately withdrawn.

A second news program developed by commercial television for school viewing began on August 14, 1989 when Ted Turner's Cable News Network made its program "CNN Newsroom" available to all high schools in the United States. Although the Turner organization had intended to carry advertising, in a shrewd turnabout, the "CNN Newsroom" was provided via cable free of charge and free of advertising to all high schools. Also, in contrast with Whittle Communications' preparation, the Turner organization developed its news program in cooperation with the National Association of School Administrators and hired a number of distinguished consultants. However, no receiving equipment has been provided to the schools.

More than a dozen prestigious educational organizations have been opposed to the Whittle proposal. In New York, the Board of Regents have prohibited schools in the state from using the program; and Harold Raynold, Jr., the Massachusetts commissioner, advised his state schools against it. William Honig, State Superintendent of Public Instruction in California, is vigorously opposed to Channel One. Meanwhile, the Action for Children's Television (ACT), founded to encourage diversity and eliminate commercial abuses in programming aimed at younger viewers, has launched a major assault against commercial television in the classroom.

The opponents argue that commercial advertisements are in no way educational and that daily uncritical viewing is no substitute for creative instruction. They state that it is more important for students to learn how to solve problems and articulate ideas than to be fed predigested news excerpts. Others have feared that such approaches may encourage the government to decrease spending on public education or to buy into technological fixes and burden schools with online video and computer services than to increase teachers' salaries and the quality of instruction. All critics agree that the classroom should not become another market to exploit.

State of the Art: Computer-Assisted Instruction

Research has often found that the introduction of new technology usage tends to peak initially and then recede toward a baseline level as the technology loses its novelty. Clark, for example, argues that similar "novelty effects" account for discovered benefits of computer-assisted instruction (CAI).[8] Using data from early meta-analyses of CAI studies, he notes that at the elementary and secondary school levels "the advantages for computer delivered instruction diminish to significant levels with time." However, Kulik et al. have observed that "long-term studies provide better control for novelty effects, but the short-term studies may provide better control over extraneous factors. In short-term studies, for example, criterion tests may measure more exactly the material taught by the competing methods."[9]

Moreover, a review of CAI evaluations used in meta-analyses found that three-quarters of the studies had evidence of serious design flaws and that there was a tendency to overstate effects.[10]

In any event, it seems clear that the eventual dominance of computer-assisted instruction, and microcomputers in particular, is not dependent on research findings regarding its instructional effectiveness, but is more directly related to powerful economic factors. Thus, there is increasing evidence that cost effectiveness may ultimately be decisive in the widespread implementation of CAI. Although cost-effectiveness of CAI remains relatively unexplored, the limited research available suggests that differences in costs seem to be correlated with differences in effectiveness. For example, a study by Levin et al. found substantial cost and effectiveness differences in eight alternative approaches to CAI.[11] They found "both actual costs and those estimated for fully utilized systems differed by a factor of 4 between the lowest cost and highest cost interventions." Interestingly enough, they found a substantial underutilization of CAI capacity. This finding suggests that there may be a greater potential for increasing cost-effectiveness by fuller utilization rather than searching for alternative interventions which may be more cost-effective.

A social learning analysis by Carnoy et al. suggests that only slight research effects can be expected as long as CAI continues to follow the traditional implementation patterns.[12] They note that only a small proportion of time is spent by the student with the computer in typical interventions and is extremely small in comparison with the total amount of time that a student is engaged in cognitive activity. Also, they point out that "typical studies evaluate the effects of one hour per week or about 30 hours per year of computer use. This is little more than the average student's weekly exposure to television."[13] Moreover, the curriculum in CAI tends to be the same as traditional programs of study. Nevertheless, there is no question that CAI does have significant advantages in achieving traditional goals of instruction. Effectiveness findings from comparison group studies range from mildly negative to extremely positive. Recent evaluations of CAI applications report consistently positive and generally high achievement gains at all educational levels. Carnoy et al. conclude their assessment by saying that "the philosophy of learning by doing being implemented in experimental cases of programming instruction for children should anticipate a very slow process of learning" and

> Papert's LOGO philosophy, while placing valuable emphasis on the need for active mental engagement in effective learning, promotes a fundamental misconception about how children learn. Intellectual development does not proceed as LOGO practice might suggest, from a child's interaction with environments in which he/she finds himself/herself, which are created by other humans. By stressing unguided learning of LOGO, its proponents, in effect, ask each child to "reinvent the wheel" before he/she can energetically and confidently employ the powerful algorithmic tools of modern software to explore expanding domains of computer-mediated creativity and learning.[14]

Research on the effects of computers is still in its early stages and there is a need for studies which pinpoint more precisely those aspects of computer applications that determine instructional effectiveness and the relationship of specific types of programming and the motivational effects of computer use.

By the late 1980s, virtually all schools had some computer-assisted instruction, but, to date, with few exceptions, CAI in schools has consisted of little more than electronic page turning or, in effect, using computers for instructional objectives which could have been accomplished just as easily by other means. Drill and practice was still the predominant mode in most schools and computer literacy and computer programming (mainly BASIC and/or LOGO) were the two subjects most frequently taught despite the prevailing doubt of teaching students BASIC.[15]

On the other hand, there have been many innovative CAI applications, such as intelligent tutoring systems. However, little use has been made of such sophisticated CAI in schools nor has there been much use of word processing whereby students might learn to improve their writing. There are few teachers with adequate CAI knowledge to enable them to use computers more creatively. Even those teachers who have learned to program for CAI tend to develop drill and practice materials. It is clear that educational technologists with training in both instructional design and CAI could influence a more imaginative use of computers in the schools.

State of the Art: CAI Software

Although CAI hardware is highly sophisticated, the "big" breakthrough in CAI instructional software is yet to be made. In a review of 163 microcomputer courseware programs by the Educational Products Information Exchange (EPIE), Bialo and Erickson report severe design flaws in most of the software currently available.[16] For example, they observed that over two-thirds of the software "either had no objectives stated or had objectives that were unclear or developmentally inappropriate." Futrell and Geisert observed that courseware producers seemed to provide more "bells and whistles" than aspects which have shown to be effective in the classroom.[17] It is clear, as Roblyer states, "that most software is being designed based on marketing priorities, rather than to meet identified needs of specific students."[18] Simultaneously, these prevailing design flaws are contributing to the problems teachers are encountering in integrating software into their other classroom activities.

Since courseware could be easily sold regardless of its effectiveness, many courseware producers have not had any incentive to assume any responsibility for good courseware design. Perhaps more cost-effectiveness studies will eventually convince educators that they will have to exercise stricter criteria in their software purchases or that they will have to develop some type of national design and development guidelines for software producers. It is clear that the software problem probably constitutes the greatest impediment to the development of CAI.

State of the Art: Instructional Theory and Design

Most instructional theories which underlie current models of instructional design were developed more than two decades ago and are highly inadequate in prescribing instruction for interactive new technologies. Unfortunately, there has been a tendency to adopt those theories and instructional designs which were seen as compatible with particular philosophical or instructional goals. Although there have been promising developments in cognitive science, they still fall short of providing the kind of instructional design models needed for effective instruction. Today there is an urgent need for a linking science (or theory) between cognitive science and instructional development.

Lesgold has made an approach toward a theory of curriculum for use in designing intelligent instructional systems. He notes the weakness in current approaches to instructional design by stating

> there is no clear method for differentiating how to present material to remediate a problem discovered after a lesson has been taught from how it should be presented when taught initially. Second, the knowledge that represents the "glue" connecting the contents of related lessons is not clearly specified, nor is it assigned to be part of the content of any specific lesson.[19]

State of the Art: Interactive Multimedia Systems

New interactive multimedia systems are just emerging and include such products as video notebooks, video editing, simulations, adventure games, talking books, and tutorials. A multimedia application typically involves a computer-controlled videodisc and/or a CD-ROM player. Ultimately, there will be video computers with many multimedia capabilities built in or available as modules.

Some interesting projects have been undertaken in recent years to explore the potential of interactive multimedia applications. For example, the Academic Computing and Information Systems of Stanford University is sponsoring the Shakespeare Project. Stanford's Professor Larry Friedlander, who has been teaching Shakespeare for many years, has completed a graphical simulation of theatrical performances on a computer and has successfully demonstrated a prototype of a videodisc-based system to explore still and moving images of theaters and performances. Other notable interactive multimedia systems developed in recent years include Sam Gibbon's Voyage of the MIMI II, a television series and supporting print and computer materials in the area of science and mathematics education for students in grades 5-7, the CD-ROM Encyclopedia product by Grolier, and Bernard Frischer's travel system for teaching the classics at UCLA. Interactions of hardware, software, and interface innovations are introducing new changes in educational environments and producing new types of curricula.[20]

State of the Art: Intelligent Tutoring Systems (ITS)

A well-understood technology for intelligent tutoring systems is still in the process of development. More experience is needed and more ITSs need to be built in order to explore the many possibilities. According to Burns and Capps, the required expertise must be integrated as the foundation for ITS. These include the following:

1. Content expertise in the expert module,

2. diagnostic expertise (determining what learners know and need to learn),

3. instructional and curriculum expertise in the instructor module,

4. expertise in creating instructional environments,

5. human-computer interface expertise,

6. implementation expertise, and

7. evaluation expertise.[21]

The goal is to integrate all this knowledge into a single ITS. The hope is to achieve through artificial intelligence an interactive, flexible system for the purpose of effective learning.

Future Prospects for Educational Technology

Another aim of this chapter is to attempt to explore the prospects for the future of educational technology in this and the next century. The most frequent failing of technological futurists is to predict the future with little or no reference to the past. As a consequence, they have usually been overly optimistic and have proclaimed the inauguration of a new era, only to be scaled down subsequently to size. In light of the past history of educational technology, there has been a one-sided emphasis on media or an excessive concentration on hardware rather than on the process of educational technology. Moreover, an understanding of cognitive processing is important, but the realms of feeling, motivation, art, and values are equally vital if we are to understand human learning. It is still not clear how this gap in contemporary educational technology will be filled, but perhaps a speculative, imaginative component will ultimately be realized in the century ahead.

Nickerson comments that

a question for the immediate future and beyond that will require the collaborative attention of technologists and educators is that of how to couple computer-based tools with other teaching/learning resources so to support an integrated approach to specific subject matter in the classroom.[22]

Landauer believes "that by 2020 a good portion of the cognitive tasks now performed by people will be capable of performance by machine."[23] However, Feurzeig thinks that

the prospects for advancing education through information technology require, for their success, a great deal in the way of nontechnological developments. These include such things as creating the necessary human resources, primarily skilled teachers who like to teach and who are knowledgeable in the subjects they teach and in the use of computer tools they teach with.[24]

Feurzeig looks to the distant future and envisages

a process of change that will require a time span of generations from the time of the creation of the first technology-based educational programs to the production of a critical mass of young people who are comfortable and competent with computers and with the richness and variety of learning experiences they make possible. These men and women will become in turn, the creators and teachers of the next wave. This is not a short-term development, but it should be underway by 2020.[25]

Malcom observes that "technology in education may not live up to its potential in the near term because of hardware costs, software limitations, and development costs, and lack of preparation of teachers to take advantage of the present capabilities."[26] However, Malcom assumes "that by 2020 we will have overcome these impediments and started to realize real productivity increases in education as a result of the technology."[27]

It is not easy to predict the future of educational technology. Probably the easiest prediction to make is that things do not usually turn out the way they are predicted. In the past, extravagant claims have been made for films, language laboratories, television, and teaching machines. Most of these have failed to solve educational problems. Today, of course, we are being seduced by the educational claims for the computer.

The changes that have taken place in psychology since the middle of this century have opened up new, exciting prospects for educational technology. The concept of an empty organism has been replaced with internal structures, and consciousness and thought have been brought back into central stage. A particularly important implication for educational technology is a better understanding of the chemical and neurological foundations of mind. There has also been a continuous advance in the biological and cognitive areas as well as many other areas of psychology which have direct application to educational technology.

It is the view of this author that the cognitive approach to educational technology offers the best possibilities of progress for the future. However, it will be essential to build a stronger bridge between the cognitive sciences so that we may eventually obtain better answers to questions about learning, perception, memory, or language. In the words of Gardner,

> the ultimate goals of cognitive science should be — precisely — to provide a cogent scientific account of how human beings achieve their most remarkable symbolic products: how we come to compose symphonies, write poems, invent machines (including computers), or construct theories (including cognitive-scientific ones).[28]

Gardner says that cognitive scientists are on the spot, but

> if we heed the lessons entailed in our scientific history and lurking in our philosophical backgrounds, if we attend to but are not stymied by the reservations aired by shrewd skeptics, if we recognize the limitations of all inquiry but do not thereby encounter a failure of nerve, there are clear grounds for optimism.[29]

A look into the distant future sees the focus of educational technology becoming increasingly centered on the applications of the methods and principles of what is now termed neuropsychology, a specialty that embraces both the experimental investigations of brain-behavior relationships and the functions of the brain in processing information. At this juncture, neuroscience can be considered one of the border disciplines of cognitive science. However, there is an increasing realization that the solution of their problems is more likely to follow from a closer interdisciplinary collaboration. But, in any event, neuroscience, in the view of this author, holds some of the most important implications for the future of educational technology.

Finally, this author does not see any quick, revolutionary changes in educational technology the remainder of this century. The more dramatic changes are likely to occur in the next century, but any change in educational technology will be evolutionary rather than revolutionary. Past history has clearly shown that there is a consistent, serious lag between the ability to establish the level of behavioral change desired and the ability to achieve it. Moreover, it has rarely been pointed out that or recognized as a problem that information and knowledge are not identical or synonymous, as it is frequently assumed. For example, computer information systems are not just objective recording devices. They also reflect concepts, hopes, beliefs, attitudes. Thus, the communications revolution has within it the poison seeds of the past. Instead of creating a "new future," modern communications may mask the underlying forces of politics, power, or greed.

It is the particular futuristic bias of this author that the educational technology of the future can generate humanistic experiences provided some persistent conceptual, methodological, and political problems can be solved within the foreseeable future. There is hope that educational technology A.D. 2001 and beyond will begin to develop into something far more exciting and creative than it is now.

Notes

[1]Marjorie A. Cambre, "Instructional Television: An Update and Assessment," in Donald P. Ely et al., eds., *Educational Media and Technology Yearbook*, vol. 14. Englewood, Colo.: Libraries Unlimited, 1988, 41.

[2]See A. Dorr, *Television and Children: A Special Medium for a Special Audience*. Beverly Hills, Calif.: Sage Publications, 1986.

[3]See M. J. A. Howe, ed., *Learning from Television: Psychological and Educational Research*. New York: Academic Press, 1983.

[4]See M. Meyer, ed., *Children and the Formal Features of Television*. New York: K. G. Saur, 1983.

[5]See D. Zillmann and J. Bryant, eds., *Selective Exposure to Communication*. Hillsdale, N.J.: Lawrence Erlbaum, 1985.

[6]ITV Futures Planning Group, *Learning Technology Issues for the Future*, unpublished monograph.

[7]PBS discussion draft. Meeting Educational Needs through Public Television and Learning Technologies: A Long-Term Plan (prepared by PBS Elementary and Secondary Service and submitted to the Corporation for Public Broadcasting in fulfillment of contract #1706/80606). Washington, D.C.: Corporation for Public Broadcasting, 1 July 1987.

[8]Richard E. Clark, "Evidence for Confounding in Computer-based Instruction Studies: Analyzing the Meta-analyses," *Educational Communication and Technology Journal* 33 (Winter 1985), 249-62.

[9]James A. Kulik et al., "Effectiveness of Computer-Based Education in Elementary Schools," *Computers in Human Behavior* 1 (1985), 59-74.

[10]Clark, "Evidence for Confounding," 249-62.

[11]Henry M. Levin et al., *Cost-Effectiveness of Alternative Approaches to Computer-Assisted Instruction*. Stanford, Calif.: CERAS, School of Education, Stanford University, 1986.

[12]Martin Carnoy et al., *Education and Computers: Vision and Reality*. Stanford, Calif.: CERAS, School of Education, Stanford University, 1986.

[13]Ibid., 63.

[14]Ibid.

[15]See A. Bork, *The Microcomputer Revolution. The Computer: Extension of the Human Mind*. Conference Proceedings, July 1982. Eugene, Oreg.: University of Oregon, 1982, 12-29.

[16]E. R. Bialo and L. B. Erickson, "Microcomputer Courseware: Characteristics and Design Trends," *AEDS Journal* 18 (1985), 227-36.

[17]M. Futrel and P. Geisert, "A Call for Action to Improve the Design of Microcomputer Instructional Courseware," *Educational Technology* 25 (1985), 13-15.

[18]M. D. Roblyer, "Fundamental Problems and Principles of Designing Effective Courseware," in David H. Jonassen, ed., *Instructional Designs for Microcomputer Courseware*. Hillsdale, N.J.: Lawrence Erlbaum, 1988, 9.

[19]See Alan Lesgold, "Toward a Theory of Curriculum for Use in Designing Intelligent Instructional Systems," in Heinz Mandl and Alan Lesgold, eds., *Learning Issues of Intelligent Tutoring Systems*. New York: Springer-Verlag, 1988, 118.

[20]See S. Ambron and K. Hooper, eds., *Interactive Multimedia*. Redmond, Wash.: Microsoft Press, 1988.

[21]Hugh L. Burns and Charles G. Capps, "Foundations of Intelligent Tutoring Systems: An Introduction," in Martha C. Polson and J. Jeffrey Richardson, eds., *Foundations of Intelligent Tutoring Systems*. Hillsdale, N.J.: Lawrence Erlbaum, 1988, 18.

[22]Raymond S. Nickerson, "Technology in Education: Possible Influences on Context, Purposes, Content, and Methods," in Raymond S. Nickerson and Philip P. Zodhiates, eds., *Technology in Education: Looking toward 2020*. Hillsdale, N.J.: Lawrence Erlbaum, 1988, 315.

[23]Thomas K. Landauer, "Education in a World of Omnipotent and Omniscient Technology," ibid., 19.

[24]Wallace Feurzeig, "Apprentice Tools: Students as Practitioners," ibid., 98.

[25]Ibid., 118.

[26]Shirley M. Malcom, "Technology in 2020: Educating a Diverse Population," ibid., 228.

[27]Ibid.

[28]Howard Gardner, *The Mind's New Science*. New York: Basic Books, 1985, 391.

[29]Ibid., 392.

Select Bibliography

Chi, Michelene T. H., et al., eds. *The Nature of Expertise*. Hillsdale, N.J.: Lawrence Erlbaum, 1988.

Clark, Richard E. "Current Progress and Future Directions for Research in Instructional Technology," *ETR&D* vol. 37, no. 1 (1989), 57-80.

Glaser, Robert, and Miriam Bassok. "Learning Theory and the Study of Instruction," in Mark R. Rosenzwig and Lyman W. Porter, eds., *Annual Review of Psychology* vol. 40. Palo Alto, Calif.: Annual Reviews, 1989.

Hunt, Earl. "Cognitive Science: Definition, Status, and Questions," in Mark R. Rosenzwig and Lyman W. Porter, eds., *Annual Review of Psychology* vol. 40. Palo Alto, Calif.: Annual Reviews, 1989.

Nickerson, Raymond S., and Philip P. Zodhiates, eds. *Technology in Education: Looking toward 2020*. Hillsdale, N.J.: Lawrence Erlbaum, 1988.

Part V
Appendixes

Appendix A
Acronyms

AAACE	American Association for Adult and Continuing Education
ACE	American Council on Education
ACER	Advisory Committee on Education by Radio (1929)
ACUBS	Association of College and University Broadcasting Stations (1925) (Became the NAEB in 1934.)
AECT	Association for Educational Communications and Technology (Originally the DVI, then DAVI. Became the AECT in 1970.)
AED	Academy for Educational Development
AER (T)	Association for Education by Radio (and later) Television (1940) (Merged with the NAEB in the mid-1950s.)
AERA	American Educational Research Association
AI	Artificial Intelligence
AIR	American Institutes for Research in the Behavioral Sciences
AIT	Agency for Instructional Television (Originally part of NITL, became NCSCT, then NIT (C). Formed as AIT in 1973.)
ALA	American Library Association
APRS	Association of Public Radio Stations (1973)
CAI	Computer-Assisted Instruction
CAR	Computer-Assisted Learning
CAT	Computer-Assisted Teaching
CATV	Cable Television
CBE	Competency-Based Education
CBE	Computer-Based Education
CBIV	Computer-Based Interactive Video
CBS	Columbia Broadcasting System
CBT	Computer-Based Training

CCC	Civilian Conservation Corps
CCC	Curriculum Computer Corporation
CEDaR	Council for Educational Development and Research
CIT	Commission on Instructional Technology
CL	Computer Literacy
CLAS	Computerized Lesson-Authoring System
CMI	Computer-Managed Instruction
CML	Computer-Managed Learning
CMLS	Computerized Mastery Learning System
CMPE	Commission on Motion Pictures in Education
CPB	Corporation for Public Broadcasting (1967)
CRT	Cathode Ray Tube
CRT	Criterion-Referenced Test
CS	Cognitive Style
CS	Conditioned Stimulus
CTW	Children's Television Workshop (1967)
DAVI	Department of Audiovisual Instruction (1947) (A department of NEA, formed originally as DVI, reformed as the independent AECT in 1970.)
DoD	Department of Defense
DOT	Division of Telecommunications (of the AECT)
DVI	Department of Visual Instruction (of the NEA) (1923) (Became DAVI, then AECT.)
ED	ERIC Document
EDRS	ERIC Document Reproduction Service
EDUCOM	Educational Communications Interuniversity Communications Council
EFLA	Educational Film Library Association
ERIC/CIR	Clearinghouse on Information Resources (Syracuse University)
ERN	Educational Radio Network (a division of NETRC) (1962)
ETRC	Educational Television and Radio Center (1952) (Became NETRC in 1959, then NET.)
ETS	Educational Television Stations (a division of the NAEB) (1963) (Merged with the "new" PBS in 1973.)
ETV	Educational Television
FAE	Fund for Adult Education (1951) (Created by the Ford Foundation. Fund for the Advancement of Education [1951] also created by the Ford Foundation.)
FCC	Federal Communications Commission (1934) (Superseded the FRC.)

FRC	Federal Radio Commission (1927) (Incorporated into the FCC.)
FREC	Federal Radio Education Committee (1935)
FWLERD	Far West Laboratory for Educational Research and Development
GPNITL	Great Plains National Instructional Television Library (1962) (Originally part of NITL.)
HEW	Federal Department of Health, Education, and Welfare
HumRRO	Human Resources Research Organization
IAMCR	International Association for Mass Communications Research
ICA	International Communication Association
ICAI	Intelligent Computer-Assisted Instruction
IER (T)	Institute for Education by Radio (and, later) Television (1930)
IGE	Individually Guided Education
IT	Instructional Technologist
ITFS	Instructional Television Fixed Service
ITV	Instructional Television
IVD	Interactive Videodisc
JCET	Joint Council on Educational Telecommunications (1950) (Originally the Joint Committee on Educational Television, later the Joint Council on Educational Broadcasting. Now the JCET.)
LITA	Library and Information Technology Association
LRC	Learning Resources Center
LRDC	Learning Research and Development Center
MACOS	Man: A Course of Study
MCAI	Microcomputer-Assisted Instruction
MECC	Minnesota Educational Computing Consortium
MET	Midwestern Educational Television (network) (1961)
MF	Microfiche
MF	Microfilm
MicroSIFT	Microcomputer Software and Information for Teachers
MIS	Management Information System
MIT	Massachusetts Institute of Technology
MPATI	Midwest Program on Airborne Television Instruction (1959) (Incorporated into GPNITL in 1971.)
MPPDA	Motion Picture Producers and Distributors of America
NACRE	National Advisory Council on Radio in Education (1938)
NAEB	National Association of Educational Broadcasters (Formed as the ACUBS. Became the NAEB in 1934.)

NAVI	National Academy of Visual Instruction (Merged into DVI in 1932.)
NBC	National Broadcasting Company
NCCET	National Citizens Committee for Educational Television (1952)
NCCGBC	National Coordinating Committee of Governing Board Chairmen (of PTV stations) (1972) (Merged with the "new" PBS in 1973.)
NCER	National Committee on Education by Radio (1931)
NCSCT	National Center for School and College Television (Originally part of NITL. Became the NCSCT in 1965, then NIT (C), then AIT.)
NEA	National Education Association
NER	National Educational Radio (a division of the NAEB until 1973)
NET	National Educational Television (Originally the ETRC. Became NETRC, then NET in 1963. Merged with Station WNDT [now WNET] New York in 1969.)
NETRC	National Educational Television and Radio Center (Originally the ETRC. Became NETRC in 1959, NET in 1963.)
NICEM	National Information Center for Educational Media
NIT (C)	National Instructional Television Center (Originally part of NITL. Became the NCSCT, then NIT in 1968, and AIT in 1973.)
NITL	National Instructional Television Library (1962) (Originally a division of NETRC.)
NPACT	National Public Affairs Center for Television (1971) (Became a unit of Station WETA in 1974.)
NPR	National Public Radio (1970)
NSF	National Science Foundation
OTA	Office of Technology Assessment (U.S. Congress)
OTP	Office of Telecommunications Policy (1970) (part of the White House)
PBS	Public Broadcasting Service (1969) (The "new" PBS, incorporating ETS and NCCGBC, was formed in 1973.)
PCEB	Preliminary Committee on Educational Broadcasting (1927)
PIDT	Professors of Instructional Design and Technology
PLAN	Program for Learning According to Needs
PLATO	Programmed Logic for Automatic Teaching Operation
PLOT	Piagetian Logical Operations Test
PSI	Personalized System of Instruction (Keller)
PSSC	Public Service Satellite Consortium (1975)
PTL	Public Television Library (1973) (Originally the ETS Program Service [formed in 1965].)
R&D	Research and Development

RAM	Random Access Memory
RISE	Research and Information Services for Education
SAT	Stanford Achievement Test
SDC	System Development Corporation
SITE	Satellite Instructional Television Experiment
S-R	Stimulus-Response
SUN	State University of Nebraska
TFC	Teaching Film Custodians
TICCIT	Time-Shared, Interactive, Computer-Controlled Information Television
UCIDT	University Consortium for Instructional Development and Technology
USOE	United States Office of Education
VCR	Videocassette Recorder
VIAA	Visual Instruction Association of America (Merged with DVI in 1932.)
VTR	Videotape Recorder

Appendix B
Doctoral Programs in
Educational Technology

University of Alabama	Ph.D.
Arizona State University	Ph.D.
Arizona State University	Ph.D. or Ed.D.
United States International University	Ed.D.
University of California Los Angeles	Ph.D. or Ed.D.
University of Southern California	Ph.D. or Ed.D.
Florida State University	Ph.D.
Nova University	Ph.D. or Ed.D.
University of Florida	Ph.D. or Ed.D.
Georgia State University	Ph.D. or Ed.D.
University of Georgia	Ed.D.
Northern Illinois University	Ed.D.
Southern Illinois University	Ph.D.
Purdue University	Ph.D.
Iowa State University	Ph.D.
University of Iowa	Ph.D.
Kansas State University	Ph.D. or Ed.D.
University of Kansas	Ph.D. or Ed.D.
Johns Hopkins University	Ed.D.
Boston University	Ed.D.

From Jenny K. Johnson, ed., *Masters Curricula in Educational Communications and Technology: A Descriptive Directory*, 3d ed. Washington, D.C.: AECT, May 1989.

Lesley College......................................	Ph.D.
Michigan State University...........................	Ph.D.
St. Cloud State University...........................	Ed.D.
University of Minnesota.............................	Ph.D.
University of Nebraska.............................	Ph.D. or Ed.D.
Teachers College, Columbia University...............	Ed.D.
New York University...............................	Ph.D. or Ed.D.
State University of New York Buffalo.................	Ph.D. or Ed.D.
Syracuse University................................	Ph.D. or Ed.D.
North Carolina Central University...................	Ph.D. or Ed.D.
Kent State University..............................	Ph.D. or Ed.D.
University of Toledo...............................	Ph.D. or Ed.D.
Oklahoma State University..........................	Ed.D.
University of Oklahoma.............................	Ph.D. or Ed.D.
University of Oregon...............................	Ph.D. or Ed.D.
Pennsylvania State University.......................	Ph.D. or Ed.D.
Temple University.................................	Ed.D.
Pittsburgh University..............................	Ed.D.
Memphis State University...........................	Ed.D.
East Texas State University.........................	Ed.D.
Texas Tech University..............................	Ed.D.
University of Texas Austin..........................	Ph.D.
Brigham Young University...........................	Ph.D.
Utah State University..............................	Ed.D.
University of Virginia..............................	Ph.D. or Ed.D.
Virginia Polytechnic Institute & State University.........	Ed.D.
University of Washington...........................	Ph.D. or Ed.D.
University of West Virginia.........................	Ed.D.
University of Wisconsin Madison....................	Ph.D.

Index

This index is to significant individuals, organizations, and subjects in the field. Most instances of the appearance of names, etc. are listed unless the mention is simply in passing. Entries are to page number, and, when a page number is followed by the letter "n," the reference may be found in a footnote on that page.

Printed in the United States
221840BV00003B/22/A

9 781593 111397